LEE COUNTY LIBRARY
SANFORD, N. C.

In Memory
Yet Green

IN MEMORY YET GREEN

The Autobiography of Isaac Asimov

1920–1954

LEE COUNTY LIBRARY
SANFORD, N. C.

Doubleday & Company, Inc., Garden City, New York
1979

Cover and title page of "Nightfall" from the September 1941 issue of *Astounding* reproduced by permission of The Condé Nast Publications Inc., copyright 1941 by Street & Smith Publications Inc., copyright © 1969 (renewed) by The Condé Nast Publications Inc. "The Weapon" copyright © 1942 by Fictioneers, Inc.

ISBN: 0-385-13679-x
Library of Congress Catalog Card Number 78-55838

COPYRIGHT © 1979 BY ISAAC ASIMOV
ALL RIGHTS RESERVED
PRINTED IN THE UNITED STATES OF AMERICA

Contents

IV *The War and the Army—in That Order*

V *Into and out of Manhattan*

VI *Two Careers, but Where Next?*

Introduction

I remember once, when I was twenty-nine and beginning to feel that, really, I was on the threshold of old age, I began for the first time to wonder if I ought to write an autobiography.

The point against doing so was that nothing of any importance had ever happened to me. The point in favor of doing so was that I was a pretty good writer and that I might weave such a spell of words that no one would notice that nothing had ever happened to me.

On the whole, though, I decided against it because I had other things to do, and because I could detect no real craving for it on the part of the public.

Now a great deal of time has passed and I am actually beginning my autobiography, and a monstrously long one it will be. This is it.

What has changed? It *still* remains a fact that nothing of any importance has ever happened to me and that it will take all my writing skill to obscure that point.

Why, then, am I doing it? Ah, at twenty-nine, I had never published a book. Now I have published two hundred. There seems to be a widespread belief (according to my editor, the beauteous Cathleen Jordan) that no one can possibly write two hundred books of both fiction and nonfiction, in dozens of categories at all age levels, without being, somehow, an interesting person.

Besides, it might be helpful to ambitious young people or to curious not-so-young people to see How I Did It.

I pointed out that this had been exactly my idea in writing *The Early Asimov* (Doubleday, 1972) and *Before the Golden Age* (Doubleday, 1974). In each of these books I included copious autobiographical passages. Cathleen said, however, that those passages had pertained almost exclusively to my literary life and she wanted a well-rounded tale that included my nonliterary life as well.

I said, "What nonliterary life? How can a person turn out two hundred books and have a nonliterary life?"

Fortunately, she explained it carefully to me so that I could understand what she meant.

She said, "Shut up, Isaac, and get to work."

So here it is.

In memory yet green, in joy still felt,
The scenes of life rise sharply into view.
We triumph, Time's disasters are undealt,
And while all else is old, the world is new.

ANON.

PART
I

Out of Russia
and into Brooklyn

1

My Birthplace

1

To begin with, I was not born in the United States, but in Russia. At the time I was born, the Russian Empire had already died and was replaced by a variety of Soviet Socialist Republics, the three chief being the Russian Soviet Federated Socialist Republic (R.S.F.S.R.), the Belorussian Soviet Socialist Republic (Belorussian S.S.R.), and the Ukrainian Soviet Socialist Republic (Ukrainian S.S.R.). The old-fashioned names for these were Great Russia, White Russia, and the Ukraine, respectively.

Two years after I was born, these units, together with others, were combined to form the Union of Soviet Socialist Republics (U.S.S.R.), which took in virtually all the territory of the old Russian Empire except for some far western provinces lost in the course of World War I and the Russian Revolution.

Strictly speaking, then, I was not born in Russia, nor in the U.S.S.R. either, but in the Russian S.F.S.R. (Great Russia). The place of my birth was just sixteen kilometers (ten miles) east of the border of the Belorussian S.S.R. That was where my parents lived and their parents for an indefinite number of generations.

This was in itself rather unusual since my family was Jewish and, in theory, Jews were not allowed to live on the holy soil of Great Russia, which had been the Russia of Ivan IV (the Terrible) and Peter I (the Great).

Beginning in 1772, however, under Catherine II (the Great), Russia had annexed large tracts of what had made up the vast, amorphous, and anarchic kingdom of Poland. Until that time, White Russia and the Ukraine had been Polish and the Poles had allowed Jews to live there. Indeed, they had welcomed them as a useful middle class of merchants. The Russians, naturally, annexed the Jews with the territory.

The Russian Tsars did not try to drive the Jews out; they remained a useful middle class. They were confined, however, to the ex-Polish territories of White Russia and the Ukraine, as well as to the Baltic provinces that had been annexed from Sweden, and these constituted "the Jewish Pale."

In a nation as inefficiently ruled as Russia, however, Jews could drift beyond the pale now and then and, every once in a while in a fit of rigor, they would be pushed back.

In the time of Nicholas I, who ruled Russia from 1825 to 1855, things got a little sticky. Nicholas was a traditionalist, who was determined to maintain the autocracy in Russia (and in as much of the rest of Europe as he could manage) against the rising tide of democracy that had been unleashed by the French Revolution. Among other things, small deviations from the traditional Jewish Pale were to be corrected and Jews living outside it were to be moved back in.

That struck my ancestral town for, as I said, it was sixteen kilometers east of White Russia and therefore sixteen kilometers outside the pale. What happened then my father told me, for late in his life he began (at my request) to write me letters telling me what he could remember of his ancestors and of his life in Russia.[1]

Apparently, there was at the time a "good landowner" (and for Jews to remember a Russian landowner as "good" must have meant he was saintly indeed) who owned many square miles of land on both sides of the White Russian/Great Russian border. On hearing that Jewish settlements beyond the White Russian border must be broken up, he carried the border sign from a position west of the town to a position east of the town, thus transferring it into White Russia and allowing the Jews to remain.

This was clearly illegal, but Tsar Nicholas, autocrat though he might be, was far away in St. Petersburg, 415 miles almost due north of my birthplace, and the landowner was on the spot. Since autocracies are usually tempered by inefficiency, bribery, inertia, and any of a dozen other ameliorative influences (or they would be unbearable), it was the immediate power that prevailed and not the Little Father far away.

2

The town I was born in is named Petrovichi, pronounced "peh-TRUV-ih-chee." I didn't know about the final *i* until I was an adult, for my father, although he spelled it as I have just given it, when I asked him, always pronounced it "peh-TRUV-ich."

When I was a child, he would talk of it frequently, saying, "Back home in Petrovichi—" He never said, "Back home in Russia—" I always assumed that Petrovichi was a huge city or perhaps a whole province, and later on I was quite disappointed to find that it was a small hamlet of no consequence whatever.

My father would occasionally come across maps of Europe or of

---

[1] He wrote the letters in his own idiosyncratic brand of English, but in quoting from him, I will, of course, do a little polishing, since it is not my intention to make him a figure of fun.

Russia in my schoolbooks, or elsewhere, and he would always greedily try to find Petrovichi. He never did. He would pause in dismay over what had happened to the western boundary of Russia, astonished at the huge losses to Poland, at the independence of Finland and the Baltic states.

It was very odd. As a Jew, he had no cause to love Russia or Russians, and yet he was Russian. He could speak Russian, he read the Russian literature, and he somehow identified with Russia.

But then he would begin looking for Petrovichi, and compounding his annoyance at his not finding it was the fact that he invariably found the small towns that surrounded it. He would find Khislavich, Mstislav, Klimovichi, and Krichev, for instance. (I still remember those odd names because of the disgust with which he pronounced the syllables, but of course, I have checked the map for the spelling.)

He would call my mother and say, "Look, they have these hamlets and hick towns and Petrovichi they don't have."

I would say, "Maybe they're bigger than Petrovichi, Pappa."

He would look at me with horror and say, "They were smaller. They were nothings. I don't understand why they don't have it." He may have suspected a cartographical conspiracy.

Later on, as I grew older, I took up the search, wondering if perhaps it were all a mirage, if I had been born in an open field or a trackless desert. Then during World War II, I bought a large map of Europe into which I intended to insert colored pins and follow the ebb and flow of the armies. Studying the section of Russia that was under dispute at the time, I was amazed to find Petrovichi. It was the first time I had ever seen it on a map. I put a pin in it of a color I didn't use otherwise, and no matter where the European fronts were, that pin stayed. After all, I needed all the evidence I could get that I had really been born somewhere.

Then, in 1967, a new edition of the *Times* Atlas came out, distributed by Houghton-Mifflin, one of my publishers, and I obtained a copy. I turned to the map of the southwestern U.S.S.R. and there were all the towns my father had despised over forty years before, and nestling among them was Petrovichi, safe and sound.

The *Times* Atlas gives its exact location—53.58° North Latitude and 32.10° East Longitude. That's all I know about it. Except for its location and its geographic position with regard to other towns and cities, I can find nothing, not even its current population. It is not included in Webster's New Geographical Dictionary, for instance.

I daresay I could, if I wished, obtain Soviet reference works that might help me, but I am not willing to carry my efforts that far.

Petrovichi's position represents an extreme for me. Obviously, I have never made my permanent abode farther east than my place of birth, since I was brought to the United States early in life and have never again left it for longer than a few weeks.

It is also true that I have never made my permanent abode farther north than my place of birth. Its latitude is that of Hamburg, Germany; Liverpool, England; Edmonton, Alberta. It is farther north than the territory of any of the states but Alaska, and I have never been in Alaska.

3

Before the "good landowner" had fiddled with the boundary line, Petrovichi was in the Smolensk-guberniya—that is, in the Smolensk district of Great Russia. "Guberniya" is a term no longer used in the U.S.S.R., I believe, and one would now speak of the Smolensk-oblast instead.

Smolensk, the chief town of the district, is 55 miles due north of Petrovichi. It is an ancient town on the upper Dnieper River, and was founded in the ninth century. It was long the object of border warfare between Russia and Poland and switched hands for the last time in 1654, when it became Russian. There was a great battle there in the course of Napoleon's invasion in 1812. Smolensk's present population is something like 220,000.

After the boundary-line shift, Petrovichi was part of the White Russian Mogilyov-district. Mogilyov, 75 miles due west of Petrovichi, is also on the Dnieper River, about 110 miles downstream from Smolensk. It did not become Russian until 1772, and its population is very nearly equal to that of Smolensk.

Nearer than either of these cities was the town of Roslavl, which was just 30 miles due east of Petrovichi. It served as Petrovichi's market town, and its population is about one quarter that of either Smolensk or Mogilyov.

After the Russian Revolution, Petrovichi was reinstated as part of the Smolensk district, although there was no longer any restriction as to Jews living there. By the time I was born then, I was born in the Smolensk district of Great Russia, and I manage to identify with it slightly.

On April 12, 1961, for instance, Yuri Alekseyevich Gagarin became the first man to orbit the Earth in a manned satellite. It turned out that he was born in Gzhatsk, a town 155 miles northeast of Petrovichi, but *also* in the Smolensk district. I felt an absurd local pride over that, just as someone who had been born in Cincinnati might feel rather pleased that the first man on the moon was born in Wapakoneta, Ohio.

One more word about the physical location of Petrovichi. Since no one I have ever met has ever heard of Roslavl, Mogilyov, or Smolensk, locating it in that fashion doesn't help. The best I can do is to say that I was born in a town just 250 miles southwest of Moscow. Or—if Moscow were located in New York City, I would have been born in Fredericksburg, Virginia. There!

2

My Ancestors

1

The earliest ancestor concerning whom my father could talk was his great-great-grandfather, who, like my father, was named Judah. My father gives no dates, for the very good reason that he probably knew none. Assuming twenty-five years to a generation, this early Judah must have been born about a hundred years before my father or, roughly, in 1800. The United States was then an infant nation and White Russia had been firmly under Great Russian rule for only a generation.

I suppose that even if I went to the U.S.S.R., I could dig up no information about the early Judah, or of anyone earlier still. No records were kept in the ordinary sense, and if the Jewish community kept its own records, they would be in Hebrew, with the dates given according to the liturgical calendar. Even if I were to imagine that I could manage to have someone translate all this, I feel rather sure that the records were destroyed in the course of World War II.

Perhaps if I stuck to it long enough (as Alex Haley did in the heroic epic he describes in *Roots*) I could find astounding details concerning my family tree, but let me be honest: I don't care.

I am not impressed by ancestry, since if I could trace my origins to Judas Maccabeus or to King David, that would not add one inch to my stature, either physically, mentally or ethically. What's more, what about all my other ancestors? There must have been uncounted thousands of human beings in the century of King David, all of whom in some small way contributed to my production, and every one of them but King David might have been criminals and drunkards for all I know. (Nor was King David himself entirely remarkable for his ethical standards.)

It is even possible that my ancestry might not move in the direction of ancient Israel at all.

About A.D. 600, a Turkish tribe, the Khazars, lived in what is now southern Russia. They established an empire that reached its peak about A.D. 750, stretching from the Caspian Sea to the Carpathian Mountains east and west, and from the Black Sea to what is now the Moscow region north and south. About that time, the Khazars adopted

Judaism as the state religion, a most unusual state of affairs. It was the only time, I think, it has ever happened in European history, that any nation voluntarily adopted Judaism. Undoubtedly, it was a politically inspired move designed to keep the Khazars from falling under the influence of either the Byzantine Christians or the Arab Moslems, who were busily engaged in the first part of their centuries-long duel.

About 900, the Khazar Empire went into decline and it was finally destroyed by the incursions of new nomadic tribes, the Pechenegs, from the east, and by attacks of the Russians from the north. After 965, the Khazars were through as an organized power, but Judaism may have remained, and it may well be that many East European Jews are descended from Khazars and from those peoples they ruled rather than from the ancient people of Israel. And it may be that I am one of the Khazar-descended Jews.

Who knows? And who cares?

It may further be that if one goes rooting among one's ancestors and is not careful to pick out only those one wants to speak of, one can find oneself to be a thoroughgoing mongrel.

My mother looked like a typical Russian peasant woman. I've hardly ever seen a small Slavic woman of the lower classes who didn't remind me, more or less, of my mother. In fact, so much did my mother look Russian that, on occasion, when she would announce to some Russian official that she was Jewish (she would have been in trouble if she had tried to deny it and was caught doing so), she had to produce her passport to prove it—though why anyone in Russia at that time should try to fake Jewishness passes my understanding. It would be like someone in the old South claiming to be a black when he wasn't.

My mother had blue eyes, and in her youth, light hair. Though my father was brown-eyed and brown-haired, there must have been a recessive blue-eyed gene there too, for my brother, my sister, and I all have blue eyes. My hair was brown, but both my brother and sister had reddish hair. My brother's daughter has bright red hair and blue eyes; my own daughter has blond hair and blue eyes. What's more, I've got high Slavic cheekbones.

Where did all this come from? Surely not from any Mediterranean people, or from any Turkish people either. It had to be of Slavic origin and Scandinavian beyond that—plus a bit of Mongol to account for my B-type blood.

And where did the Slavs, Scandinavians, and Mongols come into it? I'm sure that my father would have rigorously denied any Gentile intrusion, either legal or illegal, into the family tree; at least he would have denied it after he regained the breath he had lost in the horror of hearing such a suggestion. So I never suggested it.

I'll just make do with what my father told me and make no attempt to go beyond that.

2

The early Judah, together with his family and his descendants (said my father), "were dealers in rye that is planted in our part of Russia in the fall. The seeds are kept warm under a layer of deep snow in the winter, and this kind of rye is called *azimy khleb*." (In English I think this means "winter grain.")

Jews in those days were known, in biblical fashion, by patronymics —that is, as so-and-so, the son of so-and-so. I myself would be Isaac, son of Judah, according to this system or, in Hebrew (transliterated), I would be Yitzkhak ben-Yehudah.

This is an inefficient system of naming people unless you live in a small and stable tribe, and as governments and economies become more complex, something must be done that makes it easier to alphabetize and classify. Therefore, in one country after another, Jews were forced to accept last names Gentile fashion (as Gentiles once had to do, for names like Thomas Johnson betray an original patronymic system there, too).

Forced to accept last names, there was a tendency to make up pretty or flattering ones, and usually in German, since in the Jewish Pale, Germans were among the landowning aristocrats, and the Jews themselves spoke a medieval German dialect—Yiddish. Thus there would be Goldstein (gold stone) or Goldberg (gold mountain) or Rosenbaum (rose tree) or Finkelstein (diamond) or Bernstein (amber) and so on.

Of course, human nature and human bigotry being what it is, these beautiful names in no way beautified a despised people. Rather the people denatured the names, which became "Jewish" and therefore objects of ridicule.

In other cases, last names were chosen from occupations. This has happened everywhere. In English, we have Smith and Miller as obvious examples. The early Judah came to be known as Azimy, from the grain he dealt in. This is clearly a derivative of the word *zimy*, which is Russian for "to winter." I suppose this family name would be roughly equivalent to "wintering" in English.

At some later time, someone in the family felt that Azimy was too un-Russian a name and therefore lacked appeal. The Russian patronymic ending "-ov" was therefore tacked on. ("Ivanov" is the Russian equivalent of "Johnson," "Petrov" of "Peterson," and so on.) Consequently, the name became "Azimov." The nearest English equivalent would be "Winterson."

The name, of course, was spelled in the Cyrillic alphabet used in Russia, and looked like this—АЗИМОВ. In Yiddish, which used the Hebrew alphabet, the name looked like this (reading from right to left) in the printed letters אזימאוו and like this in the cursive script ||ICN'ƆIC

When my father came to the United States, however, he had a problem on his hands. For the immigration authorities, he had to spell his name in English, and though he was perfectly at home with the Cyrillic and Hebrew alphabets, the Latin alphabet, in which English is written, was strange to him.

He managed to make do with his memory of signs and inscriptions on imported objects, but made one mistake. A product that was familiar in many Russian households was a sewing machine, and the sewing machines were largely imported from the United States. They were, in fact, Singer Sewing Machines (named, as it happens, for Isaac Merritt Singer, one of the early manufacturers of the sewing machine).

The word "Singer," with the usual unvoiced *s* sound, meant nothing in Yiddish. The word *zinger*, however, is Yiddish for "singer" and that made sense. This was particularly so since the German *s* is pronounced like the English *z*, and if any lower- or middle-class Russian did have acquaintance with the Latin alphabet, it was almost always in connection with German.

Consequently, the Singer Sewing Machine was universally pronounced Zinger among the Russian Jews, and my father was quite certain that *s* was the Latin alphabet way of signifying the *z* sound. He therefore spelled the family name "Asimov" and it stayed so. The name is *pronounced* as though it were spelled with a *z*, but it is spelled with an *s*, and I am absurdly offended when the *z* is put in.

I tell myself that this is so because recognition value is important for me. People have to tell at a glance that a book is by me, and if my name is spelled in more than one way it will create confusion, hurt sales, and help impoverish me. But that's nonsense. I just want my name to be what I'm used to its being, that's all.

In Russian and in Yiddish, the name has always been pronounced with the accent on the second syllable, with the initial *a* like the *a* in "father," and the final *v* halfway to an *f*. It is pronounced "ah-ZEE-muf." In English, however, the accent shifted to the first syllable and it became "AZ-ih-mov."

I have always had trouble with the name. It is an indescribably simple one. Six letters; three vowels and consonants in alternation; all the vowels short; the *s* pronounced like a *z*. Nevertheless, when I was in the Army and we were subjected to a company roll call and some new sergeant was trying to bend his limited literacy to the task, I could only wait in silent martyrdom.

There would seem no name this valiant soldier would not tackle, no matter how long and how rich in consonants. If there were a soldier named Wrziewyloczszky, he would plunge headlong into it without hesitation and come out the other side with broken teeth but with some version of the name clutched between them.

Then he would come to a name that even he dared not tackle and there would be a simple silence. After I waited three seconds to make sure it *was* a silence, I called out "Here!" I was never wrong. It was always my name that defeated the unconquerable and smashed the invulnerable.

To this day, I get postcards asking me how to pronounce my name, with details concerning the Homeric wagers being made on various alternatives. Usually I say something like this:

"There are three very simple English words: "Has," "him" and "of." Put them together like this—'has-him-of'—and say it in the ordinary fashion. Now leave out the two *h*'s and say it again and you have Asimov."

Really! What the heck is the difficulty?

3

Petrovichi was what was called a *shtetl*, a little town in which a Jewish community was concentrated. It was ingrown and there were a number of Asimovs in it. I presume, in fact, that any Asimov in the United States probably had an ancestor who came from Petrovichi, and who is therefore some distant cousin of mine.

The Asimov could be spelled differently, it could be Azimov, Asimow, Azimow, Asimoff, Azimoff. The final *w* is simply the German way of transliterating the Russain *v* sound, since the German *w* is pronounced *v*. In the United States, nevertheless, the final *ow* gets to be pronounced as in the word "how," thus distorting the name considerably.

Not very many years ago, I found that not all Asimovs are of the Petrovichi line—or, indeed, are even Jewish.

One of the constituent republics of the U.S.S.R. is the Uzbek S.S.R., in central Asia, south and southeast of the Aral Sea. Its capital is Tashkent, a modern city of one and a third million, but its most famous city is Samarkand, which, six centuries ago, was the capital of the empire of the great conqueror Tamerlane. The Uzbeks, who make up two thirds of the population of the republic, are Moslem in religion.

As it happens, the family to which Muhammad belonged are the Hashimites, and I wouldn't be surprised if among some groups of Moslems, the variant name Asim was, for that reason, popular. Attach the Russian patronymic to it and it becomes Asimov. Apparently this is not an uncommon name in the Uzbek S.S.R.

Now that my name has become known in the U.S.S.R. through my writing, there seem to be Uzbeks who think that I am of Uzbek origin, and, in fact, I met one traveler who told me that he was solemnly assured by an Uzbek that the American writer, Isaac Asimov, was a brother of someone who lived in his town. Well, it's very flattering to be claimed in this fashion, but it isn't so. I'm a Petrovichi Asimov and not an Uzbek Asimov.

4

According to my father, the early Judah Asimov "was one of the great scholars."

There is no reason I shouldn't believe this, for there is nothing inherently impossible in his being a great scholar. I might even argue that since I myself can be considered a great scholar,[1] it seems only reasonable to suppose that I came by it honestly and inherited my brains from a line of scholars.

However, I have heard many Jewish people talk about their ancestors in eastern Europe, and one and all of them (no exceptions, regardless of their present apparent IQ) were descended from a long and unbroken line of great scholars.

I'm sorry, but I can't believe it. I look around now and see among Jews I know a fair share of klutzes and shlemiels, and I can't believe that this is the first generation in which they have appeared.

The only conclusion I can come to is that it is all a pious fraud. The Jews of eastern Europe can't lay claim to dukes and earls in their ancestry and can only find impoverished and oppressed people, eking out a living under the forever-threatening fall of the ax. Since one needs *some* pride, the ancestors become scholars.

So the early Judah Asimov is reported to have been a scholar, and,

---

[1] Whenever I say something like this, some people seem to be shocked and they call me "conceited." No one, however, not even these people, calls me a liar.

who knows, it is possible he may have been. According to my father, the early Judah Asimov accumulated some money, left his family, and became the equivalent of an itinerant preacher, traveling to those various towns he could reach on foot in order "to tell the Jewish people that they should mend their ways, and become more pious."

That is all my father knew about my great-great-great-grandfather.

5

Judah Asimov had two sons. He may have had other children as well, but my father knew of only those two. The elder was Abraham Ber and the younger Moses Jacob. It was Abraham Ber who was my father's great-grandfather and therefore my great-great-grandfather.

Abraham Ber must have lived to a good old age, for he lived long enough to see the birth of his great-grandson, my father.

My father says, "He died when I was about three years old, and I remember that somebody brought me to his bed that he might bless me, and he gave me some kind of a red jelly, but I cannot visualize his face." (That means that Abraham Ber must have died about 1899).

My father goes on: "The stories I heard about him were that he was a natural-born smart man, and that he was a great scholar. That goes without saying." (Of course!) My father also says, "Like his predecessors, he was a dealer in rye and other products, and he was well known in town as a great and charitable man."

Charity is another great attribute, quite rivaling scholarship. This was a time when governments did not consider themselves responsible for the welfare of their subjects—and if the Tsarist government did, it would certainly draw the line at Jews. Therefore, impoverished Jews had no recourse but the charity of those other Jews who were better off.

Abraham Ber Asimov had twelve children by his first wife. The first eleven died in infancy, and only the twelfth survived. It was this twelfth, named Mendel, who was my father's grandfather, and my great-grandfather.

My father says, "Imagine how much my grandfather meant to him," meaning Abraham Ber.

I can imagine it. Abraham Ber must have spent perhaps fifteen years, mourning one child after another, giving up hope of ever having one as comfort in his old age, and then having little Mendel—and waiting for him to die, and with each year of the child's survival becoming more and more hopeful and yet afraid to hope, lest even now the boy be snatched away.

My father, however, does not speak of the boy's mother, who had to go through twelve pregnancies and twelve childbirths in order to salvage one child. But then, women, until quite recently, were given no mind in this sort of thing. Thus my father, in reciting the names of his ancestors, speaks only of the male ancestors. He gives no female names, not even that of his own mother.

Then again, when I was young, my father, who loved to tell me stories and parables designed to improve my mind and spirit, would occasionally expound on a biblical verse. (He knew the Bible by heart—for *he* was a very great scholar, too, in the *shtetl* sense—but in Hebrew, of course.) He would recite the verse in Hebrew, then translate it into English—or Yiddish, if he couldn't think of an English word—which was all right, since I am bilingual and speak and understand both English and Yiddish with equal ease.

One time, I remember, he chose a verse which, in later life, I discovered to be Proverbs 10:1, which goes, in the King James Version: "A wise son maketh a glad father; but a foolish son is the heaviness of his mother."

Having translated it, my father then said, with a Talmudic singsong to his voice, "*Why*, if the wise son makes his father glad, does a foolish son make his mother unhappy, and not his father? The answer is that if the son is wise, the father keeps him by himself, but if the son is foolish, he sends him to his mother and doesn't bother with him."

I thought about that, being about ten at the time, and then I said, "Isn't that unfair, Pappa? Why should the mother get him only if he's bad? Why shouldn't they both have him, either way?"

My father had no answer at all. In his whole life, he had never heard such a heretical notion as equality between the sexes, and I think he didn't understand my point any more than if I had delivered it in Swahili.[2]

6

As for Abraham Ber's younger brother, Moses Jacob Asimov, he, too, lived into my father's lifetime. In fact, he outlived his older brother, and my father remembers him when "he was very old and half blind." He, too, was a scholar, of course, and for many years he was a cantor at the town synagogue.

"When I remember him," said my father, "he was already on a

[2] The proper interpretation of the verse, with its father/mother antithesis, lies in the fact that the essence of Hebrew poetry lay in parallelism of statement, but I didn't know enough at ten to be able to explain this to my father and he would have laughed at me, anyway, if I had tried.

pension of ten rubles a year, but if they allowed him, he would still perform as a cantor. He couldn't believe that anyone could perform better than he could."

In fact, it must be that my father told me about this great-granduncle of his, for I distinctly remember him telling me, when I was young, of a very old blind man who had once been a cantor and who continued to insist on singing on appropriate occasions even though his voice had altogether decayed. He would sing in his quavering, cracked voice, and out of respect for his age, no one would stop him, even though the sound was horrible enough to scrape the wallpaper off the walls.

One time, though, Gentiles were present, and the embarrassment then became too keen. Someone approached the old man and said, "Moses Jacob, please stop. There are Gentiles present and it is not fitting."

Whereupon Moses Jacob turned his old blind eyes this way and that and said, "Gentiles? Gentiles? I see no Gentiles," and kept on singing.

To me this is an important story for two reasons. First, it indicates that the ability to sing may be an inherited trait among the Asimovs. At least I remember that my father constantly sang in cantor style (lots of quavers and grace notes in an intensely minor mode) and did it pretty well.

And I can sing pretty well myself, either baritone or tenor, depending on how I feel. I like to sing tenor better, because I associate the tenor's melting notes with the juvenile lead in the movies and he's the one who always gets the girl. Baritone does sound more manly, I admit, and perhaps I do that better.

What really gives me pause about the story, however, is that I fully intend to continue writing as long as I live, and I wonder if I, like my great-great-granduncle, Moses Jacob, will continue to do so long after senility has deprived me of any writing ability, under the delusion that I can still do it. I have visions of my editors drawing straws to see who gets to tell me that I'm embarrassing the Gentiles.

Well, what the heck! Great-great-granduncle didn't listen, and I won't, either.

7

My father dismisses Moses Jacob's progeny very briefly. He says, "He had two daughters and so no Asimov was born of him." Having two daughters, apparently, is like having two horses. You don't count them.

Abraham Ber Asimov, who had twelve children and one survivor, by his first wife, was finally a widower. He married a second time and had a son named Judah, the second in the family of that name. My father says, in patent disapproval, "He was not only not a scholar, but he was a very average man."

This one, you see, my father saw with his own eyes. It is easier to be a scholar if there is an insulating period of decades between the man who is the subject of the description and the man who is doing the describing.

"In my time," said my father, "he married and had a daughter. While I was in the United States I heard that she became a physician, but I do not know anything more about her."

After the Revolution, you see, women could be educated and could even enter the professions. Still, she was only a woman and my father clearly wasn't interested.

In any case, it was Mendel Asimov, the only surviving son of Abraham Ber by his first wife, and my father's grandfather, who was the person on whom the Asimov stock was to depend.

My father says of Mendel, "He was not a scholar. He was not ignorant in the reading of Hebrew and in praying, but he did not study the Talmud." In other words, in American terms, he went to high school, but he never went to college. However, says my father, "What he missed in his studies, he made up in his cleverness."

Mendel's first-born was Aaron Menahem Asimov. He must have been born about 1865 or so. He was my father's father, and therefore my grandfather.

3

My Parents

1

Aaron's first-born was a girl, who died an infant. His second child, born after the death of the girl, was my father Judah, the third of that name[1] in the family.

My father was born on December 21, 1896. That sounds precise, but I wouldn't swear to the exact date. In the first place, the Russian Government didn't bother to keep birth records in those days, except perhaps in the important cities. If my family itself kept the record, they kept it according to the Jewish calendar, which is a lunar calendar, and the dates of which are not easy to match with the ordinary calendars of the Christian world.

Then, too, the Russians at the time of my father's birth (and of mine, for that matter) used the Julian calendar, which differed by thirteen days from the Gregorian calendar used by the West, and this introduces another complication.

In any case, when my father went to the United States, he had to produce documentary evidence of birth and it had to have a birthdate on it according to some European calendar. He got the birth certificate, and the day was according to the best of his memory under pressure. It seems to me it could have been off by a month or so in either direction, but what's the difference? The exact day would matter only to an astrologer and I wouldn't give an astrologer the time of day.

Though it means nothing, Joseph Stalin was also born on December 21, but in 1879. My father, therefore, assuming his birthdate is correct, was born on the day Stalin turned seventeen.

2

My father, it appears, was the apple of the eye of his grandfather Mendel. My father was a bright and precocious boy and, as he said, "I was so loved by him that he would, without giving it a moment's thought, have given his life for me or killed somebody for me."

[1] When my father came to the United States, the transliteration of his name dropped the final "h" in Judah. His official papers made him Juda, and on numerous occasions he had to sign himself in that fashion. That didn't seem to bother him, and in later years everyone called him Jack anyway.

My father entered Hebrew school at the age of five. There were ten boys at school (no girls, of course), and my father remained there till he was sixteen. Afterward, he received advanced instruction in the Talmud from the rabbi. That was the extent of his formal education.

My father, in his childhood, had a Gentile girl of about twelve or thirteen who took care of him. She had been in the house for four years, spoke Yiddish like a Jew, and even learned all the prayers in perfect Hebrew so she could supervise young Judah at his homework.

Once when my father was eight, the young girl came to Hebrew school to bring him his lunch and found my father crying. She rushed back with the story, not to his father, Aaron, but to his grandfather, Mendel, figuring that she could count on old Granddad for the heavy artillery.

Off rushed Mendel to school, convinced that the rabbi, having been displeased by some failure in scholarship on the part of young Judah, had thereupon struck him. This was a common action on the part of the rabbis, who, being instructed by the Bible not to spare the rod, never did.

Once Mendel reached the school, he did not bother to find out the facts of the case. These he considered irrelevant. What counted was that the rabbi had struck his grandson and that the rabbi must therefore be dismembered. The only thing that saved the rabbi was my father's top-of-the-voice screaming that it hadn't been the rabbi; the rabbi had intervened to save him; it had been another boy, taller, older, and stronger, who had been annoyed that little Judah had known an answer he didn't know, and who had therefore thoughtfully chastened him with his fist in order to teach him respect.

Slowly, Mendel understood, but he was not going to let the rabbi off easily. He explained to the rabbi very distinctly that if *anyone* struck young Judah while said young Judah was under his, the rabbi's care, the rabbi would be held responsible.

Thinking about that story, it occurs to me that my father must have deserved the beating he got. My father doesn't say anything that would lead me to think that *he* thought so, but I remember my father when he was much older than eight, and he had the most offensive way of being right. Worse that that, he acted offensively right, even when he was wrong. It would never occur to him at any time in his life to save another person's face, or to let some small error go if it were unimportant.

No, sir, however small someone's error might be, or even if the error were only imaginary and it was my father who was wrong, he would charge in immediately with all his troops, with all machine guns blazing, and with all his planes circling overhead.

Following in my father's footsteps, of course, I was rather like that when I was young and you can bet that many people found it very difficult to be fond of me. However, I changed as I grew older (or, at least, I like to think I did).

At another time, my father, being eleven by then, and having been scolded by his father, went straight to his grandfather and reported the incident. Whereupon Mendel came to Aaron and dressed him down without inquiring into the rights and wrongs of the case. My father found himself very embarrassed at this. He found he couldn't stand having his father scolded and he made up his mind never to carry tales to his grandfather again—and he never did.

In 1916, Mendel (who, by then, must have been in his seventies) fell sick at a time when my father, then nineteen years old, was in Borisoglebsk on some business matter. It was 450 miles southeast of Petrovichi. He received a telegram to return immediately, but by the time he reached Petrovichi, his grandfather was dead.

My father always schooled himself never to show emotion, but he wrote me of this more than fifty years after the event and, in his careful understatement, I can still hear his sorrow. He says, "I could not forgive them that they had not called me home sooner, but I was told that when he first became sick they hoped for a quick recovery, and then he went so rapidly that under no circumstance would I have been able to reach him while he was still alive—and in this way my beloved grandfather was taken from us, and I was not around to see him at his death."

3

As for my father's mother (my grandmother), my father says, "She came from a family in which her mother counted for more than her father. Her father was a very simple man but a very honest and pious one. My grandmother, his wife, lived to a great old age, passing, I believe, the hundred mark. She had eight children, three girls and five boys, with my mother the oldest."

Nowhere, however, does my father tell me his mother's name. I learned it from another source. It was Anna Chaya.

My father was one of six children who survived infancy, he being the oldest. I know of three younger sons, since he talked of them occasionally in my younger years. They were Ephraim, Samuel, and, the youngest, Abraham Ber. The youngest had something wrong with one of his legs apparently.

My grandfather, Aaron, never raised his hand to any of his children, but only reasoned with them, according to my father. I can well believe this, for my father never raised his hand to his children that I could remember, but only reasoned with us.[2]

However, that didn't make life so entirely wonderful, because my mother, who was a terrible-tempered woman, did not follow the same philosophy my father did. She raised her hand to me any time she felt she needed a little exercise and then she reasoned with me, in addition, and at the top of her voice, for hours at a time.

In doing so, she made use of an extensive Yiddish vocabulary of derogatory terms, which were colorful and expressive and, for the most part, incomprehensible to me. I must admit that I liked the sounds, which were full of Russian gutturals and sibilants, and I repeated some of them once in front of my father when I was annoyed.

My father, terribly shocked (for he *never* used bad language), said, "Isaac, where did you hear such terrible words?"

I said, "Mamma says it all the time."

My father, doubly shocked, said, "Mamma *never* says any such words." I know he believed it, because he was such a terrible liar that he had long since given up trying to lie—yet when my mother used those words, my father *must* have heard them, for everyone for blocks around did.

Anyway, at one time, my grandfather *did* strike my father, full in the face with his open hand, and at a time when my father was already a grown youth of eighteen. It's a long, complicated story, which ended with my grandfather Aaron and a fellow townsman with whom he was having a dispute, standing before the town rabbi, who was, of course, the Supreme Court of Petrovichi in his single person. My father was an observer.

The rabbi's decision went against my grandfather, and my father, outraged, denounced the decision. Whereupon my grandfather struck him for being disrespectful to the rabbi, saying, "The decision is made and we must not question it."

Fortunately, I never had the opportunity to commit this kind of *lèse-majesté*, so that my father was never compelled to strike me on principle.

My grandfather was, apparently, quite well-to-do by the standards of Petrovichi. He dealt in all kinds of grain, particularly buckwheat, owned a mill that was in constant operation, owned horses and cows, and passed for a rich man. When my father was still quite a young boy, not long after he started Hebrew school (at the age of five), he began to be given little jobs to do in connection with the family business.

[2] For my part, a moderately hard blow would have been preferable to some of the reasoning I got, because it would have been over much more quickly.

It was only natural. He would someday inherit the business, and the earlier he began to learn its ins and outs, the more proficient he would be and the easier his life would be.

It seemed normal to my father, then, that when I was a little boy, I be put to work in what was then our new family business. However, it was not something I planned to inherit, and I never really threw myself into it wholeheartedly.

4

My mother, whom I have already mentioned, was named Anna Rachel, and her maiden name was Berman. She was born (officially, but give or take a little) on September 5, 1895, and she was roughly a year older than my father.

She was a small woman, about four feet, ten inches in height. My father was five feet, nine inches in height—average height, you see, though when I was young, I thought he was a tall man, and when the time came that I discovered he was not six feet tall, I was rather crushed.

The children of the family did not particularly outdo these hereditary starting points. I grew to be just my father's height, five feet nine inches, and my brother is perhaps half an inch shorter. My sister is five feet even.

My mother's father, my maternal grandfather, was, according to my father, "a great scholar in Talmud, even among the many great scholars that our home town had. Petrovichi was known through the whole area surrounding our town for its great scholars, but even so, your mother's father was spoken of with great reverence. It was enough for someone in a scholastic agrument over a certain point of doctrine to mention that your mother's father explained it this way or that—and that would end the argument at once."

My mother's father was Isaac Berman, and I was named for him.

Isaac Berman was married twice. By his first marriage, he had a number of children of whom my father named only three: David, Mordecai, and Joseph. Mordecai died young.

Joseph was the first member of either my father's or mother's family to go to the United States. I do not know in what year exactly he came to the United States, but it must have been before World War I.

When Isaac Berman's first wife died, he married a second time to a woman named Tamara, and it was she who was my mother's mother.

My father said about her, "She was like any other Jewish woman of that time. She was not educated, because Jewish education was for men, but she was very smart. In town, if they wanted to speak of some woman's cleverness, they would say, 'She's another Tamara.' "

Isaac Berman had, by his second wife, Tamara, four children in his old age. The first was a girl, my mother, Anna Rachel, and then three sons. Isaac Berman died in 1901, when my mother was six years old.

Apparently my father did not want to mention things he considered disgraceful, but from another source I learned that he was divorced before he died. "Your grandmother Tamara," I was told, "had divorced him because he didn't want to give up his learning and to occupy himself with the trivialities of her business."[3]

After Isaac Berman's divorce and death, it fell upon my mother to help with the business and to act as surrogate mother for her three younger brothers. Tamara married again, too (no one stayed unmarried in the *shtetls*) and had another set of children so that my mother had two sets of half siblings, one by her father's first wife and the other by her mother's second husband, as well as full siblings of her own.

My mother's stepfather owned what we would call a general store, and my mother, together with a younger half sister, along with a Gentile girl employee, eventually ran the store. According to my father's admiring account, my mother did so with great efficiency and intelligence, with a smile for everyone, and a quick wit, so that she was beloved by all—at least so my father says, but he was always very prejudiced on my mother's behalf.

But that was my mother's fate in life. Coming to the United States meant for her only a shift in counters. For nearly all her life, her world was bounded by customers and merchandise and by profits made up of accumulating pennies.

5

However things might have been for Jews in other parts of Russia, things apparently went reasonably well in Petrovichi—at least according to my father's gold-misted memories of a half century later. He said, "When I think of Petrovichi, I recall the inhabitants to have been always happy. I can't say that we had very rich people there, but among the more wealthy ones were my father and my mother-in-law. We never experienced pogroms, or anything like that."

It's not surprising that, under those conditions, my father failed to be terribly anti-Russian after he came to the United States.

[3] That strikes home, because I know quite well that I wouldn't want to give up my learning in order to occupy myself with the trivialities of any business. Fortunately, my learning turned out to be profitable as Isaac Berman's did not, so I was never in a position of having to leave it to a resentful wife to support the family.

It was even possible for Jew and Gentile to be friendly. My father said, "In the Gentile part of the town there was a boy who became very friendly with me and who was a couple of years older. In Petrovichi, there was a Church school where they taught religion and where the children were taught to sign their names and read a little. My Gentile friend used to come to me for help with his reading."

My mother and father were born on the same block in Petrovichi but on different corners. My father went to Hebrew school with my mother's younger brothers, and when he came to play with them after school, he said, "I noticed that the brothers had a sister. I was very young when I started to like to talk to her, but she used to dress up and go away with girlfriends, giving me the impression that she didn't care for me."

My mother, being a year older, undoubtedly felt annoyed at the hobbledehoyish attentions of this kid who hung about with her baby brothers. If my father was, as a youngster, what he was as an adult, he could not possibly have been a suave wooer. I visualize him as dogging my mother's footsteps to the point where she couldn't turn suddenly without falling over him. She married him in June 1918 and may well have done so as the only way of getting rid of him.

Once, I remember, my sister said to my mother, "Mamma, did you have a lot of boyfriends when you were young?"

My mother cast a ruminative eye backward into her life and said, "Let's see now. Maybe five, maybe six—and I married your father, so you can imagine what the rest were like."

As far as I know, however, my father, who fell in love with my mother at puberty, if not before, never wavered. He did not, in the time I knew him, ever look at another woman, say a flirtatious word, make an off-color remark, or in any way indicate that sex, in even its mildest form, existed for him—except, of course, in connection with my mother, since he did, somehow (but I presume in the usual fashion), have three children by her.[4]

As for my mother, she was an earthy creature. Whereas the thought of "fooling around" is inconceivable in connection with my father, I would readily believe it of my mother, if she had been given a chance—but, of course, circumstance saw to it that she never was.

I wouldn't dream of telling an off-color joke to my father. (He refused to laugh at any jokes at all, in fact, considering them foolish and

---

[4] There is no question that those children were his; the family resemblance is too strong to admit of any doubt. To this day, if I unexpectedly come across a full-length mirror in a dim light, my heart jumps because I think I am looking at my father. My brother resembles my father even more closely than I do, and I can trace some of my father's lineaments even in the face of my beautiful daughter.

undignified.) I would tell them freely to my mother and she would laugh her head off.

In any case, they remained a devoted couple throughout their entire marriage, though when I say "devoted" I merely mean inseparable. They were certainly not cooing lovebirds. I rarely heard either one utter an affectionate expression to the other. And a kiss or a squeeze in public? Never!

6

World War I, somehow, didn't seem to affect my parents. My father was not taken into the Army, which is puzzling. Since he was nearly eighteen when the war broke out, strong, and in good health, I don't see how he escaped. My father never said a word about it, and I never felt like asking him. It is possible that money changed hands and that his family bought immunity for him. I don't know this; it's just a guess on my part.

My mother used to travel to Vitebsk, about 120 miles northwest of Petrovichi, in order to buy merchandise for the store. Why Vitebsk, when Smolensk was closer, I don't know. During the war, this grew increasingly dangerous as soldiers became more common along the route and as defeat after defeat drove the government ever closer to disorganization and revolution.

On March 16, 1917, the Tsar abdicated, and Alexander Kerensky established a socialist government. It was attacked from both sides. Kerensky tried to continue the Russian role in the war, but elements among the army officers and aristocrats wanted the Tsar back, while the Bolsheviks under Lenin wanted an end to the war and the immediate communization of the nation.

In September 1917, General Lavr Kornilov decided to take the Russian capital, now called Petrograd (the Russian version of the German, St. Petersburg), and restore the Tsar. Kornilov ordered an army northward from the front, but the soldiers wanted to go home, so that his army disintegrated and the effort failed.

At just about this time, however, my mother went to Vitebsk on one of her periodic journeys, and when she returned to the train station, there was Kornilov and his army. My mother, being a small woman, with a girlish air and a quick, conversational wit, could usually manage to talk herself out of any fix by enlisting the co-operation of the men about her.

She managed to find that not all trains had been commandeered by Kornilov but that one train was actually going to Roslavl. Somehow she managed to have all the stock she had bought transferred from the train she was going to take to the train that would actually move, and she reached Roslavl with herself and her merchandise intact. My father "happened to be that day in Roslavl" with his horse and wagon, and he got her home.

That was it, though. My father laid down the law. She was to go traveling by herself no more; it was too risky. By that time, it had become understood by the whole town that they were going to marry, and that was enough to give him the right to order her around. In any case, it *was* too risky, for Russia was falling into revolutionary chaos, with the German Army moving steadily eastward and with counterrevolutionary armies (the "Whites") amusing themselves by killing helpless Jews (always safer than attacking an armed enemy), and with no one able to predict what would happen in Petrograd.

Then, in October 1917, my father fell ill with typhoid fever, and for three weeks the rest of the world receded from him.

My mother visited him every day, although my father's mother warned the young girl that there might be contagion and that she might herself fall sick. This sounds as though my grandmother was a very considerate woman, and so she might have been, but in this case, I think she was merely trying to keep my mother away. She did not approve of my mother and she did not approve of my father's infatuation. Whether this was because she felt my mother to be too small and therefore not likely to be strong enough to be a good wife and mother, or whether she was just one of those mothers who didn't want to give up her first-born son to any woman, I don't know.

In any case, my mother disregarded the warning and my father says, "I think Mamma was destined to help and work for everybody, and to worry constantly. That was how she was when she was young, and that is how it is now."

True enough. I remember her worrying. It was not just concern for others; it was a terrible fear that something had happened or would happen, and it created a dreadful prison for the children, particularly for myself, since I was the oldest and bore the brunt of it.

Any time I was leaving, I had to announce the time I would be back and then *be* back at that time, or "Mamma would worry," meaning she would go mad and drive everyone about her mad. Fortunately, I have always been timebound (or I became timebound as a result of this), and I *did* always come back when I said I would. Of course, that made it worse, since on those rare occasions when, through circumstances beyond my control, I was late, my mother was convinced I was dead. ("If Isaac says he'll be at home at five o'clock, he'll be home at five o'clock, and if it's five minutes after five o'clock, I know something happened to him.")

My younger brother and sister were never as reliable as I was in this respect, and my mother was always holding me as a mark to shoot at ("Why don't you come home when you're supposed to? Isaac always comes home. If Isaac says he'll be home at five o'clock . . .").

I hated it and I always thought that when I was finally out from under, I would throw all that stuff out the window and come and go as I pleased and everyone could just wait.

Fat chance! It was ingrained too deeply. To this day, I am on time everywhere—on the minute if I can manage it. I arrive when I say I will arrive; I return when I say I will return; and I invariably drive my nearest and dearest into fits when I am five minutes late because "You're always so on time, I thought something terrible must have happened to you."

Worse yet, I expect others to be on time and fall into a fury when they prove to be late, or, in the case of loved ones, into a panic. The fact that I'm thoroughly aware of what a pernicious effect my mother's attitude produced on me somehow doesn't prevent me from adopting the same attitude toward others.

That is why it is always a little difficult for me to laugh freely at the follies of mankind. If I look closely enough, I find I share them all.

7

In any case, while my father was sick, the October Revolution took place and the Bolsheviks took over control of the country, or as much of the country as wasn't in the hands of the Germans, the Finns, the Poles, the White Russian bands, the Allied Expeditionary forces, and local functionaries.

When my father had recovered sufficiently to be aware of his surroundings, he asked for a newspaper, and discovered to his astonishment that it was full of unfamiliar names. My mother had to explain the new revolution to him. Russia had become Soviet Russia without his knowing anything about it.

Petrovichi was taken over by a Soviet functionary. The Gentile boy, whom my father had once helped learn to read, had left town as a teen-ager, and he now returned as commissar. My father said, "When we met we became friendly again, just as though we had never parted. He was now a big shot, but I influenced him."

It was a time of inflation, of rising prices and declining food stocks, but my father managed to organize the Petrovichi inhabitants into a

co-operative attack on the problem. He set up an organization for buying and distributing food and, in doing so, he kept constantly falling
afoul of the local authorities, who saw in it the attempted establishment of a private business which, in the early years of the Bolshevik
Revolution, was strictly forbidden.

My father spent much of his time, therefore, having to prove that
it was indeed a community endeavor and that the only money he drew
out of it was for operating expenses. He also had to explain why Gentiles were not involved and succeeded in demonstrating that they had
been invited to join but had refused to do so. And because he was
clearly engaged in useful work, he was not called into the Red Army,
and he continued to run the co-operative for five years.

My father also helped organize a library in the town and he and
my mother took part in amateur theatricals. Apparently my mother had
unexpected talent in this direction. According to my father: "Mamma
learned her lines very easily. She did not depend on the prompter, who
used to read in a low voice to keep the actors from making mistakes.
Mamma did not need anybody's help. She learned the lines and did not
make any mistakes. She was the best."

My father, who was an excellent reader[5] and who would read
books aloud as part of his library work for those whose reading ability
was limited, also took part in the plays but was, apparently, not as
proficient as my mother at it.

According to my father, he and my mother "played as amateurs in
more than ten plays and we were so good that they used to come to
see us play from all the surrounding villages and towns."

There's no sign of anyone in my family having been a writer,
though perhaps they might have been if the opportunity had come
their way, but obviously both parents were used to being on the stage
and must have had some talent for it.

I myself have never acted on the stage, but I do make a substantial
part of my living as an after-dinner speaker, and I'm very good at it.[6]
Apparently I come by it honestly.

My father says that toward the end she was acting at a time when
she was "in the seventh month with a baby and nobody could have told
that she was pregnant at that time."

That meant she was acting in the fall of 1919, for the baby she was
carrying was I. That nobody could tell she was pregnant was probably

[5] I can vouch for my father's ability in this respect, for he would, on rare occasions,
recite, from memory, short stories of Sholem Aleichem (in Yiddish, of course), and
it was always delightful for me to listen to him.
[6] Once again, this may be conceit, but it is not a lie.

true enough, for I was a very undersized baby. (My father's mother very probably said, "I told you so.")

When the time came for my mother to bear her first-born, it happened that there was no doctor in Petrovichi. In general, in the small *shtetls*, there would be no doctor, and sickness meant a visit to the nearest city, or (at great expense) to bring a doctor to the *shtetl*— whereupon everyone in the *shtetl* would bring to the doctor all the illnesses they had been saving up for him.

In 1915, my father had arranged to have a real doctor come to Petrovichi, and had arranged to have an apartment for him. This was a Dr. Gugel, "a real doctor for the first time in our town," my father said. After the revolution, however, a hospital was opened in the region, but not in Petrovichi itself, and Dr. Gugel went off to the hospital, leaving Petrovichi without a doctor again.

4

My Infancy

1

When my mother went into labor, there was no one to help her, therefore, but a midwife, and the process took three days and two nights, during much of which time she walked the floor, leaning on my father. The result of all that was myself, and I was named Isaac after my mother's dead father. (A Jewish child is, by tradition, named after a dead relative.)

The date of my birth, as I celebrate it, was January 2, 1920. It could not have been later than that. It might, however, have been earlier. Allowing for the uncertainties of the times, of the lack of records, of the Jewish and Julian calendars, it might have been as early as October 4, 1919. There is, however, no way of finding out. My parents were always uncertain and it really doesn't matter.

I celebrate January 2, 1920, so let it be.

My mother was twenty-four when I was born and my father was twenty-three. I weighed 4½ pounds at birth. As my father says, I was "a tiny baby, but a live one, with open eyes and working hands, closing and opening constantly. You were a very quiet baby who cried very little."

They must have been pretty uncertain as to whether I would make it, however. Babies who died in their first year were very common in that place and at that time. Although, in the Orthodox Jewish tradition, circumcision should take place eight days after birth, the rite did not take place in my case until five weeks after birth—about February 7, 1920, if my birthdate is correct.

According to my father's golden memories, I was "the healthiest possible" baby for two years and then I got double pneumonia. That must have been toward the end of 1921.

The treatment consisted largely of "cups"—a device in which a small glass cup was dampened with alcohol and a small piece of lighted paper was placed inside. The cup was then upended and placed on the body. The paper went out almost at once, but not before consuming enough of the oxygen in the cup and heating the air enough to create a partial vacuum as it cooled. The skin was drawn into the cup, and surface circulation was in this way encouraged.

Whenever the encouragement of such surface circulation helped conditions, cups were helpful. Otherwise, their only value was in that they encouraged the patient and those watching around the bedside into feeling that something was being done. On the whole, though, such treatment is largely useless, and it went the way of that other great specific of a half century ago, the mustard plaster.[1]

I was also treated by being wrapped up in a complicated way to encourage sweating. Finally, after seven days and nights, during which my parents worked over me in relays without stopping, the crisis was reached and passed, and I recovered.

In later years, my mother told me about the incident with what may have been a number of dramatic additions. She told me, for instance, that there had been an epidemic of pneumonia in town and that seventeen infants had fallen ill and that sixteen had died. I, apparently, was the only survivor.

She told me that the doctor had given me up and said that I would die and that my mother must accommodate herself to this fact. My mother further told me that *her* mother had told her not to concern herself about the matter—it was only a baby and there would be others.

I was, however, my mother's only child at that time and she had gone through a bad time to have me, and was rather fond of me and wouldn't give me up. So she sent her mother away and never forgave her for characterizing me as "only a baby" (and indeed I never heard my mother say a kind or loving word about her mother). She also sent the doctor away and then (she says) she held me in her arms without ever letting go until I had recovered.

2

I have only one memory of this early period of my life. It is the vague impression of a book. I recall sitting in a chair, turning the pages of a book, and loving it. Then I seem to recall wanting the book again, and looking about for it vaguely, but not finding it and wondering where it was.

Years later, I told this to my mother in an effort to place the memory and she said, "I remember the book. You were two years old at the time and you loved it."

I said, "But where did it go? I remember turning the pages and then I couldn't find it."

[1] Even so, when I was a little boy of five or six, here in the United States, I witnessed my mother being treated with cups. It was quite frightening, for after the cups were taken off, the skin on my mother's back was covered with puffy round red marks.

"Sure," she said, "because every page you turned you tore out."

From this I deduce that when infants are destructive, they don't mean to be.

My father tells a story which, I believe, refers to this same book. He says that near the house we lived in "was a single house where two old maids lived. Mamma used to visit them when she was in her teens and once they presented her a book containing pictures of all kinds of animals and birds from different lands, with descriptions under each picture. Mamma gave the book to you to play with and read to you the names of the birds and the animals. After a while you could open any page and little Isaac could name them all, and not by reading, because he had not yet learned to read."

Of course, I had to say the names in Russian, I suppose, and I daresay I could speak some Russian in those days, but nothing lingers. My parents spoke Yiddish to each other in the United States and I picked that up and I can still speak and understand it virtually as well as English. Furthermore, I am bilingual in the sense that I understand Yiddish directly and don't have to translate it in my mind in order to understand it—or, for that matter, to speak it. And I never confuse the two languages, either. I can shift from one to the other, but always deliberately, and never accidentally. I presume this is true for other bilingual, or multilingual, people.

My parents did not speak Russian to each other, unfortunately, although they could easily have done so, for they could each speak Russian fluently. They did not choose to. Had they done so, I would have learned Russian and that would have been an infinitely more practical language to have in my repertoire than Yiddish is.

They were, however, anxious to have me learn English, and I arrived in the United States young enough to make English my native language, and an unaccented one (if we don't count Brooklynese as an accent). On the whole, I am satisfied. Of all the languages in the world English is (in my opinion) the best, the richest, literarily the greatest, the most useful. If I had to have one language, it is English I would want, and if Russian would have in any way interfered with my total use of the English language as a tool, then it is well lost.

Yet how I wish I could speak a little Russian, too.

But what happened to the book of my childhood about birds and animals that I loved so much and that was my one memory of my years in Russia?

"We could not take the book with us," said my father, "when we left for the United States because nothing of the book was left but shreds of paper. But what could you do to a baby you love so much?"

So he didn't hit me for tearing up the book.

3

There are other passages from my Russian years that I *don't* remember.

My father says, "We were very happy with our new baby. When you were six months old, on a Saturday afternoon, a whole lot of our friends walked out to the forest about two miles from the town. Of course, Mamma and I were among them, and all the way there I carried you and danced with you, holding you up high in the palm of my hand. You were the only baby among us."

That must have been rather a high point in my father's memory of young married happiness, for I remember him on occasion saying to my mother, "You remember, dear, the day in the forest?"

Heaven only knows what they did there. I never had the nerve to ask, but I can rely on my father's stern morality and on the general prudishness of Orthodox Judaism. It was *not* the carrying out of some fertility rite.

I must say that when my father said that to my mother and imitated that happy day with his hand held high, I did not appreciate it. In fact, I can't understand how my mother could have allowed him to do that. What if he had dropped me?

Then there's the time I fell into the pond behind the house (or so my mother tells me). I toppled off a windowsill, apparently, and my mother described with great and impossible dramatics the manner in which she rescued me from imminent drowning.

Then, too, I seem to recall being handed by my father to some strange woman, once. This must have been in Russia, for I was unable to explain what was bothering me and therefore was at a stage where I could not talk much—so this must be another Russian memory after all.

My father was holding something which, as I look back on it, must have been the harness, or part of the harness of a horse, so I suppose he had to go somewhere (presumably with my mother) and was leaving me with some baby-sitter.

I objected and I remember crying strenuously while the strange woman (who might have been a grandmother or an aunt, perhaps) kept me clutched to her ample bosom and took me off somewhere. The point is that I remember my emotions exactly. I was not frightened, I was not angry. I was merely trying to say, "I want to be with my father. Can I be with my father?"

Since I didn't know how to say that I made the only sound I knew how to make and wailed. The memory of that soothed me a bit when I had wailing children of my own and encouraged me to take the wailing as a mere comment.

4

On June 17, 1922, my mother gave birth to my sister, who was named Manya. When she reached the age of discretion, she decided on Marcia, which is now her name. In this book, I will refer to her only as Marcia, in accordance with her wishes.

5

Leaving the Soviet Union

1

It might well have been that my parents, my sister and I, along with unborn siblings might have settled down to live in the U.S.S.R. the rest of our days. By 1922, the nation was at peace. Both war and civil war were over; the days of Tsarist pogroms were over as well.

My father showed no signs of wanting to be a government functionary and was content to run co-operative ventures in Petrovichi and would probably have continued to do so. He and my mother were undoubtedly clever enough and flexible enough to avoid undue trouble and might well have escaped the danger that came as a result of the fall of Trotzky and of the purges of the 1930s.

I, myself, would undoubtedly have gone to school there and have done well. I would surely have managed to obtain a university education and would have tried my hand at writing. I have no doubt that in the end I would have proved able to turn out publishable material. I might well have ended as a science-fiction writer in the U.S.S.R.

However, in June 1941, the Nazis would have invaded the Soviet Union. I would have been twenty-one at the time and I imagine the chances would have been enormously good that I would have joined the Army, either as a volunteer or as a draftee. And the chances would also have been good that I would have died in the early months of the war or, what was worse, been taken prisoner, and have died slowly rather than quickly.

That it didn't come to that was the result of circumstance, and there was nothing terribly dramatic about it.[1]

The key was Joseph Berman, my mother's older half brother, the son of Isaac Berman by his first wife. He was living in Brooklyn, New York, and in 1922, he remembered his little sister in Russia. I daresay he read of the disturbances in Russia and imagined our plight to be far worse than it was.

He therefore sent a letter to the Petrovichi rabbi to ask if his sister,

[1] I am sometimes asked to give the details of how we left the Soviet Union, and I get the distinct feeling that the questioners will be satisfied with nothing less than having my mother jumping from ice floe to ice floe across the Dnieper River with myself in her arms and the entire Red Army hot on our heels—but it just didn't happen.

or any of her family were still alive. The letter was given to my mother, who answered, and there soon followed another letter from Joseph Berman inviting us all to come to the United States.

Uncle Joe (as I came to know him in later years) was reasonably well off and could easily demonstrate to the American Government that he could guarantee that his sister and her family would not become charges upon the public. That, and permission from the U.S.S.R., was all my parents needed to get into the United States, for entry through the Golden Door was still fairly unrestricted.

When my mother received the letter from Uncle Joe, there was a family council, and the decision was that it might be well to go. It would mean leaving the home in which they had been happy all their lives, going to a strange land, with strange ways, and a strange language. They would, however, have Uncle Joe to cushion the shock and they were not immune to the general notion among Europeans in those days that in the United States everyone became rich.

Then, too, they might not have the chance again, for the invitation might not be repeated. My parents decided to go.

2

The problem was to get permission from the Soviet Government. That was not easy to do. Aside from the fact that the Soviets had inherited the bumbling tradition of the Tsarist bureaucracy, and had added a few refinements of their own, to want to leave the new paradise of the workingman was a rather insulting commentary on its value. The mere wish to leave had an anti-Soviet flavor to it, and the Soviet Government at that time (and at this time, too) did not feel secure enough to accept such wishes casually.

Fortunately, there was my father's childhood friend, whose homework my father had done for him, and who was now a high functionary over the entire region. (What happened to him, I wonder, since then? My father didn't mention his name and I'll never know.)

My father's friend had his headquarters at Klimovichi, forty miles southwest of Petrovichi. There went my father, in order to obtain a formal letter to the functionary next higher up. The letter would have to say that my parents wanted to go to the United States of America to join their brother and that in his view there was no objection to this and that he would appreciate any help, within the law, that the higher-up could give him.

This was, in itself, a not entirely unrisky thing to do, yet my father's friend gave him the letter and let him read it before it was sealed, and thus proved his friendship in a very real way. That childhood help in schoolwork certainly paid off.

Off went my father to Gomel, 120 miles southwest of Petrovichi, to run the gauntlet of the next higher-up.

"I came there in the evening," said my father. "He and his wife were just sitting down to their supper. They invited me to have supper with them, but I politely excused myself and accepted only a cup of tea. After their meal, which took much longer than I thought I would be able to endure, I handed him my friend's letter. He read the letter long enough to send me out of my mind and what I felt at the time I don't think I could describe. Then he pocketed the letter and told me to see him at 9:30 A.M. at his office.

"At 9:30 A.M. I was at the door of his office and was taken into him at once. He said, 'You need for your petition a federal stamp costing six rubles, which you can get at the post office.'

"I turned to leave and he stopped me. 'Where are you going?'

" 'To the post office for the stamp,' I replied.

"'But how will you leave? Everyone is permitted entrance, but no one is permitted exit.' "

My father then said, "If I did not die right there, I hope to live a little longer, but I did not show how scared I was, or at least I thought I didn't. I asked in a calm voice, 'Then how can I get the required stamp?'

"He picked up a piece of paper with a number printed on it and said, 'Now go. The soldier will permit you to leave.' "

Apparently the official was just having a little pleasant fun with my father. What is the use of being a great, important official if one can't indulge in a little genteel sadism? This is not a particularly Russian characteristic. I have encountered this sort of thing among the insect authorities of the American bureaucracy also.

The next step was to get to Moscow, and here there was trouble, for my father was running low on cash. He said, "Usually, my credit was good with anybody who knew me, but once the word was out that I was going to go to Moscow for a passport to the United States, even my best friends would not risk their rubles."

I'm sure that not one of them thought my father would go abroad without paying his debts. They must have thought that my father would be imprisoned or executed and that in that case the authorities might not be thoughtful enough to give him time to pay his debts first. So my father sent a telegram to my mother, who instantly wired him the money. My father said, "Mamma was my true friend."

It took my father nearly a week to get the passports, during which time he stayed with a friend (and his friend's brother) who had "one room with one bed with no heat, no wood or coal to be gotten, and the temperature way below zero." (That was zero on the Centigrade scale, so it may have been +10, let us say, on the Fahrenheit scale.) "I slept on the floor, covered only with my coat and without taking off my clothes for almost the week that it took me to get the passports."

He added, "All there was to eat was black bread and herring—we could not even get onions for it."

While in Moscow, he changed thirty rubles in gold for a quantity of paper money—more than the official exchange value—and even as he walked away, the police arrived to search for black-market dealers. He said, "I walked on very quickly."

He was also intrigued by a smart city fellow who tried to sell a large diamond to another city fellow for ten thousand rubles. The second fellow went home to get the money and the first one turned to my father and said, "I'm in a hurry. Here, you can have it for nine thousand rubles and when that man comes, he will pay you ten thousand."

My father, who till now had taken everything as an honest business transaction, said, "Now it dawned on me the diamond was plain glass," and he walked away very quickly again. The big city is a dangerous place for country bumpkins.

3

But he got the passports and I have them with me right now. They are dated December 13, 1922, and are bilingual. On the left-hand side of each page the information is given in Russian, and on the right-hand side in French, the language of international diplomacy.

My father's name is given as Azimy on the French side and it adds, "*avec ses enfants: Ayzik de 3 ans et Mania de 6 mois*" ("with his children: Isaac, aged 3 years, and Mania, aged 6 months"). My mother had her own passport.

The passports had, of course, photographs of my father and mother respectively, looking incredibly young and pretty. My father had had hair. In fact, a picture of him, taken at the age of eighteen, shows him not only with hair, but also with copious, tightly waved hair. Unbelievable!

He began to go bald in his late twenties, and my mother began to go gray. By their thirties, my father had only a dark fringe of hair around a shining pate, and my mother was white-haired.

Both were inherited characteristics, and the baldness, in particular, seemed to strike all the male Asimovs, as far as I know. I took it for granted all through my youth, therefore, that I would turn either bald or white or, most likely, both, by the time I was thirty-five at the latest. It didn't happen. I wasted a lot of regret-in-advance over nothing.

4

Once he got the passports, my father then rushed back to Petrovichi, sold everything we had, and, on December 24, 1922, I began the first, the most arduous, and the most important journey of my life.

The first stop was Moscow again, in order to visit the offices of the White Star Line and arrange for passage. By the time we reached the town of Pochinok, halfway to Smolensk, at a time when "the frost was very severe," poor little Marcia was coughing and was obviously very sick. The only available room was unheated and it took all my mother's blandishments "and a few rubles" to have a fire made up. There was no doctor, of course, for the only one in town was celebrating Christmas somewhere out of town.

In the morning, Marcia seemed a little better, so we made it to Smolensk. We went to the inn where my father usually stayed when he was in Smolensk and asked for a doctor. The innkeeper, fearing contagion, at once ordered us out of the inn. My father pleaded for the chance to see a doctor first, and the doctor, when he arrived, assured the innkeeper that it was not a contagious disease. (How can a condition that involves coughing not be contagious? I wonder if a few more rubles changed hands.)

By nighttime, however, Marcia began to choke, and it seemed clear she might not survive the night. My father went to the other side of the town to a pediatrician and leaned on the bell till a woman answered. The doctor, alas, was at a meeting of the Smolensk Soviet and it would be impossible to disturb him. My father, however, wept and pleaded with her and in the end she found she could not steel her heart to it all and went for the doctor.

The doctor came to the inn, reached it at 1:00 A.M. and prescribed medicines and treatment. He then refused all payment and asked only that my father pay the driver of the horse and buggy that had brought him.

After a week in Smolensk, during which time Marcia recovered with marvelous celerity, we set out again and reached Moscow. This was my first and only time in Moscow—at the age of three. My dramatic mother tells me she went about with me carefully buttoned up inside her coat to keep me from freezing solid since the temperature dropped to —40. Where she kept Marcia, I don't know.

The officers of the White Star Line sent my father to the Latvian consulate to get a visa, since he would have to take the ship at Riga. (Riga had been a Russian port before World War I, but was now the capital of the independent nation of Latvia.)

This was done, and finally, on January 11, 1923, we crossed the boundary of the Soviet Union and entered Latvia. From that day to this, none of the four who departed returned to the U.S.S.R.,[2] and we have never again seen our home town.

5

Once the Asimov family was in Latvia, it quickly turned out that our troubles were not yet over. The original plan was to take a ship from Riga and to travel through the Baltic and North seas to France, from which a transoceanic liner could be taken to the United States.

On the day, however, that we entered Latvia, the French Army occupied the Ruhr in Germany. Expecting all kinds of troubles and disorders, France temporarily closed its borders and we had to be rerouted. We had to move on to Danzig, then a "free city," and take a small ship to Liverpool, England.

The ship was smaller, less comfortable, and rocked a great deal more than the planned ship from Riga would have. In the stormy winter seas, my father, whose first voyage by ship this was, went out like a light. For the duration of the voyage, he remained helplessly seasick, and my mother had to take care of him and of the two children.

When we arrived at Liverpool, it turned out that some necessary papers that would make a visa to the United States possible had, of course, been delivered to Cherbourg in France, where the original ship had been slated to go. Fortunately, the Hebrew Immigrant Aid Society in Liverpool, learning of the rerouting, had sent for the papers for all the immigrants affected and they had arrived only the day before.

That meant the four of us could now board the good ship *Baltic* for the trip to the United States.

That wasn't a good trip, either. There was an enormous storm; my father said, "It started while we were on the ocean and the ship was bending from side to side. We had a trunk in the cabin with us and it was sliding from one wall to the other with a big bang. I walked out on

---

[2] Oddly enough, it was just as we left the country that the U.S.S.R. formally came into existence—on January 1, 1923.

the deck and when I looked on one side I thought the ship was reaching for the sky, and when I looked on the other, it seemed to me that we were heading down into the sea."

My father apparently had his sealegs, though, as a result of the Baltic passage, and he survived it. It was my mother's turn to be seasick, and my father had to take care of the children. Fortunately, Uncle Joe had sent a small sum of money that had reached us, with the papers, in Liverpool, and my father at once found how different life was outside Russia. In Russia, to get a favor or a little consideration, rubles had to change hands. On the ship, it was altogether different—*dollars* had to change hands.

My father had one clear memory of biting into a biscuit someone had handed him and finding it contained a dead insect of some sort. Since my father's passion for cleanliness was little short of a disease,[3] he rushed indignantly "to the only steward that spoke in Yiddish and showed him the biscuit with the dead fly inside. He asked me to see it. I gave it to him. He didn't even look at it, just threw it in the garbage pail, then turned to me and said, 'What is it you are telling me?' I thought that I could tell him a lot but it was better to keep quiet so I turned around and walked away."

I have one vague memory that may be part of the trip to the United States. I recall a sheet being let down from a height and a motion picture shown on it—with people crowding about it. It was the first motion picture I remember seeing and I remember nothing about it, but I think the event took place on the *Baltic*.

6

On February 3, 1923, the *Baltic* docked in New York, and the day after, we all disembarked. My mother was twenty-seven years old, my father twenty-six; I was three.

My father, with myself in his arms, came down to Ellis Island and, after a while, noticed that my mother, with Marcia in her arms, had disappeared. He said, "They brought me with you in my arms into a large room where the noise was impossible. Some swarthy fellows were jumping one over the other and fighting—but it turned out later they were Italians and that was a game they were playing."

It was after that had distracted his attention that he realized that my mother and Marcia were gone. He rushed about, inquiring after

[3] He once refused to eat any part of a bread I had placed on the steps, even though I pointed out that it was thickly wrapped in wax paper. "Heat can get through, so germs can get through" he said, and no amount of my scientific explanations of the essential difference between forms of energy and material objects would sway him.

them, and it was only after some time that he discovered the sexes had been separated as a matter of course and that no one had bothered telling him this.

As for me, I increased the general joy of the situation by choosing Ellis Island as the place to have measles.

It was not till February 7 that the family was reunited. When my father finally caught sight of my mother and Marcia again, Uncle Joe was with them. My father was not allowed to speak to them, though, until he was asked by an immigration official what he intended to do in the country. My father said that he would take any honest work that was necessary to support his family; that nothing would be too hard for him. It turned out that that, more or less, was the answer they wanted.

Uncle Joe told him later that he had sent a letter with full instructions as to what to expect in Ellis Island, and how to answer the various questions, but if the letter was sent, it arrived in Petrovichi after we had left.

It didn't matter. We made it. And just in time, too. The year 1923 was the last year in which immigration into the United States was relatively unrestricted. On May 26, 1924, fifteen months after we had entered, a new quota law was passed that restricted immigration to a certain percentage of the numbers arriving from given nations in 1890. That was just before the flood of immigration from southern and eastern Europe began and it was deliberately intended to cut off that flood and favor the entry of the more easily assimilable immigrants from northwestern Europe.

Had my parents remained irresolute as to Uncle Joe's invitation, and had they allowed a year and a quarter to pass before deciding to leave for the United States, the decision would have done us no good. We would never have gotten in.

6

Van Siclen Avenue

1

Now we were in the United States. We settled down in New York City's borough of Brooklyn, where I was to spend my formative years, and to this day I speak with a pronounced Brooklyn accent that nobody can fail to recognize.

It is overlaid with a lifetime of education and I can, with very little trouble, enunciate carefully and make use of an enormous vocabulary and yet the Brooklyn in me will shine through. Not the most careful effort in the world will wipe it out completely.

Without any effort at all, I can peel off the overlay of learning and speak pure lower-class Brooklynese, complete with all its peculiarities of pronunciation and intonation. Another peel, and I can speak, quite effortlessly, the Yiddish-accented English of someone not long off the boat, the kind my parents spoke. One last peel and I can speak Yiddish itself.

We moved into the East New York section of Brooklyn, and the first apartment we lived in was located on the ground floor at 425 Van Siclen Avenue, between Sutter Avenue and Blake Avenue.[1]

East New York was heavily populated with Jews and Italians at the time and much of it was the respectable home area of quite poor people intent on making their way up in the world. Our own particular apartment was nothing lavish. There was no electricity; we used gas jets. There was no central heating; we had a cast-iron stove, which my mother started with paper and kindling.

Fortunately, I didn't know that this represented slum living. It was home to me, and I was happy. My memories start here, for I remember the stove well, and I was particularly fascinated by it. I was always on hand to watch the fire start, or to watch my mother knead dough and make noodles, with the knife going so fast that the roll seemed to sepa-rate into fifty pieces simultaneously.

It was not, however, a happy time for my parents. For the first

[1] I feel a little silly giving statistics of this sort. I mean, who could possibly care what the exact address was? Yet these are among the questions I am sometimes asked: "Exactly where did you live when you first came to the United States?" I hope, though, that no one is thinking of making a pilgrimage to the site. It was lower class when I lived there and it has gone downhill steadily ever since.

time in their life, they were functionally illiterate, since all around there were signs they couldn't read, even very fundamental ones, such as street signs and store-front signs. They could not even make out the letters and get some notion from the sound.

My father told me that a short time after he came to New York, he saw a sign in Hebrew letters on a store front in the distance, and he rushed toward it in order to read and prove to himself that he *could* read. He got there and the sign said, as he pronounced the Hebrew letters, "Vindehz Gefikst." It was a kind of Yiddish-flavored sign announcing that a glazier inhabited the premises but it did my father no good at all.

In Petrovichi, my father had been a leading citizen, both socially and economically, and so had my mother. In Brooklyn, they were "greenhorns."

The flavor of the word has been lost now that it has been a long time since the United States has been buried under an annual flood of immigrants. It was a bitter insult, however, delivered with contemptuous laughter by those who were not greenhorns—say, those who had been in the country for five years.

To be a greenhorn is, of course, not just to be unacquainted with the language of the country. It is to be unaware of the subway system details, to be unhelped by guiding signs, to be unable to ask for advice from anyone who didn't speak Yiddish (or Russian) and no way of being sure whether some particular person did or did not speak it. It was not knowing any of the simple customs of the country, what you asked for in a store, how you paid, how you ate, what you ate.

Every greenhorn was embarrassed and humiliated fifty times a day through an ignorance that was not his fault. All self-respect was gone, all feeling of intelligence. It was as though one were the focus of laughter—and this was from other Jews.

Gentiles were no problem in a way, for to them the difference between a greenhorn Jew and a nongreenhorn Jew was too small to take notice of, and a Russian Jew didn't care what Gentiles thought anyway. To a true Orthodox Jew, a Gentile was totally unimportant—except to the extent that he might be dangerous. All that counted to a Jew was his status among Jews, and my parents went from top to bottom in the space of time it took them to go from Petrovichi to Brooklyn.

It was no wonder that it took them years to stop speaking longingly of Petrovichi. It was only when they were sure I was getting advantages I couldn't possibly have had in Petrovichi that they were finally reconciled.

In theory, Uncle Joe was our cushion. I imagine he got us the apartment. I imagine he helped my father find work to do. He must have instructed my parents in the ways of the country. He could even have been counted on for financial help in an emergency.

He was married and his wife's name was Pauline and they had a son named Martin. In addition to an Uncle Joe, I had an Aunt Pauline and a Cousin Martin and, in the first few years of my life in Brooklyn, they were an important part of the family.

In theory, also, my parents would have had to be grateful to Uncle Joe, since he had made it possible for them to come to this country; he had sent them money; he had met them at the ship; and he continued to be there to help.

It didn't work that way. Both my father and mother found it difficult—indeed, almost impossible—to accept help and instruction from my uncle and aunt. My father undoubtedly felt far more educated than my uncle was in the only way that counted in my father's own social milieu. My father was a scholar who knew the Bible and the Talmud Commentaries thoroughly, who could quote endless miles of Hebrew. My uncle, I'm sure, had none of this.

Yet my uncle acted as though *he* were the man who knew, and in a hundred ways the world seem to prove that this was so. And my mother was made to feel by Aunt Pauline (who might even have been native-born—I don't know) as a total boor.

I am quite certain that both Uncle Joe and Aunt Pauline had no intention whatever of being patronizing, or of humiliating my parents. Intentions, however, don't count. It's what they did. I doubt that they could have avoided doing so, however they tried. I doubt that my parents were justified in feeling humiliated. Still, an unjustified feeling of humiliation hurts just as much as a justified one—maybe worse, if deep in your heart you suspect you are being unfair to an apparent humiliator who doesn't really deserve your resentment.

As for myself, I was completely unaware of this until years later when my mother told me tales of how cruelly Aunt Pauline had treated her. I didn't understand of what the cruelty consisted until more years had passed and I was able to look back on it and understand that my mother simply hated the feeling of having to be instructed in fundamentals.

Naturally, as the years passed and my parents learned their way around the new world and became less greenhorny and even began to learn the English language, they drifted away from Uncle Joe and Aunt Pauline. We never broke off relations, but kept them friendly and proper. However, we saw less and less of them.

This was too bad. Relatives are exciting to children, and we saw so little of these, that, in effect, I could relate only to the immediate nuclear family.

2

I was a spindly little fellow in Van Siclen Avenue. I had never been particularly big ever since my undersized birth, and my mother told me that I had lost weight on the trip to the United States and was so thin and weak by the time we came to Brooklyn (the measles didn't help, I'm sure) that I virtually had to learn to walk all over again.

Although I was only three, I spoke a high-pitched voluble Yiddish, and because I looked even younger than three, my volubility was the more amusing. It became a game with the women in the neighborhood to say, "Isaac, how do you feel?" (in Yiddish, of course) in order to hear me answer, "*Nishkusheh,*" which means "Not bad."

It dawned on me before long, though, that it was useless to give that answer when they pushed the button, because the laughter puzzled and offended me. I asked someone what "*nishkusheh*" meant in English and the next time I was asked, I said, "Not bad," and they stopped asking.

I was a little greenhorn myself. It never occurred to me at first that there was anything wrong with standing on the curb and urinating into the gutter. Undoubtedly, this was standard in Petrovichi, where indoor plumbing must have been unknown. It didn't occur to my parents to stop me from doing this.

I found out that it was wrong when I took up my position next to a woman sitting near the curb on a folding chair, and discovered that she hastily moved some distance away, while muttering angrily under her breath. The fact that I still remember this now, over half a century later, is indication enough to me of the profound impression it made. I didn't do it anymore after that.

If my body was undersized and weak, my mind didn't seem to be in a bad way. My mother came upon me wrapped in thought as I was standing at the curb one day (it's her story, for I don't think I remember it) and said, "What are you doing, Isaac?"

"Counting automobiles as they pass, Mamma," I said.

There weren't very many automobiles then, so that I wasn't forced to strain my counting ability—but I've been counting things ever since. When I am in a public place and bored, I find even today that I cannot stop myself from beginning to count light bulbs, repeated decorations, holes in soundproofed ceilings, and so on.

You don't really change so much as you grow older.

3

What I remember most of all about my stay at Van Siclen Avenue was my incredible longing to understand what the various signs I saw all about me meant. I had learned English almost at once, of course, picking up words and phrases like blotting paper, but that wasn't enough.

Perhaps my interest in the signs arose out of the fact that I knew my parents couldn't read them and that it made them unhappy not to be able to do so. Since they couldn't help me, I had to take my curiosity and my ambition to the older boys on the street. This meant I had to endure a certain amount of impatience and teasing, but I managed.

After I had learned the names of a few letters, I suddenly realized that I knew them all, for we had a rope-skipping game that went to the singsong tune of "Ay-bee-see-dee-ee-ef-jee; aich-eye jay-kay-elemenoh-pee," and so on. That meant I had the alphabet, and I just had to fit the shapes to the letters.

When that was done, I started dogging after my unwilling teachers to get them to tell me what each letter sounded like, and they told me that. I was amazed to find that most of the sounds were those of the names—that em sounded "mmmm" and en sounded "nnn" and pee sounded "puh," and so on. It was very easy to remember.

They also showed me how to write the various letters, in script, of course, and I remember learning how to make *m*'s and *n*'s and *u*'s first. I therefore promptly wrote a long series of those letters in random order, convinced that anything you wrote made sensible words.

I showed it to one of the more co-operative of the older boys (and by an older boy, by the way, I mean someone aged eight) and asked him what it said. He laughed. I endured that and continued to ask him what it said and he finally told me, "It says 'mmummumunnnunum-mum.' "

That instantly taught me that letters had to go in certain orders and only certain orders, so I studied the signs to see what made certain orders correct. When I sounded out a word and it seemed to make sense, that was a triumph. When I could see that the sign that read V-a-n S-i-c-l-e-n, sounded out to "Van Siclen," which I knew was the name of our street, I was overjoyed. When I worked out a word I was uncertain of I checked it with an older boy and he either confirmed or corrected. I began to gather a reading vocabulary.

To this day I remember the sudden surge of triumph when I realized there must be such things as silent letters. My mother was going somewhere on the elevated and took me with her (it was always an exciting experience to stand high in the sky and look down on buildings and then see a train coming into the station). Once on the train, I amused myself by studying the sign on the window just opposite my seat. It said CONEY ISLAND.

Carefully, I spelled it out with no chance of any help, for my mother couldn't read it. It seemed to spell out "sohnee issland" and it made absolutely no sense. I didn't know what a sohnee might be and I had never heard of an issland.

Of course, I knew that a c was sometimes pronounced as though it were a k, but I didn't know what a kohnee was either.

And then there was a flash of insight. I had heard people speaking of something that sounded like "konee iland" and I suddenly realized that that was what CONEY ISLAND said. Not only did this teach me that the s in "island" was silent and that this might therefore, by extension, mean that other words had silent letters, but I also knew how people determined what train to take to get where they wanted to go.

Life, however, is not always a series of triumphs. When I first came across the word "ought," I couldn't pronounce it. I consulted my older-boy mentors, they pronounced it in a thoroughly improbable way, which I was nevertheless forced to accept. Having learned to pronounce it, I asked what it meant, and no one could tell me clearly—but such failures were unusual.

As a result of this, by the time I was five years old and had not, as yet, started school, I knew how to read. Of course, I could only read very simple passages and only haltingly, but I could read without anyone having taught me to do so in any formal way.

Eventually I felt secure enough in my ability to demonstrate it to my parents. They were astonished. They had, of course, been unable to teach me themselves (my father had reached the point where he could read English about as well as I could) and they had not known what I was up to.

Naturally, my father asked, "How did you learn all this, Isaac?" and I was at a loss over how to explain the process. The easiest way to get out of it was to say, "I don't know. I just figured it out."

That gave my father the idea that there was something strange and remarkable about me; something he clung to for the rest of his life. Many years later, he looked through one of my books and said, once again, as on that day so long before, "How did you learn all this, Isaac?"

By then, though, I had learned better answers to the question.

"From you, Pappa," I said.

"From me?" he said, astonished. "I don't know any of this."

"You didn't have to, Pappa," I said. "You valued learning and you taught me to value it. Once I learned to value it, all the rest came without trouble."

Of course, being admired by your father (when he was a father like mine) wasn't all ice cream and chocolate cake. Once he got the idea that I could do anything, I had to bring back perfect test papers or be greeted with patriarchal disapproval.

"*If*," he would say, with the Talmudic intonation he used when he was trying to demonstrate something by impressive displays of logic, "a person can only get a 65 and he brings back a 65, that is wonderful and he is to be praised. If another person, however, can bring home a 100 and comes home with a 95, then he has done wrong and should be ashamed."

It was clear that he expected me to bring home a 100 every time, and I didn't always. Poor Pappa! He was always convinced I was lying down on the job and that perhaps being knocked around rabbi-fashion would teach me better, but he couldn't bring himself to hit me.

4

What he did on that long-ago day when he found out I could read, however, was to buy me a small dictionary, "so you can look up words and know how to spell them."

My first thought was that it was surely impossible to find some one word among all the incredible number, but after I studied the book for a while, the workings of "alphabetical order" became plain and I asked my father if that was how the words were arranged. My father, who might have told me this to begin with, had clearly held back the information to see if I could work it out for myself, and was terribly pleased.

After that, he would have me look up words for people so that I could be admired. (I didn't mind, for I found out quickly that I had no objection to being admired.) I remember that when Uncle Joe was visiting one time, my father who, to the end of his life, never learned that boasting was an odious habit,[2] said, "Isaac can find any word in the dictionary."

Uncle Joe looked upon my skinny little body and my stupid face (to this day, no one who doesn't know me estimates me as extremely intelligent at first glance—sometimes I have to *tell* them) and said, "Impossible!"

Thinking that that was the word I was being asked to find, I found

[2] Neither did I, except that I learned to do it ingratiatingly—I think.

it at once. I didn't know what it meant, but fortunately the spelling was sufficiently straightforward to allow it to be found. Uncle Joe must have been terribly impressed, but he managed to restrain his enthusiasm, something my father complained about afterward to my mother.

5

In February 1925, shortly after my fifth birthday, I entered kindergarten. If you want further statistics, the school was PS 182.

My stay in kindergarten produces very little in the way of memories for me. In fact, school in general produces few memories that involve my schoolmates.

The trouble was that I was always primarily interested in the subjects being taught rather than in the boys and girls who filled the other seats.

This has often proved embarrassing, since people who were my schoolmates at some point in my life from beginning to end sometimes meet me and recall themselves to my memory—and I draw a blank.

And yet, if I think hard, out of the five-year-old memory-section of my brain comes the name of Sophie, as the girl my age who lived next door and with whom I walked off to kindergarten the first day, each of us with a handkerchief pinned to our outer clothing in the beautiful hope that we would not use our sleeves to wipe our noses with.

There was another girl in the kindergarten also, who was having trouble following the directions required to produce an intricate patriotic display. We were supposed to center a red circle on a piece of cardboard, pasting it down neatly with such paste as was left over after we had carefully drenched our clothes with most of it.

Having completed that part of our task, we then pasted a smaller white circle, neatly centered, on the red circle, and a still smaller blue circle, again neatly centered, on the white circle. We thus ended with a beautiful red, white, and blue design intended to make our little hearts beat with national pride.

The girl I refer to, a pretty little dark-haired, dark-eyed cutie, couldn't quite make everything center. I helped her after I was through with mine and we both ended with little masterpieces.

When my mother arrived to take me home, she admired my design with appropriate maternal pride and I pointed out the little girl's design and, placing vanity above gallantry, told her that I had also made that one.

"Why?" said my mother.

And I smiled and said in a bashful voice, "Because I like to look at her."

That, as far as I know, was the first stirring of my heterosexual fascination with women that has endured to the present moment and that shows no signs of slackening, thank goodness. Ever since kindergarten, I have liked to look at women, and, as time went on, to engage my other senses as well.

6

In the ordinary course of events, I would have stayed in kindergarten one year and entered first grade in February 1926, after my sixth birthday.

My parents, however, couldn't bear to wait that long. They felt that since I could read, the sooner I got started putting the ability to use, the sooner I would sharpen and extend it. They didn't want it to fade and shrivel through lack of exercise. (They were perfectly right.)

In September 1925, I remember, my mother took me to school. My father was working and couldn't come, but Uncle Joe came along as my mother's interpreter. At the time, I hadn't the faintest idea what they were doing, and it was only in later years, consulting my memory of various incidents, that I was able to deduce what must have happened.

My mother, backed by my Uncle Joe, was assuring the school authorities that I was born on September 7, 1919. Considering the uncertainty of my birthdate, it was less of a lie than it looked, but it was a little of a lie, because, allowing for all uncertainties, I couldn't possibly have been born that early.

Still, once that birthday was accepted, I turned six years old on September 7, 1925, and it was on September 8, 1925, that the fall semester started. I was eligible, therefore, to start first grade on that day, and I did.

The reason that I know that this is what must have happened is that when I was in the third grade, the teacher (for some reason I cannot remember) had the children recite their birthdates. In all innocence, I said January 2, 1920, and the teacher frowned and told me it was September 7, 1919.

I have always been quite certain of what I *know*, however, and I became very emphatic about having been born on January 2, 1920. So energetic did I become in the matter, in fact, that the school records

were changed accordingly. If that had not been done, my official birthday would have been September 7, 1919, for all time.[3]

[3] As a general rule, I don't want to hoist little red flags in my autobiography and say
things such as "and believe it or not, this ended by having a remarkable influence on
my life." That's a silly thing to do. Let me, however, make one exception—this one
—for as we shall see, believe it or not, this act of mine in changing back my birthday in the third grade was to have a remarkable influence on my life. And don't
worry, it won't escape you. When the time comes, I'll point it out.

7

Miller Avenue

1

About the time I entered the first grade, probably a little before, we moved to 434 Miller Avenue, on the corner of Sutter Avenue.

It was only a block and we were moving up in the world as well as up that block—literally as well as figuratively. Instead of being on the ground floor where the world could look in your windows at its lazy ease so that the blinds had to be forever down, it was one flight up. Instead of three rooms, there were four. In the new apartment there was also a gas range instead of a wood-burning stove, and electricity instead of gas jets.

For me, though, it was a traumatic experience. It was the first move in my life that I was aware of as a move, and I remember hurling myself, crying, on my parents' bed and holding onto it, as though to keep our apartment in place.

I quickly got used to most aspects of the change and came to see them as improvements, but I never grew to like the gas range. Indeed, to this day I am discontented with them and can't help but feel that the "ovens" attached to such things, whether heated by gas or electricity, are shoddy imitations of the real thing. The real thing, of course, is the cast-iron stove with the blazing fire inside and the flat stove lids that could be lifted with a special hooking device to show the fire burning beneath, and with a stovepipe stretching up and into the wall.

I also found it hard to get used to the toilet. In Van Siclen Avenue it was flushed from a water reservoir near the ceiling. You pulled a chain and down it came. It never occurred to me to wonder how it filled up again. When, in later apartments, the reservoir was behind the seat, or even nowhere in sight, I always felt uneasy, fearing that there might be no flushing.

I remember, too, that sitting on the toilet seat was always a dull and boring chore, so I would practice my reading. We had no books in the house but there were always some sort of boxes or cans in the bathroom with writing on them.

What I remember most clearly is the box of Bon Ami, a powdered cleanser, which I pronounced as I had always heard it pronounced, "bah-NAM-ee." I would make out as much of the advertising spiel as I could and was particularly impressed by the picture on the can, which was that of a just-born chick with the broken eggshell behind it and the legend "Hasn't Scratched Yet."

I knew Bon Ami was a scouring powder and I was very impressed with the thought of the people who made it being very conscientious and checking on all the users to make sure it had never scratched. I was quite convinced that if they ever discovered a scratch, the legend would be changed to "Scratched Only Once."

I suppose we are born with an instinctive assumption of honesty that must be beaten out of us by life, more or less painfully.

Years later, when I was studying French in high school, I burst into laughter on discovering that the French people, when they wanted to say "good friend," said *bon ami* and didn't even pronounce it correctly.

2

Staying in the neighborhood by moving only one block was a comfort to me. Sutter Avenue and Blake Avenue were the extremes of my world. Everything else seemed unbearably distant.

In those days, I remember, my father worked for a living as any human being did and stayed home on Sundays. That was a big day because it meant I could crawl into bed with him in the early morning and he would tell me stories. He told me, of course, the only stories he felt suitable for me—those from the Bible—and here he improvised improvements and dramatic detail.

One passage I remember particularly. Moses was bringing on the plagues of Egypt and an obdurate Pharaoh was being gradually broken down. Finally, after the first-born had died, Pharaoh had to find Moses to tell him to get his people out of the land immediately and on any terms. My father said, "But Pharaoh couldn't find Moses because Moses had said that Pharaoh wouldn't see him anymore. Pharaoh rushed to Sutter Avenue and everybody said Moses was on Blake Avenue. He rushed to Blake Avenue and everyone there said Moses was on Sutter Avenue."

I got the idea at once. Good Heavens, Pharaoh simply scoured his dominions from end to end looking for the man.

Blake Avenue reminds me, by the way, that the Roaring Twenties were the last decade of the immigrant, and I caught it. Blake Avenue, for instance, was lined with pushcarts in those days. Each morning, the small enterpreneurs, too poor to own even the smallest store, would bring their stock on a pushcart, which they urged forward by muscle-power for who knows what distance to a particular spot that was theirs by common consent. There they spent the day hawking their fish or their vegetables or their needles and thread, or whatever it might be, to the hordes of housewives who drifted along this spread-out, noisy, smelly, one-long-line department store.

There was the iceman, too, who was a familiar figure because re-frigerators were unheard of, and there was no apartment without an icepick. Whenever the iceman appeared, the kids would flock around to watch him chop the ice with practiced blows of the pick, producing perfect cubes. (A cubic foot of ice cost ten cents, and for that dime he would place it on his shoulder—all sixty pounds of it—with a rubber pad between it and his shirt, and carry it up several flights of stairs and put it in the icebox.

For the children, the year was divided into seasons—exactly when the divisions fell or how anyone knew about it, I don't know. There would be a time when everyone was playing with marbles ("shooters" we called them), and then one day all the marbles disappeared, and ev-eryone had tops, or checkers, or something else.

The girls had "jacks," with which they played intricate games in which they bounced a ball and picked up set numbers in time to catch the ball as they came down. This they did with incredible agility, but that was a "girls' game" and we didn't play it—probably because boys weren't agile enough.

Most streets were paved only down the middle so that on the curb side there was a strip of bare soil ("dirt" we called it, and that's what it distributed over us). We would dig a shallow hole at one end, toss mar-bles at it, trying to get into it while striking enemy marbles away from the hole by flicking our own marbles against them and getting a free shot at the hole if we succeeded in making contact.

With checkers, we had a remarkable game called "skelly," one of which I never tired. The sidewalk was marked off into natural squares by the cracks introduced to allow for expansion and contraction with temperature change (not that I knew that was the reason—I thought that that was the way God created sidewalks, and didn't question it).

At each corner of these squares we marked off a numbered little square, 1, 2, 3, 4, in order. At the center of each side of the sidewalk square were more little squares numbered 5, 6, 7, 8. At the very center of the sidewalk square was a very little square—just large enough to hold a checker comfortably—numbered 9, and this was surrounded by a considerably larger square, the corners of which were attached to the corners of the small No. 9 square by straight lines. This central structure was the "skelly." (This could, conceivably, have been short for "skeleton.")

From a distance you flicked your checker toward the 1-square. Eventually, you flicked it into the 1-square without touching any of the lines, then went on to the 2-square, the 3-square, and so on. Meanwhile, one or more other players were doing the same, each going in turn, each getting a second shot if he landed within the proper square, or struck another's checker (driving it farther from its goal, with any luck).

There were complications. Getting into the 9 was very difficult, since if you landed in the space between the large square and the small square (or were hit into it by an enemy) you had to start all over at 1. You were safe if you landed on any of the lines, though, and loud were the arguments as to whether a checker was on the line or in the space.

Once you reached 9, you worked backward to 1 again and were now only partially in fear of the skelly, for if you got into it, you only went back to 9. However, if by some mischance you got into the central 9 it-self in the course of your backward journey, you had to start all over again from 1. This hardly ever happened, but when it did, the game had to be suspended for five minutes while all the contestants jumped and yelled with ear-splitting excitement.

No game of skill has ever excited me as much as skelly did, and I could play it for hours. I wasn't bad at it, either. Of course, all that crouching on the sidewalk made all of us filthy, but I don't recall that fact ever bothering any of us, or our parents either. We were all sup-posed to wash our hands before eating (at least I was), but baths were once a week. (It seems to me, looking back on it, that I must have smelled rather bad much of my young life, but since everyone around me undoubtedly smelled just as bad, none of us ever noticed.)

There was one serious catch, however. The whole fun of the games we played was to win one's opponent's marbles, or checkers, or tops, or whatever it was we were playing with. That was called "playing for keeps." If I lost a piece of paraphernalia, however, my parents strongly resisted replacing it. It quickly became apparent to me, then, that the joy of winning the next fellow's checker was small indeed, compared with the pain of losing my own.

I therefore steadfastly refused to play for keeps. What I wanted to do was merely win for the honor of winning, and I did not want to con-fuse this with material gain. This was called "playing for fun." Most of the young fellows, however, were adamant in their view that "playing for fun is no fun," so I was reduced to playing with only a few people who either didn't mind just going through the motions or who were desperate for a game and couldn't find anyone else.

My father, of course, approved of my refusal to play for keeps. In fact, he was dubious about my playing for fun, even, since he felt that my time could be spent much more instructively practicing my reading or studying or trying to think great thoughts.

He was particularly dubious of the more energetic street games. We used to play "punchball," for instance. This was a variant of baseball, played without a lot and without a bat. All you needed was a street (we called it a "gutter") and a rubber ball. You hit the ball with your clenched fist and from there on it was pretty much like baseball.

To my father, any boy who played ball in the street was a "bum" and was clearly in training to become a "gangster." If I went out to play with them, it would elicit the remark, "Are you going out to play with those bums again?"

He didn't forbid me outright, you see, but he would load me down with his Talmudic aphorisms. "Remember, Isaac," he would say, "if you hang around with bums, don't think for a minute that you will make a good person out of the bum. *No!* That bum will make a bum out of you."[1]

The result, of course, was that I didn't play punchball often, and that introduced a vicious cycle. Since I didn't play often enough to develop real skill, I was an undesirable choice for a team, and I played less than ever.

Fortunately, I developed a series of solitary ball games. I would throw a ball against a wall or against the small flight of stairs leading up to a porch. Ordinarily the ball struck and came back to me with one bounce on the sidewalk. That was zero points, and if it took a bad hop or, through sheer clumsiness, I didn't catch the ball, that ended the game. If, however, the ball caught a projection on the wall, or the point of the step, just right, it returned to me without a bounce and that scored 1. The idea was to see how high a score you could build up without ending the game. I grew very skilled at that and could bounce my ball for hours without missing, racking up scores of over 100.

All these games were, of course, extremely inconvenient to pedestrians who had to walk around skelly games, or to automobiles (there

---

[1] Once, in recent years, I had occasion to repeat that saying of my father's, explaining the conditions under which he had delivered that warning to me. My good friend Lester del Rey, the science-fiction writer and editor, said to me, "So why do you still hang around with bums, Isaac?" And I said, "Because I love you, Lester." And that was the *only* time Lester ever let me (or anyone) have the last word. He was too busy laughing, and let it go.

weren't very many in those days, remember) that had to drive slowly through punchball games while enduring catcalls.

The noise, inseparable from the games, the cheers, the arguments, the screaming, must have been unbearable to people trying to carry on ordinary occupations. The thunk-thunk-thunk, steady and unwearying over the hours, of my ball against a wall must have driven many a person insane, too.

I don't recall ever being annoyed at the noise, whether I was part of a game or not. It was an inseparable part of the world.

And, of course, it was pleasure. I have never been able to work up much sympathy for those who mourn the plight of the city children crowded into their nasty streets. When I think back on the children of my childhood, all I can remember is that those nasty streets belonged to us and that the boisterous competition and the noisy excitement were the very breath of life to us.

It may be different now, I suppose.

3

There I was at PS 182 (I forget exactly where it was, but it was only three or four blocks from home) in grade 1A1. The initial "1" meant it was "first grade," and the A meant it was the first semester. You went from 1A to 1B, then to 2A, and 2B, and so on. We never called them semesters, however. We called them "terms."

Furthermore, each grade was divided into several classes. No. 1 was for bright youngsters, No. 2 for slow youngsters, and Nos. 3, 4, etc., for the vast stretches in between. So the fact that I was in 1A1 meant that I had already been included with the bright students, presumably on the basis of the judgment of my kindergarten teacher.

I suppose there were advantages in thus segregating youngsters according to the presumed level of their intelligence. Bright classes weren't held back by dull youngsters, and dull classes could move more slowly and do better in that way.

It did categorize a youngster (sometimes unfairly), however, and anyone in the "2" class was bound to feel humiliated. He might, if left to himself, stop thinking of himself as "dumb," but his schoolmates from the other classes would never let him do so. They informed him of his dumbness constantly, not willing to allow so vital a piece of information to be lost to the world.

I went to segregated schools throughout my childhood, of course, since the student body was always heavily Jewish. My teacher in 1A1, however, was a plump black woman. I think she was the first black woman I had ever seen. (I seem to recall a black boy among the children in Van Siclen Avenue, but the only memory I have of him is of his having an accident that cut his forehead and noting with astonishment that his blood was the same color it would have been if his skin had been lighter. It meant, I deduced, that he wasn't black all the way through.)

Since I had never been told anything at all about blacks, I accepted my teacher as someone with a different complexion, as I would have accepted a redhead as someone with a different color of hair. She was a warm, comforting teacher who smiled readily, and she was delighted with me when she discovered she didn't have to teach me to read.

She was, in fact, too delighted with me, for ignoring the fact that I was equally delighted with her, she got rid of me. After about a month in her class, she had me put ahead into 1B2. (That was the only time I was ever in the 2 classification, and it was done so that I wouldn't be too disadvantaged at beginning a class a month late.)

4

One of the big excitements in school was the terrific question at the end of each term: Will you be "promoted" or "left back?" Being left back was an unspeakable disgrace that would bring shame on your parents. Fortunately, few children were left back. (Nowadays, I think no one is, which may be a good thing, since children who were left back were so endlessly humiliated at being with other children younger than themselves that they tended to resign from the human race and never learn anything again.)

What happened, on rare occasions, was being "skipped." That meant being shoved ahead a grade in the course of the term. That had its good and its bad, of course. (Doesn't everything?)

The good was that you weren't held back by the others so that (a) you yourself didn't become frustrated and bored and (b) you didn't get beat up by the other kids for showing your angry contempt for them, and (c) your parents were very proud and wrote letters to all their relatives and friends, thus making themselves and you well hated.

The bad was that you were younger than the rest of the class and got to thinking of yourself as younger. Thus, when people ask me if I was a child prodigy, my invariable answer is, "Yes, I was—and still am." It made it difficult to make friends on an equal basis, of course, destroyed friendships that had already been formed, and encouraged an obnoxious and insufferable air of superiority that surrounded one with universal hostility.

At the time I was skipped, however, none of these things bothered me. Thanks to the skip and to my mother's lie about my age, I was a year younger than anyone else in 1B2, 5½ years old to their 6½. But what did I care about that? What did bother me was that I was lonesome for my nice black teacher. (For some years after I kept hoping I would have another black teacher, but I never did. Never. She was my one and only.)

I still remember her squeezing into my seat with me and moving her finger along the words as I read: "Dickie Dare went to school. On the way he met a cow. 'How do you do?' said Dickie Dare. 'Moo, moo,' said the cow."

Dickie Dare went on to meet a sheep, a pig, and a goose, who went "baa, baa," "oink, oink," and "s-s-s," respectively. Why children in the city slums should be told about meeting animals on their way to school is a mystery. School books tend to be at least half a century behind the social facts I guess.

My black teacher was not there in 1B2 and neither were any of the children I knew. What's more, I had come across addition in 1A1 and got the idea instantly, but in 1B2, the children were subtracting and that was a complete mystery.

I was very frightened at that, for at that time (and today, too) not understanding upsets me. I managed to get the idea, though. After listening to the different children stumble out the fact that $3-2=1$ and $5-3=2$, it dawned on me that what they were doing was the reverse of addition, and a great relief flooded over me. I could do that.

What was worse was that the classes were staggered, and 1B2 was let off for lunch half an hour earlier than 1A1 was. Ordinarily, my mother was waiting there at the school gate to take me home, feed me, and then bring me back to school. (There was no school cafeteria in those days—at least not in PS 182.) Now I came out and, of course, she wasn't there. After all, she had not been told I was to be skipped, and, for that matter, neither had I.

My first reaction at finding that my mother wasn't there and that I was not to go home in security was, of course, to cry. The crying meant nothing. I was not frightened or unhappy. It was just the appropriate response to being alone, present in the young of the species as an instinct, I suppose.

I went walking home, wailing, and a man, his heart touched at the sight of a five-year-old boy walking down the street crying, stopped and

said, "Are you lost, little boy? Where do you live?" (That is the purpose of crying, I suppose, and its survival value; it rouses the protective
instinct in adults.)

I stopped crying at once, looked up at him in indignation, and
said, "Of course I'm not lost. I know where I live." (What did he think
I was? A little kid?) Having put him in his place, I resumed my wailing
and continued to walk down the street.

I walked into the apartment, and my mother, who had counted on
another ten minutes before having to leave for school, stared at me in
panic. "Isaac, what are you doing home? How did you get here?"

I told her. She prepared lunch quickly and got me back to school,
but from that day on, she never called for me again. Once it was established that I knew the route and could negotiate it without disaster,
that was it for young Isaac. And, of course, once I knew in advance that
my mother would not be there, there was no point in crying.

The next morning, though, I carried through a little plan I had
worked out. I returned to 1A1 and took a seat in the back of the room,
hoping no one would notice me. Fat chance! The teacher saw me,
asked what I was doing there, and paying no attention to my sobbing
response that I wanted to stay with her, she put my hand firmly in hers,
walked me down the hall, and deposited me in the room in which 1B2
held forth.

And now I found to my horror that the 1B youngsters were doing
something with numbers I couldn't understand at all. To say that
$7-3=4$ was quite understandable once I gave it a moment's thought is
one thing, but $7\times3=21$ left me completely in the dark. I couldn't
imagine what you could possibly do to 7 and 3 that would get you 21.

What's more, for homework we got a series of multiplication problems, and I went home deeply troubled. I might have asked the teacher
to explain after class, but I couldn't very well do that. If I had gotten
home five minutes late my mother would already have alerted the
police of all five boroughs.

At home, I tried to explain to my mother that I couldn't do the
homework and, of course, I started to cry. My mother was unable to
understand exactly what the homework was or why I couldn't do it. My
father would, of course, have been able to help me, but he was at work,
and my mother thought it would be quicker to get outside help. She
therefore called in a neighboring girl, aged twelve (that is, I found out
in later years that she had been aged twelve; at the time, I thought she
was a grownup).

The girl began drilling me in $2\times1=2$; $2\times2=4$; $2\times3=6$, and so
on. Rather quickly, it began to seem very familiar. I asked her to wait a

moment and got the five-cent copybook my mother had bought for me when I started 1A. On the back of the book were reference tables telling me that there were 12 inches to a foot, 16 ounces to a pound, and so on. There was also a large square array of mysterious numbers that were numbered 1 to 12 down the left and 1 to 12 across the top, with numbers that increased erratically and symmetrically rightward and downward.

"What is that?" I asked.

"That," she said, "is the multiplication table."

"In that case," I said, "I know how to multiply," and I sent her home. Having had nothing better to do, I had memorized the numbers almost as soon as I got the book, and from what she told me, I had seen how the multiplication table worked.

It took me a bit of thinking, however, before I penetrated the fact that multiplication was repeated addition and could see the sense behind it.

At the end of the term, it was clear that I didn't belong in the "slow" category, and I was promoted to 2A1, which I entered at the beginning of February 1926.

8

The Candy Store

1

While I was in the second grade, a great change came over our lives.

During our first three years in the United States (where, by second-grade time, I had already spent half my life), my father did as he promised the Immigration Service official he would. He had turned his hand to anything honest that would enable him to support his family.

I remember he worked as a knitter in a sweater factory, and I even have a dim memory of being taken there by my mother when she once had to take something to him. The factory was on Stone Avenue, near the edge of Brownsville, which was an even more depressed area than East New York, and I remember being quite uneasy as the bus (or trolley, I don't remember which) passed street after street after street. I had never been taken such a distance in my conscious memory and I was awed at the vast number of streets in the universe.

(I remember my father telling me of a similar feeling when he first came to New York. He watched elevated trains pass by from some vantage point and he told me that his thought was, "Where do they get the people to fill all those trains?")

The factory had intricate machines in which there were hundreds of thin metal extensions (if my memory does not play me false) like the keys of a hundred typewriters, all moving in complex combinations as they automatically wove a pattern into the sweater. There were also conical spools from which the wool was taken as the machines worked. I was fascinated and envied my father for being able to watch it all the time.

While my father worked there, all was well, I suppose, but I think the factory must have gone out of business, from some fugitive remarks that linger in my memory. In any case, my father wasn't a knitter anymore.

He tried his hand at being a door-to-door salesman of various things. There were definitely sponges among the products he sold, because I remember him telling me about that; and vacuum cleaners, because he had his sample cleaner in the house for a while; and maybe other things.

My father was not, however, the salesman type. He was entirely too argumentative and did not know how to ingratiate himself. Add to that the fact that his command of the English language was still very weak and you can see that this was not his field.

I don't recall, though, that we were ever in danger of being thrown out of the apartment for failure to pay rent, or that there was ever any undue shortage of food, so whatever the difficulties, he managed to support us.

In 1926, though, in search of some sort of security, he put what money he had been able to accumulate into a candy store that existed at 751 Sutter Avenue, between Miller Avenue and Bradford Avenue. It was, in point of fact, just around the corner from our apartment.

Candy stores were a product of the times. They required no education or skill and could be run by a greenhorn as easily as by a sophisticate. You sold discrete objects like pieces of candy, glasses of soda, newspapers, packs of cigarettes, and so on. You bought all these in quantity for a certain sum of money, and you sold them, one by one, for, in total, a slightly larger sum of money.

Candy stores were incredibly convenient for a poor neighborhood. You could get small items there, sometimes on credit. You could change money, get stamps, buy *one* cigarette (for a penny; a pack of twenty cost thirteen cents in those days, and some packs sold for ten cents), and sit and talk with your friends while sipping a soda for half an hour.

As for the owner, he was his own boss, and he could make a living provided he was willing to open the store at 6:00 A.M. and close it at 1:00 A.M.

Naturally, my father couldn't do this all by himself, but he didn't expect to. My mother had spent her time in a similar store in Petrovichi much of her life and she took up the task again. She went to sleep earlier than my father did, and he spent the last hours in the store alone, carefully washing all the glassware, going over the transactions of the day and entering them in the books, and getting everything neat and ready for the next day.

He made up for that late hour by taking a nap every afternoon from 2:00 to 4:00 P.M., and that afternoon nap became a fixed constant in the life of the family. We children were not allowed to make noise, and since breathing constituted noise, we were encouraged to stay out of the apartment altogether. In fact, it was my duty to stay in the store, if I weren't at school, in case my mother had errands I could run for her.

At four o'clock it was my duty to wake my father, a task I performed in the most direct possible way. I would stick my head in the door and shout, "Wake up, Pappa. It's four o'clock." My father would invariably say, "I'm not sleeping," even though I had startled him awake in midsnore, and he would scramble into his clothes.

2

Despite her work in the store, my mother had to take care of two small children, too, but she was used to that sort of thing. It meant that she could not learn to be a gourmet cook or develop much in the way of a culinary repertoire, but that would not have occurred to her anyway.

She did lots of frying because that took little time, and lots of boiling because that took little supervision. We had boiled beef and boiled chicken frequently and I found it delightful, for soup always came with it. When she added potatoes, lima beans, barley, and anything else that wasn't green or orange, I loved it. When she indulged her penchant for putting carrots, peas, or cabbage into it, I loved it a little less.

Along with the beef (or chicken) and soup, we were served with thick slabs of pumpernickel bread. Under her watchful eye I had to eat a mouthful of bread with every mouthful of meat or chicken, and if I ever (on purpose) finished my bread in advance so I could have some of the meat or chicken in my mouth undiluted, she would slice off another piece of bread for me. I think it was her feeling that a meal without an overflowing supply of bread was so lacking in essential nutrients that it would kill me.

There were also lots of delicacies, such as chopped liver with hard-boiled eggs and onion, which she made herself. (She would chop the liver in a wooden bowl with a special chopping knife. It was very simple. She would just go chop-chop-chop at a steady five-per-second rhythm for half an hour. When I try it, even now as an adult, my arm falls off after twenty seconds.)

She did the same thing with white radish in place of the liver. That lingers in my mind even more than chopped liver. The latter is a universal delicacy; the former I've eaten only in my mother's house.

My mother also made something called "ptchah," which consisted of the meat and gristle from calves' feet with chopped hard-boiled eggs and who knows what else, the whole forming a thick soup that set into a hard jelly when it was cold. It was an acquired taste, and a great deal of it had to be forced down my throat before I got to the point where I loved it so much that I objected to anyone else eating any of it.[1]

And, of course, she made that ultimate delicacy, chicken fat ("schmaltz," we called it). She would render big lumps of the fat every time we had boiled chicken, along with chopped onion, and then strain off the onion and the hard, charred bits of skin. The fat itself was wonderful, but the leftover onion and skin were what I was waiting for.

In between meals, we had bread and butter, or bread and cream cheese, or bread and chicken fat, or occasionally bread and jelly. In addition, we would have salami sandwiches, or, on rare occasions, expensive corned beef sandwiches. Whatever we ate there were those thick slabs of pumpernickel bread, though occasionally we might have rolls or bagels. And, on Saturdays, of course, we had a braided egg-bread called "khalleh," which was to ordinary bread what diamonds are to rhinestones.

And there was smoked salmon, sturgeon, whitefish, herring, gefilte fish, dill pickles, and much, much more.

You don't adopt this dietary, by the way; you must be born into it and introduced into it gradually. Anyone who was not used to the food of the East European Jew and who ate a quantity of it at one time would undoubtedly die of pernicious dyspepsia at once. One helping of stuffed derma (with the intestinal wrapping—you've got to eat that, too) would alone slay its thousands, no doubt.

Since I was weaned on it, I didn't appreciate the utter indigestibility of it. I ate it with delight and in as large a quantity as I could manage. The result is that I can, today, eat anything. I have seen, with my own eyes, people stare at unfamiliar food and pick at it and decide that the taste doesn't agree with some hidden standard they carry in their taste buds. Not me. I am omnivorous.

Of course, as I think of my childhood diet, I can't help but conclude that it was totally lacking in essential minerals and vitamins, so that despite the fact that I invariably cleaned up everything in sight, I remained bone thin through all my youth.

I had to eat ravenously, by the way, because my parents always told me about the starving children in Europe and how they would long for the crust of bread I seemed on the point of throwing away—so I would eat it. After all, why should the starving children of Europe get it? Now that I look back on it, I don't understand the force of the argument.

[1] The Russian Tea Room in New York is one of my favorite restaurants and it has something called "studen," which is clearly a cousin of my mother's "ptchah," rather like skim milk is a cousin of heavy cream.

My mother did not keep a kosher house. We never ate meat and dairy products at the same meal—out of simple habit (because both of my parents were brought up in households that *were* kosher)—and we never ate pork products for the same reason.

Just the same, my mother didn't have separate dishes for meat and dairy, and she looked for ways to break away. She introduced bacon into the house to my utter horror. I wasn't horrified, you understand, at its being nonkosher, for I knew nothing about that, but only because it looked so funny. I assumed it was very fatty corned beef, *so* fatty as to be useless. And when she fried it up, I was repelled by the smell—but only for a while. Faced with it, I first endured, then pitied, then embraced.

As a matter of fact, despite my father's deep and thorough religious education, he was not religious. In Russia, prior to the revolution, there was an insistent vein of secularism blowing from the West, and many young Jews were trying to rid themselves of the trammels of Orthodoxy and to become "modern." My father was one of these.

While he was in Russia, he could not deviate from Orthodoxy in the slightest, for he would have offended his father, and this he could not do. Once he was in the United States, however, that was it. He lived a secular life.

I was brought up myself without any religious training to speak of (just one short period for a specialized reason), and I was spared the great need of breaking with an Orthodox past and, after having done so, of playing the hypocrite for the benefit of pious parents, as so many of my generation had to. I was simply a freethinker from the start, a kind of second-generation atheist, and in that respect my life has always been a liberated one. I have been grateful for that always.

3

The worst aspect of the candy store was that, in some respects, it made me an orphan. A candy store is open every day of the week. The hours are just as long on Sundays and on ordinary holidays as at any other time.

As long as we lived in a Jewish neighborhood, we could (indeed, we *had to*) close the store during the first two days of Passover, during the two days of Rosh Hashonah (New Year), and during the one day of Yom Kippur (Day of Atonement). Naturally, we closed at sunset on the holiday's eve and opened at sunset on the day of its end.

Those rare closings were exciting times, for the mere fact that the store was shut gave everything a kind of incredible holiday atmosphere.

We would all eat at the same table at the same time, which was in itself a sort of monstrous departure from the usual. At Passover there would be the thrill of eating matzo, which was rather tasteless by itself but terrific with anything else. With chicken fat it was divine.

My father was quite capable of leading the formal Passover meal (the Seder), and I recall the *one* time he did it—in 1928, I believe— talking endlessly in Hebrew, spilling ten drops of wine, one for each of the plagues of Egypt, filling the wineglass for the prophet Elijah, and leaving the door open for him. (I watched carefully, but he was as invisible as Santa Claus.) I myself had to recite the Four Questions in Hebrew, with my mother prompting me.

What I liked then (and like now, when on occasion I attend a diluted American version of a Seder as an adult) is the food. There is chicken and beef and chopped liver and hard-boiled egg, and horse-radish, and soup, and, most of all, sweet port wine.

There was no drinking in my parents' house ever. Drinking was always considered a peculiarly Gentile disease, and an upright Jew merely took a few sips now and then on ritual occasions. Sweet port wine on Passover was one of those occasions. My father filled his glass full on the occasion of that one Seder, but gave me only a quarter-filled glass and let me dip my sponge cake in it. (My mother made the best sponge cake ever invented.)

Childish habits persist. To this day I do not drink. I love sweet wines, such as port, cherry heering, even cream sherry and some kinds of brandy and liqueurs and will occasionally have a little if it is available at a host's table. On a very few occasions, each special and to be detailed in this book, I have even overindulged, but in general I am extremely abstemious, and I can honestly say that never, not even once in my life, have I ever *bought* a drink.

Still, the Jewish holidays were very rare occasions, and because of the store, my father was no longer home on evenings and on Sundays. It meant that never again, after I was six, could I be with him on a Sunday morning, while he told me stories. It meant I could never have dinner with him. I always ate with my mother and sister and *we* had to finish quickly, so that my father could take his turn and so that *he* could linger.

I retained the habit of eating quickly and with concentration for the rest of my life. I almost never talk while eating and I almost never pause, with the result that the food disappears almost magically. This is the height of bad manners, I am well aware, but I can't help it. I can force myself to delay by keeping a conscious eye on what I am doing, but as soon as I forget, things go back to normal and the food vanishes.

Generally, I read during meals. My father was not there. My mother was busy cooking and serving (she ate on the fly). So I wasn't reproved for what is another example of bad manners. Indeed, since it was a sign of studiousness, I think my parents rather approved than otherwise, and that habit also lingers to this day.

All in all, my family was never together, and I never interacted with any of them except in the context of the candy store. It was in that respect that I was orphaned in a functional sense.

In another sense, matters were quite the reverse. My parents were *always* home; I *always* knew where they were, so that I was too densely sheltered.

Then again, we could have no social life. We could neither visit nor be visited except on rare occasions, so that I interacted with almost no one *but* my immediate family. That, too, twisted and distorted my life and my personality in ways that must be all too apparent even now.

Despite all that education and experience can do, I retain a certain level of unsophistication that I cannot eradicate and that my friends find amusing. In fact, I think I sometimes detect conspiratorial plottings among my friends to protect me against my own lack of sophistication. I don't mind. I suspect that I am never quite as unsophisticated as they think I am, but I don't mind.

4

But let me not overdraw. I had *some* life outside the family and the candy store.

For one thing, there was a movie house, the Sutter Theater, immediately across the street from the store. Every Saturday afternoon, my mother got rid of me for three hours by giving me a dime and watching me narrowly while I crossed the street, to make sure I wasn't run over and squashed flat without her being aware of it at once.

Usually she sent me over as soon as the doors opened, which could be up to half an hour before the festivities started. It was always a children's matinee, which meant that the place was full of kids from five to fifteen, all squealing and shouting and running around. Looking back at it, it seems to me that the place must also have been filled with the stench inseparable from imperfectly washed humanity.

All is a matter of custom, however, and my ears and nose were blissfully unaware of anything unusual.

Eventually, the projectionist would arrive and walk up into the booth at the back of the movie, and the childish din, loud enough before, split the walls now. And then, eventually, the light would go out and there would flash on the screen something like *The Claw of the Panther*—Episode 6: "Attack of the Cat Men," and sheer pandemonium would drown out the credits (assuming anyone dared take credit for what followed).

Of all things the movie house supplied us with, the favorite with us were the serials (which we called "episodes," because that was the word we saw). These included incredible adventures, frequent fist fights, a masked villain whom we knew would eventually be unmasked as one of the ordinary characters of the charade, and an impossible cliff-hanging ending each week to be resolved at the start of the episode to be shown the next week.

Usually, the ending was a complete cheat. One episode would end with an explosion that clearly killed the hero. The next episode would begin with the same explosion except that the hero was clearly well away from it. But we didn't care.

In addition, there would be, for the same dime, a short comedy, a cartoon, coming attractions, newsreels, and two features. The whole thing was silent, for I began going to the movies just before talking pictures were coming in—and this was great because you could make all the noise you wanted without interfering with any understanding of the picture. There were numerous subtitles, which everybody read aloud in complete lack of synchronization.

The whole thing was sheer hell, but only in retrospect. It seemed like heaven then.

5

The candy store had delectable offerings of its own. For one thing there was the candy itself, of which there seemed to be endless quantities—but concerning which the law was instantly laid down. Candy could not be eaten—repeat—could *not* be eaten—without permission.

We quickly found out that permission was very rarely given. Before a meal, we couldn't have it because it would spoil our appetite. After a meal, we couldn't have it because, having eaten so much, it was disgustingly greedy to want more.[2]

I had better luck with sodas, for some reason. Every once in a while, my mother would make a chocolate soda for me. The soda fountain in the store could make cherry sodas, vanilla sodas, strawberry

---

[2] And yet I distinctly remember envying the boy whose father owned a bakery until he told me he envied me. Only then did I realize his chance at cake was about what mine was at candy.

sodas, pineapple sodas, and so on, and there were bottled sodas, too. And if you added a dollop of ice cream, you had an ice cream soda. For a penny or two, if you were a pauper or a masochist, you could have a small or a large plain seltzer. What I wanted, however, was a chocolate soda, undiluted with ice cream.

You could never get that anywhere but in a candy store because chocolate sodas were never bottled. Now that there are no candy stores to speak of, and no soda fountains, there are no longer any chocolate sodas of the kind I remember.

I have a theory that chocolate sodas are called "egg creams" by some people. At least some people assume that since I was brought up in a candy store in the old days I must be an expert on egg creams, and when I tell them I never heard of an egg cream, they doubt my sanity. Therefore, when I found a place recently that said it supplied egg creams, I ordered one, and found that it tasted like an inferior chocolate soda to me.

Even better than a chocolate soda, however, was a "malted." This was milk and ice cream and malt and syrup (chocolate syrup by my preference) all whipped up into a thick, bubbly consistency in an electric mixing machine. It was then poured into a large glass, with half remaining in the mixer for addition afterward, and you could watch the bubbles very slowly and viscidly breaking at the top.

On the peak of Mount Olympus, the gods and goddesses drank nectar—which I always visualized as a pale imitation of my mother's malteds. Fortunately, since my mother was convinced that malteds were a very healthful drink, I got at least one a day.

Then, of course, the candy store had magazines. Most of them meant nothing to me, but on a string in the window, my father had small paperbacks on incredibly cheap paper that detailed the adventures of Nick Carter, Frank Merriwell, and Dick Merriwell. It was the last decade of the dime novels, which were being killed by the category pulps that were taking over.

I wanted to read those adventures and my father carefully explained to me why I could not.

"Junk!" he said to me. "Junk! It is not fit to read. The only people who read magazines like that are *bums*."

Bums representing those who were the dregs of society, apprentice gangsters, I realized that I wasn't going to have much chance. I said, "You sell them to other boys."

"I have to make a living. If their fathers don't stop them, I can't stop them."

"*You* read them, Pappa."

"I have to learn English. You learn it in school, but I don't go to school. I have to learn it from these books."

He had me at every turn, but I kept hankering after them, and my father felt that temptation would overcome me if he didn't find a substitute for me. Consequently, before I was seven years old, he managed somehow to get a library card for me—at the Watkins Avenue Branch (I think), wherever that was.

From then on, I could go to the library, a constant activity of mine for many years, since it was the only way I could get books. *Buying* books was unheard of.

My father and mother, knowing nothing of English-language books, could in no way guide me in my selections, but they felt I could not go wrong, since they were certain that the libraries contained only wholesome books and nutritious literature.

Left to myself, I read voraciously and undiscriminatingly. I was allowed to pick out two books each time I went, only one of which could be fiction. My parents had to take me, and as I finished the books quickly, they had to take me often.

With the candy store in operation, it became increasingly difficult to take me, but my needs were so great that eventually, out of desperation, they simply gave me two nickels and trusted me to go to the library by bus, there and back, alone. It was my first brush with independence.

The candy store had a public coin telephone. Since it could perfectly well be used by us for our own social needs (except that we had none), or for someone to call us (but who would?), it could be considered our own phone, the first we ever had. I remember that first phone number. It was GLenmore-8999.

The chief use of that phone was to serve the neighborhood. In those days few people in our neighborhood had private phones. Therefore, they came into our store to make a call and that was good, because perhaps they would stop to buy something once they were inside. Besides, the phone company paid us a small rental for the use of the place.

Second, if our phone rang and someone in the neighborhood was needed, my father would run to wherever his apartment was and call him: "Telephone at the candy store for so-and-so." Then whoever it was would run to answer.

There was no charge for this. It was a courtesy for customers, which meant that people had to stay customers to get the courtesy. If the call was for someone we didn't know, or someone who hadn't been in lately and had fallen from grace, the answer was, "Sorry, I'm alone in the store and there's no one to send."

One other item of importance in the candy store was tobacco. As I look back on it, it seems to me that I might very well have found myself smoking in my teen-age years since cigarettes were always available.

My father, however, set his face against smoking as fervently as against candy-eating—for me, that is.

He himself was at one time in his life a heavy smoker—so my brother says, and he claims he was assured of this by my mother. For myself, I cannot for the life of me remember my father with a cigarette in his mouth. If indeed he smoked, the thought of it is so distressing that I have blocked it out of my mind utterly.

6

I went through the second grade without trouble. In fact, it became my custom at the start of each term, throughout my grade-school years, to read quickly all the books given us on the first day. I managed to complete them in two or three days. In the case of the arithmetic books, I would work out enough of the problems to make sure I got the point.

Then, for the rest of the term, I did not have to "study." I would do my homework as soon as I got back from school, and just as quickly as I could, and then I was through. My test marks were always very good, except that whenever I got a 95, my father would put on his sorrowful I-must-explain-this-to-you-for-your-own-good expression and tell me, "*If* a person can only get 65 and he gets 65 . . ." and all the rest of it.

My father never seemed aware that something he was telling me might be something he had already told me before. He would tell me the same story or read me the same lesson any number of times and I would listen patiently. When I grew older and less reverent, I would sometimes recite the stories along with him, but I never noticed that this in the least discommoded him. He would keep right on going.

Occasional 95s in tests did not prevent me from bringing back steady A's in schoolwork on the monthly report cards, which one of my parents had to sign as an indication they had seen it. Those A's were not the whole story, though.

Early in my school career, I turned out to be an incorrigible disciplinary problem. No, I wasn't destructive, or disobedient, or difficult in any way. The point was that since I understood what the teacher was saying as fast as she could say it, and very often I already understood before she could say it, I found time hanging heavy on my hands, so I would occasionally talk to my neighbor.

That was my great crime. I talked in school.

Schoolchildren were supposed to be absolutely silent except when called on. They were not only supposed to be absolutely silent, they were supposed to sit bolt upright with their hands clasped on their desk.

Most of the children talked and tittered, or made faces in order to induce someone else to titter—but my particular talent was that of getting caught at it. I would be ordered to stand up and I would be lectured in public and, in general, made to feel very bad. It never cured me of my reprehensible evil, but it made me feel bad.

My first report card from 1B2, I remember, gave me an A in schoolwork and a B+ in deportment.

My poor mother didn't know what "deportment" was, and neither did I. Nor was she aware of what a B+ signified, except that it wasn't an A. She came to school late that afternoon, therefore, in order to find out what it was all about. She had the report card and talked to the teacher (what an agony of embarrassment that was for me!). She was told (I overheard) by the teacher, who tried to put it in terms my mother's imperfect command of English would make comprehensible, that I "talked a little bit too much."

My mother then signed the report card without a word, went out of the school, and waited there till the day was over. (This was before the candy store had been bought.) I came out and she walked me home in absolute silence while I desperately made comments on the weather. Then when we got home, she removed my pants, and she proceeded to spank me into one big bruise.

That didn't cure me either, and before long she gave up on me. She just made sure that the schoolwork came back with A's and let the deportment take care of itself.

Of course, the teachers couldn't do anything with me, either. Although I continued to whisper and titter, thus proving myself to be a creature of incredible wickedness and of Satanic evil, I was still the smartest pupil in the class and so I had to be accepted. Some of my teachers must even have had a suspicion I might conceivably amount to something and they therefore hesitated to take extreme measures such as poisoning my milk and cookies.

7

I couldn't very well be that smart without knowing I was that smart. I had begun to suspect that I was not as other children were even before I went to school. Once I was in school, there was no way in which I could avoid the knowledge.

Each day, it became increasingly evident to me that where I saw something at once, the others had to have it explained. Furthermore, whereas once I saw something, it was safely inside my head never to be lost again, the others would forget and have to have it explained again.

It never occurred to me to hide the fact. All kids are showoffs as a matter of course. If one child beat another in any game whatever, the natural tendency was to jump up and down and say, "I won! I won! You stink and I won!" Furthermore, children would go about saying, "I can beat you anytime," and "I'm the best marble shooter on the block." If you didn't say things like that, you would probably build up enough internal pressure to damage your inner organs severely. And if you were told that saying it was bad manners, it would make no more sense to you than if it were said in Sanskrit.

In a hundred different ways, involving everything *but* schoolwork, I had to listen to others boast. I had to get my own back. Since I knew that I was the smartest pupil in the class (and so did every other pupil in it), I said so on those occasions when it seemed appropriate to make the information known. Even when, as the result of skipping, I ended up the youngest pupil in the class by better than two years, I was still the smartest and knew it and made sure *they* knew it.

It had its difficulties. The larger, older, stupider classmates occasionally found me wearisome and decided that I would probably be a much more likable person if I were kicked into submission now and then. I had a certain amount of applied brightness as well, however. I found that if I picked out the biggest dumb youngster in the class and did his homework for him, he would constitute himself my protector.

Another point that helped save my life was the very fact that I was a disciplinary problem. The fact that I was periodically kicked into submission (in words, anyway) by my teachers somehow lessened the pressures within my classmates. I daresay the other kids decided anyone as sinful and wicked as my teachers held me to be couldn't be all bad, and it made it easier for them to resist the impulse to eradicate me.

The result of all this was that I never learned to develop that lovable quality called "modesty." I continue to be aware of my virtues and to inform others of them if it seems suitable to do so (and it frequently seems to me to be suitable to do so). I lay no claim to virtues I do not possess, however, and perhaps that may be considered a palliative.

Besides, I don't call my lack of modesty "immodesty," as perhaps I ought. I call it "cheerful self-appreciation."

This is not to say, of course, that my passage through grade school was one long scholastic triumph. I managed to trip up badly on one occasion or another. In one case it was not my fault, but I was badly embarrassed just the same. This is the way it happened.

By the time I reached 3A1 (which I entered in February 1927) I had accumulated enough of a lead over my classmates to be skipped once again. This time they put me right into 3B1 and didn't bother testing me out with the slow class.

But now the same thing happened as in the previous skipping. The class was doing something of which I was utterly innocent. They were studying geography, and I knew no geography. Until then, the only map I had ever looked at in detail was a map of New York City, which we had studied in an earlier grade. The five boroughs of Manhattan, Brooklyn, the Bronx, Queens, and Richmond made up, I thought, all of the United States, and I pored over my own fifth of the nation— Brooklyn—with a great deal of pride.

Beyond the five boroughs that made up the United States, I knew, vaguely, that there was another nation called Europe, since that was where my father said we came from—and that was it.

In 1B, at least, when I knew no multiplication, I wasn't called on. In 3B, however, when I knew no geography, the teacher had no hesitation in calling on me. She knew I had just arrived from 3A and she might have spared me the needless humiliation—but, on the other hand, she might have heard rumors about me and decided that it would be good for my soul.

The subject under discussion was the continent of North America, and a young man had just explained (in response to questioning) that Florida (of which I had never heard) was a peninsula (a term with which I was unfamiliar) on the southeastern portion of the United States.

The teacher then called on me and asked me to locate Yucatan, and I drew a complete blank. Since I do not *look* bright even under the best of circumstances, my expression when I feel stupid is dumb beyond the dreams of Simple Simon. The class, therefore, which did not know me, responded in the usual manner and with the true sympathy one child feels for another who is under the harrow. They laughed very loudly.

When the afternoon was over, I asked the teacher if any of the new books I had been given would tell me where Yucatan was located. She pointed out the largest of them and said it was the geography book. That night, I went over every map in the book in detail, and you can bet I was never caught again on *any* geographical point.

8

Sometime in 1927, Marcia caught the chicken pox. My parents could not stay with her because they had to stay in the store, and Marcia demanded company. I was elected. It was my duty as a big brother to take care of my little sister. So I did. She was indoors a week and, except when I was at school, so was I.

But you know the result. As soon as she was well and could run out and play, I got the chicken pox. At once I demanded that she now return the compliment and stay with me and keep me amused. Not a chance! She never came near me, and I was in this way introduced to the injustice of the world.

But what the heck, I survived. Nor have I too much to complain about in the matter of health. I am hardly ever disabled through infectious disease. I almost never run a fever. I rarely even catch cold.[3]

Nor have I suffered much in the way of physical accident. At about this time, I cut my left thumb (the dorsal surface, I believe doctors would say) when a penknife with which I was playing slipped. I ran home dripping blood, and my mother, placing her thumb tightly over the cut on the thumb, ran me to the nearest drugstore.

We waited for the pharmacist to turn his attention to us. He didn't for quite a while, since selling cough drops is bound to take precedence over a bleeding child, and eventually my mother lifted her thumb carefully to see what the progress of the bleeding was. The bleeding, it turned out, had stopped, so she took me directly home without treatment and bandaged it. There was no problem, but I still have the scar on my left thumb today.

At about this time, too, I briefly made the acquaintance of a remarkable youngster. He was roughly my age, rather smaller than I was, and a little swarthier in complexion. I discovered, somehow, that he had the ability to tell stories that held me enthralled, while he discovered, simultaneously, that I was an audience most willing to be enthralled.

For some months, we sought each other out so that we could play the roles of storyteller and audience.[4] He would rattle on eagerly while we walked to the library and back, or while we just sat on someone's front steps.

For the first time, I realized stories could be invented, and that was a terribly important thing to learn. Until then, I had naturally assumed that stories existed only in books and had probably been there, unchanged, from the beginning of time, and that they were without human creators.

[3] I have had my medical problems, however, which will be mentioned in due course but without undue detail. My own feeling is that there is very little of interest in the medical misadventures of someone else, and I don't want to bore you.
[4] It is hard to believe, as I look back on it, that *he* was the storyteller and *I* was the audience, but that's the way it was.

Of the tales my friend told me, I have only the dimmest of recollections. I seem to remember that they involved the adventures of a group of men who were forever facing and overcoming dangerous villains. The leader of the group, an expert in the use of all conceivable weapons, was named Doddo "Weapons" Windrows, and his lieutenant was one Jack Winslow. Another character was a black who spoke in what my friend (and I) conceived to be the way blacks spoke, and a Chinaman who spoke in another variety of ludicrousness. (By now, you see, we had been to the movies often enough to absorb the casual racism of the times. We didn't know there was anything wrong in it— and how hard it is to shake vicious habits learned in childhood.)

Whether my friend actually made up the stories, or retold me material he had read, with adaptations, I didn't know. At the time, I had no doubt whatever that he was inventing it as he went along, and looking back on it now, his enthusiasm seems to me to have been that of creation and not of adaptation.

Both of us were careful never to let anyone overhear us in our enjoyment of the process. My friend once explained that the other kids would laugh at us. I suppose he felt his stories weren't first-rate and that while I seemed to appreciate them, others might not. Like any true artist, he did not care to expose himself needlessly to the possibility of adverse criticism.

As for myself, my chief fear was that my father would become aware of what was going on. I was quite certain that my friend's tales would come under the heading of "cheap literature" and that I would be forcibly rescued from their baneful influence. This I most earnestly did not want to happen, and insofar as I recognized that my friend's stories were akin in spirit to the tales to be found in sensational magazines, my hunger for those magazines sharpened.

Ah well, it didn't last long. The storytelling spree could not have gone on for more than a few months before my friend's family moved away from the neighborhood and, of course, took my friend along. He never returned; he never visited; he never wrote. I never knew where they had moved, and contact was broken forever.

It seems to me now that my storytelling friend could not possibly have gotten such pleasure out of telling stories without having tried to become a writer as he grew older. I know something about that particular compulsion and I am certain he would have tried. And if he had tried, it would seem to me that he must have succeeded.

And yet I remember his name—it was Solomon Frisch—and I am not aware that there is any writer by that name. Can he have used a pseudonym? Is he dead? I don't know. But wherever you are, thank you, Solly; those stories meant a lot to me.

9

The candy store had not yet become the all-devouring entity it was eventually to become. My father was just past thirty and he was still young enough to carry the load all by himself for a limited period of time. In 1927, and again in 1928, my mother, myself, and Marcia spent two weeks of the summer in the Catskills.

We stayed in a town called Parksville, at a resort owned by a family named Siegel. It was not a fancy resort; it was little more than a farmhouse with some cottages about it.

I hated it.

I didn't like the country. I didn't like the food. I had some passing interest in watching the cows being milked, but I didn't like the way the cows smelled and I didn't like the danger of stepping into cow plop. Nor did I like milk given me to drink fresh from the cow. It was warm and it smelled and tasted funny.

Finally, I was furious because a calf—a little baby cow—was carried off in a truck. (Goodness, I still remember the calf in the open truck, with dabs of cow manure stuck to it here and there, mooing mournfully as it was carried off.) The mother cow bawled for a whole day and when I innocently asked why they didn't give her back its baby, they told me that the calf was to be slaughtered. I was horrified;[5] I counted the hours till I could get back to the sweet and gentle city.

10

The year 1928 had several high points for me, at least one of which concerned me very nearly.

Once a year of school had confirmed, extended, and intensified my ability to read and write far beyond what I had managed to attain on my own, the next step was to teach someone else how to do this. I needed a victim and they were not easy to come by. The other children in the neighborhood were either older than I, so that they knew how to read (in some more or less stumbling fashion) or younger than I, but

[5] What a hypocrite I was! And am! Do you think I would give up eating meat because I can't bear the thought of animal slaughter? Do you suppose that I'm not crazy about veal and eat it as often as I can? As long as I don't *witness* the slaughtering, I'm fine. If it's done without my knowing it, it doesn't bother me— which is the trouble with the whole world.

inaccessible. The only possible subject for immolation at the burning altar of my desperate desire to teach was my sister, Marcia. She was both illiterate and accessible.

So I began to teach her, possibly during her siege of chicken pox, though I can't remember this clearly. Poor Marcia was a most unwilling pupil, but I had no intention of being foiled out of the fun of teaching just because she would rather do something else.

I got a slate and chalk and made up my own letter cards and word cards, which I would shuffle and then have her identify. Under my merciless browbeating and thanks to her own native intelligence, she learned how to read and write before she ever went to school. In fact, she was better at it than I had been, for she had a firm and dedicated teacher, which I had not had.

In September 1928, it was time for her to enter school. My father went to school to register her (he, instead of my mother, because he was planning a coup). I went with him to show him where to go once he got inside the school.

Some teacher was registering the new students who were waiting in line—all of them scared into catalepsy. The greenhorn parents who accompanied them seemed equally scared. When it was Marcia's turn, my father marched her up to the desk and said in what was by now clearly understandable (though heavily accented) English, "I would like to have my little girl enter the second grade."

The teacher looked up in surprise, and adopting the natural tone one of them would take to a greenhorn, said, "Are you crazy, mister? Children enter school in the first grade."

My father was not frightened. He had frequently dealt with Russian officialdom and he took this hectoring attitude as the small change of the profession. He said, "But my little girl can read. Give her something to read."

The teacher laughed scornfully and opened a second-grade reader. "Here," she said, "read this, little girl."

Marcia rattled it off unhesitatingly, and into the second grade she went.

That same month I passed another kind of milestone.

My father came to the United States with every intention of making it his permanent home, and that meant citizenship. He took out his "first papers," a declaration of intent, after he had been in the country for three years, and in September 1928, when he had been in the United States for 5½ years, he received his "second papers"—the real thing—and became a naturalized citizen at the age of thirty-one.[6]

[6] My mother did not become a citizen until 1938, ten years later.

On my father's citizenship papers, as on his passport, his two children, both minors, were mentioned. That meant Marcia and I automatically became naturalized citizens on our father's papers. I have thus been an American citizen since I was eight years old.

11

Something that was less important, but more noticeable, to me, was that my father did a little moonlighting. How he managed it, I don't know, considering all he had to do in the store, but he actually had taken up part-time duties as a bookkeeper at the local synagogue.

He had had bookkeeping duties in Petrovichi in his father's business and in his co-operative ventures, which he ran after the revolution. He even kept meticulous and detailed books for the candy store, even though for the income he commanded in those days there was no income tax to make it a necessity.

I suppose he welcomed the opportunity to exercise his expertise in this direction, especially since it gave him the opportunity to indulge in his beloved disputations over the Holy Books and to display his knowledge of the Talmud. After five years of being a virtual illiterate, he could once again shine as a learned scholar.

If he were going to be a secretary at the synagogue, he felt he would have to attend services now and then. He had his regular seat in the synagogue in row J, and he would attend Sabbath services on Friday evenings now and then and take me with him.

He would be there in his hat and prayer shawl but would never sit with me in the seat until the services started. Before that (and he was always early, since the social period before services was the best part) he would be speaking to others somewhere in the aisles or in the back. I was always craning my neck to look for him since I feared he might forget I was there and leave me in the strange place.

It was indeed a strange and fearful place—the balcony where the women sat (for it was an Orthodox synagogue, and the sexes were segregated), the ceremony with which the scrolls of the Torah were brought out and taken from their velvet covers and opened to the appropriate verses, the intonations of the prayers in an incomprehensible language, the wailing of the cantor. I even remember the blowing of the shofar, or ram's horn, on the high holiday period of 1928 and the difficulty the blower had in making it sound.

What fascinated me most was Hebrew, for here again I was illiterate. It was a language written in letters I didn't know, letters that were both more complicated and prettier than the by-now prosaic letters of the Latin alphabet.

My father, of course, read the Jewish newspapers, in particular *The Day*. (The most important of the Jewish newspapers was *The Forward*, but my father disapproved of its politics and wouldn't touch it.) The Hebrew block letters had therefore been tantalizing me for some time.

I asked my father if Hebrew had an alphabet the way English had and he showed me the letters in order and told me their names. I asked him how they were sounded. He told me the sounds of the consonants and which letters were used as vowels in Yiddish (Hebrew itself has no vowels, but uses little "diacritical marks" for dullards who need the help). Once he had done that, I said, "Good. Now I can read Yiddish."

My father laughed and handed me the copy of *The Day*. I bent over the first column (fortunately, I knew the words went from right to left in Yiddish—and in Hebrew, too) and began to read. It wasn't at all difficult because once I pronounced some of the letters in my mind, I would recognize the word, since I could *speak* Yiddish fluently.

My father was once again astonished (I really don't know why; by now, he should have expected it) and sent me to Hebrew school. For about half a year, I attended Hebrew school on certain days of the week (every day of the week, except Friday and Saturday, in fact) after ordinary school was done.

I learned to read Hebrew with the help of the diacritical marks. Hebrew books intended for accomplished readers didn't have them,[7] but I never got to the point of being an accomplished reader.

I learned a considerable Hebrew vocabulary and some of its grammar. I even remember memorizing and reciting a speech in Hebrew at some ceremony to which parents were invited. Someone had to stay in the store, but my mother came, and sat there, beaming, while I pronounced the ancient syllables.

But it all came to an early end when we moved—synagogue, Hebrew school, and all.

I wasn't sorry, for I wasn't terribly interested in Hebrew school, and it was always a chore to remember to wear a hat. I still know a very little bit of Hebrew, however, and I can still read it with the diacritical marks, even though I can't really understand it.

That was the beginning and the end of any religious training I have ever received.

[7] In English, for instance, the experienced reader would at once recognize and read FRSCR ND SVN YRS G as "Four score and seven years ago."

9

Essex Street

1

By the end of 1928, we had lived on Miller Avenue for three years and we had owned our candy store for a little over two years. That was enough.

My father, on a number of occasions, would find that a candy store had grown dull, or perhaps he thought he might locate a more profitable one. He would therefore employ an agent who specialized in such things. The agent would suggest places and my father would then visit those stores, study their books, stay a day to observe how the business went, and so on.

Sometimes he would take me, and that I would always find terrifying. I never wanted to leave the old place. New stores always looked dangerous to me; new neighborhoods unnatural and ominous; new people monstrous. To this day, this remains true for me. I don't like to travel; I like to stay put; I have very little sense of adventure.[1]

Finally, my father found a likely prospect, and in December 1928 we left the old apartment and store and moved half a mile eastward to the corner of Essex Street and New Lots Avenue. The exact address was 651 Essex Street. It was still East New York. It was still a Jewish neighborhood.

The store was indeed a better store. It was larger and the clientele were apparently better off. One thing I had never seen before was a slot machine. People would throw nickels into it, pull the lever, and I would watch with fascination as the three wheels whirled. I never had any impulse to try it myself, though. The whirling wasn't worth a nickel to me and I could clearly see that the wins did not balance the losses, except for the slot-machine owner (who paid us a small percentage for keeping it there).

Sometimes the intricate mechanism would go wrong and a repairman would come and take the thing apart. I would watch and marvel at the many parts and would be overcome by an earnest desire to take

---

[1] This tendency may be helped along by the fact that I find so much change and adventure inside my head that I don't feel the necessity of going through the trouble of dragging my physical body over the obstacles and through the underbrush.

apart, carefully and delicately, the entire machine. It was then my notion to line the parts up in order of decreasing size. I knew, however, that I had no desire whatever to put them together again thereafter.

My attraction to mechanical objects was purely destructive, never constructive, and I realized it. In my whole life, therefore, I never fooled myself into thinking I wanted to be an engineer or an auto mechanic or anything of the sort.

2

In the new store, we lived upstairs and not around the corner. There was a staircase in the back of the store that led directly up to our living quarters.

There were numerous advantages to this. The store and the apartment were all there was to the building so that we rented the entire structure and we did not have other people sharing it with us. There was no one for us to annoy and no one to annoy us. It was very simple to go up and down the stairs, so we saved on commuting time, so to speak, and my father did not have to go through a stretch of the outdoors in bad weather just to eat or take his nap.

On the other hand, it was a small apartment, and we were back to three rooms. Worse than that, far worse, we were just above the store, so that if my sister and I had the slightest discussion, there'd come a banging on the radiator pipes, or a yell up the stairs, or, worst of all, the sudden, physical presence of my mother.

Her complaint was always that the customers were astonished and perturbed; that they looked up at the ceiling saying, "What is that?" as though an earthquake were taking place instead of a discussion. The impression *we* received was that all the customers came from homes where the utmost decorum prevailed at all times and that for them to hear voices raised in discussion shocked their sensibilities to such an extent that they would certainly never return. They might even report the matter to the police.

My mother, always short-tempered, would sometimes explain her views by hitting us on such parts of our bodies as she could reach, thus invariably giving rise to outcries far worse than those she was correcting.

In a cabinet in the kitchen, she kept a length of clothes rope that was specially hardened and sharpened for the purpose of beating recalcitrant mules and little children, and when she was *very* angry, she would light into us with that. It was much worse than spanking. In a spanking, the pressure is spread over the palm of a hand. When that rope curls around you, however, with all the pressure concentrated into a narrow region and with the extra speed induced by the leverage effect of its being farther from the pivot, it really *smarts*. It takes a long time to rub the pain away.

In later years, when my mother would look back on my childhood and marvel at what a good boy I had always been, I would say, "What kind of good boy could I have been, Mamma? You were always hitting me with ropes."

"With ropes?" she would say, stupefied.

"Sure," I said, "you had a rope that you kept in the closet and when you got really mad at me you would whip me with the rope. How could I have been a good boy if you had to hit me with ropes?"

And she would say, "*Never. I never* hit you with ropes." I think she even believed it.

The fact is she struck me even when I grew to tower over her four feet, ten inches. She would order me to sit down and then she would attack me like an enraged lioness. By that time, however, I was large enough and she had grown old enough for it to have become easy for me to fend her off with my elbow and she would end up wincing and complaining that I was an unnatural son who was hurting her.

I said, reasonably, "It's because I'm getting too big to hit, Mamma." So she stopped. I must have been about fifteen by that time.

3

When we moved into that apartment, by the way, the old owners had not yet completely removed their possessions and, for just a few days, there was an overlap. One of the things they had left behind was a typewriter, and I believe it was the first typewriter I had ever seen.

It is really astonishing, as I look back upon it, to recall my reaction. I scarcely knew what a typewriter was. If I did know, there could be no reason why I should want to use one—and yet I felt the strangest yearning toward it. I would stare at it and touch the keys and carefully depress one and watch the letter move up.

Somehow I had the dim hope that it might be left behind and that it might become ours by default and that I could then use it. What purpose it could possibly serve, I didn't know, but I wanted to use it.

If I were a believer in psionic power (which I am *not*), I would think that the force of my ultimate fascination with typewriters and my endless use of them in years to come had somehow sent a message backward in time to my nearly-nine-year-old self.

4

At the time we moved I was in 5A. After we moved I could no longer go to PS 182, where I had gone for nearly four years. We were out of the neighborhood and there was no busing. The new neighborhood school was PS 202, which was a newer, cleaner, and better school—but it meant I was totally uprooted.

There's something I remember that I can't swear belongs to this particular move, but it may have. As I recall, I got into an argument with another young man of my own age in the playground, as we were lining up to be led into our classes.

He maintained that 202 was much better than 182, and I denied it, naturally. He said that the smartest boy in 5A in his class was smarter than the smartest boy in 5A in 182; and I said he was full of something-or-other-that-I-wasn't-allowed-to-say-at-home, because I was the smartest boy in 5A in 182, and I was certainly smarter than the smartest boy in 5A in 202.

It was a terrible boast to make, for it might well have ruined my stay at the school if I had turned out to be engaged in unfounded boasting. And how could I know? After all, could I be certain that the brightest boy in class in this new school might not be a prodigy who would far outshine me?

I was indeed to meet such superprodigies in time, but fortunately for myself, this wasn't to be one of those times. I moved smoothly into position as brightest boy in the class and there was no real argument about it.

5

I was being put to work more and more in the store. I had always done what I could from the beginning. I had watched the newsstand to pick up the pennies left there and to make sure no one took a paper without paying. (If even a seven-year-old calls out, "That's two cents, mister"—which is what the morning papers cost those days—it takes a hardened criminal to walk away without paying.)

In the new store, however, I was being placed behind the counter to dole out penny candy, or to sell a pack of cigarettes or a cigar or a newspaper. I would deliver papers on occasion (we didn't have a regular delivery). I became the one to run and call people to the phone, which meant I sometimes got a nickel as a tip. (Tips, though, I turned over to my father. It was understood, after all, that I had no use for a nickel, since I was supplied with all my necessities free of charge.)

About the only thing I didn't do was to fool around with the ice cream, or make malteds. (I did make ordinary sodas.) Somehow I never learned how to dish out ice cream, make sundaes, ice-cream sodas, or malteds in all my years in the candy store. I can't believe it was because I was too stupid to learn how, so I can only suppose it was because it was the one task in the candy store I was determined not to do, and you can't learn to do what you're determined not to do.

My father let me get away with it.

Still, the increasing duties managed to break off my relations with my peer group. In the first place, I couldn't very well keep friends if I had to say constantly, "I have to go watch the store."

Second, there was a vast social gulf raised between myself and the rest. If one of them came in for a piece of candy for a penny, and could stand at the counter, taking his ease, and deciding slowly, while I had to wait patiently for him to make up his mind and then give him whatever he asked for on demand, it made me his distinct social inferior— and I felt it.

The reason why I was suddenly put to increasingly onerous duties in the candy store was not merely the result of my growing older (I was a big boy of nine by now), nor was it any weakness in my father.

He turned thirty-two at just about the time we bought the Essex Street candy store, and had worked hard all his life, as had all his family, and he had the work-hard ethic. I remember his chopping his own ice in that candy store to put into the ice-cream storage container (we did not yet have an electric freezer for it) and then adding rock salt to bring the freezing temperature to the required point where ice cream would remain hard. He would have to mix the chopped ice and the rock salt by thorough pounding with the thick end of a baseball bat. I remember him wrestling carbon-dioxide cylinders into and out of the basement so that the carbonated spouts of the soda fountain would work.

No, there was nothing wrong with him. The trouble was with my mother. Sometime in midfall of 1928, during our last months at Miller Avenue, she became pregnant.

It was not a planned pregnancy. It was an accident, and if it had occurred a half-century later I have a strong suspicion an abortion would have been performed, if only because a baby *and* a candy store were an incredible combination. As it was, abortions were unthinkable, and there was nothing to do but go through with it—which is a good thing, for everyone was, and has always been, pleased with the result, including, particularly, myself.[2]

This meant that through the first half of 1929, my mother was becoming steadily less capable of putting in her usual sixteen-hour day of unremitting toil, and I had to substitute. Furthermore, my father had to look forward to my mother's being inevitably wrapped up with the demands of an infant for some time after birth, so I had to know my way around the store sufficiently to be able to take over as second in command.

That was the beginning. For a period of many years thereafter, I was tied to the candy store. Since I also had to go to school (and do *well*, for my father had no intention of allowing me to use my home duties as an excuse for falling short), it meant that many years were to pass for me with little or no leisure.

I might have rebelled inwardly at this and, once I escaped, I might have made up my mind never to live so again—taken to sleeping late, learning how to loaf, and so on.

However, I either started working too young or found too much compensation in work, for I was imprinted for life. When the time came that I could have all the leisure I wanted—I found I did not want it. In fact, I could not take it even when others insisted. I am forever and always in the candy store, and the work must be done.

I even know the precise reason for it.

My father, who was forever bustling about the store, hauling cases of soda bottles or bundles of newspapers, would occasionally find me sitting down, lost in a book, and would immediately inform me that I was lazy and that lazy people would come to a bad end. He would then find some chore for me to do in order to preserve me from disaster.

I always defended myself against the imputation of indolence. I never disobeyed my father, but my respect for him was not carried to the point of accepting libelous remarks in silence.

And I *still* defend myself. I kept trying to disprove my laziness for so long that I forgot that leisure was not necessarily laziness. Whatever within me was needed to relearn that fact has atrophied past saving.

So I still work seven days a week and ten hours a day, when I can, as though I were still in the candy store. When circumstances force me to stop for a while, I get uneasy as though I hear a voice within me saying, "Who's watching the store?"

[2] When I stated the pregnancy to have been accidental in *Before the Golden Age*, my brother (the result of that pregnancy) asked me, in a rather challenging manner, what made me think so. I said, "Mamma told me," and you never heard anything so unanswerable in your life.

Of course, it is writing at which I now work, but the memory of my father is with me constantly and it is that, more than anything else, that has made me so prolific. I am still trying to dodge the imputation of laziness.

It's also there that we may find the reason, more than any other, that makes me insist on doing all my work solo, and never employing a typist, a secretary, a researcher, or anything else. The candy store was a family operation and we had no helpers—so I allow myself no helpers now.

6

But never mind that. In the spring and summer of 1929, I had no way of knowing what the candy store was to do to me. All I knew was that my mother was getting fat and tired and that I couldn't play with the kids at all. About the only thing left for me to do that could be called playing was, when things were slow in the store, to bounce a ball against the wall (but not when my father was napping), provided I kept an eye on the doorway and came into the store if more than two people entered.

This forced me the more firmly into the world of books, and I became an assiduous librarygoer.

I read omnivorously and without guidance. I would stumble on books about Greek myths and fell in love with that world. When I discovered William Cullen Bryant's translations of the *Iliad* and the *Odyssey* I took them out of the library over and over. Unaware that they were classics I was *supposed* to read and should therefore avoid, I enjoyed them and read and reread them, often beginning again as soon as I had finished, until I had almost memorized them. (I was so ignorant that it was years before I discovered that Achilles was not pronounced ATCH-illz.)

I read Dumas and Dickens and Louisa May Alcott and, indeed, almost the entire gamut of nineteenth-century fiction. Because so much of it was by British authors, I became a spiritual Englishman and a conscious Anglophile.

I read E. Nesbit's books and Howard Pyle's and George Mac-Donald's. I even read Eugene Sue, which carries the Romantic Era to the extreme edge of endurability and had me constantly in tears. But then I was crying all the time in those days. I wept over Beth in *Little Women*, over Raoul, Athos, and Porthos in *The Man in the Iron Mask*, over Smike in *Nicholas Nickleby*, and eventually learned, in my frequent rereadings, which chapters to skip.

I had to read nonfiction too, because at least one of the two books I was allowed had to be nonfiction, and I would read *anything* rather than nothing. I found, by experimentation, that history and science fascinated me, so I picked out every book I could get on those subjects.

And, because I had (and still have) a retentive memory and instant recall, everything I read remained with me and was at my service and made schoolwork all the easier. It was to be many, many years before I learned anything in school that I did not already know.[3]

What I *didn't* read was what the libraries of the 1920s and 1930s were poor in, and that was contemporary fiction. Or, if the libraries did have them, then I discovered them too late, after my literary tastes had solidified. Most twentieth-century *serious* fiction is beyond me.

Mysteries and humor are another matter, of course. Of all twentieth-century writers I should say the two I have read most carefully and thoroughly, and have reread most assiduously and with undiminished delight, are Agatha Christie and P. G. Wodehouse.

7

Even my library foraging was not enough for me back in 1929, and I kept studying the magazine racks in the candy store with steadily increasing desire. In that particular respect the spirit of rebellion was growing slowly higher within me.

The Nick Carters and Frank Merriwells had died out, and it was the pulps that now attracted my attention—the detective stories, the Westerns, the adventures, and so on. Even such magazines as *Paris Nights* or *Spicy Romances* (which were daring-for-the-1920s forays into the realm of soft-core pornography) caught my eye and filled me with strange and uncertain emotions as I stared at feminine legs and breasts on the cover paintings.[4]

What attracted me most, though, were the science-fiction magazines.

In the spring of 1926, the first magazine ever to be devoted to science fiction exclusively was placed on the newsstands for sale. It was entitled *Amazing Stories*, and the first issue was dated April 1926.

[3] In fact, it all *still* remains with me and is *still* at my service. People frequently ask me how I do all the research needed to write my dozens of books on dozens of subjects, and it's hard to explain that at least some of the research was done when I was a youngster, and that it is filed away in accessible locations in my mind. As to *how* I manage to remember and recall, I can't tell you. I have always been able to do it, but I don't know how, except that it's easy and causes me no trouble.

[4] Instinct told me, however, that paternal lightning would flash full force if I even let on that I knew that *Paris Nights* existed, let alone tried to get permission to look inside.

I never saw it. Perhaps my father did not get that particular maga-zine in the Sutter Avenue store; or perhaps my eyes weren't attuned to it yet. In the Essex Street store, however, I came across the magazine and began to long for it, and to sneak looks inside.

Unfortunately, my father was adamant about keeping me from reading any magazine. The pressures built, however, and everything conspired against him—even school.

In February 1929, I entered 5B1, and my teacher was a Miss Mar-tin. She was the best teacher I had had since the first grade—and for many years afterward—and I loved her more than any other. She was unfailingly good-natured and never scolded shrewishly. She read to us from books and, in fact, introduced me to Hugh Lofting's books about Dr. Dolittle which, for some years to come, were nectar and ambrosia to me.

Furthermore, she was clearly fond of me and didn't mind that I was my usual disruptive self in her class. Her liking wasn't reflected in the marks I got. For two months running, I remember, I brought back my report card with an A in schoolwork and a D (in *red*, for failure) in deportment. Fortunately, my parents knew what deportment meant now, and merely lectured me.

But despite my deportmental villainy, Miss Martin liked me. For one thing, she gave me the chance to recover from a particularly pain-ful setback I had had in 5A1.

Not long after. I had joined PS 202, the school's semi-annual spelling bee came up. Every class within a certain range would send out its representative, and the bee would be held in the auditorium. The students all loved it because it was exciting. After all, you could root for your own class and laugh and hoot like fiends if anyone missed. (The old hand-on-the-shoulder, "Well played, old man," was totally foreign to us.)

Naturally, I was sent into the fray by 5A1. I hadn't been there long, but I had already proved that I was death on spelling. I could spell any word I had ever seen.

So there I was on the stage.

It wasn't as though I had never been on the stage before. Every schoolchild gets his chance, whether he wants to or not, because every class is bound to have a class play, and every youngster in the class is somehow involved. If he misses in one term, he gets it in another.

I, too, had been in plays. I had once played a Russian soldier in a play that was set in Russia. As I recall, the little heroine, a poor girl, was so unhappy with her lot that her fairy godmother told her she could change places with anyone, just by shaking hands with them. The little girl then met a series of other people, all of whom seemed to be better off than she was, but she always found something about them that made her shrink away. The princess who enters is frightened of thieves, so the little girl thinks that if she were only a soldier she wouldn't be afraid of anyone.

That was my cue to enter (age seven, I think, at the time), with my woolen hat's earflaps coming down and buttoning under my chin to represent a soldier's helmet, and my arms crossed over my chest to indicate resolution and valor. I had but to appear and the entire audience did what they always seemed to do when I appeared—they burst into loud laughter. Fortunately I was used to it, and I delivered my lines with *sang-froid*. By the time I had detailed the hardships of a soldier's life, the heroine wouldn't shake hands with me.

But that was a play—in a familiar school before familiar fellow pupils.

Now, two years later, I was in a contest, facing strangers in a strange school. And it was a competition that was particularly unfair. Victory was only what I expected and would give me no great pleasure. Defeat, however, would be an unthinkable humiliation. I had nothing particularly to win; everything to lose; and there was no fun in it.

My teeth chattered, my body shook—not so much out of fear as out of tension. When it was my turn, I was asked to spell "weigh." I stood up and said, "Weigh, W-I-E-G-H, Weigh," and knew I was wrong the minute I transversed the two vowels.

I went down and walked back to my seat, with hoots and catcalls ringing in my ear. I had missed the first word.

Even if everyone at school had not made it their mission to remind me of this now and again, I would not have forgotten.

When the time came for the next term's spelling bee, I was in 5B1 and Miss Martin said, "Is there anyone in the class who would like to represent us in the spelling bee?"

Two or three hands went up; mine stayed firmly down. Once was enough for one lifetime.

Miss Martin looked at me. "Aren't you volunteering, Isaac?"

The class looked at me. I said, "I missed last term, Miss Martin. I don't think the class wants me."

Miss Martin said to the class, "Isaac has the best marks for spelling this term, and I think he can win. How many in the class want him?"

Once she expressed her preference, of course, all the little syco-phants raised a cry on my behalf, and I was forced to be the 5B1 representative in a bee that included all the classes in the fourth, fifth, and sixth grades.

I was nervous again, but this time, at least, I had the comforting knowledge that I could not do worse than the term before. As soon as I had spelled the first word correctly, I was ahead of the game. And once I was ahead, I calmed down and was certain I would win.

It wasn't quite that easy. By the time the period ended, another boy (from one of the sixth-grade classes) and myself were still on our feet. We had to fight it out in a tie-breaking session a few days later in the principal's office.

We were both shaking with tension and barely able to enunciate, and the principal kindly tried to ease the situation by telling us that we would have two tries at every word. When I spelled "customer" C-O-S-T-O-M-E-R, my face went into a spasm of unhappiness.

The principal said, "Try it again, Isaac," and I got it right the next time.

After a few more words, the other boy spelled "disappointment" D-I-S-S-A-P-O-I-N-T-M-E-N-T. I tried to keep my face frozen. The principal gave him another chance and, after some hesitation, he spelled it *the same way*. I was astonished.

The principal said, "Can you spell the word, Isaac?" Of course I could, and did, and I won. I didn't really enjoy the victory, however, because I had been the first to miss, and if it had not been for the relaxation of the rules, the other boy would have won. I have never forgotten this.[5]

I got a fountain pen as my prize, the first one I had ever owned. Till then the only pens I had were those with steel points that you fitted into a wooden holder and dipped into an inkwell. Every desk had an inkwell, which the teacher filled out of a tall ink bottle when necessary and which, sooner or later, got all over the clothes of every pupil in the class (sometimes accidentally, sometimes maliciously).

I don't recall that we had any spelling bees after that. I don't know why they were stopped, but I was tremendously relieved. I would certainly have been class representative if they had continued, and I didn't want to be. The second time out I had a failure to make up, but afterward I would merely have been defending champion with nothing to gain and everything to lose.

One final gift of Miss Martin's came when the class was over and the summer vacation had begun. In the final days of the class, she announced that she would take a few selected members of the class, those who had done very well in both work and deportment, on a visit to the Statue of Liberty.

[5] There are disadvantages to a too-good memory. It is difficult for me to remember things to my own advantage, by adjusting details.

It was clear I wouldn't make it, for that pair of D's in deportment placed me out of the running under even the most liberal interpretation of what "good marks" might be.

That bothered me for several reasons.

First, I had never gone *anywhere* without my parents, except to the local library, and it would be thrilling to do so. Second, I wanted to see the Statue of Liberty. Third, when my parents found out (and somehow they would, I was sure) that selected members of the class had been chosen for this outing and that I hadn't qualified, I would be in for a sticky half hour.

So I sat there, looking disappointed, and Miss Martin, ever an Isaac enthusiast, said to the pupils, "Class, shall we make an exception for the brightest pupil in the class even if his deportment is bad?" Once again all the little sycophants cheered, and I got to go.

She was *such* a softhearted teacher. I saw her once or twice during the next year, but then I left PS 202 and I never saw her or heard from her again. Still—thank you, Miss Martin, wherever you are.

The outing was on July 2, 1929, something I cannot forget because I was 9½ years old that day. The weather was perfect; the Statue of Liberty was impressive; we all went spiraling up endless stairs without feeling particularly tired, and of course there was the ferry ride before and after. It was a great success, but from that day to this, although I have seen the Statue of Liberty innumerable times from a distance, I have never actually been on Liberty Island (or Bedloe's Island, as it was called in 1929) again.

8

I returned from that trip with a heightened feeling of being grown up. I had had a most unaccustomed taste of freedom and I was in no mood to undergo tyrannical oppression, and I actually wanted to have a showdown with my father over the science-fiction magazines.

And I could now make out a good case for it. As long as I had only *Amazing Stories* to fight about, I was in trouble, for there was nothing in the name of the magazine that would impress my father. In 1929, however, Hugo Gernsback, the publisher of the magazine, had been forced out, and had immediately begun a competing magazine, which he named *Science Wonder Stories*. The first issue, August 1929, was on the stands when I came back from the trip to the Statue of Liberty.

As soon as I inspected it and found out that it, like *Amazing Stories*, was science fiction (the expression "science fiction" had not yet been invented, by the way, but was soon to be—by Gernsback), I saw at once that I had an opening, for the new magazine had "science" in the title.

I had read enough about science to know that it was a mentally nourishing and spiritually wholesome study. What's more, I knew that my father thought so from our occasional talks about my schoolwork.

I picked up the magazine and, not without considerable qualms, approached my formidable sire. (It is hard for me to believe that at the time he was only thirty-two years old. I took it for granted that he was infinitely old—at least as old as Moses.)

I spoke rapidly, pointed out the word "science," showed him the paintings of futuristic machines inside as an indication of how advanced it was, and (I believe) made it plain that if he said "No," I had every intention of mounting a rebellion and introducing a resolute campaign of guerrilla warfare.

I have a feeling that even so I would not have won out over my father's incredible obstinacy. (I never knew my father to give in or compromise over any point in which he was wrong; he was sometimes willing to retreat a little if he happened, by accident, to be right.)

However, what I didn't know was that my mother was just about ready to have the new baby. My father had this on his mind and just lacked the patience to argue something that at the moment seemed unimportant. So, like Pharaoh after the tenth plague, he gave in.

I then collected other science-fiction magazines to read even though they didn't have the word "science" in the title. I planned to maintain with all the strength at my disposal the legal position that permission for one such magazine implied permission for all the others, regardless of title. No fight was needed, however; my harassed father conceded everything.

Well, not everything. For some years, my father held the line at science-fiction magazines, whereas I kept pushing for the "hero" magazines in particular. The magazine that was the center of the sharpest fight was *The Shadow*.

That magazine came out twice a month and featured a crime fighter who became a passion all over the nation. I would sneak peeks into the magazine when my father wasn't looking and I *knew* I wanted to read it, but he said "No," and that was that. Since I had my science-fiction magazines, I was not prepared for all-out war.

The thing was that my father liked *The Shadow* and would always take it upstairs with him during his afternoon nap. He would read it for the ten minutes or so it would take him to fall asleep, and just before he drifted off he would slip it under his pillow.

That's where I would come in. When my father slept, he slept *soundly,* both figuratively and literally, for he snored, and while he snored you knew he slept. Under cover of the snoring, I would sneak in and filch the copy of *The Shadow.* I knew exactly when he was supposed to wake up (it was my job to wake him, remember), and there was no chance he would wake up before then, so five minutes before it was time, I replaced the magazine. Then I woke him up.

This went on for quite a time, and I read *The Shadow* under conditions of excitement and deadly peril for months, and, of course, that made it all the sweeter.

Once, I remember, my father got dressed and started down the stairs, *leaving the magazine under his pillow.* Usually he took it down to avoid exposing me to a temptation that would destroy my soul if I succumbed, but this one time he didn't. I waited breathlessly to make sure he would get all the way down, for once he got involved with store work, there was no chance he would remember the magazine. He was only halfway down, however, when Marcia called out, "Pappa, you forgot your magazine," and he came up to retrieve it.

I was never closer to sororicide than at that moment.

In the end, of course, I was caught, and as I looked up and found my father silently watching me, I prepared for battle. But my father gave me no chance. "Well, Isaac," he said, "rather than have you *steal* and learn to be a gangster, you can read the magazines."

That lost me about three quarters of my fun, but I kept on reading them on principle. My father would look at me sorrowfully whenever he caught me reading them, and those looks stabbed me to the soul, but principle was principle. I kept on reading.

Yet, as I look back on it, I think he was right. If he hadn't closed off that outlet and others, too,[6] I would not have had to turn to the library.

Eventually my brother was old enough to become interested in what my father would consider trashy reading. By then my father had lost some of the verve of youth and, having expended himself on the battle with me, he let him read whatever he wanted. By then the comic books were on the newsstands, and my brother wasted enough time on them to appear less bright in school than I did, though I'm sure he is just as intelligent as I am.

[6] We got our first radio after we bought the Essex Street store, but my father kept it on top of the telephone booth, where only he could reach the dials. I, in particular, was forbidden to stand on a chair and fiddle with them myself. Still, he liked "The Eddie Cantor Show" on Sunday nights, and I was always in the store to listen, praying that customers wouldn't come in.

9

Toward the end of July 1929, my mother went off to the hospital, and Marcia and I were told why. For a week or so, some neighbor fed us and I hated it, because my experience was entirely limited to my mother's cooking (except for those occasions at Siegel's place in Parksville, which I also hated).

Another neighbor went into the hospital at the same time for the same purpose, a neighbor with whom my mother was particular friends. They were delivered on the same day, July 25, 1929—my mother of a boy and the neighbor of a girl. My mother lived; the neighbor died.

We kept it from my mother. Even we children knew what had happened, but we were told by my father in unusually emphatic terms that we must not say a word about it. Indeed, when my mother came home from the hospital with the new baby, she was still ignorant of the tragedy.

When one of the neighbor's older children arrived to look at the baby, my mother asked, querulously, "Where is your mother? They wouldn't let me see her in the hospital."

In all innocence, the child said, "My mother died," and *my* mother proceeded to have fits of hysterics all over the place. I had never seen that happen before, and it was a very frightening thing.

10

I participated in the naming of the new baby. It was the first time in my life such a thing had happened, and I had very strong feelings about names.

For instance, for as long as I could remember I have been extraordinarily fond of the name Isaac. I don't know why; perhaps it is one aspect of being pleased at being me, generally. In any case, I have never willingly allowed nicknames. Ike, Ikey, and Izzy are all abominations, and I correct all who call me that, except for very old friends of whom I am very fond. If a correction in their case doesn't take, then I correct no more but endure it. These represent no more than a handful of people, I assure you. Sometimes I am called "I," which may even be written "Eye." That I won't fight over, but it is still not the name of choice.

While we were still on Van Siclen Avenue, old-timers were instructing my mother on How Not to Be a Greenhorn. The suggestion was made that she ought to do something about my name. Isaac, they explained, would be a terrible stigma. It would be entirely too Jewish and it would keep me from advancing in the new land. What would be an appropriate name, they said, would be Irving. It would keep the initial "I," so that my mother could still console herself with the pious thought that I was named for her dead father, while it would give me a name that would enable me to hold my head up among the Gentiles.

I didn't know at the time that it was all folly. Irving is an old aristocratic English name. Once, however, enough Jewish youths were named Irving, it became a Jewish name, with all the disadvantages thereto appertaining.

I didn't have to know. When my mother tried to call me Irving, I set up a howl of objection. My name was Isaac, I would answer to nothing else, and that was the way it was going to stay. And so it *has* stayed. As far as I know, it has never in any way proven a stigma or kept me from advancing, since my Jewishness did not need the name to be self-evident.

In fact, simply because it is an uncommon name, it has made it possible for those of my readers who, for one reason or another, feel close to me to use it as a way of signifying familiarity and affection without much fear of ambiguity.

I wanted my brother to be called Solomon. I still remembered Solly Frisch, and I wanted him to have the honor. My father, unaware of the origin of the suggestion, was attracted to it. It was a classic Jewish name and no living member of the family bore it. It was thus understood, when my mother went in the hospital, that if a boy were born, his name was to be Solomon.

What we didn't count on was that the woman in the bed next to my mother was planning to call her child, if it were a boy, Stanley. My mother liked that name, which was (if she but knew) another fine old aristocratic English name. What's more, she must have taken the strictures of the old-timers more seriously than my father or I did, and she did not wish to add another stigma to the family. Stanley it was, therefore, to my profound indignation.

What made it worse was that my mother, for years, called him "Standely" with an extraneous *d*, and no amount of coaching on my part could get her to omit it. (There were other parental idiosyncrasies of pronunciation I couldn't eradicate. My mother spoke of "birthsdays" and wouldn't drop the s despite anything I could offer in the way of logic, reasoning, and ridicule. My father, who never used coarse language, was reduced to saying "Nots" when driven past endurance, and nothing I could say would induce him to say "Nuts.")

As to my father, he customarily referred to the new baby as Shlaymele, which is the Hebrew version of "Solly" in our dialect of the language. Still, Stanley it was, and there was no fighting it.

When Stanley grew to mature years, he tended more and more to drop the second syllable, and now he consistently uses the first syllable only. He is Stan Asimov.

11

Once Stanley was born and my mother had recovered somewhat, she returned to the store full time. Fortunately for her, while Marcia and I had been breast-fed (what else, indeed, was possible in Petrovichi?), Stanley, in this new land beyond the sea, could be bottle-fed and was. Moreover, he was bottle-fed, for the most part, by *me*.

There were only two alternatives possible. Either my mother helped run the store and I helped care for little Stanley, or my mother devoted herself full-time to the kid and I to the store.

For myself, I preferred to take care of Stanley. For one thing, I liked the baby, and for another he was no particular trouble. Except when he needed changing (which my mother took care of), he either drank his milk or slept. Unlike his older siblings, he was over seven pounds at birth and was well developed, so he did very well indeed. He stayed in the carriage and I propped myself in a chair leaning back against the brick wall of the house, reading—and set to go into the store if I were called.

Or else I could wheel him around the block a dozen times or so with a book propped against the handle of the carriage. No problem. No trouble.

One embarrassment I can recall in connection with this was once, when he had grown big enough to want to stand up in the carriage, I amused him by starting and stopping the carriage so that he would sway back and forth and laugh. A woman scolded me for doing so, feeling I was endangering the child. When I got home, I complained to my mother that some strange woman had scolded me "for just doing this." I demonstrated it, and Stanley immediately tumbled out of the carriage—and don't think I didn't get a hiding promptly.

On another occasion I stopped at a plant nursery that existed on one of the other sides of the block. A bud of some sort hung over the fence, and I plucked it and examined it as I continued walking. I thought nothing of it, but when I reached the store, the owner of the nursery was there ahead of me.

"Did you take a flower?" my father asked.

"Yes," I said, frightened, "but it was just a bud."

"Why?"

"I wanted to see what was inside."

My father paid up and said not another word. He knew he didn't have to. I had just never known that flowers weren't free. Now that I had learned that wasn't so, he knew I wouldn't do it again.

12

It was about that time, too, that I became aware of the outside world as reflected in the newspapers, which I began to read.

My first experience with the newspapers—the Sunday *News*, to be exact—was while we were still living on Miller Avenue. The comic supplement was a powerful attraction, and I loved reading it. My favorites were Moon Mullins and Winnie Winkle. For some reason, I still remember the Rinkeydink Club, of which Perry Winkle was the leading member. The other three members were Spike, Spud, and Chink.

I even have dim memories of my mother reading the comics to me before I could read. In a way, this was impossible, since my mother couldn't possibly read English at that time. I can only presume that, going by the action, she made up her own conversation.

But matters besides the comics were beginning to penetrate. In 1928 I was aware that there was a presidential election on, in part through the four-page newspaper that was distributed in grade school.

It was Al Smith of New York vs. Herbert Hoover of Somewhere Else. Naturally, I was for Al Smith because he was from New York. So were all the other kids at school, so it seemed clear to me that Hoover didn't have a chance. I was devastated when Hoover won. In fact, I couldn't believe it, and was convinced that there had been some crooked work somewhere. I wondered if perhaps Al Smith could be president of New York, at least.

My clearest memory of that election is of a radio set up over the front door of some store on Sutter Avenue with a crowd of people standing about in front of it listening to the election returns.

Then in October of 1929, came the stock market crash that put an end to the prosperity of the 1920s and introduced the Great Depression. The economic situation slid steadily downhill and, as my father's customers found themselves with less and less money, things turned bad for the store as well. Our second candy store, after half a year of moderate promise, showed clearly that it was to be no more a highway to riches than the first had been.

Just the same, the Depression taught us the value of the candy store. There were bread lines and soup kitchens and people selling apples on corners, but none of that was for us. Even people with jobs had to dread the possibility of a layoff, and once laid off, there was the near impossibility of finding another job. None of that was for us, either.

We could not be fired. We had a job and a place to live. The job might be sixteen hours a day and seven days a week, and the profits might be small, but it represented security. All through the Hoover administration we never missed a meal, and there was always money for necessities.

10

Junior High School

1

I passed through the sixth grade smoothly. In 6B1, I had as my teacher a Miss Growney (I believe that was her name), who was at the opposite pole from Miss Martin. Miss Growney was considered "strict," and she regularly scolded us in unmeasured terms.

I had entered her class with the greatest misgivings, fearing that with my well-known proclivities for antisocial whispering, I would be in constant trouble—and so I was. Miss Growney, however, seemed to have a perverse affection for me, possibly because she was pleased at having such a bright little boy in her class, so she was never as hard on me as I thought she would be.

And as for her short temper—well, that was old-home week for me. She was very much like my mother in that respect.

Then, in June of 1930, my stay at PS 202 came to an end after not quite two years. I was 10½ years old now, and once the summer vacation was over, I would enter junior high school.

Summer vacations were never easy times for me. Theoretically, they were vacations, but not for me. It just meant I worked in the candy store all day instead of only from 3:00 P.M. on. During the school year I got away from the store, and the school itself offered me no problems in exchange (except for my periodically being punished for my many terrible transgressions).

So I loved school and found the summer tedious. This was at no time more pronounced than the summer of 1930, when I was looking forward to the excitement of junior high school and feeling very adult about it. It seems to me I spent that entire summer doing only two things:

First, I wheeled Stanley around the block endlessly while reading the *Iliad* endlessly.[1] Second, I carefully computed the number of hours until school began.

I think that was the first time I ever computed hours to some zero time, but I've been doing it ever since. I would routinely compute the

---

[1] I even told myself stories designed to continue the *Iliad* after Homer had left off. I was Achilles, and although Homer clearly indicated that Achilles was slated for an early death, he never died in my daydreams.

number of hours until the next issue of some desired science-fiction magazine would appear on the stand and watch the number diminish as I grew more excited. Even today, you can ask me at any time, when I am out of town for any reason, how many hours it will be till I'm back at my typewriter and I'll tell you.

And though I thought, at some times during the summer, that vacation would never be over, it was. On the last day of vacation I remember sitting on my father's newsstand (which I could do when the papers were mostly gone) drumming my heels against it, with myself in a delirium of joy because the next day would be Monday, September 9, 1930, and I would start junior high school.

The junior high school I went to was East New York Junior High School 149, on Sutter Avenue between Wyona and Vermont streets (I think), quite close to where I used to live on Van Siclen and Miller avenues. Had I still lived there I would have been able to walk to school.

As it was, there was the far more exciting necessity of having to go to school by bus. It meant that every weekday I would have to take the bus twice, once going and once coming. It meant my mother would have to entrust me with two nickels, one for the bus going and one for the bus coming.

For the first time since I started school five years before I would not be coming home for lunch. That meant I would have to buy something to eat or take lunch with me. Since my mother didn't have time to make lunch for me early in the morning, she gave me a quarter with which to buy hot dogs, french fries, corned beef club sandwiches, and other foods guaranteed to pickle the stomach. I loved it.

2

Junior high schools cover the seventh, eighth, and ninth grades, and you could traverse them in one of two ways: You could take a full three-year course: 7A, 7B, 8A, 8B, 9A, 9B. You could also go through in two years by taking a "rapid advance" course, if you were considered bright enough. You could go through RA, RB, RC, and RD, where the "R" stood for "rapid advance," of course. RA was the equivalent of 7A plus 7B, and RB was the equivalent of 8A plus 8B. RC and RD were 9A and 9B, respectively, allowing for some extra brightness. Naturally, I was placed in the rapid advance course.

That meant that at the end of my first year of junior high school, having completed RA and RB successfully, I had also completed both seventh and eighth grades. When I received my promotion in June

1931, which meant I was officially in RC, which was the ninth grade, I was the equivalent of a high-school freshman.[2]

I had expected this promotion, of course, and I arranged with my mother that I would not go directly home. I ran to the library instead and came up against the librarian's desk with a thud.

"I want an adult library card, please," I panted, handing her my children's card.

I was still a week short of being 11½, and was very skinny and looked younger still. The librarian said to me gently, "You can't have an adult card till you're in high school, little boy."

"I *am* in high school," I said, and presented her with my report card. She consulted another official and for a while both looked at me as though it must surely be against the law for anyone looking like me to be in high school, but in the end I got my card.

This meant I could roam at will among the mysterious stacks containing adult books. The card was stamped "H.S.," however, which still restricted me to two books at a time, only one of which could be fiction.

3

Fortunately, I had my science-fiction magazines, too, and they were wonderful. To be sure, I couldn't keep them. They had to be sold, or, if not sold, returned to the publisher. Consequently, it was my habit to grab them as soon as they came in and to read them with a very light hand, so that when I was through they would close neatly, as though they had never been read.[3]

I felt a little put upon that this was necessary, and even more put upon that I could not keep the magazines permanently. It meant I could not save the serials, for instance, and then read the parts all together. On the whole, though, I was fortunate beyond belief.

If my father had not owned a candy store, and if he had made an equivalent living in any other line of endeavor, it simply passes the bounds of belief that I could possibly have *bought* science-fiction magazines. They cost a quarter each (one of them, an at-that-time inferior magazine called *Astounding Stories*, cost twenty cents), and my father simply would not have given me seventy cents a month in order that I

[2] Grade schools are usually Grades 1 through 8, and high schools Grades 9 through 12. Junior high schools, when they exist, combine the last two grades of grade school with the first year of high school.
[3] I also learned to read newspapers that way. To this day, I can read the Sunday New York *Times* and, when I am through, you will not be able to tell that it has been in any way disturbed.

might buy science-fiction magazines. Nor would my mother, at that time, have let them accumulate in the tiny apartment.

As a matter of fact, I was never allowed any money to spend as I wished. About the only luxury I could legitimately need money for was an occasional movie, and then I would say, "Mamma, can I have fifteen cents for a movie?" (The price had gone up since the Sutter Avenue Theater days, but on the other hand, the pictures now talked.) She would give it to me and off I would go, or she wouldn't give it to me and off I wouldn't go.

Once, when we were still living on Miller Avenue, my mother had the idea of giving me ten cents a week allowance. I was to be allowed to spend that dime on any unbelievable luxury I wished. I think that started because I was going to Hebrew school at the time and some of the other kids had allowances and I called this to my mother's attention. Perhaps she didn't want me to make a poor appearance before the other kids, so I got my dime.

I specifically asked what the limits on the spending were and I was told there were none. It was my dime and I could do as I pleased with it. So I decided to start a stamp collection, and saved up several dimes and then used them to buy a thousand "mixed foreign stamps" (which meant that most of them were duplicated examples of the most common French and German varieties) and a little stamp book to put them in.

As soon as my parents saw me carefully arranging my stamps and discovered that I had lavished immense sums on them (actually, I think it was a quarter), they rescinded the allowance. When I was told that I could spend the dimes as I pleased, I think they meant by that that I was to save up and buy myself underwear.

In later years, my father gave me an allowance of a dollar a week, but ostentatiously put it in a little mechanical savings bank, unwilling to have me spend the money on incredible foolishness like stamps. When enough had accumulated, he bought me an insurance policy that was to mature twenty years later.

Of course, everything has its bright side. If I couldn't afford to buy science-fiction magazines, neither could my friends at the junior high school. I could, at least, read the stories even if I couldn't keep them, and I discovered that I owned a valuable commodity—the ability to *tell* the stories.

I took over the role of my story-telling friend of Miller Avenue days, and now it was others who listened to me. Of course, the stories weren't my own, and I made no pretense that they were. I carefully explained that I had read them in science-fiction magazines.

During lunch hour, we would sit on the curb in front of the school, each with our sandwiches, and, to anywhere from two to ten eager listeners, I would repeat the stories I had read, together with such personal embellishments as I could manage. It increased my pleasure in science fiction and I discovered, for the first time in my life, that I loved to have an audience. I found that I could speak before a group, even when some of them were strangers to me, without embarrassment.

There was one story that particularly impressed me, and that I told with particular éclat, I remember. It was called "World of the Red Sun" and it appeared in the December 1931 issue of *Wonder Stories*.[4] The author of the story (I discovered years later) was Clifford D. Simak. It was his first published story.

My interaction with my fellow junior-high-school students, even those I knew best, was, however, limited to school hours. Thanks to the candy store, I rarely saw them afterward. That meant I could never reinforce the friendship with social nonschool camaraderies.

I was sufficiently extroverted so that I could fit in cheerfully, if temporarily, especially if I had something to offer (like the stories I told). But no one sought me out.

The result is that I remember almost none of my classmates at any level—even in college. There are many who remember me (I was loud-mouthed and eccentric enough to be remembered), and it always embarrasses me to be unable to return the compliment.

As a matter of fact, this has set up a pattern that I have kept throughout life. I am universally friendly in all work settings, yet engage in surprisingly few social interactions outside work—not at all because I am morose and antisocial, but because the social function in me atrophied at an early age.

Perhaps I am all the more friendly at work for that reason, dragging in the energies that would otherwise be expended socially—so that I routinely invade my publishers' offices, for instance, with loud cries and totally inappropriate madness that utterly disrupt the workaday atmosphere.

4

It was about then, also, that, for the first time, I began to try to write stories of my own. You would think, considering my literary interests as just described, that those first stories would have been science

[4] *Science Wonder Stories*, with which I initiated my science-fiction reading had a sister magazine, *Air Wonder Stories*. They lasted as separate magazines for about a year, and with the June 1930 issue, they were combined as *Wonder Stories*.

fiction, but you would be wrong. I had a most exalted notion of the intense skills and vast scientific knowledge required of authors in the field, and I dared not aspire to such things. Instead, I aimed elsewhere.

The 1920s, you see, were the heyday of series books—books about given characters who appeared in book after book indefinitely. There were the *Tom Swift* books, which were in a way a kind of mild Jules Vernish sort of thing, and for younger readers, *The Bobbsey Twins; Bunny Brown and his Sister Sue,* and so on.

In addition, there were *Roy Blakely, Pee Wee Wilson, The Darewell Chums, Poppy Ott,* and so on. Most important of all, at least to me, were *The Rover Boys.* There were three of them—Dick, Tom, and Sam—with Tom, the middle one, always described as "fun-loving."

My friends might not be able to afford science-fiction magazines, but some of them had obtained one or another of these books, and occasionally they could be persuaded to lend one to me. I would read and return it, and I had to do so rather on the sly. If my father had caught me reading one of those books, he would undoubtedly have confiscated it and I might not have persuaded him to return it to its original owner.

One of the books, I remember, I managed to keep. It was *given* to me because it was rather dilapidated and I somehow kept it secure and read it over and over again. It was *The Rover Boys on the Great Lakes.* In it were not only the three Rover boys, but also Andy, the villainous sneak, and his father, the reformed jailbird, and Mr. Crabtree, an oily confidence man, and Dora the Heroine, and her well-intentioned but weak mother, who seemed to be a sitting duck for old Crabtree.

One book just wasn't enough, but what was I going to do about it? Buy books I couldn't; and to borrow books seemed very difficult.

A year or so earlier it had occurred to me in the case of a library book concerning the Greek myths that if I *copied* the book I could then have it permanently. I obtained a nickel copybook and with the fountain pen I had won in the spelling bee, I began to copy it.

It took me just a page and a half to see that there were two flaws in my plan. I could only keep a library book for two weeks, and it was going to take me two years to copy it. Second, my hand was going to fall off in another page and a half. I gave up.

Now, though, it occurred to me that the mistake was in copying. What I ought to do was to write a different and *new* book, one that was all my own. I wouldn't have to depend on a library book for that, so it wouldn't matter how long it took, and I need write only as long as my hand stayed on.

I got another nickel copybook and sat down in the corner of the kitchen and got to work.

I wish I knew what date that was because that was the very first time I ever engaged myself in original composition that had not been a command performance for a schoolteacher. There is no way I can know or ever find out, but I was still in junior high school at the time and I think in RC. That would make it the fall of 1931, most likely, or just before my twelfth birthday.

What I was going to write was a series book, the first of many, I decided (apparently I always had the instinctive knowledge that I would be prolific), and I called it *The Greenville Chums at College*. I had seen a book called *The Darewell Chums at College*, and it seemed to me that by substituting Greenville for Darewell I had made all possible concessions to the need for originality.

I wrote two chapters that evening, making it up as I was going along (something that is still my system), and my mind was full of it the next morning. That day at lunch, I said to one of the youngsters who was particularly assiduous in attending my story-telling sessions: "Hey, let me tell you a story."

And tell him I did, in full detail, and just about word for word, up to the point where I had faded out. He was listening, rapt with attention, and when I stopped, he demanded I continue. I explained that it was all I had so far and he said, "Can I borrow the book when you've finished reading it?"

I was astonished. I had either neglected to make it clear to him, or he had failed to understand, that I was *writing* the book. He thought it was another already printed story I was retelling. The implied compliment staggered me, and from that day on, I secretly took myself seriously as a writer. I remember the name of the young man whose remark unwittingly did this for me. It was Emmanuel Bershadsky.

I never saw him again after I left junior high school, but thank you, Emmanuel, wherever you are.

Still, *The Greenville Chums at College* did not continue forever. It petered out after eight chapters.

The trouble was that I was trying to imitate the series books without knowing anything but what I read there. Their characters were small-town boys, so mine were, for I imagined Greenville to be a town in upstate New York.[5] Their character went to college, so mine did.

Unfortunately, a junior-high-school youngster living in a shabby neighborhood in Brooklyn knows very little about small-town life and even less about college. Even I, myself, was forced eventually to recognize the fact that I didn't know what I was talking about (especially

[5] There *is* a town named Greenville in upstate New York. Naturally, I didn't know that at the time, but I have been there in recent years.

when the plot made it necessary to describe what went on inside a chemistry laboratory). After eight chapters I had to quit.

Just the same, from that time on, I never stayed away from my copybooks for long. Every once in a while I would drift back to try my hand at writing again. Nothing lasted very long for quite a number of years, but I never quit altogether.

5

It wasn't just science fiction and series books that I longed for, nor even the hero pulps or library books. Something else I saw on my father's newsstand was *The World Almanac*, and I began laying siege to him. What I wanted was that the next time *The World Almanac* appeared, one issue was to go to me to *keep*.

The World Almanac, in those days, cost 50 cents. My father got it wholesale, naturally, for 37½ cents. It is a good commentary on just how tight things were in those days that my father hesitated. I think I swung it when I explained that *The World Almanac* came out toward the end of the year and that my birthday was on January 2, and that I wanted it for a birthday present.

In our family, we didn't worry about birthday presents, or any kind of presents. Christmas presents certainly did not exist; we never so much as recognized the existence of Christmas itself (except that we got a long school vacation then); but we didn't fudge the situation by giving Chanukah presents either. It seemed useless to give each other presents—especially the kind of trivial objects that counted as presents. After all, the important things never count as presents. No one, for instance, would accept the fact that one had been fed, housed, and clothed all year as a birthday present. No, what was needed was something silly, and for something silly there was never any money.

It might have been different if we had collateral members of the family or close friends. If presents came in, some would have to go out, and the whole ritual would begin. However, the candy store made social relations impossible and, by the time we had moved to Essex Street, we saw Uncle Joe and his family only very occasionally—and they were our only relatives.

I knew, nevertheless, that birthday presents existed, at least in theory, and I laid claim to *The World Almanac* on that ground. My father finally bit the bullet and got it for me. Specifically, he got me *The 1932 World Almanac* as a present for my eleventh birthday.

I never had any present out of which I got such mileage. I admit it cost my father more than the book itself. He had to get me a sheaf of graph paper, and a thick colored pencil, blue on one side and red on the other.

With all that I got to work. I had been counting automobiles when I was four years old. Now, seven years later, I took advantage of all the people who were counting and measuring the world over in order that a book like *The World Almanac* might be filled with endless columns of tiny figures.

Actually, I could only work when I wasn't at school, or doing homework, or working in the store, or watching Stanley, so it took me a long time, but I ended by making scores of bar graphs and circle graphs and line graphs of various collections of statistics. There were populations and areas and national debts and mountain heights and death rates and everything else.

I didn't care what it was, just so long as I could arrange it all in order and make a pretty picture out of it. And, given my tenacious memory, I got a lot out of it that has remained with me all the rest of my life.

6

I was in JHS 149 for only two years and then I was finished with it. This time I was graduated.

I had left PS 182 in mid-stream because my family had moved. I had been transferred from PS 202 to JHS 149 without ceremony. But when I finished JHS 149, I was subjected to graduation ceremonies for the first time. It was in June 1932, and I was 12½ years old.

The school held the ceremonies at a fancy auditorium somewhere in Brooklyn. My father gave me a fountain pen as a graduation present to replace the old one that I suppose I had managed to use up. More important, he and my mother actually managed to shake off the candy-store duties (I don't remember whether they closed the store or hired a temporary store sitter) in order to attend the graduation. They took it very seriously.

I remember only two things about it. First, the glee club sang "Gaudeamus Igitur," which included the line "Glorious youth is with us." I was at once overwhelmed with a sharp and sorrowful pang at the thought that I was graduating, that I was twelve years old, and that youth was slipping fast away.

The other thing I remember was that two awards were given out, one for excellence in biology and the other for excellence in mathematics. Both winners marched forward and onto the stage and were covered with glory in the sight of their proud parents. And I knew that somewhere in the audience my father's face was setting into lines of grim disapproval, since neither winner was I—and both he and I took it for granted that I was the smartest boy in the school.

Sure enough, when we were all home, my father, in awful patriarchal tones, demanded to know why it was that I had won neither prize.

"Pappa," I said (for I had anticipated this and had had time to work out the best way of putting it), "the kid who won the mathematics prize is lousy in biology. The kid who won the biology prize can't add two and two. And as for me, I was second in line for *both* prizes."

That was quite true, and it took me neatly off the hook. Not another word was said.

PART
II

Education—
in and out of School

11

Entering High School

1

Having graduated from junior high school, the next step was high school, of course. In general, pupils those days went to the local high school and as far as East New York was concerned, Thomas Jefferson High School was the local institution. It was a perfectly good high school, but my parents were thinking ahead.

In eastern Europe, you see, the most prestigious profession a bright Jewish boy could get into was the rabbinate. When a young man became a rabbi, his family was proud, and his social prestige, within the Jewish community, was enormous. Of course, he remained poor, and was nobody at all outside the Jewish community, but there was no real way he could be anything at all in the Gentile community, anyway.

In the United States, where social opportunities were greater, it was less valuable to be a rabbi and more valuable to be something that would involve an income and general prestige. The obvious profession for a boy was medicine, and for a girl it was to marry into medicine.

Every immigrant Jewish family in the United States could ask as its share of heaven on Earth to have every son a doctor and every daughter married to a doctor. One of each would be a minimum desire.

My father took it for granted that I was going to be the Asimov family's doctor; and if my father took that for granted, I did, too. I didn't know any better, for one thing, and for another I had the best motive for ambition in the world. If I didn't do *something*, I was going to inherit the candy-store business, and I sure as anything didn't want to do that.

The only trouble with the ambition for doctorhood was that it was well known that too many Jewish youngsters had the same idea, and the medical schools were not anxious to become more Jewish than the general population was. In fact, there were plenty of medical schools whose administrators were quite willing to err on the side of caution and to allow the student body to be almost or entirely ethnically pure in the direction of white Christianity.

It made sense, therefore, to go to schools with particular prestige. This would tend to deodorize your Semitism before you accosted the dainty nostrils of the admission boards.

The word was that Boys High School of Brooklyn was just such a school. It was well known to be excellent in mathematics, and although it had a football team, it was the mathematics team that could be counted on to win. This was very impressive to my father, who was proud of his own computational ability and who would keep a close eye on what I was doing in arithmetic, since that was the one subject in which he felt himself to be my superior.[1]

It was therefore to Boys High School that I applied for entrance and it was there I went. I think three boys of the JHS 149 class went there, no more. It seems to me that this move had important consequences in a direction my father would never have thought of.

Thomas Jefferson High School was coeducational; Boys High School, as the name implies, was not. I didn't give the matter any thought then, since girls were still a matter of being pleasant to look at, as they had been in kindergarten, but I did not yet think of them in connection with anything more than that.

Yet had I gone to Jefferson High and spent my early teens there, I would undoubtedly have discovered that girls existed for more than looking at.

And there was the real harm of skipping grades. I was getting into the second year of high school at the age of 12½, and the normal age at that level was 15. A 15-year-old girl might look very interesting to a 13-year-old boy, but a teen-age girl can barely see a boy her own age as anything but disgustingly juvenile, and nothing on earth would have forced her to notice, let alone be friendly with, a 13-year-old boy.

Had I gone to Jefferson, then, I might easily have spent my time in frustration and despair and my schoolwork might have gone to the devil. It was a narrow escape, all the more so since I hadn't any idea that I was escaping.

To be sure, there were difficulties in going to a boys' school. It meant that I had very little day-to-day contact with girls, and that introduced complications and had an effect on me that shows itself to this day. Still what did happen was, in my opinion, ease itself compared with what would have happened in Jefferson.

2

In September 1932, then, I entered Boys High School, but spent the first half of the tenth grade (or, as we called it, "the third term")

[1] This only lasted until I began to study algebra. I found that problems that required subtle reasoning if you tried to solve them arithmetically, became childishly simple if you used the formal techniques of algebra. My father, when I showed him how that was done, indignantly rejected that as cheating on the grounds that any fool could solve problems with algebra so that it destroyed the value and use of intelligence—nor could I ever argue him out of that viewpoint.

at Waverly Annex. This was a small, ramshackle school that served as one of three reservoirs intended to keep the student body at Boys High itself from overflowing its bounds. (I don't remember the exact location of the Annex.)

The Annex contributed a column to the high-school newspaper (a "news from Waverly" thing), and I volunteered to write it. It was the very first bit of writing I ever did that was published anywhere.

I don't remember how many columns I did, but I do remember that on one occasion there was a ministir brought about by the fact that I had naïvely reported that we had been let out early one day, when that was against regulations. The head of the Annex found he had to do some explaining, and from then on he read my column before I was allowed to pass it on to the newspaper office.

It was during this third term that the presidential campaign of 1932 was carried on, and I was much more alive to events this time. I had never forgiven Mr. Hoover for defeating Al Smith, and since everyone I knew blamed Hoover entirely for the Depression, there was no question but that I was supporting Franklin Delano Roosevelt (who, like Al Smith, was from New York) with all my heart.

This time my side won, and I was delighted. I never deserted Roosevelt either. His election made me a "New Deal Democrat," and I've never wavered thereafter. I have considered myself a "liberal" ever since.

In February 1933, a month before Roosevelt became President,[2] I finally transferred to the main building of Boys High and entered the fourth term.

Boys High was (and still is) located at Marcy and Putnam avenues in Brooklyn, about 3½ miles west of the Essex Street candy store, and I reached it by streetcar, I believe. In 1933, Boys High, like all the schools I had attended up to that point, was a ghetto school in that its student body was very largely Jewish.[3]

My coming to Boys High meant a distinct change for me. Things weren't as they used to be. For one thing, I discovered that in high school, school wasn't confined to school hours, and that meant a new disadvantage that I had never before had.

I had assumed, for instance, when I was in the Annex, that once I went to the main building, I would join the staff of the school paper. It

[2] And just a few days after that, Adolf Hitler became Chancellor of Germany, though that fact didn't register with me at the time.
[3] It is located deep in Bedford-Stuyvesant, so it is still a ghetto school, though of a different kind. The student body is almost entirely black and, since it has recently become coeducational, it is now Boys and Girls High School.

seemed natural to me to do so, since I had no doubt of my writing ability at all. That, however, was never to come to pass.

For one thing, I found that working on the paper meant all kinds of after-school activity, and I *couldn't* work after school. I had to get back to the candy store. For another thing, the students on the staff of the paper were all considerably older than I was and infinitely more sophisticated. They seemed, to my abashed self, to be very cynical and worldly wise, and they knew much more about politics than I did. I was overawed and backed away.

The result was that I *never* worked on a school paper, either in high school or in college.[4] But as always, all was for the best. I would have made a rotten reporter. Newspaper work would have been the wrong turning for me.

3

The main building supplied me with a worse shock by far. Through all my seven years of school so far, right up to Waverly Annex, I had been the "smartest kid in class" and very probably the "smartest kid in the school." I had accepted that as a basic law of the universe, and it came as a disconcerting boot in the rear end to find this wasn't so any longer.

Boys High's reputation for scholastic excellence was deserved, and there were easily a dozen students there who consistently got higher marks than I did. One student averaged 98 per cent each term, and I was sufficiently overawed by this to remember his name even though I don't recall ever having spoken to him during our stay together at the school. It was Karl Hill. In comparison, I was only too pleased to get a 93 average. I generally got less than that.

After the initial shock and embarrassment, however, I shrugged it off. All the rest were much older than I was, and besides, young as I was, I had grown old enough to realize that "smartness" is not exactly, or entirely, equivalent to high marks. It was quite clear to me that some of the youngsters who did very well did so only at the cost of a great deal of sweating over their books. I, of course, continued to depend on what I could get by understanding-at-once-and-remembering-forever. I

[4] When it was Stanley's turn to enter high school, he was much more self-possessed than I. In his day, it became less fashionable to have students skip grades, so he entered high school at the normal age. What's more, he managed to find the extra time, even though he had duties at the candy store (which shows that my own failure to manage must have been at least as much through cowardice as through duty). He therefore worked on school papers, rose to an editorial position, and made newspaper work his profession.

had to, as long as so much of my out-of-school time had to be spent in the candy store.

My father was far more annoyed than I was at my failure to be at the tiptop of the class. He was particularly irritated at my failure to be elected to Arista, which was the school's honor society. My school marks qualified me, but—very rightly—this was not enough. You had also to engage in extracurricular activity in order to show yourself a well-rounded person. This I could not do, because extracurricular activity was out of the question.

I never explained this to the school authorities, because I didn't want to seem to be begging to get in. I also never explained it to my father, since it would have saddened him without helping the situation in the least.

A subshock, by the way, came when I discovered I was not a mathematician. What I had studied in the field had all seemed so easy to me that I assumed I was a mathematician. I took it for granted that I would get on the Boys High Math Team and knock them all dead with my lightning long division. Then I saw the kind of problems the Math Team solved as a matter of course. They might as well have been in South Martian.

The members of the Math Team were no brighter than I was, if as bright, but they had a feel for mathematics that I didn't have and would never have—so that went by the board just as newspaper work did.

And that, too, was good. It is important in life to recognize at the earliest possible moment what your field is *not*. It would be dreadful to waste a sizable portion of an at-best limited life assailing impregnable barriers when, in another direction, the door is open.

12

Decatur Street

1

In early 1933, my father gave up his second candy store at Essex Street. It had seen us through the Hoover administration, but the lure of El Dorado was on him again.

This time, it seems to me, the lure was a disastrous one. We had a candy store on Church Avenue for a month, but apparently it was not as represented, or my parents found they had overestimated their own ability to handle it. In any case, they had to give it up and move twice —once into an apartment in that area, and once out of it again.

It was all a very traumatic period and I find it interesting that almost all trace of it has vanished from my mind. Through a wise provision of nature, we tend to forget the unpleasant—at least to a greater extent than the pleasant.

About the only thing I remember was that my mother, faced with a store larger and more complicated than she could handle, and an apartment in which everything was jumbled in the middle of the rooms, simply gave up, went into her bedroom, and closed the door.

My sister and I, scared witless, proceeded to straighten up, pulling furniture here and there as quietly as we could, putting the dishes in place, storing things in drawers and cabinets as nearly as we remembered they should go, and then dragged the boxes and paper out in the street.

When my mother came out of the bedroom, looking haggard and beaten, she stared in amazement at the neatness of it all and burst into tears of joy. That was one of the few times I remember us being good children.

I don't count the Church Avenue store as one of our candy stores. It was just an experiment that failed at once and that cost my father perhaps half of his painfully stored accumulation of capital. He had to retreat from his attempt at moving toward a big-and-busy store and find himself a candy store at the same level as the first two.

This candy store, which I count as the third, was at 1312 Decatur Street, on the corner of Knickerbocker Avenue. It was about 2¼ miles northwest of Essex Street and was one third closer to Boys High than the old location was, which was an advantage for me.

Another advantage was that it was just on the northeastern border of Brooklyn. One block farther north was Irving Street, along which ran the local boundary with Queens. This meant I was able to wangle a library card out of the Ridgewood branch of the Queens Public Library, and for several years I could go to it as well as to the local branch of the Brooklyn Public Library, thus getting twice as many books as I would have otherwise.

What's more, by the time we were in the new store, my father gave up the fight. Either he decided I was incorrigible or he felt that my mind had been formed and could resist, so that junk reading would not turn me into a *bum*. I therefore read all the pulp magazines that interested me; not only the science-fiction magazines and *The Shadow*, but also *Doc Savage, Operator 5, The Spider, G-8 and His Battle Aces*, and so on.

The move also meant that, for the first time in the ten years since we had come to the United States, we moved out of the East New York section of Brooklyn. We had moved to Ridgewood.

2

Leaving East New York was inconvenient in one way. It meant that for the first time since coming to the United States, we did not live in a Jewish neighborhood. Ridgewood was heavily Catholic at the time, I believe, and had a strong admixture of Germans. And now I was old enough to begin to understand and experience anti-Semitism, both in terms of the names I was called in the street and the subtler ways in which I was made to feel an outsider; and in terms of the infinitely more dangerous form epitomized by Hitler's Nazis in Germany.

I did not feel particularly Jewish, however. I did not observe any of the rituals. Since my father's brief flirtation with the synagogue in Miller Avenue, I had not gone into one.

On January 2, 1933, nearly at the end of our stay at Essex Street, I had turned thirteen. Even unbelieving Jews often saw to it that their sons went through a bar mitzvah—the occasion on which a young man accepts Judaism independently, rather than having it thrust on him by his parents. I did not undergo the rite.

Nor have I ever felt any guilt over this, nor any urge to make up the lack. I have never felt anything but comfortable over my lack of religion.

However, Hitler's anti-Semitism was not a religious persecution, but one against anyone who could be defined as a Jew by those who were professional Jew-haters. Under those conditions, I qualified perfectly and the world grew a distinctly more dangerous place each year for me and for all Jews.

It made me more than ever a liberal and a New Dealer, for liberals were openly anti-Hitler and conservatives seemed to me to be rather complacent about the Hitler phenomenon and to be interested in other things.

3

In the Decatur Street store, as in the previous one, the apartment was upstairs, but it could not be reached from the store. We had to go outside to go upstairs, which was a pain in the neck. Furthermore, there were two other tenants, one downstairs and one across the hall from us upstairs. Another pain in the neck.

It was, however, a roomier apartment than any we had yet had. What's more, we were now in the full American technological swim. We had an electric refrigerator, and not an icebox, and in the store, the icecream was kept in an electric freezer. (I remember worrying about this iceless cooling. I didn't see how it was possible.)

What's more, we had a radio *in the apartment*, and we could play it ourselves.

Of course, we could not play it when my father was napping. Not that it would disturb his sleep, but we found, as we grew larger, that my father preferred no one to be in the house when he was napping. He valued his privacy.

Nor could we play it when my mother napped. She didn't mind our being in the house, but there was no way we could play the radio, for it could not be made loud enough for us to hear it with our ear against the loudspeaker without its being loud enough for her to hear it two rooms away.

Within those limitations, however, I listened to all the quarter-hour adventure serials, from "Little Orphan Annie" and "Jack Armstrong" to "Buck Rogers in the Twenty-fifth Century" (the last being my favorite, of course).

The real excitement came in the evening comedy shows, however. Eddie Cantor, my favorite in the Essex Street days, was replaced by Jack Benny in Decatur Street.

My parents occasionally listened, but I had long since come to realize that their senses of humor didn't jibe with mine. My father would not laugh at a joke on principle, and if I ever caught him smiling at anything on the radio, he would shrug his shoulders and say, "Ah foolishness."

My mother was willing to laugh, but erratically, and not always at the same things I laughed at. For instance, an impertinent youngster asked Eddie Cantor what he did for a living, and Eddie, in the skit, was supposed to be indignant and say, "Don't talk to me that way. I'm old enough to have five daughters." Whereupon the youngster said, snottily, "I asked your job, not your hobby."

I laughed wildly, but my mother said indignantly, "What a terrible boy. His mother should be ashamed of herself to have him talk like that."

No use trying to tell her that it was probably an actor, playing a boy's role, and reading from a prepared script.[1]

4

The candy store had a kitchen in the back, for it differed from our previous stores in being a luncheonette. We served cake, pie, milk, coffee, and a variety of sandwiches, and my mother would usually cook up something hot for about a dozen people besides the family. It was the only thing on the menu, and people who wanted a hot dish took pot luck.

My mother made elaborate pot roasts, meat-ball dishes, and a variety of other things, and for a while the family ate unusually well, but it was too much. She just wearied of it and gradually let the luncheonette practice dwindle, serving only the old customers with sufficient lack of interest to make them all drift away except for one never-say-die gentleman who was back every lunchtime for whatever my mother had for the family, quite indifferent to the fact that he was the only one eating there.

Finally, my mother, with as much tact as she possessed, informed him that she would not serve him anymore. Her full supply of tact was insufficient. He was mortally offended and we never saw him again for any other purchases either.

The kitchen in back was convenient because it was comfortable and enclosed and one could eat in peace, for if it grew busy in the store one could always hear and emerge, and as long as things were quiet, one could take one's time.

I liked it because it had no windows. Why it should be, I don't

[1] I, of course, knew enough about sex to be able to get the joke and laugh. I had learned about sex at the junior high school in the usual manner. I overheard the older kids talking about it—this was called "picking it up in the gutter." I also saw the pornographic comic books that were passed around from hand to hand and that completed my education as far as the little-boy level was concerned.

know, and psychiatrists may make what they like of it (for I will not ask them, and I will not listen if they try to tell me), but I have always liked enclosed places. For instance, the ersatz rooms in department stores fitted out with furniture on sale always looked far better to me than real rooms did. They seemed warmer and cozier, and I never knew why till it dawned on me that they had no windows.

Again, when I used to take the subway, I would envy the people who ran the newsstands on every station (now mostly gone), for I imagined they could board it up whenever they wanted to, put the light on, lie on a cot at the bottom, and read magazines. I used to fantasize doing so, with the warm rumble of the subway trains intermittently passing.

Well, the room in the back of the store, with the curtain drawn across the opening, and the smell of food permeating it, and my plate full and a book open beside it, and the electric light on over the table (even if it was broad daylight outside), and nobody else there, and the store quiet—who could possibly want more? Certainly not I.

Looking back on my childhood now, I know perfectly well it was a deprived one in many ways, but the thing was, you see, that I never knew it at the time. No one is deprived unless and until he thinks he is.

5

The Decatur Street store was the first with a newspaper route. It was not a terribly large one, but papers had to be delivered both morning and afternoon, and I was the one who had the job. It meant getting up not only in time to get to school at the required moment, but also in time to deliver the papers first and *then* go to school, which meant an extra hour.

It also meant being home from school in time to make the afternoon delivery, which further decreased the possibility of extracurricular work at school.

I never had an alarm clock, or rather I had the best one in the world, for if I wasn't down at the set time, my father would be on the street, shouting up at the window. If it took me more than five minutes after that, I got lecture 5A on responsibility and punctuality and on the deadly spiritual dangers of being a *fulyack* (a sluggard).[2]

Those papers went out every day, including Sunday (when, how-

[2] Ever since, to the very present time, I have awakened in time for the morning newspaper delivery, and it is a point of pride with me that though I have an alarm clock, I never set it, but get up at 6:00 A.M. anyway. I am still showing my father I am not a *fulyack*.

ever, there was only a morning delivery) so that there were thirteen deliveries a week. What's more, the papers had to be delivered with a faithfulness the post office would do well to envy. At least, neither rain, nor snow, nor heat, nor dark of night stayed me from the swift completion of my appointed rounds. My father saw to that.

In fact, I only failed him on one day (barring the rare occasions on which I was sick in bed, and that was not often at all). That one day was February 9, 1934, when the temperature dropped to —14 degrees Fahrenheit, the coldest day the Weather Bureau had ever recorded in New York City, and a record that has not been surpassed to this day.

I bundled up and started out but I had not gone half a block before I turned back. It took a lot of cold to push me into telling my father I couldn't make it, but a lot of cold was what we had. I thought the papers might well be undelivered that one day, but my father thought otherwise.

"Watch the store," he told me, and off he went and delivered the papers. Of course, he had been brought up in Russian winters, but it still made me feel rotten to think that the cold that had stopped me had not stopped him. I therefore forebore to suggest that it was not the kind of day on which it was essential that anyone go to school. (In those days schools were never closed whatever the weather—these days, a heavy dew or a light mist is enough.)

I walked the four blocks to Halsey Street, waited for the streetcar to come in its own good time while I chattered and shivered and stamped my feet and tried to shrink into my clothes. (By then, though, the temperature had risen to a mild —10, I imagine.) I got on the streetcar just before I froze solid, and I had barely thawed out when I had to get off to walk the three blocks to the school. There was a long line of frostbitten youngsters at the nurse's office—but I was spared that.

6

Another thing about Decatur Street was that by that time I had finally become old enough for my parents to be willing to let me out after sunset. Well, they weren't exactly willing, but the vociferousness of my insistence finally overcame their conviction that if I vanished into the darkness I would somehow find some river, fall into it, and drown—or do something else equally disastrous.

As soon as I won the right to be out till nine or even ten o'clock, my sister won the same right, even though she was 2½ years younger than I. I felt it profoundly unjust that she wasn't imprisoned until she reached the age at which I was liberated.

My father was unsympathetic. He said, "All right. So let's go back in time 2½ years and let you out at that time." Then he laughed. At *that*, he laughed.

Night was a wonderful time in Brooklyn in the thirties, especially in warm weather. Everyone would be sitting on their stoops, since air conditioning was unknown except in movie houses, and so was television without exception. There was nothing to keep one in the house. Furthermore, few people owned automobiles, so there was nothing to carry one away. That left the streets and the stoops, which were thus full, and the very fullness served as an inhibition to street crime. People were everywhere, talking, laughing, gossiping, and the roadways were relatively empty.

I would walk all over the neighborhood, daydreaming. In later years I channeled the daydreams into material for fiction, but in Decatur Street, I still hadn't reached that stage of practicality, and my daydreams were just invented and thrown away.

As to what those daydreams were, I can scarcely remember. Some were megalomaniac in nature. I think I used to imagine, in great detail, waking up someday to find that I could play the piano beautifully, and surprising everyone with my ability; or being a master swordsman *à la* d'Artagnan; or in other ways demonstrating an unexpected and impressive virtuosity.

Oddly enough, I'm quite certain I never imagined myself to be a prolific writer.

Then, too, I would imagine myself a character in some book I had read and would continue it past its ending. I've already mentioned I had done this with the *Iliad*. I remember also doing it with Louisa May Alcott's *Little Men* which somehow impressed me more than her *Little Women*. —Perhaps that was because I read *Little Men* first.

My good friend and fellow writer, Frederik Pohl, whom I was not to meet for some years yet, but who was growing up in Brooklyn contemporaneously with me, was more systematic about his walks. He got himself a street map of Brooklyn and began taking long walks. It was his ambition, he said, to walk through every single street in Brooklyn, and mark them off on the map as he walked through them till every one of them had felt his step.

I don't know that he ever completed this monumental task, for there are hundreds of miles of streets in Brooklyn, but the point was that he was not afraid to walk anywhere. There was not a street in the borough that he imagined would be unsafe, and probably none of them was. Nowadays, of course, only a person intent on suicide would harbor Fred's ambition.

It never occurred to me to take on such a task, but there were other ways of indicating that I (and my father) thought the streets safe.

Even when we lived in Essex Street, and I was a preteen-ager, he thought nothing of sending me to the bank. This was always a complicated transaction because he had to deposit the week's earnings in cash, together with any excess in coins. He would wrap this excess in special paper marked with the coin and the total worth. For instance, 50 pennies were wrapped up in rolls marked "50¢," 50 dimes in rolls marked "$5.00," and so on. The paper had to be wrapped tightly and the paper pressed in on either side. When my father was finished they were as tight as though they contained a solid bar of metal, and as heavy. (I could never do it. My rolls were always mushy and useless.)

All this I had to deposit. I also had to withdraw a quantity of coins of those denominations in which he was short (mostly nickels, whereas pennies were the usual superfluity). Week after week, I would go to the bank to make a complicated deposit and an equally complicated withdrawal. My father never worried that I would make a mistake, or that I would get lost, or that I would let anything inveigle me into doing anything but going straight there and straight back—and he was never disappointed.

What he never thought of and what I never thought of was that a skinny subteen-ager, carrying several hundred dollars in bills and coins in a brown paper bag to the bank and then quite a bit in coins coming back from it, might be waylaid and held up. I just went there and back, swinging the bag, and was never afraid—though thinking back on it, I get shaky with ex post facto terror.

7

Being out evenings gave me a chance, finally, to talk to girls more intimately than I had ever had occasion to before. Living immediately across the street was a girl a year older than myself who was named Mary, but whom everyone called Mazie. I was thirteen and she was fourteen when we met, and I thought she was an amazingly beautiful woman, for fourteen seemed quite mature to me. (Actually, she looked like Ann Dvorak, the movie actress—at least to me.)

I did a great deal of following after her and hanging around her stoop at night and talking to her. I even went to the movies with her on occasion (Dutch, of course, for negotiating any money out of my parents for anyone other than myself was quite out of the question).

Aside from the excitement of being with Mazie at the movies were the movies themselves. On a hot summer day, it was a miracle, and a heavenly one at that, to step into coolness, for the movies were the only places where air conditioning existed. Returning to the heat was a purgatory.

Nothing ever came of this first puppy-love affair of mine, but it was useful, for it gave me practice talking to girls, and this particular girl was always pleasant and subjected me to no embarrassment at any time. Eventually, she married Danny Metta, one of the other boys who hung about the stoop (for I was not the only one who noticed that she was pretty).

8

Another puppy-love affair that began about the same time was between myself and baseball.

I was never particularly interested in sports as a participant, since there was never any chance that I would be good at it. I was too light and too skinny for contact sports, and I was nearsighted besides.

My nearsightedness was recognized for what it was by the time I was in junior high school, and I was then fitted out for glasses, which I have worn ever since. It came as no great shock to me. My father wore glasses, and my mother wore glasses, and I guess I couldn't have avoided them. My sister and brother also wore glasses eventually. In fact, of the five of us, my eyes are the least bad.

Once I had eyeglasses, my vision was normal (in fact, rather better than normal when the lenses are correctly fitted). However, I then had to fear damaging my glasses, so sports were out.

Nor was I a particularly enthusiastic sports spectator. For one thing, I didn't have the money to get tickets to see games.

When I began to read the newspapers, however, I could not help but see the sports pages, and baseball attracted me, largely because the teams represented the cities, and New York City, toward which I felt strongly patriotic, had the Giants and the Yankees. Naturally, I wanted them to win.

Once I had a radio of my own, I found I could listen to baseball games, and I soon learned to understand the rules, get the names of the important pitchers and hitters, and, in general, I became a wild fan.

Of course, I did things the complicated way. At the beginning of each season I somehow managed to get a ten-cent copybook (large, thick, with white pages—nothing but the best), and I filled each double-page spread with a table for the National League on one side and the American League on the other. I had room not only for total wins and losses, but also for a double-entry arrangement that would show me how many times each team beat every other team, or was beaten.

It was then my aim to listen to the news every evening, find out all the scores, enter them, work out percentages, places in the standing, games behind, and so on. I worked out everything even though I could have found it all in the paper the next morning. I had to do it *first*.

The Giants were my idols. Carl Hubbell, their ace pitcher, was king to me, and Mel Ott, their cleanup hitter, could do no wrong. The odd part was that Brooklyn had a team of its own, the Dodgers, but when I first became aware of baseball the Giants were contenders (they won the National League pennant in 1933 and then went on to beat the Washington Senators in the World Series), and they captured my heart. By the time I found out there was a Brooklyn team, it was too late; I was imprinted.

Since virtually everyone else in Brooklyn was a Dodger fan, I had nothing but trouble. I was a minority of one, and every single male customer my father had was in a perpetual stage of anger with me over my high treason. My father was very upset. I couldn't make him understand that these were just friendly arguments designed to spice up the game. To him, every argument meant a possibly lost customer, and over and over again he would order me to shut up.

Shut up? Refuse to defend the Giants against the cowardly attacks of a bunch of depraved Dodger fans? Never!

The year 1934 was the most exciting baseball year ever for me, and it broke my heart. September opened with the Giants in first place by seven games. Nothing but a miracle could keep them from the pennant. The miracle happened. They went on a losing streak, lost, lost, lost, and LOST. Crucially, they lost two of the last four games to the despised Dodgers, and this after the Giants' manager, Bill Terry, at the beginning of the season had said, "Are the Dodgers still in the league?" when asked about the Brooklyn team's chances at the pennant. Wow, did that remark come back to roost!

The St. Louis Cardinals took the pennant that year. They were called the Gashouse Gang and they were the most colorful team in baseball history, but the only colors I wished for them were black and blue. They had a remarkable brother-team on the mound, Dizzy and

Daffy Dean. Together, and almost without help, they proceeded to win the World Series over the Detroit Tigers in seven games. I think that in my whole life I never hated anyone in sports with so malignant a hatred as I did those Dean brothers in September and October of 1934.

The baseball mania receded slowly after that Heartbreak Peak, but I remained quite intensely interested through the rest of my teen-age years.

9

Nor was it only my Giants fanaticism that proved a liability to my parents' efforts not to lose customers; they were also constantly afraid that my other eccentricities would do the same.

Let me list some of my eccentricities.

When I was walking anywhere I was invariably lost in thought. As a result, I was only sufficiently aware of my surroundings to keep from being run over and from colliding with trees. It wasn't that I failed to recognize people I passed—I didn't even see them.[3] The trouble was that every customer I ignored in passing felt pained and reported it indignantly to my parents. I was constantly being hounded to say hello to everyone I passed. My attempt to explain that I didn't see them was met with profound disbelief.

My mother also reported to me that I had to do something about the way I walked home from the library. It seems that I had reached the point where I was allowed three books, and it was routine for me to read one of them on the way home. This didn't make it particularly hard for me to walk, since I never saw anything anyway, even if I weren't reading a book. It made it a little difficult crossing streets, but I usually peeked over my book at such times and I was never run over, so what was the difference?

I had to do something with the other two books, however, and the easiest way of disposing of them was to place one under each arm. Well, would you believe that I was reported to my mother for walking down the street with a book under each arm while reading a third? And would you believe my mother ordered me not to do that? It was apparently too eccentric to be endured by the customers.

Naturally, I ignored the order.

Just one more. Once I was walking home from the trolley-car stop in a snowstorm. It wasn't very cold and the flakes were big and fat and I noticed that while they were white against the buildings, they were

[3] This is still true to this day. If a friend doesn't call after me, or physically grab me, I will walk right past, unseeing.

black against the white clouds. I found this fascinating, and as I watched the falling bits of black, I noticed that they made interesting swirls against the sky. I watched those swirls and got home, taking a bit of time, since I couldn't walk quickly while watching the sky.

Would you believe that some customer had seen me and raced on to the store to report that I was walking down the street with my head tilted back and my mouth open? And would you believe my mother was furious with me?

One eccentricity I had that no one knew about, because I was careful not to talk about it, was my love of cemeteries.

In exploring the Decatur Street neighborhood, I found that three blocks to the southwest lay some cemeteries. The nearest was Trinity Cemetery, a small and crowded Catholic cemetery that didn't interest me. Another, though, was a large Protestant cemetery, the Cemetery of the Evergreens, just beyond Trinity. It was perhaps two thirds the size of Prospect Park (Brooklyn's largest) and was very much like a park that was unobtrusively interrupted here and there by gravestones.

I found that wandering about in it was delightful. It had the advantages of a park without the disadvantage of being full of people. I had been in parks; in fact, when we were younger, and before we had the candy store, a rare treat was that of taking a trolley to Highland Park and picnicking there. Highland Park was, actually, just on the other side of the Cemetery of the Evergreens, but I didn't bother trying to go there.

Cemeteries are, of course, full of the remains of dead people, but that didn't bother me. Whenever I could get a few hours off in the summer, I would take whatever it was I was reading at the time, preferably a science-fiction magazine, and go off to the cemeteries. (In 1933, *Astounding Stories* had been taken over by Street & Smith Publications, Inc., and under the editorship of F. Orlin Tremaine it scaled new heights and became far and away my favorite science-fiction magazine.)

Sometimes I would explore new avenues in the cemetery, and before long I had a whole series of favorite stone benches where I could sit under trees with no signs or sounds of human life or human artifacts in any direction.

In fact, the only thing that ever intruded into this lonely Eden (it was remarkably like being in a room with the blinds pulled down—just as cozy and separated from the world) was once when the caretaker stopped me as I went in—he knew me well by that time—and asked me, in a rather embarrassed tone of voice, not to whistle as I walked through the cemetery, because it offended the occasional mourners there. For a moment I was astonished that there would be mourners there; what could they be mourning? Then I remembered, apologized, and whistled no more.

That was another thing. I whistled constantly. Other people might chain-smoke or chew gum; I whistled.

I whistled popular songs of the day. I whistled Gilbert and Sullivan. I also whistled Italian operatic selections. This undoubtedly bothered the people I passed, and that would occasionally be reported to my mother, and she complained about that.

The whistling mania has decreased with age, but it never has vanished. In fact, I even sometimes absent-mindedly *sing* in public. This is all usually interpreted by others as signifying that I am happy (and they sometimes say so in what seems a pettish annoyance, as though I have no right to be). And they are right. I am usually happy.

Fortunately, none of the complaints lodged against me did anything to repress my ego and individuality, because no matter how many times I was reported, and how many times my mother stormed at me for risking the family welfare by being eccentric, I nevertheless continued to do exactly as I had been doing. I had gathered the notion somewhere that my eccentricities belonged to me and to nobody else and that I had every right to keep them.

And I lived long enough to see these eccentricities and others that I have not mentioned come to be described as "colorful" facets of my personality.

10

I'm afraid I was also eccentric at school. It was no longer just a matter of whispering to my neighbor. I was beginning to have a novel and dangerous thought. More and more it seemed to me I could think faster than the teacher.

I worked it out carefully. If I said something with a perfectly straight face that was designed to evoke laughter at the teacher's expense, and if I didn't laugh, but just looked surprised—I could plead innocence. There would be nothing to do about it.

It worked for a while, but after that while, teachers refused to accept pleas of innocence, no matter what. I'd get kicked out of class.[4] I'll give you my favorite example.

In English we were studying *Abou Ben Adhem* by Leigh Hunt, which is sufficiently short so that I can quote it in full here in the unlikely case that you've never seen it or have forgotten it:

[4] And I deserved it. I was a smart-alecky teen-ager, but I've learned better since. Mostly. Sometimes I forget.

Abou Ben Adhem (may his tribe increase!)
Awoke one night from a deep dream of peace,
And saw, within the moonlight in his room,
Making it rich, and like a lily in bloom,
An angel writing in a book of gold:—
Exceeding peace had made Ben Adhem bold,
And to the Presence in the room he said,
"What writest thou?"—The vision raised its head,
And with a look made of all sweet accord,
Answered, "The names of those who love the Lord."
"And is mine one?" said Abou. "Nay, not so,"
Replied the Angel. Abou spoke more low,
But cheerly still; and said, "I pray thee, then,
Write me as one that loves his fellow men."
The angel wrote, and vanished. The next night
It came again with a great wakening light,
And showed the names whom love of God had blessed,
And lo! Ben Adhem's name led all the rest.

It seems to me that no one who had studied the psychology of English teachers (and their pupils must do so if they are to survive) could fail to see what the first question would be. I didn't fail to see it, and I was prepared.

Our teacher said, "Now, class, *why* did Abou Ben Adhem's name lead all the rest?"

My hand shot up. He said, "Yes, Asimov?"

And I said, with a polite note of uncertainty, "Alphabetical order, sir?"

The class roared and I placed an astonished look on my face, and the teacher lifted his arm and pointed to the door.

I got up. "But what else could it *be*, sir?"

"Just report to the principal's office," he said.

Oh well.

None of this ever hurt me scholastically, though it may possibly have contributed to my not making Arista.

What *did* hurt me scholastically was a particularly unpleasant discovery I made in high school. Until then, all scholastic subjects had been the same. Whatever schoolbook we opened—history, geography, arithmetic, grammar—it was all interesting, it was all fun, and, most of all, it was all easy.

I suppose I could be excused for thinking that this was a universal law of nature. Then, in high school, I found that one of my classes was on economics, and I found, further, to my deep surprise, that I *hated* economics. I'll tell you something worse: I found to my deep embarrassment that I didn't *understand* economics and that nothing my teacher could say would help.

I don't know whether I hated it because I didn't understand it, or refused to understand it because I hated it. I would like to say that it was because I had a bad teacher and for that reason both hated and couldn't understand it. That, however, isn't so. I had had lots of bad teachers and they had never stopped me from loving and understanding a subject—but to this day I find economics both a bore and a mystery.

My dream of universal brilliance was shattered, and not by that only. As time went on, I found that there were subjects upon subjects that proved to be hate objects to me and that were therefore foggy and impenetrable to me (or vice versa).

If you think I knuckled down and forced them into my head by sheer perseverance, you're crazy. There were too many subjects I liked and caught at once for me to waste time with these cultural villains. I just let economics go, as I let other things go later on, convinced that they were not for me and that my failure to understand them was Nature's way of telling me so.

A good thing! Without even knowing, I was being forced down the path that, if I had had the brains I thought I had, I would have taken deliberately.

11

I got one kick in the pants that nearly ruined me, however.

In February 1934, just a week or so before that day of record cold, I entered sixth term.

As a startling innovation, the school offered a special course in creative writing for those who chose to take it, and I jumped at the chance. I had been writing, on and off, ever since I had worked on *The Greenville Chums*. I don't remember any of the details at all, except that I remember being occasionally driven to attempt to write poetry.

What's more, in class, I always eagerly grabbed at any opportunity to write something for the English teacher—essays, fiction, whatever— and I usually got high marks. Then there had been the weekly reports I had written at Waverly Annex.

Now at last there seemed a chance for me to demonstrate my literary prowess, for I saw the class only as a chance to shine. It never occurred to me that I might learn something. I felt I already *knew* how to write.

Shine? I don't think I ever voluntarily put myself into a position to make such a prize jackass of myself. The whole thing was an utter fiasco.

There I was, fourteen years old, with not even the experience of life one might expect of an average fourteen-year-old, because I had been hidden away in my father's candy store. What's more, I had no knowledge of contemporary literature at all because I had received no guidance, and my self-driven library reading had consisted almost entirely of nineteenth-century fiction.

Everyone else in the class was, however, fifteen or sixteen years old and terribly intellectual in the literary sense. I was outclassed.

I remember that one of my first tasks was to write a descriptive essay, and I determined to describe a beautiful spring day. It might have been a good idea if I had described spring in Brooklyn and talked about windows being opened and rugs being shaken out of them; of the cheery laughter of children as they killed each other over a dispute in a game of punchball.

I was entirely too stupid to do that. I decided to describe a spring day in some never-never pastoral land full of larks and daisies. What's more, as though that were not enough, I fatuously raised my hand as a volunteer when the teacher (Mr. Newfield, his name was, I think) asked for someone to read what he had written.

I had not read more than two paragraphs before Mr. Newfield could endure no more. "This is shit!" he said, sending me back to my seat.

Everyone laughed, of course, and I was stricken to the heart. It was worse than spelling "weigh" W-I-E-G-H. I was acquainted with the monosyllabic word for feces, had heard it often, and had occasionally used it myself, but I had never heard a teacher use it in class before. I had the feeling that if the principal found out about it, Mr. Newfield would be fired (and I rather suspect, as I look back on it now, that he would have been reprimanded, at least) and that only the most intense emotional misery could have forced that word out of him.

I never wrote *anything* in that class that anyone seemed to take seriously or that anyone seemed to find the slightest hint of talent in.

I never came closer in my life to giving up; to deciding I really didn't have it after all; that I had been a temporary prodigy; that I had burned out and, having been a rising rocket, would now have to settle down to being an endlessly falling stick.

And yet, thank goodness, I didn't give up entirely. I may have turned away from mathematics and from economics at the first hint of difficulty, and would do so for other subjects yet untried—but I was unable to give up on writing altogether.

I was helped out by a final stroke of luck in the class.

We were finally given our major assignment, the writing of anything we chose—essays, fiction, poetry—for submission to the *Boys
High Recorder*, the school's literary semi-annual. In fact, I suspect the
entire purpose of the creative writing class was to squeeze out material
for the *Recorder*. After all, it is very difficult to get anything written by
a high-school student that wouldn't make duller reading than the blank
page would.

Naturally, everyone in the class submitted a piece. They had to.
Not to do so would be the equivalent of getting a zero in the final examination. So I wrote something and submitted it too.

What I wrote was an essay entitled "Little Brothers,"[5] which was
my attempt to do a humorous essay as nearly after the style of Robert
Benchley (an idol of mine) as I could manage. I doubt that anyone in
the world (even I myself, after I grew a few years older) could find in
that essay any hint of Benchley or, for that matter, any hint of successful humor, but it was *intended* to be humorous, and there is even a
chance that a fourteen-year-old reader who, like myself, had led a
sheltered life, might find it humorous.

Everyone else in the class wrote pieces that were marinated in
Weltschmerz and sprinkled thickly with crumbs of heartbreak, then
frozen in a sauce of iced pessimism. In the first place, there had been
now four years of world Depression, and pessimism seemed the only
possible way of looking at life. Second, these deep heart-wrung sighs
seemed like great literature to them. (It might have seemed so to me,
had I read contemporary literature myself.)

Some of the pieces were accepted, of course. After all, the *Recorder* had to be filled somehow. Among the pieces was mine!

"Little Brothers" was my first acceptance. It was a nonprofessional
acceptance and it involved no money, but except for those little pieces
about Waverly Annex, it was the first thing I had written ever to see
print. It is the earliest of my writings ever to have survived to this day.

Mr. Newfield was not a tactful man. When I expressed my surprise
and pleasure at having turned out a masterpiece fit to appear in a periodical with the exalted standards of the *Recorder*, he said, "It was the
only thing anyone submitted that was supposed to be funny, and I had
to have something funny."

[5] Since I take this book seriously as a sort of "reference guide to Asimov" I am
going to footnote each piece of fiction I refer to and tell you where to find it, if
you wish to read it. Needless to say, you don't have to read it. In the case of "Little
Brothers" you will find it in *Before the Golden Age* (Doubleday, 1974) on page
454 of the hard-cover edition. I give the page number only because the item is not
listed in the Contents.

It was rather like winning a ball game merely because the other team didn't show up, but, as Charlie Brown of "Peanuts" would have done under those circumstances, I rejoiced anyway. I considered myself on a one-game winning streak and the whole course became worthwhile.

I suppose that everyone who has ever become a success in his own eyes sometimes falls prey to the temptation to wish he could show off to the people in the old hometown, or to the friends of his youth, or to someone in the past who didn't recognize his potential and cry out, "See! You were wrong! Nyah, nyah!" That sort of thing.

I never felt such a temptation at all. I should hope I am above such things; that I am too fine, too noble a fellow. And so I am—with one exception.

For years, I wished that I could somehow transport my older self into that rotten creative writing class and say, "*Now* what do you think?"

What spoiled that thought was the sneaking suspicion that there might have been half a dozen youngsters in that class who made it literarily, who became great writers, who were much greater and more respected than myself. I didn't remember any names, and it was perhaps better not to know.

As it happened, I didn't keep my copy of the *Recorder*; or, if I did keep it, I lost it somehow. So I couldn't tell how many geniuses had sat in that class with me, and I remained in uneasy uncertainty for decades. When the time came that a copy came into my possession (one that I still possess), I forced myself to look at the Contents page.

I went down the list and not one name was familiar to me. Not one! Except my own, of course! I am now quite certain that I am the only person who was in that creative writing class who went on to become a professional writer and a successful one.

What a relief!

13

Entering College

On January 2, 1935, I turned fifteen. By that time, I had reached a height of five feet, nine inches in my shoes (or perhaps a quarter inch less as yet) and was able to look my father right in the eye. I confidently expected to grow to be taller than he was, but I was wrong. As it turned out, somewhat to my discomfiture, that was it. I got that quarter inch but no more. To this day, I am but five feet, nine inches in height—average for the American male.

I was extremely skinny and probably weighed no more than 125 pounds. For years I remained skinny, though I slowly gained.

At fifteen, I began to shave (only twice a week at first), and I was also in the full flower of my acne. The pimples started coming shortly after I was twelve, heralding the arrival of puberty along with the cracking voice and so on. I had been a really good boy soprano and I regretted letting that go, but since I became a pretty good baritone (and even a tenor if I wanted to tighten my vocal cords a bit) I was consolable in that respect.

The coming of acne was something, however, I could have done without. It got worse and worse as the years passed, reaching its peak in my late teens and not vanishing till I was over twenty. It left its marks. If you look closely, you can see the pockmarks on my cheeks and temples.

It might have left more serious psychic scars if I had been involved with girls in my late-teen years, as I ought to have been. Unfortunately (or, rather, fortunately), the stress of school and the candy store left me no time for girls during my acne years. Except for my utterly platonic conversations with Mazie, there was nothing.

What did occupy me in the early part of 1935 was the approaching end of high school. I was going to be graduating in June and there was no question but that I would have to start college in September. The question was: Which college?

To begin with, the college would have to be in New York City, for I would have to commute. For the sake of the candy store, I had to be home evenings and weekends, college or no college.

If we confined ourselves to New York City, the obvious choice was City College. It had two great advantages. First, it was tuition-free. Second, anyone living in the city could enter without question if his grades were good enough—and my grades were good enough. My entrance into City College was therefore assured, so when the time came I applied and was accepted.

But—and this was a big "but"—City College had a student body that was largely Jewish and largely radicalized by the increasing menace of Hitler. It was well known that medical schools hardly ever accepted a graduate of City College—and I was intent on medical school (at least my father was intent on it on my behalf).

On the other hand, the most prestigious college in New York City, and therefore the most prestigious one to which I could commute, was Columbia College, and it was equally well known that graduates of Columbia College were kindly looked upon by medical schools. One might even get into Columbia University's College of Physicians and Surgeons, which was, to a medical student, something like playing the Palace was to a vaudevillian.

The difficulties were that it wasn't likely that Columbia College would accept me, and if they did, it wasn't likely that my father could muster up the tuition money. However, time enough to worry about that when and if we had to. The first step was to apply to Columbia College. There was very little charge for a mere application, and we would see what would happen.

I sent in my application, and at least Columbia didn't reject me out of hand. They were willing to grant me an interview. (Grades were fine, but they weren't enough. A Columbia student must be a gentleman, and I imagine the prime purpose of the interview was to see if I were too Jewish to give at least the appearance of a gentleman.)

2

The date fixed for the interview was April 10, 1935, one of the few exact dates I remember for the period before I was eighteen.

At that time, I had never gone to Manhattan alone. In fact, the only times I had ever left Brooklyn, after arriving in the United States twelve years before, were to go to Parksville in 1927 and 1928 (and, in 1931, too, when Stanley, two years old, accompanied us). Less extended trips occasionally took me, with the rest of the family, to Radio City Music Hall on some Jewish holiday and, of course, to the Statue of Liberty six years before. Then there were occasional forays a few blocks into Queens to go to a local library or to the farther end of the Cemetery of the Evergreens.

Except for that, Brooklyn and the universe were coterminous for me.

My father, I think, had visions of my ruining my chance of getting into Columbia by getting lost in the confusing subway system and of arriving late for the interview—or not arriving at all. He therefore actually abandoned the store to my mother and came with me. Naturally, once at Columbia, he waited outside the building I was supposed to enter because he didn't want to ruin my chances by having me appear to be a baby who could not be trusted to travel on his own.

He might have saved himself the trouble. I ruined my chances entirely on my own. I made a very poor impression. I was bound to. I don't think that I ever made a good first impression on anyone in my life until such time as my name had become independently impressive. After that, of course, there came to be no such thing as a first impression. People saw me through the haze of my reputation and thought me far better than they would possibly have thought me if they had encountered me under some other name.

The trouble is, and always has been, that at any first interview, I am too eager, too talkative, too nervous, too lacking in poise and self-assurance, too obviously immature—even *now*. And in my teen-age years, there was, to add to it all, my acne. It is no great crime or dishonor to be pimply, but it is no great advantage either, and it doesn't improve the impression you make.

All in all, then, the poor man who had to face me and decide if I were Columbia material must have been dreadfully disappointed. I simply didn't match my transcript, and that was all. It was probably the poorest match he had seen in years, and he must have decided on the spot that I wasn't for Columbia College. I have never held that against him (whoever he was, for I don't remember), for it was the only decision he could possibly have made.

I could tell I was going to be rejected, and my expression showed it, but he semireassured me. The rejection was only for Columbia *College*. I was so naïve in those days that I knew nothing beyond the mere name "Columbia." I did not realize that Columbia *University* was a huge establishment of which Columbia *College*, the elite undergraduate school, was but a small part. However, I found this out in the course of the interview.

My interviewer may have been sufficiently impressed by my scholastic record not to want to lose me to Columbia altogether. He may also (I like to think) have been impressed by the intelligence that must have been apparent to a sufficiently shrewd observer even through my pimply and adolescent uneasiness. He therefore suggested I apply to Seth Low Junior College[1] instead. This was another undergraduate college of Columbia University and was by no means elite. I had never heard of it at the time and, in my entire life since, I have never met anyone who has ever heard of it—unless he, too, had been a student there.

Seth Low Junior College was located in Brooklyn and had the same scholastic standards as Columbia College (the interviewer said). What's more, in the third and fourth year of college, I would be allowed to take courses with the Columbia College students.

In order to save my face, the kindly interviewer stressed the fact that Columbia College had a minimum age of sixteen as one of the entrance requirements and that I would be under sixteen even in September and that was why I could not enter. That was quite true, for I had read it in the booklet they had sent me. I had, however, taken it for granted that colleges would not refuse a bright enough student even if he were under sixteen. Prodigies were prodigies.

Afterward, I checked the requirements for Seth Low Junior College and it set sixteen as an entrance requirement there as well, so I saw the excuse for what it was—a well-meant lie.

The interviewer didn't say something that I eventually found to be the case, which was that the Seth Low student body was heavily Jewish, with a strong Italian minority. It was clear that the purpose of the school was to give bright youngsters of unacceptable social characteristics a Columbia education without too badly contaminating the elite young men of the College itself by their formal presence. Those were the days when racial quotas weighted in favor of the elite were as American as apple pie.

Seth Low Junior College was not what I wanted, but what could I do? I nodded as cheerfully as I could manage and said he might alter my application to have it apply to Seth Low.

I tried to put a good face on it to my father when I came out of the building and stoutly maintained that Seth Low "was just as good," and my father stoutly agreed that it would get me into medical school just as surely as Columbia College would, but I didn't believe it, and neither did he. We each said it to cheer up the other. We each failed.

[1] It was named for the president of Columbia University in the 1890s, who, before that, had been mayor of the independent city of Brooklyn, and after that, the mayor of the conglomerated city of Greater New York.

We went home glumly, and my father took advantage of one of his rare absences from the store to stop in to see a movie with me. That was so rare an event that I remember what it was. It was *Richelieu*, with George Arliss, Edward Arnold, and Cesar Romero. Being imbued with Richelieu as the villain of *The Three Musketeers*, I had difficulty adjusting to a story in which he was the hero.

We also stopped in at a museum (I don't remember which one) and there we saw Albert Einstein, who happened to be looking at the exhibits also. He was unmistakable and he was the one scientist who was a legend to everyone (and especially to Jews) in his own lifetime. Everywhere he went, a small crowd of the curious followed, standing off at a respectful distance, with no one, *no* one, daring to do anything as crass as asking for an autograph. My father and I followed along with the crowd, being quite satisfied just to stare. It was the only time I ever saw him, and it is for his sake more than for my Columbia interview that I remember the exact date.

3

My failure at the Columbia interview took a lot of the steam out of my high-school graduation. In fact, so much of a flop did my school career seem after the remarkable beginning in grade school that I remember nothing at all about the graduation. Not one thing. Well, maybe one thing.

It seems to me that only my mother attended. (My father must have been as downhearted as I.) My mother sat in the balcony and I gave her strict instructions to stay in the balcony till I came up to get her. (The direction of instructions had clearly swung over by now and was from me to her, rather than vice versa.)

As soon as everything was over I rushed for the stairway to the balcony and found a thick and steady stream of people coming down. It was impossible to move upward against the current. I had to wait till all were down. When all were down, to the very last person, my mother, who had loyally followed instructions, appeared at the head of the stairs, wondering what had happened to me.

I, of course, received my copy of the *Senior Recorder* for the graduating class of June 1935, but I didn't keep it—or it was lost. In recent years I have managed to get a copy and I will try to preserve it now.

In the *Senior Recorder* of that year is the photograph of an incredibly young, skinny, and toothy Isaac Asimov (or at least it is incredible now, as I look back on it). My father saved a print of that picture for some reason and had it in the mirror over the bureau in his bedroom.[2] Otherwise, when I came across it again years later, I simply wouldn't have recognized it.

The photograph was used on the book jacket of *Before the Golden Age*.

Each photograph of each student had something written underneath, in italics, by some anonymous wit who probably did not survive the strain and who perished to universal applause. Underneath mine, the villain had written: "When he looked at the clock, not only did it stop, but it started going backwards."

This is an allegation I repel with the scorn and contumely it deserves.

In the statistics they included under my picture, they listed "Columbia" as the college I intended to attend. It was a white lie, for what I meant by Columbia was Columbia University, of which Seth Low was a part. To this day, if someone asks me where I went to college, I say "Columbia." I never say "Columbia College," because that would be a lie outright, but I don't prevent anyone from thinking that is what I mean. My excuse to myself is that if I said, "Seth Low," everyone would say "What's that?" and I was in no mood to spend the rest of my life making explanations. The real reason, however, is that no matter how hard I try to be absolutely straightforward (and I do try), a little bit of phoniness *will* creep in now and then, and this is one of the little bits.

It also says "surgeon," presumably as an indication of my intended profession, but to that all I can say is "What!"

I knew that I (in response to my father's sternly pointing finger) planned to be a doctor, but I don't recall ever wanting to be a surgeon particularly. Yet I must have, since they got the information from the students themselves, who had to fill out a questionnaire for the *Recorder*. It must have been another bit of phoniness; I apparently thought that "surgeon" sounded more impressive than "doctor."

It also says "Honor Roll 5 times" and lists of my other accomplishments as well. It says I was "Grade Advisors Assistant" in 1933. I remember that. The work consisted largely of getting large volumes of

---

[2] I say *his* bedroom, for from the Decatur Street store on, my mother and father always had separate bedrooms—till retirement at least. This was not a sign of estrangement, for they were never estranged, no matter how strenuous their discussions of policy became. Since my father and mother kept radically different hours, however, it made a lot of sense to have separate bedrooms so that neither woke the other at the wrong time.

school records from the storage vats and returning them there. They had to go to the various teachers who entered marks into them. Dull work and not very rewarding.

Then too, I was on the "Repair Squad," something I have no memory of. I can't even imagine what it could possibly have been. And it says "Psychology Club." I presume I was a member, though why I should have been I can't say. I must have felt I had to join *some* club; it may even have been required that I do so. I suppose the Psychology Club met at a time that made it possible for me to attend, but I doubt that I attended often.

Finally it says "Typist for Biologist '35" and behind that lies a story.

4

Ever since I had been close to my first typewriter when we had moved into the Essex Street store, I had longed for one. I wrote, whenever I wrote, in pen and ink, and that was difficult, arduous, and most of all, unglamorous. Writing, I more and more came to realize, should be done on the typewriter.

The difficulty was that there was no way in which I could get my father to get me one. It cost too much money.

That sounds awful, I know. Why should I put pressure on my poor father? If I wanted a typewriter so badly, why didn't I go out, earn money somehow, and buy one for myself? Ah but how could I? I was already working every day in the candy store, and, alas, that was unpaid labor. Nor, as I explained earlier, did I ever get an allowance that I was allowed to keep.

The attitude I might have taken was that my work had earned me a chance at the typewriter, but that never occurred to me. My work earned me a chance at food, clothing, and shelter. A typewriter would have to come out of my father's superfluity, and of that there was none.

Except that he *did* get me a typewriter, and it must have been some time early in 1935. How is it possible that I could forget so important a date as obtaining my first typewriter? I don't know, but I've managed. Early in 1935 is all I can say, and I based that only on the notation in the *Senior Recorder* that I was a "typist." Before I obtained my *Senior Recorder* in recent years and found that notation, I used to say that I got my first typewriter in 1936; but that was wrong.

My father didn't go hog wild. He didn't buy me a new typewriter. He inquired among his customers and found a place where they would sell him an old but serviceable typewriter for a small sum of money. He bought me an Underwood No. 5 for ten dollars. It was a tremendous bargain, but even so, finding the ten dollars wasn't easy. How old it was I don't know, but it worked perfectly. What's more, it was a full-size model and not a portable. (Portables are convenient but not as comfortable for long-continued use as full-size models are.)

However, getting the typewriter and listing myself as a typist did not make me any more of a writer than I was before, nor increase my importance in the school by one iota.

The photograph and its accompanying information and witticism is the only indication in the *Senior Recorder* that I attended Boys High. I am not mentioned in any of the listings of Halls of Fame, in any of the historical items, in any of the statistics. Nowhere.

On page 54 of the *Senior Recorder* is a list headed "Class Statistics," which includes the best in this category and that. "The Best Literary Man" is listed as Martin Lichterman.

In the *Recorder* of Spring 1934, the one in which I had my essay "Little Brothers," Martin Lichterman had two items. One was a piece of fiction called "Oh, To Leave It All." Yes, the title adequately describes it. It is about a man of fifty-seven who is in apparently terminal illness and who considers suicide but changes his mind at observing the beauty of spring.

I guess there's no question but that it is better written than my piece. However, Mr. Lichterman did not become a professional writer.

5

I don't remember much concerning the summer of 1935. It did not have the excitement of the summer of 1930, when I waited to enter junior high school, or the summer of 1932, when I waited to enter high school.

I knew I was going to be allowed to enter Seth Low—but I also knew that I was really going to go to City College, and I desperately didn't want to do that.

Seth Low meant tuition fees—as high as those of Columbia College, by the way—but where my father might conceivably have scrabbled money together for Columbia, I knew he would not for Seth Low. That meant I would have to find a scholarship.

I had applied for a state scholarship, which was open to a certain number of boys and girls resident in New York State on the basis of overall scholastic averages in high school, but it was clear that my overall average simply wasn't high enough to earn me those one hundred dollars per year. Economics helped see to that. So did some other sub-

jects, somewhat less hateful, in which I functioned only at the B level
—my single course in physics, for instance, which had been poorly
taught, and my third year of German, where my lack of talent in languages had finally become unmistakably evident.

This was very embarrassing to me, especially since I had to face my
father, who was far less willing to give up that smartest-kid-in-the-class
bit than I was.

The summer, however, was not a complete loss. For one thing, my
interest in science fiction was becoming stronger and more realistic. I
tried, for the first time, to write an actual letter to *Astounding Stories*.

It was a perfectly ordinary letter. I commented on the most recent
issue I had read. I praised and denounced stories and authors, with the
usual lordly condescension of the critic,[3] and I asked for trimmed edges.

Years later, an organization named "First Fandom" was being organized, with membership extended to those who had been active as
science-fiction readers and fans prior to 1938, and I received a request
to join. I replied sadly that although I had read science fiction avidly
for years prior to 1938, I had not been active. At once they came up
with that 1935 letter in *Astounding Stories* and declared that qualification enough. I have been a member ever since.

In *Before the Golden Age*, I mention this incident and say, "It
must have been a handwritten letter, for in 1935, I didn't know how to
type and, for that matter, I had no access to a typewriter."

That wasn't so. That passage was written before I got my copy of
The Senior Recorder with its evidence that I was already a typist, and
though I introduced changes in galleys to take what it said into account, I somehow missed this passage.

6

And, of course, there was the typewriter. Once I got the typewriter,
I had learned how to type by myself—with my father's help.

Naturally, I knew how to type in the sense that I knew how to put
the paper into the machine, and I knew that if you struck the key
marked *f*, and you got an *f* or, if you also struck the "shift," an *F*. I
knew how to make a space, a back space, how to return the carriage,
and so on. What I didn't know was how to touch-type. I didn't think
that was necessary. I sat at the typewriter and typed by the hunt-and-
peck method.

I was at it every day until my father, coming up one day for his af-

[3] I was going to say "unqualified critic," but I hate unnecessary adjectives.

ternoon nap, stopped to watch his son type. He frowned and said, "Why do you type with one finger, instead of with all your fingers like on a piano?"

I said, "I don't know how to do it with all my fingers, Pappa."

My father had an easy solution for that. "Learn!" he thundered. "If I catch you typing with one finger again, I will take away the type-writer."

I sighed, for I knew he would. Fortunately, there was Mazie, who lived across the street and for whom my pure and puppyish passion still continued. She was taking a commercial course in high school and knew how to type.

I asked her how to type and she showed me how to place my hands on the typewriter keys and which fingers controlled which keys.[4] She watched while, very slowly, I typed the word "the" with left-hand-first-finger, right-hand-first finger, and left-hand-middle-finger. She then offered to give me periodic lessons.

An excuse to be alone with her every once in a while was just what I was looking for, but I had my pride. No one was ever allowed to teach me any more than I required to begin teaching myself. "That's all right," I said, "I'll practice."

And I did. I've been typing fairly constantly ever since, and I can now do ninety words a minute for hours at a time. (To be perfectly truthful, I've sacrificed accuracy for speed, and I don't pretend I don't make errors. I just strike over or x-out. My editors don't mind, or, if they do, they maintain a discreet silence.)

Naturally, when I first began to type, I used both sides of the paper, single-spaced, and no margins. Eventually, I learned to use one side and to double-space, but to this very day I can't bring myself to leave respectable margins, and I tend to use typewriter ribbons and carbon paper until they are quite, quite dead. It is not a matter of economy; I have no reason to economize in that direction. It's just that I've never recovered from having to extract money for paper and typewriter ribbons from the candy store.[5]

Once I was typing, of course, I had much more incentive to write. I remember distinctly that the first piece of fiction I ever wrote on the

---

[4] Sometimes, when I tell the story, I say that she showed me where to put my hands—but that is an ambiguous statement that lends itself to a horrible and untrue misconstruction.

[5] I told this story in *Before the Golden Age*, and the copy editor, who was struggling with my inadequate margins (for it is the margins in which the copy editing corrections must be made), wrote in the margin of this passage: LEARN! Alas, it did not work. I am older, more set in my ways, and I fear no person today as I feared my father then.

typewriter involved a group of men wandering on some quest through a universe in which there were elves, dwarves, and wizards, and in which magic worked. It was as though I had some premonition of J. R. R. Tolkien's *Lord of the Rings*. I can't for the life of me remember what it was that inspired me in this direction. I had read *The Arabian Nights*, the E. Nesbit fantasies (particularly her stories about the psammead), and all sorts of books of magic and legendry, but none of them stick in my mind as sufficient.

I wrote better than forty pages, both sides, single-space, no margins, and I imagine that I must have turned out nearly thirty thousand words before I ran down. But run down I did, and it cured me. I had my fill of fantasy and I didn't try again for years—and never in any lengthy way.

The next item of fiction I tried to write, possibly in 1936, was, at last, *and for the first time*, science fiction. Again, it was a long-winded attempt at writing an endless novel, just like the fantasy earlier, and, indeed, just like *The Greenville Chums at College* five years earlier.

I was bound to get weary of such endless, meandering efforts, and therefore, as soon as I found myself mired in literary quicksand, which sooner or later I always did, I quit. The science-fiction novel died just as my previous efforts did.

What I now remember about my science-fiction epic is that there was a great deal of talk about the fifth dimension at the start and that later on there was some catastrophe that destroyed photosynthesis (though not on Earth, I think). I remember one sentence, and one sentence only. It was "Whole forests stood sere and brown in midsummer." Why I remember that, I don't know, but that is the earliest existing Asimovian science-fiction sentence.

The manuscript still existed some years later. I remember looking at it once (perhaps as late as 1940) and noting that, on the whole, my vocabulary was more complex in that story than in later stories that I actually published. I was still naïve enough at that time to think that this spoke poorly for the stories I published—as though I had declined in literary ability as my style had grown more direct.

Indeed, it is rather embarrassing, as I look back on it now, to realize how little I learned about writing through careful study and intelligent consideration of what I read, and how much I made my way forward through mere intuition. Until I was a published writer, I remained completely ignorant of the fact that there were books on how to write and college-level courses on the subject that one could take.

After I did find out these things existed, I avoided them—perhaps because of the ever-present memory of that horrible course in creative writing in the sixth term of high school.

Of course, I sometimes say, quite emphatically, that it is a good thing I never took courses or read books on how to write. I say that it would have spoiled my natural style; that it would have made me observe an artificial caution; that it would have hedged me about with rules that I could not have followed without wearing myself out.

All of that, however, is probably simple rationalization designed to resign me to things as they are.

7

The summer of 1935, which I spent dreading the coming of City College, was also the summer of another kind of beginning. My brother, Stanley, was going to start school.

My father was then almost thirty-nine and my mother was just turning forty. They no longer felt young at all, and the years at the candy store had made them far more middle-aged than the years alone would have. Consequently it meant that I was the one who took Stanley to school that first day, made sure he knew the route, saw him to his class, called for him at lunch, took him back, then called for him at the end of the day.

I think that was the only day I had to do it. Stan was always level-headed. He knew the way just as I did when I was skipped into 1B, and managed to walk home as accurately as I did—and without crying about it.

Of course, it is always the fate of the younger child not to have to bear the brunt of his parents' neuroses. My parents—my mother, especially—trembled over my well-being so extremely, especially after my babyhood experience with pneumonia, that I couldn't help but absorb the fear and gain an exaggerated caution for myself. (That may be why I won't fly, for instance, and why I do very little else that would involve my knowingly putting myself into peril.)

By the time Stanley came along, however, my parents were far more complacent and indifferent to the possibilities of danger. The result is that Stan is a far more stable individual than I am. He flies, plays tennis, and in all possible ways is a normal, respectable human being.

On the other hand, Stan claims that, as my younger brother, he has suffered untold agonies not at the hands of my parents, but at the hands of *me*. He says that I had a cutting tongue, that no one in the world could beat me when it came to the quick whiplash retort; that I had no hesitation in using it on everybody—especially on him—and that he was in a perpetual state of frustration about it. He further claims that if my mother beat me, or my father denounced me, or my sister screamed at me, I must surely have deserved it every time because each one had to get back at me in the only way they could, after being put on the rack by my "joking remarks." And finally, he insists that I insert this passage somewhere in my autobiography to counteract what he otherwise feels will be a saccharine portrait I will paint of myself. So here it is.

Naturally, I don't remember anything of the sort and insist that Stan must be speaking of someone else, except that I do seem to recall my father saying to me, now and then, in a resigned way, "Again with the jokes?"

I would think that I would remember more of my brother's first days at school, but the day after he started school, Huey P. Long (America's most dangerous demagogue till Joseph P. McCarthy came along) was assassinated and I lost myself in the newspapers.

Besides, it turned out that my brother was not particularly interested in talking about school or in seeking my help. He went through his school career methodically, lacking my erratic brilliance, but getting along with his schoolmates, doing well in his studies, involving himself in extracurricular activities such as newspaper work. On the whole, if you discount that erratic brilliance I mentioned, his school career was far more successful than mine.

At home also, he showed none of my erratic brilliance. By not engaging my parents in disputes over every point of principle, his life was quieter at home and he got his way more often (of course, he benefited by my victories, for he didn't have to fight for what I had already gained).

The saying in our family has always been that "Isaac is the smart brother and Stanley is the good brother." It didn't mean that Stanley wasn't smart or that I wasn't good, it was just that I was smarter than I was good and Stanley was gooder than he was smart. It's perhaps a sad commentary on human nature that "good" is never sufficiently valued. It is almost traditional that the charming ne'er-do-well is more likely to be loved by his mother and to get the beautiful girl than the good and steady fellow.

Well, it was quite clear to me that I was always my parents' favorite. They went for the spectacular brightness and underrated Stan's goodness. The fact of the matter is, however, that everyone today loves Stan, really, including me; and I don't think everyone loves me. In fact, I think everyone swallows hard and *forgives* me.

14

Seth Low Junior College

1

It was not long after Stan's entry into the first grade that the time came for me to go to college. I had acceptances from both Seth Low and City, and I had to go to City College.

I stayed there three days, hating every moment of it, and I remember only two things about those three days. We had a physical examination, and since I was still as skinny as a stick, I was put down as PD, where everyone else's card had WD. I asked that PD meant and I was told "poorly developed." Everyone else, obviously, was "well developed"—another punch in the solar plexus.

The other thing I remember was that we were all given an intelligence test. I've taken intelligence tests periodically in my life and I have always done remarkably well. I am rather cynical about the value of such tests[1] but there's no question that academic people are impressed by them, and I always welcomed them. Getting a high mark in such tests made my scholastic life easier, and I welcomed that even though the feat of getting such a mark was trivial.

I don't know the score I made in the City College examination, and I was never even sufficiently stirred by curiosity to want to know, but about a month after I took the test, I received a letter asking me to come in for further testing because I had astonished them. But by then I was no longer in City College, and I was glad they would have no opportunity to test me further. "Poorly developed" indeed!

What happened was that on my third day at City College, a letter arrived from Seth Low Junior College. I was away at school, and my father, sensing something urgent, opened it, and found they were inquiring as to why I had failed to show up for registration. My father called Seth Low at once and explained that we lacked the money for tuition. The Seth Low people (I don't know who it was he spoke to) at once offered a one-hundred-dollar scholarship for the freshman year, to be repaid at our leisure, and a job with the National Youth Administration (NYA) that would net me a further fifteen dollars a month.

[1] See my essay "Thinking About Thinking" in my book *The Planet That Wasn't* (Doubleday, 1976).

Together, this would nearly pay the first year's tuition, and my father could not resist this. Off I went to Seth Low Junior College after once again maintaining my position that a letter addressed to me was not to be opened by anyone else. My father shrugged that off as a trivial matter.[2]

Seth Low Junior College was located in the Boro Hall section of Brooklyn, about 4½ miles due west of the Decatur Street candy store, and I took the subway to get there. In those days, of course, subways were clean and safe, charged five cents a trip, and were terribly crowded. If you want dirt and danger you have to pay for it, so nowadays the fare is fifty cents and no one takes the subway who can avoid it.

I was the first person, I believe, to enter Columbia University who had been born in the 1920s, and I remember the registrar remarking on this when I gave her my birthdate. How dull that moment of registration would have been if my mother's lie had remained on the books and I had had to say I was born in 1919.

I tried to turn over a new leaf when I went to Seth Low. I was impressed at being in college and I wanted to be a good boy and to stop being a disciplinary problem.

I don't think I succeeded, for every once in a while the director of the junior college (I think his name was Allen), who took a personal interest in me since it was his decision that gave me the scholarship, and who was a very gentle and diplomatic soul, would meet me in the hall and talk to me. He talked about the best ways of getting along with others, how to avoid annoying others by too obvious assumptions of superiority, and so on. He did so in so general and subtle a fashion that it never occurred to me to take it personally. In fact, I wondered why he bothered to tell me all that. It wasn't till after I had left Seth Low that, thinking back on it, it suddenly occurred to me that he meant *me*.

Once I received a message to come to Dr. Allen's office. I spent an uneasy few minutes trying to think what I had done. I couldn't think of a thing and went in very puzzled. Dr. Allen said nothing; he just whipped out a comb and combed my hair. That astonished me, too. I used to comb my hair at the beginning of the day in a sketchy sort of fashion, and it never occurred to me that the process required renewal at intervals during the day.

---

[2] In my family, and perhaps in immigrant families generally in those days, mail was so rare a phenomenon and so likely to contain bad news that the first hands to reach it opened it regardless of the minutiae concerning its addressee—and generally opened it in a state of incipient hysterics, too.

2

I made a friend at Seth Low.

This wasn't usual for me, but don't get me wrong. I made friends as anyone would, and talked to people in amicable fashion, but usually other people didn't mean very much to me. If I saw someone I knew, I would greet him, and if I didn't see him, I didn't notice.

But by a *friend*, I mean someone I sought out and who sought me out, so that we were together a good deal, enjoying each other's company and conversation.

It had happened before. In PS 202, I had made friends with a classmate named Morris Samberg, and we saw each other occasionally even out of school hours. We went on to JHS 149 and to Boys High together.

In Boys High, we had a falling out. I don't remember the occasion, but after over a year in which we studiously ignored each other, it seemed to me that I was no longer angry and that the only reason I behaved in an unfriendly manner was because I was too proud to make the first move. It occurred to me that that was all that was stopping Morris. Well, someone had to move, so I walked to him one day and said, "I don't even remember what the argument was, Samberg. Let's be friends," and held out my hand. He was delighted to shake hands and we were friends again.

But then, after high school, we went our separate ways.

In Seth Low, I met Sidney Cohen, who was perhaps a year older than I was. We took our classes together, we ate lunch together, and we saw each other whenever we could outside of school. It was a good friendship and we got along very well indeed. As in all good friendships, there was a symbiotic relationship between us. I sometimes gave an impromptu lecture on the schoolwork, if Cohen happened to be shaky on some point; and he served as patient audience and as steadying influence. He was a lot like my brother—less brilliant and more sensible than I was.

Nor was it all classwork we discussed. We talked endlessly about all the facets of life that impinged on both of us in common, and particularly on the news events of the day.

We were great on the news events and exchanged views on them vigorously each day. We generally agreed with each other in our estimates of the situation, which caused each of us to have a high opinion of the other's sagacity. Cohen was, perhaps, more aware of Jewishness than I was, but we were both equally aware of Hitler.

This was the closest friendship I ever made, but even here social relationships remained meager. We both commuted, we both lived in Brooklyn. He, however, lived in East New York, and we were far enough apart to make visits back and forth inconvenient. We almost never saw each other except at school, therefore. Nor did we talk on the telephone except on rare occasions, since neither of us were part of a telephone society.

During the summers, however, we would send letters back and forth. Innocently enough, I discarded his letters after I had read them but, as it turned out, he saved mine (at least for a time). When he discovered I had not saved his, he grew angry over the matter, but not permanently so. His anger surprised me, for at that time it never occurred to me to save *any* letters—what good was a letter once it had been read? Nor did I prepare, let alone save, carbons of my own letters.

3

I remember some of my courses in Seth Low.

I took a course in English composition, and when we were asked to write a piece of fiction, I proved I had learned nothing from my high-school experience. I wrote an incredibly long story (intended as the first chapter of an interminable book) set in Nazi Germany. I don't think the professor read all the way through it. It couldn't have taken many pages for him to come to the conclusion that it was worthless, though he didn't express himself as graphically as Mr. Newfield had.

I also continued my German. In high school, it had been my intention to take French and Latin, and I had indeed taken two years of French. When the time came to take Latin, however, it turned out for some reason known only to the Fates that too few people were willing to sign up for Latin. There was no Latin class, and German was the only other language offered. As it happened, I was again forced into the right path. German proved simple, for my knowledge of Yiddish guided me sufficiently to lessen its horrors.

I was never very good at foreign languages.

Vocabulary, to be sure, never offered a problem. I picked up words with no trouble and I still know almost every French and German word I ever learned.[3] What stopped me cold was grammar, however. That remained pretty much a problem area to me. Even English grammar was a pain in the neck, though I mastered it by brute force. By the time I got to the third year in the high-school course, I was embarrassed to

[3] For that matter, I have a surprisingly large Latin and Greek vocabulary, just from my interest in English etymology.

discover that even German, which had been so simple at the start, was beginning to overbear me with its complexities. Latin, with its cases and conjugations and subtleties outdoing even those of German, would have thrown me for an utter loss. I know, because there came a time when I obtained a Latin grammar and decided to teach myself the language and discovered almost at once that had I taken Latin as a school course, I would have hated it.

I took a course in contemporary civilization, too, and also zoology. It was zoology that I planned to make my major.

I was taking a "premedical course," after all, and it was standard in such a case to take either zoology or chemistry as the major. It seemed to me that zoology was closer to medicine so, in the first year of college, I took a general course in zoology.

It is hard to believe it as I look back on it, but I actually dissected animals in that course. We started with earthworms, frogs, and dogfish. Predictably, we got so used to dissection that we would eat our lunch in the biology lab, with the stench of formaldehyde in our nostrils and with animal fragments strewn about. As I recall, Sidney Cohen was much better at dissecting than I was. I put that down in those days to my greater squeamishness, but I eventually found out that I was poor in every laboratory course I ever took.

My most horrifying memory of that zoology course is the dissection of a cat in the second semester. Each of us had to find a homeless alley cat, bring it in, and chloroform it. And I did it! I did it!

To this day, when I think of chloroforming that cat, I turn physically sick—and in fact, as I type this, I feel nauseated.

The point is, I love cats. Everyone in my family loves cats. We never had a dog when I was a child, and I, for one, dislike dogs of all varieties. (My brother, the normal one in the family, eventually got a dog.)

When we were kids, some homeless cat would periodically adopt us and it would become our cat until at some time it would wander off or have to be given away. And when that happened we would take weeks to recover.

And yet I killed a cat. There's almost nothing I have done that I'm more ashamed of. I could argue that it was necessary for the course; that I would have failed the course if I had refused; that it might have aborted my medical career. The answer to that is that I should have done just that. I should have refused to kill the cat, dropped the course, and aborted my medical career, if necessary. I should have realized that a career that involved killing a cat wasn't really for me.

But I didn't realize it. I did what I was told, in true cowardly fashion, and I *deserve* to feel sick over it every time I think of it.

Since I gave up zoology as a major, however, I like to think that I wasn't totally insensible.

Of course, there were other reasons for giving up zoology than my dislike of animal experimentations—reasons that were less important but more persuasive. My sharpest memory of the course is, as you might expect, a trifle—but it turned the scale.

Our zoology lectures were given us by Dr. Elftman (I think) in an old-fashioned room with a tile floor. At one point during one of those lectures, I needed a handkerchief and pulled one out of my pocket. In the same pocket was a glass marble. I had it there because it was a pretty marble and I liked to look at the light through it.

It came out with the handkerchief and went bouncety-bouncety-bouncety all over the tile floor.

Elftman waited patiently while the class held its breath and I, red-faced, struggled to retrieve the marble. When I had done so, and silence had fallen, Elftman said, contemptuously, "Well, this is a *junior* college." The dam broke and the other students laughed—and laughed—and laughed.

A small thing, and not worth remembering, except that it helped sour me on zoology. I ended the course with good marks, but the incident of the dropped marble, even more than the killing of the cat, made it easy for me to consider switching majors when the appropriate time came, and that, in turn, helped deflect the current of my life for (I believe) the better. So though I wasn't thankful to Elftman for his contempt then, I am now.

4

My first year at Seth Low, at least at its Brooklyn campus, was also my last. That first year was Seth Low's tenth year and *its* last. Columbia University simply put an end to it. Why, I don't know, but I'm not paranoid enough to think it was on account of me.[4]

I was not particularly depressed by that. I had done well in that Seth Low year of 1935–36, and was back to smartest-boy-in-the-class form, which cheered me up. (In fact, my class average in the four years of college was just about A—, with equal numbers of A's and B's and

[4] Once again, I had a narrow escape. If I had not been skipped in first and third grades, I would have reached the stage of applying for college one year later, in 1936. Columbia, without Seth Low to fall back upon, would undoubtedly have rejected me outright, and there would have been no escape from City College.

one or two C's. This was by no means record-breaking or even particularly startling, but it was reasonably good. I didn't have to slink around.)

Then, too, the ending of Seth Low didn't leave its students homeless. Columbia University may not be notable for its loving kindness,
but it wasn't quite as heartless as all that. In the second year, we were
told, we would be moved up to the main campus at Morningside
Heights in Manhattan. I had the dim feeling that this meant we would
become full-fledged Columbia students, and that satisfied me, too.

5

If there was something that worried me as my freshman year in
college came to its close, it was the matter of finances. The hundred-
dollar scholarship I had received the year before had been a one-shot,
for the freshman year only. What was to be done for the sophomore
year?

Fortunately, my father managed to persuade one of his customers
to arrange a summer job for me and so, in June 1936, I went to work at
the Columbia Combining Company. It was the first time in my life
that I worked as an unskilled laborer in a paying job, and also the last
time. I got it at the cost of lying a little about my age.

It was a *thoroughly* unskilled job. What I had to do was to help
pull out lengths of rubberized fabric from a huge roll suspended on
hooks at one end of a long measured-off table, cut fixed lengths of it,
pile one length on top of another (with each end of the length held
down by an iron bar), put down a length of slick paper every ten
lengths, then fold them up ten lengths at a time. We would then pile
them onto a handcart, appropriately marked, and they would be taken
out into the universe somewhere.

All that varied was the type of roll we worked with, the number of
lengths we pulled out, and the length of the lengths we pulled out.

Mind you, I only *helped*. I had a superior, a couple of years older
than I, who counted the sheets, saw to it that they were laid exactly
one on the other, and ordered me to move each sheet this way or that
until the adjustment was correct.

It was very dull work, but it brought in the breathtaking sum of
fifteen dollars per week (a full fifteen dollars, for there were no payroll
deductions in those days—no withholding tax—no Social Security). I
might have earned more, but I had to beg off overtime, since, job or no
job, I had to put in as much time as possible in the candy store.

Except for walking endlessly back and forth along a twelve-foot-long table, I remember only one incident out of the ten weeks or so I was on the job.

Some of the men had to wash pretty thoroughly at the end of the day, and change from their work clothes to their street clothes. One of those men, rather slim, rather *macho*, seemed to take pleasure in speaking roughly to me and in watching me respond with a nervous look. I was the youngest person there, still only sixteen, and they were blue-collar workers, only lightly educated, and hard-bitten. To me, they were an utterly unknown quantity and therefore frightening.

One time, after he had taken his shower, and before he had put on his street clothes, this man approached me with no clothes on in what, looking back on it now, was clearly intended to be a seductive manner, and said, "What about it? I'll go easy on you."

I thought he was offering to fight me, and I scrambled back in haste and fell over some rolls of fabric, at which humorous feat everyone laughed. I got to my feet and made for the door, but they called me back and said, "He's just joking, kid," and I came back, but cautiously.

Nothing more happened in that way for the remainder of my job's duration, though I took care to remain far away from this particular man. I assume now that everyone there thought I knew what the man was suggesting and that in running away I had tried to avoid that suggestion. It was not so.

I had heard of homosexuality in a dim and vague manner, I think, but it certainly didn't come to mind at the time. I was merely trying to avoid (so I thought, then) getting beaten up by a hard-muscled and sadistic brawler. It was only long afterward that, remembering the incident, I was suddenly afflicted retrospectively, with an entirely new terror.

He may, of course, have been joking, but, remembering his walk, I don't think so.

6

The summer came to an end at last, and it had been a hot summer. It was during that summer that New York experienced its hottest day on record—106° F. on July 9—but I don't remember it. I certainly don't remember it the way I remember the coldest day 2½ years earlier.

I was skinny, then, and relatively unaffected by heat. My father, however, had grown fat and now weighed well over two hundred pounds. I remember him sitting outside the store on hot, muggy days when the customers had momentarily thinned out, trying to catch his breath and muttering that he was completely unmanned.

Still, the hot summer brought me $150 or so that I had made at the summer job. Add to that the $15 a month I expected to make at my NYA job and we could struggle through for another year.

In September 1936, then, I began my second year at Columbia, and now I was taking courses at Morningside Heights. It meant a new extension of my physical world. For the first time in my eleven-year-long school career, I attended an institution that was not in Brooklyn. Every day I walked a few blocks to the subway station and took it to the end of the line at Fourteenth Street and Eighth Avenue, where I changed to another subway line, went up to 116th Street, and then walked to class through (and up) Morningside Park, which had several flights of stairs in it. (That's why the western side was called Morningside Heights.) I then retraced my steps in the evening. The whole trip took a little over an hour each way, about eleven hours per week just traveling.

It wasn't completely wasted time, however. I read the newspaper, for instance, and by now I was fiendishly interested in politics as well as baseball, and the time was rapidly approaching when F. D. Roosevelt would be running for re-election. Or I read books or, in a pinch, did some studying.

Columbia was the most elaborate institution I had ever attended, with its numerous buildings spread out over blocks and blocks of Manhattan. I was strangely detached from it all, however.

Since I was not at a dormitory, I was never on campus except to go to classes, and I did so in the most economical way possible, walking straight to the building in which the classes were held and then straight out of it. There was many a building I never entered at all in all my years at Columbia.

Nor was there ever a feeling of being part of an organic whole, I was at all times a visitor and the students who passed me as I moved from one building to another were strangers to me. My own mood in all this was so like what it had been at high school that there was scarcely any inner awareness that I was in college.

Besides, I wasn't in Columbia *College*. The fact that I was at the Morningside campus and went from course to course with the sophomores of Columbia College did not make me one of them after all. I was not allowed to register at the college. Along with the other Seth Low rabble, I was eventually put into the category of "university undergraduate." I was not an undergraduate of this college or that college, but of the entire university taken as a whole. But this had always been the fate of the Seth Low student after the second year. It was just that I experienced the fact a year early (if not quite the title—I was still theoretically Seth Low, even though Seth Low was defunct in my second year). It was disappointing and freshly humiliating, but I suppose I should not have been so simple as to expect anything else.

I took my first course in chemistry in my sophomore year and fell in love with it. The teacher (whose name I have forgotten) was interesting and the chemical demonstrations were delightful. I enjoyed the laboratory infinitely more than I did the zoology dissections and was both fascinated and relieved to be working with chemicals rather than living things. I might have begun to have a glimmer of myself as a professional chemist even then, were it not that the assumption that I was going to be a doctor of medicine overrode everything.

It was the immediate fascination of working with chemicals and the ease of the subject that drew me to chemistry, rather than any abstract consideration of the importance or value of science in general or of that science in particular. I wasn't complicated enough to grow philosophical over such matters, but I was simple enough to know what I liked.

What made chemistry easy was that not only had I had it, on a simpler level, in high school, but also, as it happened, I had read chemistry texts on the college level under the delusion that they were "library books" so that I had given myself a formidable head start.

What was not wonderful was the new course I was taking as part of my zoology major. It was embryology, and it consisted, in very large part, of looking through microscopes at slides of embryo sections of chicks at each day of their twenty-one-day period of development, and then drawing what one saw.

I was under a double handicap here. No matter how I adjusted my microscope focus and my light and my slide, I never saw what the embryology text told me I would see. I saw clearly, of course; there is nothing wrong with my vision; I just don't have that kind of visual imagery that sorts out tiny details. Then, if I had seen it, I would have been unable to draw it anyway. My artistic inability is of the towering sort that could have produced a Sistine Chapel if every fault could have been turned into a corresponding and equal virtue.

Toward the end of the semester, the teacher announced in a warm and jovial manner that everyone in the class was passing the laboratory part of the course. He added, even more warmly and jovially, "except one."

With a sinking heart and a desperate effort to try to recall if there happened to be someone in the class who drew embryos even worse than I did, I called out, "Who's the one?"

And with a kindly manner, he said, "Strange you should ask that," and got the dutiful laugh of everyone else in the class.

Fortunately, I was spared an overall failure. My reasonable work in the lecture portion of the class raised my final mark to a snappy C—.

That was enough, however. The killed cat and the dropped marble had brought me to the edge, and the embryology professor's pleasant sense of tact pushed me over.

I switched majors. I never took another course in the biological sciences. Chemistry was my new major, and that remained permanent. And for the first time I began to doubt whether I really wanted to go to medical school, with its dissections and microscopes.

15

Windsor Place

1

While I was in my sophomore year, we had another change of candy store. In December of 1936, my father sold his third candy store and bought his fourth. The new candy store was at 174 Windsor Place, in the Park Slope section of Brooklyn, about 4.8 miles southwest of Decatur Street.

It was farther west than any other residence we had ever had in Brooklyn, and it was only two short blocks west of Prospect Park. I always described the location as being "on the other side of Prospect Park," for whenever I said I lived near the park, the person I spoke to would always say, "On Flatbush Avenue?" and I always said, "No, on the other side."

All our candy stores were alike in essentials, but I remember this one best. Unlike the Essex Street store and the Decatur Street store, it was not on the corner of the block, but was in the middle, as the Sutter Avenue store had been.

When one entered the door, one found the store broader (left and right) than it was deep. Near the left wall was the cigar counter, with the cash register at the end away from the door. That cash register marked the nerve center of the store, and my father was usually behind it and a little to the left, where a bare patch of counter was the place where money was handed in and change handed out.

The cash register was an old-fashioned one, with the amounts that were rung up showing on white tabs that moved up into the glass-enclosed top. There were separate keys for penny units from 01 to 09, for dime units from 10 to 90, and for dollar units from $1.00 to $3.00. I don't think it was conceived that any spendthrift would be so lost to reality as to find ways of spending more than $3.99 at one time.

From an early age I was allowed free access to the cash register and I quickly learned how to play chords on it. You could strike, at the same time, one of the dollar units, one of the dime units, and one of the penny units, so that if someone paid you $1.64, the tabs marked $1, 60, and 04 would show up. You could not push down two or more of the keys in a particular unit.

Then, of course, there was the "No Sale" key, marked in brown to distinguish it from all the whites and with which no other tab could be punched. "No Sale" would open the cash register if it were necessary to give someone two nickels for a dime, or to poke around for something you had placed there for safekeeping.

Making change, with or without a sale, was an art my father much valued. It had to be done speedily and correctly, and it must have been a great relief to my father when he found that I caught the essence of making change at once and could be relied on to make no errors. He never showed that relief, however, for he strictly maintained the notion that proficiency was merely to be expected and that praise would rot my moral fiber.

Looking back on it now, I am amazed that my father let me have full use of the cash register. There were foolproof ways of withholding some of the money for my private profit. I never did it, because it never even occurred to me to do it (so that I didn't suffer the agonies of temptation), but how did he *know* that it would never occur to me to do so?

On the wall behind the cash register were the vertical slots in which packs of cigarettes were kept in a definite order so that my father could speed service by reaching for the desired brand without looking. In those days, all the cigarettes were "regulars," of course. There were no king-size, no filter tips. The individual packs were all $.13 except for a few mavericks, which were $.10.

We kept an open pack out of which we would sell individual cigarettes for a penny apiece. And, of course, an occasional millionaire would buy a whole carton of them and we would stand around reverently to watch my father ring up a purchase price of some $2.50.

There was a hinged top to the cash register, and when that was lifted, certain meters were revealed that indicated sums of various kinds. My father usually set one of them to zero at the beginning of the week, and it amused me to keep an eye on it to see how the week's intake was running.

At right angles to the cigar counter was the candy counter, laden with a wide variety of penny candies in three rows, each in its open box. Some were a penny apiece, some two for a penny, some even five for a penny. A few were lavish enough to be two cents apiece. There was a fourth row up on top where we kept the nickel candy bars for wealthy kids.

Waiting on the candy counter, which was my exclusive job in even the very first candy store, and which I never entirely outgrew, was a tedious task. The typical youngster with three pennies to spend could buy candy in any of a thousand combinations or more (I mean that quite literally), and it took him a long time to decide how best to make his investment. I had to wait, more or less seethingly, for him to make up his mind.

Behind the candy counter was a small enclosed area where we kept reserve supplies of candy and cigarettes, and where there was a toilet. It was the one niche of privacy in the store, but only my father could use it freely. For the rest of us, it was there for paternally begrudged emergencies.

Next to the candy counter was a small aisle, and across from it, in the right half of the store, was that vanished piece of Americana, the soda fountain. There was the refrigerator with its large cylindrical containers of ice cream; the containers of various syrups, which could be pumped in squirts into glasses and over ice cream; the electric stirrers that made the malted milks; the faucets out of which carbonated water would emerge; the platform for clean glassware; and the sink for washing the dirty glassware.

It was my father's special domain, and I never tried to evict him.

Before it were four stools where, every once in a while, a youngster would sit endlessly while very slowly sipping a soda. He could not properly be evicted while his soda glass remained unempty, and some kids had the art of drinking steadily yet leaving the glass unempty for half an hour at a time.

On the right wall was the magazine stand which, of course, I knew by heart. Next to it was the telephone, and in front of the telephone, one table with four chairs. Strictly speaking, the table was for people to sit at with sodas and malted milks, but we discouraged its use. It was more important as a surface on which to put together newspapers and deal with packages of magazines.

Next to the door was an ice container in which we kept bottled sodas cold, taking them out fresh and dripping for store consumption. If anyone wanted to buy bottles to take home, they got dry ones at room temperature. Outside the store was, of course, the newsstand, which had the newspapers and some of the more popular magazines.

There were times when we had a pinball game in the store (always lucrative but troublesome, since it attracted groups of teen-age idlers), and eventually we had a rack for paperback books.

All told it was a rather small store, the smallest we had yet had, with not much room for toys, stationery, and miscellany—but it was a good one. It had a large newspaper trade, and that meant we had a much larger newspaper delivery route to cover. There was always a hired boy to deliver the papers (but I was always there as a fail-safe mechanism). I also had to collect paper bills rather extensively once a month, and hated that job.

We were on a street through which many people went and returned on their way to and from the local Catholic church, located not much more than a block away. The neighborhood was heavily Irish, which meant we were extraordinarily busy on Sundays. In fact, we marked off Sundays from 6:00 A.M. to 1:00 P.M. by the Masses, and we all had to be on our mark and ready as the human flood crested past our store at the conclusion of each Mass.

It was also a very conservative neighborhood, with the people at best uneasy in the presence of a Jew and at worst downright hostile. The Catholic newspaper, the *Tablet*, sold in large numbers, and occasionally I could not forebear to read it, and it infuriated me. It was violently anti-Roosevelt, and (at least in those days) was filled with a thinly veiled anti-Semitism. While very aware of the Communist menace, it didn't seem to be much aware that Hitler existed.

Of course, Hitler did exist and was becoming more powerful yearly. Between the growth of that menace and my new awareness of hostility in the immediate surroundings, I entered a period of deep and worrying insecurity. Yet I must add at once that we were never actually mistreated in Windsor Place or, except once or twice, made to feel seriously uncomfortable.

Considering all that, there was even less feeling of being an organic part of a neighborhood in Windsor Place than in any of the earlier stores. There was no chance of social, or even particularly friendly, relations with customers in general. I, for one, felt resentful of them as a class because of the false position of "servant" in which I found myself. I had to wait on them and be polite to them and smile and be obsequious. This never came easy.

I conceived of the particular customers of the Windsor Place store as rich people (lower middle-class, actually, I now realize, but they seemed rich to me then—there was one person who was known to make five thousand dollars a year). What's more, they seemed stodgy and uninteresting.

I knew them by face and, just barely, by name in some cases. I do remember a teen-aged red-headed girl named Eileen who attracted my attention for a brief time in a way that none of the others did. I talked to her occasionally, but nothing further took place.

It was the first time I had ever lived quite so near a park. What's more, to the west of us, at a somewhat greater distance, was Greenwood

Cemetery, the largest in Brooklyn. I sometimes went there. I never liked it as well as Evergreens, however, so that I gradually deserted it for the park.

We lived across the street from the store. This meant a little more independence for us youngsters since now my mother could not hear every footfall overhead. However, her preternatural sense of hearing did allow her to hear us on those occasions when our philosophical discussions grew particularly exciting. She would yell at us from the street and a dread silence would instantly fall. Later she would tell us that for blocks around people had been stopping and saying, "What's that noise?" She was referring to our discussions and not to her shouting, though it's my private opinion that it should have been the other way around.

The new neighborhood was even more bound up in baseball than the old one had been (they were all Dodgers fans here, too), and my own mania continued unabated. In fact, within a few months after arriving at Windsor Place, I attended my first baseball game. It was, I believe, the Memorial Day doubleheader at the Polo Grounds. As I recall, Carl Hubbell had ended the 1936 season with sixteen straight victories, and had started the 1937 season with eight straight victories, and I went, hoping, to see him take his twenty-fifth win over two seasons without a loss (an unprecedented feat)—and he was knocked out of the box and lost.

I didn't know whether to be indignant over having missed twenty-four victories in order to be treated to a defeat, or fearful that it had been my own presence that had "jinxed" him.

Not long after we moved into the neighborhood, the new main branch of the Brooklyn Public Library opened at Grand Army Plaza, a mile and a quarter away along the western edge of Prospect Park. I walked there and back periodically, going there at a half run and coming back at a stroll—and reading.

I daresay I must have gone, occasionally, in cold or cloudy weather, but when I remember those walks I remember only mild sunshine, for some reason.

The new building was white, simple, and impressive, very twentieth-century, but my style of reading continued as always—that is, immersion in nineteenth-century romanticism and its later imitators.

I never discovered twentieth-century realism. I never read Hemingway or Fitzgerald or Joyce or Kafka. Even in poetry, I clung to meter and rhyme and never discovered post-Victorian poetry. Or if I saw some by accident, I found it repelled me.

I might as well admit that this was permanent. To this day I am a stranger to twentieth-century fiction and poetry and I have no doubt that it shows in my writing.

Why was this? For one thing, I was entrapped in science fiction and, to a lesser extent, in other pulp magazines, and I never quite emerged. I wanted excitement and action in my stories rather than introspection, soul-searching, and unpleasant people. So if I did reach for fiction in the library it was likely to be a historical novel by Rafael Sabatini or a Cape Cod novel by Joseph C. Lincoln. (Usually, when I discovered one book by a prolific author I found I liked I would methodically go through all the others by him I could find.)

For another, I found myself shifting to nonfiction more and more. My interest in historical fiction intensified my interest in history itself, as my interest in science fiction intensified my interest in science. I devoured H. G. Wells *Outline of History* and his *The Science of Life*. I read endless histories of Greece because of my fascination with Homer, and endless histories of France because of my fascination with Dumas.

In nonfiction, the contemporary output was open to me, of course, and I had no hangups as far as the twentieth century was concerned. To this day I never tire of reading books about the Civil War if they are satisfactorily pro-Union, or books about the World Wars and Hitler if they are satisfactorily anti-Nazi.

I also read James Jeans and Arthur Eddington and because of them swallowed whole anything I could find on new developments in astronomy and physics.

I was attracted to almost anything I could find in the humor section, but nothing satisfied me as much as the essays of Robert Benchley and the verses of Ogden Nash.

My reading reached a peak in its aimless variety in my late teens. Later on, I began more and more to read for school or for my work, and eventually my reading for amusement became restricted to murder mysteries and an occasional history—and even that could be regarded as a professional interest.

2

My interest in political and world affairs was now such that I could (and did) time the events in my personal life by the events in the greater world outside.

For instance, the last notable event that took place during our sojourn on Decatur Street was the 1936 Presidential election on November 3. I had spent a miserable few months following *The Literary Digest* poll, which predicted a Republican landslide. It seemed to show

168 IN MEMORY YET GREEN

that the Republican candidate, Alfred M. Landon, would carry every state outside the Solid South and the border states. There seemed no reason to disbelieve this, since *The Literary Digest* had polled an immense number of people whom it had drawn out of telephone directories and automobile registration lists.

What's more, the poll was accurate, for if only those people voted who were prosperous enough to own telephones and automobiles, Landon would indeed have won in a landslide. Fortunately for the Democrats, the less prosperous could also vote even if *The Literary Digest* didn't think them worth counting.

On November 3, I took a nap in the afternoon because it was my intention to stay up and listen as long as Roosevelt had any chance at all of being re-elected. It is an indication of how old I was getting that my mother was willing to let me do this.

Of course, as it turned out (and I couldn't believe my ears), Roosevelt won everywhere. Landon carried only Maine and Vermont, and I stayed up all night just glorying in the gathering figures. Naturally, I had made up an elaborate state-by-state checkerboard of my own. I recorded the electoral votes and then went on to record the figures and award the states this way or that once I considered a plurality to be insurmountable. I remember hesitating over New Hampshire.

After that election, *The Literary Digest* went out of business and a new group of pollsters came in who sampled fewer people in more representative groups.

Then, after we arrived at Windsor Place, the first world event of note was the capture and imprisonment of Chiang Kai-shek of China by the Young Marshal, Chang Hsueh-liang, a competing warlord, on December 12, 1936. This started a train of events that led to a renewed war between China and Japan in 1937. (Japan had begun its invasion of China in 1931, while Great Britain and the United States confined themselves to speaking loudly and doing nothing.)

3

Our new apartment across the street was distinctly more commodious than any we had yet had, but in no way more distinctive. All the apartments I lived in as a child as an adolescent had, as I remember them, nothing that was not entirely utilitarian. There were no heirlooms, nothing precious brought from Russia, nothing that was a favorite item that we could not bear to part with.

There were chairs, tables, sofas, beds, all bought cheaply, all characterless. When they wore out, if we could persuade ourselves to the expenditure, we replaced them with other items equally colorless.

As a matter of fact, I hated anything new because for a long while after it arrived, my parents would be reluctant to allow it to be used lest we "wear it out." We could make do without sitting on a chair, but to get in a new radio and be told not to use it vitiated the very reason for its existence and drove me wild.

Of course, a larger apartment meant more room for me. For a while I shared a room with Stanley, but some time after we moved to Windsor Place, he contracted the mumps and was taken out of the room and not returned. After that, for the first time in my life, I actually had a room of my own.

The privacy was virtually nil, for it was a railroad apartment and there were four rooms in a line: living room, my room, Marcia's room, my mother's (plus Stanley's) room. The kitchen and my father's room could be reached directly from the hall (there were no other tenants on the floor, so the hall was ours too), but anyone wanting to go from the living room to their bedroom had to go through *my* bedroom. Still, at least there was no one actually *in* the room with me.

Then, too, I was even given a closet all my own and permission to keep my magazines there. After seven years of reading science-fiction magazines, I found myself more enamored of the stories than ever. They were, as a rule, every bit as exciting as the pulp adventures of the "Shadow" and "Doc Savage," which I also read, and, in addition, brought me into a fantastic world beyond anything earthbound literature could offer.

The horizons in science fiction were limitless, and the excitement of outer space, of time travel, of the far future seemed a continually unsurpassable delight. It was the pleasure of magic combined with the discipline of science. It was just enough of a slipping of bonds to give freedom, and not enough to seem folly and anarchy. It was the use of imagination to give the effect of a roller coaster loop-the-loop, with the use of the laws of nature to keep you on the track and bring you safely home.

And now, with my delights in science fiction almost unbearably high, I finally reached a new plateau. I rebelled, at last, against putting each one back on the stand after I had read it. I had *kept* the August 1936 issue of *Astounding Stories*. By the time we moved into the new place, I had five issues of that magazine and a couple each of *Thrilling Wonder Stories* and *Amazing Stories*. It wasn't a large closet, but it was such a luxury for me.

The sight of all those magazines there inspired me to prepare a little index-card system in which I listed all the stories alphabetically by title. I included the author, the length, a brief review and opinion, and a rating from no stars to five stars in half-star units.

That really made me conscious of stories, as literary items, as never before and, after six years of writing amorphous, disconnected, unending—and therefore dying—fictional items, it finally occurred to me to write a *story*.

The day on which this happened was May 29, 1937. I remembered the date a few years later and jotted it down, and still have the jotting, so I know. It was the first time I ever began a story with the vague thought of actually attempting to get it published when it was done. And getting *paid*, too. I was nearly 17½ at the time.

The story I began to compose for the purpose, the first story in the list I eventually kept, was entitled "Cosmic Corkscrew."

In it I viewed time as a helix (that is, as something like a bedspring). Someone could cut across from one turn directly to the next, thus moving into the future by some exact interval, but being incapable of traveling one day less into the future. (I didn't know the term at the time, but what I had done was to "quantize" time travel.)

As far as I knew then, the notion of helical time was original with me. It is difficult for me to remember what particularly inspired the story. I think it began with my discovery, in the books I read, of the neutrino. The existence of the neutrino had been postulated five years earlier and it had not been detected. Indeed, at the time it was thought it might never be detected.

Of course, the reason it wasn't detected was that it had neither electric charge nor mass, so that it offered no handle to the detecting techniques of the time—but that was prosaic.

What if the neutrino could not be detected because it went off into the past or the future? I had a vision of neutrinos flashing through time, backward and forward, and thought of them as a vehicle for time travel.

That turned out to be typical of my science fiction. I usually thought of some scientific gimmick and built a story about that. In this case, the time-as-helix notion came only afterward as a way of limiting my hero's freedom of action and creating the plot complication.

My protagonist made the cut across time and found the Earth deserted. All animal life was gone, yet there was every sign that life had existed until very shortly before—and no indication at all of what had happened to bring about the disappearance. It was told in the first person from a lunatic asylum, because the narrator had, of course, been placed in one when he returned and tried to tell his tale.

In this story, I had the full panoply of pulp style, for I knew nothing else. I read enormous quantities of pulp magazines, to say nothing of the florid fiction of the nineteenth century and, without even thinking about it, I loaded down my sentences with adjectives and adverbs and had my characters crying out, and starting back, and shrieking madly, and screaming curses. Everything was in jagged, primary colors.

But as far as possible I was interested in realistic science, or the illusion of it. Even in that first story, I went to some trouble to explain about neutrinos as authentically as I could, for instance, even if I did introduce the time-travel angle out of left field.

With time, the pulpish aspects of my writing became subdued and faded out, though perhaps not as rapidly as they would have were I better acquainted with contemporary writing by literary masters. My concern for realistic science stayed, however, and I quickly became and remained a writer of "hard" science fiction.

As for "Cosmic Corkscrew," I worked on it, on and off, through the summer and then stopped when the school semester began, and I left it only partly done in my desk drawer.

4

My earnings of the previous summer together with my NYA job carried me through the sophomore year in satisfactory fashion. The two together paid most of my tuition, and there were few other expenses of consequence. Each day I spent ten cents on carfare and twenty-five cents for lunch. As for textbooks, I didn't buy them. I made do with the lectures or I would borrow my friends' texts at crucial moments or, on occasion, get used copies, which I would give back when I was through. Laboratory fees and other occasional expenses couldn't be avoided, of course.

My NYA job during the sophomore year was rather interesting. I worked for Professor Gregory Razran of the Psychology Department. (Cohen and I took his course in psychology—we took almost all our classes together—so I knew Razran well.)

I remember several incidents in connection with my work for Razran.

Razran was interested in preparing a table of the lengths of the hypotenuses, given the lengths of the two sides of a right triangle—or, mathematically, the square roots of the sums of given squares. It was useful in some sort of statistical work, and a table would have been handy in those precomputer days.

He had several students working on it, including me, and since it meant working with numbers, it was right up my alley. I threw myself into it, apportioned the work (doing my own fair share), checking the work of others, designing and preparing a master chart, and so on.

Nobody, however, has ever said I had the knack of working with people. I find it difficult to follow orders from someone who is my superior since I would much rather do things my own way. I find it equally difficult to avoid giving precise orders to someone who is working under me and do not like to let him do anything *his* way. (Is this inconsistent on my part? Certainly, but it always seemed to me, unfortunately, that my way was better than any other.)

What happened in this case was that the others involved in working out the table complained to Razran that I was being high-handed and, to keep the peace, Razran asked me to stop trying to run the project. I was horribly embarrassed, and handed over the master chart (which I had been keeping at home, so that I could work on it at all hours) to the other students. I then asked that I be given a different job to avoid the friction. I was given one (I forget what it was) that did not involve my working with anyone, and then I had no trouble.

The sequel to the story is this:

In the summer of 1937, Razran asked where the master chart was, and I answered, in surprise, that I handed it over to the protesting students. But Razran didn't have it, it turned out, and couldn't get it. No one seemed to know what had become of it. It might be that Razran eventually found it, but my impression is that the project was never completed.

It *would* have been completed if he had left me in charge, though, and the master chart would eventually have been safely in his possession. I didn't say, "Serve you right!" but I thought it, and I was mean enough to grin over it when he wasn't looking.

Another memory is this one:

While I was working for him, one of his graduate students came wandering in and asked me for help. He didn't know who I was but I was there and alive and that was enough.

It seemed he was devising a maze that he intended to use to test students for some dark purposes of his own. He had a board with innumerable nail-heads on it and if you touched any of them with a wired metal stylus, a circuit would be completed. Some nailheads would light a green light and some a red light. The trick was to try to go from one end of the board to the other lighting only the green lights. Naturally, you had to begin by doing it hit-and-miss, but each time you repeated the attempt, you got it more nearly right, and in the end you could follow the winding path of the green lights rapidly and surely.

The student timed me and when I learned the path, he decided I had done it too quickly so that it must be too easy. He added winds and twists in private and then brought it back and timed me again. Then he added more winds and twists until finally he thought, from the time it took me to solve the maze, that it was difficult enough for the average student.

Then, on a later day, he showed Razran the plot of the green-lighted pathway when I happened to be in the room working on my NYA job. Razran looked at the pathway in astonishment and said, "Why is it so complicated?"

"It has to be," said the student, "or it's solved too easily."

"Did you check it on someone?"

"Certainly."

"On whom?"

And the student pointed to me. "On him."

Razran clicked his tongue in exasperation, and said "Here, take it back, start all over, and use somebody else to test it on so that you'll end with something reasonably simple."

When he left, I said, "I'm sorry, Dr. Razran. If I had known he was looking for an average student, I'd have *told* him I was above average."

"It's all right," said Razran, "you're below average in plenty of ways." And I guess he was right.

One thing I recall with disappointment. The first slide rule I ever saw was in Razran's office. I picked it up and fiddled with it curiously.

"What is this, Dr. Razran?" I asked.

"A slide rule," he said.

"What does it do?" I asked.

"That would take too long to explain," he said with irritation, and took it away from me.

I have never forgiven him for that. If he had simply said, "It's to multiply and divide" and had showed me how to multiply two by three and no more, I would have worked out the rest for myself. It would have taken him ten seconds and, because he wouldn't, he lost me three years in which I might have used the slide rule.

One last incident that puzzled me at the time was this:

Sidney Cohen and I were standing on 116th Street, talking, when

Razran passed by. We said, "Hello, Professor Razran," in chorus (and in the approved polite manner of students who were aware that they had not yet been graded).

Razran stopped, looked at us, shook his head sadly, and said, "I *wish* that when I saw one of you on campus I didn't always see the other one." And he passed on.

We watched him in astonishment until he turned a corner, and then Sidney said to me, "Why did he say that?"

"I don't know," I answered. "Maybe he thinks we ought to make more friends."

Then we walked on and forgot about it, or at least Sidney did, for long afterward, when I recalled the incident to him he drew a complete blank. (It's the curse of a good memory that one often doesn't forget trivial incidents that are, perhaps, better forgotten.)

Years later, when I looked back on that remark, I suddenly put a scandalous construction on it and found myself moved to fury. How could Razran have dared misconstrue my utterly non-sexual friendship with Sidney? And how many others had made the same misconstruction?

5

An event, equally trivial, stands out in my mind as having taken place in the summer of 1937.

My father was taking his nap in the apartment across the street and my brother—then eight years old—was throwing the ball against the wall as I had once done when I was his age.

My mother called to him to stop, but he was obviously caught up in the game. He was a good kid and never made trouble, which of course made my mother all the more impatient that he didn't obey her now. She did what any good officer does: She called on the non com.

"Isaac," she said, "go over there and stop him."

I was in no mood to hit him (I would have had to chase him and catch him first), and yelling might not work, so I tried strategy. I walked over slowly, with a pleasant smile on my face, very much the seventeen-year-old big brother.

"Hey, Stan," I said, "throw me the ball and I'll show you a trick."

My brother watched me warily and then—obviously deciding I intended no harm—tossed me the ball.

Whereupon I promptly tossed it onto the unreachable roof of the candy store.

Poor Stanley burst into tears, and in exactly half a second my clever trick turned into pure garbage in my mind. I began to apologize and to ask forgiveness and to try to hug him, but he would have none of it. He just left me.

I remember it still. I have never forgotten it. It takes me the smallest effort to jump the intervening decades, see the store, the street, my brother at eight, and his face crumpling at the deceit I had practiced on him. Thirty-two years later (at a time I will describe in due course) I finally brought the matter up, apologized once again, and said "If you don't forgive me, Stan, I'll carry this to my grave."

He frowned and said, "I forgive you, I forgive you, but I don't remember it at all."

He probably forgot it after half an hour; *I* carried the scar for a third of a century. It is surely better to be wronged than to do wrong.

I think it was also in the year 1937 that my Grandfather Aaron died. When he fell sick, my father's younger brother, Abraham Ber (who had taken to calling himself Boris), took him to Moscow for medical treatment, and there he died. I have no idea when either of my grandmothers died.

News from Russia was very slim and intermittent. Worse yet, my father and mother discussed what news there was, but never talked about it to me. It was a life I had not shared and they hugged it to themselves.

16

My Diary

1

With the new year of 1938, a turning point came in my personal life that might have seemed of the most trival character.

I started a diary.

In itself, this was not remarkable. I believe that almost any youngster who is reasonably articulate and introspective sooner or later tries his hand at a diary so that he might record his momentous acts and thoughts. Why should I be an exception?

In most cases, I suspect, a diary lasts for a few days, a few weeks, a year at most. Sometimes, though, it endures, and in my case it did. It is still going on today, and dozens of annual diaries stand side by side on my shelf like good and faithful soldiers, each of them, with one or two exceptions, in the same style, for I am an orderly creature of habit.[1]

My diary did, of course, trail off in some ways. I began with the intention of recording everything of significance each day. And I did—at least what I regarded as significant. I reported the news each day in incredible detail and from a very partisan pro-New Deal and anti-Nazi slant. I also reported baseball games in even more incredible detail. In fact, my baseball record took up something like one third of each page, and the entire first year is written in very small handwriting top to bottom and left to right with no margins anywhere.

As time went on, however, I grew less interested in baseball and less preoccupied in converting my diary page into a compendium of newspaper headlines. I wrote in a larger hand, rarely filled the page, and eventually my diary became a kind of compact literary and social record of my life.

Whether I wrote at length or briefly, however, it was never my intention to say anything in the diary that it was no one's business but my own to know. I relied on my memory for any secret or disgraceful items.

This, I suppose, is not traditional. Girls especially are supposed to

[1] In one way they differ. The price went up by stages. My first diary cost me $.50, my most recent $2.85 plus tax. I'm not complaining, mind you. It is a lot easier for me to come up with $2.85 plus tax now than it was for me to locate $.50 in 1938.

write diaries in which they record their inmost erotic fantasies. Maybe they do, but I didn't. The result was that I never had to lock my diaries away. Anyone was welcome to read them, and no one ever did after a first attempt.

Even I don't read them for pleasure. They are a series of reference books for me, a way of finding out when something happened and in exactly what order things happen.

Why should this matter? Well, I'm an orderly person and it is my experience in life that people who describe events of which I had personal knowledge almost invariably get the story wrong in almost every detail, sometimes missing or inventing important portions of the story.

One of my motives in starting a diary was, in fact, to be able to have some documentary evidence to help out in the numerous arguments that started when I said, "That's not the way it happened. It was *after* you did this that I did that. . . ."

I don't know that the diary helped, though. I found that the people with whom I had the arguments would develop a pettish way of saying, "I don't care what your diary says."

The diary came in handy, in a systematic way, when I wrote *The Early Asimov* (Doubleday, 1972) but that was only a limited autobiography—limited in time to the eleven years during which I wrote only for the magazines, and limited in subject almost entirely to that writing.

Now I'm going to use it again for a much broader view in every respect.

When I first turned to my 1938 diary in connection with *The Early Asimov*, I received a horrible shock. I had always taken it for granted that I was an extraordinarily clever eighteen-year-old, far in advance of my age. The sad truth, though, is that my 1938 diary sounds as though it were written by a very ordinary eighteen-year-old boy.

It was very disappointing.

The worth of the diary, however, is that it instantly proves that my own memory, excellent though it is, and inordinately proud of it though I am, is not to be relied on in all respects.

For instance, on January 1, 1938, the first day of my diary (a Saturday), I record that my mother and I took advantage of the holiday (which meant a slow day in the store, especially since it was drizzling icily all day) to see a play on the Yiddish stage.

When I was little, my parents would frequently take me to see Yiddish shows. It undoubtedly brought back those days in Russia to them when they had acted in such shows.

I understood the shows perfectly, of course, and I enjoyed the musicals, particularly because they were funny and because the tunes were invariably catchy. ("Bei Mir Bist Du Schön" came from one of those musicals and I knew it and could sing it, in Yiddish, a decade before the Andrews Sisters grew famous with it.)

The serious dramas, however, I found inexpressibly dreary. They dealt, very frequently, with long-suffering and noble immigrant parents and their ungrateful Americanized children (so that all the immigrant parents in the audience wept and had a wonderful time and all the ungrateful Americanized children in the audience shuffled their feet uncomfortably). Another common subject was that of the good, plain Jewish wife who scrubbed floors to send the husband through medical school, and then got thrown over for some painted, uncorseted floozie. That filled me with ennui, too.

The thing is, though, that without my diary, I would have sworn on the grave of Isaac Newton that Yiddish plays were a thing of my childhood, of the 1920s, and possibly of the early 1930s. At any suggestion that I had gone to see one with my mother when I was about to turn eighteen and a junior in college, I would have scoffed.

"If that had happened that late in my life," I would have said, "I would have remembered it."

Well, I don't. Even when I look at it on the diary page, I don't remember it. So much for my fancy memory.

The various aspects of Yiddish culture never really permeated my life, however. Up to the age of thirteen I lived in a Jewish neighborhood, but because of the candy store (and I scarcely remember the years before) we didn't participate in the neighborhood social life. There were the Jewish holidays but, except very briefly in 1928, no synagogue, no Hebrew school, and eventually, for myself and my brother, no bar mitzvah.

I have dim memories of my mother "blessing the lights" when I was very little, the traditional task of the Jewish woman, but later on, especially after we moved into a Gentile neighborhood in 1933, we did not observe the Sabbath in any way, or the dietary laws, either.

Little by little my parents took to speaking English, even to each other. The result was that Marcia's knowledge of Yiddish is much sketchier than mine, and Stanley has no Yiddish at all.

When I was very young, even as late as when I attended Hebrew school in 1928, I accepted all the tales of the Bible, the existence of God, and every other formal aspect of religion as a matter of course.

This slipped away quietly, however, as I realized through my reading of science (and of science fiction, too) that much of the Bible represented nothing more than a collection of primitive legends. There was no trauma about it, no soul-searching, no internal crisis, no troubled discussions with my parents or anyone else. There merely came a time, probably before I was thirteen, when I found myself accepting atheism as matter-of-factly as I had previously accepted religion. Nor have I ever wavered in this point of view since. The universe I live in consists of matter and energy only, and that doesn't make me in the least bit uncomfortable. I am quite certain that death is followed by nothingness, and that doesn't make me feel uncomfortable either.

As for Russian cultural influences? None at all.

In the Nazi ferment of the 1930s, it was impossible to think of ourselves as anything but Jews, even if we abandoned Judaism. We might have been born in Russia, but we weren't Russians.

Then, too, if there were Russian enclaves in the city (Gentile Russian)—and, frankly, I knew of none—they would certainly represent the "White Russian" outlook, the pre-Soviet Tsarist days, and with that my parents would feel nothing in common.

As for myself, not speaking Russian, I couldn't even penetrate Russian literature in the original. I tried reading some of the Russian novels in translation, but the culture shock was too great for me and I never managed to finish any. Even *War and Peace* palled on me, although I tried on three separate occasions to read it.

2

The other item on the page mentions my playing chess with my brother and sister.

I had known how to play checkers from childhood, for my father had been a big checker player in Russia and had taught me the game— but according to the Russian rules. The American rules were different, and when I learned the latter and tried to teach it to him, he refused to have anything to do with the new version. He probably felt that the checker game rules *he* knew had been delivered on Mount Sinai to Moses straight out of the mouth of God, and that people who played the American game were heretics.

Chess, however, was a mystery, and when I watched people playing the game at Columbia and asked them to explain it to me, they said it would take too long. So I did as I had often done before. I took a book out of the library and learned the rules of the game as best I could. I then cut up a piece of cardboard into squares, marked each one with the conventional symbol of the various pieces, used them as chessmen, and taught my sister how to play.

Eventually I persuaded my father to invest in a set of real chessmen, and the game proceeded more smoothly. Marcia and I played quite a bit, and Stanley, who watched us, finally asked for a game, too. He had learned the moves just by watching and I found I had considerable difficulty beating him.

Indeed, he went on to become a much better chess player than I ever was. He was still a mere wood-pusher in comparison to real players, but he was good enough to join chess clubs and have fun.

As for me, I abandoned chess early on. I quickly made the humiliating discovery that just about anyone could beat me—old ladies, little kids, trained chimpanzees, anybody. Why, I don't know. It may be that I lacked patience; that I was too accustomed to seeing things at once. If I looked at a chessboard and didn't see the good move at once, I would make *any* move and get beaten.

It's really depressing to think of the vast number of things I'm not very good at.

3

By the time I was eighteen, I was old enough to stay up with father till he closed the store, if I wished to.

By midnight the work was done. Few people arrived after that and my father did not welcome them when they did. Generally, he would lock the store and shake his head if anyone arrived, indicating the store to be officially closed. Only if a particularly important customer arrived would he open on an emergency basis.

It took him an hour to get everything set for the next morning. He would sweep the floor, wash all the dishes that needed washing, arrange a tray with cigarettes, matches, and other necessaries to take outside in the morning so that as his regulars passed on their way to the subway station entrance one block to the northwest, he could hand them papers and, if necessary, cigarettes.

He knew everyone's paper and cigarette brand and they always had the money ready. My father was very proud of the efficiency with which he had everything planned out and, ideally, he hoped to get rid of everything on the tray, with nothing left and no additions for which he would have to scramble inside the store. He never allowed me to close the store by myself because he knew that I would not adjust the tray properly—to say nothing of knowing that I wouldn't sweep and wash with the proper devotion.[2]

What he spent most of his time on, though, was the matter of balancing the daily books. It wasn't for the sake of income tax; it was for the love of adding figures in columns and making comparisons of day to day and week to week and month to month. It meant he was forever saying dolefully, "Last week was the worst week in two months" or "This is the worst June 14 we ever had." For some reason he never reported "best" statistics.

Of course, everything had to balance. Income had to equal outgo plus profit, which meant carefully recording how much had been rung up on the register (there were meters inside you could read) and how much had been paid out in bills. Subtracting the second from the first told you exactly how much cash there ought to be in the cash register and in other places in the store. Since no one ever touched the cash register but my father, my mother, and myself, there was no question of theft. Any discrepancy could only be a matter of forgetting to take some bill into account, or of making a mistake in addition.

Time after time, my father would linger over the register and I would say, "What's the matter, Pappa?" and he would mutter, "I'm out a dollar."

It didn't matter whether he was a dollar over or a dollar under (or any other sum), he would stay there till he had straightened it out. My own remarks to the effect that surely it didn't matter were greeted with scorn.

In later years, after money had begun to come more easily, I would visit the old folks and, staying one night with my father, I found him looking for that missing dollar again. I said, "Pappa, forget it. Here's five dollars."

To which his comment was, "Don't be a wise guy. If you gave me

---

[2] Once—in 1937, I believe—there had come one of those rare times when my father was really down with the flu and he simply could not get out of bed for nearly a week. My mother and I struggled with the store alone. But just as my father took to bed, the news of a particularly juicy multiple sex-murder broke and people flocked to the store for the newspapers. Even those customers who couldn't read could look at the pictures of the murdered model, since the *Daily News* and the *Daily Mirror* found it necessary to print every undraped photograph of her they could find in order to keep their readers (or lookers) informed. (Those were the days before the modern girlie magazine had sated everyone with intimate anatomy.) Those people who flocked to the store bought other things as well, and when my father finally staggered to the store, he looked at the income the register told him we had made and his eyes bulged. "What happened?" he said. Whereupon I said, cheerfully, "It's always like this when you're not in the store, Pappa." But my mother told him the truth.

a million dollars, that dollar would still have to be found. The books must balance."

He never told me why, though. It taught me a lesson. In later life, when I had occasion to balance accounts, I never bothered about trifling discrepancies. I just made arbitrary corrections and let it go. My father did enough searching for both of us in his lifetime.

When I stayed with him, he would often regale me with reminiscences of his days in Russia, usually adding improving tales designed to make a better person of me. He filled me with aphorisms such as:

"*If*, Isaac, you should have a chance to take ten thousand dollars that is not yours, you should not take it. Why? Because someone might find out and you would be punished? No! Even if you should be sure that no one would ever find out, you should *still* not take it."

I would think it over to try to catch his reasoning and I would say, "Because God would know! Right?"

And my father would brush that aside. "Never mind God. *You* would know. You would know that you had done wrong, and you mustn't do it."

Then at some later time, he told me of how his father had once purchased bushels of grain from a certain peasant. To keep track of the number of bushels, my grandfather had thrown a shiny new ten-kopeck piece into a dish, one for each bushel.

"Can you imagine," said my father, "a peasant who could resist stealing ten-kopeck pieces? Naturally, he took some and there was a short count so that my father profited greatly since the bushel of grain was worth far more than ten kopecks." And he laughed heartily at the memory.

I frowned and said, "That was dishonest, Pappa."

"Why?" he said. "Who told the peasant to steal?"

"Your father knew he would and he let him do it."

My father fell silent. The peasant was the natural enemy of the Jewish merchant. Once drunk, the peasant would beat up and plunder any Jew he encountered and feel justified and pious for doing so. Yet the force of my remark was plain.

This was one of the few stories my father never repeated to me after a first telling.

4

Each successive store had seen me tied down more than before, and the Windsor Place store saw the last freedoms go. It was my fault, really. It seems that the *Daily News* put out a very early "pink" edition (so called because the front page was that color), one that was so early it came out the evening before its actual date. That had always been so, but we ignored it, largely because that edition wasn't delivered directly but had to be collected at some key stopping points.

In Windsor Place, however, the clientele was much more keen on the news of the day than had been true in the earlier stores. Furthermore, these were exciting times. In 1936, civil war had started in Spain; in 1937, Japan had mounted a renewed invasion of China.

I myself was following the news with agonized absorption, becoming ever more fearful of Hitler's might; ever more contemptuous of the Western powers for failing to take a stronger stand against Germany and Japan. The point was that I wanted to be able to read the pink *News* every night, in order to keep up with events.

I therefore suggested we get it, using as my justification the fact that customers occasionally wanted it. The papers would have to be picked up at "the circle"—that is, the traffic circle at the corner of the park where Prospect Park West and Prospect Park Southwest met.

That was only four blocks away, and three of those were immune to weather vicissitudes because one could walk through the nearby subway station, one end of which was within a block of the store and the other end of which was at the circle itself. I volunteered to go there every evening at 8:00 P.M. and pick up the necessary twenty-five papers and bring them back.

It turned out not to be worth it. In my eagerness to get the news I committed myself to being nailed down each evening. I *had* to be there, and I *had* to be there before the truck came. It killed my evenings.

5

On the lighter side, we had a cat in the early years at Windsor Place. We often had cats, both before and after this one, but this one was the best cat we ever had and the one most nearly a member of the family. Like all the cats my family had, its name was "The Cat."

It was a female cat who was a nymphomanic and who had kittens at every opportunity. She once left us for three days in search of who knows what nameless orgies and came back, very much the worse for wear, after we had given up and decided she had been kidnapped. (I secretly thought she had been taken by some college student for a zoology class, but I didn't tell my parents that. It would have distressed them.)

While she was at the store, however, she was a model of decorum, at least as far as her attitude toward the rest of us were concerned. She treated us with amused contempt and was willing to accept food from us, but allowed no other familiarities, and treated the newsstand as her own. She would always stretch out on top of the pile of *Times*es and blink lazily in the sun. She did not budge at the approach of customers, whom she preferred to ignore in godlike indifference. Nor did my father ever disturb her. He would flick out a *Times* from underneath the top one and the cat would settle sharply downward by the thickness of one newspaper without any sign of concern. We always kept the kittens until they were in danger of losing their kitten cuteness and then we would labor to place them with various customers.

At night in good weather, my father, if he felt expansive, would decide to walk the two blocks to the park and back and would say, "Come on, Cat."

The cat would follow. There was no leash, of course, and she always followed with circumspection, as though she were interested in her own affairs only and ended up at my father's heels by pure accident.

When they reached the park, the cat would vanish inside and my father would wait for about five minutes and then he would call out, "Come on, Cat," and the cat would reappear and walk him back. The cat stayed out all night, living her life of wickedness and shame, but she would always be waiting at the entrance of the store when my father came down in the morning to open it.

My clearest memory of that cat is of one warm and sunny morning when the cat was sitting on the newsstand and a tomcat walked jauntily down the street across the way. Our cat's yellow eyes saw him and followed him with distinct interest, and I could see the almost sensuous workings of her feline mind. So, with my customary stupidity reaching temporarily monumental heights, I moved in front of her and placed my face so that it was between her and the object of her carefree lust.

The cat looked at me wearily and craned her neck so as to see around me. I moved my head to put it in the way again and the cat, moving far too quickly for me even to begin to duck, unlimbered her right front paw and handed me a slam on the left check that staggered me.

I left in a hurry with the knowledge that the cat was far more intelligent than I was. She might have unsheathed her claws and sliced my cheek into four pieces, but she did not. The blow was hard, but velvet-smooth. She just gave me what I deserved, but no more than that.

The cat's one fault was her undying hatred of dogs and her inability to take a live-and-let-live attitude toward them. Since many of our customers had dogs and since they brought their dogs with them, we were under the perpetual necessity of snatching up the cat and holding her tightly till the dog was gone, while we felt her muscles writhing angrily in our grasp as she made every effort to get loose and grind the dog into chopped meat. My father clung to the cat longer than he would have clung to me, I think, if I had threatened the welfare of his customers, but in the end she had to go.

On January 13, 1938, she attacked not a dog but the dog's owner, and after that there was no choice. She was handed over to the SPCA while I was at school, and all of us, my father and I most of all, did not recover for a long time.

6

In my junior year at Columbia, my courses included qualitative analytic chemistry, quantitative analytic chemistry, intermediate physics, calculus, English literature, medieval history, and possibly a few other things.[3]

By all odds, English literature was the most unusual of the courses, for we had as our teacher Professor Lyon.

Of all the teachers I've ever had, Lyon seemed at first glance the most mannered and affected. He spoke with extreme preciosity, he dressed like a dandy, he held himself carefully, his gestures looked as though they had been rehearsed before the mirror. He was sixtyish when I first encountered him, but he had clearly been theatrically handsome when young, and he acted as though he still were.

He lectured in the grand manner, walking slowly up and back, striking poses, using no notes but affecting a theatrical delivery that made it seem he was satirizing a Shakespearean actor, but he wasn't. I got to know him fairly well and I never caught him in any other pose. If he were phony on the surface, he was at least phony all the way through—and it wasn't phony, it merely seemed so. In reality, he was a gentle, kind-hearted fellow who always tried to help me.

But never mind that. When he lectured, he allowed no interruptions. In grade school and in high school, of course, there were no lectures as such. Even in most college classes, though the professor lectured, we did not hesitate to interrupt and ask questions, nor did the professor hesitate to turn the lecture into a dialog. There was always the feeling of give and take—but not in Lyon's class.

[3] Sidney Cohen refused to take calculus with me, proposing sociology instead. I scorned that emphatically, so for three hours a week we separated, I to differentiate and integrate and he to do whatever is done in sociology.

That was one long monolog and nothing more. Fortunately, it was always an interesting monolog, which he would lace with reminiscences concerning theatrical performances he had seen.

I myself greeted those reminiscences with delight for, except in the Yiddish theater, I had never seen any performances on the stage. I had never seen either Shakespeare nor Gilbert and Sullivan (my two great dramatic enthusiasms) done professionally up to that time.

For that matter, I had never even seen burlesque (it was a secret wish of mine to see that, too), and now it seemed I never would, for Mayor Fiorello LaGuardia of New York, in a fit of self-righteous Puritanism, had banned burlesque some short while before.

But I could always listen to Lyon, who on one day went into polychromatic raptures over a play he had once seen. With graceful gestures of his hand, he described the scenery, the heroine in her diaphanous costume, the glittering bespangled gorgeousness of the sofa on which she reclined in luxurious abandon, and so on.

"Gentlemen," he said, "I am sorry for you, but never in your life will you see such a vision of beauty, such a glory of grace, such a . . ."

And from my place somewhere in the front row, I said, casually, "Not as long as LaGuardia keeps those places closed."

Well! One didn't interrupt Lyon to begin with, and one certainly didn't interrupt him in order to imply he was describing a sleazy burlesque show to us. So the class went into hysterics.

I wasn't counting on that. I had expected a snicker, and then a ten-minute-long series of cutting comments from Lyon. I was prepared for that. I got such comments from my mother for matters that brought me far less satisfaction. Some things are worth a reasonable amount of hot water.

But hysterics? Literally hysterics? Every time Lyon held up his hands to quell the monsters, they broke out again and he had to give up. He was literally unable to finish his lecture and had to dismiss the class.

I sat there stricken for quite a while after Lyon and the rest of the class left (except Cohen, who sat there shaking his head at me). Surely there could be no possible consequence for this but permanent ejection from the class and, possibly, just possibly, expulsion from college. After all, Lyon was a valued professor speaking to a Columbia College class and I was a university undergraduate interloper.

I finally dragged through my remaining courses of the day and carried on, somehow, waiting for the ax to fall and wondering how I would explain to my father. ("Again with the jokes, Isaac?")

Nothing of the sort happened. When the next class opened, he smiled at me and nodded in his lofty way. I can make no pretense at analyzing the psychology of it. I don't know if he admired my courage, or the successful "theater" of my remark, but I was a favorite of his from that moment and got an A in the course.

7

Marcia finished high school on February 4, 1938. Like myself, she got out at the age of fifteen. She did not go to college. It was not as customary then as it is now for girls to go to college, and education for women was not something that fit in with my parents' background.

Marcia went to business school instead and before she was sixteen had her first job. She went on to become a crackerjack secretary.

8

I tend to think of Brooklyn in the 1920s and 1930s as idyllic and crimefree, but that, of course, is only in comparison with the situation now. It was not crime zero.

On February 16, 1938, when my father woke and looked casually out the window to see what the weather was like, he noticed that the night light in the store was out. It might have burned out, of course, but he was dressed and downstairs in a hurry to see. The rest of the family, awakened by my father's unusual excitement, remained at the windows. I saw him get to the door and walk in immediately, instead of fiddling with the lock for a time—and that was the giveaway.

"Break-in," I said.

And it was. Three hundred dollars of cigars, cigarettes, and tobacco were gone, along with the radio, the electric clock, and sixty dollars in cash. Say four hundred dollars altogether, counting the damage to the door.

Quite a bit for a family for which every five-dollar expenditure required a council meeting.

The merchandise was replaced before the day was out, and the door was fixed and reinforced, too. By the end of the week we had a new radio and clock, and a burglar alarm was installed. After that, the whole process of closing and opening the store had one additional delight. My father would set the alarm, close the door, then open it to see if it was working. R-ring-g-g would go the alarm at 1:00 A.M.

In the morning he would open the door and rush to insert the key

and turn off the alarm, and in the interim, r-ring-g-g it would go at 6:00
A.M. No one ever complained as far as I know, but since I have always
been a light sleeper anyway, I never missed them.

It was the first ripoff we had ever suffered, and my father didn't
stop talking about it for months. No matter how well things went in
the store[4] and how favorable the balance was, he would say, "If we still
had that four hundred dollars . . ."

One of our customers walked in as the burglar alarm was being installed and said, "Aren't you locking the barn door after the horse has
been stolen?" (The purpose of aphorisms is to keep fools who have
memorized them from having nothing to say.)

"We've bought another horse," I said, taking the chance that my
father would scold me for talking back to a customer.

Aunt Pauline and Cousin Martin were over that afternoon to commiserate. There was still a tenuous connection between the two
branches of the family. Indeed, Cousin Martin dropped in periodically
over the next few years, but my best memory of him is of that afternoon. We sat in the living room and talked Shakespeare—*Hamlet*,
specifically. As I recall, I was made very uneasy by the fact that he
seemed more familiar with the play than I was.

[4] They went pretty well at that. At least there was no need for me to get a summer
job in 1937 or in 1938. My NYA job was enough and the store could handle the
rest of the tuition and miscellaneous expenses in my junior and senior years.

17

Astounding Science Fiction

1

In the spring of 1938, *Astounding Stories* gained a new editor: F. Orlin Tremaine was out, and in his place was John Wood Campbell, Jr., who was then not quite twenty-eight, and who, through the early and mid-1930s, had made a name for himself as one of the greatest science-fiction writers of the period. Certainly he was one of my favorites.

Campbell instantly began to remold the magazine closer to his (and, inadvertently, my) heart's desire. For one thing, he changed the title to *Astounding Science Fiction*, which, to me, was a promising sign of further improvement.

The excitement of the change persuaded me to begin writing letters again. After all, I was carefully reviewing, recording, and tabulating the stories in every science-fiction magazine that came out, and it seemed silly not to let the magazines themselves, or *Astounding* at least, reap the benefit of my thoughts—and, through them, the world at large.

I wrote a letter to *Astounding*, therefore, commenting on the stories, rating them, and, in general, taking on the airs of a critic.

What's more, the editor printed the letter in the letter department of the December 1937 issue, and I had the extreme pleasure of seeing my name and address (as well as my immortal words) appearing in semimicroscopic print at the back of the magazine.

After that, I wrote other letters and, indeed, began to write them monthly.

One of the reasons for that, as it happened, was that the mechanics of the process had been simplified for me since by now I was a fast and proficient typist.

Part of the credit belongs to my NYA work, which during my junior and senior years was for J. Bernhard Stern, a sociology professor, who used me as a kind of miscellaneous typist, working up passages from books, collecting statistics, and so on, all for a scholarly volume on which he was working.

When my sister became a proficient typist through her studies at the business school, I had her test my speed, and it turned out I was typing at the rate of fifty words a minute. (Of course, I refused to deduct for errors, since I was not a professional secretary and my work did not have to be letter perfect.)

2

For years *Astounding* had been published regularly on the third Wednesday of each month—at least officially. Magazine deliveries took place on Tuesdays and Thursdays, so that *Astounding* actually appeared at my father's store the day before the third Wednesday. Each month, on the day it came, I was there waiting for the bundle so that I could cut the bundle and extract the magazine at once.

This was always to my father's great annoyance, since he had a definite procedure for handling the magazines, as he did for everything. He would cut the bundle, take all the magazines apart in neat little stacks, count them to make sure he had the right number of each, place each little stack in the right place in the newsstand, removing, as he did so, any previous issues of that sort left over. He put the previous issues in another place to stack up and return to the distributor. All this was simple, but it took time, and my father preferred to cut the bundle when things were slow in the store and not, as I invariably did, the instant they arrived. (He always liked it better when I had to be in school at the time the *Astoundings* arrived, and he always saved me my copy.)

On Tuesday, May 10, 1938, the day I expected *Astounding* under the new second-Wednesday-of-the-month dispensation my father was particularly annoyed because, having cut the bundle, I didn't find any copies of my magazine. It had been cut for nothing, he complained.

If he was annoyed, I was terrified. On May 11, my diary begins, "Another day has gone by, and no *Astounding*. I never realized before how much these science-fiction magazines mean to me."

My terror, of course, was that *Astounding* might have ceased publication. On May 12, in desperation, I invested a nickel for a phone call to Street & Smith, Inc., the publishers of *Astounding*. I was solemnly assured by whoever it was at the other end that the magazine had *not* ceased publication. I decided it would probably arrive the next Tuesday, having returned to the older schedule.

There was nothing to do but wait for Tuesday, which I did in a rather distraught way. It sounds silly to have taken on so about a magazine, but each person has his own standards of what, exactly, counts for much or little in his life. I would stand there behind the cash register, handing out packs of cigarettes, and making change, and I would find myself staring at the magazine rack at the other end of the store and deciding that as long as *Astounding* wasn't there in its accustomed place, life was not worth living.

And on Tuesday May 17, *Astounding* didn't come.

3

I had spent days planning my course of procedure in this case. I picked up tips now and then, when delivering an order or calling someone to the phone, and I had been saving them of late, feeling that they were *my* money. I had enough to make the subway trip to Street & Smith, Inc., and to buy a copy of *Astounding* there if I wished.

Choosing my mother as the softer touch in this case, I argued her into giving me permission to take off two hours that otherwise I would have to spend in the store—choosing two hours during my father's afternoon nap, so that I would not have to ask his permission as well. (Fortunately, it was finals week, and I had no classes to attend, merely exams to take.)

Then off I went. I might have been over eighteen by now, but a sheltered life is a sheltered life. It was one of the first times I had ever taken a subway ride into Manhattan on my own, except to go to school. I was going to wander about streets I did not know in order to make my way into strange buildings and ask questions of strange people. It made me uneasy.

I got there. It was not a really difficult task. The Street & Smith offices were at 79 Seventh Avenue, not far away from a subway station I passed through every day going to and from school. I placed my case before the elevator man, who gave me directions, and on the fifth floor I met a Mr. Clifford, who explained to me that the publication date had been changed from the second Wednesday to the third Friday. When I craved certainty, he showed me a printed schedule, and there was *Astounding* listed under Friday, May 20. Assuming it would actually come Thursday, May 19, it meant I had two more days to wait.

On Thursday, May 19, the June issue of *Astounding* came, and although it was raining that day, the sun shone brilliantly for me. It was the day of my chemistry finals, but I bothered with no last-minute studying. Until the moment I had to leave for school, I read the magazine. (It's all right. I did well in the exam.)

4

The whole incident would be unimportant (even allowing for the nine days of anguish) were it not for consequences.

I had not entirely forgotten "Cosmic Corkscrew," which I had begun just a year before and which I had worked at in very desultory fashion for a few months. In the spring I had even taken the manuscript out of the drawer and thought about it, and, on occasion, had written a page or two, or had rewritten a passage.

Now, however, after the incident with *Astounding*, I was galvanized into activity. In the first place, the days during which I had imagined the magazine to be lost forever had revealed to me the extent to which science fiction had seized upon me. It made me realize something that until then had been only subliminal—that one of my ambitions in life was to be a science-fiction writer.

I did not want to be simply a writer, you understand. Nor was I interested in making money. Neither of these two items ever occurred to me. What I wanted was to write a *science-fiction* story and to have it appear in a *science-fiction* magazine. That would be to join the company of the demi gods whose names I knew and idolized: Jack Williamson, Nat Schachner, E. E. Smith, Edmond Hamilton, John W. Campbell, and all the rest.

In the second place, my visit to Street & Smith had somehow reduced the great gulf that separated myself and the demi gods. Street & Smith, and therefore *Astounding*, had become attainable. It existed in a real building in real space, a building I could reach and enter and it contained people who would speak to me.

In the third place, my junior year at college was completed and I would have more time on my hands.

With all these factors meeting, I took "Cosmic Corkscrew" out of the drawer again, read it over, and determined to complete it.

To do so, I had to overcome some obstacles. The January 1938 issue of *Astounding* contained a story called "Dead Knowledge" by Don A. Stuart that had a scene describing a mysteriously empty city, much like the mysteriously empty city I had begun writing about in my story half a year earlier. In addition, I had become aware that P. Schuyler Miller in his story "The Sands of Time," which appeared in the April 1937 *Astounding* just before I started "Cosmic Corkscrew," had involved a kind of helical structure of time.

I was in two minds whether to continue the story or to abandon it and try something else. I thought about it for a while and then decided that the overlaps were unimportant. The story as a whole was quite different from either "Dead Knowledge" or "The Sands of Time," and so I moved forward.

What's more, I continued to move forward even though the July issue of *Astounding* was again delayed. I did not go into a tailspin this time because an advertisement in *Doc Savage*, also published by Street & Smith, dealt with the July issue of *Astounding*, which it described as being "now on the stands," so I knew it would come eventually. In fact, I hastened my writing, so as to finish the story before I could possibly learn, for certain, that the magazine had died. In that case, I did not think I would be able to write at all.

5

I finished "Cosmic Corkscrew" on June 19, 1938. It was actually the first piece of fiction I had ever completed with a view to possible publication. The next question was what to do with it. I hadn't the faintest idea as to how one went about submitting a story to a magazine. Nowadays, there are many youngsters who don't know, and all of them (it sometimes seems to me) write to me for advice. I wasn't even smart enough at that time to write to anyone for advice.

I knew I might mail it, but even if I could figure out what I was supposed to say in the letter, there was a problem. As I said in my diary, "If I mail it, it will cost a mint of money as the damn thing weighs four ounces."

Mail was three cents an ounce in those days, so that the "mint of money" came to twelve cents.

We counted the pennies in those days. Just a few days earlier my father had refused to have a plumber fix a leaking gas pipe because the job would cost three dollars and he went shopping for a more reasonable plumber.

Again, through sharp bargaining, my father managed to get someone to agree to fix a fountain pen for thirty-four cents, this to include the cost of mailing it to us, thus saving ten cents in subway fare. It was only after he returned and he had explained that he managed this low price by leaving out a new clip for an additional twenty-five cents that he found out he had made a mistake. I told him, rather forcefully, that a fountain pen was useless without a clip, and he called up to have that added to the tab.

None of this, at the time, seemed to represent the cruelty of poverty to us. We were used to it. We were aware at all times of the exact amount of money we had in our pockets, right down to the penny, and every outgo, however small, was carefully considered.

It did not escape me that a round-trip subway fare would cost me ten cents, or two cents less than to mail the story. Furthermore, the subway fare would enable me to check once again on the lateness of *Astounding*.

On June 21, with the July issue still not at the store, I discussed the matter with my father.

I had till then kept the matter of my writing entirely to myself. I had viewed it as merely a hobby, a way of spending my time doing something interesting. It was for my own amusement only. I had told Emmanuel Bershadsky about *The Greenville Chums at College* seven years before, but I can't remember ever telling anyone else about anything I was writing. I certainly didn't tell my parents, and I don't think they were really aware that I was writing.

I had the instinctive feeling even then that I would not welcome criticism. Even when I came to my father with this purely tactical problem of how to submit a story, I did not offer to let him read it. Nor did he ask to read it; but if he had done so, I would have refused. (I haven't changed since those days. I still don't discuss my stories when they are in the process of being written, and I still don't welcome criticism.)

Of course, as to such collateral matters as *submitting* a story, I was willing, even eager, to seek advice, and my father's suggestion was that I not only make the trip by subway, but also that I hand the manuscript to Mr. Campbell himself.

The thought was a frightening one. It became even more frightening when my father further suggested that necessary preliminaries included a shave and my best suit. That meant I would have to take additional time, but the day was already wearing on, and I didn't have very much time. I had to be back for the afternoon newspaper delivery, just in case the delivery boy didn't show up.

I compromised. I shaved, but did not bother changing suits, and off I went.

I was convinced that for daring to ask to see the editor of *Astounding Science Fiction* I would be thrown out of the building bodily, and that my manuscript would be torn up and thrown out after me in a shower of confetti. My father, however, who had lofty notions, was convinced that a writer (by which he meant any one with a manuscript) would be treated with the respect due an intellectual. He had no fears in the matter, for had he himself not braved the Soviet bureaucracy? Maybe so, but it was I who had to brave Street & Smith.

I put off the crisis by stopping in to see Mr. Clifford again, and he explained that the new publication date was the fourth Friday every month.

There was now no excuse to delay any further. I went into the main building and asked to see the editor. The girl behind the desk spoke briefly into the phone and said, "Mr. Campbell will see you."

I was astonished. I had asked to see him only because my father had told me to, but I was convinced that this was just my father's lack of sophistication. I assumed I would be asked to leave the manuscript with the receptionist, and this I was prepared to do.

What I did not know was that Campbell's invitation was what would have happened in many cases of this sort. John Campbell was a most unusual fellow who loved to talk and who would seize almost anyone as an audience. Furthermore, and this may have been a crucial point, he knew me from my recent letters—my name was familiar to him—and that meant he certainly wouldn't turn me away.

What if I hadn't written those letters? What if I didn't live on the subway line? What if I lived—I wouldn't say in Nebraska—but in Westchester, Jersey City, Staten Island; anywhere that made Campbell reachable only by spending more than ten cents in fares?

In that case I would not have traveled to Street & Smith, but would have mailed the story. Or if I had gone there, without having written letters to the magazine, he might conceivably not have seen me after all. And without personal contact, everything might have been different.

But it wasn't different; it was the way it was. The receptionist directed me through a large, loftlike room filled with huge rolls of paper and enormous piles of magazines and permeated with the heavenly smell of pulp.

And there, in a small room on the other side, was Mr. Campbell.

18

John Campbell

1

John Campbell was not quite twenty-eight years old at the time I first met him. Under his own name, and under his pen name of Don A. Stuart, he was one of the most famous and highly regarded authors of science fiction, but he was about to bury his writing reputation forever under the far greater renown he was to gain as editor.

Campbell[1] was a large man, an opinionated man, who smoked and talked constantly, and who enjoyed, above anything else, the production of outrageous ideas, which he bounced off his listener and dared him to refute. And it was difficult to refute Campbell even when his ideas were absolutely and madly illogical.[2]

We talked for over an hour that first time, on June 21, 1938. He showed me forthcoming issues of the magazine (actual *future* issues in the paper flesh), and he, too, assured me the magazine would not die. I found there was a letter of mine in the July issue that was about to hit the stands and another in the August issue. He smiled when I pointed them out excitedly and said that he knew.

Campbell told me about himself, and about his pen name—which occasioned me a little embarrassment. It had been Campbell himself, under the Stuart pen name, who had written "Dead Knowledge," one of the two stories that overlapped "Cosmic Corkscrew," an overlapping I decided to ignore when I didn't know that Stuart and Campbell were the same person.

I was too shamefaced (or cowardly) to say anything about that, but if I had, it wouldn't have mattered. Campbell never quibbled about minor overlappings as long as the stories and major ideas were different and valuable.

---

[1] In later years, much later years, I would sometimes address him as "John," but always uneasily. I never got over my early awe of him, and he was always "Mr. Campbell" when I addressed him and "Campbell" when I wrote of him. In this autobiography, I will speak of people as I addressed them in life—first names only when I actually used first names, last names when I used last names.

[2] And illogical they certainly seemed to be to *me*, for he was always an idiosyncratic conservative in his view on life, whereas I was an idiosyncratic liberal—and we never agreed on anything. Yet although he stood somewhere to the right of Attila the Hun in politics, he was, in person, as kind, generous, and decent a human being as I have ever met.

Campbell, on that first day, told me that when he was seventeen, his father had sent in one of his manuscripts to *Amazing Stories* and that it would have been published had the magazine not lost the manuscript and had he himself not lacked a carbon copy. (I was behind him by a year in age, but at least I brought the story myself and, despite all my innocence of things literary, I had the good sense to make and keep a carbon.)

Campbell promised to read my story that night and to send a letter, whether acceptance or rejection, the next day. He promised also that in case of rejection he would tell me what was wrong with the story so that I could improve.

He lived up to both promises. Two days later, on June 23, the manuscript came back. It was a rejection.

As my diary put it: "At 9:30 I received back 'Cosmic Corkscrew' with a polite letter of rejection. He didn't like the slow beginning, the suicide at the end."

Campbell also didn't like the first-person narration and the stiff dialog. He pointed out that the length (nine thousand words) was inconvenient—too long for a short story, too short for a novelette. Magazines had to be put together like jigsaw puzzles, you see, and certain lengths for individual stories are more convenient than others.

2

By that time, though, I was off and running. The joy of having spent an hour and more with Campbell, the thrill of talking face to face with an idol, had already filled me with the ambition to write another science-fiction story, one that was better than the first, so that I could have occasion to meet him again.

In fact, by the time I returned to the store on the day of that visit, I had worked out another story in my mind, one I intended to call "Stowaway," and I waited only to hear from Campbell before starting it. His letter of rejection, when it arrived, was so cordial and helpful that it did not in the least dampen my spirits, either.

Rather the reverse, for I began "Stowaway" as soon as the rejection came, being careful to use the third person, begin quickly, and make it the proper length—six thousand words.

What happened to "Cosmic Corkscrew" after that I don't really know. I abandoned it and never submitted it anywhere else. I didn't actually tear it up and throw it away; it simply languished in some desk drawer until eventually I lost track of it. In any case, it no longer exists.

This seems to be a source of discomfort for many of my readers.

They seem to think that the *first* story I ever wrote for publication, however bad it might have been, was an important document. In fact, once I revealed that I had written eight chapters of *The Greenville Chums at College* when I was eleven, there seems to have been a certain impatience with me on the part of some of my fans for not having carefully preserved that too.

All I can say, Gentle Readers, is that I, too, am sorry. I, too, would be curious to see what those old productions looked like, and I have no doubt that I could get such things published as curiosities, but how could I tell it *then?* There was no way of my knowing in 1938, let alone 1931, that my first tries at scribbling might have historic interest some day.

In fact, there are a number of stories that I wrote in the late 1930s and early 1940s that I never sold, and every one of them no longer exists. I swear to you, though, that however sad this makes completists, they represent no literary loss whatever. In fact, I suspect that in order to have truly served humanity, it is not so much that I should have saved those stories I lost, but that I should have lost some of the stories I saved and published.

3

On June 23, 1938 the July 1938 *Astounding* finally arrived, and I found it an anticlimax. I have this to say in my diary: "Somehow this business of contributing seems to have spoiled some of my joy in *Astounding*. When I read *Astounding* now, I'm consumed with jealousy. I think that even if one of my stories is ever accepted that I won't return to my old enjoyment. . . . However, maybe I'm unduly pessimistic."

I wasn't. The loss was permanent. The bliss that the science-fiction magazine brought me, which had increased to an almost unbearable height after I had started keeping, saving, and cataloguing the magazines in 1937,[3] slowly faded, and never returned to that peak again.

I had eaten of the fruit of the tree of knowledge when I went to visit Campbell, and I had been ejected from Eden.

Yet I can't very well complain. I might, with far greater justice, say that I had emerged from a chrysalis into a far better form and world, for if I left one Eden, I entered another, that of writing. And this Eden, in one shape or another, I have never left, nor has it ever palled on me.

---

[3] The absolute height came with the September 1937 *Astounding*, in which the first installment of E. E. Smith's "Galactic Patrol" appeared.

A strange change came over my diary, too. Until the day I visited Campbell I filled every page (with very few exceptions) from top to bottom and left to right—leaving no margins—with microscopic writing. After that day, I rarely finished a page and I totally omitted the detailed baseball analyses, which I suddenly outgrew and to which I never returned. I wrote more briefly and succinctly, because I wanted to spend more time on writing "Stowaway" and the stories that followed.

Almost at once, you see, I gathered that ideally all the writing I did should be for publication; that anything I *had* to write for personal reasons, whether diary or mail, would have to be brief. I have followed that principle ever since.

4

My letters to *Astounding* were bringing me into the wider world of science fiction in ways other than the fact that they probably got me an interview with Campbell. On June 27, 1938, for instance, I received a letter from R. R. Winterbotham, a minor science-fiction writer who lived in Salina, Kansas. He noted that I carefully rated all stories and asked if I might send him my rating for his.

That was an embarrassing request, for I had eight of his stories in my files and I didn't like any of them very much. It rather spoiled the fun of publicly denouncing stories when I stopped to think that the writers were living people who would read the denunciation and be hurt. It also occurred to me that the time might come when readers might publicly say hurtful things about my stories, if I ever managed to get any published. Quite suddenly, and even before I was actually published, I found myself viewing critics from the standpoint of the professional writer, and I decided that I didn't like them. I have never changed my mind concerning them since.

I answered Winterbotham as politely and as kindly as I could, and this started a correspondence between us that lasted several years.[4]

The letter from Winterbotham served to put me to work on "Stowaway" with added ardor. It had taken me only five days to complete a first draft of the story, but I prepared a final copy in greater lei-

[4] In the years since those old times I have received letters from young fans eager to begin correspondences. I have never been able to do so, out of sheer lack of time. One or two—*only* one or two, I am glad to say—have taken umbrage and have asked me sarcastically how I would have felt if my letters to the established authors of my day had been so callously rejected. All I can say is that I don't know how I would feel, since I never intruded upon them. In some cases, they (the authors) wrote to me and themselves started the correspondence, but I never suggested such a thing to them, let alone demanded it.

sure and wasn't done till July 10. It dealt with an expedition to Callisto that encountered animals that killed by means of an intense magnetic field, animals that could be approached only by someone wearing a non-ferrous spacesuit.

Where "Cosmic Corkscrew" had taken me thirteen months to complete, "Stowaway" had taken me only eighteen days. I found my speed—double quick. I wrote, you see, in the tradition of the pulps. Since the word rate was extremely low (one cent a word was tops in science fiction at the time) and a short story netted you only sixty-five dollars at most, and only half that usually, it was impossible to spend much time on any one story and still make even the most meager of livings.

I wasn't planning to make a living at writing, of course, but I knew nothing else but the pulp tradition. A letter from Winterbotham on July 15, for instance, in response to my questions, assured me that he had received rejections, too (he enclosed two of them as samples) and said that he had written *forty-three* stories before he had gotten one accepted. He advised me not to spend too much time revising a story.

I felt that to be good advice. From that day to this, almost everything I write goes through the typewriter just twice—first draft and final copy. If after two typings the result proves unsatisfactory, it has always seemed to me it is better abandoned. There is less trouble and trauma involved in writing a new piece than in trying to salvage an unsatisfactory old one—in my own case, at any rate. In the very few cases that I tried salvaging, it never did either myself or the story any good.

5

On Monday, July 18, 1938, I traveled to Campbell's office a second time. Now I had "Stowaway." Once again I stayed with him for over an hour, and this time he actually gave me a copy of the August issue of *Astounding*, which I thus had, without charge, three days before I would have had it on the newsstand. I asked him, rather diffidently, if he minded my bringing in my stories personally, and he said it would be perfectly all right "provided you don't come on make-up day."

Naturally, I asked when make-up day was, but he wouldn't tell me. Perhaps he wanted to leave matters open to refuse me for any reason by pretending it was make-up day.

I was quite certain that "Stowaway" would be rejected, but by the time I got home I had my next story all plotted in mind. It was to be "Marooned off Vesta" and, I said in my diary, "I will try to inject a bit of humor in this one and lay off the heavy drama."

That, incidentally, was the marvel of Campbell. It didn't matter that he rejected you. There was an enthusiasm about him and an all-encompassing friendliness that was contagious. I always left him eager to write further.

I have written of Campbell in other books and therefore I have received numerous letters from youngsters in their teens who ask me to remember what Campbell did for me and asking me, therefore, to do the same for them. It is a reasonable request for, having benefited from Campbell's bounty, it is only fair and just that I pay it back—not to him, since I cannot, but to other youngsters coming after me in my footsteps.

The trouble is I cannot do that either. I am not Campbell. In some ways, I have passed beyond him, but in the essential characteristics that made him my literary father, I am but a pygmy to him. I don't have his ability to bestow enthusiasm and self-confidence; I don't have his endless fertility of mind. Most of all, I don't have his capacity to help others along miles of successful pathways while remaining behind himself.

In other words, he was the quintessential editor, who fertilized and nourished a whole generation of writers, and I am only a writer, completely wrapped up in myself. Campbell could point out what was wrong with a story and describe precisely what ought to be done to correct it. I can't even do that for my own stories, which, if they are wrong, must remain wrong forever if the correction is to come out of my mind alone. How much less, then, can I talk intelligently about someone else's stories.

In the case of "Stowaway," Campbell was slower than he had been before. When Wednesday's mail did not bring rejection, I was upset. I was afraid Campbell had decided it wasn't worth reading; or, having read it, that it wasn't worth returning.

On July 22, however, back it came after four days. I said in my diary concerning the letter that accompanied it:

". . . it was the nicest possible rejection you could imagine. Indeed, the next best thing to an acceptance. He told me the idea was good and the plot passable. The dialog and handling, he continued, were neither stiff or wooden (this was rather a delightful surprise to me) and that there was no one particular fault but merely a general air of amateurishness, constraint, forcing. The story did not go smoothly. This, he said, I would grow out of as soon as I had had sufficient experience. He assured me that I would probably be able to sell my stories but it meant perhaps a year's work and a dozen stories before I could click. . . ."

It is no wonder that such a "rejection" letter kept me hotly charged with enormous enthusiasm to write. It merely sped me further on my way with "Marooned off Vesta," which dealt with three men on a wrecked spaceship and the manner in which an improvised rocket-drive was set up to bring them to the nearest asteroid.

Many years later I asked Campbell (with whom I had, by then, grown to be on the closest of terms) why he had bothered with me at all, since the first story was surely utterly impossible.

"Yes, it was impossible," he said frankly, for he never flattered. "On the other hand, I saw something in *you*. You were eager and listened and I knew you wouldn't quit no matter how many rejections I handed you. As long as you were willing to work hard at improving, I was willing to work with you."

That was Campbell. I wasn't the only writer, whether newcomer or old-timer, he was to work with in this fashion. Patiently, and out of his own enormous vitality and talent, he built up a stable of the best science-fiction writers the world had, till then, ever seen.

Even today, it is almost inevitable that anyone, listing those science-fiction writers who are the most respected in the field will mention (in alphabetical order, so that we can avoid invidious distinctions and yet keep me first) Isaac Asimov, Arthur C. Clarke, and Robert Heinlein. All three of us (still alive, still active) were Campbell discoveries. Others, either discovered by him or developed by him after their discovery, include Poul Anderson, Hal Clement, L. Sprague de Camp, Lester del Rey, L. Ron Hubbard, Theodore Sturgeon, A. E. van Vogt, and many others. The one great writer who made it in the early 1940s and was *not* a Campbell discovery was Ray Bradbury.

Nor would Campbell ever accept credit; at least, not from me. There were times, years later, when I would try to express my gratitude to him and to tell him that but for him I would never have become what I was.

And he would shake his head violently and say, "You're all wrong, Asimov. I helped hundreds of writers exactly as I helped you. Why aren't they all Isaac Asimovs?"

But it was he who was wrong. I'm sure he helped hundreds of writers but not quite in the way he helped me. I can't help but think I was "teacher's pet." Perhaps it was because I came in each time I had a story. Perhaps because I listened closely and tried so hard to follow his suggestions. I don't know. Once he praised me for always putting in my own interpretations into the story.

He said, "If I give a story idea to a writer and get it back exactly as I told it to him, I don't waste any more story ideas on him. I want it to grow and develop inside him. I want more back than I give. I'm selfish that way."

If I gave back more than I received from him, that was just my incapacity at following suggestions. I did my best to make it *exactly* what he wanted, imagining that was the way I'd sell him. If I had been a cleverer writer, then, more adept at controlling what I wrote, I might not have made it—at least not with Campbell.

6

For "Stowaway," unlike the case of "Cosmic Corkscrew," rejection did not mean oblivion. On August 3, 1938, I worked up the nerve to visit the offices of *Thrilling Wonder Stories.*[5] These were located at 22 East 48th Street in Manhattan and was the only other science-fiction magazine I could reach. (The editorial offices of *Amazing Stories* were then located in Chicago.)

I left "Stowaway" with the receptionist, therefore, along with a stamped, self-addressed envelope. That was what I had expected to have had to do in Campbell's case that first time, but he had spoiled me now. I left the offices of *Thrilling Wonder* rather peeved with the editor.

From mid-July 1938 onward, by the way, I began to live for the mail (something I still do), since from that time on I almost always had *something* out, *something* that would bring me back either a rejected manuscript or a check.

Mornings, therefore, if I weren't at school, I would sit outside the store and wait for the mailman. (My return address was always the store, never the house we happened to live in.)

Once the mailman reached and delivered mail at the house across the street, just before the point at which he crossed to deliver the mail for 174 Windsor Place, he always took out our mail and held it in his hand. A large manila envelope meant a rejection, of course. The lack of such an envelope meant, conceivably, a letter of acceptance or a check —or nothing at all.

Eventually, the mailman caught on to what I was waiting for and would call out as he crossed the street, "Nothing today, Isaac," or "Bad news, I think, Isaac."

It spoiled my fun, rather, and I longed to be able to tell him to say nothing and let me find out for myself, but I was always afraid of irritating a mailman in any way. I didn't want him refusing to deliver my mail.

[5] The old *Wonder Stories* had changed owners and title with the August 1936 issue.

"Stowaway" bounced back from *Thrilling Wonder* on August 9, and in due course from *Amazing* as well, and I retired it for the nonce.

The stowaway of the title, by the way, was named Stanley. I suppose it was only natural that I use my brother's name. He turned nine years old on July 25, just a week after I submitted the story for the first time, and was now almost as old as I was when he had been born.

There were no girls in "Stowaway," any more than there had been in "Cosmic Corkscrew" or than there were in the new story "Marooned off Vesta" that I was writing. But then, women were very much an unknown quantity for me. I had made eyes at Mazie in Decatur Street, but that had been a very minor thing, and since we had come to Windsor Place there wasn't even that.

Boys High and Columbia were entirely masculine so that I didn't even encounter women my own age at school. In 1938, when I was writing my first stories, I had yet to have a formal date with a girl. In short, the circumstances of my life were such that it never occurred to me to put a feminine character in my stories.

When I first explained this in *The Early Asimov*, it elicited irate letters from a few of the more advanced feminists among my women readers who would not accept my youthful ignorance as an excuse for ignoring women in my stories.

And I ignored them not only in my earliest stories but to some extent even later on. I eventually had dates, and I eventually learned about women, but the early imprinting had its effect. To this very day, the romantic element in my stories tends to be minor and the sexual element virtually nil.

7

On July 30, 1938, only eight days after Campbell's second rejection, I had finished my third story, "Marooned off Vesta." I had no intention, however, of taking that down to Campbell at once. For one thing, I did not want to bother him too much, and once a month, I felt, was all I could inflict on him without wearing him out. Second, I was not sure it was a wise thing to let him know how quickly I had written the story. Perhaps he would feel I ought to have taken more pains.

I decided, therefore, to wait several weeks—but without any intention of wasting my time. I could always write additional stories.

Except that I couldn't. My old second-hand Underwood No. 5, which had given me good service for three years, was breaking down, and on August 2 it was clear that it would have to be repaired.

My father's passport picture, 1922, I think, at the age of twenty-five.

My mother's passport picture, 1922, at the age of twenty-six.

Me in 1934, I think, at the age of fourteen, standing outside the candy store on
Decatur Street.

My father in 1915, at the age of eighteen,
with a full head of hair. Unbelievable.

Stanley, at the age of three (1932), outside the Essex Street store. Behind him is the icebox in which my father pounded ice and salt to keep the ice cream cold.

My high school graduation photo—fifteen years old—1935.

June 16, 1940. Cyril Kornbluth at left, I at right.

September 13, 1940, me and my mustache, at the age of twenty, superimposed on a page of Marcia's diary.

Thursday, November 1, 1945   D day 12/24

305th Day—60 days to follow

CLEAR
CLOUDY
RAIN
SNOW

6 A.M. — My last few minutes as a civilian are whiskering away. God knows where I'm heading now. I feel sick.

1 P.M. Still a civilian but have very little to go. I passed my physical. Defective vision, otitis (inflamed ears or semi-circular canals or what have you) & "nutritional tremor" according to the psychiatrist. Waiting x-ray, fingerprinting, placement interview etc! My mind is easy. I'm planning it and to have little trouble. A guy's going in from NYU, 25½, married, New Yorker, looks like Marty Goldstein, & a P.Y. (went to NYU — names Bill (Faber). I'm writing cards to mamma & Gertie which I will mail at the first opportunity. I haven't seen _____.

3:20 P.M. This is the last half hour as the induction ceremony is to take place at 3:50. My number will be, I think, 45012053. Don't see this guy Faber around. Maybe he's been rejected. I imagine interviews etc will take place after induction.

4:45 P.M. I am now in the army. I've been sworn in and am sitting now in the B.Y.O. waiting to be taken to Fort Meade (near Baltimore). We will be there "about five days."

Two pages from my diary:
Thursday, November 1, 1945,
the day I entered the Army;
and Thursday, May 20, 1948,
the day I became Isaac Asimov, Ph.D.

---

35 2/4

Thursday, May 20, 1948

141st Day—225 days to follow

CLEAR
CLOUDY
RAIN
SNOW

9 A.M. — Here goes nothing!!

10 P.M. — Here comes something & writes Isaac Asimov, Ph.D. In fact, I had a swell time — gave my little turn, answered all questions thrown at me, was very nicely and fairly treated, formality was at a minimum. After an hour and twenty minutes, I was led out — five minutes after I was called in and passed with honors and enthusiasm.

Tupley & Jordan were waiting for me. After I called up Gertie & the folks, they & Jordan took me out and got me dead drunk on five manhattans. It took Tup & Joe 3 hours & 4 cups of black coffee to sober me up. It's the second time I was ever really drunk, the first time being my last weekend in the Army.

I've got 4 tickets to commencement and on June 1, I will be a Ph.D. officially.

Oh, yes, I had supper with Boselow & his girl Eileen; nobody let me pay anything, for the drinks or for the meal.

At home, everyone feels great.

I got a letter from Sturgeon asking us to come over again. Also a letter from de Camp.

My parents and I
in Prospect Park in 1941.
I am twenty-one, my father is forty-four,
my mother forty-five.

Ordinarily, my father would have seen to it that it was repaired, but he reasoned that the repair would be expensive, that the machine would break down again for an additional expensive repair and that it might, therefore, represent long-term economy to invest in a new machine. Second, the mere fact that I had written and submitted two stories had made me, in my father's eyes, a literary man, and the rejections had not tarnished that image. As a literary man, he felt I deserved the best.

On August 4, therefore, we went to the Boro Hall section of Brooklyn, where the borough's largest department stores are to be found, and there we spent four hours comparison shopping before we bought a late-model Smith-Corona portable typewriter, the first new typewriter I ever owned.

It cost sixty dollars, though from that sum we can deduct seventeen dollars as a trade-in for the Underwood. In other words, after three years of use, we got back seven dollars more on the old typewriter than we had spent for it, which, of course, made us feel good.

My father felt so good about it, in fact, that he was willing to have lunch in a cafeteria on the way home. I carefully recorded what we bought and the price thereof, for we did not often eat out. I had a salami on roll for ten cents and my father had whole wheat bread and baked beans for fifteen cents.

The new typewriter was delivered on August 10, while I was in the cemetery reading the new issue of *Amazing*. It was there to gladden my heart when I returned and, of course, the old Underwood was gone.

The fact that the new typewriter was a portable meant that I didn't have to keep it permanently on the desk, but could stow it in its case and place it on the floor and out of the way when it was not in use. The fact that it was new meant that the key action was very easy and that typing could be faster and yet less tiring. The disadvantage of a portable, of course, was that it was light enough to slide across the desk as I typed and I had to find a piece of sponge rubber to place it on.

8

With the new typewriter, I quickly completed two additional stories, my fourth and fifth, "This Irrational Planet" and "Ring Around the Sun." With "Marooned off Vesta" that meant I had three stores set for submission.

Of the three, I felt "This Irrational Planet" to be the weakest, so I did *not* submit it to Campbell. I submitted it directly to *Thrilling*

Wonder Stories on August 26, 1938, and it was not rejected till September 24. Campbell had spoiled me, and the four-week intervals between submission and rejection appalled me. I even called during that interval to make an indignant inquiry—not knowing that a mere four-week wait was brief indeed for anyone but Campbell.

But at least the rejection, when it came, was typewritten and was not a printed form. What's more, it contained the sentence, "Try us again, won't you?" That encouraged me. Perhaps I had underestimated the story. Buoyantly I tried Campbell, and he rejected it in six days. Five other magazines rejected it afterward. I never did sell it, and "This Irrational Planet" is also nonexistent now. I don't even remember the plot, except that I'm pretty certain that the planet of the title was Earth itself. The only other information I have about it is that it was quite short, only three thousand words long.[6]

The other two stories written in the same month were reserved for a better fate, but it didn't seem so at first.

On August 23, I visited Campbell on the third of what I was determined to turn into a monthly trip, but this time I was disappointed. Campbell was on vacation. It had never occurred to me that people take vacations (it still doesn't), and it had never occurred to me to call first and find if he were in and could see me before making the trip. With phone calls a nickel apiece it wasn't the sort of thing I would think of.

Rather dashed, I tried to hand the manuscripts to the receptionist, but she urged me to try again the following week. On August 30, therefore, I came back. He was out to lunch (I didn't think that people take lunches either—and still don't) but I waited, and when he arrived we went down to his office together for our third interview. I gave him both stories and he pointed to a pile of manuscripts that had accumulated during his vacation.

"I've got to skim over these," he said, "and put aside the hopeless ones for rejection."

"Is that personal?" I asked, timorously.

"No," he said, "I don't consider you hopeless."

But, on the other hand, he didn't consider me very hopeful either. At least, both stories were back in my hands on September 8 with a very brief letter indeed. I told myself that the postvacation pileup made it impossible for him to write at his usual length, but I was badly shaken.

[6] Those stories of mine that I never sold and that no longer exist were all short. They total just about fifty thousand words. Since I have published an estimated total of a little over three million words of fiction, the lost works amount to less than 2 per cent of the whole.

The very next day I shipped off "Marooned off Vesta," which I felt to be the better of the two, to *Amazing Stories*, and for a period of six weeks it seemed to have vanished. As for "Ring Around the Sun" I mailed that to *Thrilling Wonder Stories* on September 28, and it was back on October 4.

By that time, I had completed another story, my sixth, "The Weapon," which I submitted to Campbell at our fourth meeting, on September 28, and which came back on October 4.

By October 21, 1938, then, I had completed six stories, five of which I had submitted to Campbell and which he had rejected. The stories had piled up four other rejections among themselves, so that the box score was six stories, nine rejections, no sales.

I might have been dejected by this were it not for my monthly trips to Campbell.

19

The Futurians

1

In that same fateful summer of 1938, an event took place that led to my entry into science-fiction fandom.

For nine years I had been reading science fiction, following it faithfully, and of late performing my own peculiar statistical analysis of it. I knew that there were other readers, because I read their letters in the magazines, but I knew no other readers personally.

What I did not know was that here and there, groups of science-fiction readers were forming clubs of one sort or another and even publishing little periodicals (usually on primitive mimeograph devices) called "fan magazines," or "fanzines" for short. In May 1934, *Wonder Stories* even sponsored a national organization called "The Science Fiction League." I read about it in the magazine but that seemed to exist in another dimension as far as I was concerned.

Then, on August 2, 1938, I received a postcard from Jack Rubinson, who had been at Boys High with me and who had been in my graduating class. He too was a science-fiction reader. He had read my letters in *Astounding,* and he wanted to begin a correspondence.

I was willing, and on September 6, he sent me a large envelope containing the first fanzines I ever saw. My judgment, according to my diary, was that they were "fairly interesting."

With very few exceptions, that is all fanzines can possibly be, even for dedicated science-fiction fanatics. Most of them are written indifferently well and are extremely ingrown. They are house organs essentially, the house consisting of ten or fifteen fans. If you weren't one of those ten or fifteen, most of a particular fanzine will seem to you to be written in some strange foreign language.

On September 12 came the next step. I received a card from Rubinson telling me of the club he belonged to—the Greater New York Science Fiction Club, which met periodically in Queens.

My heart yearned for it and I replied at once, begging him to tell me when the next meeting of the club would take place, so that I could attend and join. I intended to do this despite the fact, as I said in my diary, that it would mean "double carfare."

I got my invitation to attend a meeting. The invitation arrived on

September 15, 1938, but in between something had happened at that club that I knew nothing of. Let me explain.

Though science-fiction clubs were small, they were contentious. The membership tended to consist of intelligent, articulate, argumentative, short-tempered, and opinionated young men (plus a few women) who got into tremendous power struggles.

You might wonder how power struggles can possibly arise in small clubs devoted to something as arcane as science fiction, and I wonder, too—but it happens. There are arguments over what happened to the thirty-five cents in the treasury, who is to run the fanzine, and other equally momentous problems. I believe there were even arguments as to how best to "control fandom" or, on a lesser scale, the world.

When the arguments overflowed the possibilities of word-of-mouth, letters flew from fanzine to fanzine—long, articulate, venomous, libelous letters, which often degenerated into threats of lawsuit that never materialized (largely because no lawsuit could ever result in substantial damages when no one being sued was worth more than $1.65, clothes, pocket change, blood chemicals, and all).

Naturally, it didn't take a club long to split up into two clubs, with each then proceeding to put out competing fanzines. The main task of each fanzine was to vilify the other group with an intensity and a linguistic fluency that Hitler might have studied with profit.

This may sound as though I'm exaggerating but, honestly, I'm not. If anything, I lack the words (competent writer though I am) to describe the intensity of the tempests brewed in the microscopic teapots of science-fiction fandom.

Let me refer you instead to something else. Back in 1954, Sam Moskowitz, one of the most active of the fans of the 1930s (and a dear friend of mine for many years), recalled those days and wrote a book the subtitle of which was *A History of Science-fiction Fandom*. It dealt with the period from 1935 to 1938 chiefly, and yet Sam found enough to say to fill a closely printed book of 250 pages.

In that book, endlessly and (forgive me, Sam) unreadably detailed, are all the feuds and quarrels of the period among people known only to themselves, over issues unexplainable to others. The title Sam gave the book, without any intent of satire at all, I believe, was *The Immortal Storm*.

Science-fiction writer L. Sprague de Camp (another dear friend of mine) has, in this connection, developed a theory of human contentiousness that I rather like. He points out that in the long history of human groups in the food-hunting stage, a multiplying tribe was always in danger. A group of fifty could not cover any more ground than a

group of twenty-five could, and would not find any more food. Therefore, the fifty might starve where the twenty-five would not.

If the fifty were full of loving kindness and brotherly affection and
could not bear to break up, they would be in serious trouble. If they
were contentious individuals who tended to split up, each smaller
group, staking out a territory of its own, might survive. Hence contentiousness had survival value and flourished, and still exists among mankind despite the fact that ever since agriculture became the most important activity of man, co-operation, and not contentiousness, has been
required.

Sprague says that if the contentiousness of small groups is to be
studied seriously, no better start could be made than to read and study
(however painful that might be) *The Immortal Storm.*

And yet let me emphasize that, despite the contentiousness, the
fans learned to love each other somehow and friendships were formed
that not all the vicissitudes of the decades could break. There is, to a
science-fiction fan, no stronger bond that can exist than that which is
covered by the phrase "fellow fan."

2

The Greater New York Science Fiction Club, concerning which
Rubinson had written me, was suffering from this contentiousness.
There was one faction, led by a fan named Will Sykora, along with
James Taurasi and Sam Moskowitz himself, that wished to confine the
activities of the club to science fiction, without any admixture of poli-
tics.

Another group, one to which Rubinson apparently belonged, felt
that the world situation was such that it made no sense to imagine science fiction as existing in a vacuum; it could not remain above the
strife.   .

Remember that 1938 was a hectic and fearful year in Europe. In
March, Hitler had taken over Austria without a fight (and Austrian
Jews entered the hell of Nazi oppression). In the months following,
Hitler, facing a fearful and hesitant France and Great Britain, de-
manded the border sections of Czechoslovakia (the "Sudetenland")
that were populated by German-speaking individuals.

By September the demand had brought Europe to the brink of
war. Peace was saved only by the craven surrender of Great Britain and
France to Germany at Munich. Helpless Czechoslovakia was dismembered and handed over to a brutal enemy by her "friends" and "allies."

As payment, Hitler postponed his war for not quite a year and then fought it under conditions much more favorable for himself.

With that in mind, the group to which Rubinson belonged wanted to use science fiction as a way of fighting fascism, and it was almost impossible to do this in those days without making use of Marxian rhetoric, so that these activists were accused of being Communists by the opposition.

In between the postcard I received on the twelfth and the one I received on the fifteenth, the final split took place. The Sykora group renamed itself the Queens Science Fiction Club, while the activists called themselves the "Futurian Science Literary Society," a name that was quickly shortened to Futurians.

The Futurians were, perhaps, the most remarkable science-fiction club that ever existed. Among the group that formed it or later joined for longer or shorter periods after its formation were people who in later life were extremely important to science fiction as writers or editors or both. They included Frederik Pohl, Donald A. Wollheim, Cyril Kornbluth, Robert W. Lowndes, Richard Wilson, Damon Knight, and James Blish, for instance.

It included me, too, for that matter, for the September 15 postcard was from Fred Pohl and I was invited to attend the first meeting of the new club at a place in Brooklyn on the following Sunday.

I was delighted. I knew nothing of the split-up, nothing of the existence of the two factions or of the nature of either. I naturally thought that I was being invited to the club that Rubinson had mentioned and that its meeting in Brooklyn, rather than Queens, was a lucky break that made it easier to reach.

Once I learned of the split, much later on, I did not, you understand, feel either cheated or hoodwinked. As a matter of fact, had I known of the issues involved, I would, of my own accord, have joined with the Futurian group, the members of which have been, by and large, among the most intelligent (if sometimes erratic) people I have ever known, and the surviving members of which are all still my friends.

Fortunately, the meeting was on a Sunday afternoon, the slowest time of the week (no afternoon papers), so I obtained my mother's permission to desert the store and sent off a postcard accepting the invitation.[1]

On Sunday, September 18, 1938, I traveled to the meeting place

[1] There was a great deal of postcard correspondence in those days since postcards cost only a penny.

and, for the first time, took part in any grouping of science-fiction fans. Here is what I had to say in my diary:

"I attended the first meeting of the Futurians and boy! did I have a good time. Attending likewise were such famous fans as Don A. Wollheim, John Michel, Frederik Pohl, 'Doc' Lowndes. . . . Dick Wilson was also there. . . . Jack Rubinson was also there. Altogether there were twelve.

"We enjoyed a three-hour session of strict parliamentary discipline. You know, motions, and amendments, and votes, and objections, and so on.[2] This was a meeting of organization in which we settled details, adopted a constitution, elected officers, and so on. Next time, we will proceed to the business of speeches, debates, and so on. Dues are ten cents a month with a twenty-five-cent initiation fee, which I paid. I also spent a nickel on a chance (they were raffling a book) but I lost.

". . . We have an organ called 'The Science Fiction Advance' which comes out once every two months. . . .

"After the meeting we all went down to an ice-cream parlor where they bought $1.90 worth of sodas and banana splits and sandwiches. I didn't get anything, though. There I had an uproarious time, especially with Wollheim who has taken a liking to me. They all know me from my letters to *Astounding* and *Amazing* and I got along famously."

I attended almost every meeting of the Futurians thereafter, for a year or so. On Sunday, October 2, I was there and "had more fun than last time." After the heavy work of parliamentary discussion, we relaxed by playing Ping-Pong.

The third meeting, on October 16, was a disappointment. It was in Manhattan's far north, at 190th Street. That was new territory to me and I managed to get lost. Some of the members were missing and contentiousness was setting in again, for Wollheim and Michel had already discovered after two meetings that the Futurians were not ideal and they wanted to reorganize. I myself had learned how to be contentious too, for, as I said in my diary, "I opposed it like hell."

The Futurians were the occasion for my first argument with Campbell. During my fourth visit to him, on September 28, I was, of course, filled to overflowing with the glories of that meeting and told him all about it and about the Futurian philosophy as expounded by Wollheim, the most articulate of the Futurians.

That was when I found out that Campbell was (my diary says) "a hidebound conservative." I argued with him but "was afraid to extend myself for fear of antagonizing him."

I went away distressed. The meeting had begun most promisingly,

[2] I had never encountered this sort of thing before and I was fearfully impressed.

for he had said "Hello, Mr. Asimov," and had shaken my hand as though he were meeting me as an equal—and then I went and argued with him.

3

My letters in *Astounding* had not yet ended their usefulness. On September 1, 1938, I received a letter from Brainerd, Minnesota.

It was from Clifford D. Simak, who was at that time a minor science-fiction writer. Back in 1931 and 1932, he had published about five stories, one of which (though I only found this out much later) was "The World of the Red Sun," which I had so enjoyed in junior high school and which I had retold to the classmates gathered around me.

In 1938 he had returned to the field, and his first story after this return was "Rule 18," which had appeared in the July 1938 issue. I had "hated it," my diary says, and in my letter to *Astounding* I gave it a very low rating.

Now Simak was writing to me to ask details so that he might consider my criticisms and perhaps profit from them. (Would that I could react so gently and rationally to adverse criticism—but I grew to know Cliff well in later years, though we rarely met, and I learned that gentle rationality was the hallmark of his character.)

I reread the story in order to be able to answer properly and found, to my surprise, that there was nothing wrong with it at all. What he had done was to write the story in separate scenes with no explicit transition passages between. I wasn't used to that technique, so the story seemed choppy and incoherent. The second time around I saw what he was doing and realized that not only was the story not in the least incoherent, but also that it moved with a slick speed that would have been impossible if all the dull bread-and-butter transitions had been inserted.

I wrote Simak to explain and to apologize, and adopted the same device in my own stories. What's more, I attempted, as far as possible, to make use of something similar to Simak's cool and unadorned style.

I have sometimes heard science-fiction writers speak of the influence upon their style of such high-prestige literary figures as Kafka, Proust, and Joyce. This may well be so for them, but for myself, I make no such claim. I learned how to write science fiction by the attentive reading of science fiction, and among the major influences on my style was Cliff Simak.

My correspondence with Cliff continued over the years.

4

On September 27, 1938, I registered for my fourth year at Columbia. I was taking integral calculus now and Sidney was taking more sociology while I was doing that. After calculus, I would go around to the sociology class, where the professor held court after the lecture was over. When that was done, Sidney and I would have lunch.

It made for dull listening, generally, for I never have been impressed by the soft sciences. On October 10, I found the sociology professor (his name was Casey) had made a table on the board in the course of his lecture in which he divided people into rationalists and mystics. Under mystics he had listed mathematicians.

I studied that for a while and then, even though I was not a class member, I interrupted the postlecture session by saying, "Sir, why do you list mathematicians as mystics?"

He said, "Because they believe in the reality of the square root of minus one."

I said, "The square root of minus one is perfectly real."

He said, "Then hand me the square root of minus one piece of chalk."

I said, "The cardinal numbers are used for counting. The so-called imaginary numbers, like the square root of minus one, have other functions. If you hand me a one-half piece of chalk, however, I'll hand you a square root of minus one piece of chalk."

Whereupon Casey promptly broke a piece of chalk in half and handed it to me with a smile. "Now your turn," he said.

"Not yet," I said. "That is one piece of chalk you're handing me."

"It is half a regulation length of chalk."

"Are you sure?" I said. "Will you swear it is not 0.52 times a regulation length or 0.48 times that?"

By now Casey realized it was time for hard logic if he was to win the argument, so he decided that since I was not a member of the class, I would have to leave the room at once. I left, laughing rather derisively, and after that I waited for Sidney in the hall.

Not wanting to be separated from Sidney for more than one period, I agreed to take a course in the History of Philosophy with him. That was a terrible mistake. It began well, with several of Plato's *Dialogues*, but I understood neither the lecturer nor the later readings, and I have rarely been so inflicted by ennui in any course I ever took.

Things were much better in organic chemistry and in medieval history, of course.

I remember that in medieval history the professor once asked the class to volunteer arguments for and against the social value of monasticism. I eagerly offered one I didn't think the other students would think of.

"Against monasticism," I said, "is the fact that since the monks were celibate there was a tendency to remove from the gene pool those genes that were clearly adapted to determining a capacity for education and learning."

The professor smiled slowly and said, "Don't overestimate the celibacy, Asimov. I think the genes managed to find their way into the general pool."

The class laughed and I'm afraid I was shocked. It was my first introduction to the thought that a vow of celibacy and celibacy itself might not necessarily go together.

My biggest disappointment, however, was integral calculus. Until now for thirteen years, all the way from arithmetic to differential calculus, I had understood math without any trouble—even if I weren't mathematician enough to join a math club. In integral calculus, I found suddenly that I had to sweat it out.

It was a horrible and embarrassing situation to get a B in a math course. I realized I had encountered my ceiling of comprehension in mathematics and I took no more courses in the subject.

5

In the fall of 1938, the political discussions between myself and my father reached their peak.

After all, my father had no one else to talk to. He and my mother rarely saw each other except in the context of the candy store, and usually when one was in the store, the other was in the house. Nor could my father talk to the customers. To a man, they seemed to be Republican or conservative Democrat, and he had a deadly fear of offending them with his own liberal views.

So he would talk to me.

Each day he and I would go over the news in those slow intervals when customers happened to be few and far between, my father analyzing past events and predicting future events with a doctrinaire certainty that was typical of him. I was a good deal more uncertain, but we ended in the same place—no faith at all, even before Munich, in the ability of Great Britain and France to face up to Hitler.

With respect to the United States, we disagreed. I took it for granted that if, somehow, President Roosevelt (whom we both revered) could move the United States into active opposition to Hitler, that would be it. I was absolutely certain that the United States could quickly defeat any nation or combination of nations, and I was endlessly frustrated at the fact that our isolationists were allowing the danger to rise to the point where it would be many times more expensive to defeat the enemy than might otherwise have been true.

My father, on the other hand, seemed to be activated by a kind of atavistic Russian patriotism. This was made the stronger by the fact that when he had left the Soviet Union, its government had claimed to be building a classless society in which there would be no racism of any kind and therefore no anti-Semitism. My father desperately wanted to believe that was so.

And since, as he insisted on believing, there was no anti-Semitism in the Soviet Union, he felt he could rely on the Soviet Union to be the ultimate destroyer of Nazism. As for the United States, he decided that the detectable anti-Semitism in our neighborhood proved that the United States would move hesitantly, if at all, in the fight against Nazism.

There, then, was the crux of our arguments. He saw events leading up to an ultimate clash between Germany and the Soviet Union; and I to an ultimate clash between Germany and the United States. We both saw Germany as the loser (and, as it happened, we were, in the end, both right).

We shared the same reaction to the situation in the Far East—one of irritation with Japan. We saw Japan as a small nation that was achieving success only because the west was divided against itself, and we both feared that her aggressive actions in China, not dangerous to us in themselves, would make it more difficult to defeat Germany by distracting either the Soviet Union, the United States, or both.

PART III

Advanced Degrees and Elementary Love

20

My First Sales

1

As October wore on, I continued to hear nothing from *Amazing Stories* about "Marooned off Vesta." Since the editorial offices were in Chicago, I couldn't telephone. Since I didn't value the magazine highly and was concentrating entirely on *Astounding,* I didn't even bother to write them.

But then, on October 17, 1938, I received a form letter from *Amazing* informing me that a sister magazine, *Fantastic Adventures,* would soon be published. They were asking all their contributors for stories suitable for it and I was dreadfully flattered that they considered me a "contributor." I replied at once, promising stories, and inquiring, as diplomatically as I knew how, as to the fate of "Marooned off Vesta."[1]

The news wasn't long in coming. On Friday, October 21, exactly four months to the day after my first visit to Campbell, I returned from school to find my mother beaming, and my sister (who, two days before, had finished business school) laughing. I was sent upstairs, where my father was just waking up from his nap. He had a letter to me from *Amazing* (which he had calmly opened), and it contained a letter of acceptance.

The letter was signed by *Amazing's* editor, Raymond A. Palmer, a small gnome of a man who became, in this way, the very first editor to buy one of my stories. In later years, he became very famous as one of the first flying-saucer enthusiasts, and for years afterward, he published a variety of mystical periodicals and books, none of which are of any value to anyone interested in the merely rational.

As it happens, I never met him in person.

For years, I kept that letter of acceptance framed on the wall. It had been written on gray paper with a thoroughly dead ribbon so that the words could barely be made out. This, too, had its uses.

After all, I didn't like to call attention to the letter. I was proud of it, delighted, overjoyed, but the good usages of society dictate a certain

1 *Thrilling Wonder* also had a new sister magazine, by the way, one called *Startling Stories,* the first issue of which reached me on October 18. This meant not only more reading, but also a greater need for stories by the publishers and, therefore, a greater chance at sales.

modesty. And yet since the words could scarcely be seen, everyone who visited me would look at the frame and say to me, "Why do you have an empty frame on the wall?"

I would mutter, "Oh it's just a letter," and then they would go up to it and read it.

In the vicissitudes of time, that letter and that frame have disappeared, and I'm dreadfully sorry.

On October 31, the check arrived. Payment was at the rate of $.01 a word, and since the story was 6,400 words long, the check I received was for $64. That was not much, perhaps, but it was the first money I ever earned as a professional writer,[2] and it wasn't so little, either. It was, after all, the equivalent of more than four months of my NYA earnings and would pay more than one month's tuition.

My parents took it big. That one sale had instantly made me a famous and established literary figure as far as my father was concerned, and he sat down to write formal letters.

The first went to Uncle Joe, whom, as it happened, my mother, Stanley, and I had visited just a month earlier. I suspect my father wanted to rub it in a little bit, getting across the notion that we-might-be-despised-greenhorns-but-look-at-what-we-have-done. With the same thought in mind (undoubtedly) he also sent off letters to the people we had known in our previous neighborhoods—all of them written in Yiddish, in stiff, old-country style.

I found it embarrassing and told him so, but it didn't help. Thereafter, on similar occasions over the next year or so, he sent off his letters again. Each time my objections became louder and finally my father stopped.

2

Not everything was great, however, quite apart from the dreadful atmosphere of Western surrender hanging over the world that Munich autumn. There were medical problems.

In those days, we had never heard of regular medical checkups. The thought that we would have a doctor go over us and then pay him good money to tell us there was nothing wrong with us would have struck any one of us as insane. If something hurt, *then* you saw a doctor —and only if it hurt very badly or if it kept on hurting for a long time.

[2] In this book, I am going to pay considerable attention to the details of the money I received for stories and other things. Perhaps I should be noble enough to rise above such sordid things as money, but the fact is I couldn't and didn't. The money I earned—or didn't earn—has influenced my pathway through life, and I must go into the financial details if the pathway is to make sense.

It was only if Nature the Great Healer (who didn't charge) wasn't on the job that you sought out some helper.

My father was particularly reluctant to see doctors.

"What is he going to tell me?" he would demand when we urged him to see to some malaise from which he suffered. "He's going to tell me to take a rest and go down to Florida for a vacation. I can't take a vacation and I can't rest. I have to work in the store."

The same went for teeth, of course. Only for a bad toothache did you see a dentist, and by that time the easiest treatment was a yank. Anything less drastic (such as root-canal work, something I had never so much as heard of in my youth) was too expensive.

The result was that both my father and my mother ailed and aged before my eyes. The change in hair added to the aging process in each case.

I remember my father in Van Siclen Avenue in his late twenties, with hair that was already retreating from a widow's peak and the beginning of a bald spot behind. By the time we were in Windsor Place, he had only a fringe of graying hair around a vast expanse of baldness. Furthermore, by 1938, he weighed 230 pounds.

As for my mother, her hair was graying in Van Siclen.[3] By Windsor Place, her hair was pure white and she had full dentures. My father had lost many teeth, but not all of them.

I was usually in excellent health and saw a doctor or dentist as infrequently as anyone else in the family. When younger, I had had some experience with a dentist and I didn't want to repeat it. One of my baby molars was extracted without anesthetic. The dentist, a faceless, nameless figure I remember with hatred, may have thought it would come out easily, but it did not. It was firmly fixed and he had to use his full strength. The pain was indescribable.

This was not exactly a see-your-dentist-regularly advertisement, but I did go now and then to have a twinge looked to and a filling inserted.

On October 11, 1938, I went to the dentist for a general inspection. He found a small cavity but then insisted on taking X rays—the first time I was ever exposed to them. On October 13, when I went back for the results, he informed me that hidden between my teeth, where casual examination would not uncover them, were *eight* cavities, and that to flush them to their lair and deal with them would cost me the unheard-of sum of fifty dollars.

---

[3] I remember that when I was five I once asked why her hair was turning gray and she said it meant she would die soon. She was just teasing but I began to cry bitterly and was inconsolable for a while. This was another memory of mine that my mother insistently denied in later years, but believe me, it happened.

I staggered home and there was a dismal gathering to decide what to do. The cavity that had been easily found could be dealt with, but the cavities between my teeth would have to wait. Even the check from *Amazing* didn't solve the problem, since that would have to be earmarked for school expenses.

What I did do was to get a second opinion from another dentist who, in my opinion, was incompetent. He found only one cavity between my teeth and I was only too glad to believe it. He remained my dentist, working very cheaply, for a few years, and I paid dearly for that "very cheaply" later on.

3

My father kept complaining of chest pains and aching shoulders. My mother clung firmly to the opinion he had indigestion, but by November 7, he had had indigestion too long, especially in the chest and shoulders, where indigestion rarely lingered.

The doctor was sent for (three dollars for a house call those days), a specialist was consulted (an incredible fifteen dollars), and the diagnosis was clear: My father had angina pectoris.

It turned out to be a relatively mild case, but it was a bad blow for a man who was, as yet, not quite forty-two years old. Uncle Joe and Aunt Pauline came the next day to commiserate and the atmosphere was rather like that of a funeral.

My father, however, went about things firmly. He had orders to lose weight, and this he did. Overnight he changed his habits. He abandoned cigarettes and adopted a rigid dietary regimen from which he never departed, so that within a year he lost seventy pounds. He took whatever medication he had been given dutifully and followed all orders, and lived out a normal life-span.

My own reaction, once the immediate panic had settled down, was that it was now clearly impossible for me to go to medical school. I was in my senior year, and Sidney and I were already filling out applications for various medical schools, but how on Earth could I go? How could I find the money or the time if my father was going to be disabled and placed on the sidelines? I was going to have to run the store.

I told my father this and he told me to stop talking nonsense. He was not going to be disabled and I was going to go to medical school.

He had to do considerable arguing, for when I decided that I could not go to medical school, I was relieved—clearly relieved.

As I passed my college years and approached the time when I would have to enter medical school, I grew steadily less enthusiastic about it. By my senior year I was, in fact, enthusiastic about *not* going to medical school.

The trouble was that first, I could not possibly say this to my father, and second, I had no alternate course of action to suggest.

So things went on.

Within limits, of course. I could scarcely apply to medical schools outside the city. It was clear to me that I would have to continue to commute and work in the store, all the more so now that my father had a bad heart. Furthermore—I must be truthful—I didn't dare leave the city. I might have been going on nineteen, but in my whole life I could never remember having spent a night away from my parents and family—and I was scared at the prospect. I would have to someday, I knew, but I was not yet ready.

There were five medical schools in New York City—Columbia, Cornell, New York University, Long Island University, and Flower—and before the year had come to its end, I had applied to all five. So did Sidney Cohen. He, however, was far less unsophisticated than I was, and he had applied to a number of medical schools outside the city. He did not fear leaving town.

<h1 style="text-align:center">4</h1>

If my father's condition was bad news, if the prospect of medical school was turning me sick with apprehension, I could not turn with relief to my science-fiction writing. The sale to *Amazing* could not cast a golden glow over the world forever. The fact was that it had not altered the world. I had not suddenly been converted into a steady winner. In fact, as far as Campbell was concerned, nothing seemed to change.

I continued my monthly visits—there were visits on October 28 and November 22, for instance. I continued my monthly submissions, and he continued his monthly rejections. I told him of course, of my sale, and he always asked with interest if I had made any additional sales, but he would not buy any stories himself unless they met with *his* approval. What other, lesser magazines did was irrelevant.

In fact, on November 4, I received back my seventh story, "Paths of Destiny," with a comparatively curt note to the effect that it was "hackneyed." It was the unkindest rejection I had yet received, and I was horrified. I wrote Campbell a letter of apology and said I would try to do better.

On November 12, *Amazing* rejected my sixth story, "The Weapon." Even the fact that they had already taken a story of mine obviously didn't mean that they would automatically buy anything I sent them. (I had thought, just possibly, that it might indeed mean that.)

When I saw Campbell on November 22, he was as friendly as ever. His curt rejection of a hackneyed story had not soured him on me. However, the story I then submitted, my eighth, "Knossos in Its Glory," came back in four days. This time, however, as though to make up for his roughness before, he said my work "was definitely improving, especially where you are not straining for effect."

Neither "Paths of Destiny" nor "Knossos in Its Glory" ever sold, and both were gone forever. I remember nothing at all about the former, but "Knossos in Its Glory" was an ambitious attempt to retell the Theseus myth in science-fiction terms. The minotaur was an extraterrestrial who landed in ancient Crete with only the kindliest of intentions, and I remember writing terribly stilted prose in an attempt to make my Cretans sound as I imagined characters in Homer ought to sound.

There was no question but that my morale was slipping. By December 3 I had written another story, "Ammonium," and having reread it after completion, I decided "it is definitely the rottenest story I have ever written. Therefore my enthusiasm for writing is at its lowest ebb since last June."

Nevertheless, I started another story that day, which I called "Ad Astra." Looking back on that day now, I can see that this, more than anything else, was what made it certain I would make it in the end. Depression is inevitable at times, self-doubts cannot help but arise—but these must not be allowed to translate into writer's block. Every story is a new ball game.

On December 21, 1938 (which happened to be my father's forty-second birthday—but we never celebrated birthdays in my family, and I gave it no particular thought), I visited Campbell for the seventh time and submitted "Ad Astra."

Campbell was as genial as ever, said I could handle words and had good ideas, but lacked "umph." That didn't help me because I did not know what "umph" was. Campbell told me I would get it in time whether I knew what it was or not.

"Ad Astra" is the first story for which I remember the exact circumstances of the initiating inspiration. I was working for Bernhard J. Stern for a second year at NYA, and since he was writing a book on social resistance to technological change, he had me reading a great many books that might conceivably be of use to him. My orders were to take note of any passages that dealt with the subject and to copy them down.

It was a liberal education for me and I was particularly struck by a whole series of articles by astronomer Simon Newcomb, which I read at Stern's direction. Newcomb advanced arguments that demonstrated the impossibility of heavier-than-air flying machines, and maintained that one could not be built that would carry a man. While these articles were appearing, the Wright brothers flew their plane. Newcomb countered with an article that said, essentially, "Very well, one man, but not two."

Every significant social advance roused opposition on the part of many, it seemed. Well, then, shouldn't space flight, which involved technological advances, arouse opposition too?

Yet I had never read a science-fiction story in which such opposition was described. Either the public role did not enter into the story at all or, if it was there, it was described as wildly approving—rather on the line of the public reaction to Lindbergh's solo flight across the Atlantic in 1927, eleven years before (which I just barely remembered).

I determined therefore to write a story about the first attempts to reach the moon, and to have opposition to space flight play an important role. It was because of that that I used "Ad Astra" as the title. This was from the Latin proverb "Per aspera ad astra" ("through difficulties to the stars").

I had no great hopes for the story, to be sure. I was not expecting that my present difficulties would carry me to the stars.

In fact, when the February issue of *Amazing* came out on December 9, it carried the announcement that "Marooned off Vesta" would appear in the next issue, and yet I said in my diary, "It ought to thrill me but it doesn't. Somehow, the story only gives me a heartache when I think that I have made no sales since."

As 1938 drew to a close—my first year as a professional writer—my score was as follows:

I had written ten stories, of which I had submitted nine to Campbell and had gotten eight rejections, with the ninth pending. From magazines other than *Astounding,* I had received a total of seven rejections. Total score: fifteen rejections, one sale. Total earnings for the year: $64.

That one sale kept looking smaller and smaller.

5

My monthly visits with the Futurians did not cheer me either. One and all, the Futurians had writing ambitions, and one and all had been writing. Almost all of them were going to make it in time; but they had not yet done so.

My own sale was the first, and I had been gleeful over it—a tactical error. Furthermore, most of the Futurians were school dropouts, and I was forging steadily ahead toward my degrees—another tactical error. At any rate, my happy relationship with them faded a bit.

Nor was there much triumph to be found in the medical-school situation (assuming I would consider acceptance a triumph rather than a disaster). Of the five local medical schools to which I had applied, it was clear that Columbia and Cornell were hopeless, for the word was that they would take only a few Jewish students in each class, and that none of these would be from New York City.

Indeed, only Long Island University seemed a likely target. My premedical adviser strongly urged me to apply to half a dozen or so medical schools outside the city. He offered to recommend those which would offer the most likely chances. I refused, however. I did not wish to leave New York City, and I didn't want to put myself in a position to be tempted to do so. Besides, I rather gloomily assumed that Long Island University would take me.

And, to be sure, I got a call for an interview, and on December 14 I was there with a haircut, with my pants pressed, with my shoes shined.

My father was enthusiastic, assuming that a call to an interview was as good as an acceptance. I was not. I remembered the fiasco of my Columbia interview nearly four years before, and I felt that if I were to be accepted, it would have to be in spite of the first impression I was bound to make.

I was right. I found myself one of a party of ten (one of whom was a woman). I waited while several were interviewed for over ten minutes apiece. Then I was called, and my interview took only five minutes. It was quite clear to me that they didn't have to take a very searching look at me to see that a pimply faced, not-yet-nineteen-year-old, with no charisma or self-possession, did not offer them much prospect.

My only chance was that my grades might more than compensate for my interview impression, but they did not. Long Island University rejected me. I was later interviewed by New York University and by Flower and I thought I did better there, but I was fooling myself. Both rejected me, and so did Columbia and Cornell, who did not even require an interview to be convinced of my unsuitability.

My father was terribly upset at all this, but I explained that this was but a set of preliminary applications in the middle of the senior year, when one didn't really expect to get accepted. There would be another chance toward the end of the senior year and then it would be another story. I didn't really believe this, but it cheered him up.

6

By December 29, I had waited eight days to hear from Campbell concerning "Ad Astra" and now a letter arrived—clearly one that was not large enough to hold the manuscript.

The first pang of ecstasy faded quickly, however, for it didn't contain a letter of acceptance. Campbell simply asked me to come to the office after January 4 for a conference over the story. I didn't know whether that meant he wanted to take it, after getting a few things straightened out, or whether he simply wanted to discuss it in detail before giving it back. That latter possibility didn't seem to make sense, but I did not dare let myself believe the former without qualification.

I couldn't help but hope, however, and I finally talked myself into such a pitch of excitement that when, the next day, "Ammonium" was rejected by *Marvel Science Fiction* (another one of the new science-fiction magazines that were now springing up), I dismissed it airily. To be sure, *Marvel* was a rotten magazine and a rejection from it was a disgrace, but I knew "Ammonium" was a poor story and I was concentrating on "Ad Astra."

I was at Campbell's office on Thursday, January 5, 1939, the first permissible day, having had to work through a full week of uncertainty and, as I suppose was inevitable, what I encountered was neither the best I could hope for nor the worst I could fear.

Campbell was not rejecting the story, but he was not accepting it after a small discussion, either. What happened was that he liked the business of opposition to space travel, which he had never encountered before in a story any more than I had. He wanted me to rewrite the story entirely, making that central.

It was rather frightening. I had never had to rewrite a story before to meet an editorial request and I found it much harder to do that than to write the story in the first place. If you write an original story, each word must please you; no more than that. If you rewrite, each word must not only please you but somehow do what an editor told you he wants done.

Nevertheless, it was exciting. It took me nearly three weeks to fulfill the assignment, but in all that time I felt as though I had half sold a story to Campbell.

For one thing, it meant that on January 10, 1939, when the March *Amazing Stories* hit the stands, I greeted "Marooned off Vesta"[4] in

---

[4] See *Asimov's Mysteries* (1968). Incidentally, just because I tell you in what book you can find each of my stories, doesn't mean that you are required to look them up and read them. But you may if you want to, you know.

print without a feeling of disappointment and anticlimax. I could enjoy it for I had made a half sale since.

My father ordered ten copies so he could send them out to various people, with Uncle Joe on top of the list. I, myself, was no better. I took a copy to school and showed it to everyone, and was openly disappointed that my name was not on the cover. It was my first appearance as a professional writer—eight days after my nineteenth birthday.

For a long time I saved the March 1939 *Amazing*, along with other magazines in which my stories appeared. With the years, however, the space required for such souvenirs became larger than the space available. Eventually, therefore, I simply excised the stories from the magazines and discarded the non-Asimov portion. It was a difficult thing to do, but I try to pride myself on my businesslike lack of sentimentality.

Then, still more years later, I regretted, in print, my failure to save at least that very first issue of a science-fiction magazine containing a story of mine in it. Even a nonsentimentalist should have done that. The well-known science-fiction fan, Forrest J. Ackerman, discovered the regret and kindly sent me a copy in excellent condition as a birthday present. I still have it and I intend to keep it until it disintegrates—or until I do.

Amazing Stories, in those days, printed little autobiographical squibs written by the authors of the stories in the issue. I had performed that service for *Amazing* at the editor's request and it appeared on page 126 of the magazine. It is my first autobiographical essay in print and attempts to be lighthearted.[5] One paragraph reads:

"There are more stories on the way, some in a state of partial completion now, and I hope and hope again that this first story does not prove to be a flash in the pan. If it does, it won't be because I didn't try."

I didn't have to worry. It wasn't a flash in the pan.

7

When I took the revised "Ad Astra" to Campbell on January 24, he was kind enough to tell me that one of his correspondents had told him that "Marooned off Vesta" was the best story in its issue.

Then, too, on January 30, 1939, I received a postcard from Jack Williamson, one of my science-fiction idols. He was the writer who had written "Legion of Space," which was one of the best science-fiction thrillers I had ever read up to that time. The postcard read:

[5] The attempt was a miserable one. When I reread it, many years later, I found it exquisitely embarrassing.

" 'Marooned off Vesta' is a nice yarn. Welcome to the ranks."

Years later, when Jack and I were talking at a convention, I reminded him of his kindness to a mere beginner, and he didn't remember sending the card. *I* did, though, on his behalf, and in time I managed to express my gratitude in a useful way.

When the mail came the next day, on January 31, I was upstairs. My father called me down yelling, "Isaac, a check! A check!"

That was how I discovered the system used by Campbell in accepting stories. Though his rejections were usually accompanied by long and useful letters, his acceptances consisted of a check only, without a single accompanying word. It was his feeling that the check was eloquent enough. In this case it was for $69, since the story was 6,900 words long and *Astounding*, like *Amazing*, paid $.01 a word in those days.

It was my good fortune that I began trying to sell science fiction at a time when new magazines were being issued. One of the new magazines was entitled simply *Science Fiction*, and it was edited by Charles D. Hornig, who had previously been editor of *Wonder Stories*. The first issue of this magazine reached the stands on January 12, 1939, and on January 19 I sent them "Ring Around the Sun" for their consideration. The consideration was good, for on February 4 I received an acceptance —the second in five days.

Science Fiction paid only $.005 a word and, moreover, paid on publication rather than on acceptance. (A magazine that is sufficiently shaky financially never knows if it will be around for publication, so why throw away money?) That didn't matter, however. I was counting acceptances, not dollars.

I had reached the point now where I attracted the attention of a would-be agent. It was Fred Pohl, who was only nineteen himself, but who had a great deal of self-confidence (deservedly so, for he was, and is, one of the most intelligent people I have ever met). He offered to help me sell my stories and to rewrite my rejects, the proceeds of which, if they sold thereafter, would be split sixty-forty in his favor. I refused at once, and firmly. I said, in my diary, "I don't need any help, and I flatter myself I can do my own writing."

I then proceeded to write an eleventh story, "The Weapon Too Dreadful to Use," which I did *not* submit to Campbell. Either I did not wish to push him too hard immediately after I had made a sale to him, or I suspected the story wasn't good enough for him and didn't want to spoil the impression "Ad Astra" had made. In either case (and I don't really remember the motive), I decided to try it on *Amazing* first. It was also a $.01 market after all, and I owed them another chance now that I had made my Campbell sale.

I mailed "The Weapon Too Dreadful to Use" to *Amazing* on February 6, and on February 20 I got an acceptance, the third in three weeks. This time there was a check with it for $64.

I must have thought I had now gotten the range, but somehow that's not the way it works. Having reached some sort of peak of delight, I promptly descended into a slough of despond. On February 21, I visited Campbell, submitted a new story, "The Decline and Fall," and it was back in my lap on February 25, just as though "Ad Astra" had never happened. On the last day of the month, I received a rejection for "The Weapon" from *Thrilling Wonder*.

The May 1939 *Amazing* appeared on the newsstands on March 10, and I was rather flabbergasted to find it contained "The Weapon Too Dreadful to Use."[6] It had appeared only six weeks after acceptance.

That rather took the bloom off the acceptance, however. I didn't have to be particularly experienced to realize that they had a hole in that issue that had to be filled right away with a story of the proper length, and my story may have been of the right length rather than of the right quality.

It *was* a rotten story, as Fred Pohl carefully, and convincingly, pointed out to me. (I was rather impressed that Fred could see what was wrong with it, and I grew considerably closer to him than to any of the other Futurians.)

I am even more impressed, in hindsight, that Fred was able to make me sit still for criticism where others (always excluding Campbell) could not. But then, Fred spoke quietly, unemotionally, and briefly, and confined himself to purely technical advice that I invariably found helpful. I don't know how he knew so much about the nuts and bolts of writing. He was almost exactly my age and intelligence, but I guess he had given the matter of writing a lot more thought than I ever had—and had read widely in contemporary literature.

Amazing at that time tended heavily toward adventure and action, and disapproved of too much scientific exposition in the course of the story. I, of course, even then was writing the kind of science fiction that involved scientific extrapolation that was specifically described.

What Raymond Palmer did in this case was to omit some of my scientific discussion and to place in footnotes a condensed version of passages that he could not omit without damaging the plot. This was an extraordinarily inept device, at which I chafed at the time. I took

[6] See *The Early Asimov*.

the only retaliation available to me. I placed *Amazing* at the bottom of the list as far as the order in which to submit stories was concerned.

As I look back on those days of the late 1930s, it is clear to me now that science fiction was approaching a fork in the line of its progress. Science-fiction pulp, which I had been reading with such love and avidity, was declining, and a new generation of writers was arising, writers who had some feeling for science.

Amazing was still slanted toward mad professors with beautiful daughters, toward malevolent monsters and hectic action, and it would even continue to have some commercial success with it.

Campbell, however, was pushing for quieter, more thoughtful stories, in which the science was realistic, and in which scientists, inventors, and engineers talked and acted like recognizable human beings. That was the direction of progress, and it was the one in which I tended of my own accord to move. Since that was also the direction in which Campbell drew me, my progress was rapid.

Thanks to Campbell, science fiction was entering what has ever since been called its "Golden Age," and thanks to the accident of my being there at the right time—and in the right place—and with the right impulses—I was able to become part of it.

8

On March 4, 1939, I began my most ambitious writing project up to that time. It was a novelette named "Pilgrimage" that was planned to be longer than "Cosmic Corkscrew." It was my first attempt to write "future history"—that is, to do a tale about a far future time written as though it were a historical novel. It was also my first attempt to write a story on a galactic scale.

I was very excited while working at it and felt somehow that it was an "epic." (Winterbotham, however, was rather dubious when I described my planned treatment of it in a letter to him.) Although it was 12,600 words long, I had it finished rather quickly and took it to Campbell on March 21.

It was back in three days with a comment to the effect that "You have a basic idea that might be made into an interesting yarn, but as it is, it is not strong enough."

But things had changed. For one thing, I was no longer accepting rejections as a matter of course. Since I had revised "Ad Astra" and made it acceptable, why could I not do the same for "Pilgrimage?" Of course, it had been Campbell who had suggested the revision in the for-

mer case, and it would have to be I who would do it in the latter case—
but that is what I did.

On March 27, I visited Campbell on my way back from school and
managed to extort from him an agreement to have me revise the story
in such a way as to emphasize those parts he favored. The story involved an Earth that was under the heel of reptilian invaders from
outer space. Earthmen occupied parts of the Galaxy but they could not
be roused to try to rescue the home planet.[7]

For one thing, Campbell wanted me to add a religious angle—to
have human beings travel to Earth as Moslems make pilgrimages to
Mecca, so as to make my title, which had no religious connotation to
begin with, particularly apt. It may even have been my title that had
given him this idea.[8]

The second version of "Pilgrimage" was submitted on April 25,
and I thought, based on my experience with "Ad Astra," that a revision
had to be accepted. No, it didn't.

Campbell wouldn't take it, but this time *he* asked for a further revision. I tried again and the third version was submitted on May 9 and
rejected on May 17. Campbell admitted that there was still the possibility of saving it, but, after three tries, he said I should put it to one
side for some months and then look at it from a fresh viewpoint.

I had never before worked so hard on a story, and I was dreadfully
disappointed—but there was nothing I could do.

I had grown a little nervous by now as to the fate of "Ad Astra." I
had heard at one of the Futurian meetings that fellow fan Milton A.
Rothman of Philadelphia had sold two stories to Campbell and that
they would appear under the pseudonym of "Lee Gregor."

The reason for the pseudonym, it appeared, was Campbell's gentle
suggestion that Anglo-Saxon names would go down better with the
readers.

In this he was completely wrong, of course; what he really meant
was that Anglo-Saxon names would go down better with *Campbell*.

I knew that "Ad Astra" would soon be coming out and I wondered
if Campbell might suggest a pseudonym for me. I was prepared to refuse, completely and unequivocally, even if it cost me sales to him.

[7] The reluctance of the human planets to oppose an occupying aggressor was clearly
influenced by the situation in Europe where, even as I wrote the story, Hitler occupied the rest of Czechoslovakia in direct and brutal defiance of the Munich pact.
[8] While there on that day, by the way, I met, for the first time, fellow writer
Horace L. Gold. He had written "A Matter of Form," which had appeared in the
December 1938 *Astounding* and which had been an excellent story. It was one of
the fringe benefits of my visits to Campbell that others visited him and that I met
some of the most important names in science fiction in this way, now and then.

However, he never did. Perhaps because my first sale was to *Amazing,* which didn't care, and because my name had already appeared, as such, on a Table of Contents, the issue did not arise.

If that were so, it is a good thing my first sale was to *Amazing.* I am sure I would not have knuckled under in this matter, but I was thankful I did not have to go through the meat grinder.

21

College Graduation

1

The period of useless revisions of "Pilgrimage" was a depressing time for a number of reasons. Rejections of my stories were coming from every magazine once again; and from every medical school I was once again being rejected as a candidate. And then, on April 20, 1939, Sidney Cohen was accepted into Long Island University Medical School.

Sidney's acceptance was a blow. It wounded my self-esteem and temporarily ground me under a rankling sense of injustice. He had made it and I hadn't and yet all through college it seemed to me I had been doing better than he had.

If he had gotten into a school outside New York City, I could have told myself that I would have made it too, if I had applied in the boondocks. The fact was that we had both applied to this particular school, we had both been interviewed—yet he had been taken, and I had not been, though his marks were, on the whole, lower than mine.

My failure couldn't even be blamed, conveniently, on my Jewishness. Sidney was as Jewish as I was, and had a quintessentially Jewish name.

I dreaded telling my parents, but I had to. They would have found out soon enough. They knew Sidney, knew he was applying, and were keen to know how he made out. When I told them the news, my father turned grim and angry, and my mother burst into tears.

My parents, I suppose, had been betrayed by me. There was no gentler way of putting it. In my thirteen-year school career I had consistently been "smart"; I had been at the top or near the top of the heap all through; and somehow it had all been a fraud. I hadn't made it.

Nor was there anything I could do. I couldn't console them by telling them I didn't want to go to medical school. They wouldn't have really believed me; they would have considered it sour grapes. If I had managed to convince them, they would have accepted that as another betrayal, for they would say that because I didn't want to go, I had so behaved at the interviews as to be certain of rejection.

It took me awhile to get over my envy of Sidney—not envy of

medical school, which I didn't want, but envy at his being successful and I a failure in something we had both tried for.

But I got over it. A little painful (and embarrassing) thought about the matter and I could see that Long Island University knew what it was doing. Sidney had made a good impression on them and I had not. Sidney was always quiet, grave, dignified; and I, no matter how I tried, was loud, grinning, frenetic.

Besides, what right had I to be envious? Was Sidney envious of my having sold science-fiction stories to magazines? He had never showed any envy but had been unselfishly delighted at my success.

Then, too, the consequence showed the decision to have been a good one. Sidney did very well in medical school, and I (I am convinced) would have done poorly. I might never have finished, which would have been a much more horrible failure, and even if I had doggedly driven myself to graduate, I am quite certain I would always have been unhappy and that I would have been a lousy doctor.

I have no way of proving that this is not a matter of sour grapes, but I honestly feel this to be a truthful and considered judgment. As it was, I was forced by circumstance into a path much more appropriate for myself; and painful though the forcing was, I survived.

As though to emphasize my failure, by the way, on April 27 I received a registered letter from Albany to the effect that enough vacancies had opened to allow me to receive what was left of a state scholarship. Since 3½ years of the 4 had passed, only $50 was left for me.

In place of medical school, in other words, I had wangled the tail end of a scholarship. My father was openly contemptuous and I felt more ashamed than before.

But fifty dollars is twice twenty-five. I accepted it.

2

Nor was there anything in my writing career to counterbalance this spring of my discontent. My work on "Pilgrimage" had filled the better part of three months to no effect, and a couple of my older stories had collected a rejection each.

I had tried to reach Hornig of *Science Fiction*, and he had written to say that he was attending a meeting of the Queens Science Fiction League on May 7, and if I were to attend also, we might meet. This was the organization I might have joined the previous September, had I not been headed off by the Futurian splitaway.

I attended and met Hornig for the first time.[1] He was dark-complexioned, needed a shave, and was a fellow sufferer of acne. I seized the occasion to hand him two stories, "The Decline and Fall" and "Knossos in Its Glory."

I also met Eric Frank Russell, an English writer whose novel *Sinister Barriers* had been featured in the first issue of a new magazine, *Unknown Fantasy Fiction*. That first issue had appeared on February 1, 1939. It was a sister magazine to *Astounding* and was also edited by Campbell.

Unknown was a magazine the like of which had never appeared before. It contained adult fantasy, some humorous, some terrifying, all well written and most thought-provoking. Campbell had conceived of it precisely as a vehicle for *Sinister Barriers*, which he bought for the excellent story it was, even though he felt that it did not quite come under the classification of science fiction.

Russell was tall, long-faced, somewhat withdrawn, and I found myself rather abashed in his presence.

Otto Binder was there, too. He was the active half of a team that included his brother, Earl. They wrote under the pseudonym of Eando (E. and O.) Binder. In the late 1930s he was the most prolific of the science-fiction writers, but he rarely appeared in *Astounding*. He was about ten years older than I was, frank, boyish, and genial. In the January 1939 *Amazing*, he had published "I, Robot," a short story about a sympathetic and noble robot that had made a great impression on me.

I was most excited, though, at meeting Jack Williamson for the first time. He was stoop-shouldered, very quiet, and, apparently, shy, but it was clear he had a golden heart.

It was an exciting day—the first I spent with fellow writers as well as with fellow fans. And I was *treated* as a writer rather than as a fan. The Sykora group ignored my association with the Futurians and did not order me out—as they might have done were I simply a fan.

But exciting or not, Hornig bounced the two stories at once: I got them back on May 9. And, of course, Campbell bounced "Pilgrimage" for the third time and ordered me to put it aside "a couple of months."

[1] In *The Early Asimov* I say, concerning Hornig, "I have never, to my knowledge, met him." This was wrong. In preparing *The Early Asimov* I went through my diary rather sketchily, searching only for literary information. For this book, my autobiography, I have carefully read every word of every page of my diary (and this was a job I found often difficult and often embarrassing), and I have caught myself in a few earlier mistakes—such as this one. There is one whopper of a mistake yet to come.

That meant that at least I would have the chance to start a new story, my fourteenth.

The memory of Binder's "I, Robot" was clear in my mind, and meeting him three days before had stimulated that memory, so on May 10 I started to write my own story of a sympathetic and noble robot, one that served as a nursemaid for a little girl. I called the story "Robbie," and on May 23 I took it in to Campbell.

3

By now I badly needed something to raise my spirits, for even breaking through the "Campbell barrier" with the sale of "Ad Astra" had not converted me into a successful writer.

When Fred Pohl once again urged me to let him be my agent, I agreed on a three-month tryout period. I reserved Campbell for myself, however, which was an unfair restriction on Pohl, but I couldn't help it. I simply couldn't give up my visits to Campbell. There was also to be no revisions by Pohl of my rejections and no sixty-forty split.

Fred Pohl became a close friend of mine after this, but there was always a shell about him I could never penetrate. He was taller than I, just as thin, had light hair that already looked as though its presence were temporary, and he had a pronounced overbite that gave him a rabbity appearance. His quiet voice was never raised in anger, and he smoked incessantly.

Nevertheless, I never knew anything about his personal life, his parents, his siblings if any, his childhood—except in small, inadvertent allusions over the course of the years. He had a girlfriend at the time I met him, but he never spoke of her particularly.

He did not go to college; in fact, I don't think he finished high school. He was an educational casualty of the Depression. It was a matter of money, but I didn't know the details. I had the impression he had to live by himself and somehow support himself, but he didn't say why or, for that matter, how.

His aborted education was a tragic thing. It didn't stop him in any way. He taught himself all he had to know in a dozen different directions, from science and mathematics to practical politics. He was interesting, clear and logical, bright and rational. It has always seemed to me that the only person in the world he couldn't impress was himself. To himself (and this is only my impression) his status as "high-school dropout" was something from which there seemed no recovery. Too bad!

On May 25, 1939, he came to my home in the evening and I gave him the collection of stories I had written but had not yet sold. I also showed him "Robbie," which was at that time still with Campbell. He read it and said, "It's a good story, Eye, but Campbell won't take it."

I asked why not. He said it was too reminiscent of "Helen O'Loy" by Lester del Rey, which had appeared in the December 1938 *Astounding*, and which also dealt with a sympathetic and noble robot, albeit one in female guise.[2] Pohl also said that the ending, in which the mother was suddenly converted from being antirobot to being prorobot, was weak.

As a matter of fact Campbell *did* reject "Robbie," and the news of the rejection reached me first from Pohl himself, who, exceeding his role as my agent, inquired of Campbell as to its fate. Campbell told him it was rejected. When the manuscript still did not come back, I could stand it no more and, on June 6, I visited Campbell and had the news confirmed. What's more, Campbell's reasons were exactly those that Pohl had predicted, and I was impressed by Pohl's acumen.[3] Later on, *Amazing* rejected "Robbie" because it was too reminiscent of Binder's "I, Robot," which was good judgment on their part, too.

It was at my June 6 visit to Campbell's that I was introduced to a tall, thin, thirty-one-year-old man with a neat, small mustache, a well-bred air, and a precise manner of speech. It was L. Sprague de Camp, one of my favorite science-fiction writers. He wrote not merely science fiction, but fantasy and nonfiction articles as well. I liked his nonfiction even better than his fiction. He had a two-part article, "Design for Life," in the most recent two issues of *Astounding*, and I had enjoyed it greatly.

It was a pleasant meeting and a fruitful one, for we have been good and close friends ever since and never, I think, in all that time has one cross word passed between us.

4

At the end of May, while I was still waiting to hear about "Robbie," my last tests were taken and passed at Columbia, including a heavy "comprehensive examination" in my major—chemistry. I passed them all, of course, and it meant I was done with college.

[2] Lester has always been one of my favorite writers. In the May 1939 *Astounding* a story of his, "The Day Is Done," reduced me to tears when I read it on the subway on April 29. These days, Lester never stops talking about it and I am forced to say that I wept over the bad writing, but that's not really so. It was a terrific story.
[3] By that time, too, Pohl had had a chance to read my stories and he told me "they were the best set of rejections" he had ever seen. That didn't do anything to hurt my opinion of his acumen, either.

It was an anticlimactic finish thanks to my inability to get into medical school, and I didn't value the graduation at all. I refused to attend the graduation ceremonies, which were held on June 7, 1939, but asked, instead, to have my diploma mailed to me. It arrived on June 10, and I put it in a closet.

The only time I ever took it out was nearly three years later, when it was time for me to register to vote for the first time. I had a clear memory of my mother registering to vote for the first time in 1938, shortly after she had obtained her own citizenship. I had accompanied her to the polling headquarters at the neighborhood elementary school and she had been required to take a literacy test. I remember her sitting there at the children's desk as she took the test.

Since I did not want to do that if I didn't have to, I dug out my college diploma and took it with me. I felt they wouldn't test my literacy with that piece of evidence in my favor. As soon as I was up before the clerk behind the desk, I presented my birth certificate, my father's citizenship papers (mentioning me on their face), and my college diploma. It turned out he had no intention of giving me a literacy test; that was only for people who seemed on the face of it to be doubtful; so he stared at my diploma and said, in a shocked voice: "Did you take that diploma out of its frame just to bring it in here?"

"No," I answered, indignantly, "it was just rolled up in the closet."

And he stood up and said, "Do you mean to say that after your parents sacrificed to send you to college, you didn't even frame your diploma?"

Well, I never did. In fact, I don't even possess it anymore. My bachelor's diploma is as gone as "Cosmic Corkscrew."

The degree I was awarded was a B.S., a Bachelor of Science. At the time I thought that was only natural, since my major was chemistry. Many years later, however, I discovered that this was a second-class degree. The gentlemen of Columbia College got a B.A. (Bachelor of Arts), for which university undergraduates such as myself did not qualify.

When I discovered this, I was dreadfully annoyed. I had never appreciated my second-class status as an undergraduate, and the thought that even in graduation I was pettily discriminated against irritated me mightily. After all, I had taken the same courses as the Columbia College students had taken, and had competed with them directly for marks. I might have received the reward of this.

There *was* something I could do about it. I was annoyed enough to stop all contributions to Columbia. I haven't paid out one cent to the university since. Petty? No pettier than they.

This was not the end of the discrimination, by the way.

At the time I went to Columbia, there was something called "University Extension," which gave evening courses for any person who wished to attend and who could pay the fees. It was essentially an adult-education device and was a valuable service to the community and to all people who wanted to learn something.

Nevertheless, it was considered by regular undergraduates to be *déclassé*. We looked upon it as a kind of glorified night school.

In years to come, University Extension was replaced by the School of General Studies. This school gathered up other disregarded miscellaneous classifications, among other things, the "university undergraduate" group. That meant that I automatically became an alumnus of the school of General Studies, and that also irritated me when I found out what it was.

Some day a biographer,[4] working through the Columbia records, and coming across the fact that I am an alumnus of the School of General Studies, will solemnly record that I worked my way through Columbia's extension courses at night.

Well, not so!

5

Once I completed college, I was faced with a problem.

Virtually all my life I had taken it for granted that I would, in September 1939 (or in September of whichever year I finished college), start my studies at a medical school. Now I was not to do it. Well then, what *was* I to do?

There was no point in ending my education and looking for a job. I doubted that I could find one any more advanced than my old summer job cutting rubberized fabric three years before, despite my education and my high IQ.

Nor did it occur to me for even a moment that I could simply try to write for a living. It had been just a year since I had begun to submit stories, and in that year I had received three checks, totaling $197.

It was a respectable feat, all things considered, but I couldn't live on that, and so far I had no indication that things would ever get better in that respect.

So I had to continue my education, and the only path that seemed open to me was to continue on with my chemistry and go for my master's degree. I wasn't sure to what end I would do this, but it would

[4] You wouldn't think that with this autobiography out there'd be any need for a biography, but undoubtedly there'll be someone who will consider this record of mine so biased, so self-serving, so ridiculous that there will be need for a scholarly, objective biography to set the record straight. Well, I wish him luck.

serve to stave off the evil day when I would have to make a harder decision. I therefore filled out the necessary blanks at school.

I did not, at that time, think that my application was anything more than a matter of going through the motions.

22

Convention Summer

1

I wrote two stories in June 1939. One was "Half-Breed," nine thousand words long, and the other was "Secret Sense." The first I gave to Pohl to peddle, feeling he ought to have a fair chance—but only on the provision he not submit it to Campbell. The other I took in to Campbell on June 21 (the first anniversary of my first visit to his office), and it was back in my hands in six days.

On the way out on that June 21 visit, however, I had a way of celebrating. I passed a pile of July 1939 *Astoundings*. It was due to reach the store the next day, but it had "Ad Astra" in it—the first story by Isaac Asimov ever to appear in *Astounding*—and it was more than human flesh and blood could endure to pass the pile and leave it untouched. That was me playing the Palace—so I helped myself to one issue, and discovered at once that Campbell had changed the title to "Trends."[1] It was a better title.

Although "Trends" was the second story I sold, it was the third to appear. Both earlier stories were, however, published in *Amazing* and, somehow, I find it difficult to count them. It was to Campbell I was always trying to sell my stories, and it was in *Astounding* that I always wanted them to appear, so that "Trends" always seems to me to be my first *significant* published story. This is rather ungrateful of me toward *Amazing*, but I can't help it.

The July 1939 issue of *Astounding* is sometimes considered by fans of the period to have marked the beginning of science fiction's "Golden Age," a period stretching through the 1940s. In that period, Campbell's views were in full force in the magazine, and the authors he trained and developed were writing with the full ardor of youth. In that period too, *Astounding* was just about the entire field. There was no competition to speak of in quality anywhere, inside or outside the magazines.

The fact that my first story for *Astounding* appeared in that issue is undoubtedly a minor factor in marking that as the first issue. What counted much more was the fact that the lead novelette in that issue was "Black Destroyer" by A. E. van Vogt, a first story by a new author

[1] See *The Early Asimov*.

who quickly became a reader favorite. In the next issue, August 1939, there was the first story, "Lifeline," of another new author, Robert A. Heinlein, who became the quintessence of all a "Campbell author" ought to be.

In time to come, Van Vogt, Heinlein, and I would be universally listed among the top authors of the Golden Age, but Van Vogt and Heinlein were that from the very beginning. Each blazed forth as a first-magnitude star at the moment his first story appeared, and that status never flagged throughout the remainder of the Golden Age. So it also was with some of the other authors.

I, on the other hand (and this is not modesty, for I have none), rose only little by little. I was virtually unnoticed for a while and came to be considered a major author by such gradual steps that despite the healthy helping of self-appreciation with which I was (and am) blessed, I myself was the last to notice.

I'm not sorry. It was more fun that way.

Incidentally, among those who liked "Trends" was a young man named Damon Knight, who is now a respected elder statesman in our field. I received a letter from him on June 26, and he asked for my autograph. He was the first person ever to ask for one, and I don't think he knows that—or will know it until he reads this book. I had forgotten it myself until I came to that page in my diary.

2

Almost immediately after the publication of "Trends," something even more exciting took place—a special kind of science-fiction meeting.

The idea was Sam Moskowitz's, the Sam Moskowitz who was one of those against whom the Futurians had revolted—a tall, round-faced, serious fellow, whose most noticeable characteristics were a loud voice and an encyclopedic knowledge of science fiction.

Most of the science-fiction clubs in the United States were made up of impoverished teen-agers. Sometimes, members from one club visited another city as guests of a club there, making the trip in jalopies or a bus. It occurred to Sam to organize a "World Convention" that *all* science-fiction fans from everywhere in the world (if they had the time and money) could attend.

"The First World Science Fiction Convention" took place on Sunday, July 2, 1939, in a hall on Fifty-ninth Street between Park Avenue and Madison Avenue. I had heard about the planned convention from the Futurians who, of course, wanted to attend. Moskowitz, along with the others who were organizing the convention, felt, however, that the Futurians planned only to disrupt the convention, and it was their intention to exclude them and prevent them from entering.

I did not know whether this exclusion principle included me. At the time of the Futurian revolt, I was not yet a member, and Sam Moskowitz did not know me. He had seen me during my visit to the Queens Science Fiction League the month before, but I had been there as a writer and I was anything but a disruptive influence.

Still, solidarity was solidarity, and it was my intention to stay with the Futurians. I arrived at 10:00 A.M. and found them in an Automat across the street from the meeting house. All were present but Fred Pohl, who was late because of some dental problems.

Finally, we decided to make the attempt, crossed the street, walked up the steps, and there facing us was the burly Sam Moskowitz (whom to this day I wouldn't dream of crossing, and with whom I have been good friends for a long time) and a number of cohorts.

It was useless to try to fight, really, and the Futurians turned and left and remained for the rest of the day across the street. I, however, continued walking up the steps, determined to adopt the role of author rather than fan. No one tried to stop me. I just walked in.

For a moment I hesitated, feeling I ought to join my friends in exile—but I couldn't. The hall was full. I saw Campbell there and others whom I either knew or suspected to be persons of consequence, and I could not resist. I stayed at the convention (and I have suffered pangs of guilt over this ever since).

The morning was an informal session where everyone introduced themselves to each other. I met Frank R. Paul, the famous science-fiction illustrator, who was guest of honor. I also met such authors as Ross Rocklynne, Nelson S. Bond, Manly Wade Wellman, Harl Vincent, and John D. Clark.[2] There were well-known fans such as Forry Ackerman, Jack Darrow, and Milt Rothman. I met Mort Weisinger, the editor of *Thrilling Wonder Stories*, who had rejected everything of mine he had seen, but whom I had never met before.

Also present were people I had already met, such as Campbell, Hornig, de Camp, and Williamson.

At lunchtime I went out and joined the Futurians. They did not berate me for my treason. Rather, they considered me a spy in the enemy's camp, though what good it did them to have a spy, I couldn't say. I told them everything that had happened, then went back in.

[2] Some I met only that one time and never again. Some became lifelong friends. It's impossible to tell in advance how it will turn out.

Leslie Perri, which was the name under which Pohl's girlfriend worked as a writer and illustrator, went in with me.

In the afternoon we saw the motion picture *Metropolis,* a silent movie that had been made in 1926. I thought it was awful.

Afterward there were speeches by the various editors. Weisinger, as a part of his statement, said, "I didn't know you fellows were so sincere!" and that made *Time* magazine, which ran two columns on the convention in its next issue.

The various notables in the audience were introduced to the general membership, and at about 7:00 P.M. John Clark called out, "How about Asimov?"

There was shouting and I stood up in pleased confusion. I made my way toward the stage and I remember receiving a healthy shove forward by a grinning John Campbell as I passed.

Leslie Perri made gestures and faces at me as I passed, but I didn't know what she meant. Later, she told me with exasperation that she had meant I ought to make a stirring appeal on behalf of the Futurian exiles—but that had never occurred to me. I just blushed prettily, thanked the audience for their applause, and referred to myself in an agony of insincerity as the "worst science-fiction writer unlynched."

Shortly thereafter it was time for me to go home, and I left.

According to my diary, "I had a simply marvelous time."

The next Futurian meeting, on July 4, had many outsiders as guests, since there were a number still in town though the convention had ended. It was the chance for the exiles to have a microconvention of their own. I met David A. Kyle for the first time at that meeting.

3

I was almost out of my teens at this point but I had not yet had what might be called a "date." I had not formally taken a girl anywhere at my expense. There's no puzzle to this. I had no money, I had no time. I knew no girls.

Nevertheless, I was attracted to girls; I was not unconscious of their existence. One thing I *could* do was to write letters. I could always wangle the necessary stamps.

As a result of my letters to *Astounding,* I got an occasional letter from other readers, and when the letters came from girls, I always answered with particular interest. Correspondences arose with several of them from distant cities, including one girl named Mary Byers. The letters were perfectly pure, of course—on both sides—but I found it interesting just the same.

Then, on July 7, 1939, at about 1:00 P.M., the store phone rang and it was for me. I didn't get many phone calls, so my first reaction, when I answered, was one of apprehension. It turned out to be Miss Byers, who was visiting New York, was in a hotel room in Manhattan, and who said she would like to see me.

I was anxious to see her, and I said I would try, but I had no hope of being released from the store for this purpose. My mother, to be sure, was horrified, but my father, out of some obscure feeling (perhaps) that we-men-must-stick-together, was on my side. I went.

I spent an hour and a half with Miss Byers in her hotel room talking. We did nothing more, and, for my part, it never occurred to me that anything more was conceivable. I liked it, however. I said in my diary, "I would have liked to spend much more time with her." It wasn't quite a date in the usual meaning of the word, but it was the closest approach yet.

Afterward I received a letter from her saying that everything she had said to me was strictly confidential. I kept it so, and now I have no choice but to continue to do so, for I transferred nothing of what she said to my diary, and none of it remains in my memory.

4

The excitement of the convention lingered, but could not obscure the fact that July was a disastrous month. Even Pohl's intervention could not alter the continuing flood of rejections. I submitted two stories to Campbell and both were rejected, while *Amazing* also rejected one.

Then, quite unexpectedly, I had bad news from Columbia. On July 13, I got a letter informing me that my application for graduate work in chemistry was *turned down*. I had not conceived such a thing was possible.

The catch was that I had not fulfilled my undergraduate requirements. As a premed student with a chemistry major, all I needed was inorganic chemistry, qualitative analysis, quantitative analysis, and organic chemistry. All these I had had and in all these I had done quite well. As an undergraduate student aiming for graduate work in chemistry, however, I needed all those courses *plus* physical chemistry. Since I hadn't taken physical chemistry, I was out.

I went to Columbia the next day to see Professor Mary Caldwell, the graduate adviser. She was a sweet and gentle person who suggested that I might take a regular graduate course, including physical chemistry, but without credit. Then, if I did well enough, the school might let me enter, retroactively, so to speak, and give me credit for what I had already taken.

It was a gamble, of course. It would mean that if I didn't do well enough to suit the department, I could just be kicked out without credit and all my time and tuition would be wasted. I favored taking the gamble, but my father, unusually cautious on my behalf (perhaps my failure at medical school had cured him of expecting too much of me), suggested that I spend a year simply on physical chemistry and then apply again.

I decided to let the decision rest till September when the time came to register.

5

If July were bad, August was worse.

Two months had passed since the third version of "Pilgrimage" had been rejected. Campbell had told me to wait several months, and two months might be called "several."

I got to work, therefore, on a fourth version on August 1, and by this time the story, which got longer with each revision, was 18,000 words long. It was done in a week, and I took it in to Campbell on August 8. This time Campbell hesitated over it for an entire month, and I eventually found out why. He was waiting for a story by Robert Heinlein. He had to know what it would be like before he could make a decision.

Heinlein's story was a short novel entitled *If This Goes On*—and it had a religious theme. "Pilgrimage" also had a religious theme, which had been inserted in an earlier version at Campbell's suggestion. Campbell felt he could not use two stories in rapid succession each with a religious theme. When Heinlein's story came in, it proved a good one, and "Pilgrimage" therefore came back on September 6, and this time it was rejected permanently. Nor did Campbell give me a song and dance; he explained exactly why he had rejected it.

I didn't blame Campbell. I accepted the fact that Heinlein was a better writer than I was and I could scarcely expect an editor who could only use one story to accept the worse and reject the better—but it didn't make me happy.

As though it weren't enough that my writing was at low ebb and that I had added failure at graduate school to failure at medical school, there was catastrophe in the great world outside. All summer long, Europe had been going through a mounting crisis over Hitler's designs on Danzig and Poland. I spent hours every day listening to the latest bulletins on the radio (and recording them in my diary), alternating in dread of another bloodless victory for Hitler, and in dread of another world war.

And, of course, as we all know, Hitler sent his army into Poland on September 1, 1939, and World War II began.

As of that fateful September 1, I had, in fifteen months, written seventeen stories, sold four, and had three published. It was now over half a year since I had made a sale, and Pohl gave up on me. His labors had netted exactly nothing for me, and therefore for him, and he ceased as my agent. It was a completely friendly separation—no hard feelings at all.

And then, on September 2, in between all the war bulletins, I got word of a sale at last. It was only to *Science Fiction,* so it was only $.005 a word, and payment on publication, so heaven only knew when I'd get the money. I still hadn't been paid for "Ring Around the Sun," and that had been bought in February.

It didn't matter, however. A sale was a sale. I needed the psychological lift, all the more so since the early news of the war was of steady German victories. The story they bought, by the way, was "Ammonium," one of my worst, in my own opinion.

The progress of the war made it almost impossible for me to write. I spent too much time with my ear against the radio and my heart in my boots. I managed to write an eighteenth story, "The Brothers," but it was rejected all around, even by the most piddling magazines. And then for three more months, I wrote nothing at all, the longest hiatus since my first visit to Campbell a year and a quarter before.

It was not only the war that occupied my thoughts; it was also the developments at Columbia.

23

Entering Graduate School

1

Toward the end of September, I was going to have to register if I intended to do graduate work, and on Monday, September 25, 1939, I spent some time at Columbia getting the details. I had decided that my father's idea was perhaps the practical route. I would take just physical chemistry (3 points), plus the attendant laboratory course if I had to (2 more points). The cost would come to $67.50 for the semester, and I would be able to swing that—and lose it, if needs must.

The next day, the twenty-sixth, I went down to register. I waited two hours to get into the chemistry office in order to fill out the forms. Dr. Caldwell was there, and with her was Professor Harold Clayton Urey, a Nobel laureate, the head of the department, and, of course, its most eminent member.

I gave him my name. He shuffled the papers and said, "What are you doing here? You're not accepted into graduate school."

I explained that I needed physical chemistry to meet the requirements and that I wanted permission to take that alone. He snapped at me, "Take it in Extension," and motioned me out.

I left gloomily. Sitting on the bench outside was a man in his late twenties, with an oval face and a high forehead, waiting his turn. (His name, I later discovered, was Lloyd Roth.)

"What happened?" he said, surprised at my short stay.

"I got kicked out," I said.

"What are you going to do?"

"Figure out something and come back."

I studied the Graduate School bulletin and discovered that there was something called an "unclassified graduate student" defined as "one with a bachelor's degree but without all the prerequisites." It went on to say that "normally" he would be allowed full graduate standing as soon as he filled out all the prerequisites.

Very well. I had to go home now, but the next day I planned to go back, demand to be made an "unclassified graduate student" and, if they refused, demand to know the grounds.

I was back the next morning and walked in when it was my turn.

Urey looked up and scowled. "What are you doing here, Asimov?" he said gruffly. "We sent you away yesterday."

I said, working up what courage I could muster, "I've come back to register as an unclassified graduate student."

"What!" he said, looking surprised.

I showed him the passage in the bulletin. "I've got the marks," I said. "I've got my bachelor's degree. I'm willing to take the missing prerequisite at my own risk. I've got the money to pay for it." (My father had given me a blank check.) "On what grounds would you exclude me?"

Urey thought a while and said that the department's decision was against me, that's all. However, if it would satisfy me, he would put up to the entire committee the specific question as to whether I could take physical chemistry only. I was to come back at 4:00 P.M.

I left, quite in despair, for I felt that was just Urey's way of shifting responsibility. The committee wouldn't go against him, and if they refused to give a reason, how could I force them to?

Lloyd Roth was, by coincidence, outside again.

"What happened?" he said.

"I got kicked out again."

"What are you going to do?"

"Figure out something and come back."

I made the rounds of various professors, who were sympathetic, but unanimous in their profession of helplessness. One was a Professor Crist, who said there was no hope and that I had better apply for graduate work at New York University or Brooklyn Polytechnic Institute. He explained that the requirements had been changed this year and that I would have had no trouble last year.

I shook my head and said that I was being excluded on a technicality and that I would not give up on Columbia unless bodily thrown out. And then I muttered, "I miss everything by one year."

I don't know what the devil I could have meant by that. If anything, I gained by one year. One year later and I wouldn't have made it into the United States; one year sooner and Campbell would not have been editor when I submitted my first story to *Astounding*. It was just an exclamation of silly self-pity, but it seemed to affect Crist.

Nor do I know what made me so stubborn about Columbia. I had been there four years and they hadn't treated me so well that I should want to stay. For my purposes, New York University or Brooklyn Poly would have done just as well. It was, perhaps, my failure to get into medical school. I was determined not to face my father with a second failure, and I dug in my heels.

I went down to the chemistry office at 4:00 P.M. and the committee was indeed meeting. There were Urey and Caldwell and three other members of the department, including Crist. I had not known that Crist was a member of the committee, and obviously that had to work in my favor, for I had inadvertently impressed him both by my determination and my pathos. I wish I could say that I had done this through shrewd and clever policy, but the fact is it was entirely accidental.

I felt I had Crist and Caldwell on my side. I would have to win one other—assuming they would dare vote against Urey, and I had given up on Urey.

One of the committee members said, "Aren't you a premed, Asimov?"

"I was," I said, "but chemistry has always been my choice in case I didn't get into medical school. I didn't try very hard to get into medical school; I only applied to five places."

"And if you take graduate chemistry courses, is that just a way of marking time till you apply for medical school again?"

(Aha, that was what they were holding against me.)

I said, as firmly and as bluntly as I could, "No, sir. I'm in chemistry permanently."

(That was a white lie. I suspected I would have to apply to medical school again to satisfy my father, but I had no doubt that I would be rejected again. I was quite positive it was chemistry for good.)

There was a bit more quizzing and then I was sent out while they considered my case. I think that by now Lloyd Roth was haunting the place just to see what happened to me.

"What happened?" he said.

"They're thinking."

"What happens if they decide against you?"

"Figure out something and come back."

(Actually, I was running out of hope, but I had to keep up my spirits somehow. Roth sat down to wait with me.)

I was called in and Urey said, "All right, Asimov, we're giving you your chance."

Then he explained the terms. It was rather like Dr. Caldwell's suggestion of two months before, and I suspect it was she who had pushed for it.

The terms weren't easy. I wouldn't be allowed to take physical chemistry alone; nor could I fill the term out with peripheral courses, spending money but marking time and allowing myself to concentrate on the essential topic. I would have to take a full collection of graduate courses, along with physical chemistry, and with every course but physical chemistry having physical chemistry as a prerequisite. That meant that all my professors in the other courses would lecture on the assumption that the students (including myself) already knew physical chemistry.

Furthermore, I would be on probation only, and if, at the end of the year, I was not up to snuff, I would be kicked out *without* credits. In other words, if I then wanted to apply to another school to continue graduate work, I would have to start all over, for Columbia would not provide the necessary transcript to show that I had taken certain graduate courses and completed them satisfactorily.

What is more, by "up to snuff" they did not mean merely passing my courses. I would have to maintain a *B* average.

"Now, what about it, Asimov?" said Urey.

Looking back on it, I am quite sure that they deliberately presented me with an impossible hurdle in order to have me back down and get rid of me that way. As it happened, though, I cared nothing for conditions. My aim at the moment was to get in and wipe out the medical school failure. If there were difficulties afterward, that would be—afterward.

"I'll do it, sir," I said. "The conditions are fair and I thank you for the chance." (If I were going to do it, I might as well do it with style.)

I came out and Lloyd Roth was waiting.

"What happened?" he said.

"I'm in," I said.

In later years, Roth told me he dined out on that story for months.

On Thursday, September 28, I registered—as a graduate student on probation. I began my fifth year at Columbia and was *still* a second-class citizen there—first Seth Low, then university undergraduate, now probation.

Attending Columbia on the graduate level was different, in some ways, from the situation in my undergraduate years. I was now confined almost entirely to a single building, Havemeyer Hall, and its annex, Chandler. In a smaller volume of space and with a smaller student body involved, I grew to know my peers a little better. There was some camaraderie—but only some.

I was still commuting, after all. I still saw my fellow students only *in* class. There was no social interaction.

Columbia was still nothing more than high school had been to me. In fact, simply because never in my school career had I ever lived on campus and because never had school been a social as well as an educational unit, I lost the major chance of intimate relationship with people of my own age level on a large scale.

Without my even being aware of it, this threw me steadily on my own resources and prepared me for the nature of my career.

2

My friendship with Sidney had not ended. On June 29, for instance, he and I had gone to the World's Fair together. It had opened shortly before with its Trylon and Perisphere, and with its General Motors exhibit, which showed clover-leaved highways that seemed like science fiction then and are so taken for granted now.

On September 30 he visited my home, and we were almost on equal terms again, he in medical school and I in graduate school. He brought his microscope and I spent some pleasant moments looking through it at slides he had also brought.

The microscope had cost him $160, and his books were expensive, too; one of them—just one—cost $18. Add to that $610 in tuition fees and it struck me quite forcibly that I had had a narrow escape. If I had gotten into medical school there would have been no way in the world I could have met the expenses.

3

One of my courses, by the way, was synthetic organic chemistry, which was taught by Professor Robert C. Elderfield, thirty-five years old at the time. A brilliant chemist and a good lecturer, he brought out the worst in me, nevertheless.

One of my chief difficulties in life is an overproficiency at the game of verbal lunge-and-riposte. I'm quick with a cutting answer and short on judgment. All through school it had caused me problems. It did nothing to endear me to my fellows, and, on occasion, it exasperated my teachers.

With most teachers it wasn't too bad (although I'd been kicked out of class for impertinence as late as my sophomore year in college), but every once in a while I would get a teacher who baited his students. It's not a very sporting thing for a teacher to do since the students are in a bad position and must suffer more or less in silence lest their marks suffer. And that would have been exactly what I would have done if I had known how.

Elderfield was a baiter, and the first time he baited me, I responded in kind, and at once. I don't remember the actual give-and-take, but from then on, Elderfield marked me as his quarry and no lecture passed without an exchange between us. It wasn't that I didn't have my full share of cowardice, or that I didn't understand my own peculiarly shaky position as a probationary student. It was just that, given my choice between saving my career and answering back, I answered back every time. That sort of thing always made trouble for me.

The lectures in synthetic organic were, however, only a minor adjunct to the laboratory course connected with it. That laboratory, together with physical chemistry, which I was desperately trying to understand, took up most of my time.

On October 7, 1939, I took the first half of a general test of knowledge in various fields, one that lasted two hours and twenty minutes. On October 14, I took the second half. I thought of it at the time as an "intelligence test." Whether it was or not, I don't know.

On December 9, we were given the results. This is the first test of this sort to which I was given the results. I recorded them and here they are:

Subject	Chemists' Norm	My Mark
Mathematics	570	610
Physics	580	580
Chemistry	640	640
Biology	550	710
History	440	650
Literature	420	590
Fine Arts	450	490
Verbal Factors	460	690
Overall Average	514	620

In each of the eight parts, 500 counted as the overall norm for college graduates. In addition, there were norms given for specialists in each of the eight parts.

I was not below the chemists' average in any field, though only at the average in physics and chemistry. In biology, I was well over even the biologists' norm, which was 640, and in history I was equally far above the historians' norm, which was 580.

I chafed considerably at all this. If I were such an all-around bright fellow, why could I not get into medical school and why, then, was I on probation as a graduate student?

Looking back on it, it seems quite obvious to me that the blame rested on my wise-guy personality, which offended people and made them undervalue my brightness. Unfortunately, I did not see this at the time.

4

Getting into graduate school did not change the downward trend in other directions. Two stories were rejected in October 1939. Campbell rejected "The Brothers" and *Amazing* rejected "Stowaway," which I had rewritten slightly and retitled "Magnetic Death."

And as though it weren't sufficient that I had no writing money coming in, NYA turned me down for a job. It was the first time they had done so since I had entered college.

By the time October 21, 1939, rolled around, I could, if I wished, celebrate the first anniversary of my first sale, but I didn't wish. Since that sale I had received two additional checks, the last nearly nine months before—and school bills were piling up.

Salvation came from an unexpected quarter, and Pohl's stint as my agent paid off. To be sure, he had sold not one of my stories, but he had on occasion spoken of the possibility that he might edit *Marvel* or some brand-new magazine. I had listened politely but hadn't believed him.

Yet at 9:00 P.M. on October 27, 1939, he suddenly showed up at my apartment, soaked in the rain he had walked through, and said, "What will you take for 'Half-Breed'?"

"Half-Breed" had been written in early June and had been rejected by *Amazing*. I had then submitted it to Campbell, who had been interested, but who had rejected it on the grounds that the readers would not like it because I pictured another species (the Martian-Earthling half-breeds of the title) as superior to human beings. What he really meant was that *he* did not like it for that reason. He always fobbed his own prejudices off on his readers; I had begun to gather that about Campbell.

I stared at Pohl in stunned wonder and he explained. He was indeed going to be editor of a new magazine. He had not yet decided on a name (eventually it was called *Astonishing Stories*), but he needed stories quickly for the first issue. He had handled "Half-Breed," knew it well, and didn't mind having another species superior to human beings. The magazine would only pay $.005 a word, but it would pay on acceptance, and since "Half-Breed" was nine thousand words long, that would mean $45.

Naturally, I accepted this with great glee, and on October 31, I visited him at his new office on East Forty-second Street. He was working on a very small salary, but he was delighted at being an editor, and I was delighted at having him be one. Even when he talked of cutting "Half-Breed" and tightening it up, I managed to work up a hollow smile, though it would have meant cutting the payment accordingly.

On November 8, he came to the house again, and this time he brought the check for the full $45; there had been no cuts after all. He also brought the glad news that there would be a second magazine, *Super Science Stories*, which he would also edit. Both would be bimonthlies but would come out in alternate months, so that the effect would be a two-named monthly. (And each magazine was to sell at the price of $.10.)

Though Pohl might be a good friend, he wasn't an automatic market. I visited his office again the next day and he handed back "Pilgrimage" with the comment that the ending was weak. I handed him the various other stories, which he knew well, and asked him to reread them. On November 16 he told me he would take "Stowaway" and I received a check for $32.50 on the twenty-eighth.

Financially, it wasn't much, only $77.50 for the two sales, but psychologically it was what I badly needed. They were two sales after a long dry spell. To be sure, they were to a personal friend, but I already knew that personal friendship cut no ice in the hard and competitive world of magazine publishing, and Pohl had rejected several of my stories.

5

At about this time I was facing an ethical problem, one that I had been dreading since the interview that had led to my provisional acceptance into graduate school.

I had said then, to the assembled committee, that I was in chemistry permanently. On the other hand, my father fully expected me to apply to medical school again, and I shrank from offending him.

I went to see the premed adviser of the year before and put the situation before him frankly. He looked grave and finally suggested I apply. It was my intention to ignore Columbia and Cornell as automatic rejectors in any case and to apply only to the three schools who had at least interviewed me in my first round: New York University, Long Island University, and Flower. The adviser suggested I apply to one out-of-town school as well and, much against my will, I added the University of Virginia to my list.

Before the end of November, the four applications went out and my father was very pleased. I didn't dare think of what might happen if any one of the med schools accepted me. It was not only that I might find myself in a career which, by that time, I knew perfectly well I detested, but also that I would prove myself a liar to the committee. And if I were accepted in medical school and refused to go, my father would neither understand nor forgive.

The only things I could hope for were rejections all around, which would quiet my father, make an at least technically honest man of me, and save me for chemistry, which I now viewed as my profession. For the next few months I lived under the sword of Damocles.

24

Irene

After seven years in classes containing nothing but boys, (and, in college, a very occasional older woman sitting in as part of her Extension work), I suddenly found myself at the desk next to a very pretty blond young woman, just turning twenty-one. Her name was Irene.

I saw her for the first time on October 4, 1939, and felt myself attracted. As the weeks passed, the attraction grew stronger. It turned out that she was not only very attractive, but also, in chemistry at least, the brightest student in the class, and that meant she was a brighter chemist than I was.

Fortunately, that didn't bother me. Rather, I found it made me admire her the more. I did not feel unmanned when I turned to her for advice on some knotty point in physical chemistry, nor when she explained something I had been unable to see for myself. (Of course, it did help a *little* that I was brighter than she was in every scholastic field *but* chemistry.)

The crucial moment came on December 6, 1939, when she had obtained a good yield of a desired compound in a separatory funnel (a conically shaped glass vessel), which she suspended in an iron ring just a trifle too large for it. She said, "That's a nice yellow color; I must have a good yield."

With my usual ineptitude in the laboratory, there was no chance of my getting an equally good yield, so I lifted the separatory funnel, held it to the light, and admired it enviously. Then I put it in the ring and it went right through, hit the desk, and shattered.

Strictly speaking, it was not my fault. She had selected the ring. Nevertheless, who had asked me to lift the separatory funnel?

I rushed out to buy a new separatory funnel for her (it cost $1.60), but there was no way of replacing the yield. She would have to start the chemical procedure all over. I couldn't apologize enough, but she shook her head, said it was her fault, and quietly began again.

That was it. I decided I was in love.

The time was to come one day when I would be perfectly at ease with women; when I could laugh, joke, leer, and, in general, do, without trouble, whatever it seemed appropriate to do. That "one day," however, was not to come for a good long time.

For Irene, I could do nothing but languish. I took to sitting next to her in the various lectures we shared, particularly physical chemistry. I would lie in wait for her, sit in the library with her, dog her footsteps, and try to ingratiate myself. She was a kind of new Sidney Cohen, but a kind who was infinitely to be preferred.

She was, of course, perfectly aware of my mooning about after her, but she didn't mind it too much as long as I didn't make it too uncomfortable for her—and I didn't. She was, throughout our friendship, perfectly proper in her behavior and never encouraged me to take liberties —and I never did. She also took care never to hurt my feelings or abash me, and I'm very grateful to her for that.

When December 12 turned out to be unseasonably mild, I suggested a walk along the Hudson River, and she agreed, so we walked for an hour or so till the next class. At least she walked; I skipped, or my heart did, at any rate.

When Christmas vacation came, we separated for two weeks—and shook hands. She gave me her address, however. I asked for it for a particular purpose, for I wrote her a letter, asking her to meet me on January 2. That would be my twentieth birthday, but that was not the point. It would also be a day when we would have the afternoon off, and I planned a date.

Irene answered very kindly and properly and the meeting actually took place. I did everything I thought ought to be done. I brought a box of candy, which she accepted. We ate at a neighborhood cafeteria (something we had done on occasion before), and then I took her to Radio City Music Hall to see *The Hunchback of Notre Dame*. We stopped for pie and cocoa afterward, and it was over.

It was all very prim, but I had planned it and I had paid, and this, on my twentieth birthday, was my very first date. I considered it so at the time, and ever since.

2

Thanks to Fred Pohl, my science-fiction career was taking on new life. On December 23, 1939, the first issue of *Astonishing* reached the store and it contained "Half-Breed."[1] It was the fourth science-fiction magazine to contain a story of mine. It was the longest story of mine to be printed up to that time and was listed in the Table of Contents as a novelette.

[1] See *The Early Asimov*.

Much more than that, my name was on the cover of a magazine for the first time. It was modestly placed. Of the three names on the cover, mine was the least prominent.[2] Still, there it was in the lower right-hand corner, and I was infinitely pleased.

My father saved a copy to give to an old friend, for the next day, quite by coincidence, there was a visit from a Mr. and Mrs. Boris Revsin. He had been on the ship with us, coming over, and his father had worked for my grandfather Aaron. He was the one remaining link (other than Uncle Joe, of course) with the days in Russia that were now seventeen years in the past.

He was a feeble link indeed, for his heart was bad, so bad that he had to stay in the store, being unable to climb the flight of stairs to the apartment. Indeed, he and my father, from what I could overhear, spent their time swapping heart stories.

I also gave a copy of the magazine to Sidney Cohen when he next visited (we had been swapping visits regularly since we had separated the previous May). What's more, on January 3, 1940, I received a letter from a reader praising "Half-Breed" highly and demanding a sequel. It was the first sequel request I had ever received.

So 1939, my second year as a professional writer, ended on an upbeat note as it had begun, with a long desert in between. Nevertheless, I had received four checks, totaling $210.50, better than three times what I had earned in my first year and enough to pay over half my tuition.

3

Nor was "Half-Breed" the only sign of renewed motion on the writing front.

Since October 2, I had written no stories. Ten dry weeks had passed, with nothing but some desultory attempts at a tale concerning the induction of Earth into a Galactic Federation, once our planet had worked out space flight. I called it "Homo Sol."

It was desultory because my mooning over Irene, my concern over my schoolwork (which was not going remarkably well and over which hung the possible abrupt cessation of my probation if my marks weren't good enough), and the desolate news abroad (Poland was gone, Finland was under attack by the Soviet Union, and the Western

[2] The other two were Polton Cross and Frederic Arnold Kummer, each of them far better known than I in those days, though both faded out of the science-fiction scene in the 1940s.

powers maintained a static front in what was called the Phony War)
all kept me from my typewriter.

My frequent visits to Pohl, however, stirred up guilt feelings within
me over my neglect of Campbell. I visited him on December 20, 1939,
and spent 2½ hours with him. I told him about "Homo Sol" and he
liked the idea. I had never seen him display quite such enthusiasm over
any of my suggestions. We discussed it in detail and I went home in a
state of eager turmoil.

What I didn't completely understand at the time was that I had
inadvertently pushed one of his buttons. He was a devout believer in
the inequality of man and felt that the inequality could be detected by
outer signs such as skin and hair coloring. Though he treated all men
kindly and decently in his personal life, and although in his treatment
of me, for instance, I never detected any trace of anti-Semitic feelings,
the fact is that, in theory, he felt that people of northwestern European
extraction were the best human beings.

In science fiction, this translated itself into the Campbellesque thesis that Earthmen (all of whom, in the ideal Campbell story, resembled
people of northwestern European extraction) were superior to all other
intelligent races—even when the others *seemed* more intelligent on the
surface. It was because I broke this rule that he rejected "Half-Breed."
It was because he saw an opportunity to demonstrate this rule that he
was interested in "Homo Sol."

He did not quite explain this rule to me, and at that time I didn't
thoroughly understand it and had no conscious intention of applying it.
Nevertheless, when I got home I tore up the few pages I had done of
"Homo Sol" and began all over again. By the end of the year, it was
done.

On January 4, 1940, I visited him and submitted the story.

On that occasion, I met no fewer than three authors for the first
time, all of whom were to be closely associated with Campbell in the
decade just beginning.

One was Theodore Sturgeon, who had published two stories thus
far, "Ether Breather" in the September 1939 *Astounding*, and "A God
in a Garden" in the October 1939 *Unknown*. He was a mild, blond
fellow with a thin, elfin face and soft blue eyes. He was a few years
older than I was, but had gotten a later start.

Then there was L. Ron Hubbard, a well-established pulp writer
whose first story in *Astounding* had been "The Dangerous Dimension"
in the July 1938 issue, and whose two *Unknown* lead novels, "The Ultimate Adventure" in the April 1939 issue and "Slaves of Sleep" in the

July 1939 issue, I had enjoyed tremendously. He was a large-jawed, red-haired, big and expansive fellow who surprised me. His heroes tended to be frightened little men who rose to meet emergencies, and somehow I had expected Hubbard to be the same.

"You don't look at all like your stories," I said.

"Why? How are my stories?" he asked.

"Oh they're *great*," I said, enthusiastically and all present laughed while I blushed and tried to explain that if the stories were great and he was not like his stories, I didn't mean he was *not* great.

Finally there was Willy Ley, who had already published several nonfiction articles on rocketry in the magazine. He spoke with a thick German accent, which was, in itself, not calculated to endear him to me at the time, but he had left Germany as soon as Hitler had come into power and was a dedicated anti-Nazi. Besides, there was something lovable about him—a kind of intense but unpretentious rationality that I found absolutely irresistible.

Over "Homo Sol" there began a struggle between Campbell and myself, though, of course, I didn't understand its nature. Campbell was intent on making me stress the superiority of human beings without actually telling me this was what he wanted. I, on the other hand, never thought it was necessary to make human beings superior (in fact, considering what the world of 1940 was like I thought human beings were bound to be outclassed by the average extraterrestrial intelligence), so, of course, I missed the point. It was almost "Half-Breed" over again.

By January 16 he was still ruminating over it and I visited him to inquire. He handed it back and requested a rewrite. "More dialog," he said, and we talked over a few other points.

I rewrote and, on February 2, had the second version in his hands. On February 23 he asked for another revision, dealing with the last half only. What could I do? I agreed and the third version wasn't submitted till March 25. The three versions had taken me three months to do—not surprising, considering the tensions I was under at the time.

The strain of those months was relieved a little by the fact that on February 7, the March 1940 issue of *Future Fiction* (a sister magazine of *Science Fiction*) arrived, and in it, at last, was "Ring Around the Sun."[3] This introduced me to two economic facts of life about fringe magazines. First, when a story is paid for on publication, there is no hurry to publish. "Ring Around the Sun" was published exactly a year and three days after it was bought. Second, payment on publication easily translates to payment long after publication. I didn't get my check for $25 until May 3, and then only after I had written a letter to a magazine called *Writer's Digest* to ask what one ought to do about it.

[3] See *The Early Asimov.*

Anyway, I now had five published stories, and on February 22 the number jumped to six, when the April 1940 *Astonishing* appeared with "Stowaway." Pohl had, without consulting me or even telling me, changed its name to "The Callistan Menace."[4] In this he had done no worse than Campbell had done in the case of "Trends." Campbell's change I had thought for the better, Pohl's I thought to be for the worse.

On March 25, Pohl told me he would take "Robbie," and this was my eighth sale, and my third to him. He also requested a sequel to "Half-Breed." It was the first time any editor had ever requested a specific story from me.

He was, in fact, in an excellent humor, for his magazines seemed to be doing well and he had received a raise. So jubilant was he that he paid for my lunch—and I think that was the first time any editor had ever bought me lunch.

I picked up my check for $35 for "Robbie" when I visited Pohl on February 12, 1940.

Then, on April 12, I visited Campbell again after he had had the third version of "Homo Sol" for over two weeks. I talked about other things for a while, cravenly staying away from the real point of interest, until he finally said, "Oh yes, your story? You haven't got it yet?"

My heart sank. Was this to be another "Pilgrimage"—three strikes and out? I remained abashed and mute and he said, "It's up in the accounting room now."

The "it" he was asking me if I had yet got was the check and not the story. He had bought it—my second sale to Campbell in nearly two years of trying. It came just in time, too, for it just covered what I still owed on my tuition in that first year of graduate work.

The clearest thing I remember about that check is an incident that took place that evening in the candy store. I had placed the check on the cash register, so that my father could deposit it when he next went to the bank (after I had endorsed it over to him, of course), and I was engaged in dealing out cigarettes, collecting payment, making change, and so on, as I had done every night for eleven years now.

One customer took offense at my neglecting to say "Thank you" as I made the change—a crime I frequently committed because, very often, I was working without conscious attention but was concentrating deeply on the plot permutations that were sounding hollowly within the cavern of my skull.

The customer decided to scold me for my obvious inattention and for my apparent lack of industry.

[4] See *The Early Asimov*.

"My son," he said, "made fifty dollars through hard work last week. What do you do to earn a living besides standing here?"

"I write," I said. "And I got this for a story today," and I held up the check for him to see.

It was a very satisfactory moment.

4

During January of 1940, I was deeply concerned as to my future. The first semester of graduate school was coming to an end, and I did not know what my marks would be, nor how they would be viewed by the committee. I was only an average student at the graduate level, since, for the most part, I was facing students who were true specialists in chemistry and were (a number of them) illiterate in every other field of intellectual endeavor. Concentrating everything into one narrow front, they could outpunch me there. I feared the worst and had to prepare fallback alternatives.

If I were kicked out of graduate school and were *then* accepted by a medical school, would a medical career be bearable? I didn't have to come to that decision, really. On January 31 I had an interview with a New York University School of Medicine official, just ten days short of a year after the first one. It went better, I thought, but I came out convinced they weren't interested—and I was right. In the end, everybody rejected me all around for the second time—with the University of Virginia Medical School leading the bunch. The medical school alternative was finally and forever washed out.

I was desperate enough to adopt an even more miserable (potential) option. I actually sent off an application to a *dental* school. In the Jewish immigrant tradition, a dentist was a failed physician. Since both used the title "doctor," the joke went that a suspicious Jewish mother would ask a prospective suitor, "Pardon me, are you a dentist doctor or a doctor doctor?" Getting into dental school would undoubtedly have humiliated my father and reduced me to quivering dementia, but there was nothing to worry about; nothing came of that, either.

And then, just to scrape bottom, I even applied for a civil-service job as a chemist. And that came to nothing.

While all these options were coming to nothing, however, I took my final examinations and on February 3, 1940, got my grades.

In Physical Chemistry, I got an A. That was the great news. It was the lack of physical chemistry that had put my status in doubt, and there were only three students out of over sixty who got straight A's and I was one of them. (Irene was another, needless to say.) In advanced organic I got a *B+* and in synthetic organic (Elderfield's course), where laboratory performance was a major factor, I got a *C*. In my three chemistry courses I clearly maintained a *B* average, and that *A* in physical chemistry had to be impressive.

That left only my one physics course in doubt. I had never taken college physics and at the graduate level it was simply incomprehensible. For one thing, it required more mathematics than I had in my armory. I feared failing, but my mark was *"m.u.,"* meaning I had to take a makeup examination. I could only hope that the committee would attach a great deal of importance to physical chemistry and very little importance to physics.

I had to sign up for the spring-semester courses, ordinarily a routine procedure, but at the moment, not so for me. I stepped into the chemistry office and, to my relief, Urey was not there. He would have been difficult to face. Instead I found Dr. Caldwell and Dr. George E. Kimball. The latter was one of my physical chemistry instructors.

There was no sign of any tendency to abort my studies. They calmly signed me up for courses for the spring semester, and I felt safe for the remainder of the school year.

In fact, it turned out better than that. My resolute acceptance of the work they had piled on me, and my showing in physical chemistry despite that, must have convinced the committee they had been mistaken in me.

On April 5, 1940, quite unexpectedly, and with myself having done nothing to spur it on, I received a letter from Columbia telling me that my probation was lifted and that I was a regular graduate student as of September 1939.

It was nearly five years (almost to the day) since my disappointing interview and my shift from Columbia College to Seth Low, and for the first time I was no longer second-class. I could, at last, look my classmates in the eye. Four days later, I flunked my physics makeup examination without even seriously trying. I handed in a blank book because it no longer mattered. I lost credit for it, of course, but with the probation lifted I refused to struggle hopelessly any longer in that particular direction.

5

One of my great worries during the January period of Damoclean suspense was that I would suddenly be cut off and would then never see Irene again. I used that as an argument for having another date, and on January 30, 1940, we went to see *The Grapes of Wrath*.

On February 9, I took her to lunch, and in the course of a long conversation she told me I was the "cleverest" fellow she had ever met. I hugged that to my bosom for months. It was not exactly a declaration of passion, but it had been a long time since I felt "cleverest," and I was glad that was her opinion on the subject. The same day we walked arm in arm and I felt myself to be drowning in happiness.

On February 22, in fact, when I took her to see *Pinocchio*, we actually held hands through part of the movie and then again when we went to the Hayden Planetarium afterward. (I think that was my first visit to the planetarium.) I considered that hand-holding to be vastly more important than the fact that "The Callistan Menace" appeared in print that day.

By April 2, I reached a pinnacle of a sort. We were on the back steps of the chemistry building, the part called "Chandler." She was holding her books, I holding mine. I thrust my books at her, saying, "I want to tie my shoelaces."

She took them in her other arm and, since she was momentarily unable to fend me off, I kissed her. It was the feeblest kiss you can imagine, contact being maintained for about a second and I caught only the corner of her lips, but it was the first time I had ever kissed a girl with libidinous intent and the effect was something like that of being sandbagged.

Irene maintained her composure. She handed back my books, said, "That was mean," and we continued walking.

On April 27, I made progress in another direction. Irene was walking down Broadway with me on the way to the cafeteria for lunch when she suddenly said, "If you really want to splurge, I know where we can get two luncheons at thirty-five cents each."

I said hollowly, "Money's no object."

She broke the rest of the bad news. "You'll have to tip the waiter a dime."

I stopped walking and stared at her. "Waiter? I've never been in a real restaurant. I'd be afraid."

"It's time you learned," she said, firmly, so I went to a tearoom with her and spent eighty cents and found out what it was like to be waited on by a waiter.

I found out in the course of that spring that she was dating four other young men as well (no, I didn't spy on her; she *told* me), and it occurred to me that probably none of them were afraid of restaurants and all of them had more money than I did. "Cleverness" was all I had going for me, and it wasn't enough.

But it was all coming to an end anyway. Whereas I was prepared to go to school forever, if need be, scraping up the necessary money on a hand-to-mouth basis, she was not. One year of graduate school was what she wanted, with a master's degree at the end, and a job—and by April, she already had the job. She had been interviewed by Hercules Powder in Wilmington, Delaware, and had been offered one, and she was going to take it.

That meant good-bye in a month or so. My spirits really dragged.

We had one last date, the best of all, on May 26. I met her at Penn Station at 12:35 P.M. and we took the subway to the World's Fair. We spent all afternoon and all evening there—an absolutely idyllic time for me, for we were away from school, away from the store, unreachable by anyone. For eleven hours I existed in a kind of carefree bubble with her, a bubble set in the never-never land of the Fair.

The only untoward thing that happened was that (at *my* suggestion) we took a roller-coaster ride. In my fantasy, I thought she would scream and hang on tightly to me and that I could (perhaps) kiss her when that happened.

I was in high good spirits over my fiendishly erotic plan as the car climbed slowly to the peak. As it passed that peak and began to drop, I turned to her—and discovered, for the first time in my life—that I had severe acrophobia. I was afraid of heights and went out of my mind at the sensation of falling.

How was I to know? I had never lived higher than one story up, and when in the upper stories of higher buildings, it never occurred to me to look out the windows straight down.

I clung desperately to Irene till the roller-coaster ride was over and by then I was half dead out of sheer agonized terror. As nearly as I could tell, Irene didn't mind it at all.

Then, on May 30, she visited the store and had dinner with the family and left—and that was it. The romance, which had lasted about half a year and that had, from beginning to end, been as nearly platonic as possible, with a quick peck on the corner of the lip as a high point, was over.

It took me a while to stop mooning about after Irene had left. Thinking back upon myself during that period of calf love aborted, I find it amusing—unless I actually read my diary, when it all becomes pitiful and exquisitely embarrassing.

It could have had no other end, though. We wouldn't have suited each other.

25

Growing Up

1

My course work went better in the second semester of graduate school after I had dropped that miserable course in physics. To be sure, physical chemistry laboratory was not exactly easy. As always, I was not deft.

At one time, I remember, I received a fairly low mark on one of my lab reports—one that dealt with the elevation of boiling points in solutions. I was not overly surprised at this, since my expectations in lab courses were never exuberantly high, but I thought I might as well see Professor Joseph Mayer, under whom I was taking the course, and attempt negotiation.

I took my paper with me and he went over it patiently. I was quite prepared to be told that I had done the experiment sloppily or that I had collected my data thoughtlessly. That wasn't it, however. Professor Mayer looked up at me and said:

"The trouble with you, Asimov, is that you can't write."

For a horrified moment, I stared at him. Then, no longer interested in negotiation, I gathered up the report and, before leaving, said to him, as stiffly and as haughtily as I could, "I'll thank you, Professor Mayer, not to repeat that slander to my publishers."

That was really a minor incident, however. I passed all my courses (only a B in the second semester of Physical Chemistry, but the pressure was off) and planned to go ahead for a second year. I was no longer planning for a master's degree only. With medical school finally a dead issue, I intended to go on for a Ph.D.

My absorption with school and with Irene helped insulate me just a little bit against the world's tragedy, which was deepening monthly. The spring of 1940 was a time of tremendous Nazi victories. Hitler took over Denmark and Norway in April; Holland, Belgium, and Luxembourg in May; and by the end of May was busy beating France and penning up the British Expeditionary Force in Dunkirk.

Irene's mind was sufficiently wrapped up in chemistry to make her impervious to such things. When Germany invaded Holland and Belgium on May 10, and I came into the library with the news, perturbed and unhappy, Irene said, "Isn't it terrible the way those countries behave?" and went on studying.

Most of us, however, talked over the war news every chance we got. The country was split into interventionists and isolationists, and so were the students. The Jewish students were interventionist, of course, and were breathless with horror over the Nazi victories. So were some of the Gentile students (the brighter ones, so it seemed to me).

Lloyd Roth (not Jewish, despite his last name) was one of the most voluble observers and one of the keenest, too, it seemed to me. We had been good friends ever since he had watched me bounce in and out of the committee room. Milton Silverman (he *was* Jewish) was another one with whom discussions were long and thorough.

As for the isolationists, I don't remember any of their names. We didn't speak. It seemed clear to me that even when the isolationists were able to bore single-mindedly through their books and do reasonably well in chemistry, they were stupid in every other field. I admit there's a chance I was prejudiced, however.

2

As for science fiction, I spent the spring of 1940 writing "Half-Breeds on Venus." It contained my first attempt at love interest, and the heroine was inevitably named Irene. It was not completed till June 1, 1940, and on June 3 I took it in to Pohl.

By that time, the July 1940 *Future Fiction* had arrived, with my story "Ammonium" in it. Its title had been changed to "Magnificent Possession"[1] and this one appeared only nine months after agreement to purchase. Again, "payment on publication" proved to be payment considerably after publication.

I didn't like "Magnificent Possession" when I read it in print. The nine-month wait had wiped out much of its memory, and it read as though some other writer (not a very good one) had written it. On my 0 to 5 star scale, I gave "Magnificent Possession" 1½ stars.

On June 14, I visited Pohl and he handed me a check for $62.50. This represented a payment of $0.00625 per word for "Half-Breeds on Venus"—which was the longest story I'd yet sold since it was all of 10,000 words long.

This was the occasion for a rather revolutionary development. On the next day, June 15, it was decided, for the first time, that the money I made writing belonged (at least in theory) to me. Until then I had

[1] See *The Early Asimov.*

handed all my checks to my father. It wasn't as unjust as it sounds, of course, since he paid my tuition, and the tuition came to more than the checks did.

Now, however, it began to look as though the checks would come in at a rate great enough to pay the tuition, so it was decided that I ought to have a savings account of my own. Then I could pay my own tuition and keep anything that was left over and, of course, if I ran dry, my father would pitch in.

On that day, therefore, I opened a savings account with $60 from Pohl's check, and I have had money in the bank ever since.

The fact that "Half-Breeds of Venus" was a sequel made the notion of writing sequels seem like a good idea. A sequel to a successful story must, after all, be a reasonably sure sale—or so I reasoned. Therefore, even while I was working on "Half-Breeds on Venus," I suggested to Campbell that I write a sequel to "Homo Sol."

Campbell's enthusiasm was moderate, but he was willing to look at such a sequel if I were to write it. I began it on June 3, just as soon as I was done with "Half-Breeds on Venus" and, since it was summer vacation and I had more time to sit at the typewriter, I completed it on June 11 and took it in to Campbell at once.

On June 19 it was back on my hands. Sequel or no sequel, Campbell rejected it. Of course, it was a sequel only in that I used the central character once again. The human-nonhuman confrontation was lacking, which probably didn't help it as far as Campbell was concerned.

3

One thing I could do to console myself for the loss of Irene was to grow a mustache. This, my first attempt at facial hair, was actually begun on May 16, 1940, and by the time a month had passed, it was long enough to require trimming at the barber's.

The mustache was a failure. Not that I lacked the hair for it; there was plenty of that. It was just that it had no distinctive color. Though my hair was brown, there is red hair and blond hair on my mother's side of the family, and in my facial hair I apparently got it all.

The mustache had red hair, blond hair, brown hair, and even a bit of black hair, so that its overall color was like nothing that had ever been invented. As far as I know, no one liked it. I couldn't even fall back on the traditional love of a mother for something no one else will accept, for she hated it more than anyone

I clung to it stubbornly, however, perhaps as a sign that I was very slowly growing up—only very slowly, however. Despite the fact that I was almost at my first graduate degree, I remained younger than my years in every respect but that of my intellect.

Nevertheless, I was beginning to slip the leash, to take tentative steps on my own.

I took Marcia to the World's Fair, for instance, on July 3, 1940; I was man of the family then, and the experienced guide who had been there before. We stayed till 7:00 P.M. when it started to rain lightly, and I thought that that might be a good time to call home and report.[2]

When I called, it turned out that Stanley (who was soon to turn eleven) was in the hospital. He had imperfectly climbed the picket fence about the school playing field and had gouged himself on one of the pickets. We raced home (or at least sat down while the subway raced), but it wasn't serious. The abdominal wall was intact and a few stitches saw him through.

The next day, in fact, I took Marcia on another venture in another direction. We went, by ourselves, to the Brighton Theater to see Clare Boothe's *Margin for Error*, and enjoyed it very much. I believe it was the first professional theatrical performance in English that I had ever seen. It was a matinee.

What counted for me, though, was a discovery I made after it was over. The Brighton Theater was nearly on Brooklyn's southern coastline on the Atlantic Ocean, and when I ventured a block or two south of the theater after coming out, I found myself staring, in awe, at the ocean. I had not seen the open ocean (as opposed to sections of the East River crossed by the subway or elevated lines, and those portions of the harbor surrounding the Statue of Liberty) since I was a very little boy.

It doesn't seem possible to live in Brooklyn and avoid the ocean, but I had managed. The various places in which I had lived in Brooklyn over the previous seventeen years had all been in the interior. It's hard to think of a place as small as Brooklyn having an interior, but from Windsor Place, Coney Island and the seashore was six miles due south, and I had no occasion to go that six miles.

But on that Independence Day of 1940, I found myself gazing at the sea with a wild surmise, rather like Balboa discovering the Pacific. I walked onto the beach with Marcia in tow, getting sand in my street shoes and approaching as close to the water line as I dared. I then investigated lockers.

2 My mother was never happy unless I reported in at crucial moments, and I've kept that habit all my life. It is a bad habit. It ties me to the phone, and if forgetfulness or circumstance get in the way, everyone is sure something terrible has happened.

The next day, after taking Stanley to a hospital for a checkup on the stitches (taxicabs both ways, I noted with awe in my diary), I prepared for the beach. I got shorts and sneakers and off I went. I invested 28 cents in a locker and spent 2½ hours on the sand.

Such decision, so rapidly and resolutely carried out, was something new for me and meant more in the way of adulthood than my approaching master's degree, or my lily-pure love affair, or even my mustache. I even spent about half an hour in the water. I couldn't swim but I moved out slowly, slowly, until I was up to my neck and then allowed myself to move up and down with the gentle swell.

Nor could I learn to swim thereafter. I simply could not, either then or since, manage to get my feet off the solid ground without terror. Provided someone stood near me, ready to save me, I could do the dead man's float, but I could never do more than that.[3]

I learned something else that day on the beach. Exposure to the sun turns me brick red. Mind you, this doesn't mean that I burn. Ten minutes' exposure will do it. I get so red, so violently crimson that everyone is convinced I have a third-degree burn, but I don't. There is no pain. (If I stayed out long enough, there would be, of course.) Then I gradually fade back to white. I may develop a very light tan en route, but nothing much.

Since I don't swim, and don't particularly want to look as though I had been dipped in red ink, my infatuation with the beach was a short-lived one, and I have foresworn it—but it served its bit of liberating service.

4

June and July were sad and upsetting months. I was in the throes of misery over having lost Irene; and overseas, France had been battered into subjection by the Nazis. (That seems to put things in the wrong order, but at the time, the personal loss seemed to outweigh the looming danger to the world.)

The discovery of the beach was not much of an alleviation, nor was a trip to the World's Fair with Fred Pohl on July 12. (I got into a show called Twenty Thousand Legs Under the Sea thanks to a press pass he had somehow wangled, and I saw female breasts deliberately—

[3] The fact is I'm a total failure in everything that requires skillful use of muscular co-ordination—well, almost everything. When Stanley got a bicycle at the age of eight and learned how to manipulate it almost at once, I tried, too. Don't ask for the disgraceful details. To this day I'm the only person I know who can't ride a bicycle.

and three-dimensionally—exposed for the first time in my life. I was relatively unmoved. They were, after all, behind a glass partition, and I wasn't so unsophisticated as to be unaware that if breasts are to be bared, you don't want them to be behind a glass partition.)

Pohl, of course, like the other Futurians, was always knocking about the countryside to visit out-of-town fans. He was going to Washington and (since he knew the reason for my woe) he urged me to come with him, telling me he would drop me off at Wilmington and then pick me up the next day.

That fired me, but I wanted to do it on my own. I had gone to the beach by myself; I would go to Wilmington by myself.

I went to Penn Station and got the necessary timetables so that I could plot out the logistics. I then stopped off at the offices of *Science Fiction* and badgered them for the check for "Magnificent Possession." I got it the next day, July 19, 1940, and that was what I needed. I deposited only part of it in the bank, holding out ten dollars for the projected trip.

It was to be a double-barreled trip, actually, for I planned to go to Philadelphia first to visit a fan with whom I had been corresponding, and then from there go to Wilmington (having made the arrangement with Irene, with whom I was also corresponding).

I left on Saturday, July 27, very early in the morning, and I was back on the evening of the next day. It was the first time I had ever left New York City entirely on my own and the first time I ever spent a night away from home (in a YMCA in Philadelphia).

Unfortunately, I chose uncomfortable days, for the temperature rose to over 100 on both Saturday and Sunday. I could not sleep at the Y, not for one moment. Then, when I finally got to Wilmington and met Irene, I found that Wilmington was *really* dead on Sunday. Even the movie houses were closed. Irene and I had to go to Philadelphia to see a movie, and then separated, she to return to Wilmington and I to New York.

The trip served an excellent purpose. Heaven only knows how long I would have luxuriated in despair if I hadn't been brought to Earth by reality. The fact was that it required absence to keep me pumped up to the necessary pitch of woeful inflation. The matter-of-fact presence of an unemotional Irene punctured the whole thing and I found to my surprise that the parting, so soon after the reunion, broke me up far less than the one on Memorial Day had done.

I had healed. I was in one piece and alive. What a relief!

This is not to say that I had sworn off women. Not by any means.

Rather, my half-year pursuit of Irene, whatever its fecklessness, had taught me just enough to make me less feckless.

But not more successful. I had too many handicaps to overcome and I did not overcome them. In the first place, I had no money; and if I couldn't spend money, and couldn't provide more than an occasional cafeteria or movie, I was scarcely a thrilling date. Then too, I lacked time, and having to cut everything to suit the candy-store schedule was a drag. What's more, I had no car, couldn't dance, lacked sophistication in every way, and wasn't even good-looking.

The result was that over the next year and a half, though I was frequently attracted to this girl or that, this girl or that was never attracted to me.

I had nothing but "cleverness" going for me, and although Irene found that interesting, the sad fact was that few other girls did; and, if they did, the bemusement lasted only a moment or two.

I remember once, for instance, sitting in a park, rather late, with a girl. We were playing a game that consisted of defining a phrase that consisted of two rhymed words and those rhymed words had to be guessed. Thus "a happy conveyance" could be a "jolly trolley," or a "merry ferry" or a "gay sleigh."

Finally the girl said, "I'll give you one that will stump you: 'Happy holiday, Your Holiness.'"

I thought for a minute or so in deep silence and then said, "*Gut yontiff*, Pontiff." (*Gut yontiff* is Yiddish for "good holiday," and of course the young lady was Jewish.)

She said, "Oh you *are* smart," and, in a fit of glee, threw her arms about me and kissed me. It was the first time I had ever been voluntarily kissed by a young woman without my having made any move in that direction—but nothing came of it. She regained her poise at once and that was that.

5

The summer of 1940 was not successful as far as my writing was concerned, either.

I was reading *Unknown* with a great deal of pleasure and I hungered to write for it, even though I felt that the writing level in that magazine was even higher than in *Astounding* and was therefore well beyond me.

I tried, though. I wrote a short story called "The Oak," in which an oak tree forecast the future by the rustling of its leaves. It was the first time I ever tried writing a fantasy, and it was terrible. I submitted it to Campbell on July 16 and got it back on my next visit. I never did sell it.

Then in the first half of August I went back to science fiction and wrote a 10,500-word story called "Twins." It dealt with two identical twins, one raised on Earth, one on Ganymede, and the manner in which their adventures on Mars turned their mutual contempt to mutual admiration.

Campbell didn't like that one either, but I didn't get it back till September 3, because in the interval, Campbell's wife, Doña (whose maiden name, Doña Stuart, was the source of Campbell's best-known pseudonym), had given birth to a daughter on August 29—their first child.

I wasn't exactly setting the world on fire in any direction.

When I submitted "Twins," on August 15, Campbell handed me a copy of the September 1940 *Astounding*, a few days earlier than it would have reached the stands. He didn't usually do that, but this was the issue in which "Homo Sol" appeared.[4] It was my eighth published article.

I read the story, of course, for my own stories always interest me. In doing so, I am always aware of any changes forced on me by editors that go against my natural predilection, and in this story those changes were particularly noticeable and particularly bothersome.

For instance, in the story I made certain distinctions between the emotional reactions of Africans and Asians as compared with those of Americans and Europeans. Campbell had suggested the passage rather forcefully and I had included it reluctantly, since I wanted to sell the story.

Then even after I had made a number of changes to please him, Campbell had, on his own hook, inserted several paragraphs that did not ring true in my ears. They were in his style, not in mine, and even if no one else could tell that, I could. What's more, they emphasized, with approval, Earthman's proficiency at warmaking.

It was August 1940, remember. Great Britain was standing alone against the victorious Nazis. Everyone was expecting a Nazi invasion attempt daily. I was in no mood to find racist and militaristic remarks in *my* stories, however mild and innocent they might seem.

After that, I did my best to wriggle out of such situations. When Campbell suggested bits of business here and there, either in preliminary discussions or during a request for revision, I would agree, but then if *I* disapproved, I would just forget to include it, or I would twist

[4] See *The Early Asimov.*

it into something I found inoffensive. I'm not sure I always succeeded, but I did almost all of the time certainly.

For one thing, I began omitting extraterrestrials from my stories so that I would not always be forced to make human beings their superiors and set off what I considered an unfortunate analogy with situations on Earth. For another, I began to lean toward robot stories, since I didn't mind making human beings superior to robots.

In a way, then, my unhappiness over "Homo Sol" paved the way for my two most popular groups of science-fiction stories.

The appearance of "Homo Sol" did not change my luck with Campbell, however. In the euphoria that followed the appearance of the story in one of the very best issues of *Astounding* the Golden Age was to produce (it had the first installment of Van Vogt's "Slan" and it also had Heinlein's classic "Blowups Happen"), I began work on another story, "History."

I wrote it during the first two weeks of September, which was precisely the period during which the great Blitz on London began. For night after night as I wrote, London was bombed, blasted, and burned, and there seemed no way in which it could endure. Great Britain would have to give in, it seemed. Certainly I could see no hope for her.

Yet, apparently, I still clung to a certainty that Hitler would be defeated. In "History," I made a brief reference to the fact that he died on Madagascar (presumably in exile, as was the case with Napoleon and Kaiser Wilhelm II).

Campbell rejected "History," but once again, Fred Pohl came through. On September 4, he had accepted "Twins" (asking for some revisions, which I made), and on October 11 he accepted "History." The two stories, together, netted me $85.

By the end of October, I had written twenty-four stories and had sold twelve. It sounds good, but only two of the sales had been to Campbell, which, somehow, were the only sales I counted. Despite all my sessions with him, all his patient advice, all his helpful suggestions, I had produced only two out of twenty-four stories that met his standards.

It was depressing, and I was depressed. I had been writing and trying to publish for nearly 2½ years now and there was no sign at all that I would ever be anything more than a minor science-fiction writer, making at best a few hundred dollars a year for as long as I had the persistence to continue trying and trying and trying.

But Campbell hadn't given up hope. He still willingly devoted time to me; he still willingly discussed stories with me. And if he had not abandoned me as hopeless, why should I despair? So I continued to try.

6

Futurian meetings continued to be held, but many of the Futurians had moved into a kind of community apartment they called "The Ivory Tower." It was about an hour's walk from the candy store and I would, on many an occasion, walk there and back. Usually it was for the purpose of borrowing a book from their combined store, or returning a book I had previously borrowed. Sometimes it was just to talk.

It was no great chore; I liked to walk. They had no telephone, however, and there was no way of knowing whether anyone was there. Usually there was, but there were occasions when, having walked an hour to reach the Ivory Tower, I found no one home and had to walk an hour to get back. That too was no great chore.

The reverse was less chancy. They knew the candy store was there and that the chances were enormous that I would be there, too. If I weren't—no loss, my parents were there, my parents knew them, and my parents were good for chocolate malted milks. Fred Pohl and Cyril Kornbluth were the most assiduous visitors and they never refused malteds—or any other delicacies, for that matter. (Well, why should they?)

Cyril Kornbluth was, by the way, perhaps the most brilliant and certainly the most erratic of the Futurians. He was perhaps more brilliant than I was, and he was certainly more erratic than I. He was only about seventeen at this time, and a college dropout, I think. He had a pudgy face and a dryly sardonic way of talking, as though he hated the whole world. Maybe he did.

7

On September 23, 1940, I registered for my second year of graduate work, and my sixth year at Columbia. I signed up for two courses of advanced inorganic chemistry and a course of food chemistry.

In order to get a Master of Arts degree and get permission to do chemical research toward a Doctor of Philosophy degree, one had to take Comprehensive Examinations. These consisted of three sets of tests, given on three separate days, each test lasting most of the day.

One had to take a certain minimum number of courses to qualify for the Comprehensives, and it was quite possible to do so after one year of graduate work—if one were bright enough and had worked hard enough.

Irene, for instance, came in from Wilmington to take her Comprehensives at the end of September. After they were over, I met her on October 5 (as had been arranged on my July trip to Wilmington) and we went to the movies. That was our last date.

Irene passed her exams, of course, and went back to Wilmington having qualified for her M.A. As for myself, I wasn't ready. I decided to take another semester's work before chancing it.

And at just about the time I was registering and getting set to renew my course work, the candy store was the object of crime again. This time it wasn't a break-in, but a stick-up. Just before midnight, when my father was alone in the store, two men came in with guns. My father didn't argue at all. He emptied the register for them and they walked off with thirty-two dollars.

My father, and the rest of us, were very relieved that they had not hurt him in any way, and also that there was seventy dollars elsewhere in the store that they did not know about and that they left behind. The rest of us were more relieved about my father, but I think he was more relieved at having retained the other seventy.

8

London was holding out, but there seemed no end to the bombing, and I kept expecting every day to read that an exhausted Britain was offering peace terms.

And in the United States, Roosevelt was running for an unprecedented third term.

I was in a continuing state of terror. I was afraid that Roosevelt might not be able to overcome the third-term tradition and that Wendell Willkie, the Republican candidate, might become President. Willkie sounded pro-British and anti-Nazi, but if he were elected, he would surely be a prisoner of the Republican Party, which was isolationist and committed to neutrality. At least that was my opinion.

I managed to vote in that election, in a way. I was still two months short of the minimum voting age of twenty-one, but Milton Silverman, who was a couple of years older than I and whose voting residence was in another state, received an absentee ballot. He had it spread open, ready to mark it, when I suddenly asked if I could mark the presidential vote for him.

"Certainly," he said, and handed me the pencil.

I placed a dark X against Roosevelt's name (which suited Silverman, whose voting intentions were identical with mine). I was very pleased with that, and infinitely more pleased when Roosevelt won the election.

And then, on October 16, 1940, the United States initiated the machinery for its first peacetime draft. Registration was confined to those who were over twenty-one, however, and, temporarily, I was not affected. On October 28, Italy invaded Greece.

26

Making My Literary Mark

1

There were touches of brightness in that generally gloomy literary autumn.

In the September 1940 *Super Science Stories*, my story "Robbie" appeared.[1] Fred Pohl had once again displayed his penchant for changing titles. He called it "Strange Playfellow." I had accepted "The Callistan Menace," but this one I rejected. My title "Robbie" made the robot-nursemaid the center of the story, whereas "Strange Playfellow" made him merely an oddity. When the time came that the story was introduced into one of my collections and was anthologized several times, I insisted on the use of "Robbie" as the title. Except for that one first appearance in the magazine, it has *never* been called anything else.

Better yet was the appearance of the December 1940 *Astonishing*, which reached the stands on October 24. It contained "Half-Breeds on Venus"[2] as the lead novelette, that is, as the first story in the magazine —the position of pride. It was my tenth published story and the first time I had taken the lead.

What's more, I had the cover. I don't mean that I had my name on the cover—that much had happened twice before. I had both the title of the story *and* my full name on the cover; and what's more, the cover illustration depicted a scene from the story. That was the first time that, in *that* sense, I had made the cover.

It was a very satisfactory forward step.

I took others. After reading "Robbie" in cold print in the magazine, I decided I liked it more than any other story I had written yet. It also occurred to me that robot stories would not involve me in any superiority/inferiority hassle with Campbell. Why not, then, write another?

Furthermore, clever devil that I was, I remembered Campbell's penchant for introducing religious motifs into stories where nothing of the sort had originally existed (I had had that trouble with "Pilgrim-

[1] See *I, Robot* (Gnome Press, 1950; later Doubleday).
[2] See *The Early Asimov*.

age"). I decided to push his buttons, therefore, by putting in a bit of religion to begin with.

My notion was to have a robot refuse to believe he had been created mechanically in a factory, but to insist that men were only his servants and that robots were the peak of creation, having been created by some godlike entity. What's more, he would prove his case by reason, and "Reason" was the title of the story.

On October 23, I presented the idea to Campbell, and he was immediately enthusiastic (as I had judged he would be). We talked it over and I went home to begin the story. His last words to me as I went through the door were, "Remember, I want to see that story."

He didn't see it right away. In this case, pushing Campbell's buttons was easier than pushing the typewriter keys. I made four starts in the course of the following week, and tore up each one after a couple of pages. Ordinarily, when I had this kind of trouble with a story, I took it as a sign that the idea was not one I could handle and I would drop it. There were several stories that soured on me in those early years, stories I quickly abandoned as soon as I caught the taste of the souring.

This time, though, I dared not quit—not after having sold Campbell on the idea so effectively. On October 31, therefore, I crawled back to him with my troubles.

He listened carefully and then gave me one of those pieces of advice that were worth untold gold.[3] What he said was, "Asimov, when you have trouble with the beginning of a story, that is because you are starting in the wrong place, and almost certainly too soon. Pick out a later point in the story and begin again."

For me, that was good advice. I started later in the story and had no trouble thereafter. Ever since then, I have always started my stories as late in the game as I thought I could manage, and if I had trouble getting off the ground, I would make myself start still later. And what about the portion of the story that comes before the beginning? That can be made clear in the course of dialog or, if necessary, in a flashback.

I submitted "Reason" to Campbell on November 18, and he took it at once, for on November 22, a check for $67 arrived.

It was my third sale to Campbell and it was the first time he had taken a story without asking for a revision. He told me later, in fact, that he had liked it so well that he had almost decided to pay me a bonus.

---

[3] I try never to give literary advice myself, for the simple reason that every writer has a different technique and that what works for one may not work for another. Fortunately, Campbell's advice always just happened to match my way of working. That was his talent. It certainly isn't mine.

2

Increasingly, science-fiction fans were beginning to recognize my more-than-fan status. On November 28, 1940, I received a letter from one Scott Feldman, who invited me to a meeting of the Queens Science Fiction League on December 1. He asked me, rather apologetically, to come alone, and it was quite obvious that he feared I would bring the dreaded Futurians with me.

I was far too eager to go to the meeting to make an issue of such a thing and I went without any of the Futurians.

I enjoyed myself. L. Sprague de Camp was there, Malcolm Jameson, Arthur J. Burks, Harry Walton—all authors whose works I had read and admired. It did strike me that the Queens Science Fiction League attracted more important people than the Futurians did, and I found that I was not entirely without the sin of snobbery. Therefore, while not abandoning the Futurians, I signed up for membership in the QSFL also.

Scott Feldman was, at the time, an officer of the club, a thin young fellow with a dark mustache. He said he had met me before, at the World Science Fiction Convention in July 1939.

"I congratulated you on your stories," he said, "and you said, 'What's there to congratulate? I've only published three.'"

That was embarrassing, for I am not usually that ungracious, but although I didn't remember the incident, it had to be true, since three was the correct number at that time.

I tried to make up for it by being *very* gracious this time and when Scott showed signs of wanting to talk about the art of writing, I at once began to give him several paragraphs of good advice. He had trouble interrupting my blaze of condescension, but he finally managed to explain to me that although he was only eighteen he had published many nonfiction articles in various magazines that were *not* science fiction; that, in fact, he was making his living that way. That gave me another reason for adopting a life policy of never offering advice on writing.

Making up for that double embarrassment, however, was the fact that I won a science-fiction quiz given to the membership, the prize being Thorne Smith's "Turnabout." One of the questions was: "What is the name of the youngest well-established science-fiction author?" (By "well-established," it was carefully explained, it meant someone who had published more than five stories in the professional magazines.)

The answer was "Isaac Asimov" and I was happy, for I was the youngest in a new category. *Still* a child prodigy!

3

Just about this time, another Futurian was becoming an editor. Donald Wollheim was planning to edit two magazines, *Stirring Science Fiction* and *Cosmic Stories*.[4] His magazines were starting on a micro-budget, unfortunately, and the only way they could come into being was for Wollheim to obtain at least some of the included items from his fellow Futurians for nothing.

I was one of those he approached. Since I was a wild fan of the P. G. Wodehouse stories (I still am), I knew and believed in "the code of the Woosters" as enunciated by Bertie Wooster, surely the most lovable of all Wodehouse's creations. It was, "Never let a pal down."

If Wollheim wanted a story for nothing, I would give him a story for nothing. I didn't want to be an utter fool, however, so I offered him "The Secret Sense," which I had written a year and a half before.

It seemed to me to be a clearly nonsalable story. After Campbell had turned it down, I hadn't even bothered offering it to anyone else (though Pohl, then my agent, sent it to England, and got it rejected at a distance of three thousand miles).

Wollheim, however, took it, and told me it would appear in the first issue of *Cosmic*. That, I thought, was that.

But, as it happened, in that same fall of 1940, a new magazine called *Comet Stories* came into the world. It was going to pay a full $.01 a word, and its editor would be F. Orlin Tremaine, who had preceded Campbell as editor of *Astounding*.

That was good news, for I had liked the Tremaine *Astounding* and I approved of any new magazine that would pay top rates. I therefore visited Tremaine one or two times and offered him stories. Unfortunately, he rejected them all.

When I visited him on December 23, 1940, however, shortly before *Cosmic Stories* was to appear, Tremaine spoke with some heat concerning Wollheim's magazines. While he himself was paying top rates, he said, Wollheim was getting stories for nothing and, with these, could put out magazines that would siphon readership from those magazines that paid. Any author who donated stories to Wollheim, and

---

[4] Wollheim was the most forceful and articulate of the Futurians. He was rather plain and, at that time, acne-ridden, but there were few who could stand up against his dour wit.

thus contributed to the destruction of competing magazines who paid, should be blacklisted in the field.

I listened with horror, knowing that any day now *Cosmic Stories* would appear, with "The Secret Sense" in it. It was a story, to be sure, that I had felt to be worth nothing, but it had never occurred to me that I was undercutting other authors by setting up unfair competition. Was I going to be blacklisted?

I could see no other course of action but to own up to what would soon be quite evident anyway, and to plead ignorance. In addition, I stressed very strongly that I had *not* given the story to Wollheim for nothing. I had been paid. And so I had been, but I did not volunteer to tell Tremaine how much I had been paid, and he did not ask. I of course said I would never do such a thing again now that the economics of the matter had been explained to me, and he seemed mollified.

What had happened was this. Shortly after I had given the story to Wollheim, I discovered that some of my fellow Futurians would have their stories appearing under pseudonyms. I had made no such stipulation, and it suddenly occurred to me that even though the story might be worth nothing, my name was worth something.

On December 5, therefore, I had written to Wollheim asking him to run my story under a pseudonym. If he insisted on using my name, on the other hand, would he make me a token payment of $5.00?

Wollheim chose to use my name, and on December 12 I received a check for $5.00 from him, but he accompanied it with a remarkably ungracious letter. He told me that I was being paid an enormous word rate because it was only my name that had value and that I was receiving $2.50 a word. That was only what I myself had suspected, but considering that he had come to me *asking* for a story and that he had accepted it freely, he might have spared me the snarl.[5]

After the unpleasantness with Tremaine, I couldn't help but feel that Campbell might take the same annoyed attitude toward the new magazines and those who contributed. I therefore told him the whole story before he had a chance to bring it up. Nor did I conceal from him the amount I had been paid. Campbell shrugged it all off and didn't seem in the least perturbed. I presume he felt quite secure and didn't think *Astounding* could be in any way hurt by a magazine that could

[5] Wollheim was not, in those days, noted for the suavity of his temperament. Together with his biting wit, he had a terrible temper. I doubt that anyone was involved in so many controversies, and such voluble ones, with other fans. When one of his letters appeared in a fan magazine, the paper on which it was printed invariably scorched.

only print stories that were unsalable in any professional market. (What other stories would be given without payment?)

The first issue of *Cosmic*, dated March 1941, reached the newsstands on January 7, 1941. At least nine items in it (including mine) were by Futurians. "The Secret Sense" was my twelfth story to see print,[6] but, understandably, I got no pleasure out of it.

Even the sale of "Reason" did not guarantee future sales to Campbell. In December, I wrote "Christmas on Ganymede," which dealt with a comic Christmas celebration involving Ganymedan natives who didn't understand what it was all about. I was trying to be funny, of course.

I had this terrible urge to be *funny*, you see, and had already indulged in humor in more than one story. Writing humor, however, is harder than digging ditches. Something can be moderately well written, or moderately suspenseful, or moderately ingenious, and get by in every case. Nothing, however, can be moderately humorous. Something is either *funny*, or it is *not funny at all*. There is nothing in between. The target for humor is nothing but a bull's-eye.

I submitted "Christmas on Ganymede" to Campbell on December 23, but he didn't want it. It had missed the bull's-eye. I then tried it on Fred Pohl and he seemed interested, but not until he was preparing his Christmas issues, which meant acceptance (and payment) the following July. I was patient, since there was nothing else I could do, and for half a year it remained in limbo.

4

Although 1940 was, on the whole, a disappointing year, I did surprisingly well financially. I had received checks for nine stories, for a total payment of $384. In this, my third year as a professional writer, I had earned considerably more than in my first two years combined and, indeed, had earned just about enough to pay my tuition, all of it.

5

My meeting with Campbell on December 23, 1940, was of extreme importance to me. Handing in "Christmas on Ganymede" was of small account. It was rejected, and it deserved to be. What was far more important was that I wanted to write another robot story. This time I wanted to write a story about a robot that, through some mistake on the assembly line, turned out to be capable of reading minds.

[6] See *The Early Asimov.*

Again, Campbell became interested and we talked it over at length
—what complications would arise out of robotic telepathy, what a
robot would be forced to lie about, how the matter could be resolved,
and so on. At one point, Campbell said:

"Look, Asimov, in working this out, you have to realize that there
are three rules that robots have to follow. In the first place, they can't
do any harm to human beings; in the second place, they have to obey
orders without doing harm; in the third, they have to protect themselves, without doing harm or proving disobedient. Well . . ."

That was it. Those were the Three Laws of Robotics. Eventually I
phrased them like this:

THE THREE LAWS OF ROBOTICS

1. A robot may not injure a human being or, through inaction,
   allow a human being to come to harm.

2. A robot must obey the orders given it by human beings except
   where such orders would conflict with the First Law.

3. A robot must protect its own existence as long as such protection does not conflict with the First or Second Laws.

These Three Laws of Robotics have been used by me as the basis
for over two dozen short stories and three novels (one a juvenile) about
robots. I am probably more famous for them than for anything else I
have written, and they are quoted even outside the science-fiction
world. The very word "robotics" was coined by me.[7]

The Three Laws revolutionized science fiction. Once they were
well established in a series of stories, they made so much sense and
proved so popular with the readers that other writers began to use
them. They couldn't quote them directly, of course, but they could simply assume their existence, knowing well that the readers would be
acquainted with the Laws and would understand the assumption.

I never minded that. On the contrary, I was flattered. Besides, no
one could write a *stupid* robot story if he used the Three Laws. The
story might be bad on other counts, but it wouldn't be stupid.

And yet I heard the Three Laws first from John Campbell and I
am always embarrassed to hear myself given the credit. Whenever I
tried to tell Campbell himself, however, that he was the originator, he
would always shake his head and grin and say, "No, Asimov, I picked

[7] I didn't realize this until many years later, for at the time I first used the word, I
thought it was a word actually used by scientists in this connection. It was, after all,
analogous to "physics," "hydraulics," "mechanics," "statics," and various other
words of this form used to denote a branch of physics-related science.

them out of your stories and your discussions. You didn't state them explicitly, but they were there."

It's true I had a remark that sounded like the First Law even in "Robbie," but I think Campbell was just trying to do what he always did—let the writer have all the credit.

Or perhaps we were both right and, as Randall Garrett said many years later, both of us invented the Laws as a result of our peculiar symbiotic relationship.

6

On January 2, 1941, I turned twenty-one. I was now, in legal theory, an adult, but nothing changed, of course. I was still in the candy store, still completely under parental control, still quite incapable of supporting myself, even though, as a minor, I had earned a total of $658.50 as a writer.

Irene was thoughtful enough to send me a birthday letter and, more surprising, Mary Byers, the fan with whom I corresponded and with whom I had once visited in her hotel room and engaged in an hour and a half of conversation, came to New York.

She had been promising to do so for quite a while and I know she expected me to socialize—and I was torn. I would have been delighted to converse with her some more, but I knew that she was no wealthier than I was and I had a nervous feeling that she might expect me to put her up for the night or help with the expenses. Well, I would have been pleased to do so, but there was no way to put her up in our place and I had no money with which to help with the expenses.

However, when she arrived in town on that birthday day, there was no way in which I could refuse to see her, and when I did, it turned out, as I noted with great relief in my diary, that "she's got plenty of money—$61."

I devoted the next few days to showing her around the science-fiction world of New York. I took her to visit Campbell and Pohl on the third, to a movie on the fourth, and to a meeting of the Queens Science Fiction League on the fifth.

The meeting was an exciting one. Dick Wilson, a Futurian, together with a friend of his, were denied admission by the unforgiving group centered about Moskowitz and Sykora. They nevertheless entered, quietly, when no one was looking, and sat in the back, bothering no one. When they were spotted, however, contentiousness won out over rationality, Moskowitz and others advanced to throw them out and, in the ensuing fracas, the owner of the building evicted us one and all.

Scott Feldman resigned from the club immediately in embarrassment, and he came home to the store with me in gloomy fashion. We dropped Mary off at her hotel on the way, and then Scott and I talked fairly far into the night.

Scott and I became friends that evening, and we discussed many things. He alluded to an active sex life, even though he was some three years younger than I, and I was very envious of that (though, of course, he might have been unable to resist the opportunity of trading on my obvious innocence and gullibility by exaggerating the situation enormously). He also talked of his plans for becoming an agent someday.

It seemed peculiar to me that he should have this ambition, for he was a very facile and skillful writer. Why should anyone who was a writer want to be anything else?

For instance, he was as fond of Wodehouse as I was, and he could write in the Wodehouse style to perfection. He once showed me a story he had written, and if he had told me Wodehouse had written it, I would have believed it. What gave it away, if anything, was that it was *funnier* than Wodehouse would have made it.

At that time Wodehouse was in detention, having been captured by the Nazis when they took France. He had consented to do some broadcasts for them in humorous vein in exchange for gentle treatment. It may not have been a very heroic thing to do, but how many heroes are there? He was in his sixties, not a very politically minded person, and was reasonably eager to be well treated. However, there was bitter feeling against this in Great Britain, since Wodehouse gave the impression that he was feeling no pain, while London was being demolished by Nazi bombs.

Scott Feldman, however, wrote letters to Wodehouse, expressing sympathy, and Wodehouse received them, apparently, and was grateful.

But back to these early January days. On January 6, I helped Mary move out of the hotel and into the YWCA and then left her. I didn't know what her plans were, but I had done my bit, introduced her to the science-fiction world as I had promised, and felt I could now retire. Besides, I had to. Classes were beginning again.

On January 12, however, a telegram arrived from her grandmother in Ohio, begging me to send her back. It came in the middle of the night, and there I was with everyone in the family staring at me round-eyed, while I kept saying, in desperate affirmation of innocence, "But I didn't do *anything*. I just took her places."

That was absolutely true. It had all been perfectly platonic, and I hadn't seen her at all in a week. I sent a letter to her grandmother to that effect and then called the YWCA and spoke to Mary. She seemed unmoved by the telegram. I had opened the door for her into the science-fiction world and she had stepped through it, and she needed me for nothing more. She had every intention of staying in New York and becoming a Futurian.[8] Well, that was her business, and I stepped out of her life.

7

Meanwhile, I was spending the month writing two stories. One was rather unusual, for it was my first attempt at collaboration.

Fred Pohl, after all, was not merely an editor. He was, like myself, a budding writer. He has since become a giant in the field, but in those early days he was struggling along with only the same sort of meager success I was having. Alone, and in collaboration with other Futurians, he turned out stories under a variety of pseudonyms. The one he used most frequently was "James MacCreigh," and under this name he appeared in the minor magazines.

Under this pseudonym, Pohl had written a short fantasy called "The Little Man on the Subway," which he apparently had hopes for, but couldn't seem to get just right. He asked me if I would rewrite it, and the request flattered me. Besides, I still dreamed of getting into *Unknown*, and if I couldn't do it on my own, maybe I could do it by way of a collaboration.

I took on the task and did it virtually at a sitting on January 18, 1941. Doing it easily didn't help, though. I submitted it to Campbell for *Unknown* on January 27, and he rejected it promptly.

The trouble with writing for *Unknown* was that there were virtually no fallback markets. Rejection ended everything, and I handed it back to Pohl with considerable embarrassment.

Meanwhile, though, I was also working on "Liar!," the story over which Campbell had drawn the protective curtain of the Three Laws of Robotics. I took it in to Campbell on January 20, and a check for $70 arrived on the twenty-fourth. At last I had gotten the range. It had taken me 2½ years to sell him two stories to begin with, and now it had taken me 2 months to sell him two more. I was making progress, and my bank account now stood at $150.

In "Liar!," by the way, I introduced my first successful female character. She was a "robopsychologist," and the story centered about her.

[8] And she did, all the way. Eventually she married Cyril Kornbluth and had two children by him.

She was more intelligent and more capable than any of the men in the story and I was very fond of her and wanted to write more stories about her.

The notion of using a woman scientist did not arise out of Irene, strangely enough, but out of Professor Mary Caldwell, my gentle and understanding graduate adviser.

The character in "Liar!" was nothing at all like Professor Caldwell in appearance or behavior, but I called her "Susan Caldwell" just the same.

After the story was accepted, I had qualmish second thoughts. It didn't strike me that Professor Caldwell would like the use of her name and I didn't want her annoyed with me.

On my next visit to Campbell on January 27, I found him out with the flu but I talked to his secretary, Katherine Tarrant,[9] and explained the situation to her.

She said, with a sigh, "I suppose you want me to go through the manuscript and change the name wherever it appears."

"Yes," I said, eagerly. "Would you?"

"What name do you want instead?"

Desperately I thought of a change that would involve the fewest letters. "Calvin," I said.

It was done and Susan Calvin has been the heroine of some ten stories of mine so far.

This brings up one of the reasons why I don't take critics seriously. Some critics, in discussing my robot stories, make much of the name "Calvin," assuming that I chose it deliberately for its associations with John Calvin, the predestinarian, and his gloomy, doom-ridden work ethic. Not at all! I was merely trying to introduce a minimal change in Caldwell, for the reasons I explained.

8

More and more I was drifting away from the fan world and entering the writer's world. Sprague de Camp, whom I had met on a number of occasions now, both in Campbell's office and at fan meetings, wrote to invite me to attend a "war game" at Fletcher Pratt's.

---

[9] Katherine, whom I invariably called Miss Tarrant in those days and for years afterward, was usually in the office when I talked to Campbell, sitting quietly and almost unnoticeably in the background, but not missing a thing. Years afterward, she would enjoy herself by describing those early days to younger writers. Invariably she would tell them, in detail, how I sat there in adoring admiration of Campbell, drinking in every word he said. I always thought I listened with a cool self-possession, but perhaps that was not how it appeared to others.

Pratt was well known for his popular historical writings and for his books on naval strategy, as well as for his science fiction. (He had written some excellent *Unknown* novels in collaboration with de Camp.) De Camp, whose wife had just given birth to their first son, addressed me as "Dear Isaac," which flattered me out of my eyeteeth.

Fletcher Pratt had devised a war game that made use of warship models carefully designed to scale, including everything from destroyers to battleships. The moves were all designed to scale as well, making use of the actual speeds of such ships, with those speeds being progressively reduced after it was hit one or more times. The shells and torpedos had to be aimed in an announced direction and with an announced range, and referees had to mark off the direction and ranges, then announce whether a hit had been made.

The rules were far too complicated for me to play a good game on my first try, on January 24, 1941. The three destroyers they gave me were promptly blown out of the water when I unwarily approached a cruiser, and I sat out the rest of the game on the sidelines perfectly happy. While watching, I had Cokes and peanuts and, in a fit of attempted adulthood, I forced myself to drink two beers as well. I hated the taste, and have almost never repeated that experiment.

At the games was Fletcher Pratt himself, a little gnome of a man who couldn't have been more than five feet four, with a retreating forehead, a bald head, and a commanding personality. There were several writers present also: Sprague himself, L. Ron Hubbard, John D. Clark, and Willy Ley, with all of whom I now talked on terms of easy camaraderie. Ley was particularly friendly.

9

Despite all this, I continued to write letters to the various magazines.

There was, for instance, another new magazine that had come out in late 1939. It was a quarterly named *Planet Stories*. I wrote them one letter, which appeared over the printed name of "Isaac Asenion." They had undoubtedly gotten that from the written signature, where the *i* looked to them like an *e*, the *m* like an *ni*, and the *v* like an *n*. I can see that and would have sympathized with the typesetter who had made the mistake were it not that my name was also typewritten, and *correctly* so.

It was a very embarrassing item, since it also indicated that my name was not very well known as yet. I wrote a rather angry letter to *Planet* over this, which was printed (with my name spelled correctly).

The editor's comment was, "There, there, Mr. Asimov, don't you cry! Things will be better by-and-by." I didn't find that amusing, either.

It gave me the grisly feeling that I was fighting over trivialities, and I began to enjoy less the writing of letters. Yet I did write them, and often quarreled with readers who objected to something or other in one of my stories—until I received a letter from the writer Nelson S. Bond (whom I had met at the World Convention in 1939 briefly, and never again), saying that since I was now a professional, I ought to stop slugging it out in fan columns. I took that seriously and from the moment I received that letter, I stopped writing letters to the magazines, except for very occasional ones that did not involve fannish comments. I have always been grateful to Bond for this word in season.

The whole episode with *Planet Stories* would now be totally forgotten were it not that my good friend Lester del Rey, who never forgets anything that by any chance is better forgotten, has, for decades, thought it exquisitely humorous to refer to me as "Asenion" even though no one in the world but he and I know what he's talking about.

10

I finished the first semester of the year with an A in each of the three courses I had taken, and in February I went on to the next semester. Among other courses, I signed up for one in thermodynamics, which was to be taught by my old nemesis, Urey.

There was the uncomfortable feeling that before the spring was over I was going to have to take my Qualifying Examinations. This was not to be the somewhat simpler Comprehensives that offered the dead end of a master's degree, which Irene had taken, for instance. They were longer and more detailed examinations, which brought you the master's degree *plus* permission to go on for chemical research toward the Ph.D. It was not something I looked forward to.

It was about now that an incident, unrecorded in my diary, took place. In the course of an uproarious cafeteria lunch with the other students, the demand arose that I have cherry pie for dessert along with the others. I demurred because of the expense, but someone at once offered to pay for it—which should have put me on my guard at once, but didn't.

What they were planning was to put a pyridium pellet in the pie, the pyridium's red color to be masked by the cherries. Pyridium is a mild antiseptic that works on the excretory system and colors the urine red until it is washed out.

That evening when I urinated prior to going to bed, my heart bounded in terror, for I was clearly urinating blood. I didn't want to report this fact since it would destroy my mother's sanity in one blow. I therefore stayed awake all night, checking my urine at half-hourly intervals and watching it grow slowly less bloody. By morning it was almost normal, so I forgot about it.

The next day, all my dear friends gathered around to try to elicit from me what had happened, hoping for details of terror and emergency medical treatments. However, I had my mind on other things, and no hints, however broad, managed to bring back the night's events to my mind. Finally, in sheer frustration, they broke down and confessed and asked if anything had happened and I said, "Oh you're right. I thought I was bleeding."

They were very chagrined and there were some harsh comments about my idiotic failure to react sensibly. Apparently there had been a school of thought among my merry friends that I should have been dosed with methylene blue in blueberry pie. That had been vetoed because it had been assumed that blue urine would have given away the show. How wrong they were and how badly they overestimated my practical good sense. Red I at least interpreted as blood—serious but understandable. Had my urine turned blue, I would undoubtedly have gone into some kind of fit.

11

I was still dying to break into *Unknown*. On February 3, 1941, I dashed off a fifteen-hundred-word short-short that I called "Masks." I haven't the faintest idea what it was about. My diary tells me it was inspired by Robert Louis Stevenson's "Markheim," but that doesn't help me.

On February 10, I visited Campbell and handed him the story, and on my next visit, a week later, I got it back.

What I didn't know was that this rejection represented a landmark.

"Masks" was the twenty-ninth story I had written. Of those twenty-nine stories, I had sold sixteen, and four more were going to be sold in the future. That meant that nine stories were never to be sold and no longer exist. "Masks" was the ninth. It was also the last. Since February 1941, I have never written a piece of fiction that has not, in one way or another, seen print.

It took me thirty-two months of submission and rejection to reach that point. And, of course, an ultimate sale doesn't mean that a story doesn't pick up rejections en route.

Later in the month, for instance, I wrote a story called "Hazing" and realized it wasn't good enough to try out on Campbell. I submitted it to Fred Pohl on February 24, and I had a postcard from him the next day, turning it down. I then sent it to *Planet* but they turned it down too, taking over a month to do it in. Yet it was eventually sold.

I had better luck with the next story, which I wrote during the last few days of February. I called it "Super-Neutron" and submitted it to Pohl. He took it at once and I made $30 out of that.

A rather peculiar fact is that during the first two months of the year, I was writing a long and complicated outline of a science-fiction novel, at Pohl's request. I discussed it with Pohl when I was done and he approved it with some suggested changes, which, in turn, I approved of. On February 13, 1941, I actually started the novel, calling it *Hostile Galaxy*.

But I never finished it. It just didn't go and I gave it up. On March 5, I said in my diary, "It's hack! My heart isn't in it."

The peculiar thing, though, is that I don't remember a thing about it. Not a thing. Indeed, until I began to go through my diary, word by word, for this autobigraphy, I would have sworn that in the course of the first decade of my professional writing career, I had never as much as dreamed of writing a novel, let alone that I'd begun one.

The April 1941 *Astonishing* arrived on February 25, with my story "Twins." Pohl had changed the name to "Heredity,"[10] and I've let that stand ever since. It made the cover; the second time I had managed this.

I learned something from that story. Scott Feldman said he didn't like it. "Why not?" I asked, surprised, for he generally liked my stories.

"You introduced two characters at the start," he said, "and you let them disappear."

Lesson: Don't let sympathetic characters disappear without a good excuse made plain to the reader.

12

More important was that on March 20, the April 1941 *Astounding* came out with "Reason,"[11] and the May 1941 issue, a month later, with "Liar!"[12] I don't know whether Campbell did this deliberately, but the presence of two robot stories, back to back, helped establish the series. (It was usually called the "positronic robot" series, because the electric currents in the brains were flows of positrons rather than electrons. I did that just to make the brains sound part of a futuristic tech-

[10] See *The Early Asimov.*
[11] See *I, Robot.*
[12] See *I, Robot.*

nology, but some of the less sophisticated readers thought that this was based on sound science and would ask me to give them additional information on how it worked.)

Even more important still was my visit to Campbell on March 17, 1941. I went to him with an idea for a story, as I usually did, but this time he turned it down impatiently. I don't imagine there was anything more wrong than usual with my idea, but Campbell had an idea of his own. I don't know if he was saving it specifically for me, or if I just happened to be the first author to walk in after the idea had occurred to him.

He had come across a quotation from an eight-chapter work by Ralph Waldo Emerson called *Nature*. In the first chapter, Emerson said: "If the stars should appear one night in a thousand years, how would men believe and adore; and preserve for many generations the remembrance of the city of God. . . ."

Campbell asked me to read it and said, "What do you think would happen, Asimov, if men were to see the stars for the first time in a thousand years?"

I thought, and drew a blank. I said, "I don't know."

Campbell said, "I think they would go mad. I want you to write a story about that."

We talked about various things, thereafter, with Campbell seeming to circle the idea and occasionally asking me questions such as, "Why should the stars be invisible at other times?" and listened to me as I tried to improvise answers. Finally, he shooed me out with, "Go home and write the story."[13]

In my diary for that day I said, "I'll get started on it soon, as I think the idea is swell, and I even envisage making a lead novelette out of it; but I don't delude myself into thinking it will be an easy story to write. It will require hard work."

On the evening of March 18, 1941, I began the story.

It was a crucial moment for me. I had, up to that moment, written thirty-one stories in not quite three years. Of these I had, as of that time, sold seventeen stories and had published fourteen, with a fifteenth about to come out.

---

[13] Here and elsewhere I have always spoken with complete candor about the role of others in the genesis and development of my stories—particularly Campbell's role. Nevertheless, I am a little sensitive when people overestimate the importance of such contributions. It is one thing to say, "I think people would go crazy if they see the stars for the first time in a thousand years. Go home and write the story." It is quite another to go home and actually write the story. Campbell might suggest but it was *I* who then had to go home and face the empty sheet of paper in the typewriter.

Of those thirty-one stories, published and unpublished, sold and unsold, only three were what I would now consider as three stars or better on my old zero-to-five-star scale, and they were my three positronic robot stories: "Robbie," "Reason," and "Liar!"

My status on that evening of March 18 was as nothing more than a steady and (perhaps) hopeful third-rater. What's more, that's all that I considered myself to be at that time. Nor did anyone else, as far as I know, seriously consider me, in early 1941, as a potential first-magnitude star in the science-fiction heavens—except, maybe, Campbell. The Golden Age was in full swing and it contained, already, such brilliant stars as Heinlein and Van Vogt and such scarcely lesser names as Hubbard, de Camp, del Rey, and Sturgeon. Surely no one could possibly have thought I would ever be considered comparable to these—except, maybe, Campbell.

With that background, I put a piece of paper in the typewriter, typed the title, which Campbell and I had agreed should be "Nightfall," typed the Emerson quotation, then began the story.

I remember that evening very well; my own room, just next to the living room, my desk facing the southern wall, with the bed behind me and to the right, the window on the other side of the bed, looking out westward on Windsor Place, with the candy store across the street.

Did I have any notion that after thirty-one stories ranging from impossibly bad to mildly good, I was going to write the best science-fiction story of all time? How could I?

Yet some people think exactly that of "Nightfall." Thirty years later, when a poll was conducted of the members of the Science Fiction Writers of America, "Nightfall" finished in first place by a healthy margin. Other polls, under other conditions, also put it in first place; and, if we restrict matters to just my own stories, there is almost a general consensus that it is certainly the best story I ever wrote.

I know perfectly well that my reputation for simpering and bashful modesty is nonexistent, and that I am widely known as a man who thinks well of himself. Please believe me, then, when I tell you that I *don't* consider "Nightfall" the best science-fiction short story ever written. In fact, I don't even consider it the best *I've* ever written. I've written at least three shorts (probably more) that I consider better than "Nightfall."[14]

But I was in happy ignorance that the story I was now writing was in any way different from those I had been writing all along. I was sur-

[14] It is not my intention to keep you on tenterhooks. My own three favorite short stories are, in order: (1) "The Last Question," (2) "The Bicentennial Man," and (3) "The Ugly Little Boy." They will all be dealt with, in due course, in the second volume of this autobiography.

prised and pleased, though, by the fact that, despite my initial apprehension, the story moved easily. By March 20, I had nearly 5,000 words
done and I said in my diary, "This is absolutely unprecedented. It is
absolutely impossible that this keep up. I never had anything write itself so easily." By April 8, I had finished.[15]

On April 9, I took it in to Campbell. It was 13,300 words long and,
except for "Pilgrimage," which, in the course of its many revisions, had
reached a total of 18,000 words, it was the longest story I had yet written.

Two days later I got a note from Campbell saying that he planned
to take "Nightfall" but wanted a few minor changes made. I rushed
over to his office and we discussed the changes—which didn't seem too
difficult. Mostly it was a case of speeding the beginning.

While there, Campbell, who, among his several hobbies, was an
amateur photographer, took three pictures of me. He showed them to
me eventually and, while I don't possess a copy of them, I remember
them. They showed me as bony-faced, for I was still gaunt at that time,
certainly weighing not more than 135 pounds, with a thick mustache
and with a pimple at the end of my nose. In later years, Campbell
would whip out the picture and show it to people who knew me
well—as a plump, clean-shaven, and pimple-free fellow—and say,
"Who's this?" They never had the slightest idea.

By the eighteenth, I brought in the revised version and Campbell
said he would take it home to read. Willy Ley was visiting him, he said,
and Willy would read it, too. That didn't bother me. I had been attending the monthly war games regularly now and Willy Ley was an
old friend whose taste in science fiction I trusted.

On April 24, the acceptance came through. It was the fifth story I
had sold to Campbell, and the first of novelette length. What's more,
Cambell had awarded it a bonus. He paid $.01 a word plus $.0025 a
word bonus, for a total of $166.[16] It was by far the largest payment I
had yet received for a single story.

15 Events in the outer world were growing grimmer, however. To be sure, the
Greeks had been humiliating Mussolini's bumbling army and driven the Italian
troops far back into Albania. As I was finishing "Nightfall," however, the Germans
had unleashed another lightning attack, this time against Yugoslavia and Greece,
and it was clear almost at once that it would be yet another great victory for the
Nazis and that for the second time in twelve months a British army would be driven
off the European Continent.
16 He didn't tell me he was paying me a bonus. I found myself staring at a check
that was for the wrong amount and in my favor. Very regretfully, I called Campbell
to tell him he had overpaid me and that's when I found out about the bonus. The
deciding factor had been Willy's report. He had said to Campbell after he read it,
"From what you told me about the story, I knew it would be good, but I didn't
know it would be *this* good."

27

Master of Arts

1

The spring of 1941 was decision time at school. I could put off my try at the Qualifying Exams no longer.

On Saturday, April 26, with the sale of "Nightfall" a glowing and fresh memory, I took my first set of Qualifyings. These were three tests, each two hours long, with hour-and-a-half intermissions between. There was to be a similar ordeal on the next Saturday and then again on the Saturday after that. It was absolutely backbreaking!

I staggered out of the first of the initial triplet of tests, the one on physical chemistry, with the cold grip of disaster clutching my heart. In my diary I said I was "scarcely more than a quarter alive until I found all the rest in similar states of utter incapacitude." In fact, it gradually turned out that I had gotten several things right that I had no earthly business to get right.

The next two tests, one on inorganic chemistry and one on organic chemistry, were easier, though in each case I missed something I should not have missed. As I said petulantly in connection with the organic test, "I couldn't synthesize beta-naphthylamine to save my life"—and, of course, when I looked it up, it proved to be an easy task and something I should have known.

On May 3, the first test was on advanced physical chemistry, dealing with quantum mechanics, statistical mechanics, and atomic and molecular spectra. It was a total loss, for I had never studied these subjects and I had to hand in a virtually blank answer book. (That isn't as bad as it sounds. No one is expected to have a grasp on all the subjects covered and it would be a prodigy indeed who would not hand in blank answer books in several of the tests.)

The second test that day was on thermodynamics and kinetics, but I could only tackle the former. On the third part, which dealt with advanced inorganic, I managed to do respectably well, I thought.

On May 10 came the last trio of tests—two on advanced organic chemistry and a third on food chemistry. I did what I could.

On May 17, I took my language examination. A chemist has to read several foreign languages if he is to keep up with the chemical literature, and mine were French and German. This subsidiary exam was relatively easy.

On May 22, the results came through. I did well enough to get my master's degree so that as of the following graduation, I was Isaac Asimov, B.S., M.A. (and still only twenty-one). I did *not*, however, get a score that was high enough to permit me to go on for my research toward my Ph.D.

I consulted Professor Caldwell the next day and she said it would be perfectly possible for me to continue my studies and take a second whack at the Qualifyings. She assured me I had done quite well the first time and there was no reason why I couldn't go over the top the second.

It meant I was back on probation, darn it. My friends in graduate school had, for the most part, passed the Qualifying at some point and were now ensconced in laboratories, working for this professor or that, and doing their doctoral research. I was not.

I was doomed to continue studying for another semester, perhaps two, and then I would have to try again and, perhaps, end up with nothing more than the M.A. after all, despite the added expense.

Of course, *if* I passed the second time, there was no loss at all, for the courses I would have taken, I would have had to take in any case, and with them all behind me, I could then concentrate on research alone.

But would I pass the second time, no matter what mark I got? I had the feeling, justified or not, that in granting a student permission to go on for his doctorate, the marks he got on his Qualifyings were only one factor. The other was whether he had the "personality," or "temperament," or whatever, to do the research.

Elderfield was on the committee that judged the results of the Qualifyings and he and I had been at loggerheads for two years. I was sure he believed I wasn't Ph.D. material, whatever my marks might have been, and I was sure he had convinced the rest of the board to that effect, and would do the same the next time I took the test.[1]

2

I didn't think Elderfield was a minority of one in this. I didn't think he had to overcome a solid phalanx of pro-Asimov sentiment. For

[1] I must stress the fact that I had no evidence to this effect, in any way whatever, and may well have been doing Elderfield a great injustice. I am not, however, reporting the facts, of which I knew nothing, but my feelings and suspicions of the time, for as much or as little as they were worth.

one thing, I suspected he had the department head, Professor Urey, on his side.

Urey might well remember my annoying persistence a year and a half before that brought me into the graduate department rather against his will. If he didn't, I thought somberly, he was sure to remember a much more recent incident in which I had spoken up in the wrong way and at the wrong time. It came about, thusly:

In one of my talks with Campbell, he had told me of the discovery of uranium fission and of the obvious conclusion that a chain reaction could be set up, that energy could be delivered at such a rate as to produce an unprecedentedly cataclysmic explosion. He was very convincing because he was very right. Enough had come out about fission for any intelligent person, knowledgeable in atomic physics, to deduce it before scientists had self-censored themselves into silence.

Campbell even told me that Columbia had a cubic foot of uranium they were experimenting with. I grew uneasy and said I was nervous about working at Columbia under those conditions.

"Why?" said he. "Do you think you would be any safer in Brooklyn if that uranium exploded?" (Actually, he was in error here. The kind of uranium that Columbia was working with could not have exploded.)

This was the first hint I had of an atomic bomb and what it could do, and this was in February 1941. I promptly incorporated what I had learned about it in my story "Super-Neutron."

During the following spring, Urey, in the thermodynamics course I was taking under him, decided to moan about the fact that he was doing nothing toward the war effort. (The United States was not yet at war, but it was gradually mobilizing its scientific talent for the war that was sure to come.) Urey pointed out that other chemists in the department were taking over important projects and he—just an ivory-tower nuclear chemist—was doing nothing.

Why Urey should have gone through this hypocritical rigmarole, I don't know, for, of course, he was deeply engaged in the most important war project of all—the gathering work on the atomic bomb. Perhaps he was trying to cast a primitive smoke screen over his work, or perhaps he was getting some sort of perverse pleasure in thinking to himself, "Oh if they only knew."

But I knew, of course, so I listened in astonishment and said, "But Professor Urey, what are you talking about? What about the cubic foot of uranium in Pupin? Isn't that your field?"

The most astonishing thing happened. Urey turned a bright, bright red, and a spasm of anger crossed his face.

"Some people talk too much," he muttered, and suddenly, very loudly, changed the subject.

As to the people who talked too much, I don't know if he meant me or himself—but by Heaven, I was innocent. How should I have known?

Nevertheless, it was clear to me that if Urey had not exactly loved me before, he could not have any excess of affection for me after I had so effectively embarrassed him before the class. I got a B in the course, but I was sure he was ready to agree I was not Ph.D. material.

In any case, I knew for certain what was happening after Urey's gaffe. Probably the rest of the class did, too. They may have forgotten the incident, but I never did, and I was prepared for the big event when it finally happened. But I never breathed a word about the matter thereafter to anyone at any time! I had read enough thrillers to know what might happen to me if I did.

With my opinion of the attitudes of Elderfield and Urey, I faced a second try at the Qualifyings without much hope, and the master's degree they had given me seemed like a mere booby prize and worthless. When commencement ceremonies came, therefore, I once again refused to show up and receive my degree in full formality. They mailed it to me and, like my bachelor's diploma, my master's diploma went the way of all paper. I don't know what happened to it or where it is. I never valued it.

3

Life went on, however. On May 18, I saw my first opera—*La Traviata*—and duly recorded that the tenor who sang Alfredo had a voice that was weak and timid, but that he was the son of the conductor, which apparently counterbalanced that.[2]

Then, on May 24, after several false starts, I began a new story, "Not Final," in earnest. It strikes me that by talking of "false starts" I lose my chance to describe in detail the thought processes that precede the writing of a story. The truth is I cannot describe them; they are too inchoate to have a finger put on them. The undramatic fact is that I

[2] It is not my intention to give the impression by a throwaway paragraph like the above that I am a cultured person with deep musical appreciation. I have occasionally seen an opera and attended a concert, but Verdi, Mozart, Beethoven, Tchaikovsky, and other great romantics represent the height of my powers. Twentieth-century music, like twentieth-century art and twentieth-century literature, eludes me completely. In fact, the music that pleases me best is light opera, and Gilbert and Sullivan is what I am fanatical over.

just think and think and think until I have something, and there is nothing marvelous or artistic about the phenomenon.

It was just about this time that the Nazis launched an airborne invasion of the Greek island of Crete and inflicted another humiliating defeat on the British. And on the very day I began the story, the largest British battleship, *Hood*, was sunk by the Nazi supership *Bismarck*. Great Britain was also losing ground in North Africa and, on the whole, the war news was unbelievably depressing.

On May 27, however, I heard the news that the *Bismarck* had been trapped and sunk, and I dressed in a state of high excitement to rush to school and crow triumphantly over Lloyd Roth, who had flatly said that the British Navy was no longer capable of holding its own against Germany.

On June 2, I submitted "Not Final" to Campbell, and by June 7, a check for $67 had arrived. Campbell had now taken four of the last five stories I had submitted to him.

Not all the news was great, though. On June 13, I visited Pohl, who told me that *Astonishing* and *Super Science* were being suspended. I was sorry, for he and the magazines had been good to me. They had published five of my stories and were about to come out with a sixth. Indeed, on June 25, I received the September 1941 *Astonishing*, with "Super-Neutron."[3]

This was the story in which I had incorporated Campbell's news of uranium fission. I spoke in the story of "the classical uranium fission method for power." I also spoke of the metal cadmium as a neutron absorber—in fact, that point was central to the plot. It wasn't bad for a story that appeared in 1941, and I sometimes quote it in public to create an impression.

Considering the burgeoning success of my positronic robot stories, I had story series on my mind now. "Super-Neutron" was certainly intended to be the first in a long chain of very clever and very ingenious tales to be told at meetings of the "Honorable Society of Ananias."

It didn't work out that way, however. There was never a second story in that series, not even the beginning of one, not even the idea for one. However, the notion of telling a story through the conversations of a group of men around the dinner table stayed with me, and on several occasions I was to try again.

Despite my sorrow over the suspension of the magazines that had done so much for me, and for Pohl's being out of that particular job, a sober sense of reality did tell me that the magazines had served their

[3] See *The Early Asimov*.

purpose. They had kept me going till I had finally caught Campbell's range, and now I could do without them.

In fact, about the only real inconvenience was that "Christmas on Ganymede," which Pohl had been holding for half a year, now could not be used (it had not been paid for) and it was back on the market.

I had another possible site for it, though. "Hazing," which had been rejected by Pohl and by *Planet*, had been submitted by me to *Thrilling Wonder* on June 10. At my request, Pohl sent on "Christmas on Ganymede" to *Thrilling Wonder* on the twenty-third. Eventually, both stories were taken. I received $55 for "Hazing" and $54 for "Christmas on Ganymede."

I began two more stories in June. One was my second attempt at a collaboration with Pohl—again for the sake of trying to break into *Unknown*. On one of my visits to Pohl, he had said he had an idea for an *Unknown* story, something about a ghost that had to prove to a court of law its legal right to occupy a house against the wish of its living owner. I liked the idea and eagerly asked Pohl if I might write it for him on the basis of a fifty-fifty split in the earnings, if any. He agreed.

This time I was more careful and consulted Campbell concerning the idea. He was intrigued, too, but warned me that I would have to learn something about the laws governing occupancy. I chanced doing it while retaining my ignorance, wrote the story, and submitted it to Campbell on June 30. I called it "Legal Rights," but he changed it to "Legal Rites," which I agreed to at once, with considerable annoyance at myself for not having thought of it. He rejected it anyway, though, and once again I had to hand back to Pohl, in failure, a collaborative effort.

The other June story was intended to be a funny one (I kept trying to write funny ones!), which I called "Source of Power." It languished, though, and I didn't finish it till August. Other things were happening and getting in the way.

4

My increasing success with writing and my tidy bank balance (which had reached $235 now, despite the fact that I was paying my own tuition now) made it seem to my parents that perhaps I deserved a vacation. That didn't occur to me, you understand, because as a result of virtually never having had one, my vacation nerve has atrophied away. Indeed, to this day, I never voluntarily take a vacation, and I grumble when one is forced on me and try to find ways of doing some work anyway.

But it occurred to my parents, and what kind of vacation would occur to them? Why, the only vacation they had ever had during their stay in the United States—a week or two in Parksville at the Siegels, where my mother and we children had stayed in 1927, 1928, and 1931.

After some discussion, the decision was for one week—that was quite long enough for me, and if I went in June, I'd get cheaper rates— $16 a week.

Nor was it an impossible task for me to leave the store. Stanley was almost twelve now and could do most of the chores—and this was a thought that filled me with glee. What was the use of having a younger brother if one couldn't hand-him-down the dirty work? Sooner or later I would have to leave home, and he might as well be groomed as my replacement. As I recall, in fact, the one reason I was eager for the vacation was to be away from the store one whole week in order to see how it survived.

I bought tickets on June 13 ($4.45 for the round trip, I carefully noted), and on June 14 I was off. It was the ferry across the Hudson River and the train from Weehawken thereafter.

For the first time ever I was going to be away from home alone for more than that single night in Philadelphia—for a whole week, in fact.

It was a curious week. I had thought I would be terrified, but I wasn't. I remembered the place vaguely from the time, ten years before, when I had been there last, although of course it looked (quite predictably) considerably smaller and less consequential than I remembered.

The Siegels were pleasant to me and fed me well (and I was far less picky at my food than when I was young). I had good quarters and, in general, I felt reasonably at home and longed only moderately for more familiar scenes. To combat possible homesickness, I took my typewriter and did some work on "Legal Rites," which was then in progress. I also took improving books to read. There have always been sharp limits to my "vacations."

The most peculiar aspect of the week was that I was an outsider. There were not many people boarding at the Siegels off-season, and those who were there all knew each other. What's more, they were a peculiar group of people. They were all Jewish, all eastern European immigrants, and all, after two years of Nazi military victory, seemed to concentrate their hatred solely on the Soviet Union.

At every meal, the conversation turned on how happy life had been under the Tsars and how wicked the Bolsheviks were. I kept raising the point that the immediate danger was Nazi Germany but they shrugged it off. One person even said that she hoped Hitler would attack the Soviet Union and that the United States would then form an alliance with Nazi Germany and invade the Soviet Union from the Pacific side. For a while I thought this was an elaborate scheme to make fun of me, but she was serious, quite serious.

At one point when there was some discussion of the unfair treatment of Jews by anti-Semites (anti-Semites in general, not Nazi Germany in particular), a few of them reeled off some of the false attitudes toward Jews that were possessed by many who didn't really know Jews.

I nodded and said, "Yes, and that sort of thing is pretty general. Consider how we whites mistreat Negroes."

There was a horrified silence and then one of them, in an awful voice, said, "What's wrong with the way we treat Negroes?" She then went on to say about the Negroes *exactly* what she had just complained that anti-Semites said about Jews.

That week was a liberal education concerning the blindness and bigotry of people, and how the pleasures of hatred rise superior even to the instinct of self-preservation.

I am not immune to that instinct, but in my own case, a constant reading of history had shown me that persecution on trivial grounds was not the privilege of Jews alone, so that I generalized my own feelings of resistance against such things out of the narrow-minded self-preservation that would have made me oppose anti-Semitism only. And it was my reading of the history of the Civil War and the decades preceding it that engaged my feelings on the side of the blacks in particular.

As for my father's teachings, alas, though they were strong on honesty, industry, and duty, there was nothing about human equality in them. As was the case with so many Eastern European Jews (in my experience, at least), he took it for granted that Gentiles were stupid alcoholics. My own arguments that we knew many intelligent Gentiles and many stupid Jews fell on deaf ears. He chose his examples to suit himself.

On my third day at Siegel's, two teen-age girls arrived. They were Jewish refugees from Austria, the first refugees I had ever met. They were shy and withdrawn and what puzzled me was that they would not drink water. They would drink only beer. I didn't see how it was possible not to drink water, and I tried to talk to them into it. I didn't appreciate at the time the real health hazard that most water supplies in the world posed.

I tried to talk German to the young refugees and they seemed very intrigued and urged me to continue. I tried, but while I could make myself understood in German, I didn't really have an easy conversational fluency and I finally said, in English, "Why do you want me to continue speaking German?"

And they answered ecstatically, in English, "Because you have such a romantic Hungarian accent."

The amusements consisted of talking, walking, and listening to the radio. We listened to a fight between Joe Louis and a contender named Conn for the heavyweight championship. Everyone rooted for Conn, the white man (they carefully explained that was the reason), and I was in a minority of one, cheering on the black champion, Louis. Louis won.

I also played Ping-Pong and handball with the daughter of the establishment, and she won every game. I watched a tree being felled; I walked to the village to buy newspapers; and, in general, such quiet amusements seemed ample to me.

Most of the people urged me to stay another week, rather strenuously, and I compromised. I agreed to stay on through the weekend and return on Monday the twenty-third, rather than Saturday the twenty-first.

It was an unfortunate decision. On Sunday the twenty-second, the news arrived that Nazi Germany suddenly, and without warning, had invaded the Soviet Union all along its border. I went into a profound panic. I was sure that the Soviet Union would collapse and that Nazi Germany would then no longer be defeatable.

I packed at once and left for home. But when I got there, what was there to do but read newspapers and listen in horror as the Nazi columns plunged deep into the Soviet Union?

28

"Foundation"

1

Once again, as during the Munich crisis, the Danzig crisis, and the battles of France and Britain, I spent most of my time listening to the radio. I kept trying to sort out German and Soviet claims, which were immensely far apart. I wanted to believe the Soviets, but on past performance I was sure it was the Nazis who were correct.[1]

The only relief at that time came from the fact that Sprague de Camp had invited me to his apartment which, at that time, was at Riverside Drive and 149th Street. It was the first time I had ever been asked to visit the home of an established science-fiction writer. It was a matter of great excitement for me.

I showed up at Sprague's apartment at 2:00 P.M. on Saturday, June 28, 1941, and on that day I met his wife, Catherine, for the first time. They had not been married terribly long and she had given birth to their first child, a son named Lyman, only some weeks before.

A "cute little baby" I noted in my diary, but that wasn't what impressed me. Catherine was a gorgeous blonde, about five feet, seven inches tall, I should say, with an aristocratic bony structure to her face, rather like that of Katharine Hepburn, and a *grande dame* manner that didn't daunt me a bit, for some reason. She and Sprague were both thirty-four years old at the time.

When I first met Catherine, I was content merely to look at her. As I grew older and more confident in my relations with women, I began a long-continued flirtation with her. In fact, she was the first woman with whom I systematically flirted. Catherine has always reacted with innocent delight, and Sprague, from his seventy-four inch height (he looks something like Robert Goulet), watched with a secure and self-confident smile, making only occasional references to the scimitar on his wall and the precise portion of my body he planned to amputate if it ever became necessary to do so.

[1] It was in that week of the beginning of the German-Soviet war that I received a letter from Irene telling me that she was engaged to be married. It didn't matter any longer and I sent her a joyful letter of congratulations. She was married on July 26, 1941.

2

During July, I slowly calmed down. On the whole, the Germans continued to advance, and, in fact they took the Smolensk area, including Petrovichi (in which such Jews as had not fled, including, I presume, many Asimovs, were wiped out).

There was no sign of a Soviet surrender, however, or a collapse, or even an overall weakening. It was clear that the Germans were meeting a quality of resistance they had not thus far encountered anywhere, and suddenly the papers were full of such phrases as "the mighty Red Army."

The war was brought home to me a little more personally when, on July 1, there was a second draft-registration. I was over twenty-one now, and this time I registered.

The next day I registered in another way—for a summer course in phase rule at Columbia. Phase rule was one of the items I had left totally blank on the Qualifyings, and I didn't want that to happen during my forthcoming second try.

I wish that my foresight had worked as well in other directions.

Working my way through my diary shows me that I had a number of ideas for which I had not written stories. On July 5, 1941, for instance, I record the fact, "I'm trying to weave a plot around a planet of a dwarf star that has a two-minute year! I did lots of figuring on it. . . ."

Nothing ever came of it; I didn't write the story.

Too bad! Had I written it, I would have had a story about a neutron star a quarter century before any were discovered. It would have been the *first* neutron-star story ever written. What a shame!

3

But then the summer saw a slackening in my writing. There was a phase rule class every day for six weeks, and it wasn't an easy class. Then, too, I spent hours every day at the radio.

Yet although my writing languished, I was keeping up a steady drumfire of dates with this girl or that—if you want to call a date what usually consisted of a long walk or an occasional movie.

I even tried to learn how to dance. First Marcia tried to teach me, but that didn't work because she could only follow and she didn't know what it was that boys did when they led. Then I tried to take a class in it and eventually learned how to fox-trot or waltz in a very clumsy and mechanical way, and never learned any more than that.

Girls were invariably tolerant of my dancing—for one dance. They never badgered me for a second. Nor did I badger them for even the first; the music never stopped soon enough for me.

On August 9, 1941, after the usual long walk, and the conversation in the park (that was the "*Gut yontiff*, Pontiff" occasion), a girl invited me to her place. Her parents were away somewhere and we were alone in the apartment.

Nothing very serious happened since, for one thing, neither of us had a contraceptive device.[2] There was some foreplay, however, and that was my first introduction to the female body from a tactile standpoint.

I didn't get home till 5:00 A.M. (she lived many miles from Windsor Place) and I found the entire family—every one of them—out in the street waiting for me. There had been no occasion, you see, when it would have been possible for me to report home without utterly humiliating myself or, worse, being ordered to return.

My mother was horrified at my having stayed out "all night" with a girl, and I think she was ready to call the police and have me thrown in jail for the fracture of a mother's heart in the second degree. My father, however, after some moments of stupefaction at my flat announcement that I was over twenty-one and my own boss, came to my defense.

Heaven knows what went on in his mind or what he thought I had done, but apparently there was a kind of masculine free masonry that stepped in and lifted him above his own prudishness. He pulled my mother off me and kept her from calling the police (or possibly the mighty Red Army).

However, the young lady was too far off to reach easily and I suspect she felt she had better things to do than to seduce children (she was several years older than I was), and nothing more came of it.

If, however, I remained backward in sex, I rapidly learned, during that summer of experimentation, how to "kid around" with girls—that is, how to make playful sexual allusions. Once I overcame my fright at saying anything of the sort (in particular, my fear that the young woman would call the police and do my mother's job for her) I found it a fascinating game, made up of word play and riposte, which I was naturally adept at, and which I have never outgrown.

There was a girl named Phyllis Roberts in the phase rule class who was short, plump, and very bright. She was married, and was an excellent subject on whom to practice this newfound delight. She didn't

[2] Having learned my lesson, I bought my first condoms ten days later, nerving myself to the task with the greatest difficulty—and then I never got to use them.

get embarrassed when I wiggled my eyebrows at her and she could, in fact, give as good as she got.

As the class drew to its close, we decided to work out the final problems together. For that purpose, I took the subway to Queens and found her house (I thought nothing by now of wandering all over New York), and all through the afternoon we slaved away at the problems in scholarly austerity. When we were finished, she invited me to stay for dinner and about that time her husband came home. He wasn't in the least perturbed at my presence and, over dinner, I started the game.

Phyllis put her fork down and said, "Why is it, Asimov, that all afternoon, when we were alone, you acted like a eunuch, and as soon as my husband comes home, you turn into a goat?"

I hadn't noticed that, but as soon as she called it to my attention, I suddenly realized that, *of course*—the game can only be played when it is safe, when there are people around. When you're alone with a girl, the game makes no sense. You are either interested and make some real move, or you're not and you leave her alone.

It all gave me a peculiar kind of split personality. My writing was at that time and has remained ever since (with very few deliberate exceptions) quite pure. One critic, a young nun, described me in a paper she wrote on my science fiction, as possessing a "sense of decorum," which I *do*—in my writing.

In general conversation, however, I have no sense of decorum whatever. I do not use those words generally described as "vulgar" in the dictionary, but I am a sufficient master of polite English to be able to say anything vulgar that I wish to say without descending to the vulgar. It may sound innocent on the surface, but I can always grin or wiggle my eyebrows or both, if anyone is slow on the uptake, and eventually those who know me also know that nothing I say is *ever* innocent.

Cyril Kornbluth, however, my fellow Futurian, wrote very ribald stories at times, but in social conversation would not allow anything improper to pass his lips, nor would listen with equanimity to ribaldry from anyone else.

He particularly disapproved of my artlessly improper conversations, and had no hesitation in making it plain that he disapproved of everything else about me in consequence. I'm afraid I never made any attempt to placate him.

4

With all this, writing slowed to a crawl. It took me ten weeks to complete "Source of Power," and it was only five thousand words long when, finally, on August 17, it was done. I took it to *Thrilling Wonder* which, about 3½ weeks later, rejected it. (I didn't bother showing it to Campbell. I had learned well that Campbell's idea of humor didn't match mine.)

Something much more important had happened between myself and Campbell in the meantime, however.

On August 1, 1941, I took the subway to Campbell's office after class was over. On the way down I racked my brain for a story idea. Failing, I tried a device I sometimes used. I opened a book at random and then tried free association, beginning with whatever I first saw.

The book I had with me was a collection of the Gilbert and Sullivan plays. I opened it to *Iolanthe*—to the picture of the Fairy Queen throwing herself at the feet of Private Willis, the sentry. Thinking of sentries, I thought of soldiers, of military empires, of the Roman Empire—of the Galactic Empire—aha!

The fate of "Pilgrimage" was rankling me. Not only had Campbell rejected it four times, but also Pohl had rejected it twice, and *Amazing* once. Seven rejections in all. It was a future-historical and I still wanted to write a future-historical. Why shouldn't I write of the fall of the Galactic Empire and the return of feudalism, written from the viewpoint of someone in the secure days of the Second Galactic Empire? I thought I knew how to do it for I had read Edward Gibbon's *Decline and Fall of the Roman Empire* from first page to last at least twice, and I had only to make use of that.

I was bubbling over by the time I got to Campbell's, and my enthusiasm was catching. It was perhaps *too* catching, for Campbell blazed up as I had never seen him do.

"That's too large a theme for a short story," he said.

"I was thinking of a novelette," I said, quickly, adjusting my thoughts.

"Or a novelette. It will have to be an open-ended series of stories."

"What?" I said, weakly.

"Short stories, novelettes, serials, all fitting into a particular future history, involving the fall of the First Galactic Empire, the period of feudalism that follows, and the rise of the Second Galactic Empire."

"What?" I said, even more weakly.

"Yes, I want you to write an outline of the future history. Go home and write the outline."

There Campbell had made a mistake. Robert Heinlein was writing what he called the "Future History Series." He was writing various stories that fitted into one niche or another of the series, and he wasn't writing them in order. Therefore he had prepared a Future History outline that was very detailed and complicated, so that he would keep everything straight. Now Campbell wanted me to do the same.

Heinlein, however, was Heinlein—and Asimov was *not* Heinlein.

I went home, dutifully, and began preparing an outline that got longer and longer and stupider and stupider until I finally tore it up. It was quite plain that I couldn't work with an outline. (To this day I cannot—for any of my stories, articles, or books, whether fiction or non-fiction.)

On August 11, therefore, I started the story I had originally intended to write (with modifications that resulted from my discussions with Campbell), and the heck with possible future stories. I'd worry about them when the time came—and *if* the time came.

Since the First Galactic Empire was breaking down (in my story), certain scientists had set up a Foundation on a world at the rim of the Galaxy, purportedly to prepare a vast encyclopedia of human knowledge, but actually to cut down the period of feudalism and hasten the rise of the Second Empire. I called the story "Foundation" (and the stories to which it gave rise have been lumped together, consequently, as "the Foundation series").

5

August 15, 1941, was a busy day. Not only was it the last day of class in phase rule, but it was also the day I obtained a copy of the September 1941 *Astounding*, the one containing "Nightfall."[3] It didn't just contain "Nightfall," it *featured* "Nightfall." It had taken me over three years but I had finally achieved an *Astounding* cover. The cover painting was a magnificent scene from the very climax of the story, when the stars finally appeared, and all it said on the cover was " 'Nightfall,' by Isaac Asimov."

I wasn't aware at the time that the story created any unusual stir. Present in the same issue after all was the last of Heinlein's serial, "Methusaleh's Children," and another Heinlein story under a pseudonym. Also present was Alfred Bester's classic "Adam and No Eve." I suspected that "Nightfall" would be lost in the shuffle.

And yet—after "Nightfall" appeared, I was no longer a minor writer, hovering about the fringes of science-fiction fame. Finally, after three years of trying, I was accepted as a major figure in the field—and I was still only twenty-one.

The only catch was that I myself still didn't know it, which was a

[3] See *Nightfall and Other Stories* (Doubleday, 1941).

good thing. I continued to strain every nerve, thinking I hadn't made it yet, and years later when it began to dawn on me that I had, I did my best to put it out of my mind. I had decided I was better off running hard; and I liked it better, too. I'm still running hard today.

Yet in one respect, I must admit, I was dissatisfied with "Nightfall." Campbell, finding my ending lacking, had inserted a paragraph of his own very near the end that was very effective but simply wasn't me. It has been praised as proof that I could write "poetically," which gravels me, since I don't want to write poetically; I only want to write clearly. Worst of all, Campbell thoughtlessly mentioned Earth in his paragraph. I had carefully refrained from doing so all through the story, since Earth did not exist within the context of the story. Its mention was a serious literary flaw.

Also on August 15, word reached me that Malcolm Reiss, editor of *Planet*, was considering the acceptance of that oft-battered story "Pilgrimage." On the eighteenth, I went to his office to discuss the matter with him and it turned out he wanted a revision (which was to be the seventh the poor story would undergo). What he wanted me to do was to take out the religious angle. It had gone in on Campbell's insistence and it would go out now on Reiss's. I agreed; I had too much invested in the story to let it drop now.

Finally, on that same August 15, I received my first draft classification. I was 2A. That meant I wasn't subject to immediate draft (that would have been 1A) but was deferred because I was a student. The draft classification was only good for six months and my status would then have to be reviewed.

6

I submitted "Foundation" to Campbell on September 8,[4] and on September 17, I received my check—$126. It was smaller than the one I received for "Nightfall," though the two stories were nearly equal in length, because there was no bonus for this one. Campbell did not hand them out lightly.

Knowing that Campbell wanted me to write a series, by the way, I had employed a little shrewdness in keeping him from backing away. After working up a complicated problem in "Foundation," I had the

---

[4] By September my panic over the possibilities of a Nazi victory had vanished completely. The Germans were still advancing, but it was clear that the invasion of the Soviet Union was not another blitzkrieg and that they were paying an increasingly serious price. Furthermore, American help to Great Britain was increasing steadily, and I decided that Hitler would not make it.

hero muse at the end, "—the solution to this first crisis was obvious. Obvious as all hell!"

And that was the end! I didn't say what the solution was, and Campbell let me get away with it.

The idea was that Campbell would have to let me write the sequel now, and would, moreover, have to take it. How clever of me!

What I didn't quite take into account was that the second story would have to be published in the issue after the one in which "Foundation" appeared, making it a kind of two-part serial, meaning that I would have to have the second story done within a couple of months at most, or "Foundation" would be delayed in its appearance. And if that happened, Campbell would be disappointed in me.

I foolishly anticipated there would be no trouble, but once I set about writing the second story in the series, I quickly became very sorry I had been so infernally clever. When the going became hard, I couldn't abandon the story—I couldn't even put it aside to let it ripen; I just had to keep working.

I had never painted myself into quite so tight a corner before.

But "Foundation" wasn't the only bright spot in my writing career at the time. It turned out that *Astonishing* and *Super Science* had not been suspended after all, or if they had, the publisher had changed his mind. Pohl was no longer editor, but the magazines continued under another.

Pohl, out of a job, asked if he might handle some of my stories again, and I agreed on a very loose basis. He could have some stories that I didn't want to bother with anymore; but I just didn't want a regular agent. It was a very uncomfortable arrangement, and very unfair to Pohl, so it didn't last long.

It lasted long enough, though, to get "Pilgrimage" sold, for it was Pohl who submitted that story to *Planet*. He also sold my old story "Weapon" (written three years before as my sixth story) to *Astonishing*. It was only four thousand words long but he got $20 for it ($.005 a word) and, of course, kept $2.00 as his agent's fee and gave me $18.00. (And he got $18 out of the overall $180 that was paid for "Pilgrimage.")

Then, in the October 1941 *Astounding*, "Not Final"[5] appeared. It was my eighteenth published story and I was beginning to take my appearances in magazines for granted. I no longer carried them around to show people.

On the other hand, I had not said good-bye to rejections alto-

[5] See *The Early Asimov*.

gether. *Thrilling Wonder* sent back "Source of Power" on September 13, and I sent it on to *Amazing*. Rejections no longer had the power to deject me utterly, however. They were beginning to seem mere way stations to eventual acceptances—which, indeed, they had finally become.

7

On September 18, there were colored streamers in the sky over Brooklyn, fading and changing. I guessed they were the Northern Lights making a very unusual far southern appearance, and I was right. Some huge flare on the solar surface had initiated a terrific electric storm in the upper atmosphere, and the auroral streamers were sent record distances southward. It was the only time I had ever seen the aurora.

It's a pity I lack that simple faith that convinced so many people that the universe is run entirely for the benefit of individual human beings. Looking back on it now I could say that the heavens were celebrating the appearance of "Nightfall" and the initiation of the Foundation series.

8

It was registration time again—time to begin my seventh year at Columbia University, and my third as a graduate student. On September 23, I signed up for "food analysis," another branch of chemistry in which I had drawn a zero in my previous attempt at the Qualifyings.

The course was taught by Professor Arthur W. Thomas, elderly, white-haired, red-faced, and short-tempered. His lectures were rather dull, and once when I spent my time writing comic verses, he caught me grinning, scolded me publicly before the class, and then called me into his office to go into more detailed analyses of my high crimes and misdemeanors. I listened stoically. I had been hearing this sort of thing from my teachers since the first grade.

Such things made more than dull and repetitious hearing, however. They generally interfered with my much-interfered-with career. In this case, for instance (as I discovered a couple of years later), Thomas ordered the lab assistants to get rid of me. (It was they who told me of it, eventually.)

That doesn't mean they put out a contract on me. Their way of doing it was to give me difficult objects to analyze. When we were doing fat analyses, everyone else got a liquid oil; I got a solid fat and had to melt it before I could do anything else. (At first I took a sample, melted it partly, and poured off some of the liquid, but the first portion was not representative of the whole and I got answers I recognized as ridiculous. I had to get the notion of melting it all, and mixing it, before taking my sample, and the lab assistants were strangely non-helpful when I consulted them.)

Then, in doing Kjeldahl determinations of nitrogen, everyone else got starchy materials with 1 to 2 per cent nitrogen, and I was given powdered protein with 16 per cent nitrogen. That meant my first attempt drowned the analytic procedure in nitrogen excess and I had to start all over with a smaller sample.

Yet it all worked out well. In the first place, although I nearly worked myself to death, I managed to hand in good results, which must have impressed Thomas. More than that, I was far too stupid to realize I was being had. Not once did it occur to me that all the complications were not pure accident, so I never complained that I was being mistreated. That was also impressive since I imagine it was attributed to my being a good sport and *pukka sahib*, rather than to my being grossly stupid.

Furthermore, not only did I do the analyses, but also (as was my wont) I was ebullient in the lab, cracking jokes, laughing, singing, and this annoyed some of the more deadpan students, whose concentration was very difficult to keep in being.

Professor Caldwell, always pro-Asimov from the start, broke the news to me. "I think," she said in her gentle way, "that some of the students in the food analysis laboratory think you're just a little too noisy. Perhaps you should be more careful in that direction, because they're complaining to Professor Thomas."

(The idiots might have complained to me, but I suspect they didn't want me to stop singing—they wanted me out of the class.)

I thought it advisable to see Thomas and discuss the matter, and decided to see if I couldn't charm the old fellow. After all, if Elderfield and Urey could be counted on to vote against me, I didn't need any further certain anti-Asimov votes.

On December 3, I came in to keep the appointment I had made. I said (might as well get to the point), "I understand, Professor Thomas, that you are receiving complaints about my behavior in lab."

"Yes, I am," he said gruffly. "Why the hell do you sing in lab, Asimov?"

Good! I was prepared for that question. I said, earnestly, "Because I'm not in chemistry to make a living, sir. It's not my bread-and-butter. I'm going to make money writing. I'm in chemistry because I love it. It's my cakes-and-ale, and I can't help singing when I'm working. I'll try to stop, sir, but it will be an effort. It's no effort not to sing for those who complain. I don't imagine they like their work."

It was a little exaggerated, but not really far off. It was also a calculated gamble, and it worked. Thomas was impressed, and from that moment on we were buddies. It was the case of Professor Lyon all over again, except that this time it was a calculated ploy. I don't often calculate a ploy, alas; I talk first and think afterward, or not at all, as a general rule. It's a shame, because when I can bring myself to think a bit and do things the right way, I generally get the results I want.

Just the same, I cut out most of the singing in lab and behaved myself thereafter.

The check representing payment for "Pilgrimage" finally arrived from *Planet Stories* on October 7, 1941. It was for $162 (minus Pohl's agent's fee). It had taken 2½ years of trying before I sold it; and it had had seven revisions and ten rejections on the way. No other story I ever wrote had so wild a history. The check was large, only $4.00 less than the record sum I received for "Nightfall," but, considering the amount of work entailed, it was tiny.

Never again was I to agree to do more than one substantial editorially requested revision. If, after that one revision, I still couldn't make it, then I just waited for a new market—or an old market with a new editor.

Then, the next day, I received $50 from *Amazing* for "Source of Power." That was sold on the second try, and it was another of those stories (not many) that I didn't let Campbell see—and with good reason, for it was rotten.

But I was still making trouble for myself over the second story of the Foundation series. So overconfident was I that I didn't even start it right away. Instead, I coolly cut down the margin of time I would have available for writing it by deciding to shift gears and turn out another positronic robot story.

This was "Runaround," which, after a few false starts, I began on October 4, 1941. It dealt with the attempt of my heroes to make robots work on Mercury, where the environment put them irritatingly out of order. This story was the first one in which I explicitly stated all three Laws of Robotics and in which I then had the plot depend on their interplay. It took me only two weeks to write. I submitted it to Campbell on October 20, and on that same day he read it and ordered a check. I received $72 in the mail on the twenty-third.

There was no question that I had Campbell's range at last. It was the sixth successive story I had submitted to him for *Astounding* that he had accepted. (Two stories, intended for *Unknown*, he had rejected.)

And all those sales were reflecting themselves in the state of my solvency. My bank account was at $450, an astronomical sum indeed. In an emergency, I could draw out enough money to pay a year's tuition at any time.

I was becoming a quasi celebrity, too. At least Phyllis, the young woman with whom I worked out phase rule problems, told me she was talking to a chemical engineering student and when my name came up naturally in conversation, he grew very excited. Phyllis suddenly realized she had gained enormously in stature (with him) through knowing me. It was a situation that was to become so common that I ceased noticing it, but this was the first case of it and I glowed with a simple-minded pride.

9

Finally, on October 24,[6] I began the sequel to "Foundation," which I called "Bridle and Saddle." In it I explained how the Foundation had solved the initial problem and went on to describe how they had established a permanent hegemony over the neighboring kingdoms. In the first three days I typed seventeen pages, and I spoke loftily in my diary of "effortless spurts" and said, "Novelettes are so much easier than shorts."

They had better be, for October 27, when I visited Campbell, his first words were "I want that Foundation story," and at once, as though by magic, "Bridle and Saddle" ground to a halt. On October 30, I said, "my thoughts concerning the yarn have been most depressing. It doesn't seem to go."

I tried revision and that didn't help. I tried bulling my way forward and it stalled anyway. I grew panicky. I had to have it done. There was no way in which I could fail to get it in to Campbell in November, and I had to have it good enough or I would lose all credibility in his eyes. My wise-guy overconfidence had now rebounded and pinned me to the wall. I was in despair.

It was Fred Pohl, once again, who came to my rescue. I visited him

---

[6] During October 1941, the Germans were driving hard toward Moscow, were within sixty miles and were announcing that the war was all but over. They had taken the entire Ukraine and had surrounded Leningrad (and, though I didn't know it at the time, my Uncle Boris, my father's youngest brother, was inside Leningrad during the siege). I didn't believe the German boasts, however. The Soviets had endured four months, when I had (in my heart) only given them four weeks to begin with—and now I was certain they would last forever.

on November 2. (We visited back and forth constantly, as a matter of course.) We walked across Brooklyn Bridge, I remember, and while leaning against the rail and looking down at the river, I told him of my troubles with "Bridle and Saddle."[7]

His suggestions were excellent ones, but what they were, I don't remember, and I didn't record them in my diary. In any case, I rushed home, began work again, and found the story moving easily. Without Pohl I don't know if I could have managed, and then what would have happened to the Foundation series?

I finished "Bridle and Saddle" on November 16, without further trouble, and took it in on November 17. Campbell read it then and there and bought it—but again without a bonus. (How easily one is spoiled. After "Nightfall" an acceptance without a bonus felt like a rejection to me.) Even so, since the story was eighteen thousand words long, as long as "Pilgrimage," I received $180, the largest check yet.

10

Although my friendship with Pohl was deep and abiding, my connection with the Futurians generally was increasingly tenuous. I had attended a meeting as late as October 9, but pretty soon I was to drift away altogether.

Looking back on it now, my connection was always tenuous for I didn't fit the mold.

Some apparently, drank freely and on a few occasions, some may even have been drunk. I not only did not drink myself, I was also never even aware that *they* drank.

Again, there were female members with whom there were naturally, interactions. There were marriages among the Futurians, and less formal liaisons. Not only was I never involved in any of this sexual activity; again, I never even knew it was going on. In fact, I don't even think I knew there were female members.

I am not surprised, really, at the fact that I was ignorant of all this. There is a hard core of nonobservance in me. My brother, Stan, once told me that in any group, my eyes remained glazed over till my name was mentioned—and I think this rule held true not only for conversation but for all other human interactions as well.

What does surprise me is that none of the other Futurians ever attempted to corrupt me—to lure me into drinking or into sexual activity. Maybe they did and I never noticed!

[7] The reason we walked across Brooklyn Bridge, I found out decades later, was that his wife, Leslie Perri, detested me and wouldn't have me in the apartment. I don't know why.

11

Another sign of adulthood came. I could vote. I had registered (that was the occasion on which I had taken my bachelor's diploma with me and had been scolded for it), and on November 4, 1941, my father and I went gravely down to the voting booth to exercise our franchises.

It was an off-year election, but New York's mayoralty was up for votes, and I voted for the re-election of Fiorello LaGuardia, the best mayor (in my opinion) and the most colorful mayor (in anybody's) that New York had ever had.

Two days later, the January 1942 *Startling Stories* reached the stands. It contained "Christmas on Ganymede,"[8] my nineteenth published story, and I read it rather captiously. It had been tampered with editorially, not through the insertion of paragraphs, as was Campbell's wont, but through the general revision of each sentence in the direction of blah. It amounted to assiduous adjustment by a non writer. Heaven knows that the story, as I wrote it, fell short of Tolstoy, but it didn't fall as far short as it did after the editor got to work on it.

On November 17, the day Campbell took "Bridle and Saddle," he told me of a plan of his for starting a new department in *Astounding*, one to be called "Probability Zero."

This was to be a department of short-shorts, five hundred to one thousand words each, which were to be in the nature of plausible and entertaining Munchausen-like lies. Campbell's notion was that, aside from the entertainment value of these things, they would offer a place where beginners could penetrate the market without having to compete quite so hard with established writers. They would form a stairway to professional status.

This was a good idea in theory and even worked a little in practice. Ray Bradbury, who was to become one of the best-known and most successful of all science-fiction writers, broke into the field with a "Probability Zero" item half a year later. Hal Clement and George O. Smith also published "Probability Zero" items near the very start of their careers.

Unfortunately, it didn't work *enough*. Campbell had to start the department going with professionals, hoping to let the amateurs carry on once they saw what it was Campbell wanted. There were, however, never enough amateurs who could meet Campbell's standards even for

[8] See *The Early Asimov*.

short-shorts of an undemanding nature, and after twelve appearances of "Probability Zero" over a space of 2½ years, Campbell gave up.

On November 17, 1941, however, he was just beginning, and he wanted me to do a "Probability Zero" for him. I was delighted that he considered me to be at that stage of excellence where he could order me to do something for him according to measure. I promptly sat down and wrote a short-short called "Big Game." On November 24, I showed it to Campbell. He glanced over it, and, rather to my astonishment handed it back. It wasn't what he wanted.[9]

I tried a second time and did a humorous positronic robot short-short called "First Law." I showed it to Campbell on December 1, and he didn't like that either. I was chagrined, and made up my mind to try once more, but *only* once more.

[9] In *The Early Asimov*, I included "Big Game" among the list of those stories of mine that disappeared. Not so. I had had it all those years and, without knowing it, had included the manuscript with papers of mine that I had donated to the Boston University library. A young science-fiction enthusiast, Matthew Bruce Tepper, who had prepared an accurate and exhaustive bibliography of my science fiction, went through my papers at BU, uncovered the manuscript, and sent me a Xerox copy. I had the story published in *Before the Golden Age* (Doubleday, 1974).

29

Qualifying Examinations

1

All through November 1941, the Germans had been inching forward here and there on the long Russian front, but *nobody* was talking blitzkrieg any more. On November 22, the Germans took Rostov at the northeastern tip of the Sea of Azov, and then, on November 29, the Soviet forces *recaptured it.*

It is impossible to describe now what excitement that bare announcement made. In over two years of World War II, the German Army had never once lost a city it had taken, not *once.* And now they had! It was the first sign that the Germans could be not merely resisted, not merely slowed down, not merely halted, but actually *thrown back.*

And although Germany was still striving toward Moscow and was only forty miles away from that goal, her advance was so slow that it was clear to everyone that the Nazis would have to halt for the winter. Germany would be forced to spend a winter in the Soviet Union with supply lines hundreds of miles long.

I sat back to enjoy that winter. As far as I could tell, nothing in world affairs concerned me at that moment but the titanic struggle taking place in the steppes and forests of the land of my birth. In all the excitement over events in the Soviet Union, I scarcely mentioned in my diary the fact that there was in late 1941 a profound diplomatic struggle between Japan and the United States.

I didn't for one moment believe that there would be war between the United States and Japan. The United States had to concentrate on Europe and, as for Japan, what could she do? She was stalled in China and helpless. And even if the United States and Japan were to fight a war, it seemed to me that the American Navy could take care of matters in short order—so I paid no attention.

On Sunday, December 7, 1941, therefore, I sat down rather grimly to make my third attempt at "Probability Zero." It was a ridiculous story called "Time Pussy," inspired by a remark by one of my classmates in food analysis laboratory. (He was Mario Castillo, a short, round-faced, quick-witted, and pleasant fellow.) He had told me, jokingly, about a man who invented a device that cooled water so quickly that when the ice formed it was still warm.

It didn't take me long to write the story, and by early afternoon it was safely done, and I turned on the radio to relax. My father was taking his afternoon nap, but it was all right to listen to the radio (low) while he slept. Unlike my mother, he slept soundly.

But you're ahead of me. Just before 3:00 P.M. the music faded and an excited voice began to read a news bulletin. The Japanese had just bombed Pearl Harbor. I ran for my father's bedroom. As far as I can remember, I had never before deliberately awakened him in the middle of his nap, but I did now.

"Pappa, Pappa!" I shook him, madly.

He sat up with a start. "What's the matter?"

I said, "We're at war. The Japanese have bombed us."

It took him a while to gather it in. Then he turned on the little radio near his bed. He never once complained that he had been awakened.

2

And even so, life went on. I suppose the dramatic thing to say at this point was that I immediately rushed to the recruiting station to enlist, but I did no such thing. I was ready to go whenever the armed forces demanded my services, but I had no desire to anticipate their needs.

Instead, on December 8, I took "Time Pussy" to Campbell—and he was there at the same old stand, doing his job. He read the story and took it "none too enthusiastically" (my diary says).

He had three "Probability Zero" stories now, the other two being by L. Sprague de Camp and Malcolm Jameson, both senior to me in age and writing experience. Campbell wanted one by an apparent newcomer to give amateurs courage. He felt therefore that I should make the sacrifice and publish under a pseudonym.

I did so, reluctantly. I chose George E. Dale as my pseudonym. I don't know why. The name just popped into my head and I put it down.

That same day, life went on in the food lab, too. I handed in my analysis of butter fat, and Professor Thomas found my results to be on the nose and said it was an "excellent analysis." He was visibly pleased with the young man who loved chemistry so much.

And the day after that, the February 1942 *Amazing* arrived and it had my story "Source of Power" in it, except that Ray Palmer had changed the title to "Robot AL-76 Goes Astray."[1] That was a com-

[1] See *The Rest of the Robots* (Doubleday, 1964).

pletely ridiculous title but I never cared enough for the story to bother changing it back.

But life was not entirely normal. In fact, it grew horrible as the months passed by. There had been the initial rage at Japan's sudden attack and a certain euphoria in the certainty that we would now smash her, but good—something I shared, I think, with just about every other American.

What very few Americans realized was that our fleet had simply been destroyed at Pearl Harbor and that for a while, we had nothing with which to punish the Japanese. For half a year, the United States had to experience the frustration of falling back continually.

On December 6, I had looked forward to a kind of grim triumph as I watched the Nazis get their lumps in the Soviet Union. Instead it was a dreadful winter of watching the United States apparently unable to get off the ground in the Pacific.

Between remaining glued to the radio and trying to fight off the gathering depression of spirits, I was unable even to think of writing. For two months I did not write a word.

But if December was worthless as far as writing was concerned (except for the $10 I received for "Time Pussy"), the fact remained that in the course of the year 1941, my fourth as a professional writer, I had sold *thirteen* stories, better than one a month—as compared with fourteen stories I had sold in the first three years altogether.

My literary income for 1941 was $1,060 and, frankly, I found it utterly unbelievable. I decided for the first time (but not for the last) that I had reached a peak I might never be able to duplicate. After all, I could scarcely sell more than thirteen stories in any one year, and even if I sold every one of them to Campbell at top rates with a bonus thrown in I couldn't make more than $2,500 dollars perhaps, so that an annual income of $1,000 seemed about the practical limit.

I wasn't complaining, mind you; $1,000 a year was good pocket money for something I wanted very much to do.

3

Yet I couldn't lose myself entirely in the military defeats of the moment. I was sure that all would straighten itself out in the end. It was impossible for me to suppose that once the United States was finally able to exert its full strength, Japan (or, for that matter, Germany) could stand before it.

So I had to continue to try to decide what to do with my own life. My second attempt at the Qualifying Examinations was only a couple of months away and I had to take into consideration the rather strong possibility that I would be turned down again. That would mean I would have to leave Columbia.

One alternative would be to find a job, and I had made tentative moves in this direction. For one thing, Columbia University was setting up a special course in explosives. (I rather had a notion this involved uranium fission, but after Urey's reaction to my innocent remark, I knew better than to check on this with anybody.) It was not my sort of thing, for with my lack of skill in the lab, it seemed to me that working with explosives would be suicide. I applied anyway, in order to keep as many options open as possible—and I was relieved when I was rejected.

I also continued to try various Civil Service examinations, and I announced myself as willing to take jobs in Buffalo, New York, and even in Huntsville, Alabama, where jobs seemed to be available. At one point, I was ready to take a train to Huntsville in order to be on the spot if they wanted me there—but was prevented from doing so (thank goodness) by discovering that in wartime, such trips required reservations, which I didn't have. No jobs came my way, anyway.

Finally, there was the alternative of continuing my education—if not at Columbia, then elsewhere. The logical elsewhere was New York University. It could start at the level of my master's degree.[2]

On December 20, 1941, New York University accepted me as a graduate student, one who would presumably be working toward his Ph.D. I wasn't sure exactly what it meant. Would I have to retake some courses? Would I have to take a new set of Qualifyings? Would I, on the other hand, be able to start in research at once?

I had no answers for this but, for the moment, I had a fallback position as the new year of 1942 started. (I turned twenty-two on January 2, 1942, something that evoked the sad remark, "I'm growing old" in my diary.)

I made a number of trips to NYU in January and learned that I *would* have to take Qualifying Examinations, yes, but *meanwhile* I could start research. I began seeing various professors, for in doing research, the student interviews professors, rather than vice versa. The point is to have the student locate, if possible, a line of investigation in which he would be satisfied to invest a couple of years—and possibly an entire professional lifetime.

It came about, therefore, that I could take the Qualifyings at Columbia without a horrible sensation of absolute doom hanging over me. The three days for those tests came on January 24, 27, and 29, 1942—

[2] The official notification that an M.A. diploma had been awarded me came on December 17, 1941.

the whole being spread over five days rather than two weeks, as in the first case.

The first day's tests were, for the most part, advanced physical chemistry, in which I did not expect to do much. The second day was on advanced inorganic chemistry, and I thought I did rather well ("five times" as well as the first time was the enthusiastic estimate in my diary).

On the third day came the advanced organic chemistry, and it seemed to me that I botched it. The more I thought so, the sweatier I got, and the more botchery I kept committing. I ended in despair and was quite convinced that this was my last day at Columbia and that there was nothing to it now but to crawl to New York University a beaten man.

As though to underline that, the Spring 1942 issue of *Planet* arrived that day containing my story "Pilgrimage," my most conspicuous failure in the literary portion of my life. Again, the title had suffered a sea change and a particularly awful one. It was the lead novelette, my name was on the cover, but, after all the insistence that I remove religion, Reiss had renamed the story "Black Friar of the Flame."[3]

That story has always been considered by knowledgeable fans to be the worst story of mine ever to see print. I don't entirely agree; I think I have published some early stories that were even worse—as, for instance, "Secret Sense." I think, however, that the horrible title "Black Friar of the Flame" had a lot to do with the consensus.

4

Deep in multiple depression, I assumed that Columbia was ending in flames as black as that of the friar and that there was nothing to do but move full speed ahead at NYU.

On February 2 and 3, I registered at NYU, but carefully deferred payment until the news from Columbia was official. I signed up for a series of courses and, on February 4, I attended my first class there. I listened to a professor discuss the determination of carbohydrate struc ture by the great nineteenth-century chemist Emil Fischer.

Periodically, though, even while I was taking my NYU courses and finding that I could not avoid taking *their* Qualifyings in March, I would go up to Columbia to see my old friends. They kept trying to cheer me up, and Lloyd Roth offered to bet I would pass.

I said, uneasily, that I didn't gamble, and he said, "All right, no

[3] See *The Early Asimov*.

money on your part. I'll bet you a dollar against your mustache. If you fail, I give you a dollar, so it won't be a total loss. If you pass, you have to shave off your mustache." (Like everybody else in the world except me, he hated my mustache.)

I agreed.

The results were due on February 13, and on the twelfth I was at Columbia to see if I could smoke out any advance news. Nobody was supposed to give out any news until the official posting, but there was no way I could avoid learning what had happened.

Professor Thomas grinned at me and said, "Go home and write a story." Professor Caldwell said, "I can't tell you the results—but don't worry too much." Someone else said, "I mustn't tell—but don't commit suicide." Professor Victor K. LaMer scorned all subterfuge. When I met him and asked if he had any idea of the results, he said, bluntly, "You passed."

It seemed like a unanimous opinion. I can only presume that Professor Thomas, impressed by my handling of unknown samples designed to "get rid of me" and by my defense of my singing in the lab, had thrown the full weight of his opinion in my favor (he had given me an A— for the course I had taken with him) and had swayed the committee. It didn't hurt that Urey had quit his post as head of the department to devote himself entirely to war work (after his crocodile tears in class) and that none other than Thomas had taken over as acting head. (I could not have foreseen that.)

In any case, the official results were posted on Friday the thirteenth (not bad for a Friday the thirteenth) and I did the honest thing. I went to the barber's and had my mustache shaved off. My face was smooth again. I then went to New York University and dismantled my setup there.

I was twenty-two, I had qualified for research, and I was on my way toward a Ph.D.

30

Gertrude

1

While the first six weeks of the new year seemed entirely filled with Qualifyings, other things were taking place, too. Sometime in mid-January, I got a postcard from one Pauline Bloom, inviting me to attend meetings of something called the Brooklyn Authors Club. It's a sign of how sloppy I was getting about my diary entries that between my concern over my Qualifyings and over the war, I did not mention the card when it came.

I was flattered, however. I didn't know how Pauline had come to hear of me, but I took it to mean that my fame as a writer was spreading through the world and, of course, I assumed the Brooklyn Authors Club was an old, established, rich-in-tradition organization, and that an invitation from them was an accolade.

On January 19, 1942, I attended the meeting to which I had been invited and it was not at all what I expected. There were about a dozen people there, almost all of them well stricken in years (by twenty-two-year-old standards) and all of them mere beginners, even unpublished beginners. It turned out to be the kind of organization in which we read each other's manuscripts and then discussed them.

I ought to have been horrified, and I might have been at the start, but it quickly turned out to be fun. I liked to listen to the manuscripts and discuss them. Then, too, I had brought along "Legal Rites," and I read my manuscript "with expression" so everyone else was enthusiastic, which pleased me.

I also remember that some time was spent in discussing the war and in considering rumors that enemy ships were at sea to serve as bases for the bombing of New York. (This sort of thing exercised us vastly in the weeks after Pearl Harbor. There were air-raid alarms in New York and I think most people expected to be bombed.)

The meeting was sufficiently successful for me to make up my mind to attend future meetings. On February 2, I attended again, and had a good time again.

What it did for me was to get me back in the writing mood. Nearly two months had passed since Pearl Harbor and, finally, on February 2, I suggested another story to Campbell. It was to be a sequel to

"Not Final" and, after listening to the plot, Campbell suggested the title "Victory Unintentional." I got to work that very day and by February 8, I was finished. I brought it to Campbell on February 9.

On February 13, after official confirmation of my having passed the Qualifyings and right after I had shaved off my mustache, I visited Campbell in the best of spirits. He wasn't in, but Katherine Tarrant handed me the manuscript and there was no doubt about the results. A scrap of paper was attached on which Campbell had scribbled "$CH_3CH_2CH_2CH_2SH$." That was the chemical formula for butyl mercaptan, the substance that gives skunks their smell.

I had never received so brief and so devastating a rejection, but even that couldn't take away the greatness of the day. I wrote an answer on the note. "The next one will be ⟨chemical structure⟩ ." That was the formula for coumarin, which is what gives newmown hay its sweet and pleasant smell.

2

Meanwhile, I had attended still another meeting of the Brooklyn Authors Club "and had about the swellest time of my life," according to my diary. I had become the official reader by now, reading everyone's manuscripts and not my own only. It had turned out, you see, that I read with life and verve, while the others did so in a monotone.

I read my own rejected story "Big Game" to great applause, particularly that of a young man named Joe Goldberger, who attended a meeting for the first time on that day. "Big Game" so pleased him that he felt he would like to be more friendly.

He said to me at the conclusion of the meeting, "Let's get together next Saturday night and go out on the town. I'll bring my girl. You bring yours."

That scared me. The phrase "out on the town" sounded very expensive. Besides, while in the course of the nearly two years since Irene had left New York, I had had dates with at least a dozen girls, not one of them could possibly be considered "my girl." In fact, looking back through my diaries, there are girls' names mentioned that are only names now. None of them remain in my memory. (But let's be fair: I doubt very much that I remain in their memory.)

So I said, "I'm sorry, Joe. I don't have a girl."

That didn't seem to bother him. "That's all right. My girl will bring a girl for you."

The double date was for the Astor Hotel at Seventh Avenue and Forty-ninth Street, for Saturday, February 14 (Valentine's Day—something I didn't notice at the time), at 8:30 P.M.

I agreed with forced heartiness, still worried about the expense, and carefully jotted down Joe's telephone number in case I decided to back out. He may have expected that I would, for on February 13, in the evening, he called to remind me of the date.

That was the day I had passed my Qualifyings so I felt that nothing was too big for me to tackle and I told him in great glee that I would be there. Undoubtedly, if I had failed my Qualifyings, I would have backed out.

Apparently what was happening that made Joe keen on not letting me back out was that it was his girlfriend who was putting on the pressure. (I learned the story afterward and I hope I've got it straight.) Joe and his girlfriend (whose name was Lee) had been going together for quite a while and Joe seemed interested in marriage but Lee was not certain that he was the right man for her.

Lee had long wanted a chance to introduce Joe to a friend of hers —Gertrude Blugerman—in order to get Gertrude's estimate of his qualities. It seemed important to do so, however, under some color of legitimacy to avoid humiliating and angering Joe, and this double date seemed just the thing.

I became a mere pawn in this subtle plan of Lee's and didn't count. When Gertrude expressed strong objections to a blind date, Lee begged her to accept for the sake of meeting Joe and passing on his qualities. And if I turned out to be a disaster then surely even a disaster could be endured for a few hours. Then too, Joe had described me to Lee as a "Russian chemist with a mustache," and Lee had passed that description on to Gertrude and had done her best to imply to Gertrude that she would be meeting someone exotic and virile. (Russians were getting a good press in those months of the Soviet winter counteroffensive against the till-then invincible Nazis.)

The fact was, of course, that except for the place of my birth, I was pure Brooklyn; and on the day before the date, I had shaved off my mustache, being unaware that it was a selling point.

Naturally, I got to the Astor early (I am always early) and proceeded to wait. Lee caught sight of me before Gertrude did, and when Joe confirmed her horrified suspicion, she rushed back, full of apologies, and begged Gertrude to endure the evening somehow. I gather (when I was told the story in later years) that, at first glance, I struck Lee as unfit to date.

When I saw Gertrude, though, I saw at a glance that *she* was fit to date. She was five feet, two inches in height, a trifle on the plump side (which didn't bother me), with beautiful dark hair, and even more beautiful dark eyes, a generously proportioned figure, and—most of all—was the very image of Olivia de Havilland who, in my opinion, was the most beautiful actress in Hollywood and with whom I had fallen desperately in love when I saw *Captain Blood*.

Gee!

I still remember that evening. Gertrude told me on a later occasion that I seemed to be looking at her constantly and to be unaware of anything else.

Yes, indeed! She was exactly right!

Joe was in charge, so the date did not follow along the lines they usually did when I was in charge. The first place we went to was a bar.

"What do you want?" said Joe to me, expansively.

I looked uncertain and miserable, and whispered to him, "What am I supposed to have?"

He took in the situation and whispered back, "Have a half-and-half. That's very mild."

I didn't know what a half-and-half was. I said, "Sure."

So I got it and sipped it and it tasted like beer, so I hated it and just held it wondering what to do next. Meanwhile, everyone lit up a cigarette, including Gertrude, and Joe offered me one. I took it, he lit it, and now I had something in my other hand.

Gertrude watched me as I desperately sipped and tried to swallow and then, just as desperately, puffed and tried not to choke. She said, "You don't drink, do you?"

I shook my head miserably.

"You don't smoke either, do you?"

I shook my head again.

"Why are you trying to, then?"

I said, "I don't want to spoil things."

She said, "You won't spoil things."

So I put down the half-and-half and stepped on the cigarette. I felt much better after that.

On a later occasion, Gertrude told me that she had always led a most circumspect life (and so she had) and that I was the first person she had ever met who made her feel wicked by comparison. Apparently she didn't mind feeling wicked.

We then went down to Greenwich Village to see some arty movie called *The Forgotten Village* and after that we had a midnight snack.

Finally I said, "I can't stay out much later than this because I have to help with the paper delivery tomorrow morning at my father's candy store."

On a later occasion, Gertrude said that that had impressed her mightily. I had apparently made no attempt to pretty up the situation but had admitted having a father who owned a candy store. Nor did I pretend I did something more important than fool around with newspapers. It seemed very honest.

Actually, it should have seemed very stupid. If it had ever occurred to me that I might have gained ground by lying, I might very well have tried to. It just didn't occur to me, and it never does, even to this day. With all the years I now own and all the experience I now possess, I still somehow possess a foolish lack of sophistication in such things.

But I did take her home, even though it turned out she lived in Brighton Beach at the far end of Brooklyn, and I didn't get home till 4:00 A.M. (My father didn't mind what time I got home, actually, as long as I was in the store at 7:00 A.M. to help with the papers—and, of course, I was.)

3

That blind date on Valentine's day was exhilarating, but it *was* expensive, as I had feared. The whole thing had cost me $2.50, and although Joe, exuberant over the apparent success of the date spoke of another date on Thursday, I was dubious. Where was I to get the money?[1]

Yet when Thursday, February 19, came, I was there, too. Expensive or not, I wanted to see Gertrude again. I managed to get lost and showed up fifteen minutes late at the trysting place, but after that all went well. At a radio station we attended a discussion called "Brotherhood of Man: Is It Fact or Fiction?," which was free, and in which someone quoted a bit of doggerel I have remembered ever since:

> *The rain, it raineth every day*
> *Upon the just and unjust fella.*
> *But more upon the just, because*
> *The unjust has the just's umbrella.*

Then we went to a cafeteria, which was not very expensive, and then I took Gertrude home again and remained twenty minutes outside her apartment door talking with her.

It was very romantic, and I was no longer satisfied to have Joe arrange the dates. I suggested I call for her at her home on February 28, and she agreed. I was off and running.

[1] The war news did not exactly fill me with glee, either. On the very day of the date, the British bastion of Singapore—so long considered impregnable—fell to the Japanese, who now controlled all the East Asian coast south of Siberia, and almost all the western Pacific.

4

I was also off and running as far as my research was concerned.

The passing of my Qualifyings had left me with both a long-range and a short-range problem. The long-range was the matter of the draft. Although my 2A draft rating had been renewed in December, matters of judgment varied from draft board to draft board and from month to month. All of Columbia was buzzing with stories of graduate students being drafted, and increasing numbers of my friends were taking defense jobs.[2]

What was best to do under these conditions, I didn't know. And when you don't know, what can you do but adopt a fatalistic stance? I decided that something would turn up, and meanwhile there was the short-range problem of choosing a research professor.

It wasn't easy. The professors knew me and, what's more, knew me as a problem student. Elderfield, who had a large corps of research students, was out, of course. I didn't even approach him. Others seemed equally unlikely. Thomas, who was a natural choice, was not taking on research students at the moment, and Caldwell, though she expressed willingness to have me, was clearly not enthusiastic.

Roth had suggested Professor Charles Reginald Dawson, for whom he himself was working. Dawson was a young man of thirty-one who had gained his own Ph.D. just four years before, in 1938, working under Professor John "Pop" Nelson, who had taught me undergraduate organic chemistry. I had had no contact with Dawson and knew nothing about him but I was desperate enough to try anyone.

On February 17, 1942, I met him, and liked him at once. He was of middle height, slim, and nattily dressed. (All my life I have admired nattily dressed men without ever being able to achieve that state for myself. Nothing natty will fit me or, it seems, will even survive contact with me without turning into instant sag.)

Dawson was kind and soft-spoken and, it was clear, perfectly willing to take me on. He was working on an enzyme called tyrosinase, which had a copper atom as an essential part of its molecule and which acted on two different kinds of molecules: cresol and catechol. Tyrosinase could be prepared in such a way as to be more active on cresol than on catechol or, by altering the route of preparation, more active on catechol than on cresol—yet the two activities could not be entirely

---

[2] Sidney Cohen, who was within a year of his M.D., was a second lieutenant now, since he would have to serve time as a medical officer once he was graduated from medical school.

separated. Was the enzyme one enzyme with two active regions of different kinds, or two very closely related enzymes with one activity each?

Not only was this interesting to me, but also it was the ideal kind of Ph.D. problem, since *any* answer was worth a degree.

I decided, therefore, to go with Dawson.

What I didn't know at the time, but found out eventually, was that Dawson was a man with a heart of butter. He routinely took on students from whom other professors shied away as being "problems." Dawson had heard about me from Elderfield, and I believe he felt sorry for me.

In all the time I was with Dawson, I never knew him to be unkind, to raise his voice, to seem impatient, or to be anything but totally gentle. He was that way with everyone, I believe, but it must have been at considerable cost to himself, for he suffered badly from a duodenal ulcer for many years.

By February 20, I had a research room assigned me and was ready to start work.

I have only vague memories of the research room itself, a room I shared with another research student—whom I have forgotten. (I remember things and events more easily than I remember people.)

The room was none too large and was certainly none too neat and clean. It had the accumulated debris of past generations of researchers in hidden drawers and corners so that there was always the chance of coming across an unexpected treasure in the way of clamps or glassware. For the most part, though, we dealt with the particular glassware we were going to use in our everyday research. These were in conspicuous and available drawers and were kept chemically clean. There were pipettes, burettes, beakers, three-neck flasks, condensers, Erlenmeyer flasks—names that were as familiar to me in those days as "chair" and "table."

There were also more elaborate setups that came with the room. There was a large constant-temperature bath with a Beckmann thermometer in it that was capable of measuring temperatures to a hundredth of a degree, and a thermostat that kept electric lights flashing on and off under water to keep heating it slightly every time the temperature fell a bit—or allow it to cool off every time the temperature rose a bit.

The Beckmann thermometer had to be adjusted properly and the thermostat had to be kept working and I was seriously doubtful of my capacity to take care of either.

There were Warburg manometers designed to measure the uptake of tiny quantities of oxygen by thin slices of still-living tissue or by enzyme preparations in the presence of the chemicals they worked on. These swayed back and forth in the thermostat to keep their contents well mixed, and the manometer itself had to be read while swaying.

However frightening all this was, it was also dramatic and glamorous and I found myself in a state of delighted incredulity that finally, after so many years, I was actually about to engage in research.

Fortunately, that was all I had to do. The long delay in passing my Qualifyings had made it possible for all my course work to be already under my belt and for my language-proficiency examinations (French and German) to have been passed. I could concentrate single-mindedly on research—if the outside world would let me.

To be sure, I was still, in some ways, a second-class citizen. Research students were judged by their professor, and Dawson was a young man who had yet to make a name for himself. Those students who worked for older, more flamboyant, and better-known professors shone in reflected glory. Elderfield, in particular, had a much larger corps of students than Dawson's poor half dozen, and though Elderfield's students might suffer from his unpredictable whims, they felt themselves to be in a higher social stratum than I was. I felt it too, for I knew that when eventually the struggle for jobs was to come, to have been a student of a well-known professor would carry weight.

5

Fred Pohl had unexpectedly renewed his connection with *Astonishing Stories*, apparently as assistant to the new editor, Norton, over a wide range of magazines. Pohl told me that they might be interested in "Victory Unintentional," and I was delighted. I gave it to him on February 22 and, despite Pohl's thoughts that revision might be necessary, Norton took it exactly as written on March 16, and I received $70 for it—a full cent a word.

Making money had its price, of course. My huge thousand-plus income of 1941 meant that I had qualified for income tax. I made out an income-tax statement on February 6, 1942, and before the March 15 deadline, I sent in a tax payment of $24. (I have never missed a tax payment since.)

I was also making progress with Gertrude. On February 28, I called for her at her home, rather than meeting her on some neutral ground. I didn't actually get inside her apartment, but even meeting in the hall indicated a heightened measure of acceptance. To be sure, the date consisted of going to the Bronx by subway (in those days subways were perfectly safe and reasonably pleasant) and visiting Joe and Lee on their home turf.

On March 14, however, I called for her again, and on this fourth occasion, Joe and Lee played no part. I took her to the movies on my own.

On March 27, things were even better. We had a long supper at a cafeteria (not that the supper was long, but that we dawdled deliciously). Then I took her to one of Fletcher Pratt's war games. I never found out what she made of it, though that was the first occasion on which she met Sprague de Camp. For myself, however, I paid very little attention to the little ships and a great deal to Gertrude.

Afterward, it being an unusually mild evening for that time of year, we walked down Fifth Avenue, window-shopping. A crucial moment came when she said to me, during a natural turn of the conversation, "There's a question I've never gotten a satisfactory answer for: What happens if an irresistible force meets an immovable body?"

I had heard the question before, it being a common paradox among young people, but I never bothered thinking about it. I did this time.

I said, "An irresistible force would have to possess an infinite energy, and an immovable body would have to possess infinite mass, so neither can exist in a finite universe. Moreover, if we suppose an irresistible force does exist, then, by that very fact, no immovable body can exist; and if we suppose an immovable body can exist, then, by that very fact, no irresistible force can exist. In other words, the two things cannot possibly coexist in the same universe. Therefore, on two different counts, the question is meaningless."

And Gertrude reacted much as that other girl had when I said, "*Gut yontiff, Pontiff.*"

"Oh my," she said, "you *are* smart." Things were more friendly at once and when I took her to her apartment door, I managed to kiss her good night for the first time.

Gertrude, it seemed, had completed a five-year high-school course in Toronto, Canada (where she was born and where she had lived till 1936, when her family came to New York). The fifth year was equivalent to the college freshman year and she had done very well. Financial difficulties, however, had made it necessary to channel effort and, as was all too customary, the son got the best of it.

Gertrude had a nineteen-year-old younger brother at this time named John (I had not yet met him) and he *was* going to college. He was very bright and apparently did not hesitate to disapprove, on intellectual grounds, young men whom Gertrude had brought home. This was naturally embarrassing for Gertrude.

That I was going for my doctorate and had published science-fiction stories were not quite enough, since John might sneer at both. My comments on irresistibility and immovability had led her to feel, however, that I could take care of myself in any encounter with John, and that meant I had gained a much better chance of penetrating the outer door of her apartment.

6

Meanwhile, Fate was approaching from another direction as well.

Robert Heinlein was now universally accepted as the best science-fiction writer in the United States, and probably in the world. I recognized this as well and was delighted when he sent me very kind words concerning "Nightfall," for instance. The two of us began a mild correspondence and we were on a first-name basis though we had never met.

After Pearl Harbor, Heinlein was caught up in frustration. He was a graduate of the U. S. Naval Academy, but had been retired from active service for reasons of health. Although he was completely cured, regulations prevented him from rejoining the Navy, even though the United States was at war and needed naval officers badly. Heinlein came East, therefore, in order to work out some way of helping the war effort in a civilian capacity.

A classmate of his, a Lieutenant Commander Scoles, had now been made head of the U. S. Navy Yard at Philadelphia, and it was Heinlein's plan to work for him there and, perhaps, to recruit other bright and imaginative people to work there.

I knew nothing of this at the time, although in February, when Campbell told me that Heinlein had come East, he added, rather mysteriously, that I was to let him (Campbell) know at once if I were in danger of being drafted.

On March 2, I traveled to Manhattan to visit Hubert Rogers, the artist who had drawn the cover of "Nightfall," in order to pick up the original painting.[3] When I arrived, I found, to my surprise, that Heinlein was there. It was our first meeting.

On my next visit to Campbell, I was invited to his home for the first time. Campbell lived in New Jersey, so it was a major undertaking for me to get there. On March 11, 1942, I took a subway to a ferry across the Hudson, then I took another train to Westfield, New Jersey. When I got off I asked the station agent for the location of the street on which Campbell lived and he pointed and said, "In that direction." I said, "How far?" and he said, "Very far."

[3] I no longer possess that original. I don't know what happened to it.

My heart sank. I began to walk, with my eyes fixed on the horizon and hadn't walked for more than half an hour (my eyes still fixed on the horizon) when I noticed the street I was passing was Campbell's. I apologized for being late, explaining that I had had a longer walk than I had anticipated.

Campbell stared at me in wonder. "Why didn't you call?" he said. "I would have come and got you by car."

He hadn't told me that. How did I know? Cars were strange animals to me.

Campbell, Heinlein, Ley, and Rogers were there. I had met all of them before, but also present were the wives of the first three, and Campbell's infant daughter.

I was very effervescent, as I usually am, and after a while Heinlein offered me what looked like a Coca-Cola. The odor seemed strange, however, and I said, "What is this, Bob?"

He said, very straight-faced, "It's a Coke. Go ahead, drink it down."

I was ashamed to hold back and I drank it down as though it were a Coke. It wasn't, of course. It was a Cuba Libre, and the rum had been added with a heavy hand. In about five minutes I had turned red and was feeling very odd indeed. I wandered off into a corner and sat down quietly, hoping the feeling would pass.

Heinlein laughed heartily. "No wonder Isaac doesn't drink," he said. "It sobers him up."

The only other thing I remember distinctly was that Heinlein projected some photographic transparencies of a beautiful nude woman, discreetly posed, photographs he had take himself. I tried to act nonchalant.

I suppose I was under inspection—and I suppose I passed. In any case, on March 30, I received an official letter from Lieutenant Commander Scoles, the commandant of the Philadelphia Navy Yard, offering me a position at the Yard at a salary of $2,600 a year. That was unheard-of-munificence, for it meant $50 each and every week. I would have to be interviewed first, however.

It put me in a quandary. I was just beginning my research work—something I had been aiming toward for years—and I didn't want to leave that. On the other hand, I wouldn't be leaving it altogether, for Columbia, under the unusual circumstances, was bound to give me leave for the duration of the war, with the understanding I could return without ceremony when the war was over. They had been doing it for other people.

But then, too, I was afraid of leaving home and of living by myself

—yet it had to be done sometime. I had to get away from the candy store, and out from under my mother and father, who, however loving they might be, were a steadily greater burden to me with their constant interference (with the best of motives, I'm certain) in my private life.

Arguing strongly in favor of accepting the position, moreover, were two other factors. One was that the danger of being drafted was coming closer. Graduate student after graduate student was being reclassified as 1A, and friends were actually being drafted—Joe Goldberger was soon to be inducted, for instance.

Although I was prepared to enter the Army, I would welcome an honorable way of staying out, and the job at the Navy Yard would offer just that.

Second, I had an idea that, my diary states, "is so radical that I'm not even putting it down here."

I'll tell you what it was. In all my dating of girls over the previous two years the one thing that had stood in my way was always a lack of money. I was working my way up to a real affection for Gertrude and I knew that under the current situation, it would come to nothing again. All I could offer was an occasional movie and she would soon tire of dates consisting of nothing more, as all my previous dates had.

If I got the job, on the other hand, there was even the possibility of marriage (that was the "radical" idea), since I would be able to support a wife—at least I would be able to support her till the war was over, and I would tackle the problem of postwar support when the time came.

I put the matter up to my friends at school the next day. They were divided. Roth wanted me to stay, predicting dolefully that if I left, for any reason, I would get married, gain family obligations, and never return. Professor Dawson wanted me to stick it out too, and take my chances with the draft.

Professor Thomas, however, urged me to take the job, because he said that the department was bound to lose its students to the draft unless they took on war-related jobs. I passed this on to Dawson and, reluctantly, he said that perhaps I might as well leave.

I therefore sent a short letter to the Navy Yard, on March 30, 1942, asking for an appointment for an interview.

7

That same day, March 30, 1942, the May 1942 *Super Science* came out with my story "The Weapon." For some strange reason, it appeared under the pseudonym H. B. Ogden. I haven't the faintest idea why that pseudonym was chosen or, indeed, why *any* pseudonym was chosen.

So distressed was I with the pseudonym or the story or both, however, that I did not save the story and, as time went on, utterly and completely forgot its existence. It is the only story I have ever published that I did not save and which I did not have in my library, carefully catalogued, so that I could put fingers on it at a moment's notice.

When I went through my diary in the preparation of *The Early Asimov*, I missed its appearance and all I could say about "The Weapon" was, "There came a time . . . when *Astonishing* seemed interested in 'The Weapon,' but that fell through. . . ." I listed it among my lost stories.

It wasn't lost. It was published and I never rediscovered that fact until I went through my diary, page for page, in preparing this book. A science-fiction convention was meeting at this time, and I announced that I was in the market for a copy of the May 1942 *Super Science Stories* and explained the reason. Within days, Forry Ackerman sent me a copy.

It seems to me that the only thing to do is to rescue this story from the limbo of the lost, and reprint the story here exactly as it appeared (it is only four thousand words long) and put it at last under my own name.

"The Weapon"

by Isaac Asimov

The council room was in absolute silence. From a raised dais, five Martians looked down upon the Earthman standing before them. Their strange feline faces were entirely expressionless. Only their eyes exhibited signs of life. Glowing greenly, they seemed to pierce the innermost core of Preston Calvin's being.

The Chief Elder of Mars spoke from his seat in the center, "Your request for an audience has been granted, Earthman. What do you want of the Elders of Mars?"

"Assistance." Calvin's voice cut like a knife. With these Martians bluntness was the best diplomacy. "Assistance in our fight against the forces of ruthlessness and evil."

The Chief Elder's gray vibrissae twitched. "Mars does not interfere with Earth. We give no assistance."

"You are doubtless unacquainted with the facts, Excellency,"

Calvin urged. "In the name of all humanity, I beg for aid. Democracy must not lose."

"Affairs on Earth have been followed with keen interest," came the calm answer, "but every world must work out its own destiny."

Calvin's shoulders sagged. He had been warned of this emotionless superrace, this product of countless aeons of evolution, but the reality was hard to face.

He shifted his ground. "Aid us for your own sakes then, if not for ours. If the brutes win, Earth will be dominated by a cult of hate. Mars itself may not be safe from danger."

"We don't fear Earth; you should know that." There was no anger, merely the coldest indifference in the Martian's voice. "We allowed you to colonize the Jovian and Saturnian worlds, which we ourselves had forsaken long before, but Mars itself we will *keep*."

Calvin sighed. "I do not ask for material assistance. I want only a weapon. You, who are so powerful and wise, who could have had a universe yet rejected it; surely of your vast knowledge, you can spare a crumb to the younger civilization of Earth, that we, too, may wax great and flourish?"

There was a low murmur from the five assembled Elders. The Chief Elder spoke slowly in answer. "You are right—our wisdom *is* great. It is so great that we know this: Every civilization must work out its own destiny. We shall give no assistance."

Their indifference seemed impregnable, but Calvin forced himself to one last effort.

"You fear, I suppose, that I ask for a powerful instrument of destruction with which to lay Earth waste. That you would be right to refuse. The fact is, however, that I ask for the opposite— for something that played its part in your own history.

"We have studied the history of Mars and discovered a few things. Your early history, like ours, is one of war and destruction; then, overnight, you emerged into your present emotionless state, in which war and evil cannot exist. We have discovered how that change came about, and we ask for a similar change back on Earth."

A pause here elicited no answer other than a motion to continue.

"There exists a gland in the human body, atrophied and apparently useless—the pineal. There is a way, known only to you, to activate that gland and restore its proper functions. These functions, we feel sure, are to act as counterweights to the fear-and-anger-producing adrenal glands.

"A world with functional pineals would then be a world without anger or fear, a world of reason. Is Mars ready to refuse information so beneficial? It would be against reason."

"You are wrong," the Chief Elder informed him. "It is not against reason. Does Earth wish to be as emotionless as Mars?"

"No," Calvin admitted, "but to go that far is unnecessary. Yours is an extreme of hyperatrophied pineals. In great dilution, the chemical I seek would merely soften the violent emotions of fear, anger, and hate. That is all."

"You know then that it is a chemical that produces the desired effect?"

"Yes, and an inorganic one," was the answer. "A small bottle of iodine dropped in a city reservoir will restore to normal the thyroids of the entire city. The 'pineal chemical' would, no doubt, react similarly. I ask only the method of preparation of this chemical. That is all the weapon I wish."

The Chief of Mars leaned closer to Calvin and spoke very softly indeed. "Once Mars, facing destruction, found the means of its own salvation. Earth must do likewise. Were the raising of a finger all that were required of us to save it, the finger would not be raised. Earth must save itself."

Calvin's lips twisted in a wry grin as he realized that his last bolt had been shot. His hand was played; his aces trumped. He turned away in despair and left the assembly room.

His mind worked feverishly as he was whirled upward to Mars' dead and barren surface. Somehow he must snatch the knowledge from the reluctant lips of these living icebergs. Without it he could not return to a world where democracy clung precariously to its last foothold on the Western Seaboard of what was once the United States. Rather he would die in space.

It was then he thought of Deimos!

Deimos! The giant laboratory of Mars! There the scientific secrets of the race were assembled—even that of the weapon he had asked for. And he formed the mad plan of assaulting that impregnable fortress of knowledge and carrying off by force what he could not obtain by his pleas and prayers.

He refused to consider, for reasoning would have halted him. Once, before the superrace of Mars had been discovered, an exploratory expedition had attempted a landing on Deimos and had been warned away by a strange space vessel. When a second and larger expedition ignored the warnings and pressed on, they never returned.

Calvin had no illusions, then, as to the certain failure of his attempt—but he did not care. The alternative to success was martyrdom, and in his present state of mind that would have been as welcome.

The hours it took to reach the little moon passed with incredible slowness but finally its jagged crags loomed before him. As he circled it cautiously, he wondered if there were some sort of protecting screen surrounding it. That was the first obstacle, for Calvin dared not land until he could assure himself he would not be killed in the process.

He made a few adjustments and one of the two lifeboats with which the ship was equipped slid from its sheath and slowly floated down to the moon beneath. It was an old trick but an effective one.

Under the infinitesimal pull of Deimos, the boat seemed scarcely to travel, in spite of the initial push. Half an hour—three-quarters—a full hour, and then the tiny projectile hit the surface. There was a small smudge visible as it landed, a tiny cloud of dust raised by its impact, and there it lay, entirely unharmed.

A faint glow of triumph welled within him. There was no screen!

Gently, he lowered the ship and landed in a hollow, a miniature valley on the side away from Mars. The sun would not reach it for a while yet; and there the ship, hidden in the dark recess, might most easily escape detection.

He emerged, a muffled, space-suited figure, teetering uncertainly on Deimos' rocky floor. First, he impressed the surroundings deeply on his mind that he might have no trouble locating the ship when and if he returned, and then turned his thoughts toward the laboratory itself.

His problem was threefold: to find a way into the lab, to avoid notice, and to locate the pineal chemical.

First, he must locate the entrance.

He tried to move, but scarcely had his leg muscles contracted when he felt himself thrown off his feet, arch high into the air, and float downward with tantalizing slowness. When he attempted to raise himself, he went into a second crazy, tumbling somersault.

Calvin cursed bitterly. On Deimos, he was practically weightless and almost entirely helpless. It was a case for ingenuity.

Clutching an outstretched projection of rock, he pulled himself forward, using an absolute minimum of force. Over he went, heels high above his head, his grip broken. This time, however, he had made horizontal progress, and when he came to rest, it was some ten yards from where he had started.

He had no idea where he was going, nor did he care much. Obviously, remaining in one place would get him nowhere, whereas moving, he ought to stumble upon something sooner or later. That was his vague generalization. Then, in the midst of one of his weirdly flopping handsprings, he went rigid and fell flat, scarcely breathing.

The harsh, discordant tone of Martian speech sounded somewhere ahead. His receiver picked up the sounds clearly but he could understand nothing of it. He understood Martian only when spoken slowly, and as for speaking it himself—well, it was organically impossible for an Earthman to imitate the Martian sounds.

There were two of them. Calvin saw them through a cleft in the boulders at his right. He scarcely breathed. Had there been a screen? Were they searching for him? If so, he could not long hope to remain hidden.

Then, suddenly, he caught the words *rest period*, and speech halted as quickly as it had begun. One of the creatures walked speedily toward the ridiculously near horizon. Calvin envied his normal gait, while the other approached a wall of rock, touched a spring, and entered the cavity that yawned in response.

The Earthman's heart leaped in joyful astonishment. The gods of space were beaming down upon him, for there before him was the means of entrance. He felt a bit of superiority over these Martians who hid their secrets so poorly.

Laboriously, he inched toward the wall into which the other had gone. The tiny metallic lever was easily found; no attempt had been made to hide it. On Earth, he would have immediately smelled treachery in this, but he knew well that the Martians were far too powerful and far too emotionless to stoop to trickery.

He entered, as he had expected, into an airlock. The inner door opened; he found himself at the threshold of a long, narrow corridor, the walls of which shone with a soft yellow luminescence. It was perfectly straight and its lack of cover dismayed Calvin. Yet it was empty and he could do nothing but step inside.

Even the light Mars-normal gravity felt comfortable after his weightlessness as he strode the length of the corridor, his steel-shod shoes making no noise against the shock-absorbent floor. The corridor ended in a balcony, and there Calvin stood for the barest moment and gazed at the prospect before him.

The whole interior lay exposed, carved into one gigantic room, partitioned into levels and sections. Elevator shafts and supporting pillars shot up dizzying heights in bewildering multiplicity. Down below, so far that it seemed lost in haze, bulky machinery loomed. Nearer at hand an astonishing variety of apparatus of all types could be seen. And all about were scurrying Martians.

A door was ajar behind him and into it he leaped. It led into an empty room, a closet or storeroom of sorts. There he unscrewed his helmet, took a deep breath of the fresh, invigorating air, and paused to consider his next step.

For the moment he was stalemated, for the place simply swarmed with Martians. His unbelievable luck was bound to break soon, and, indeed, he was not oversafe where he was. Then, suddenly, the yellow glow of the walls faded and died and in its place a dim, ghostly blue appeared.

Calvin jumped to his feet in tense anticipation. Was this a signal that warned of his discovery? Had they been playing with him after all?

And then another change forced itself upon his attention. The busy noise that had pervaded the entire place had died down and given way to deep silence. Fear gave way to curiosity, and Calvin edged the door open very slowly and tiptoed out. The entire giant laboratory was bathed in the same weird blue light, and Calvin felt little cold fingers of uneasiness dance up and down his spine as he surveyed what was now a realm of dimly seen shadows and dark, sad-looking light.

He remembered the two words he had heard one of the Martians on the surface utter: *rest period.* This then was what was meant. His spirits rose again. His luck had held!

The next step was to locate the secret of the pineal chemical. As he glanced about at the murky expanse, so terrifying in its vastness, and so mysterious in what it hid, he first realized the immensity of the task he had set himself.

He stopped and considered. The laboratory would have to be arranged in an orderly fashion to suit the Martians. He would first have to locate the section devoted to chemistry and if that proved useless (supposing he still remained at large) he would try the biologic section.

The elevator, dimly seen in the blueness, was a short distance to the right. Fortunately, its power had not been shut off for the duration of the rest period, and Calvin descended to the lowest level at a speed that left him gasping.

Calvin drew his flashlight. He would have to use it now, daring all risk of discovery. Its thin shaft of light revealed him to be among giant structures, which stretched higher than the beam could reach. The Earthman did not recognize them, in spite of a familiarity with Terrestrial science, but they seemed to have nothing to do with chemistry. Picking his way carefully through narrow lanes running between these structures, with the flashlight pointing the way at all times, he finally emerged into relatively open space.

Evidently he was in a powerroom of sorts. At his right, a gigantic motor lay idle, even in rest giving out a terrifying aura of strength and power. Directly ahead was a small atomic-power generator. It was with some interest that he inspected this, for Earth had as yet made only the first few stumbling steps in the direction of atomic power. But his time was limited and he passed on.

He wandered into a spacious section of the laboratory occupied only by low tables on which shrouded objects lay, bulking dimly in the blue light and jumping suddenly out of the shadows as the flashlight swept over them.

The odor of formalin stung Calvin's nostrils and it struck him that he was in a dissecting room. He shuddered at the thought of what might lie under those concealing shrouds and hurried on quickly.

A little further he passed among wire cages and the sickly smell of animal life rose to meet him. Martian "womboes," Europan "Skorats," and common Terrestrial white mice squeaked and whined at the intrusion. Calvin scarcely glanced at them and passed on.

There were shelves and shelves of cubical bottles containing the quick-breeding Martian insect that had displaced the classical fruit-fly—even on Earth; rows upon rows of bacterial cultures; piles upon piles of lenses; mirrors, and other optical paraphernalia. Calvin felt as if he were in some museum, which at every turn presented something new and startling, but which never, under any circumstances, repeated itself.

He estimated having spent over an hour and a half in a vain search before stumbling upon a chemical supply room. Partitioned off by a low waist-high wall, its walls were laden from top to bottom by myriads of containers—glass, wax, and rubber—containing test solutions in infinite variety. Over all hovered the odors inseparable from chemicals, the sharp, tangy atmosphere that recalled vivid memories of chem courses back in college.

Upward went the flashlight, to be stopped short by a "ceiling" which marked the bottom of the second level. One of the ubiquitous elevators was almost at his side. He stepped in and shot noiselessly upward.

On the second level, and the third and the fourth, much the same sight met his eyes. There were hosts of other supplies necessary to chemistry: beakers, flasks, burettes, all sorts of complicated glassware, rubber tubing, porcelain dishes, platinum crucibles.

Then he reached the experimental labs and here he could not help but linger. There was a vat filled with a green, miasmic gas, evidently chlorine, connected through a series of intricately arranged tubing (at present shut off by stopcocks) into a small beaker filled with a colorless liquid. Further away a pair of yardlong burettes dripped, ever so slowly, drops of cloudy fluid into two flasks filled with a simmering purple chemical.

At the far end, almost beyond the reach of the flashlight beam, was a complicated web of glass tubing, in the center of which a beaker sat spiderlike over a small flame. A viscous, red liquid gurgled and bubbled within, and Calvin smelled the faint tarry odor that issued.

The levels through which he rose seemed endless. Past the seventeenth, he came upon the analytic labs. At the twenty-fifth he recognized organic chemistry setups; at the thirty-fifth, physical chemistry; at the fortieth, biochemistry.

It was a complete achievement worthy of the Martian supermen, yet through it all Calvin saw only defeat. All that he saw gave no slightest hint of the nature and identity of the pineal chemical, and upon not a single level had he been able to locate a single file of notes, let alone anything in the nature of a chemical library.

There was only the top level to be investigated now and it was all but empty. It was very large, more than a hundred yards in each direction as nearly as he could estimate in the blue gloom, but all that occupied it were squat, cubical structures, which stood flush against the wall.

There were hundreds of these, circling the entire room, all alike. They were a yard high, equally wide, and equally deep, and each stood on four stubby legs. The side toward the center of the room was of cloudy glasslike material, the rest were of featureless metal.

And on the top of each was etched in golden letters a single Martian ideograph, and below it a Martian numeral. Calvin understood its meaning immediately. It said "Summary 18."

Calvin's eyes narrowed—summary of what? The logical explanation would be that it was a summary of all chemical data known to the Martians, a chemical encyclopedia. He approached the cubes again with devouring curiosity, noticed further that each cube was marked by a separate number, and selected the one marked "1."

Probing fingers located a protruding segment on the upper right-hand corner of the side facing him. A slight pressure shoved it aside revealing a small lever protruding from the center of a half-moon slit. Without hesitation, he edged the lever slightly to the left. Immediately the vitreous frontal face came to life—a bright illumination from within making it resemble a television screen back on Earth.

Nor did this constitute all, for from the bottom of the screen a long column of print began working upward slowly. Calvin read it slowly and laboriously, for the language was technical. It is difficult to learn a language one cannot pronounce and recognize at once. His guess had been correct. It was an encyclopedia, alphabetically arranged.

He turned back to the lever and replaced it in the center, whereupon the movement of the queer, graceful Martian script stopped and the light went out. Again he moved it to the left, further this time, and the movement of the writing was measurably faster. Further and further he pushed the lever, and faster and faster flew the print until it became a grayish blur. Then Calvin stopped for fear of harming the mechanism and brought the lever back to center.

Now he pushed it to the right and the print moved in the opposite direction, speeding backward over the ground it had already covered, until the beginning was reached and the light extinguished.

Calvin rose with a sigh of satisfaction. It was quite evident what the next move was to be. Find the article under the Martian word for "pineal gland" and there, if anywhere, he would find the information he had come to seek.

Now that he was so near his aim, Calvin felt a weakening in his knees.

But even as he felt all sorts of clammy fears rising within him, he skimmed down the row of cubes, searching for that article, and thanking his stars that the Martians saw fit to use an alphabetical arrangement.

Upward drifted the cold, emotionless print; thousands of words on every aspect of the pineal gland. Calvin followed it breathlessly, understanding not more than a tenth, and watching, watching for the one vital fact he was after.

And then it came, so suddenly that it caught him unawares and passed him by. He laughed hysterically as he turned the machine backward, and for five minutes shut it off altogether until the almost painful sensation of relief that overwhelmed him had subsided.

Over and over again he read the short description of the chemical and its method of production. It was only bromine, an element that seawater was filled with, yet with a difference. The pineal chemical was an isotope of that halogen; an isotope that was not to be found naturally and that would exist for only a limited period when produced artificially. In terse and cryptic language the nature and strength of the neutron bombardment that produced the isotope was described, and the description sank deep into Calvin's brain.

And then he was through, all through. To return to Earth—only that was left. Surely, after having completed so much against the laboratory and all of Mars, the return need not frighten him. A sense of bubbling triumph pervaded him, a triumph that shrieked aloud with laughter and then died suddenly.

The light changed! Dull blue gave way to bright yellow with a suddenness that left him gasping, bewildered, and blinded.

Martians sprang from nowhere and surrounded him. Calvin fell back, utterly bewildered at the sudden change of the situation. Then, as he recognized the stern, immobile visage of the Chief Elder in the midst of the throng, all emotion was drowned in one flood of tearing, blistering rage.

His needle-ray was drawn, cocked and aimed in one motion, but in the icy gaze of the Martian potentate he felt his arm grow numb and lax. Struggle as he might, he could not compress the trigger finger. Dimly, he heard the gun clang to the floor.

A long silence ensued, and then the Chief Elder spoke. "You did very well, Earthman. You were a little reckless, but quick at seizing opportunity."

A look of astonishment spread over Calvin's face. "You were playing with me?" he demanded. "You allowed me to hope and to all but attain my object that you might snatch it from me in the end?" He felt it difficult to breathe. "Then Martians are sufficiently emotional to indulge in cruelty, aren't they?"

Calvin suddenly felt weak and futile.

"I knew your moves from the first," the Chief Elder was saying. "We recognized the possibility of an attempted raid on Deimos as a result of your own individual psychology, and consequently removed the screen from the satellite; showed you the means of entrance; introduced a fictitious rest hour; and refrained from interfering until you had discovered your precious weapon. The experiment was an entire success."

"What are you going to do now?" Calvin asked bitterly. "All your explanations are of no interest to me."

"Do? Why, nothing!" came the answer in slow, measured tones. "Your ship is safe. Return to Earth with your weapon."

Calvin's eyes snapped wide open. His first words were but a meaningless stutter. When he had recovered sufficiently to speak, he cried, "But you refused to give me the secret back on Mars."

"True! But we said nothing about refusing to let you take it. Earth as a suppliant for help, we would refuse, for every world must work out its own destiny. However, when Earth refuses to accept our refusal, but, in your person, attempts a plan foredoomed to failure and carries it out without a moment's hesitation, we no longer refuse. It has not been given you; you have taken it. Return to Earth with your weapon."

And finally Preston Calvin gained an inkling of the mental processes of these alien, incomprehensible people. His head bowed and with trembling voice he whispered, "You are a strange people, but a great one!"

There; not exactly a very good story, but not bad for an eighteen-year-old. I wrote it in the first half of September 1938, just as the Munich crisis was heating up to the point of war or surrender, with the Western powers surrendering. No wonder I portrayed democracy as at the point of destruction.

And I was just beginning my senior year in college and the vast chemistry laboratory on Deimos was simply my college laboratories magnified. Not one futuristic detail was I able to imagine though I *did* mention an atomic power generator and a television screen.

Oh well. I apologize for this interruption and now let us get back the spring of 1942 and the problem of the Navy Yard job.

8

The possibility of a job at the Navy Yard strengthened my confidence where Gertrude was concerned. I went to see her on April 3, 1942, and got into her apartment at last. I told her about the job offer and was as open as I dared be about the possibility of marriage. It wasn't quite a proposal, but I did bring my bankbook with me in order to indicate to her that I was a man of wealth and substance. I pointed out that I had $450 in the bank.

It never occurred to me that *she* might have money (and, of course, she didn't). I was quite prepared to take her without a cent, but I was unwilling to take on liabilities. I therefore asked her if, by any chance, she supported her father and mother. She said no. Her father, Henry Blugerman, was a superintendent at a paper-box factory and made an adequate living.

That was a relief and I guess I showed it.

Gertrude was amused by all this and took me into the kitchen to introduce me to her mother, Mary, whom I now met for the first time. Mary was just about five feet tall and quite plump. Like my parents, she spoke with a pronounced accent.

Mary and her husband, Henry, had, like myself, been born in Russia. They came from the city of Kherson on the Ukrainian Black Sea coast. Both had come to Toronto as teen-agers, before the revolution. In Toronto they had married, and Gertrude was born there on May 16, 1917. (She was a little older than I was, but that didn't bother me a bit, either then or afterward.)

I went home feeling that the marriage business was all but settled —and it was only seven weeks since we had met.

By April 12, though, Gertrude had had time to think about it. I visited her with the plan of taking her home to meet my parents but she demurred. She was not in love and, under the circumstances, she said, it would be best not to see each other again.

I was two years older now than when Irene had left and I had the strong promise of a job. This time I did not intend to take the loss of a girl without strong resistance. We were walking on the boardwalk, I remember, on a cloudy and rather dismal day, and I talked and talked.

What I said I don't remember, but whatever it was I managed to talk long enough and eloquently enough to get myself invited back to the apartment.

Gertrude's mother was surprised to see me come back, for it had been her impression I was to be given my walking papers. Perhaps she wasn't too depressed, though. According to what I heard later, she had suspected I might be a good catch.

By April 27, I was sufficiently intimate with the family to be invited to dinner and I discovered that Mary was a superlative cook. When she roasted a chicken I wouldn't swap it for all the ambrosia on Olympus.

But I didn't press the marriage business again. I simply continued to see Gertrude and to make it clear, while saying as little about it as possible, that I assumed we would be married, and finally Gertrude accepted the matter.

We continued to have frequent dates, with one odd contretemps. On May 6, I took, as usual, the streetcar that traveled in a straight line southward from two blocks east of my house to two blocks west of hers. It was a six-mile trip and took about half an hour. On this occasion, though, after the streetcar had progressed two miles, it stopped. All passengers had to get off.

I walked several blocks to the elevated train that ran on a parallel route, but it wasn't going, either. All public transportation in Brooklyn had stopped, and remained stopped for an hour.

There seemed no alternative but to walk, so that was what I did, carrying the box of candy I was taking to her. It was a four-mile walk, which was nothing for me in those days, but I was keenly aware that I was going to be late so I walked as rapidly as I could. A *rapid* walk of four miles brought me to Gertrude's place in a fairly broken-down condition, and I had to hand her the box of candy wordlessly and then sit down to recover.

When I was finally able to explain what had happened, Gertrude said with astonishment, "Why didn't you take a taxi?"

I might have told her that I had tried and that no taxis were available. Taxis didn't cruise much in Brooklyn, and those that did would undoubtedly find passengers at once when public transportation failed I would have had no chance of finding one and if I told the story pathetically enough, I would have been a hero.

Once again, though, the clever lie eluded me. I told the truth—which was that taxis had never occurred to me—and all I accomplished was to give an impression of foolish miserliness.

PART
IV

*The War and the
Army—in That Order*

31

Philadelphia

1

Life in the great world outside continued without regard to my growing expectations with regard to Gertrude and a job. In the spring of 1942, the Japanese had completed their occupation of the Philippine Islands and were busily engaged in rooting the Americans out of their last foothold on Corregidor Island in Manila Bay. Elsewhere the Japanese were advancing in Burma and had about completed the occupation of Southeast Asia and the Dutch East Indies. There was even some feeling that the British might lose India.

In Europe, the Nazis had survived the Russian winter, had suffered disappointingly few territorial losses, and now they were preparing to resume their blunted blitzkrieg. The clouds were dark in all directions.

In the smaller world of writing, Campbell had made one of his periodic experiments in advancing *Astounding*'s respectability by making it large size so that it would be displayed on the newsstands along with the slicks and so that it would get more in the way of fancy ads. It didn't work, and I hated the change myself because it upset the even line of my science-fiction-magazine collection.

In any case, several of my stories appeared in the large size. "Runaround,"[1] the third of my positronic stories to appear in *Astounding*, was in the March 1942 issue, and "Foundation"[2] in the May 1942 issue.

I was withdrawing, somehow, from all this. I scarcely mentioned the appearance of the new stories in my diaries. Where I was not concentrating my thoughts on Gertrude, I was concentrating them on the possible job in Philadelphia.

On April 10, I made the train trip to Philadelphia for the second time in my life and worked my way out to the Navy Yard in the city's southern outskirts. I was amazed at its size, at the density of its military population, at its tight security, and at the beauty of its laboratory equipment. I was interviewed and it seemed to me clear that I would get the job. I was fingerprinted for the first time.

What followed then, though, was a long delay that drove me to

[1] See *I, Robot*.
[2] See *Foundation* (Gnome Press, 1950, later in a Doubleday edition; it appears as Part II, entitled "The Encyclopedists").

distraction. It was my first experience with government red tape. I was told I would hear in two or three weeks, but it wasn't till six weeks had passed, and May 11 had come, that I received my appointment as junior chemist at the Navy Yard.

2

On May 13, 1942, I took the train to Philadelphia for the third time, and there occurred, now, a break in my life almost as deep as had occurred to my parents when they took the train and the ship to the United States.

I had till that day maintained connections, albeit tenuous ones, with people out of the past—with Sidney Cohen, with Mazie (the girl I had known in Decatur Street), with Uncle Joe, Aunt Pauline, and Cousin Martin. Contact was virtually broken in every case after I left for Philadelphia.

All my friends from college and graduate school receded into the distance. The periodic visits to Campbell and Pohl came to an end. The Futurians were gone and so was Scott Feldman, the war game, the Brooklyn Authors Club.

Even inanimate objects went. I left my magazines, my manuscripts, my diplomas, and my original painting of "Nightfall" in Brooklyn, and I never saw any of them again. Eventually they must have been sold or otherwise disposed of.

Even the candy store was gone—at least as far as I was concerned. After sixteen years of day-in, day-out work in it, I left it on May 13, 1942, and never went back to it except to visit. Stanley, who was now approaching his thirteenth birthday, took over.

Something else vanished, too. For years I had wanted an Encyclopaedia Britannica and finally my father managed to scrape together the money to buy a copy, and on March 11, it arrived. I began a project of reading it from cover to cover—not every word, to be sure, but lots of them, and at least I looked at every entry. I was in the third volume when I left, and my last words as I left were, pointing to the encyclopaedia, "Gee, now I'll never know how it came out."

The only thing I did not leave behind when I went to Philadelphia was Gertrude. I left her behind physically, but my whole purpose in going was to come back later and take her with me to Philadelphia.

3

The YMCA was full when I got to Philadelphia, but they directed me to a rooming house where I could stay the night. The next morning,

May 14, I made my way through an incredible gauntlet of security and showed up at the chemical laboratory of the Naval Air Experimental Station.

My immediate superior was Bernard Zitin, a very thin fellow, taller than I, with crisply curled black hair, an asymmetric nose, and a stammer. He was very bright and very helpful. He drove me to West Philadelphia so that I might examine possible rooms and I finally chose to move into 4707 Sansom Avenue.

It was not really an independent apartment, but a room in someone else's house. It was the only time in my life I ever lived with strangers, although I must admit the people who owned the house were reasonably good to me during the time I stayed there.

It being wartime, the Navy Yard was on a six-day week, but it was my plan to leave the Navy Yard each Saturday just as soon as the workday ended (at 4:00 P.M., for work began at 8:00 A.M.) and make my way to Broad Street Station. There I would take the train to New York, go straight to my parents', wash, shave, dash over to Gertrude's place, then return and sleep in my own bed. Sunday, I would visit Gertrude again and then take an evening train to Philadelphia to start the week again. (Of course, I would bring my laundry to New York for my mother to take care of and head out to Philadelphia with fresh clothing.)

It was a dreadful routine, but I kept it up for week after week. Because I was in New York only for the twenty-four-hour period centered about Saturday night I could never see Campbell, but that didn't matter. I didn't want to see anybody but Gertrude, and writing, which had been at a halt since February, continued to be nonexistent.

I was under the impression, after all, that the purpose of my writing had been to pay my way through school. Now there was no school to be paid. Indeed, the work I was doing was paying *me*. Why should I write, therefore? I even stopped reading science-fiction magazines, for the first time in thirteen years (I think because reading science fiction activated guilt feelings over my failure to write it.)

I tried to take advantage of my newfound independence. After all, what was to follow was the longest stretch in my life—the very longest —in which I was completely alone and not beholden to anyone; in which no one might tell me yea or nay in my personal life.

I seized the opportunity to do as I wished, therefore. Here is one example I remember. I loved soda pop, as who does not. Occasionally my mother would take a large-size soda-pop bottle, containing four glasses worth, into the house and dispense it to us. I usually got the equivalent of one glass worth.

Well, on one of my first days in Philadelphia, I bought a large-size soda-pop bottle, took it up to my room, and *drank it all* while I read a mystery. I promptly made an important discovery: One glass is about enough; each succeeding glass was less good, and the last glass was vile.

Being free to live as I wished taught me quickly enough that I wished to live soberly and reasonably—exactly as my parents had always expected me to live. It was a dreadful disappointment.

I had arrived in Philadelphia on a Wednesday night. By Saturday night I was home again, and, to my mother's dismay, did exactly as I had planned to do. I dashed to Gertrude's place immediately and stayed there half the night. It was Gertrude's twenty-fifth birthday and she seemed glad to see me. She asked me of her own accord to write to her periodically from Philadelphia, and agreed to see me every Saturday.

The next Saturday when I came home, I had to lean against the door of the living room before entering because Gertrude was there. My parents had arranged it as a surprise to me, and it was the first time she had met them. My parents were very favorably impressed with her.

The next day I casually brought up the marriage date. She discussed it equally casually, as though she were taking marriage for granted. It apparently could not be before July at the earliest. I would simply have to wait.

4

The Navy Yard was a large and sprawling place, spread out over acres and acres of what was not very far removed from swampland at the southern edge of Philadelphia where the Schuylkill ran into the Delaware.

There were numerous buildings, in some of which all sorts of construction and engineering work went on. With my usual concentration on the task immediately before me, however, and with my usual lack of curiosity concerning the rest of the world, I never had the urge to explore. I spent virtually all my time in the building that housed the chemistry laboratory and, for the most part, stayed within that lab.

Naturally, there were numerous naval personnel present, all of them in snappy uniforms with much in the way of gold braid, but I virtually never saw any ordinary sailors. The officers made me uneasy with their aura of authority and through the fact that they were reminders of the world of armed forces I was hoping to be able to avoid.

Within the laboratory, however, those present were civilian almost entirely. As for the work done in the laboratory—its purpose, I was told, was to maintain the quality and performance of hundreds of different materials used by the naval air forces, and on my work depended the safety of men and the course of battles. I strove to believe this so that I could justify to myself my not doing research and my not being drafted.

One factor that made the early days in the Navy Yard pleasant was that Heinlein was working there; I saw him every day. Sprague de Camp joined us on May 26. He was working there too. What's more, John D. Clark of the war games was in Philadelphia, engaged in work on explosives and boarding with a family within walking distance of my rooming house.

In those early days in Philadelphia, I visited John Clark often. He had a room lined with books and I remember I borrowed a book called *Under the Hog* from him and read, for the first time, a historical novel that treated Richard III sympathetically.

On May 20, I received my first paycheck. It was only for the two days of work before the fifteenth (we were paid twice a month, on the fifth and the twentieth, so it came to only $10.72, but I used it to buy a pocket mystery and a birthday present for Gertrude.

Some cracks in the pretty picture at the Navy Yard appeared, however. A young man, whom I recognized with some surprise as one of Marcia's boyfriends, appeared in the lab to do something or other with the wiring. I rather condescended to him since I was a chemist and he was only an electrician, but I caught sight of his card (which had to be filled out by someone at the lab if he were to get credit for his time) and I found he made $5.00 a week more than I did. I was quite chagrined, but it taught me an important lesson in humility—which would be great if I didn't have to be retaught it periodically.

Then too, I discovered that the young men working at the Navy Yard were as insecure about the draft situation as had been the students at Columbia. Through all my stay at the Yard I was to live from half year to half year, waiting to see if my draft status (2B now; a more effective deferral than 2A) would be maintained. The word about the Yard was that it was forever a case of "2B or not 2B."

On the positive side, work at the laboratory was full of variety. It consisted largely of testing different products intended for use on naval aircraft—soaps, cleaners, seam sealers, everything—according to specifications. There were all kinds of physical and chemical tests, and I got a wide variety of experience with a wide variety of chemical techniques.

5

By June 7, the wedding date was set for Sunday, July 26, 1942, and I had the forethought to make an arrangement with my superiors at the

Navy Yard that on Saturday, the twenty-fifth, I was to get in fifteen
minutes early on Saturday and then leave fifteen minutes early in order
to be certain of making the 5:00 P.M. train.

But meanwhile I had to get through the seven weeks remaining till
the wedding, and each weekend I was in New York. It was during this
period, I think, that a curious incident took place on the beach at
Coney Island. I never entered the matter in my diary so I don't know
the exact day—but I remember it well.

Gertrude and I had gone to the beach and spread out a blanket
and then spread ourselves out upon it. We were talking and totally absorbed in each other, and were quite oblivious to the rest of the world.

Really oblivious, for we came to at one point and found that there
was an enormous crowd all about us. No, they weren't watching us, for
we weren't actually doing anything worth watching. They were watching a police car that was just pulling away. Something must have happened that made it necessary to call the police, something that had successfully gathered a crowd—and there we were in the midst of it and
totally unaware it was happening.

We were ashamed to ask others what had happened and we were
sure that by reading the papers that evening and the next morning we
could find out. We didn't. We found nothing in the papers that would
give us a clue and, to this day, I don't know what happened no more
than ten feet from me that drew the police and a crowd. Now, *that's*
concentration.

In that period there were interconnections between Gertrude and
earlier phases of my life. I got a letter from Irene announcing that she
had become a mother on May 30, 1942. After some thought I consulted
Gertrude and she was perfectly willing to have me answer the letter
after I explained the situation. So I did, offering congratulations, and
passing along the news of my own forthcoming marriage.

Then, on Saturday, June 20, Sidney Cohen joined the two of us on
an evening foray to the amusement center at Coney Island. He and
Gertrude, whom he now met for the first time, got along very well. Gertrude wanted to go on the large roller coaster. I remembered my experience at the World's Fair and shook my head in a very uneasy way. Gertrude seemed annoyed at my hesitation and I decided it would not look
well if I played the coward—so, too cowardly to admit my fears, I went
on the roller coaster.

It was a mistake, of course. I could force myself to buy a ticket and
get in the car, but there was no way I could force myself to withstand
with equanimity the sensation of falling. I crumpled up against Ger-

trude and she held me all the way. I got off half dead and it took me a while to recover. She told me on a later day that, at that time, she had serious doubts as to my suitability as a husband.

I had another chance to prove my unsuitability the next evening. I took the train to Philadelphia and en route I discovered that I had left my identifying badge in New York. I couldn't get into the Navy Yard without my badge.

Of course, if I had used my head I would have realized that badges do get forgotten and that there must be some way of getting a temporary badge. All I could think of, however, was that I had to have my badge. When I arrived at Philadelphia, therefore, I took the next train back to New York and got home at 2:30 A.M. I picked up my badge, endured my mother's loud and prolonged comments on the matter, caught another train to Philadelphia, and got to Sansom Street at 6:00 A.M.

Naturally, I didn't bother going to bed; I went straight to work.

In time, I learned what to do when one forgot one's badge, since I managed to leave it home now and then. What happened was that one was stopped at the gate, taken to a visitor's reception center, issued a temporary badge, and sent to work. It meant getting in about half an hour late and being docked an hour's pay. Annoying, but not desperate.

Once, early on, Sprague de Camp and I were going to work together and when we got off the trolley, Sprague clapped his hand to his lapel and said, "I've forgotten my badge."

I could guess what was going through his mind. He had applied for an officer's commission and he wanted nothing on his record that would make anyone think he was not officer material. Well, I wasn't applying for anything, and I was certain that my superiors already knew (or if they didn't, that they would soon find out) that I wasn't officer material or any other kind of material either. What's more, I had already been through the I-forgot-my-badge mill and it didn't frighten me. It was very much like being sent to the principal's office.

Consequently I handed Sprague my badge and said, "Here, Sprague. No one will look at it and they will pass you through."

Sprague took it and had obvious difficulty in mastering his emotion, but master it he did, except to gulp out something like, "Kind hearts are more than coronets," and off he went. I went through the tedium of getting a temporary badge and of being docked an hour's pay (less than a dollar, actually), but that was a small annoyance. That evening, after we left the Yard, Sprague gave me back my badge. As I had predicted, no one had looked at it—so much for security practices.

Ever since, though, Sprague has been convinced that I have a warm and generous heart and goes around saying so by word of mouth and in print and, in this fashion, puzzling everyone who knows me.

6

I spent the final month of my bachelorhood with petty worries over blood tests, licenses, and so on. I visited John Clark a good deal in order to pass the dragging time and moan over the difficulties of waiting. John gave me a book to read that he said would put Gertrude out of my mind. I took it thankfully and when I got into bed that night I found it to be Balzac's *Droll Stories*. Just what I needed in the last days of my bachelorhood—sex-centered stories.

At work, fortunately, I dealt almost entirely with "Mother Asimov's pies." I was testing various plastics and other substances for waterproofness by placing weighed amounts of water-absorbing calcium chloride in aluminum pans, covering them with the film to be tested, and sealing those films with wax around the edges. I then weighed them, placed them in a humidifier for twenty-four hours, took them out, dried them, and weighed them again. It was not very demanding to the intellect, but it meant the kind of meticulous record-keeping I liked, and it kept me absorbed.

There was even a little bit of leftover science-fiction news that served to amuse me. The June 1942 *Astounding* came out shortly after I had joined the Navy Yard, and I had made the cover with "Bridle and Saddle."[3] I showed it about at the lab and it helped remind me that I was, after all, a writer.

Then, too, Fred Pohl still needed stories, and I dug up a few of my old ones for him. He passed them on to Norton, who took "The Imaginary," my old sequel to "Homo Sol." So I had made another sale, and eventually $72 came my way. This was the first money I had obtained through my writing after I got my Navy Yard job.

And in the large world outside, things continued to go badly. In June, the Germans opened a second offensive into the Soviet Union, concentrating on the southern front, and once again they were making huge gains. They were also gaining in North Africa. About the only scores for our side was that the air war in western Europe had shifted clearly in favor of the Allies, who were bombing German cities heavily.

[3] See *Foundation*, where it appears as Chapter 3, "The Mayors."

32

Marriage

1

On July 25, 1942 (Stanley's thirteenth birthday), I took the train to New York in order to keep my wedding date.

The matter of my wedding was heavily distorted by the fact of war. The Navy Yard gave me exactly eight days for a honeymoon, from Sunday to Sunday, inclusive. I couldn't exactly complain of this, considering the war crisis, but neither did I want to waste an hour of the period if I could help it. For that reason, I could not have a civil wedding since that would have meant waiting to be married on Monday.

Since neither my family nor Gertrude's family had any religion, we had no rabbis of our own, and it proved difficult to get one out of the Yellow Pages. I would have settled for a practitioner of any religion, asking only that the marriage be a legal one in the eyes of the government, but the old folks weren't quite that easygoing.

We found a rabbi. I don't remember his name. I never saw him again.

It was a small wedding. No one but the immediate families were present, which meant bride and groom, four parents, and three siblings. Total, counting the rabbi, ten. And it was to be in the Blugerman living room.

It was a difficult and embarrassing session. The rabbi chanted Hebrew over us in a cracked voice, which I suffered in resignation, while Gertrude tried hard (and not entirely successfully) not to giggle.

Nor did it go entirely smoothly. The rabbi demanded a witness and it turned out that it had to be someone who was not a member of either family.

No such creature existed within the walls of the apartment and Mr. Blugerman was forced to go into the hall and commandeer the first innocent bystander who passed. The bystander was dragged into the apartment, rather confused, and then it turned out that to fulfill his official function he had to wear a hat and he had none on him since it wasn't raining in the hall. The rabbi therefore seized my father's hat, which happened to be resting on some piece of furniture, and planted it firmly on the stranger's head.

My father, whose ideas on hygiene were complicated and, in some ways, senseless—but very firm—rose in horror to protest, remembered where he was and what was happening, and sank back in frustration. I suspect he never wore that hat again.

At another point, the rabbi raised a glass from which Gertrude and I had drunk and was going to smash it under his heel for some complicated symbolic reason and Mr. Blugerman snatched it from his hand.

But eventually, at 5:30 P.M. on July 26, 1942, Gertrude and I were man and wife (or, with equal validity, woman and husband). The marriage took place 5½ months after we had met at our Valentine's Day blind date, and I was 22½ years old at the time.

Henry Blugerman gave us $300 as a wedding present, over my protests. It just about halved his bank account and nearly doubled mine. I always considered $300 of my assets as belonging to the Blugermans, however, and as unspendable. I merely held it for their use in case of emergency.

The two families had a rather hilarious postmarital dinner at the Half Moon Hotel at Coney Island and then Gertrude and I went off to the Dixie Hotel in midtown Manhattan because that was near the place where we were to take the bus next morning to go off on our honeymoon.

The wedding night lacked a bit of complete success. Both Gertrude and I had been raised circumspectly and, not to beat about the bush in these sexually explicit times, we were both virgins. We lacked experience and were terribly nervous.

In addition, the premarital, marital, and postmarital tension had its effect on me, and I spent the week of the honeymoon suffering from indigestion. It was not exactly a gloriously romantic beginning.

2

On the morning of July 27, we took the bus to a resort in the Catskills named Allaben Acres. It was a very pleasant place and for the first time in my life, I was at a classic resort, with shows, tennis, volleyball, arts and crafts, calisthenics, and so on and so on and so on. And a *tummler* too; a master of ceremonies whose only function was to make a *tummel* (a noise) and keep anyone from getting bored.

It was a delightful place, and only two things served to mitigate its wonder. In the first place, it wasn't ideal for a honeymoon because I wanted to spend seven solid days with Gertrude and with no one else and that was impossible at Allaben Acres. In the second, the world news continued depressing in the extreme. To be sure, six weeks earlier, the United States had won the Battle of Midway, which marked the turning point of the war with Japan, but I didn't know it was the turning point and I tended to undervalue naval victories in any case since, despite the Fletcher Pratt war games, the actions of the Navy always seemed auxiliary to me. It was the war on land and the occupation of territory that I could more easily understand. And on land, the Nazi armies were pouring toward the Don River and southward toward the Caucasus.[1]

There is only one thing I remember clearly about the honeymoon that did not involve ourselves only.

On July 30, a quiz was held during the afternoon, and guests were invited to volunteer. I raised my hand, of course, and became one of the contestants. When everyone gathered in the casino for the quiz, Gertrude retired into the balcony, feeling rather nervous about watching me make a fool of myself at close quarters. She was all alone in the balcony.

I was third in line, and when I rose to field my question in the first round, spontaneous laughter broke out from the audience. They had laughed at no one else.

The trouble was I looked anxious and when I look anxious I look even more stupid than usual. The reason I was anxious was that I wanted to shine and I feared I would not. I knew that I was neither handsome, self-assured, athletic, wealthy, nor sophisticated. The only thing I had going for me was that I was clever and I wanted to show that off to Gertrude. And I was afraid of failing and of spelling "weigh" "WIEGH."

I ignored the laughter as best I could, and tried to concentrate. The master of ceremonies, trying not to grin and failing, said, "Use the word 'pitch' in sentences in such a way as to demonstrate five different meanings of the word." (Heaven only knows where he got his questions.)

More laughter, as I paused a moment to collect my thoughts. I then said, "John pitched the pitch-covered ball as intensely as though he were fighting a pitched battle, while Mary, singing in a high-pitched voice, pitched a tent."

The laughter stopped as though someone had pulled a plug out of the socket. The master of ceremonies had me repeat it, counted the pitches, considered them, and pronounced me correct.

[1] In the fighting in the Caucasus, my Uncle Ephraim was killed in action He was my father's favorite brother—or at least my father mentioned him more than he did the other two.

Naturally, by the time the quiz was over, I had won. I didn't wait to collect the bundle of lollipops that was the first prize. I just went up in the balcony and collected Gertrude.

I noticed, though, that winning the quiz did not make me popular at the resort. Many people resented having wasted their laughter. The thought apparently was that I had no right to look stupid without being stupid; that, by doing so, I had cheated.

3

On August 2, we returned to New York. Gertrude stayed in New York for an additional week to straighten out various matters, and I returned to Philadelphia alone.

I found my $72 check for "The Imaginary" waiting for me and with that, and with Henry Blugerman's untouchable $300, my bank account reached a dizzying height of $854.80. I had no qualms about marriage; I was simply rolling in money.

Also during that week I received the October 1942 *Thrilling Wonder*, which contained "The Hazing,"[2] and earlier I had received the August 1942 *Super Science*, which had contained "Victory Unintentional."[3] Of all the stories I had sold, only "The Imaginary" remained to be published, and that appeared in the November, 1942 *Super Science*.[4]

With that, it was almost as though the writing part of my life were over, after four years. I didn't entirely abandon it. I did think of a story I called "The Camel's Back," which involved, essentially, the formation of a black hole, decades before astronomers began to talk about black holes, but I never got past the first few pages.

Writing just didn't concern me. Only Gertrude and the job, in that order, did.

4

On August 8, I went to New York once again—for the thirteenth weekend in a row—and on August 9, 1942, I brought Gertrude to Philadelphia.[5]

August was, however, most uncomfortable. It was largely humid,

2 See *The Early Asimov*.
3 See *The Rest of the Robots*.
4 See *The Early Asimov*.
5 In the world outside, the Germans were pushing east of the Don bend toward Stalingrad, and the United States finally began the counteroffensive, eight months after Pearl Harbor, by landing Marines on Guadalcanal in the Solomon Islands.

rainy, or both, and the two of us were living in someone else's house. I had lived there alone for four months and there had been no problems, but why not? I was away daytimes and weekends, and was no trouble to the owners. Once there were two of us, with Gertrude home all day, and both of us all Sunday, things were altogether different. On August 15–16, I spent my first weekend in Philadelphia, alone with Gertrude, and things got very frosty, indeed. We were asked to leave.

That, in itself, didn't bother us, for we wanted to leave. The question was where.

33

Walnut Street

1

We spent several days looking for a place and finally found one just a block away, at 4715 Walnut Street. It was an apartment that we sublet from the previous tenants, who were leaving. The lease had only four months to go, but we felt that it could be renewed if necessary.

The rent was $42.50 a month, which seemed stiff to us, but we decided to handle it, since our combined assets had now topped the thousand-dollar mark. On August 31, 1942, we began moving into the new apartment, and by September 2, the move (our first move as a married couple) was completed.

For the first time in my life, I lived in an apartment of my own, with a bathroom of my own, a kitchen of my own, a living room of my own—all paid for by myself.

It had its disadvantages. It had no proper bedroom, with a bed standing in it, for instance. It had a Murphy bed, which meant we had to take it down each evening and put it up each morning (with at least a minimum of smoothing out) unless we wanted a double bed in the middle of our none-too-large living room during the course of the day— which we generally didn't.

This also meant that the first thing we had to buy for the apartment was not a bed, but a mattress. After all, you could eat out, and you could sit on the floor, but you couldn't very well sleep on the floor if you were newlyweds.

Gertrude had to do all the shopping, by the way, because I was at work every day but Sunday, and the stores were closed on Sunday. Except for those stores that were open on at least one evening of the week, I was helpless. Gertrude did well, though, with such help as I could give. Almost everything we bought then lasted us for many years.

Another disadvantage of the apartment was the fact that its four windows all faced in the same direction so that there was no cross-ventilation unless we opened the door into the hall and put a blanket across for some privacy. The summers in Philadelphia in the early 1940s were uniformly hot and humid—and miserable. The lab was air conditioned and I spent much of the day in comfort, but Gertrude didn't have that advantage.

Then, too, we had no telephone. Nor could we get one in the war years. It meant I couldn't call her from work or she me at work. It meant Gertrude had to spend rather lonely and uncomfortable hours in a small apartment six days a week.

What's more, not only did Philadelphia as a corporate entity have the reputation of being a dead town and of rolling up its sidewalks at eleven, it also seemed that all its citizens did the same.

There were strict apartment rules against playing the radio after 11:00 P.M., and careless walking about on a floor that as yet had no rugs brought banging from below. I had to sympathize with the restrictions for I believe in quiet neighbors myself, but it did seem hard, once we got a radio, that I could not hear the 11:00 P.M. news when the Battles of Stalingrad and Guadalcanal were raging. Even though I turned it on so low that I had to put my ear against it to hear, there were nevertheless instant shouts from somewhere crying, "Turn off that so-and-so radio."

The manager of the apartment building, a Mr. Moses, was one of the most unpleasant and hateful people I have ever encountered. He was, quite literally, a nonstop talker who never listened. I heard his voice droning on and on in another apartment one time and the tenant's voice finally rose to a shriek: "Will you let me *say* something, damn you?"

Little by little, the apartment was filled with furniture. We even got a rug once the manager spent some time yelling at Gertrude in nonstop fashion, ordering her to get a rug for the living room because the people underneath complained about our "jumping up and down," by which I presume they meant our walking. Within a week we found a rag rug for $15, which was just the thing—at least it was just the thing for us, but, as it turned out, it didn't satisfy the people beneath.

The neighborhood itself was not terribly different from Brooklyn, but little differences loomed large. Small stores were not so thickly strewn, and some Jewish delicacies (bagels, for instance) took some looking for.

The movies usually ran single features and started them at fixed times, once in the afternoon and once in the evening. There were no continuous showings and you couldn't walk in whenever you wanted to.

Then, too, the relatively small subway system and the intricate network of streetcars took getting used to, as did the rather duller quality of the newspapers. I quickly fixed on the Philadelphia *Record* as the liberal newspaper, however.

There were pleasant things. I was very fond of the Philadelphia Library, of the Franklin Institute, of Horn and Hardart, but I never grew to think of Philadelphia as my home. It was always a way station, someplace I was staying "for the duration." It was an interruption in the serious business of my life, which was that of getting my doctorate.

It would have been helpful if Gertrude had obtained a job, not so much for the extra money it would bring in as to get her out of that apartment and with other people. The war made jobs plentiful, but most of the desirable ones were for American citizens only at that time. The Blugermans had come to the United States on a visitors' visa and had never bothered to regularize their status so that not only was Gertrude not an American citizen, but also she could not even begin taking steps toward citizenship without returning to Canada first and then entering the United States on an immigrant basis. And as an "alien" she had to report at the post office every January and could not take any war-related job.

2

On September 5, 1942, which was my mother's forty-seventh birthday, we finally returned to New York for the weekend and established a kind of routine. Once a month we would make the trip. I would go on Saturday and return on Sunday (for the Navy Yard was as much a rigid yoke upon my neck as ever the candy store had been). Gertrude either left the preceding Wednesday and returned with me on Sunday, or went with me on Saturday and returned the following Wednesday.

I always looked forward to the monthly visits with dread, always fearing that Gertrude would refuse to return to Philadelphia with me. Things were so much more comfortable for her in her parents' house than in our apartment, after all.

And in mid-September, Lee married Joe Goldberger. Apparently, she had decided, at last, he was good husband material. Or perhaps the sight of Gertrude finding a husband as a result of that double date that had been designed only to gain an estimate of Joe from her, inspired Lee to a spirit of emulation.

The job was developing social discomforts, too.

The people at the Navy Yard were simply not like those at Columbia. At the Navy Yard, there was virtually no one with whom I could have the long conversations on war, politics, and science from a common ground of assumptions. The fellow workers at the Navy Yard tended to be conservative in politics, or, if they were not, they tended to keep their mouths shut.

About the only fellow worker with whom I found myself truly congenial was Leonard Meisel, an incredibly thin mathematician with a beak of a nose that was not unusually large really, but that seemed tremendous when attached to his stick-figure body. We were both in the car pool, driven by Bernie Zitin, which took us to work and back, and our quick verbal exchanges were hilarious. (Well, *we* found them so, and that was all that mattered.)

The Jews at the Navy Yard did not feel themselves to be in an enviable position. It seemed to some of us that there were strong feelings among some of the Gentiles that the war was being fought to "save the Jews" and that Pearl Harbor was a put-up job somehow arranged by Roosevelt and his Jewish friends. It seemed reasonable for us Jews to fear that continued reverses in the war would cause a vast increase of anti-Semitism in the United States.

In fact, some of my fellow Jews spoke to me about my effervescence in the lab. They hinted that I ought to keep a low profile, since if I made myself annoying and unpopular that would reflect on the Jews generally.

I told them to go to the devil. It was quite clear that anti-Semitism in the world of 1942 could not be blunted by the "good behavior" of individual Jews any more than the lynching of blacks could be stopped if some of them behaved like cringing Uncle Toms. So I stayed myself. Being myself did me no particular good, but I don't think it harmed the Jewish cause particularly.

A kind of crisis arose in September, however, as the first High Holiday season of post-Pearl Harbor times approached. Before Pearl Harbor, Jewish employees at the Navy Yard were routinely given time off for Rosh Hashonah (the New Year) and Yom Kippur (the Day of Atonement). The new rules after Pearl Harbor, however, made it quite clear that the only day off other than Sundays was to be Christmas. No exceptions.

Some of the Jewish employees, however, felt very strongly that they oughtn't to work on Yom Kippur, even if they worked on all other Jewish holidays. It occurred to someone that perhaps a deal could be made. If the Jewish employees were allowed to take Yom Kippur off, they would work on Christmas.

Bernie Zitin approached me on September 15 and asked how I felt about the Jewish holidays. I said, quite flatly, that I never observed them and that I had no objection to working on them. He told me what was being planned, the switchover of Christmas for Yom Kippur, and said it wouldn't work unless the petition was signed by all Jews without exception. Otherwise the attitude would be that if some Jews could work, all could.

So I signed. It was against my principles but I couldn't bring myself to interfere with the concerns of many people for the sake of my principles.

The next day, Bob Heinlein stopped in to see me. "What's this I hear about your not working on Yom Kippur, Isaac?"

"I signed a petition about working on Christmas instead," I said.

"You're not religious, are you?"

"No, I'm not."

"You're not going to temple on Yom Kippur, are you?"

"No, I'm not."

"Then why are you planning to take off on Yom Kippur?"

By now I imagine I was flushing with annoyance. "I won't go to church on Christmas, either," I said, "so what difference does it make which day I take off for nonreligious purposes?"

"It doesn't. So why not take off Christmas with everyone else?"

I said, "Because it would look bad if I didn't sign. They explained to me that . . ."

Heinlein said, "Are you telling me they *forced* you to sign?"

It seemed to me that I was going to be used as a stick to beat down the petition.

"No," I said, strenuously, "I was *not* forced to sign it. I signed it voluntarily because I wanted to. But since I freely admit I intend no religious observances I will agree to work on Yom Kippur if I am told to, provided that does not prejudice the petition."

And that's the way it was. On September 19, the Navy Yard announced that Jewish employees would be allowed to take off Yom Kippur with pay, and without having to work Christmas—and because of Heinlein's encounter with me, I had ended up volunteering to work on Yom Kippur.

On Monday, September 21, 1942, I was therefore the only Jewish employee at the Navy Yard (I believe) to show up at work.

It was no great hardship, but I must admit that I resented Heinlein's having put me on the spot. He meant well, I'm sure, and we have stayed good friends, but I have never been able to erase the memory of his having backed me into a corner.

3

During the first months of our marriage, Gertrude and I ate out. While we were in the rooming house, we had to, of course. And after we moved into the apartment, we were too concerned with buying furniture and settling in to get involved with meals at home.

John W. Campbell. PHOTO BY JAY K. KLEIN

The cover of the September 1941 issue of Astounding, featuring "Nightfall." Opposite, the first page of "Nightfall," inside the magazine.

Nightfall

By Isaac Asimov

How would a people who saw the stars but once in two thousand years react—

Illustrated by Kolliker

"If the stars should appear one night in a thousand years, how would men believe and adore, and preserve for many generations the remembrance of the city of God!—Emerson

ATON 77, director of Saro University, thrust out a belligerent lower lip and glared at the young newspa-

Professor Charles Dawson as he was when he was my research professor.

Gertrude, not long before I met her.

Navy Yard people, around 1943. From left around table: Zitin, Heiken's wife, Heiken, Bowen's wife, Bowen, myself, Gertrude, and Zitin's wife.

Above, Robert Heinlein, L. Sprague de Camp, and myself at the Navy Yard in 1944. Below, the same trio (with Catherine de Camp) a generation later, at the Nebula Awards Banquet, 1975. PHOTO BY JAY K. KLEIN

Me as a private in Hawaii in 1946, holding a borrowed pipe to look suave and man-of-the-world.

There was a small hotel in the neighborhood, the Brierhurst, with an attached restaurant in which there were meals at three levels of prices—65 cents, 75 cents, and 95 cents. We always ordered one of the alternatives at the 65-cent level, sometimes splurging to 75 cents. I don't think we ever touched the 95-cent meals.

They had the best hot rolls I ever ate. They would serve three and we would eat them and ask for three more and eat those, too. I don't remember what else we ate—but I do remember those rolls.

Then, on October 2, 1942, I came back from work and when I entered the door I found waiting for me an aroma of cooking. It was a surprise dinner and I recorded the menu: pineapple juice, vegetable soup, veal chops with potatoes and string beans, chocolate pudding, and coffee. Since I know exactly what brides' first meals are supposed to be like from my assiduous observation of events in movie comedies, I feel impelled to add that nothing was burned and nothing was raw.

It was, in fact, a good meal, and Gertrude was a good cook. She would always insist that her mother was a better cook, but these overall betters and worses are misleading. Gertrude's mother could make wonderful roast chickens, noodle puddings, and apple strudel. No one could touch her on that. Gertrude herself, however, could make Chinese-style meat or shrimp better than Chinese restaurants did, and had some chicken recipes that it was impossible to eat enough of.

After I was introduced to Gertrude's meals, the Brierhurst's offerings lost their glamor.

4

Between eating out and consuming every roll in sight, and then experiencing Gertrude's good cooking and large portions, I began to gain weight. I had weighed 153 pounds when I was married, and I had been at that weight for several years. I was under the firm impression that this weight was fixed, regardless of how I ate. What gave me that firm impression, I haven't the faintest idea.

By October 9, after I had been married just over ten weeks, I weighed 162 pounds. My weight kept going up farther, not spectacularly at any one time, but rather steadily over the years.

Of course, even when I was thin, I always had a pot belly. A sedentary life does nothing to strengthen those abdominal muscles, which are only too likely to weaken, bulge, and lie flaccid. Consequently, I always looked fatter than I was, for people judge fatness by waist measurement. My arms and legs were never fat, even when I was at my stoutest, and my face thickened only somewhat.

The abdomen was rather spectacular, I suppose, and it helped make me the butt for comment. Of course, I never served as a butt in quiet resignation, but always handed it back—sometimes with unfortunate results.

There was a girl in the laboratory, for instance, who was rather pretty, but quite thin and with a figure consisting almost entirely of vertical lines.

I was carefully pouring something from one vessel into another and I suppose I made a humorous figure as I stood there in a frozen attitude, with my rubber apron rounding the curve of my corporation.

Struck by the humor of it, the thin young woman picked up a long piece of glass tubing and, holding it spear-fashion, said, "I'm going to puncture your stomach and let out the air so that you'll look more like a man."

"All right," I said, still pouring, "and when you get the air, use it to pump up your chest so that you'll look more like a woman."

There was a loud shriek from the young woman (who could hand it out but apparently didn't like to get it back), and she picked up a large chair, heavier than she was, with the full intention of throwing it at me. I left the lab in a hurry and didn't return for most of the day.

5

Gertrude introduced me to a widened dietary. My mother (who also had her good points as a cook—her boiled beef and attendant lima bean soup seemed unparalleled to me) had a very limited scope.

Gertrude did far better. I had not only never tasted shrimp until Gertrude prepared them for me, I also had never *seen* shrimp. Nor had I eaten cauliflower till she prepared it for me. I had never eaten chicken fried in butter until she prepared it so, and I found to my amazement that the chicken did not taste buttery, but rather that it tasted better than any other fried chicken I'd ever had.

But I'm a quick learner. My food preferences widened very rapidly and eventually became more catholic than Gertrude's. I remember, once, ordering bear steak in a restaurant while Gertrude sat there and shuddered.

Gertrude also enforced more rigid rules of hygiene. I learned to shave every day instead of every other day, to take showers every morning instead of when I got around to it, and that deodorants are for always.

About the only thing I somehow never learned how to do was to comb my hair properly. It still tends to get as sloppy as the day when the head of Seth Low combed it for me.

6

Somehow we never managed to work into the social swim at the Navy Yard. We were occasionally invited to attend one gathering or another, and sometimes we even attended.

On October 17, 1942, John Hardecker (my boss's boss's boss—or my great-grandboss) was celebrating his twenty-fifth anniversary at the Navy Yard and we attended the celebration dinner. Everything went well. I had two Cuba Libres (I knew what they were now) and promptly got drunk, but Gertrude saw to it that I got home safely.

It might have helped if I could dance. Gertrude was a good dancer and, on occasion, when she danced with someone else at some party, I could see how much she enjoyed it. I, however, simply lacked the aptitude.

Once when Gertrude was in New York, I tried a little socializing on my own. I had an evening out with the boys and played poker— with chips and for money. I ended up winning $.15, but the next time I tried, I ended with a loss of $1.70—my entire bankroll.

The result of a few such experiments taught me quickly that I hated losing far more than I enjoyed winning. Therefore, even assuming a fair game at which I was an average player so that I could win and lose with equal frequency, I would nevertheless lose emotionally.

The result was that I never played poker for money again—or any other game "for money," either.

7

In October, I managed to wangle permission to have a Monday off (because I had worked one day without pay when I had started) and seized the opportunity for a two-day visit to New York. Monday, October 26, then, saw me at Campbell's for the first time in six months. Gertrude was with me and she met Campbell for the first time.

I don't think they hit it off. It always seemed to me that Campbell was not at his best with women. At least, I have never heard him make a single remark in the presence of one from which one could deduce that he had noticed she was a woman.

Perhaps that is the way it's supposed to be. It may be that I find it odd only because I never make a single remark in the presence of a woman from which one can deduce that I have even momentarily forgotten she is a woman.

In any case, nothing came of the visit in the sense that I was not inspired to return to writing. I didn't seem to be motivated. I was getting a regular paycheck.

8

Our apartment, as I said, was only sublet, and the lease was to expire on January 7, 1943. We paid that no mind, assuming it would automatically be renewed. As in so many things in life, the assumption was false.

On November 2, we got official notice that our lease would not be renewed and that we would have to be out by January 7. We went down to talk to the obnoxious Mr. Moses, to point out that we had gotten a rug as soon as we had been asked to do so, and offering to cooperate in any other reasonable way.

Nothing helped. He talked and talked and talked, and I finally said impatiently, "Oh, do the world a favor and drop dead!" and left him in midsentence.

It seemed rather a crisis and Gertrude's parents came to visit. Henry offered to talk to Moses on our behalf, which was rather amusing. Henry was a soft-spoken angel of a man whom everybody idolized. I never knew him to raise his voice, or be unkind or even unfair. To throw him to Moses, the human buzz saw, was out of the question.

I shook my head and said firmly, "It will work out." It sounded a lot braver than I felt.

34

Wingate Hall

1

It *did* work out. On the last day of November, Gertrude found an apartment much like the one we were leaving, but in a far better apartment house called Wingate Hall at Fiftieth and Spruce.

The new apartment was not far away. The kitchen was a little smaller and there were the same disadvantages as before: a Murphy bed and one-way ventilation. The rent, however, was $42.50, including utilities. We could scarcely afford more than this and we had to be satisfied.

The month of apartment hunting, which was, understandably, an anxious one of tramping about and debating possibilities, was lightened by developments in the war.

On November 8, 1942, we heard the news that a British-American fleet was landing troops in North Africa for the first large Western counteroffensive. It was not against the Germans directly, of course, but clearly that would come, too.

It was a Sunday morning when we heard the news on the radio and Gertrude and I danced wildly about the living room out of sheer joy. It evoked banging from below, but a lot we cared now; they could do no more to us than they had already done.

Later that month, the British struck at El Alamein in Egypt and the German general, Erwin Rommel, was sent reeling backward into a long, long retreat. With the Allies advancing from both ends of the African Mediterranean coastline, it was clear that the Nazis would be driven out of Africa.

Then, most spectacularly, at Stalingrad, where the Soviets had held on grimly for two months (with myself expecting the city to be lost from day to day), the Soviets launched a counterattack that for the first time saw the Nazis forced into the same kind of defeat, and retreat, and army destruction that, until then, had been inflicted only by them upon their enemies.

In the Pacific, though the only news was of endless fighting on Guadalcanal, it was now clear that ever since the Battle of Midway, the Japanese advance had been stopped. I had enough confidence in the American Navy and Air Force to believe the Japanese advance was stopped forever.

An additional item of relief on a far less cosmic scale was that my 2B rating was renewed on November 9—which gave me half a year more.

The officers at the Navy Yard, by the way, were amused, or professed to be amused, by the concern of the civilian employees over draft status. They would frequently ask one or another of us how we stood, and would then go on to ask if it were true that there had been a report that all Navy Yard employees under the age of thirty-five were to be drafted.

Usually this would create some mild panic, and finally I could stand it no more. I went in one morning and reported that I had heard on the radio that all naval officers on shore duty were to be sent out to sea to replace those with more than six months' service there—and could it be true, do you suppose?

The news spread like wildfire and there was a tremendous flap among the officers. No work was done by them that day and it took a second day, I think, before they decided that the rumor was false.

After that, the officers most likely to ask us about the draft had to withstand being asked about sea duty, and by general consent there was a truce.

2

On December 28, 1942, we moved for the second time as a married couple. It was not as easy as the move in September, when we had had no furniture at all, and could carry our belongings in suitcases, but it was still neither difficult nor expensive. It took one hour and cost $7.00.[1]

Some pleasant things had happened even during the dreary find-a-new-apartment interval. Sprague de Camp, who had been gone for six weeks to attend officers' candidate school, returned on September 9 in the uniform of a naval lieutenant, senior grade. He looked very handsome, indeed.

For the rest of the war, he and I did similar work, he in an officer's uniform, which entitled him to walk the streets as a presumed hero, and I in civilian dress and therefore entitled to slink the streets as a presumed draft dodger. I never resented it, though, for Sprague is far too lovable a person to elicit anything but affection, and never, never did he pull rank on me.

[1] Every move I have made since then has been more difficult than the one before, and more expensive. Eventually one becomes willing to suffer indescribable catastrophes rather than move, I suppose.

On December 1, we visited the de Camps' place in Lansdowne, a western suburb of Philadelphia, and Gertrude and Catherine de Camp met for the first time.

What I remember best about that meeting is that Catherine scolded me rather thoroughly over my habit of referring to "my wife" in Gertrude's presence. She said it showed an ugly tendency to view Gertrude as my property, as an appendage of myself.

My point of view in the matter was that I was proud of my achievement in managing to marry Gertrude and I referred to "my wife" only to make sure the world knew what I had accomplished. That, however, only had the truth going for it, so that it failed to carry conviction. As for Sprague, who always referred to Catherine as "Catherine," he maintained a discreet neutrality.

The next day we saw *Iolanthe.* Although I knew the various Gilbert and Sullivan plays by heart, this was the first time I had ever seen one staged, as opposed to hearing it on the radio. I was ravished with delight, and a week later we saw *The Gondoliers.*

3

When the year 1942 came to an end, it turned out I had sold only two stories in my fifth year as a professional writer, both very minor ones, and had earned only $152. This was less than one seventh what I had earned the year before and was, indeed, less than I had made in any year since my very first. I wasn't concerned, for my earnings at the Navy Yard had amounted to $1,420 that year and my total income was therefore over $1,500.

As the new year of 1943 began (my twenty-third birthday, on January 2, 1943, was my first away from home and my first as a married man) I received a couple of letters from Fred Pohl.

There was personal news—he was separating from his wife and he would soon be in the Army—but there was also science-fiction news. He wanted to try his hand at rewriting "Legal Rites" once more and resubmitting it. I agreed to that, of course.

Pohl's letters reminded me that science fiction existed, and it was as though I suddenly emerged from the influence of the lotus. All at once I felt myself a writer again.

Specifically, Pohl's mention of "Legal Rites" reminded me that I had never managed to sell a story to *Unknown,* and it was *Unknown* that was my ideal magazine. Even in Philadelphia, I managed to keep up to date in my *Unknown* reading, even though I was at least five issues behind in *Astounding* and read the other magazines not at all.

So far I had written five stories intended for *Unknown* and all had been rejected. On January 13, 1943, I was suddenly impelled to make a sixth attempt.

I began a story called "Author! Author!," which dealt with a mystery writer's fictional detective who suddenly came alive. I wrote seven pages that day with an ease I had forgotten I could manage.

Unfortunately, the nine-hour day at work (Saturday was only eight hours) had a draining effect, and I didn't work on the story every day. And when Gertrude was away, I was usually too downhearted to write at all.

It wasn't till March 5 that I finished the first draft, and not until April 4 that I had finished the final copy. It was the first story I had actually finished in fourteen months.

4

And meanwhile I kept experimenting with adulthood in various ways. My occasional poker games for pennies were an example. Then, on March 3, 1943, while Gertrude was in New York on her monthly visit, I worked up my courage and went to Philadelphia's one and only burlesque theater to see the one and only burlesque show I was ever to see.

Like drinking the full bottle of soda, burlesque turned out to be a disappointment. The theater was dirty, the dancing girls were clearly tired and unhappy. The strippers showed me nothing I didn't know was there. And as for the off-color objects sold during intermission, it was clear from what I saw of them that they were pallid indeed, even by the standards of those days.

A more serious project that March was my attempt to master the Russian language on my own. The Soviets were in high favor at the time, for during the winter of 1942–43 they had driven the Nazis back in marvelous fashion, canceling out almost all the gains the Germans had made in the previous summer.

I regretted, therefore, that although my parents could speak Russian perfectly they had never given me the chance to learn it as a child when I would have picked it up as though I were blotting paper. I bought a Russian grammar on March 17, 1943, however, and got to work to repair the omission.

The Cyrillic alphabet and the vocabulary were no problem, but the grammar was. The multiplicity of cases graveled me but I stuck with it until I reached Chapter 11. There I learned that there were two forms of each verb, depending on whether action was completed or ongoing.

You formed the former from the latter (or, possibly, the latter from the former, I no longer remember) by adding the prefix *pa* in some cases, *na* in other cases, *s* in still other cases, introducing a vowel change in yet other cases.

There were no rules as to which verbs underwent which changes. It all had to be learned by brute memory. And then, when I was beginning to suffer intensely, the chapter added with a straight face, "And some verbs are completely irregular." Thus, I recall, there were two verbs meaning "to speak," one being *gavareet* and the other *skavat*. You are *gavareet*ing now, but you *skavat*ed yesterday (or possibly vice versa).

At this point I discarded the book (actually, I threw it against the wall) on the ground that I would rather be sane than talk Russian. About a year later I repented, and began over from the beginning, going carefully and slowly—until I hit Chapter 11 and the book hit the wall again.

To this day, therefore, I know no Russian. It frequently happens that someone of Russian descent or, on occasion, an actual Russian meets me and assumes from my name and my birthplace that I speak Russian. I must then always interrupt the spate of Slavic syllables by saying, "*Nyet gavareet*" or "*Nyet skavat*"—I'm not sure which—if either.

5

On the lighter side (or at least it seems lighter now, it didn't then), the Navy Yard was in the leisurely process of revising and improving its parking lot in the winter of 1942–43. As a result, everyone had to park in an unpaved desolation about half a mile away. The rains turned the said unpaved desolation into a deep sea of mud, a sea that never really dried after a rain before the next rain came.

I remember once that we were maneuvering in Mud Lot when one of the members of the car pool, Tom Walb, who was sitting in the back seat, decided to get rid of his cigarette. He opened the rear left window and flipped out the butt just as another car passed us quickly on the left. He turned back in instant black-face.

Since Tom Walb was a short, handsome fellow, who prided himself on his fine clothes and good appearance, it followed as a matter of course that the rest of us thought the incident a very funny one and soothed his feelings by laughing uproariously.

We had to move across huge lengths of mud on foot once we got out of the car and, what made it worse, the contractors were planning to drain the parking lot (or something) and had therefore dug ditches across the desolation. They did not bother with any such boring task as marking out the paths of the ditches in any way, reasoning that anyone could see them. And so they could, until they were filled with mud and were thereby blended into the general flatness.

I was walking gingerly across the mud, wearing what was a reasonably new pair of pants, and stepped into one of those ditches one day. My leg, complete with shoe, sock, and pants, disappeared into it up to the knee, and Jack Bullen (another labmate), who was up ahead and who had recognized the ditch and who had stepped across it without wearying himself by calling back a warning, stopped to help me out by laughing.

I was furious and ran up to him red-faced. He assumed I meant fisticuffs and threw himself into a posture of defense, fists upraised. I meant no such thing, of course.

Way back on January 22, 1939, I had a fist fight with a neighborhood boy and had been properly banged up. I recognized at that time that my instinctive feeling that fist fights were not a specialty of mine was completely correct. I have tended to avoid them ever since and to achieve my results by more effective methods—if I could think of them.

This time I could think of one. I held onto one of his upraised arms to steady myself, and, lifting my muddy leg, wiped it carefully on his overcoat, which looked quite new.

Bullen was a tall, beaky-nosed fellow, very good and meticulous in his lab work, very hard-working and reliable—but totally lacking in a sense of humor. The rest of us couldn't resist kidding him and he would grow angry and seek for ways to get even.

We all had wash bottles as a matter of course. These were flat-bottomed round flasks filled with distilled water. Pressure on a rubber bulb fitted into the side would eject a thin stream of water from a nozzle for use in rinsing beakers, washing out residues, wetting filter paper, or any of a dozen other things chemists were always eager to do.

The wash bottles could also be used to send a thin stream of water down the unsuspecting neck of a fellow worker who, for some reason, had stooped. Bullen modified his own wash bottle in such a way that it ejected a stream of water farther and more forcefully than one would think possible. He would save up hurts and repay them with water when least expected. At times we would try to return in kind, but he would always win.

Once when Bullen was away for a day, someone (not me) carefully plugged his wash bottle with wax in five different places and put it back. When Bullen returned, one of us (not me) walked up casually to him, lifted a wash bottle, and let him have a trickle on his sleeve. Bullen stared disbelievingly at the other, who made no attempt to get out of range, snatched up his own powerful piece of artillery, and attempted to return the attack—and nothing happened.

He quickly dismantled it, and located and removed a wax plug. He was greeted with another squirt of water, and found that his wash bottle still did not work. The process was repeated over and over, with everyone in the lab suspending operations to watch. It was only when Bullen had located the fifth and last plug and had removed it that a truce was hastily declared.

Bullen had worked out a system of consolidating the necessary tests on the materials he was working on into one large and rather impressive structure on his desk, with a little American flag surmounting the whole. All parts of it might be going at once with five different tests being conducted simultaneously.

Therefore, when Bullen was away on vacation, his entire structure was carefully and lovingly pulled apart, every component of it washed, dried, and stacked neatly in his equipment drawer. We were all at work early on the day he came back so as to be there when he returned and caught sight of the neat flatness of his unoccupied desk surface.

He walked in with his usual rapid stride, stopped short, and stared at his desk for a long time, while everyone held his breath and risked apoplexy. He then turned and stared at each of us in turn, without saying a word. He then went to his desk and, still without a word, began slowly and methodically to re-create his structure, complete to the flag.

It spoiled every bit of our fun.

Looking back on it now, it seems to me that Bullen was much put upon and that the rest of us were entirely wrong in baiting him.

It doesn't seem to me that I ever took the lead in any of the jokes played at his expense, or even took any important part in them. There was no question, though, that as far as joking remarks and snappy repartee were concerned, I took the lead. And because I was an effervescent personality and therefore conspicuous, it was taken for granted by my superiors that I was the ringleader.

I was lectured on occasion for being the source of turmoil in the lab and, at one time, I was sent in to the offices of Hardecker himself. It was for all the world like being sent to the principal's office—and it was the same as always. No one could complain about my work, which was top-grade. It was my "deportment" everyone objected to.

On April 1, 1943, I was promoted from a Civil Service grade of P1 to one of P2.[2] It meant a salary increase, so that I moved from a salary of $2,600 per year to one of $3,200 per year. I welcomed that but it didn't seem like a vote of confidence to me.

I couldn't help but get the feeling that the Navy Yard was patiently waiting for the war to end so that they might get rid of me. This did not hurt my feelings. The Navy Yard had to be aware—since I made no secret of it—that I was patiently waiting for the war to end so that I might return to my research.

6

I didn't have to wait for the end of the war to return to my writing. On April 4, as I said earlier, I completed final copy of "Author! Author!," and on April 6, I mailed it to Campbell. It was the first time in the nearly five years since we had met that I did not take in a story personally.

The fact of mailing did me no harm. On April 12, I received the news of an acceptance in the usual Campbell fashion—a check. What's more it was a check that included a bonus for the first time since "Nightfall," almost exactly two years before. At last, after nearly three years of trying, I had managed to place a story in *Unknown*.

Since "Author! Author!," was twelve thousand words long, the check, including the $.0025-a-word bonus, came to $150. By the standards of my new P2 rating, that represented 2½ weeks' salary, and the story had taken considerably longer than 2½ weeks to write—but it had been pleasurable work.

I was back in stride at last. On May 3, I began another story, science fiction this time, called "Death Sentence," about an experimental colony of robots on a distant planet—an experiment that got out of control and a planet that turned out to be (you guessed it) Earth.

7

My neglect of my teeth over the previous years, when I could not easily afford treatment, now came home to haunt me.

During the spring of 1943, I visited the dentist regularly as he went to work on what were now twelve sets of cavities that existed in my teeth. Unfortunately, one tooth, the lower first molar on the right, was abscessed and too far gone.

[2] On that same day, Sidney Cohen completed medical school (somewhat accelerated as a result of the war) and became an interne. On that day, too, Fred Pohl was inducted into the Army.

Once all the cavities were filled there was nothing left to do but to yank the abscessed tooth. I was in dreadful terror for I remembered the pulling of my baby tooth (without anesthetic).

However, when the time came to pull the tooth, on October 18, anesthetic *was* used, and it came out smoothly. There was an unpleasant yanking and pulling sensation but no pain. To my surprise, there was no very great pain after the anesthesia wore off, either.

It was the only tooth I have ever lost (so far) and at the moment of writing, I still have thirty-one teeth in my mouth, each firmly attached to its root. In the gap produced by the missing tooth is a bridge which, thank goodness, has never given me trouble. When I think that each parent reached middle age toothless or nearly toothless, I feel quite grateful to modern dentistry.

8

The alien status of the Blugermans was more and more disturbing as the war went on. There was no telling when visitors' visas would be suspended. More and more, it seemed advisable for them to return to Toronto and then re-enter the United States as full-fledged immigrants.

The elder Blugermans, Henry and Mary, made the trip back in March 1943. Having gone through all the red tape, they re-entered the United States without trouble. There was every reason to think that Gertrude could do the same, especially since she was the wife of an American citizen. Nevertheless, I couldn't help frightening myself with visions of "something going wrong" and an enforced separation of indefinite duration.

To prevent this we took all possible preliminary precautions. We set up everything in Toronto beforehand, so that Gertrude need merely show up there, sign papers, see some friends if she wished to, and come back. On June 5, 1943, we went to New York together and the next day I returned to Philadelphia alone, knowing that I would not see her for twelve days.

While she was gone I tried to keep myself busy with letter writing, reading, even work on "Death Sentence." What I further decided to do was to suspend the shaving of my upper lip. It seemed to me that by the time I saw her again, I would have a distinct mustache and she could see what it was she had missed when she first met me. I anticipated having to shave it off quickly thereafter.

This second attempt at facial hair was the occasion for another one of my cruel ripostes at work. There was a girl in the secretarial pool, one who was quite pretty, but dark and just a little on the hirsute side. By the third or fourth day of my nonshaving, it was pretty obvious that something was wrong with my upper lip—and she decided to be haughty about it.

In a tone of voice that I could not help but take as a slur upon my virility, she said, contemptuously, "Are *you* trying to grow a mustache?"

"Why not?" I said, eyeing her coldly, "*you*'ve managed."

She burst into tears and didn't speak to me for many days. I should never have done it. What would I have lost if I had simply said, "Yes, I am." It's just that when the opponent's thrust comes, the parry and riposte come automatically and quite without conscious effort on my part.

One of the paperbacks I bought during Gertrude's absence, by the way, was one called *The Pocket Book of Science Fiction*, just out. It was edited by fellow Futurian, Donald A. Wollheim (with acknowledgments to fellow Futurians John Michel and Robert W. Lowndes). It contained stories from the magazine, such as Stanley G. Weinbaum's "A Martian Odyssey," Robert Heinlein's "—And He Built a Crooked House," and Theodore Sturgeon's "Microcosmic God."

As far as I know it was the first anthology of magazine science fiction.

9

Let me pause a moment to recall what has remained with me, ever since, as absolute idyllic periods. These were the Saturday evenings at Wingate Hall.

They were the only evenings that were not followed by early-morning risings and when we could, consequently, stay up late.

I worked out a ritual. After dinner, I went out and bought the early editions of the two Philadelphia Sunday papers I was not ashamed to read: the *Inquirer* and the *Bulletin*. When I brought them back, I placed them on the kitchen table, and Gertrude was not allowed to touch them.[3]

I showered, then made myself a hot chocolate in a large glass, hot and very rich, and placed a half pound of cookies next to it. Those cookies were of a particular type that I have never been able to dupli-

---

[3] There was a reason for that. When I read the Sunday paper, that paper, through long years of training in the candy store, ended as neatly folded as it had been when I started. Gertrude, on the other hand, like everyone else in the world, let the various parts drop here and there so that the papers were spread in spasms across the floor. I objected strenuously to this, but when she pointed out that I was no longer in the candy store and didn't have to sell the papers afterward, I saw her point and let her have her way. *However*, I arranged for that one evening to read them first myself, so that I could give them to her in perfect order and then allow her to do what she would.

cate anywhere since and that I had bought at the same time I had
bought the papers.

Slowly I read the comics of both papers, while dipping the cookies
in the hot chocolate and polishing off the entire half pound, and then
drinking the unsopped-up remainder of the hot chocolate. (This goes a
long way toward explaining my slow but steady rise in weight.)

I then gave Gertrude the comics, transferred to the living-room
couch, and read all the war news and commentary in the rest of the
papers.

All this worked best in the winter, when I would go out for the
paper of a frosty evening and then be delighted to return to a warm
apartment. Cole Porter's "You'd Be So Nice to Come Home to" was
popular in the winter of 1942–43, and I would hum it as I was going for
the papers and cookies, and look forward to returning to apartment and
wife. To this day, when I sing that song (especially the line "Under
stars chilled by the winter") I find myself back on Spruce Street, going
for the papers, and then I remember what I call "my Saturday nights"
and I ache with nostalgia.

I suppose they're not what the average person would think of as
good "Saturday nights," but those were mine.

10

On June 10, 1943, Gertrude reached Toronto and sent me a postcard from there, as I had asked her to do. On June 15, she left and re-
entered the United States as a full-fledged immigrant entitled to begin
to make moves toward American citizenship.

On June 18, she was back in New York and there I met her again.
She had cut off much of her hair (to my slight distress—for I like long
hair on a girl). She affected horror at the unexpected sight of my mustache, crowding into a corner with her hands over her eyes, but I jollied
her into letting me leave it on for a while.

On June 20, I went back to Philadelphia with my immigrant wife,
and on the twenty-seventh, I decided I'd had enough of my mustache,
and while Gertrude was still asleep I shaved it off. She didn't notice it
was gone until I pointed it out.

35

Back to Writing

1

I completed "Death Sentence" on June 27, in the midst of a searing heat wave that made life virtually unbearable in the apartment. It was only seven thousand words long and had taken eight weeks to write.

I mailed the story to Campbell on June 30, and I received a check for $90 on July 8. It was $.0125 again, but it turned out that it wasn't a bonus. *Astounding* had simply raised its rates, for it needed stories badly. Too many of Campbell's reliables were off in the Army, or in civilian war work, and were not writing.

I welcomed the check and realized that it had been a mistake to spend over a year not writing. I would need every bit of income I could get to tide us over the period after the war when I would have to return to my unpaid doctoral work.

And for a while, I thought that that "period after the war" might not be so far removed.

On July 5, Germany had begun her third summer offensive in the Soviet Union. This time it was on a very restricted front in the middle of the line. The Soviets stopped it cold, and thereafter there were no more great, successful Nazi offensives. History had finally passed them by.

On July 10, Allied forces based in North Africa invaded Sicily and, for the first time since the fall of Greece, British forces were back on the Continent. American forces, accompanying them, were there for the first time. I thought all this heralded speedy collapse of the Axis powers. As far as Italy was concerned I was right—but Germany held out with disappointing tenacity.

2

I arranged to be in New York the weekend of our first anniversary and to stay over through Monday, July 26. Not only was it our anniversary, but also John Blugerman was about to be inducted into the Army, and Gertrude wanted to have time with him. (He was six years her junior, she remembered him as a delightful baby, and there was a strong bond of affection between them. It wasn't surprising. As an adult, he was intelligent and very good-looking. It always seemed to me he looked a great deal like Cary Grant, and with Gertrude looking like Olivia de Havilland, they made a remarkable brother-and-sister team.)

On the evening of Sunday the twenty-fifth, John, Gertrude, and I walked the length of the boardwalk at Coney Island.

It became a custom with us, and for a number of years there was always at least one summer walk on the boardwalk, often with John. It was another piece of idyllicism. We sauntered, we weren't going anywhere, we could walk a couple of miles without crossing streets or encountering vehicles, we could buy foolish things to eat or play useless games. (I never went on the roller coaster again, however.)

Each year, though, we watched Coney Island decay a bit more.

3

On July 26, I visited Campbell. I couldn't very well be in New York on a Monday and not visit him. I had a third Foundation story in mind, one I planned to call "The Big and the Little." It was to deal with the manner in which the Foundation extended its grip on neighboring regions of space by making use of trade, selling little gimcracks that the large kingdoms found, after a while, they could not do without —so that they passed into economic servitude.

Campbell was willing but he badly needed short stories, so he asked me if I would do a positronic robot story first. I agreed and after I got back, I started one on July 29. I called it "Catch That Rabbit."

By now I had twenty-seven stories in print (not counting that pseudonymous "The Weapon," which I had already forgotten), and that meant that I had twenty-seven magazines filling up a shelf in the bookcase.

That, in turn, meant that room was taken up and, in small apartments, room is precious. Besides, the magazines were getting beaten up, just through reference.

I remembered one thing I had seen in Sprague de Camp's home when I had visited it: a set of three volumes of his own stories. He had taken them out of the magazines as "tear sheets" and had them bound. Why not? It was a neat and compact way of keeping one's stories particularly safe.

I consulted John Clark and found the name of a binder willing to do the work. On August 1, I carefully demolished the twenty-four magazines that were of normal pulp size and withdrew my stories. By August 30, 1943, I had the volume. It cost me five dollars.

I still have that volume. I used it in preparing those books that were collections of my early stories. I used it again in connection with *The Early Asimov* and with this book. It was the first of a long line,[1] but it is the first volume that I value the most.

Sprague's volumes had been an elegant off-white in color, but my first volume was a kind of drab green. I had asked for green, but I had had a livelier shade in mind. Perhaps that drab green was all that was available in the war years. In any case, I kept that rotten color ever since for the sake of uniformity.

I was terribly annoyed that the three stories in the large-size *Astoundings*—"Runaround," "Foundation," and "Bridle and Saddle"— could not be bound with the rest, and eventually I had to have them bound into a second, very slim volume by themselves.

It wasn't even that *Astounding's* large size (8½ by 11½ inches) was successful. It wasn't. It didn't get the advertising that was hoped for; its new place on the newsstands didn't help sales; and the wartime restrictions on paper were making that size impossible, anyway. After sixteen large-size issues, *Astounding* returned to its pulp size (7 by 9½ inches) with the May 1943 issue. What's more, as Campbell told me on my July 26 visit, even that could not be maintained. Soon the magazine size would have to be reduced further, to "digest size" (5½ by 8 inches), which, ever after, was to be standard for all science-fiction magazines except for an occasional maverick.

One thing Campbell didn't bother to tell me on that visit was that the paper shortage meant that *Unknown* would have to cease publication. Its circulation was simply not high enough and, if it were eliminated, the paper allotted could be switched over to *Astounding*, which could then continue publication as long as things grew no worse.

I got the news from Bob Heinlein on August 2, and it was a terrible blow. It meant that "Author! Author!" would not see print after all. My sixth attempt to appear in the magazine, which I thought had succeeded, had been a failure like the rest. Heinlein's news was that *Unknown* had folded "for the duration" but, as I said in my diary, "I interpret that as forever," and I was right.

It was a very fortunate thing that I had already written and sold "Death Sentence," as the disappointment of having tried so hard to make *Unknown*, of having made it at last, and then of *not* having made it after all might otherwise have set back my writing drive indefinitely.

[1] I now have over 230 such volumes—though I was too lavish with what I had bound. I could have made do with a third, or even a quarter the number if I had been more intelligently selective. Some, in fact, which contained only foreign translations, I have given to charity.

4

We had a one-week vacation coming to us in 1943. We had had one in 1942 and had used it to get married and have a honeymoon. For 1943, we could just have a vacation. Originally we planned the vacation for July, but John Blugerman's induction made it necessary to postpone it till August.

We might have gone back to Allaben Acres, but it was too far away. What we needed was a place fairly close that we could reach by public transportation, one that was reasonably priced, in the mountains, and on a lake. Eventually we chose a place called Hilltop Lodge, basing our choice entirely on the resort's own description of itself.

We set out on Saturday, August 21, and when we got there, it proved a horrid disappointment. The cabins were tiny and squalid, and worst of all they were set up on the hilltop that gave the lodge its name, while the dining room, the recreation hall, and the lake itself, of course, were down in the valley.

We tried desperately to find some other place that would take us, and when that failed, it seemed to us we had no choice but to go home. We trudged desolately up to the cabin where our luggage had been deposited—and who should come bounding down the steps but Lester Weill.

Lester Weill had been one of my fellow students in the graduate chemistry department at Columbia. He had not been one of my closest friends, perhaps, but he was certainly in the second rank. He was one of the ringleaders, for instance, among those involved in feeding me the pyridium pill in order to make me think I was urinating blood.

We stopped and I introduced Gertrude, who cheered up at once, for Lester was tall, slim, dark, and good-looking. To me he looked rather like the English actor Michael Wilding, with a mustache.

He talked to us cheerfully, told us what a great place Hilltop Lodge was, took us on a three-hour hike through the woods, played twenty questions with us, and after supper lured us into some folk dancing. We had a great day and, in fact, a great week.

The next day, Gertrude rowed me across the lake, and I rowed her back. She then took the canoeing test and passed, so she took out a canoe by herself. (She could swim like a fish, but since I was a non-swimmer, the canoe was not for me.)

The day after that, Gertrude and Lester went canoeing together, while I found a young man named Abe who could tell jokes. That meant we spent hours telling jokes to each other, with others clustered about to pitch in an occasional joke themselves but, for the most part, to serve as an appreciative audience.

There was no question but that Lester Weill made the whole difference. Once he showed up, the cabins stopped being tiny and the climb stopped being steep. By the time we left on Saturday, August 28, it seemed to me I had had the best time in my life, and Gertrude was willing to agree to that. Thank you, Lester Weill, wherever you are.

5

The summer of 1943 began my experience with the Navy Yard cafeteria. Early in our marriage, Gertrude routinely made sandwiches for lunch for me. They were wonderful and I had a delightful time eating at my desk at my ease, in air-conditioned comfort, in reasonable privacy, and reading a book. It was absolutely the best part of the workday.

When Gertrude had been in Canada, however, I ate at the Navy Yard cafeteria. The cafeteria was a half-mile away across a desolation that was a muggy Sahara in the summer, a dank Siberia in the winter, and a mudflat in spring and fall. Once you got to the cafeteria, you found it enormous (the purple haze of distance obscured the opposite wall) and crowded. Worst of all, the food was so horrible as to revolt even a person such as myself, who doesn't ask much of food except that it be there.

After Gertrude returned from Canada, I tried to return to things as they had been before, but the catch was that when I did go to the cafeteria, I generally joined the Heinlein contingent, which included himself and his wife, Leslyn (small, dark, skinny, forty, and voluble), and a few staunch cronies. I helped keep the table lively, and Heinlein didn't want to give me up just because I wanted to be comfortable.

Somehow, I couldn't resist Heinlein's pressure but went along with poor grace. The summers were really unbearable and the trek to the cafeteria required camels and an occasional oasis—and I *really* disliked the food.

Leslyn Heinlein was a high-strung woman who ate very little and who chain-smoked over the food. She used her mostly filled plate as an ashtray. Somehow she always sat across from me, and I think that watching her plate become half garbage and half butts started the process that converted me from neutrality to ardent and fanatic hostility toward smoking and smokers.

Oddly enough, it was Leslyn who found *my* eating habits repulsive. I am a quick eater and don't waste time. Once I had a salad that contained among the greens two halves of a hard-boiled egg. I like hard-boiled eggs, so I ate one of those halves. Now, I don't nibble around the edges of half a hard-boiled egg or approach the center in some uncertain and erratic fashion. I just stick my fork into the thing and transfer it to my mouth. Nor do I make a slow-motion procession of it. One moment the half egg is on my fork, the next it is gone, rather like a fly being speared by a chameleon.

Leslyn said, irritably, "Don't do that. You turn my stomach."

I looked behind me to see whom she was talking to. Then I said, "Are you talking to me, Leslyn?"

"Yes!"

"But what did I do?" I said in honest astonishment, and disposed of the other half egg.

"You did it again," she screamed.

Another incident that remains in my memory was the time we were seated at one end of the cafeteria when, from the other end, approximately 2⅓ miles away, there came a long, shrill feminine scream, something along the lines of what you would expect of a woman sawn in two.

A profound hush fell on the entire cafeteria for the first time in its existence, and in that eerie quiet my voice rang out loud and clear. "Funny!" I said, "I'm over *here.*"

Everyone within earshot laughed and we never found out what the screaming was about, though I myself suggested searching the premises for two halves of a woman.

What irritated me most, however, was (a) the food and (b) Heinlein's patriotic refusal to recognize that anything prepared for noble war workers could possibly be inedible.

When, annoyed by memories of the sandwiches I had left in limbo, I spoke eloquently of cardboard potatoes and wilted lettuce and middle-aged roast beef, Heinlein passed a ukase to the effect that from then on anyone who complained about the food would have to put a nickel into the kitty. (When enough had accumulated, I think he was going to buy a war bond.)

I objected bitterly, for I knew it was aimed at me. I said, "Well, then, suppose I figure out a way of complaining about the food that isn't complaining. Will you call it off?"

"Yes," he said.

After that, I had a mission in luncheon life that took my mind off the food, at least. I was going to find a way of complaining that couldn't be objected to. My best solo attempt, I think, was one time when I pretended to be sawing away ineffectually at a dead slab of haddock and asked with an innocent air of curiosity, "Is there such a thing as tough fish?"

"That will be five cents, Isaac," said Heinlein.

"It's only a point of information, Bob."

"That will be five cents, Isaac. The implication is clear."

Since Bob was judge, jury, and executioner, that was that.

But then someone new joined the table who did not know the game that was going on. He took one mouthful of some ham that had been pickled in formaldehyde and said, "Boy, this food is awful."

Whereupon I rose to my feet, lifted one arm dramatically, and said, "Gentlemen, I disagree with every word my friend here has said, but I will defend with my life his right to say it."

And the game of fine came to an end.

6

On September 17, I sent "Catch That Rabbit" to Campbell, and on September 24, I received my check for $93.75 (7,500 words at $.0125 a word).

Something that was more abstractly pleasant took place on September 25, 1943, when the Soviets announced that they had recaptured Smolensk and Roslavl, and on September 27, when among the many places recorded in the Soviet war communiqué as having been recaptured was Petrovichi—or at least the ground on which Petrovichi had stood—after it had remained twenty-six months in German hands.

Bob Heinlein shook my hand and solemnly congratulated me.

7

The High Holidays produced no crises in 1943. Apparently the upward turn in the war made it look as though we might not be instantly defeated if a few Jewish employees took off a day or two. At any rate, I had accumulated a few days' additional vacation leave, and I took them for Rosh Hashonah and for Yom Kippur and, no, I didn't go to temple either time.

In fact, we called Abe, the young man with whom I had so pleasantly swapped jokes at Hilltop Lodge, and suggested he meet in the city with us and with Anne (a girl whom we had also met at Hilltop Lodge) on the evening of October 8. The idea was to have a pleasant reunion, but Abe told us, quite coldly, however, that it was Yom Kippur Eve and he would be at his devotions.

I cleared my throat in embarrassment and suggested October 9—after sunset. He agreed.

We met on October 9 (after sunset) and sat down for a small snack. Gertrude and I had eaten that day, of course, but Abe had not, and we felt it only right that we make sure he broke his fast.

Abe, however, caught up in the righteousness of having cleared himself of all sin for the past year, saw fit to lecture us on our apostasy, which was so enormous in scope that we did not, apparently, even know when Yom Kippur was, let alone observe it. He was quite eloquent about the matter, and we sat silent, not knowing how to answer appropriately.

Then Abe noticed the waiter hovering nearby and said, briskly, "Waiter! Let me have a ham on rye, please."

Whereupon I made a few pleasant remarks to the effect that in my opinion God might forgive an outright atheist who made no bones about his beliefs, yet fail to forgive a hypocrite who felt himself better than other men because he beat his chest in temple and then could hardly wait to get out in order to fall ravenously upon the flesh of swine.

We spent the evening together in a civilized enough manner, but it was the end of a beautiful friendship.

8

I visited Campbell earlier that Friday and he gave me a copy of the November 1943 *Astounding,* the very first in the new digest size. It had "Death Sentence"[2] in it and it was the only magazine with a 1943 date that contained a story of mine.

On October 11, I finally began "The Big and the Little," my third Foundation story.

9

I didn't get to vote in 1942, because I hadn't had the necessary qualifications for residency. On November 2, 1943, however, I could vote. It was an off-year election, but the mayoralty in Philadelphia was at stake. I voted against the Republican incumbent, whom I believed to be corrupt, but he was re-elected handsomely just the same.

Better news that came that day was that John Blugerman was back on furlough. We quickly arranged to go back to New York the next

2 See *The Early Asimov.*

day. He was there in uniform, looking great. Apparently induction made an American citizen out of him and he didn't have to go back to Canada for re-entry or go through any other forms.

He had been accepted in Columbia Dental School and would start the following October and would be discharged from the Army for the purpose of attending (provided he served as a dental officer thereafter).

And so the year came to an end with my writing having resulted in the sale of three stories in 1943 and a total literary income in my sixth year as a professional writer of $333.75. It was over twice what I had made in 1942, but only a third of my earnings in my top year of 1941, but then I didn't really believe I'd ever have another 1941.

Besides, my earnings at the Navy Yard for 1943 were $3,050, so that my total income was over $3,300, and I had no complaints about that.

On the whole, 1943 had been far more quiet than 1942. It lacked any momentous upset for either good or evil. We had spent the entire year in one apartment, living a life of routine, by and large. I didn't mind. My final remark in my 1943 diary was, "I ask nothing better of 1944," and I celebrated my twenty-fourth birthday on January 2, 1944, quietly, but with considerable satisfaction.

10

On January 12, 1944, I got a letter from Campbell telling me that his pay rate was now $.015 per word. That was good news.

"The Big and the Little" was going along slowly, but very well—and very wordily, too. By the time I was done on January 17, it turned out to be 22,500 words long, the longest story I had ever written. I mailed it to Campbell the next day and on January 26 received a check for no less than $400—not only $.015 a word, but an additional $.0025 a word as bonus. It was an unbelievable check, more than twice as large as any other I had gotten from my writing. That one check equaled 1½ months of my Navy Yard income, though of course, the story had taken one and a half months to write.

Meanwhile, on January 21, the February 1944 *Astounding* had come out, containing "Catch That Rabbit."[3] The year had gotten off to a good start.[4]

[3] See *I, Robot.*
[4] In the Soviet Union, the siege of Leningrad was lifted that January. My Uncle Boris had survived the nine-hundred-day ordeal and was among those who were taken eastward for recovery and rehabilitation. He sent letters to my parents, who responded with packages containing food and other useful items.

36

Navy Yard Matters

1

It wasn't till February 21, 1944, when I had been working at the Navy Yard for nearly two years, that I was lifted from the task of chemical testing to something more responsible. I was given a project to head up —one on seam-sealing compounds.

These were compounds that sealed seams on aircraft (what else with that name?). They had to resist heat and cold, and not be gummy under heat, or stiff and cracking under cold. They had to be impervious to water and sunlight and various chemicals—and so on.

I would have to write to various firms that produced materials supposed to do the job we wanted done. Each would send samples of their products along with the specifications they used to describe its properties, together with the performance tests they used to check those properties.

Each product would then have to be checked by all the performance tests, and an overall specification would have to be written—a specification that was as rigorous as possible and still allow at least one product to meet it.

The chief problem for me, I knew, would be the actual writing of the report. Writing was not a simple procedure in the Navy Yard, even for an illiterate—let alone someone like myself who was an expert at writing and would therefore violate all official illiteracy rules.

Early in my Navy Yard career, I had been asked to write a letter and it was promptly brought back to me. It was not written in Navy style.

"What is Navy style?" I asked, blankly.

They took me to a large filing cabinet containing all kinds of letters written in a formal, convoluted fashion. There had to be a heading of a certain kind, and then an "in re" with a coded letter-number entry. Each paragraph had to be numbered. Every sentence had to be in the passive.

The safest thing, they said, would be to find some paragraph in some previous letter that was approximately what I wanted to say and then make use of it with minimum changes.

I could see the purpose of that. Clear, literate writers could be trusted to use their ingenuity—but what of the average employee? By using fixed paragraphs, no idiot (however deeply immersed in idiocy) could go far wrong. It was like painting with numbers. It was a little hard on the few literates in the place, but that is a small price to pay for the privilege of avoiding rapid and total collapse, so I learned how to write Navy style.

Specifications had to be written Navy style also. Every paragraph had to be numbered; so did every subparagraph and every subsubparagraph.

The main paragraphs were listed as I, II, III, and so on. If anything under a particular paragraph had to be enumerated it was A, B, C. . . . If A included enumerated items it was 1, 2, 3. . . . Under any of these was a, b, c . . . , and under these (1), (2), (3) . . . , and so on.

Furthermore, if in any one sentence you have to refer to another sentence, you located the referred sentence in its position in the specification, as, for instance, II, C, 3, a, (1).

Generally, there weren't too many indentations, or too many references back and forth, and the specifications, while rather tortuous, could be understood—given several hours of close study.

When it finally came my time to prepare the specification of the seam-sealing compounds, a certain Puckishness overtook me. Writing with absolute clarity, I nevertheless managed to break everything down into enumerations, getting all the way down to [(1)] and even [(a)]. I further managed in almost every sentence to refer to some other sentence for which I duly listed a complete identification.

The result was that no one on Earth could have plunged into it and come out unscathed. Brain coagulation would have set in by page 2.

Solemnly, I handed in the specification. I had done nothing wrong, so I could not be scolded or disciplined. All they could do would be to come back with some embarrassment and ask for simplification—and, of course, the joke would be over and I would simplify. I just hoped that none of my supervisors would require hospitalization. I didn't really intend things to go that far.

But the joke was on me. My supervisors were wreathed in smiles at this product of the satirist's art. They took it straight and swallowed it whole, and on March 7, 1945, Hardecker himself warmly complimented me on the excellence of the specification.

Years later, I was told that that specification was still preserved (under nitrogen, do you suppose?) and handed out to new employees as an example of how specifications ought to be written.

I worried, sometimes, in looking back on it, just how much, in my eagerness to play a harmless little joke, I had set back the war effort.

2

On February 3, 1944, I received a letter from Campbell that rather plaintively asked for stories, especially additional Foundation stories. (How our roles had changed!) He particularly suggested a short story dealing with the Traders, whom I had introduced in "The Big and the Little."

I therefore spent the first half of 1944 writing "The Wedge" and "Dead Hand," the fourth and fifth stories of the Foundation series. The former was the short story that Campbell requested. It was only seven thousand words long and was the shortest of the series. The latter was twenty-five thousand words and was the longest so far.

Both stories were accepted promptly. "The Wedge" was taken on April 11, 1944, for $122.50, and "Dead Hand" on August 26, 1944, for $437.50 (a new high in payment for a single story).

3

We weren't bothered much by wartime shortages, thanks to our unsophisticated way of life. Rubber and gasoline rationing didn't affect us since we didn't own an automobile. Bernie Zitin organized a car pool so he could qualify for more gasoline and use the excess for his own purposes, and I benefited by that. In the end, though, I switched to rapid transit. Zitin's comings and goings were too erratic to suit my orderly self.

It was also difficult to get alcohol, and we were issued liquor rationing stamps. Neither Gertrude nor I drank so we had no use for them at all, and this sometimes brought us a dubious popularity when we were courted for the sake of those unused stamps.

There was food rationing, of course, and shoe rationing, and we couldn't avoid that. Such matters were inconvenient—but never to the point of hardship.

Sometimes there would be rumors of particular shortages. Suddenly it would become hard to get soap because everyone talked of a soap shortage and hoarding would set in. Well, lack of soap *was* unthinkable now that I had learned to love showers, and we did our share of hoarding.

In the winter of 1944–45, there was a sudden and temporary shortage of cigarettes, and that would have pleased me if both of us didn't smoke, for the panic and fright of all the addicts would have been a source of sardonic amusement for me. Unfortunately, Gertrude smoked, and she and I would stand on separate lines to accumulate cartons.

The war seriously affected the candy-store business. It put everyone to work and nobody would run a candy store if there were any other way of making a living. Store after store closed down, therefore, and never reopened. Those that stayed open, such as my parents', became less dependent on their customers. They could close at times, for instance.

On February 22, 1944, for instance, my parents seized the fact of a legal holiday to close the store and come to Philadelphia to visit us for a day. They brought Stanley with them; he was now 14½ years old and was going to Brooklyn Technical High School. All went very well and Gertrude prepared an excellent dinner for them.

4

In the spring of 1944, Sprague lent me his six-volume *Study of History* by Arnold Toynbee (one volume at a time). After the war, Toynbee went through a period of great, though temporary, popularity. Sprague, however, was an admirer long before the rest of the world caught on. I came to be an admirer, too—temporarily.

There are some people who, on reading my Foundation series, are sure that it was influenced basically by Toynbee. They are only partly right. The first four stories were written before I had read Toynbee. "Dead Hand," however, was indeed influenced by it.

Afterward, however, as I continued to read Toynbee, my admiration waned. More and more, it was obvious to me that he was essentially a classical and Christian scholar and that the order he found in history was an imposed one produced by his seeing reflections of classical history wherever he looked. The final stories of the Foundation series were once more relatively free of his influence, therefore.

What really influenced the Foundation series was, as I said before, Gibbon's *The Decline and Fall of the Roman Empire*, which I had read and admired as a seventeen-year-old and which I never ceased to admire.

Another influence was *The Historian's History of the World*, a 1907-vintage twenty-four-volume collection of historical writings so arranged as to give a chronological account of events, nation by nation. It made for jumpy reading, but I loved it, and during the latter half of 1943, I picked it out, volume by volume, from the Philadelphia Free Library, reading it both at work and at home.

5

Paradoxically, as the war went better, the draft situation got worse. Nor was it really paradoxical. The longer the war endured, the more it seemed unfair that some young men should do the fighting and others (like myself) should sit in comfort at home. Furthermore, as victory seemed more certain, experience in fighting men seemed less crucial. There was less risk in relieving men who had borne the heat and the burden of the fight and replacing them with neophytes.

The papers therefore began to be full of all sorts of stories about the ending of war-work deferments for men under twenty-six. Since I was only twenty-four, I began to expect that I would be drafted sometime in the spring of 1944. I didn't enjoy the prospect.

On March 25, the Navy Yard made the general announcement that they would be forced to abandon those males under twenty-six to the draft, and that meant my 2B status was over. On March 27, 1944, I received the official word. I got a new draft card, with the fatal expression 1A upon it. It was the first time I had seen this since I had registered three years before.

I at once began considering the options open to me. Being an officer was better than being a private, at least as long as a shooting war was in progress, so I went down to the Naval Procurement Office to see about applying for officers' training.

They wasted little time with me. An officer behind a desk ordered me to take off my glasses. He then said, "Read the chart on the wall there."

I said, with my usual chuckleheaded honesty, "What chart?" even though I was clearly staring in the right direction.

I was out on the street within five minutes.

There was nothing to do but wait. The other under-twenty-sixers in the lab all got 1As also, and one by one we were called up for physical examinations. My call came at last on April 8, just as I was getting ready to go to New York with Gertrude. I was to report for a physical (in New York, where I was registered) on April 15.

We stayed in New York through Monday and Tuesday (things were very different from that first uptight year at the Navy Yard and it was by now easy to get a day or two of leave now and then). I seized the opportunity to do as I used to do. I visited Campbell on April 10, to submit "The Wedge" in person and to have the usual long talk.

When we got back to Philadelphia I asked the Draft Board there to have my physical transferred to Philadelphia, since I lived in that city even though I was registered in New York. It was a reasonable request and was granted at once—but it meant a month's delay and I certainly didn't object to that.

On May 5, I received my second notification of a physical, this time from the Philadelphia Draft Board. I was to report on May 18.

On that day I had my physical—which lasted from 8:00 A.M. to 4:30 P.M., a full workday. There were eleven different tests, including a "psychiatric test," concerning which I remember nothing at all. Nothing was particularly wrong with me except for my nearsightedness, which was bad enough to get me into 1AL—that is, 1A Limited. This removed me from immediate danger of being drafted, and I felt much better.

In fact, it made it possible for us to continue planning our vacation. We were going to return to Hilltop Lodge, in June this time, and we planned to take Stanley with us.

Then, on June 2, as though to compound our relief, a new draft card came with the unexpected classification of 2BL, which was even better than 2B, and set us into ecstasies.

More excitement came on June 6, 1944, when a vast British-American-Canadian armada unloaded an army onto the Normandy beaches. The radio went into such a yammer of excitement over it that work was impossible that day.

The next day, by coincidence, Heinlein, de Camp, and I were interviewed by the Navy Yard news periodical *Air Scoop*. A picture was eventually taken on June 27 to accompany the article. I still own a copy of that picture, and all three of us look unbelievably young and handsome, at least by later standards. It appeared in *Air Scoop*, along with the interview, on August 9.

6

On June 17, 1944, we left for Hilltop Lodge with high hopes, but, alas, everything went wrong. The year before it had been an unexpected success; this time it was an unexpected fiasco.

What happened was that it rained—and rained—steadily for four days. There were few vacationers present and, among them, none of value. Poor Stanley, who was with us, and, as always, good as gold, tried to be cheerful and suggested card games. We did play—but it wasn't enough. On Wednesday we gave up and went home, losing a sizable bit of our money, which was not refunded, of course.

Anyone who goes to a resort for a limited period of time always takes the chance of experiencing unsuitable weather, but among all the vacations I have ever taken, none was as completely unsatisfying as that one was.

7

On July 18, I received a copy of the August 1944 *Astounding*, with "The Big and the Little"[1] in it. The story had received the cover. On the cover, in fact, it said, " 'The Big and the Little,' a Foundation Story by Isaac Asimov." The fact that a new Foundation story, identified as such, was included in the magazine had obviously become a selling point.

It was a pleasant break in a horrible July in which we had just lived through eight straight days of over-ninety temperatures with the air conditioning broken down in the laboratory.[2]

On July 25, I called home to wish Stanley a happy fifteenth birthday, and I was greeted with the news that my parents *had bought a house*. I couldn't believe this evidence of unexampled prosperity. It was at 192 Windsor Place, just across Tenth Avenue from the candy store and a hundred yards south.

My parents planned to live downstairs and rent out the upstairs. It would mean that they would no longer be across the street from the store and would no longer be able to look out to see if "everything was all right."

It was very difficult for me to get used to the thought of my parents as property owners.

The next day, Gertrude and I celebrated our second anniversary. I arranged to get off from work at twelve, even though it was a Wednesday, and raced madly around getting two roses, a card, a bottle of wine, a box of candy, and a jigsaw puzzle, and then rushed home.

It was a surprise, for I hadn't told Gertrude I was planning this. It was lucky, too, that I did not arrive five minutes later, for she was just on the point of leaving for the movies. Eventually, after sampling things I had bought and solving the puzzle, we went to the movies together.[3] It was a poor picture but a good day.

In the outside world, an assassination attempt on Hitler on July 20 had failed, but Allied forces were steadily expanding their holdings in

---

[1] See *Foundation*, where it appears as "Part V—The Merchant Princes."
[2] The summers of 1943 and 1944, which we spent in an apartment with one-way ventilation, were real stinkers. There were thirty-eight days over ninety in 1943, which set a record for Philadelphia, and thirty-four such days in 1944.
[3] We went to the movies a great deal in those days and probably saw every picture made—good, bad, and so-so. So did everyone else, of course, since these were the days before television.

Normandy, and the Soviets had retaken virtually all the land they had lost to the Germans in two years and were coming within striking distance of Germany itself. In the Pacific, the United States was island-hopping toward Japan and was fighting on the island of Guam.

8

Gertrude took two weeks off in the last half of August, planning to spend them with her family. I didn't like having to endure her absence, but it was only reasonable. The heat of this second impossible summer in a row, and the vast disappointment of the vacation had certainly earned her a relief. She left on August 14, 1944, and I followed on Saturday, the nineteenth, to share with her a three-day weekend.

In the course of that weekend, I visited the old apartment across the street from the candy store for the last time. It was there that I had lived for the 5½ years before I went to Philadelphia and it was there I had done all my early writing.[4]

Then, on August 21, I visited Campbell and handed in "Dead Hand," the fifth Foundation story, for which the record check arrived on the twenty-sixth. Meanwhile, the fourth Foundation story, "The Wedge,"[5] appeared in the October 1944 Astounding.

To tell the truth, though, I was tiring of the Foundation series. I had written three Foundation stories in a row and for nine months those three stories had been constantly on my mind. I wanted a rest and I also wanted a chance to make use of the other writing I was doing—the Navy style—which, unless I exorcised it somehow, might well corrode my vitals.

When I handed in "Dead Hand," I suggested to Campbell that I do a short story I planned to call "Blind Alley," in which I made use of my Navy Yard experience. The story was to involve red tape, and part of it was to be told in the form of letters between bureaucrats in the Navy style, with the thesis being that it protected against stupidity but could not protect against ingenuity—if there was enough of that.

Campbell laughed and agreed, and on September 2, I began it.

It was set in the Foundation universe, at the height of the Galactic Empire, before the fall of that Empire and the beginning of the Foundation. I did that because it was easier to do so than to make up a completely new background.

It was the one story written in the Foundation universe (whether

[4] By September 1, the family moved to the new house—in time for my mother's forty-ninth birthday on the fifth.
[5] See Foundation, where it appears as "Part IV—The Traders."

part of the Foundation series or not) in which there were extra-terrestrial intelligences. In all the other stories, a purely human Galaxy is described, with no other intelligent beings present and with no unusual or monstrous animals either.

The device of an all-human Galaxy had apparently never been used before. Stories of interstellar travel prior to the Foundation, notably those of E. E. Smith and by Campbell himself, had always presupposed numerous intelligences and had used these intelligences as devices wherewith to drive the plot.

The multi-intelligence Galaxy is, to my way of thinking, more probable than the all-human one. However, I was concentrating on political and social forces in the Foundation series and I would have complicated these unbearably if I had introduced other intelligences. Even more important, it was my fixed intention not to allow Campbell to foist upon me his notions of the superiority and inferiority of races, and the surest way of doing that was to have an all-human Galaxy.

In "Blind Alley" the plot, as it worked itself out in my head, was to have a clever bureaucrat use Navy style to help save an extra-terrestrial intelligence that would otherwise be destroyed. I knew that Campbell would interpret this as a superior humanity helping an inferior race and he would have no objection to it, and as long as he didn't interfere to introduce a heavy-handed indication of this interpretation, I would be satisfied. I mailed the story to him on October 10, and a check for $148.75 was in my hands on October 20.

9

We were planning to go to Atlantic City on the weekend of September 9 and 10. So far all our vacations had been in New York City, or in some resort we would have gone to if we had lived in New York. There was nothing to indicate that we were now Philadelphians and had been Philadelphians for more than two years. Why not Atlantic City, then? It was only fifty miles away and the train could take us there and back without undue expense, leaving us a whole day and a night to enjoy ourselves there.

The only trouble was that as the weekend approached I found myself suffering from intestinal flu. Though I volunteered to go anyway rather than spoil our plans, Gertrude would have none of it.

"We can go next weekend," she said firmly. "The Atlantic City boardwalk will not blow away."

Those were her exact words. On Thursday the fourteenth, a hurricane hit the East Coast of the United States, and large sections of the

Atlantic City boardwalk blew away—so we did not get to go to Atlantic City the next weekend, either. In fact, we *never* got to go there together.

10

The presidential campaign of 1944 was on. Roosevelt was running once again, for a fourth time. This made me very happy, for it meant I would have a chance to vote for him directly, instead of by way of Milton Silverman's absentee ballot.

Vice President Henry A. Wallace had not been renominated, however, and that distressed me. Senator Harry S Truman was running for Vice President instead, and I considered him a very mediocre person and could listen only glumly when one of the Navy Yard employees (a Republican) said, "Can you imagine Truman as President if anything happens to Roosevelt?"

I couldn't.

Running against Roosevelt was Thomas E. Dewey of New York, a slick campaigner, and Senator John W. Bricker of Ohio. I had approved of Dewey when he was a district attorney in New York, but he was a Republican so I wouldn't dream of supporting him for state office, let alone for national office. As for Bricker, he was utterly beyond the pale, for he was an isolationist and an extreme conservative.

Nevertheless, I knew that Roosevelt, running for a *fourth* term, would have trouble with increasing numbers of those who felt he had been President long enough. It also seemed to me that Dewey was running a clever and effective campaign. The Philadelphia papers were strongly anti-Roosevelt and I got more and more depressed about it.

On September 23, 1944, I was back in New York and visited my parents' new apartment at 192 Windsor Place for the first time. It was not the "little palace" my mother had proudly proclaimed it to be but it was certainly the nicest place they had lived in yet.[6]

On that evening, while I was sitting in the new apartment, Roosevelt addressed the Teamsters Union, making his first speech of the campaign, and he was in top form. His good-natured wit was excoriating and when he protested against slanders aimed at "my little dog, Fala," I knew he was in no trouble. I said in my diary that day, "It was a lulu and a knockout. 'My little dog, Fala' will win the election for him."

---

[6] Another sign of the changing times was that my father was reluctantly giving up newspaper deliveries. It was impossible to get a paperboy, and he wasn't going to stick Stanley with it. Ten years earlier, he wouldn't have hesitated to stick me with it, but it was different now.

Before the election, though, on October 27, 1944, he toured the Navy Yard. More excitement built up then than anything since Hedy Lamarr had done the same thing two years before. (Myself, I was more excited *this* time.)

I was outside the building along with everyone else when the limousine passed and there was Roosevelt leaning out the window, with his big grin. Suddenly, I realized that the familiar face I had seen so often in newsreels, photographs, and cartoons actually existed and was actually affixed to a living person. I found myself going wild, jumping up and down, and screaming like a teen-age girl. I don't think I ever lost control so upon viewing anyone else in my life.

It was the only time I ever saw F.D.R. in person.

11

When I stop to think that I spent years of my life in chemical laboratories, I have to realize that I ran the risk of accidents. I never worked with really dangerous materials, with tricky explosives, or with deadly poisons—but anything can be dangerous. There could always be explosions, fires, noxious vapors, corrosive chemicals.

Naturally, I had stained my fingers and burned my clothes with acid, and I had cut myself on breaking glassware—but nothing serious ever happened to me in the lab.

Once at Columbia, I remember, a reflux condensation got away from Lloyd Roth while I was standing by. It started bubbling madly and he did the only thing one could do. The first law is GET OUT. He turned off the flame and fled fleetly, and so did I—and then I ran back in to get my books. Nothing happened to me, but if it had, I would have deserved it.

At other times, both in Columbia and in the Navy Yard, there were horror tales of explosions, of hot acid spraying, and so on. It was always on another floor, or when I wasn't there.

One time and one time only did I come close to serious damage— and it was completely my fault. I had a device that determined carbon content in steel powders. It was a quartz tube within which one placed a small alumina boat containing the powdered unknown. The tube was, in turn, placed within a cylindrical electric furnace. A gentle stream of oxygen gas was sent through the tube and into a small U-tube containing a substance that absorbed carbon dioxide. The stream of oxygen combined with the carbon in the heated steel powder to form carbon dioxide, which was added to the absorbing substance as it passed through. By weighing the U-tube before and after, the quantity of carbon dioxide, and hence the per cent of carbon in the original sample, could be determined.

On October 5, 1944, a fellow labworker gave me a fluffy white powder and asked me to determine the carbon content. I hadn't the slightest idea as to how much carbon it contained. The thing to do was to start at the safe end—with a very small amount to begin with. If there was then too little carbon to measure, a larger sample could be worked with, and so on.

I did no such thing. With criminal stupidity, I simply filled the boat. Now, if there were a lot of carbon in the sample—as there turned out to be—the combination with oxygen might be rapid enough to explode the substance.

I turned on the electric furnace and stood there with my left hand on the quartz tube where it emerged from the furnace, testing to see if it were warming up—an indication that the furnace was working.

At that point, Bernie Zitin's superior (hence my grandsuperior), J. Hartley Bowen, called, "Hey, Isaac, come here. I want to talk to you."

Rather annoyed at being interrupted, I took my hand away from the quartz tube, took two steps toward Hartley—and at that point there was an explosion and the quartz tube was shattered. Had Hartley called me ten seconds later, my left hand might well have been shattered with it.

It took me all day to recover. The realization of my incredible idiocy was even more bitter than the thought of what might have happened.

Generally, though, I was careful to a fault. For instance, Navy officers have gold braid freely distributed over their uniforms and are very proud of it. This gold braid must be cleaned now and then, and the best way to do it is to brush it with a solution of potassium cyanide.

Different members of the chemical laboratory would be more or less assigned the task at different times. Not me, however. I steadfastly and firmly refused to involve myself with potassium cyanide for anything as frivolous as cleaning gold braid. It was hinted to me several times that my refusal would make trouble for me. This was an idle threat, however. My eccentricities were such that all the trouble was already made.

I recall another time when Bernie Zitin brought in a young man of perhaps eleven and told me he was the son of a top officer and would I give him some chemicals he wanted. That wasn't exactly legitimate, but I didn't see that as worth a big hassle.

"What would you like, young man?" I asked.

"Some potassium nitrate," he said.

"Okay," I said, reaching for the reagent bottle. It was not very expensive. "What else?"

"Charcoal."

"Okay," I said. That was very cheap. I was about to ask what else he wanted when a suspicion jabbed me and I said, "Do you want sulfur, also?"

"Yes," he said, astonished. "How did you know?"

I took him by the hand and led him back to Zitin. "This young man," I said, "wishes to make some gunpowder in his home laboratory, and I will not give him the ingredients. Have someone else give it to him, if you want to." Someone did and, as far as I know, the young man did no damage with it, but the responsibility was not going to be mine.

Once there was a much more humorous incident involving a petty misuse of laboratory time and equipment.

A young lady from the secretarial pool, given to gaudy clothing and blessed with a gaudy figure to match—and therefore much superior, in her opinion, to the girls who worked in the chem lab in ill-fitting, acid-stained smocks—walked in with a piece of jewelry her boyfriend had given her. It was a bracelet of rubies set in gold, and she asked if it could be cleaned for her.

One of the girls in the lab volunteered—mainly, I think, to get her hands on the magnificent object. Having admired it sufficiently, she doused it in ethyl acetate, a mild solvent that would serve to remove any greasy crud on the bracelet and leave the gold and rubies sparkling with delight.

What happened was that all the gold dissolved and all the rubies softened and the poor technician dissolved in tears. She knew she couldn't pay for the valuable bracelet she had just ruined.

I said, soothingly, "Don't feel bad. Everything is okay," and rushed off to get the gaudy secretary.

The secretary viewed the bracelet with horror. "What have you done with it?" she screamed and the technician blanched.

I said, "Don't yell at her. The metal is probably steel with gold paint over it and the rubies are plastic. Your boyfriend can replace it very easily for fifty cents and you can clean it with a soft handkerchief if you don't rub too hard."

Off she went and the technician recovered very quickly. We never found out what the secretary did to her boyfriend.

And then there was an accident that only I found humorous—and that, in truth, wasn't at all humorous, but very nearly tragic—but I couldn't help it.

What happened was that Tom Walb, who was senior to me, was promoted to P3 and moved into more nearly executive quarters behind a desk.

One time he came back into the lab—no longer with rolled-up sleeves and a dirty smock, but resplendent in a beautiful suit, tie, and collar. He told me he was going to help himself to some engine cleaner for some purpose he didn't explain.

Engine cleaner is meant to dissolve the carbon crud around engines. It is nasty stuff—it smells bad and it is corrosive. He took one of my beakers from the tabletop, put it near a five-gallon aluminum container of the stuff, and picked up the container.

"Gee, Tom," I said, mildly, "you shouldn't be taking samples of that stuff when you're dressed like that."

Walb paused and said to me with what I thought was an offensive implication, "A person who uses the proper technique can work in a chem lab dressed in a tuxedo."

I shriveled, of course, because everyone knew (and I most of all) that I didn't have the proper technique and that no one had smocks and rubber aprons so continually assaulted by chemicals as I had.

Having put me neatly in my place, Walb then picked up the container and gave it a sharp, expertly twirled shake in order to set the fluid within it into a swirl so that it would be well mixed when he removed a hundred milliliters or so.

What he didn't know and what I didn't know was that whoever had used that container last (and it wasn't I) had not really tightened the screw top, but had merely balanced it on the lip. That should not have been done, but, on the other hand, it was a matter that should have been checked. Well, Tom hadn't checked it, and when he swirled the container, a jet of the foul-smelling corrosive stuff shot out and drenched him.

There was a loud outcry and he was dragged off immediately by a dozen hands and placed under a shower that we had available for just such occasions. Thanks to the instant action, he was not seriously damaged at all, but every item of clothing he was wearing, including his shoes, was unusable thereafter.

I am ashamed to say that I was not involved in this rescue effort. I was quite helpless with laughter. It is a terrible thing to admit, for Walb might have damaged himself seriously and permanently, but it struck me as such a remarkable example of pride followed immediately by a fall that I could not help myself. If a gun had been aimed at me with a promise to shoot if I laughed, I could not have kept from laughing.

12

Fan letters from *real scientists* were not a totally unknown quantity. On October 21, 1944, for instance, I was very impressed (my diary for that day is full of underlinings) to receive a letter from William C. Boyd, Ph.D., an associate professor of biochemistry at Boston University School of Medicine. He was not writing about any of my recent stories at all, but about "Nightfall," which had been published three years before.

Apparently it had stayed with him, and now he was writing to tell me it was the best story *Astounding* had ever printed and that it was a classic. He was the very first person ever to tell me this.

I answered the letter, of course, and a sparse exchange of letters with him continued over the next few years.

13

On November 1, 1944, I started another positronic robot story, one I called "Escape." It was my first such story in a year and a quarter, and the previous one, "Catch That Rabbit," was perhaps the weakest in the series. Certainly it did badly in the readers' column and finished last in *Astounding*'s "Analytical Laboratory" (which tabulated reader reactions).

I decided I had to try again. I couldn't let the positronic robot series end on that low note.

The new story occupied me for the rest of the year, largely because a new and monumentally silly project had caught me up. In the outside world, the Soviets were at the eastern border of Germany, the British and the Americans at the western border; and in the Pacific, the American forces were back in the Philippines. It was clear that the war was in its last stages, with our enemies facing utter defeat, and I began to view the war as a matter of history.

And why shouldn't I write that history? (It was the *first* time I ever had the impulse to write anything but science fiction since I had begun "Cosmic Corkscrew.")

My manner of gathering material was to read every book on the war and on the decade preceding it, and to copy out of each book every passage that might be of interest. (I remembered the work I did for Professor Stern when I was an NYA worker in 1938 and 1939.) It was fascinating—but time-consuming (it got in the way of everything) and useless.

It was worse than useless, for it slowed my real writing, my science fiction.

14

On November 7, 1944, I voted in a presidential election for the first time in my life. I voted for Roosevelt, of course, and assuming the worst, I felt Roosevelt would get 311 electoral votes to 220 for Dewey. Once the reports started coming in, however, Roosevelt ran consistently ahead of my estimate and by 10:00 P.M. it was all over as far as I was concerned.

Roosevelt ended with 432 electoral votes to Dewey's 99. It had been the smallest of his four victories, but only by Roosevelt standards was it anything less than completely satisfactory.

15

Jack Williamson, the science-fiction writer who had been the first to welcome me to the ranks, showed up at the Navy Yard in a sergeant's uniform, and on Saturday, December 2, 1944, Gertrude and I attended a dinner that, in theory, he was hosting. Actually, Bob Heinlein arranged it—he knowing the city better.

In addition to ourselves, Jack, and the Heinleins, there were present the de Camps, L. Ron Hubbard, and a friend of the Heinleins named Firn—nine people altogether. According to my diary, "we had a swell steak and potatoes dinner that must have set Jack back $25."

Afterward, we went to Firns' place, and the party didn't break up till 2:00 A.M.

Gertrude was wearing a costume that was very unusual for her—a low-cut dress. She was magnificently built for such dresses and I always urged her to wear them if for no other reason than that I myself enjoyed them. Generally, however, she was far too modest for this and wouldn't. On this occasion, even though I had ardently approved her choice, she kept unobtrusively hiking up the neckline. It didn't help, of course, and Hubbard and Heinlein swarmed all over her. I used this as proof of the effectiveness of the dress, but no use—she wouldn't wear it again.

The star of the evening was Ron Hubbard. Heinlein, de Camp, and I were each prima donna-ish and each liked to hog the conversation and was not overwhelmed with delight at failing to do so—ordinarily. On this occasion, however, we all sat as quietly as pussycats and listened to Hubbard. He told tales with perfect aplomb and in complete paragraphs. He sang songs to a guitar, including, as I recall, "Fifteen Men on a Dead Man's Chest" and "I Learned About Women from Her."

In after years, Hubbard became world famous for reasons far removed from science fiction and guitar plunking, but whatever he does, I remember him only for that evening.

16

Toward the end of the year, the Germans began an offensive that came to be known as "the Battle of the Bulge."

The news media went into a flap but I couldn't for the life of me see any importance to the German offensive. There were casualties, of course, and that was too bad, but the offensive could have no strategic value at all, and I said so loudly at the time. The Germans were far too beaten to do any more than make some local advances, and consume their last dregs in doing so. Even if, very unaccountably, the British and the Americans had to fall back many miles, there were still the Soviets on the eastern borders of Germany.

It was a case of everyone suddenly thinking that the Germany of 1941 still existed, and it didn't. There was, of course, talk of secret weapons, but I knew that it was the atom bomb that would be such a weapon and I was quite certain that the United States would get it first —but of that I said nothing.

By the end of the year it did, in fact, appear that Germany's last gamble had failed. I was able to end that year's diary with the satisfaction that 1944 had been a decent year all told and "let us hope that 1945 brings us back to New York." I was beginning to look forward with burnished hope to a return to research.

Even in writing, I was back in high gear. I had only sold four stories, but all of them were at the new high rates of $.015 or even $.0175 a word, and two of them had been very long. The result was that my 1944 writing earnings stood at $1,108.75, for a new record. Add to this my Navy Yard earnings and my total income for the year topped $4,300. It was the dreams of Croesus realized.

Our bank account now stood at over $2,000, and I felt that, one way or another, I could see my way through research.

17

At 1:00 A.M. on the night of January 1–2, 1945, Gertrude woke me to sing "Happy Birthday." It was pleasant, but nevertheless the year didn't begin well.

For one thing, I was twenty-five—"a quarter of a century," I noted mournfully in my diary. There's nothing so wrong about being twenty-five, and it is certainly better than never making it—but a child prodigy takes getting older worse than others do.

There was always something spectacular about my being younger than others of my achievement, but I was slowly coming to the realization that I wasn't going to stay younger than others forever. A number of people at the Navy Yard, for instance, were younger than I was yet were on a level with me.

In fact, some of the younger employees were going to pass me and attain P3 ratings, and it was quite clear throughout 1944 that there would be no promotion for me. Quite apart from my general effervescence and eccentricity, there was my penchant for talking back to my superiors.

Then, too, wherever I have been, I have always managed to offend some one particular person mortally and to induce a "get Asimov" syndrome in him. I never cared really, for the person I offended was very likely to be stupid, humorless, or unpleasant (or all three), and offending him earned me kudos in heaven. Nevertheless, they could, and sometimes did, sprinkle sand into the gearbox of my progress.

At the Navy Yard, the person I had chief trouble with was one Lieutenant Commander Mason, whom I found utterly exasperating. I presume he had finished grade school, but he never betrayed the fact in anything he said. He thought it the height of wit to allude to my Russian birth, and when I lost my temper and told him off harshly on the matter (in public) he managed to scrape together enough mentality to keep that in mind. Before long, through the workings of the revered principle of seniority, whereby an old jackass is considered more worthy of reverence than a young lion, he attained a high enough position at the Navy Yard to make it possible for him to veto a promotion of me even if anyone beneath him were mad enough to suggest one.

Then too, I was very depressed over "Escape." As the new year dawned, it had been sitting with Campbell for nearly three weeks, and he simply *never* waited that long to announce a result. By January 5, 1945, I was desperate enough to call Campbell long distance (long distance!) just to make sure he had received it. Campbell wasn't in, but Katherine Tarrant assured me it had been received and bought.

That left me in a puzzle as to where the check might be and I decided to be in New York the following Monday.

I was, and when I saw him on January 8, he explained that he wanted a revision—not much of one, but a revision. After having sold Campbell seven stories in a row without any question over a space of nearly two years, even a slight revision was a bad setback. The revision only took me a few days; I sent the story in again on the fifteenth, and on the twenty-fourth I got a check for $147—but the incident shook me.

On the January 8 visit, we discussed the next Foundation story, and Campbell said he wanted to upset the Seldon Plan, which was the connecting backbone of the series. I was horrified. No, I said, no, no, no. But Campbell said: Yes, yes, yes, yes, and I knew I wasn't going to sell him a no, no.

I made up my mind, rather sulkily (I was still brooding over "Escape"), to follow orders, but to get my own back by making the new Foundation story the longest and biggest and widest yet. On January 26, 1945, then, I began "The Mule."

On that day, I had been married 2½ years, and that may have influenced me, for the heroine, Bayta, was modeled on Gertrude—certainly in appearance. Toran, her husband, was modeled on myself, though his appearance wasn't described as similar to mine.

Bayta was, of course, the key to the whole story and was the person who defeated the Mule at the end, while Toran was definitely subsidiary and bumbled about in Bayta's wake. I suppose that was the way I viewed the family situation. I was clever academically and I had a writing talent. For the rest, I never felt that I was particularly bright in anything that had to do with ordinary living and with human interrelationships.

As for the Mule himself, his personal appearance was based on my friend Leonard Meisel, who by then was the only person at the Navy Yard with whom I could completely relax.

I worked rapidly, more rapidly than I had at any other time during the war. To be sure, the story took me some 3½ months to complete, but it ended being fifty thousand words long, approaching novel length. It was the very first story I had ever written that was so long, that had so intricate a plot, and that had so lengthy a cast of characters. And with Gertrude to inspire me, I think that Bayta was the first successful, well-rounded female character I ever had in any of my stories.[7]

It helped the progress of the writing that news in the world outside looked so good. With the new year, the Soviets opened another offen-

---

[7] I loved Susan Calvin of the robot stories passionately, but she could scarcely be considered well-rounded.

sive in the East and swooped into Germany proper. By the time I was working on "The Mule," the Soviet Army was within striking distance of Berlin, and I felt that every day I was taking a giant stride toward New York and my return to research.

18

On Saturday, February 3, 1945, there was another science-fiction dinner, including the Heinleins, the de Camps, and the Asimovs. This time, instead of Hubbard and Williamson, there were present Henry Kuttner and his wife, C. L. Moore. It was the first time I had ever met them.

Kuttner wrote fast-moving, action-filled stories when he wanted to, but he was a very quiet fellow who said almost nothing the entire evening, but sat on a couch with his wife, holding hands.

The Kuttners had a copy of the March 1945 *Astounding*, which contained "Blind Alley,"[8] and "Dead Hand" was announced in it as slated for appearance in the April 1945 issue. When that issue eventually appeared, it turned out I had the cover again.[9]

As was not true of the first dinner party, the food and service were horrible. It embarrassed Bob (who was hosting it) extremely.

The peak moment of embarrassment came when someone tried vainly to get a waiter to bring a fork, and Heinlein finally, by main force, stopped one in midflight and demanded a fork. The waiter nodded, walked over to another table piled high with dirty plates and assorted garbage, and looked over the scraps for a possible fork. We yelled out, "Never mind," and the diner who was short a fork made do with his fingers.

19

With my seam-sealer project completed in the Navy Yard, I went on to handle a dye-marker project.

A dye marker is a reddish-brown powder containing fluorescein which, when dumped in water, produces a bright and fluorescent green solution. It is kept in a plastic container that can be ripped open. If an airman is forced to leave his plane over sea and to float about on a gas-filled rubber raft, he might be able to stay afloat and alive for days, but he would be difficult to spot from potential rescue planes high in the

[8] See *The Early Asimov*.
[9] See *Foundation and Empire* (Gnome Press, 1951, later published by Doubleday). It appears in the book as "Part I—The General."

sky. By dumping the dye marker in the ocean when he sees a friendly plane overhead, a splotch of bright green is produced that is far easier to see than the boat itself.

The great task I set myself was to work out some way of devising a laboratory test that would predict, accurately, how well the dye marker would be seen from a plane. The sure way of doing it would be to have someone fly in a plane and note the ease with which different samples of dye marker could be noted. That, however, it seemed to me, would be very expensive in terms of planes, gasoline, and pilots—to say nothing of the chance of accident—so that a satisfactory laboratory test would be valuable indeed.

The only trouble was that in order to decide whether the laboratory test gave useful results, they would have to be checked from the air to begin with. Working with a batch of different samples of dye markers, you would run the lab test on each and list the dye markers in order of efficiency. You would then view them all from the air and check whether they were in the same order of efficiency. You could then check the boundary limit of effectiveness for sighting and you would be all set. No one would then ever have to fly a plane to check a dye marker again.

It was the most creative thing by far that I had ever tried to do in the Navy Yard, and I was excited. Although I had never been in a plane and although I was scared of accidents and (remembering my two experiences on roller coasters) certain that I would be very upset over the feeling of being high up and of having, perhaps, a sensation of imminent falling—I applied for permission to conduct the plane test.

On March 9, 1945, I was taken up twice in a two-motored plane. A dye marker that I predicted would be unsuitable on the basis of my lab test proved, indeed, to be unsuitable when studied from the air, and I was very satisfied at that. I wrote in my diary, "The most interesting feelings were seeing the earth tilt when we banked, an air pocket we hit, and the first take-off. I wasn't the least bit airsick."

Nor was I conscious of being terribly afraid. However, I must have been pretty tense while flying, for the next day all my muscles were stiff and sore.

I applied for a whole series of plane flights to calibrate my lab test in detail, even though my first flight hadn't made me the least bit keen on airflight in general.

Hardecker was not particularly pleased by the expense that would be entailed. He called me in, tapped my request, and said, "Can you guarantee that this will succeed?"

"No, of course not," I said, surprised. "The point of the test is to find out whether it will succeed. It may not, of course, but that would be a useful finding, too. If we knew in advance that the test would succeed, we wouldn't have to run it."

Hardecker shrugged. "If you can't guarantee success, you can't have the plane."

And that was that. I might have put up a harder fight if I had found flying more delightful.

Hardecker's reaction reminds me of an earlier time when some of the more highly placed civilians in the Navy Yard got tired of the poor quality of the coffee and sent a sample back for analysis. It seemed to have a green tinge and someone had suggested that there was copper in it.

I analyzed it and there was no detectable copper in it—or any detectable quantity of a few other heavy metals I thought might conceivably be present. I brought back my report.

"No copper?" they asked.

"No copper," I said, "and none of the other heavy elements I've listed."

They looked at me in contempt. "Then you didn't find out *anything?*"

"Finding nothing," I said, "is finding out something."

But I couldn't get that across to them.

37

The Draft

1

The war in Europe was winding up. The Americans had crossed the Rhine River in March; the Russians were within reach of Vienna, as well as of Berlin, and had taken Danzig, where it had all started 5½ years before. In the Pacific, American forces had landed in Okinawa.

That meant, of course, that the draft pressures began to increase. Once again, the conversation at work became entirely a matter of who was in what draft classification, who was being called up, who had gotten a stay of execution, and what the Navy Yard was going to do.

The Navy Yard was resigned to losing most of its younger men who were in 2B and intended to ask for deferments for only a fraction of them—presumably the most important fraction. For those persons who were 2BL nothing was to be done at all, since it was felt that the "Limited" designation would keep them out of the Army anyway. I was 2BL because of my eyes, but my draft classification expired on April 2. Then what?

There was nothing to do but wait.

Gertrude and I went to New York on our monthly visit on April 7, 1945—and I had as yet received no word from the draft board.[1]

I took the chance of stopping by at my local draft board on April 9 and inquired delicately as to my status. The girl there said they hadn't gotten around to me, but she was perfectly pleasant and there was no indication of trouble.

I went home the next day, but Gertrude didn't come back till Thursday, April 12, 1945. When I got home from work, she had not yet showed up, but just as I was preparing to leave for dinner, there was the sound of a key in the lock and I greeted her enthusiastically. We went out to dinner and had a wonderful time. Afterward, we took a walk to the local park and relaxed in the mild weather. We were feeling better than ever as we left to go home.

[1] My parents visited the Blugermans and had dinner with them on the evening of the eighth. While it was still daylight, my father went up to the roof of the apartment house and from that roof he saw the Atlantic Ocean rolling its waves in upon Brighton Beach. That was the *first* time he had seen the open ocean since he had landed in Brooklyn twenty-two years before, though at no time had he been more than a few miles from it.

And then I caught sight of the newspaper headlines at a newsstand.

President Roosevelt had died! He did not live to see the end of the war. The whole weekend was devoted to national mourning, and Gertrude and I mourned, too.

Harry S Truman was President, but I had no hopes for him.

In the middle of that three-day period of mourning I got a card from the draft board extending my deferment for another six months. I would have appreciated receiving it a little sooner so that I might have enjoyed it more.

2

The month of April ended with the Germans in collapse, with the Soviets in Berlin, and with Adolf Hitler a suicide. In the first week of May, in which I excitedly waited for the end of the war in Europe and the end of the long nightmare of Nazism, I saw *National Velvet* in the movies and *Oklahoma* on the stage. They would have filled me with hilarity at any time, but coming the week they did, I nearly burst with pleasure. The only black spot in the blaze of light was that Roosevelt had not survived a little longer to see the end of Hitler.

I kept racing ahead in the last stages of "The Mule." It was almost as though the Mule's ambitions were collapsing in time to Hitler's.[2]

On May 8, 1945, the war in Europe was over. It was V-E (Victory in Europe) Day.

For me, on a much smaller scale, the month had its victory, too. I finished "The Mule" on May 15, brought it to Campbell on May 21, and received the acceptance on May 29 in the form of a check for $875—50,000 words at $.0175 per word.

It was an incredible sum. That one check was only a little less than I had made in the first three years after my first visit to Campbell. It represented a quarter of my annual salary at the Navy Yard. Yet my comment in the diary was, "Falls flat somehow, however. Guess I'm so sure of sales these days, the thrill is gone."

Certain success evicts one from the paradise of winning against the odds.

3

I was in New York on May 21, 1945, in order to submit "The Mule," and with the war over in Europe and obviously soon to be over in Asia, it was time to be arranging my postwar life.

[2] The Mule was in no way a Hitlerian character, however. The story line worked out as it did, in fact, precisely because the Mule was not a complete villain.

I visited Columbia to check on the situation and found that I was still on the rolls and that I could return at any time, just as though I had never left. Professor Dawson remembered me with no trouble despite my absence of better than three years. Milton Silverman was still there, as was Phyllis of the phase rule class. Both were about to get their Ph.D.s.

Unfortunately, the draft situation continued its downward slide, and my recent renewal of 2BL status began to look shaky. General Hershey, who headed the Selective Service, suggested that the lists of those with mild physical defects be combed to see if they could serve as replacements—and among those with mild physical defects was none other than myself.

There was nothing to do but wait. I had seven months to go before my twenty-sixth birthday when, in all likelihood, I would be safe, for the accent had always been on those under twenty-six.

It was going to be a long seven months, though, and as uncertainty set in and intensified, I found myself unable to write or, indeed, to think of anything but the perennial "Will I or won't I be drafted?"

4

I celebrated Memorial Day 1945 by donating blood to the Red Cross for the first and only time of my life. Among my many physical fears is that of being jabbed for blood samples. These days this is routine at physical examination and, as I grow older, I have those examinations more frequently. And always I hate the blood sampling and turn my head away and grit my teeth and moan. I always threaten to faint but somehow I never have.

This time, though, I managed to work myself up to giving the blood voluntarily—a very difficult task.

I had never been blood-typed, and in this case, I wasn't exactly. I was just checked to see whether I was blood type O. Blood type O represents a "universal donor." In blood of that type there is no substance that gives rise to antibody reactions, so that in general it can be given to anybody. If one is not of blood type O, then one's blood can only be given safely to someone of the same blood type.

I was *not* blood type O.

When I was done, I was given orange juice, chocolate, and cookies. The loss of a pint of blood is trivial, but the psychology of it is not. So while I felt weak and dizzy and regaled myself with fattening material that I could, for the moment, eat virtuously, I listened to the conversation about me.

Some fat slob in my vicinity announced he was blood type O.

"Really," said someone else. "I notice they were particularly interested in blood type O. Why is that?"

"That's because," said the slob, "O blood is particularly rich and wholesome."

I was furious. My blood was just as rich and wholesome as his. The damn fool just didn't understand blood chemistry. I knew better than to try to explain the matter so I said nothing, but I burned all that day, and all that night, and all the next day and so on, right down to the present time whenever I think of it.

I'd have forgotten about the blood donation after a few months, and, thinking I had never given any, could easily have been shamed into making another donation. As it is, I have *never* forgotten the donation, and don't want ever to give another and run the risk of having the value of my non-O blood impugned again.

5

As I said earlier, the Navy Yard had reserved its limited ability to hold onto its young employees and requested deferment only for those it felt were in particular danger of the draft. Where someone was in a "limited" classification, they relied on the classification to keep him out.

Now that the Army had decided to lower its standards so that some 2BL's were eligible for the draft, the Navy Yard would be in no position to defend them because they would not have listed them as essential.

What it amounted to was that of two employees precisely equal in position, age, efficiency, and so on, the one with normal vision would be deferred and the one with bad vision would be drafted. It was a neat method of sticking the Army with inferior material—as American as apple pie.

While I marveled at the casual dishonesty of it, I was well aware that I was at the cruddy end of that particular stick.

On June 11, I was called for a physical again, to see if, on closer observation, my eyes weren't as bad as they seemed. I promptly asked for a transfer to Philadelphia and gained a month. (Every month counted, with my twenty-sixth birthday looming.)

As day after day passed, with rumors, speculations, and conflicting statements from Navy Yard higher-ups giving us endless grounds for excitement, Leonard Meisel said to me, "Won't Columbia take you back?"

I was off like a shot, working my way up through the chain of command. My thesis was a simple one: If the Navy Yard was not going to request my deferment, then the implication was that I was no longer useful to them. In that case, I said, give me my release and on that very day I would be back at Columbia engaged in important scientific research.

"Choose," I said, in effect, "deferment or release."

I got to the top and someone had to go off to Washington to discuss the situation with the Secretary of War or somebody. When he came back, the word was that deferments were out. Did I really want my release?

Wait, I said. It was Monday, July 2 (just six months to go before my twenty-sixth birthday), and Gertrude was already in New York for her monthly visit and I would welcome the chance to see her. I took emergency leave and chased out to New York with my hopes high.

They were quickly dashed. Dawson shook his head. Columbia wasn't saving anyone. Any research student whom the draft boards decided to take had to go. No chance.

It was disappointing, but at least while I was in New York, Gertrude and I managed to take our traditional walk along the boardwalk.

When I got back to Philadelphia, a letter setting a date for a draft physical in Philadelphia was waiting for me.

On July 18, I had the physical, which was a repeat of the one I had had the year before, with all the results identical. I even weighed 169 pounds on both occasions.

6

With the draft flap on, it was amazing how many other things that would ordinarily have had me quite concerned, meant comparatively little.

My father-in-law, Henry, had quit his job in May. My mother-in-law had long urged this, for she felt that a change would open the highway to success for him. He spent the next few months looking for jobs. Naturally, no high road to success ever opened.

As far as my parents were concerned, there were a variety of annoyances in early 1945. There were newspaper strikes, cigarette shortages, and so on. My father cut his finger on a broken glass and required several stitches. Young Stanley had appendicitis and was operated upon just before his sixteenth birthday.

One particularly minor irritation of that period came when I obtained the August 1945 *Astounding* and found that it contained "Escape" but that Campbell, for some reason I couldn't fathom, had changed the title to "Paradoxical Escape." I changed the title back to "Escape"[3] when I put it into one of my collections in later years.

7

Gertrude and I had no children and weren't planning to have any, at least for the duration. We rather took it for granted that we would eventually have one or two, but we felt no really great drive in that direction. For one thing, our experiences with children were not overwhelmingly happy ones.

The de Camps, for instance, had to go away for a couple of days and needed someone to stay with four-year-old Lyman. It occurred to them that we might be willing to stay at their place and serve as baby sitters.

We were *not* willing, but the Code of the Woosters is that you can't let a pal down—so we spent July 23 to 25 at the de Camp home, along with young Lyman and an elderly relative.

It was awful. Lyman was a rambunctious child who wore us out. Nor was it possible to deal with him properly. The elderly relative was a broken reed as far as discipline was concerned, and we hesitated to throw Lyman against the wall or to dribble him across the floor, as we would cheerfully have done had he been a child of our own.

There was nothing to do but reason with him, drive ourselves to frenzied exhaustion, and get nowhere. Never were we so relieved to see anyone as the de Camps on the twenty-fifth.

Oddly enough, Lyman (whose red hair gave him the inevitable nickname of Rusty) grew up to be as reserved, inhibited, and well-behaved as his father, despite the fact that in 1945 I would have bet a hundred to one he would grow up to be an outlaw. In fact, he grew up to become a delightful and highly intelligent fellow.

July 26 was our third anniversary, and just being home after that experience was celebration enough.

8

On July 27, I received a new classification from the draft board— 1AB. The added B was a bow of recognition to my nearsightedness, but it meant nothing. Anyone in 1AB was draft material, and I still had five months to go to the safety of my twenty-sixth birthday. So I requested a hearing with the local draft board, which was granted and set for August 7. I made ready to leave on the afternoon of the sixth.

[3] See *I, Robot*.

We were getting ready to go, and I remember exactly what happened.

I was reading a copy of Will Durant's *Caesar and Christ*, the third volume of his history of civilization[4] and Gertrude was ironing some clothes.

The radio stopped its regular programming for an emergency bulletin: The United States had dropped an atomic bomb on Hiroshima.

I was not surprised, mind you. I had known it was in the works since 1941. Therefore my original comment was not one of shock or awe or horror or anything like that.

Besides, something else was on my mind. Therefore, my first words when I heard the dramatic announcement were a thoughtful, "Hmm, I wonder how that will affect my draft status?"

Why shouldn't I wonder that? Japan was on its last legs and it was quite certain that the atomic bombing meant that surrender was only days away. Might the United States not stop the draft altogether in that case? It was a reasonable thought.

Until (and unless) the draft were halted, though, I remained in danger. I went to New York with Gertrude that day and on the next saw the draft board. Alas, there was no room for discretion. Since there was no appeal from the Navy Yard (and according to the latest government directives there could not be) I would have to be inducted when my turn came up. They couldn't tell for sure when that would be. I would just have to wait.

On August 14, Japan surrendered, and draft quotas were cut at once, and I felt myself hoping a bit.

At the Navy Yard, there was a sudden spurt of change. Saturdays stopped being workdays and there was a corresponding cut in salary as we changed back to a five-day week. Rationing of various kinds was called off. The Navy Yard personnel began dispersing. Heinlein was leaving. De Camp was preparing to leave.

I couldn't move, however. My actions depended on the draft. Just as soon as I knew I would *not* be drafted, I would leave at once and return to Columbia.

9

September 2, 1945, was V-J (Victory over Japan) Day, the formalities of the Japanese surrender having been completed. World

[4] I read each volume as it came out. After I had read the first one and heard he was planning a multivolume history—five volumes was the original plan—I felt worried. I knew he was in his forties and I carefully noted in my diary that I hoped he would live long enough to complete the set. He did.

War II was formally and completely over, six years and one day after it had begun.

And still I could only wait. One of the Navy Yard employees, Mel Roberts, who had grown to be a close friend of mine in recent months because we had had identical draft problems, had lost out. Even an attempt on his part to get into the Navy had failed, and on September 4, I received a letter from him. He was in the Army at last and was about to begin his basic training at Camp Lee, Virginia.

September 5, 1945, was my mother's fiftieth birthday. I called her long distance, teased her about it (to my surprise, she didn't seem to find the situation humorous), and did my best to mask my draft worries.

And then, on September 7, 1945, the eve of Rosh Hashonah, Gertrude called me up at work to tell me that my draft-board greetings had come and that I was ordered to show up for induction on the twentieth. I left work at once, dashed for home, and prepared to go to New York.

It did not escape my notice that if, in the third grade, I had kept my mouth shut and had let my mother's lie stand, and had not insisted on a change in my birthdate, then September 7, 1945, would have been my twenty-sixth birthday and I could not have been drafted. As it was, I was four months short of my twenty-sixth birthday.

It also did not escape my notice that the war was over, that millions of Americans had been drafted over the past few years and had had to face bombs and bullets while I had been safe at home; that many thousands of them had been wounded or killed while I had been safe at home; and that now I would be going off to face no more danger than the ordinary risks of ordinary life.

I was aware of all this and I did my best not to view the event as more tragic than it was. The fact remained, however, that I didn't want to go into the Army; I wanted to go back to Columbia. And I didn't want to leave Gertrude; I wanted to stay with her. So I felt terrible.

10

On September 10, I managed to see Professor Thomas, but he confirmed Dawson's statement that Columbia was as helpless as the Navy Yard to stand between me and the Army. The next day I saw the New York draft board but they refused flatly to grant me a stay of induction.

There was nothing to do but return to Philadelphia and live on a day-to-day basis, ready to seize what legitimate opportunities arose, and to go into the Army with as good grace as possible if all alternatives failed.

On September 12, I arranged a military furlough at the Navy Yard. I did not resign outright, for I wanted to remain a Navy Yard employee just in case the ball made a sudden bounce that would allow the Navy Yard, against all expectations, to request a deferment for me.

The next day I arranged to move to New York. We would have to work on the basis that I was not long for civilian life and that Gertrude would have to remain for an indefinite period without me. The logical thing, then, was to move her back into her parents' apartment.

Then, on the seventeenth, I transferred my place of induction from New York to Philadelphia—while I still lived in Philadelphia. I knew from experience that that would give me a month's delay and, if nothing else, that would give me more time to get my affairs arranged. It would make it possible, for instance, for me to be there at the time of moving, rather than leaving it all in Gertrude's hands.[5]

On September 25, we moved. Gertrude and I had lived in Wingate Hall for 2¾ years and, on the whole, it hadn't been too bad. By 2:30 P.M., the movers had emptied the apartment, and that evening Gertrude and I left, too, each of us carrying and wearing as much as we could. I went to my parents' place and she went to her parents' place in a sort of temporary neutralization of the marriage. The move (our third as a married couple) cost $34 this time.

The next day, the contents of our Wingate Hall apartment arrived at the Blugermans' place, where some was unloaded, the rest moving on to Windsor Place.

On the twenty-seventh, I opened a joint savings account at the Lincoln Savings Bank near the Blugermans' apartment. I deposited what we had managed to save during our years in Philadelphia—$3,800. Among this, and the dependent's allotment Gertrude would get, and, of course, her parents' help and mine in a screaming emergency, I had no fears that she would not be able to get by even if I remained in the Army two full years.

There was now nothing to do but wait for a new notice of induction from the Philadelphia board and, meanwhile, to live as normal and relaxed a life as possible.

I divided my time between my parents' and the Blugermans' but

[5] While we were preparing to move, we had also to deal with the problem of Gertrude's citizenship. Her visit to Canada in 1943 and her return as an immigrant were equivalent to "first papers," since she was married to an American citizen. That meant only a two-year wait for the final papers. That time was now coming, but she was assured that her more or less enforced move to New York would in no way interfere with the proceedings.

spent most of my time at the Blugermans' because that's where Gertrude was and I could not bear to be separated from her—all the more so because I would soon have to be.

John Blugerman was a civilian again and going to dental school. Henry was still trying to find a job. Gertrude was so relieved over the former and so concerned over the latter that it kept her mind off my own dilemma—which hurt my feelings a little.

So keen was I on normality, however, that on October 15—at which time I still had not received a new date of induction from the Philadelphia Draft Board—I went to visit Campbell. I had a new idea for a positronic robot story, one dealing with a robot that mimicked human flesh and blood—the problem resting with how one was to decide whether it was human or robot. I warned him that I might not be able to write it till after I was out of the Army.

Campbell invited me to lunch[6] with three friends of his from Bell Telephone. I watched with a certain horror as each of them ordered "huge steaks that cost $2.25 for steak and french fried potatoes alone." I couldn't possibly do that so "I had pot roast and stuff for $.85."

The November 1945 issue of *Astounding*, which I obtained at about this time, carried the first part of "The Mule,"[7] which Campbell was running as a two-part serial. It was the first time any story of mine had ever been serialized.

On the next day, October 16, I unexpectedly got word from Philadelphia that the Navy Yard, having become aware that I hadn't been inducted, was demanding that I get back to work. I couldn't take a military furlough unless I was in the military.

It would have made sense now to tell the Navy Yard to go to the devil and resign—but again I played for that one-in-a-million chance that the Navy Yard might somehow be able to do something. Always I tend to try to keep as many options open as possible.

11

On October 17, I had to go back to Philadelphia, after three weeks in New York. I showed up at the Navy Yard and got back to work.

It was like Napoleon's return from Elba. No one could believe my walking into the lab in civilian clothes. For me it was sheer anticlimactic hell, especially since I was back in Philadelphia without Gertrude and without a place to live.

Fortunately, one of my fellow workers, Roy Machlowitz, took me

[6] Even now I was consistently referring to the midday meal as "dinner" and the evening meal as "supper." It took me quite a while to move from this lower-class nomenclature to "lunch" and "dinner," respectively.
[7] See *Foundation and Empire*, Part II.

in. I reported in my diary that "he has a swell double room." It couldn't, in any case, be for long. Either I would be inducted in a matter of weeks and be off his neck, or, by some miracle or other, I would not be inducted and then I would, at most, stay on in Philadelphia only until my twenty-sixth birthday, now only a little over two months away.

I didn't get along completely with Roy. There was nothing wrong with him. He was intelligent, kind, and always helpful, and yet I found him hard to take. He had come to work less than a year before and we had grown friendly. In those last months at Wingate Hall, he had visited us frequently.

What bothered me was that he *disapproved* of me. He was aware of my faults and would give me improving advice concerning them. For some reason, I didn't appreciate that.

Now I was living with him, feeling very keenly the fact that I depended on his hospitality and kindliness, and very ashamed that I couldn't manage to like him better.

The first morning I was with him, as I recall, he prepared to don the phylacteries on arm and forehead and recite his morning prayers in true Orthodox fashion. I knew about phylacteries, of course, but I had never seen them in operation since I was a little boy and I guess Roy caught my look of surprise as he took them up.

"If you laugh," he said, "I'll kill you."

"Laugh?" I said. "I'm interested."

After I left Roy's place in due course, I never saw phylacteries again. To be honest, I haven't missed them.

12

Then, on October 24, I finally received my induction notice from the Philadelphia Draft Board, and the date set was October 26.

I called up at once and demanded my ten days' notice. They said that I had known for nearly two months that I was going to be inducted and I said, "Yes, but I didn't know the exact day, and I can't close out my civilian affairs without knowing the exact day, and I can't do it now with only a single day to do it in. Besides, ten days' notice is my legal right and I don't have to advance any explanations to get it."

So they altered the date of induction to November 1.

Now once again, I got ready to leave Philadelphia. I spent my last evening, the twenty-fifth, at Leonard Meisel's, so sorry for myself I couldn't stand it. Over and over I told him how happy Gertrude and I had been in Philadelphia and how now I would be gone for two years and everything would be changed—sob, sob—and I would never be happy again.

How Meisel could endure all that mawkishness I don't know, but he was patient and sweet and assured me that my stay in the Army would be over before I knew it and that things would then prove better than ever. I would get my degree, have a wonderful career, continue writing, and so on. He was completely right, but that didn't raise my spirits.

Meisel had the gift of being able to improvise on the piano and of being able to play any musical composition whose tune he knew. He therefore reinforced his words by singing jolly and merry tunes and urging me to sing. I sang, but that didn't seem to raise my spirits either.

Then Meisel had an inspiration. He remembered the kind of songs I liked best to sing, and he suddenly began beating out songs in the minor. He even took some of the happy tunes and converted them into the minor.[8]

I cheered up at once. The more lugubrious the songs, the happier I grew, and when I left, I was in fine spirits. There is nothing for which I am more grateful to Meisel than for that evening.

13

On Friday, October 26, I got another military furlough from the Navy Yard, ending the nine-day return. This time it was final and I left the Navy Yard after three years and five months.

It was my intention to leave at once after the formalities were attended to, but the girls persuaded me to stay on a little, bribing me with the offer of a rubber of bridge (a game I had learned to play with Roy Machlowitz, who was a real shark).

Leading the pack was Betty (I don't remember her last name), who was a sweet and pretty girl, large and busty. My clearest memory of her is my having once snapped the back elastic of her bra through her blouse (a very bad habit I sometimes can't resist to this day) and it broke. Betty had to rush off to the ladies' room to make the necessary repairs. When she came back, she brushed aside my voluble and embarrassed apologies. "Doesn't matter," she said, and wasn't the least annoyed. I was very fond of her after that.

In any case, by the time lunch came, ice cream and soda had made a magical appearance and it turned out there was a farewell party for

---

[8] To this day I can sing "Roll Out the Barrel" in the minor, to the pain and horror of everyone within earshot.

me in progress. I was quite taken aback because it never occurred to me that anyone would bother with such a thing.

I went back to New York with a warmer feeling than I thought I could manage.

By now, Henry had found himself a niche. Despairing of finding a new job, he had opened a business of his own, which he called the Henry Paper Box Company. It was now moving into operation as he obtained the necessary equipment, hired the necessary personnel, and so on. It absorbed Gertrude (who was acting as a kind of secretary and factotum for the new firm) completely, and she scarcely noticed my comings and goings.

On the night of the thirtieth, however, I took a room at the Manhattan Beach Hotel for five dollars, and Gertrude and I spent the night. It was our first night alone together in five weeks.

Then, on the next day, she went off to the Henry Paper Box Company. I said good-bye to Mary and John, went to Windsor Place, said good-bye to my parents and to Marcia and Stan, went to the Henry Paper Box Company for a final dinner with Gertrude, and said good-bye to her.

Then, once again, I went to Philadelphia, not knowing when or how I would see anyone again.

At least there was no war on. No one would be shooting at me. There was that consolation.

38

Fort Meade

1

Early on the morning of Thursday, November 1, 1945, I went to the induction center in Philadelphia. Once more, there was a physical. I was listed as having defective vision and otitis.[1] According to the examining psychiatrist, I also had "situational tension," which had to rank with the least surprising news ever recorded.

At 3:50 P.M. we were sworn in. The elderly recruiting sergeant had the recruits all repeat an oath, and with that we were in the Army. When it was all done, he said, "All right, soldiers, any questions?"

And a voice promptly sounded out, "Yes, Sarge: How do we get out of this chicken outfit?"

I understand that this is traditional, that no group of soldiers has ever been inducted without at least one of them asking this silly question.

In this case, it was I who asked it. I knew it was silly; I expected no answer (the recruiting sergeant rolled his eyes upward and looked pained), but one has to keep one's spirits up somehow—and my way is to joke.

I've joked under far worse conditions, and some of them will come up in this book.

My Army service number was 43012053, and that night we were put on a train and taken to Fort Meade, near Baltimore, Maryland. We went through Wilmington, which I had once visited in order to see Irene over five years before, and then passed on farther South—farther South than I had ever been in my life.

It was a peculiar feeling. For the first time in my life, I was going somewhere without my parents, without my wife, *and* without my volition. I kept watching the telephone poles slide backward outside the window and I kept saying to myself, "I can't change my mind. I can't get off the train. I can't go back home. I've got to go wherever I'm told. I have no say in the matter."

I was in prison, in a way.

We didn't go to bed till midnight that night, and by that time each of us was given a barracks bag for our belongings, and a fatigue

[1] Otitis, or inflammation of the ear canal, had been plaguing me throughout the Philadelphia years.

uniform to wear. Since we were given the fatigues at random, they weren't expected to fit, and mine were far too large.

We were awakened at 4:30 A.M. on November 2. At least some of the soldiers were awakened. I hadn't slept. When a corporal came roaring into the barracks shouting, "Rise and shine! Hubba hubba! Up 'n' at 'em!" and all the other horrible sounds I despised from the start, I waited for him to pass and then I said calmly, "Corporal, what time is it?"

I instantly learned the measure of manliness in the Army: It was how far you could recede from ordinary decency.

The corporal said, "How the hell should I know?"

Whereupon I said, "But if you don't know what time it is, how do you know it's time to wake us?"

The corporal stopped short. He was keen enough to recognize, at once, the prime enemy of any military individual—the rational mind. He said, tightly, "What's your name and serial number, private?"

I told him and he wrote it down. My first night in the Army—and I was on report.

I was quite philosophical about it. I had spent my whole life going on report—from grade school to the Navy Yard—and always for the same heinous crime, answering back.

2

Later that day, we had shots for tetanus and typhoid, and another physical examination, a very sketchy one. We had blood-type determinations and I turned out to be blood type B (which is every bit as rich as blood type O).

In the evening, I was turned loose. I found myself in a more formal uniform, which fitted reasonably well, and in a barracks with nothing to do but think. What I thought was: This is it for two years!

I was overwhelmed with such homesickness, with such an unbearble feeling of helpless imprisonment that for a few moments I thought I must collapse. I had to think of something and, bending my giant brain to the task, I realized that it was Friday and that somewhere on the post there had to be a chapel and that in it pretty soon there had to be Sabbath services.

I hadn't attended Sabbath services since I was eight, when my father had taken me, but I was in no mood to stand on principle. What I needed was companionship and something to do. So I went to chapel.

We recited Hebrew prayers and sang hymns. I couldn't manage the prayers, but I could sing hymns well enough, since I can match the notes of whoever stands next to me with almost no perceptible delay and, after a while, I get the feel of the tune and can guess the next note. I was so relieved to be doing something other than standing in the empty passage between the barracks that my voice rang out thankfully and soared above the rest so that someone tapped me on the shoulder and asked me, eagerly, if I would care to lead the singing. I shook my head in terror and sang in a whisper thereafter.

After services we had salami on khallah (the traditional white egg-bread eaten on the Sabbath) and cake and tea. I got back to the barracks at ten-thirty and was tired enough to fall asleep at once.

I frequently felt homesick in the Army thereafter, but never, *never* quite as painfully as upon the end of that first full day, when I felt as though the whole world had forsaken me, that I was lost, and that no one would ever find me again. What would I have done if it hadn't just happened to have been a Friday and I could not have sung hymns and eaten salami?

3

On Saturday, November 3, the recruits all took a sort of intelligence test given by the Army. I believe it is called the AGCT score.

There were five tests. There was one on reading and vocabulary, two on mathematics, one on pattern analyses—and all these were familiar territory to me. The fifth one was brand-new. We were taught the Morse signal for three different letters and then had to reproduce the letters as the signal sounded, faster and faster and faster.

I welcomed that, to my surprise. It was hypnotic. I scarcely had to concentrate. My fingers did it all by themselves.

The whole thing took three hours and I enjoyed it. It was something that represented what my whole life had been.

Then we sent our civilian clothes home (I called them "civvies" in the diary, for I was picking up soldier slang) and got a haircut in which the barber merely hacked off all the hair that was more than an inch from my scalp. When I finally looked too ugly to be a civilian he knew he was done.

By then, I had made the acquaintance of two nearby soldiers and discovered that every Army post had movies, first-run, at a reasonable charge. So I went Saturday night—and Sunday night, too.

4

On Monday, November 5, we were marched to a building where our AGCT scores were to be analyzed and we were to be interviewed. This was in line with the theory that the Army would place you in a position best suited for you. (If you showed great aptitude for geology you could dig trenches; for chemistry, you could be a cook; and so on.)

I waited in line as we were called and eventually I realized I had to visit the men's room and I happened to be standing right at the men's room door. I asked the sergeant who was supervising our slow advance if I could step into the men's room. Very reluctantly (for all requests by privates are to be refused as a matter of principle) he agreed, but warned me not to take too long.

I didn't, but it was long enough. When I emerged, there were loud outcries and the sergeant seized me roughly by the arm and shouted. "Here he is!"

I thought: *Now* what have I done?

I hadn't done anything. The various interviewers had just come across my AGCT score and were arguing as to who could have the fun of interviewing me. It turned out that my score was 160, and none of them had ever seen a score that high. When they settled the argument among themselves, I was interviewed with something approaching awe.

Naturally, I was very pleased and in an attack of naïveté thought this might make my Army life easier for me, perhaps even spare me basic training. My interviewer told me, unofficially, I would probably be assigned to Camp Lee, Virginia, and he somehow made it sound as though it was an intellectual's haven—the Army equivalent of an Ivy League college.

That was exactly where the glory of the 160 ended. After we were through with the interview, everyone had to shoulder his duffel bag and trot over to another area. Everyone trotted. No one seemed to be aware that he was carrying fifty pounds. No one except me. I lagged far behind, puffing, sweating, and strangling, and no one seemed to think a head full of 160 should be spared the necessity of carrying fifty pounds. No one even noticed me except a sergeant who barked, "Get a move on, soldier."

In the evening, I got my first menial detail. I was sent to the officers' club and told to empty ashtrays and trashcans and to do some general sweeping. Such officers as were present bent vacant eyes upon me now and then. They apparently couldn't see the 160 written on my forehead.

My illusions didn't last. I was a private in the Army and nothing else counted. I was the scum of the earth.

5

On the night of November 5, I managed to find a telephone and I tried to call Gertrude. She was at the Henry Paper Box Company, of course, though Henry himself was not. I told him about the results of the test and asked him to pass it on to Gertrude.

Later on, Gertrude told a friend who had let her know her boy-friend's or husband's score—which was well above the 100 average, but not remarkably so.

"My husband," said Gertrude, "scored 160."

"116?"

"No, 160. One-six-oh."

"How do you know?"

"He told me so."

The other girl snickered. "And you believe him?"

When Gertrude eventually told me this, with great indignation, I said curiously, "But how do you know you can believe me? How do you know I'm not lying?"

And she said, "But 160 is average for you. Why should you lie?"

I don't imagine Gertrude ever thought I was perfect, but she certainly never doubted my intelligence.

6

On November 6, I had further proof of just how valuable I was to the Army in view of my intelligence.

I was given my first KP assignment, and spent all day in the mess hall performing various menial tasks.

This is understandable, I suppose. Someone has to do them and it is the essence of military democracy that all menials take their fair turn.

What was a lot less comprehensible was that no provision was made for storing the outer wear of the soldiers doing KP. It was cold enough outside to be wearing a field jacket, but no place of security was provided for me to store that field jacket. It had to be left out in the open, and it was stolen. I was charged $14 for a replacement of lesser quality and was "chewed out" for the high crime of allowing it to be stolen. "Chewed out" is an Army term that means being barked at incoherently by a sergeant who, in all likelihood, was the animal who stole the field jacket.

39

Camp Lee

1

On Thursday, November 8, after having been in the Army a week, I was shipped out to Camp Lee, Virginia, where Mel Roberts had been. It was just outside Petersburg, Virginia, twenty-five miles south of Richmond and three hundred miles south of New York City.

In Camp Lee, I was put in the 62nd Quartermaster Training Company, and the next day I was on KP again. I came across a German prisoner of war and spoke German to him, while a crowd of youngsters gathered around and listened in amazement, since they had never heard anyone speak anything but English before. I also saw, for the first time in my life, an illiterate adult. Someone was writing a letter for him.

As for me, I wrote letters constantly—to Meisel, to Machlowitz, to Campbell, to Heinlein, to de Camp, to Stanley, to my parents, and so on. And, of course, I wrote a letter daily to Gertrude (except when it was physically impossible, which was rare).

My letters to Gertrude told her of daily events that I did my best to make funny—as much to cheer myself as to cheer her. They were a better record of my Army life in many ways, I suppose, than my diary was.[1]

Gertrude, alas, did not answer daily. She was quite busy at the Henry Paper Box Company (it was her candy store, I guess) and, in any case, no one in her family was much of a letter writer.

She wrote me about once a week during my stay in the Army, and they were valued letters indeed. They dealt chiefly with events at the Henry Paper Box Company, where things, apparently, went from one crisis to another. There were always frictions with the employees who were, according to Gertrude's account, very difficult and, in some cases, psychotic. There was also trouble with the union, with the landlord, and with the suppliers.

I was tempted to point out that these problems were characteristic of the life of the small entrepreneur attempting to start a family business with insufficient capital—something I had tried to warn them

---

[1] I kept my diary carefully throughout my stay in the Army. By this time I was in my eighth volume, and not to keep it up to date had become unthinkable.

against at the start. (I might be an unworldly person, but I did have the kind of experience that came with watching a candy store being run.) It had done no good.

On Saturday, November 10, assuming that the Henry Paper Box Company would be closed, I tried calling long distance and, for the first time since I was inducted into the Army, I heard Gertrude's voice. I was naturally too prudent to speak for more than three minutes. In this case, I foolishly wasted some of the precious three minutes by beginning to weep.

On November 12, I discovered that Camp Lee had an excellent library and thereafter I spent as much time there as I could. The Army was a bore and it offered endless humiliations to privates, but it did offer ways of passing the time that weren't entirely unwelcome.

My first mail arrived on the thirteenth—one letter from Marcia and one from Stanley. The next day there arrived the first letter from Gertrude—four pages, which I read and reread until the ink grew faint from repeated eye contact.

On the fifteenth, I received a letter from Machlowitz. He had seen Gertrude over the weekend and, with his usual tact, told me she seemed tired and strained. Somehow the letter gave me the impression that it was my fault. A better husband would not have consulted his selfish desires and run off to join the Army.

2

I learned new ways of life in the Army. I learned how to take showers in public—or at least with other young men surrounding me.

I did not enjoy it. I don't think I would have minded if it were young women surrounding me, but I have always found the sight of naked men repulsive in the extreme.[2] I was aware of this first at my very first Army physical when, for the first time, I saw a line of men with their genitals dangling. I wondered then (and I wonder now) how women can bear it.

Worse yet, I learned, or attempted to learn, how to defecate in public. In latrine after latrine, the seats were arranged in long rows without the sketchiest partitions between them. Other soldiers seemed not to mind, but I took to waking myself at 3:00 A.M. in order to have the latrine to myself. It never worked; I don't think I ever walked in without finding at least one other soldier there.

[2] If there is any amateur psychologist who thinks this bespeaks some hidden homosexual impulse in me, he or she is welcome to continue thinking so en route to Hell.

3

I tried to go through channels in order to see if I could avoid basic training and simply be assigned to some appropriate job in the Army. It seemed reasonable to me that this be done in view of my AGCT score, and my experience as a chemist. Add to this the fact that the war was over and that I wasn't ever going to be doing anything that required military drill and setting-up exercises.

It was amazing the way everyone agreed with me and the way in which everyone said nothing could be done. On November 19, I was officially switched into a basic-training unit, and on the next day I began the process.

There were two hours of drill, followed by two films, one on military courtesy, which I had seen before, and another warning soldiers against venereal disease. In the evening I was given a rifle—a real, honest-to-God, working rifle—and it was the first time I ever held a firearm of any kind. We had calisthenics, too.

On Thanksgiving (November 22) I had all the turkey, and everything else, I could eat, so for that one day I was fairly consoled. And in the library I found a copy of the December 1945 *Astounding*, with the second part of "The Mule," which I read with somber pleasure. It reminded me of those already distant-seeming civilian days when I was writing it. It made me remember the days when I was an individual and of some importance.

4

On November 23, I had another interesting KP session. I was given the role of stevedore this time. I drove in a truck with another soldier who was, fortunately for me, an eighteen-year-old farmboy with a kindly nature and muscles of iron. We loaded and unloaded sacks of potatoes, bags of flour, crates of oranges, chicken, meat, fish, and so on. We weren't exactly stevedores, at that. A stevedore would have worked eight hours; we worked thirteen. My partner did far more than his share of the work.

Finally, we were shown huge stacks of aluminum serving trays on which soldiers ate their meals and were told to shift them from one end of a mess hall to another. These serving trays fit together snugly so that to lift a stack that is a foot high is the equivalent of lifting a hundred pounds or more of solid aluminum.

I couldn't even begin to lift such a weight so I lifted stacks that were about two to three inches high and my partner (smaller and slighter than I) lifted considerably higher stacks.

The soldier in charge (only a private first class, heaven help us) watched in gathering annoyance and said to me, "Hey soldier, what's the idea of letting your partner do all the work?"

I unbent and said, rather snappishly (for it had been a long day and I was tired), "I'm lifting as much as I can."

"You mean that's all you can lift?" He at once lifted a pile twice as high as the one I was trying to handle. "Look at that."

And without much in the way of forethought, I said, "We're not all alike, Private. I've got a strong mind and a weak back."

You'd be surprised how amiss he took that simple statement. He didn't have a mind so weak, unfortunately, that he missed the implication.

I was promptly set to cleaning out the grease trap, which was supposed to be a very terrible job because it induced nausea. I managed.

5

The next day we had our first inspection.

In the old days, I had never been deft in the laboratory. Now I was never deft in inspection.

We were carefully told how to make beds so tight that a quarter would bounce off the blanket if dropped on it. No quarter alive ever bounced off any blanket I touched.

We were also taught to clean our rifles with a greased patch and a ramrod in order to get out the accumulated rust. My rifles invariably manufactured rust and no grease patch ever emerged unstained from any rifle barrel I put my hand on.

Eventually I learned to name every part of a rifle and to disassemble and assemble one even in the dark, but if I ever had an unrusted rifle barrel I was unaware of it.

I was in a constant state of terror that I would be punished in some vague way for having blankets on which quarters did not bounce or rifles in which rust could be sighted. The loss of furlough privileges was the least of it. My imagination conjured up visions that were more along the line of being drawn and quartered.

Hikes were another source of insecurity. We were all supposed to march briskly, with our rifles on our shoulders slanting in a perfectly vertical fashion, and leaning neither to the right nor the left. If ever I achieved that vertical stance, it was only a momentary one as my rifle shifted from a left-leaning slant to a right-leaning one or vice versa. Nor did I march briskly. After about a quarter of a mile, I drooped and dragged.

I never even learned how to salute with the proper snap.

Yet none of this ever drew upon me a reprimand. Not once was I ordered off to be hung, or even just to be strung up by my left big toe. Noncoms and minor officers passed me by to bark at some soldier on the other side of me who, as nearly as I could tell, was a model of military deportment in comparison to me. Nor did anyone ever make any adverse comment to me after looking through my rifle barrel, even though it seemed to me, as I watched tensely, that I could clearly see rust drizzling down into the officerial eye.

Many months later, a friendly lieutenant told me that the commanding officer, before basic had begun, had gone over the soldiers with his subordinates and had said concerning me, something as follows:[3]

"Now this guy Asimov you might as well leave alone. He's got a 160 AGCT score and they ain't going to use him anywhere except behind a desk so don't waste time on him. He's the kind of stupe that's okay on those shit tests, but he don't know his right foot from his left and there ain't no use trying to teach him because he ain't got any sense. I been watching and I can see that."

After that I was ignored by every officer and noncom in the place.

When I found this out, I was indignant beyond words. Not, you understand, that I quarreled with the commanding officer's opinion of me, which I thought was accurate enough and a credit to his perspicacity. What graveled me was that no one was kind enough to whisper the news to me so that I could relax. I would gladly have agreed to have continued to do my best to make beds, clean rifles, and march, but why should I not have done it with a song in my heart?

6

If I thought I did poorly on bed make-up and rifle cleaning, I hit new depths of degradation on the physical-conditioning test, held on November 27. It was the physical version of the AGCT score and again I managed to make the extreme. I was best in the company (maybe in the Army) in AGCT and worst in the company (maybe in the Army) in physical conditioning.

There was nothing I could do without falling apart. I hit rock bot-

[3] I wasn't there and I don't know how accurate the lieutenant was in making his report to me.

tom in the running test. They ran us five at a time and a fellow stood near the finish line with a stopwatch calling off numbers as each person passed the line. Somehow they matched time and soldier but I don't know how, for I was tensely waiting my turn.

Four others and I finally started off and the man at the finish line called out four times, realized no one else was passing, and shouted, "Next five!"

"Wait!" cried a medley of voices, and the time man looked up in surprise and found I was still trying to reach the finish line. I was walking.

That day we were also issued gas masks, though gas had not been used at any time in World War II. We had to march with gas masks on and I simply could not pump enough air through the absorbent. It was either strangle to death with the gas mask on, or take it off. I took if off. I would probably have been court-martialed and shot if I had been caught at it.

Later on, we were forced to smell samples of various poison gases, just in case we were called upon to fight World War I again. I held my breath till out of range.

We also spent some days on the rifle range, where for the first and last time of my life I shot firearms. I fully expected to be bothered by the noise but discovered I wasn't. When I concentrated on hitting a target neither the bang of my own rifle nor my neighbor's made any impression on me.

Firing a rifle at a stationary target, I found, was purely mechanical and required no skill, once you had properly zeroed in your sight—that is, you fired a shot after having brought the crosshairs on target. If you ended up a little to the right of bull's-eye, you adjusted the crosshairs a little to the left, and so on. Eventually you hit bull's-eye every time.

If they had let me count the shots only after I had zeroed in the sight I would have had a perfect score, but they insisted on counting the imperfect shots that took place in the course of adjusting the sight.

Then, after a break, in which I took my turn down in the pit observing other soldiers' shots, I was forced to take a new rifle at random to complete my shooting.

I said that I wanted my own rifle, which I had zeroed in perfectly, but since that was rational it merely confused the sergeant. He just pointed to some rifle lying on the ground and said, "Get started, soldier!" in the Army ape-language you get to understand after a while. Naturally, I found the sights in the strange rifle adjusted to hit the next county and I wasted shots correcting that.

In the end, I got a score of 160, which earned me a "sharpshooter" score and a special kind of gizmo to hang on my chest. I never enjoyed it, though. I would have done much better if I could have injected a few brains into the heads of the noncoms in charge. (Not likely, of course, for their heads were solid and would have quickly rejected the foreign substance even if they had been hollow.)

7

By now, one Gerald Cohen was a good friend of mine. When there was an offer of a weekend pass (that is, from Saturday noon to Monday morning) I would have been delighted to take it, had I but known how to get home. I could take the train in Washington and get to New York in four hours, but how did I get from Camp Lee to Washington?

I was on the point of rejecting the pass (if I couldn't go to New York to see Gertrude, there was no point in going anywhere) when Gerry said he was going to New York and he would show me how. I accepted both the pass and his offer eagerly, therefore.

Gerry took me down to Petersburg on December 1, therefore, took me to the bridge leading out of town, and explained how one hitched a ride. You stood there, he said, with your thumb aiming in the direction you wanted to go, and you tried to look pathetic.

"Now you stand here and practice," he said, "and I'll just step into the drugstore for a minute, then I'll come out and show you how to do it *right*."

He stepped into the drugstore and he may have come out in a minute, but by then I was gone. A car driven by a Navy lieutenant, junior grade, stopped almost at once and picked me up, so that I was off on my first furlough from the Army. The war had not yet receded so far into the distance that soldiers could be ignored. A uniform was a guarantee as far as pick-ups were concerned. In all my stay in the Army, I never had any difficulty in getting a ride.

I had only occasionally been in automobiles in my life. I had never been in a car on a modern intercity highway before. Certainly, I had never experienced hour after hour of smooth sixty-miles-an-hour driving before. No words could express my admiration for the driver. It took him three hours to reach the train station in Washington, and I stumbled incoherently in my attempts to thank him. He waved it away nonchalantly and drove off.[4]

I was down at Brighton Beach at eleven forty-five and saw Ger-

[4] Later on, I became more nonchalant myself. A simple "Thank you" proved to be enough.

trude for the first time in thirty-one days. This time she had reserved the room at the hotel, and oh my goodness, was that different from sleeping in the barracks!

On the evening of December 2, I set out on the return journey. Getting to Washington was no problem, but once there, it was useless to expect to hitch a ride late at night to Petersburg. I had to take a midnight train—and not the kind of train that made the run between the big cities of the Northeast. It was a wretched, slow, uncomfortable horror of a train on which I had to sit up all night, packed in with many other soldiers, and with civilians as well. I got into camp at 5:00 A.M. on December 3.

8

There was one drawback to the furlough and that was the fact that I had an infected right big toenail, which grew worse and worse till I could barely walk.

I had tried everything from soaking in Epsom salts to the application of some sulfa drug preparation. In the end, half the nail had to be cut away.

It was done in two installments. On December 15, the doctor swabbed it with a liquid and it grew very cold. I assumed he was using ethyl chloride, which evaporates so quickly it freezes the skin temporarily and makes it incapable of feeling pain. "He quick-froze it," I said in my diary. Sure enough, it didn't hurt.

Some weeks later, the doctor cut more of my nail off. This time he broke an ampule, squirted some liquid on the toe, and the skin turned white.

"What's that?" I asked in astonishment.

"Ethyl chloride," he said, cutting away deftly.

"Ethyl chloride! Then what did you use the first time?"

"I just washed it in alcohol."

Goodness! The first cutting had been made without anesthesia, and I had been so convinced the nail was frozen, I had felt nothing.

9

Occasionally, I walked guard in another make-believe aspect of Army life. On the night of December 10, I had the pleasure of breaking my guard shift on a bed's bare springs, with a rolled-up mattress as pillow and with all my clothes on.

The next day I got my first Army pay, $36.30. It in no way compensated.[5]

10

My mail was copious enough. Sprague de Camp was a particularly faithful correspondent, and I even heard from William Boyd of Boston University, who wrote to tell me how much he liked "The Mule." As for Marcia, she sent me a 1946 diary so that I might continue my daily recordings.

By all odds the most interesting item I read was not in any letter, though. On December 17, 1945, I came across an article in the *Army Times* for December 15, which dealt with a new Army order that allowed *the release of chemists engaged in research*.

That galvanized me into activity at once. For over a year before induction I had done whatever I could legitimately do to avoid induction; and now it was my intention to do whatever I could legitimately do to gain release.

The thought of doing something, of arranging interviews, of marshaling arguments in my mind, made a little more bearable such ridiculous activities as bayonet practice and marches in full field pack through melting snow and slush.

On December 20, I saw some sergeant in the administrative building. There had been reports that no one in administration had heard any such order, and I was selected as the soldier to see and enlighten them, since I had been first and loudest in the field. I had the clipping ready, complete with the number of the order and so on.

I was half afraid that they would tell me the whole thing was a hoax. The sergeant merely said I would need proof that I was in scientific research in civilian life.

Fine! I asked for nothing better. My Christmas furlough started the next day and I would surely be down at Columbia to get whatever documentation was necessary. The thought kept me warm awhile I was indoctrinated into the mysteries of the submachine gun that day.

11

Friday, December 21, 1945, was my father's forty-ninth birthday. I spent all day getting home on my second furlough and that was as good

[5] At home, meanwhile, Gertrude completed the necessary routine for citizenship. She went to Philadelphia on December 13, 1945, to take the tests, and early in January of 1946 she became an American citizen.

as any other way to celebrate it. I took the train from Petersburg this time and arrived at Union Station in Washington to be greeted with a fearful Christmas rush. Although I had arisen at 5:00 A.M., I didn't get home till 9:00 P.M. and spent the first night of my furlough at Windsor Place.

The next day I rushed to Columbia even though it was a Saturday, and I was fortunate enough to catch Professor Thomas. I arranged to get all the documentation I needed, then rushed to the Henry Paper Box Company to see Gertrude for the first time in twenty days. The proof of research arrived on the twenty-seventh.

The furlough lasted a total of ten days, and by and large it was active in a pleasant way, except for the fact that my father had the flu and ran a bad fever for a day or so. I alternated between Windsor Place and Brighton Beach and saw all I could of Gertrude.

Christmas itself was quiet and peaceful and I spent it serenely reading murder mysteries.

On December 26, I met with Charles Schneeman, one of the more popular and successful science-fiction illustrators of the time. It was the first time I had met him. He was a handsome man, who looked younger than his thirty-three years; talkative, energetic, full of enthusiasm.

He had written me a few letters earlier in which he had spoken without details, of a project he had in mind. Now he told me about it. He wanted to do a science-fiction strip of the quality of "Terry and the Pirates," he to do the drawing and I to do the continuity.

I was dazzled by the project (especially by Schneeman's predictions as to the money we could make on it), and before the furlough was over I had written up some continuity for a sample Sunday strip and eventually got it to him.

Schneeman prepared one strip, finally, and it looked beautiful but nothing ever came of it. Nevertheless, it was the first time that I looked beyond the routine of writing for the science-fiction mazagines themselves.

12

On December 30, I met Fred Pohl at the candy store. He had been in the Army for thirty-two months, had achieved the rank of sergeant, and had just been discharged that month. He had been in Italy and in France during the war but had not seen actual action.

He said, "My AGCT score was 156. What was yours?"

I reddened (I know I did, because I felt myself redden) and said, "I got 160, Fred."

"Shit!" he said.

He didn't doubt me for a minute. I would have been dreadfully hurt if he had—not at his questioning my ability to get the score, but at his thinking I would lie just to put him down.

He was full of news about the Futurians. He himself was divorced and remarried. His second wife, a WAC captain, was still in Europe. Dick Wilson was in Tokyo; Cyril Kornbluth had been in the Battle of the Bulge; and Don Wollheim was suing Robert Lowndes for $25,000.[6]

13

And so the year of 1945 drew to its close. It had been a dreadful year in some ways, filled first with apprehension of induction, and then of induction itself and the dull and toilsome life of a private in basic training.

I was most regretful over the fact that it might have been a very good year if the shadow of the Army had not fallen over me. My writing earnings for my eighth year as a professional were $1,022. It was the third year in which my earnings had passed the thousand-dollar mark, and it had all been done in the first five months of the year with the sale of two stories. How much might I have earned if the whole year had been as normal as 1941 or 1944? My total earning of the year, including the ten months at the Navy Yard, came to over $3,600—not as good as the year before, of course.

Still, I was in no mood to concern myself too deeply with figures and comparisons at this time. What occupied my mind almost exclusively was the prospect of discharge. On the evening of the thirty-first, I headed back to camp, the Columbia documents proving my status as a research chemist warming my duffel bag.

It had to do a lot of warming, though, for I spent the last hours of the year in Union Station in Washington waiting for the midnight train to Petersburg. When midnight struck and a cry of "Happy New Year" went up, the cry I managed to send up was rather on the hollow side.

To this day when I am in Union Station, there is still enough of the old roof pattern to remind me of that moment of the turn of the year from 1945 to 1946, and it still gives me a chill.

January 2, 1946, saw me twenty-six years old—the same twenty-sixth birthday I had groped for as a goal of safety through the first two

---

[6] The last item was not important. Someone was always suing someone in fandom, and $25,000 was a nice round figure. My impression was that it was usually settled out of court for $2.50.

thirds of 1945. It was here at last, and I was two months deep in the Army.

14

Any attempt to put through a discharge application could not be hurried. For one thing, I was told it would take at least six weeks to get action on it, during which time I would be stuck wherever I was at the time of initiation. I didn't want to be stuck in a basic-training unit, so it made sense to wait until after basic training and see what my permanent assignment would be.

Meanwhile, I was sufficiently elated at even the possibility of discharge at any time earlier than the two years to which I had considered myself doomed that the possibility of writing a science-fiction story arose. (My short sessions with Schneeman and Pohl over the Christmas furlough had helped put me into the mood.)

At the base library, the librarian was pleasant enough and told me I could use the typewriter any time she was around. On January 6, 1946, therefore, I began the robot story I had discussed with Campbell, the last time I had seen him—the one about the human-appearing robot. I called it "Evidence."

I found to my great pleasure that I could write just as quickly and easily in a camp library as at home. I even persuaded the librarian to lock me in the library during the lunch hour on January 13, and while I was in the locked building I managed to type up seven pages.

On January 17, my seventy-eighth day in the Army, I completed basic training. I don't know that it did me any good whatever, though it did cost me eighteen pounds that I could well afford to lose—even though I ate as much as I could all through that period. In fact, while I was in the Army I grew thin again for the first time since I had been married.

I was not smart enough to stick to it afterward.

15

After that there was nothing to do but wait for shipping orders to our permanent assignment.

I whiled away the time in January, seeing the camp psychiatrist, a Lieutenant George Kriegman. I had seen him first one time when I was more than usually depressed at the stupidity of life in the Army, and when my sergeant asked if I wanted to see the psychiatrist, my first impulse to deny it indignantly was drowned out by my prudent realization that if I went to see the psychiatrist I would miss out on a march. I thought I could bear to miss the march.

After that, I found I could miss out on a great many things I felt no dire necessity to experience if I visited Kriegman. I even enjoyed talking to him. There weren't many people I could talk to in the Army on an equal eye-to-eye level. Kriegman, however, was delightful. The various noncoms who worked under him were also pleasant, intelligent people, particularly Jerome Himelhoch, who had been in Fort Meade the day my 160 AGCT score had been evaluated, and who may even have been the person who interviewed me that day.

When I talked to Kriegman it became an interesting game. I would try to get Kriegman to accept my own point of view of the situation—and I never could. He was very skilled at his work and he generally forced me out of any position I tried to occupy.

I think he felt he was psychoanalyzing me, something I wasn't the least interested in having him do. What I was doing was missing as much basic training as I could.

It momentarily stopped being a game, though, when he told me he had put a hold on me, making it impossible for me to move out of Camp Lee until he was through with me.

I went into instant panic. "Come on, Doc. I don't want that. Don't freeze me. There's nothing wrong with me."

And he unfroze me at once.

Our shipping orders came through on January 24. We were going to be shipping out on the twenty-ninth, and my hope was, of course, that wherever we went, it would be closer to New York than Camp Lee was. Meanwhile, we got a weekend furlough.

For the third time, on January 25, I went through the torture of Petersburg to New York (this time I took a bus from Petersburg to Richmond), and then, on the twenty-seventh, the reverse torture of New York to Petersburg. I thought, with satisfaction, that this would be the last time I would make that particular trip.

I was quite wrong. On the morning of the twenty-ninth, groups of soldiers got into buses and were taken off here and there and everywhere (exactly where no one would say). Then I and only two others got into a bus and were taken no farther than another part of the camp! Our permanent assignment was right there with the Quartermaster Board at Camp Lee.

I was demolished with horror, but I thought about it and recovered. I might be no nearer New York and Gertrude, but I was no farther either and I might easily have been shipped to Dayton, as Mel Roberts had been (I learned from his letters), or even farther.[7]

---

[7] On the other hand, if I had been stationed a thousand miles or more from home, I would undoubtedly have used planes on furloughs and might not have developed my present reluctance to travel by air.

Then too, now that I was in Camp Lee on a permanent basis and not with a basic-training unit, I could move onward with my request for discharge.

When the new captain talked to me in order to decide what work I was to be assigned to, I spoke of my research at Columbia and said I wanted a discharge. He sent me on to a Major Connor, and I repeated this.

When the others at the Quartermaster Board asked me what it was all about, I told them all I was asking for a discharge. It seemed to awe them. I became a conspicuous character at once and the general consensus was that I had plenty of "moxie."[8]

I next tried to see the inspector general but got only as far as a sergeant in his entourage. He said I had better be at my permanent assignment for a month before applying for discharge and also said, in what seemed to me to be a threatening manner, that I could be shipped anywhere to do anything. I put that down to bluff, but it did make me feel rather uneasy.

After I got back from my fourth weekend pass on February 4, I was given a temporary assignment as a typist in the orderly room.

I discovered that being a typist was equivalent to being an aristocrat. You wore regular uniform at all times (never fatigues) and you never pulled KP. After this, I did everything I could to get a typist's position.

The best trick, when in a new place, was to walk into the orderly room and say to the master sergeant as politely as possible, "Sarge, could I possibly use the typewriter for just a little while to type a letter to my wife?"

Naturally, I wouldn't ask this unless I saw the orderly room was empty and the typewriter unused. Writing letters to a wife was a noble occupation for a soldier, and a master sergeant was not likely to discourage that. He would therefore say (with what is for a master sergeant the quintessence of courtly politeness), "Go ahead, soldier, but get your ass in gear and make it snappy."

I would then sit down, make sure the sergeant was not particularly occupied, and would begin typing with machine-gun rapidity. I would not get far before a fat forefinger would tap my shoulder. "Hey, soldier, how would you like to be a typist?"

8 What is courage, I wonder? Every one of those other fellows was less afraid of heights than I was, less afraid of guns, less afraid of rowdy scuffling—but none of them ever dared say a word to an officer.

There were never enough soldier typists to meet the demand, and none who could type as quickly as I could or (as the first sergeants quickly discovered) were as reliable as I was.

That first day as a typist, on February 4, I spent time typing out my request for discharge. I was sufficiently cautious about it to consult Kriegman on the matter. He suggested I put the request through.

But then as the days passed, and I received no permanent assignment, the rumor began to spread that I, and all the other fellows who were in similar state, were being saved for some very special test having to do with atomic bombs, either out in Nevada or somewhere in the Pacific.

I refused to believe it but, playing it safe, I marched straight to Kriegman and told him that I was now ready to be frozen. I found to my dismay that since I was out of basic training I was no longer under his jurisdiction and could not be frozen. I had outsmarted myself.

After hesitating a moment, however, I decided that I would not let myself be browbeaten by rumors. On February 11, I made it definite, handing in my request for discharge under Rule 363, which allowed the discharge of those engaged in scientific research.

16

Even in the midst of my preoccupation with assignments and discharges, there were whiffs of an earlier day.

I got a letter from Sprague de Camp on February 6, telling me that the January 20 issue of the Philadelphia *Record* had a front-page article about Heinlein, de Camp, and me at the Navy Yard. He was terribly indignant about it and the clipping he sent me showed clearly why he should be. The reporter made fun of us as blue-sky thinkers who never came up with anything and, of course, the fact that we were science-fiction writers struck him as *ipso facto* hilarious.

All the facts were wrong and Sprague sent me a copy of the letter he had written demanding an apology. I replied with a soothing letter to the effect that probably no apology would be forthcoming but what was the difference? All publicity is good publicity.

What's more, another science-fiction anthology had come out. This second one was much more elaborate than Wollheim's paperback anthology had been. The new anthology was the first in hard-cover. It was *The Best of Science Fiction*, edited by Groff Conklin, someone of whom, up to that time, I had never heard.

It was an anthology of particular interest to me in that it contained a story of mine, "Blind Alley." This was the first of my stories ever to be anthologized.

On February 25, I found a letter from Campbell, enclosing a check for $42.50 as payment for the use of the story in that anthology. The payment was actually made to *Astounding*, which owned all rights to the story. There was no legal requirement that *Astounding* pass on any part of that check to the author. Campbell, however, insisted that every penny be passed on to the authors, and he had his way.[9]

It was the first indication I ever had that a story could make any money in addition to the initial payment from the magazine. It was also the first bit of money from my writing that I had made while I was in the Army.

17

Meanwhile I actually went to a USO dance in Richmond on the night of February 9, 1946.

I danced with a very pretty girl and made a date with her for the next day. I stayed in Richmond overnight and then had the date with her. I know exactly what I had in mind and I might have carried it through. I think she was willing.

But I couldn't! After I got to her place and after I'd been there a while and made some tentative advances, I suddenly said I had to go back to camp. She looked shocked and let me go.

I did go straight back to camp rather hang-dog and ashamed of myself for humiliating the girl and humiliating myself—but I couldn't help it. I hadn't gone to bed with anyone but Gertrude in my whole life, and the thought of doing so was unbearable. (I went through my entire Army career without any extramarital ventures.)

As it turned out, my attack of fidelity turned out to be a lucky break. No sooner had I reached camp than the weather turned very bad. Had I stayed in Richmond for most of the tenth and then tried to get back to camp overnight, I would have been unable to make it by roll call on the morning of the eleventh, and I would have been AWOL. What would have followed, I don't know.

I overheard a lieutenant, the next day, being chewed out by the captain for having arrived late and thus being technically AWOL.

The lieutenant tried to explain that weather conditions made it impossible to get back in time, and he was told that, as an officer, he should have used his ingenuity and figured out a way. Of course, I

[9] In later years, I (and authors generally) were intelligent enough to sell only first serial rights to magazines. Subsidiary sales then involved money that went to the author as a matter of right and not as largesse from the magazine publishers.

wasn't an officer, but I daresay they would have found a different argument to use on me.

18

On February 17, I finished the first draft of "Evidence" and was very pleased with it, but the next day came news that was like an entirely new draft—one that was worse than the original.

It came about this way:

As of early 1946, only three atom bombs had been dropped. The first was at Alamogordo, New Mexico, in July 1945, and that was merely to see if it worked at all. The second and third were on Hiroshima and Nagasaki, in Japan, in August 1945, and those were dropped in anger and ended the war.

Now it was time to explode an atom bomb in such a way that its effects could be carefully studied. This was slated to happen at Bikini, an atoll in the Pacific.[10] The experiment was named "Operation Crossroads," I suppose because the atomic bomb placed humanity on a crossroads to death and destruction or to life and prosperity, depending on how nuclear energy was used.

Operation Crossroads was primarily a Navy operation, but the Army wanted part of it. It was their intention, therefore, to expose Army issue—food, clothing, and so on—on board various ships at various distances from the center of explosion[11] and have them all examined afterward by army personnel for radioactivity or other damage.

Including among the Army personnel were to be a number of "critically needed specialists" designed to lend flavor and importance to the Army's role, and I was to be one of those critically needed specialists. For this I had my AGCT score to thank.

If I had been less cautious; if I had applied for discharge while still in basic training; if I had accepted Kriegman's move to freeze me then —there would have been no way of including me in the project. And my discharge might have gone through.

As it was, we would still be assigned to Camp Lee, but as part of the new project we would be "attached" to Operation Crossroads. Such attachment would put us in limbo. We couldn't be promoted by the organization to which we were merely "attached," but could only be promoted after we had returned to our regular assignment. What was much more to the point, anyone who had a request for discharge in the

---

10 The atoll gave its name, thereafter, to a very brief woman's bathing suit that presumably acted upon the male psyche with all the effect of an atomic bomb.
11 These were old ships being left there with no human beings aboard, I believe.

works would find that it could not be acted on until he was unattached and returned to his regularly assigned post.

There were a variety of colorful Army expressions to describe what had happened to me, of which the mildest was that I was "screwed, blued, and tattooed."

And not so much by the Army, as by myself. Had I not insisted on having my third-grade teacher record my true birthday, I would not have been drafted in the first place; had I not insisted on not being frozen by Kriegman when I might have been, I would not have been attached to Operation Crossroads.

Oh well.

I had one more furlough to New York, my fifth, over the Washington's Birthday weekend, and broke the news to everyone there.

It was a very sad time for me. I had been in the Army nearly four months, but in that time I had gone home and seen Gertrude five times for a total furlough time of more than two weeks. I saw her roughly one sixth of the time. But now . . .

We had been told that we would be shipped out to the mid-Pacific for 180 days—half a year—and it was obvious that in all that time I would not be able to see Gertrude and very likely not even hear her voice on the telephone. In fact, I didn't even have faith in the 180-day period; it was quite likely that Army-type delays would stretch matters out longer still.

40

Hawaii

1

We went through the routine of various immunization shots, physical inspections, clothing shakedowns. I got to know some of the other critically needed specialists, and since misery loves company, we became desperately friendly.

The most intelligent and articulate one of them was Edwin C. James; but others included Stanley W. Dylewski, a charming, lively fellow, who, I suspected, was an effective ladies' man; Edwin T. Upton, a rather quiet fellow with a red birthmark on his face; Robert F. Credo, who had a wife who knew a senator; John L. Laudenberg, the youngest of us; and Sherwood W. Cross, who had a lovably rough-hewn face.

I was the oldest of the group, by the way, since only those under twenty-six had been drafted in the last year and I had been grabbed so close to my twenty-sixth birthday. It marked the official end of my career as child prodigy. (Some of the younger soldiers called me "Pop," to my enormous indignation.)

On March 1, 1946 (the day I began my fifth month in the Army), I phoned Gertrude so that I might hear her voice one more time and then, on March 2, we took off. After 16½ weeks at Camp Lee, I said good-bye to it. Under many circumstances I would have said good-bye without regret, but not this time. Even Camp Lee was preferable to Bikini.

The first leg of our journey was by train—four days—to San Francisco. In a way, that trip was my happiest time in the Army. There was nothing to do, so we seven critically needed specialists clung together like a band of brothers and, for the most part, played bridge. The love and friendship among us; the hypnotism over endless hands of bridge;[1] the bitching over common grievances made everything so warm that I almost didn't miss Gertrude.

Ed James, in particular, urged me to follow his philosophy of: F— it!

[1] Dylewski swore that we had played so many hands that they were beginning to repeat themselves, but I calculated the total number of possible bridge hands and proved there were enough different hands to keep us busy for countless trillions of years without much chance of repetition.

He would say, "What are you worried about?"

I would say, "Suppose something happens to Gertrude while I'm gone."

He would say, "What could you do right now if something does?"

I would say, "Nothing."

"He would say, "Then f— it."

I couldn't quite make myself take that attitude, but it did lighten the tension a bit.

There was a problem about sleeping. Three soldiers were assigned to every upper and lower bunk—one in the upper and two in the lower. James, Upton, and I had one set of bunks, and we tossed coins, odd man taking the upper. Ed James won and climbed above.

Ed Upton seemed unconcerned, stripped to his underwear, got into the lower bunk near the window and, as nearly as I could make out, fell asleep at once. I stripped to my underwear, got in very cautiously, and tried to hold myself in such a way as to make no contact.

I got very little sleep on that train.

We got into Chicago at 3:30 P.M. on March 3 and had a five-hour layover. We seven got out, visited a USO, then trooped over to a bar. There we sang songs (we did that a lot on the train, too, between bridge games) and the other six drank. In particular, we did a soulful rendition of "The Whiffenpoof Song."

A fellow at the bar was so taken with Dylewski, in particular, that he gave him his card and urged him to come see him after he got out of the Army and there would be a job waiting for him.

Back on the train we passed through Iowa and Nebraska. I mailed letters in Omaha. We also made up parodies of popular songs, which we referred to as the "Ballads of the Battling Bastards of Bikini." Unfortunately, I don't remember a single parody. Not one.

I found out that one of the officers on the coach with us was a science-fiction fan. He didn't know who I was, so I asked him leading questions, while the other six listened with straight faces, and finally elicited from him the fact that he read and liked Asimov's stories. After I got him to say that Asimov was "a brilliant fellow," I revealed myself.

It was funny at the time and for the moment, but it was a bad move. That was one officer who disliked me intensely thereafter—and it served me right. (Fortunately, he never did anything about it.)

On March 5, we stopped at Ogden, Utah, where I bought a postcard to which was attached a small pack of salt from the Great Salt Lake, and mailed it off to Gertrude. I usually got newspapers wherever we stopped so that I had a chance to read a wide variety in the course of the trip. The only one I specifically mentioned in my diary was the Salt Lake *Tribune*, which I called "rotten reactionary."

On March 6, we got off the train and took another to Camp Stoneman, California. I couldn't reach Gertrude that evening; the lines were all busy. The next morning I sent a telegram, which cost $.45, and, after trying all afternoon, finally put through a station-to-station call to her for $2.50 and heard her voice.

2

On Saturday, March 9, 1946, we embarked on a troopship called the *President Hayes*, which was going to take us on our second leg of our trip, and disembark us at Hawaii. That trip was to take us six days, and the *President Hayes* was no luxury liner. (This was to be my first ocean trip since I arrived in the United States twenty-three years before.)

There were about two hundred of us sleeping in the same room, with beds stacked three high. (I got an upper and was delighted to get it to myself.) It was so crowded that after waiting in the chow line for what seemed an interminable period, we gave up on dinner.

It was just as well. Once we got under way, seasickness was endemic. I didn't feel great, but I fought it down. I didn't throw up once, but considering that there were soldiers throwing up all about me, there seemed little advantage to not doing it. Everything smelled just as bad as though I were personally involved.

I decided to grow a beard for the duration of the ship voyage, together with mustache, through the simple expedient of not shaving. It was my third attempt at facial hair. By the time we disembarked, I looked like a western prospector. The beard, while still very short, was solid, thick, and dark. None of the other six, who had also decided to eschew shaving, could do well at all.

On March 14, however, I had to shave it off, since it would have been against Army regulations to keep it.

On March 15, thirteen days after we had left Camp Lee, we were in Hawaii—specifically, on the island of Oahu—in an Army Camp outside Honolulu. Once there, we had nothing to do but wait for the final leg of the trip to Bikini.

3

It was a more or less tedious wait, but it affected me not nearly as badly as the initial period of waiting in the Army. I had grown used to Army life, and besides, basic training was over, and I wasn't hounded very much.

Sometime during my stay in Hawaii, I underwent a turning point in my personality. Until then, I had always been eager and willing to display my intelligence and learning—even insistent on it. It wearied people and made me disliked and, in my saner moments, I knew it wearied people and made me disliked—but I couldn't resist.

Then, one day, I was the only critically needed specialist in the barracks, idly reading something or other, while at the other end of the room, three soldiers were talking to each other.

They were "nonspecialists" (the kind I always dismissed in my mind as "farmboys"), and they were talking about the atom bomb since that was very much in the minds of all on Operation Crossroads. One of the three took it upon himself to explain how the atom bomb worked and, needless to say, he got it all wrong.

Wearily, I put down my book and began to get to my feet so I could go over and assume "the smart man's burden" and educate them.

Halfway to my feet, I thought: Who appointed you their educator? Is it going to hurt them to be wrong about the atom bomb?

And I returned, contentedly, to my book.

This does not mean I turned with knife-edge suddenness and became another man. It's just that I was a generally disliked know-it-all earlier in my life, and I am a generally liked person (I believe) who is genial and a nonpusher later in my life. Looking back to try to see where the change began, I find it in this incident in the barracks outside Honolulu.

Why? I'm not sure I know. Perhaps it was my surrender of the child-prodigy status. Perhaps it was my feeling that I had grown up, I had proved myself, and I no longer had to give everyone a headache convincing them that I was, too, smart. (Of course, I backslide now and then, but not often.)

4

Oahu was a pleasant place. In fact, though I consciously resented being there as part of the Army, I couldn't help but enjoy it a little bit.

There was something unutterably free about always being able to wear shirtsleeves—about feeling no concern for rain. Every day it clouded up and rained now and then, but the rain never lasted for longer than a few minutes at a time and then the sun came out and dried you.[2]

There were flowers everywhere and the people were delightful, though downtown Honolulu itself was unpleasantly commercialized.

[2] This wasn't always so. On April 17 and April 20, there were steady all-day rains of the kind I was accustomed to.

We visited Waikiki beach, which did not live up to its Hollywood reputation. I was, in fact (used as I was to Coney Island), amazed at its small depth.

We took tours around Oahu and we visited the Dole pineapple plant on April 18. What I remember most vividly about the sights of Oahu, in fact, was a faucet in the lobby of the Dole plant. When turned, it delivered not water, but pineapple juice—and not just pineapple juice, but the best I've ever tasted before or since, thick and sweet. I had five cups.

We also periodically visited the USO in Honolulu, which I always enjoyed except for one unpleasant event. At one time, the song "God Bless America" was played, and everyone in the place stood up and sang along.

As it happens, however, I think the song is a disaster. The tune is one long cliché and the words are embarrassingly mawkish. So I didn't stand up and I didn't sing, and I was pretty conspicuous.

After it was over, a servicewoman who was a German refugee demanded to know why I had not stood up.

I said, "It's not the National Anthem. I don't have to stand up."

Whereupon she delivered herself of a strong denunciation of me for my lack of patriotism.

When she was all through, I said, "You don't demonstrate your patriotism by singing a bad song. If you think that's patriotism, it shows you don't know anything about it."[3]

Since I had clear logic on my side, there was nobody against me but the damn fools. Unfortunately, that category included almost everyone in the room.

On April 25, by the way, my role as bridge fiend came to a permanent end. Bridge games had continued ever since our train trip, and in one game that day I bid a grand slam that I felt absolutely confident of making, since between myself and the dummy, I owned virtually every trump. Nevertheless, through a piece of elementary miscalculation, I found myself set three. After that, I still played an occasional bridge hand, but only occasionally, and always unenthusiastically. That mishandled grand slam poisoned the game for me.

For a while, I shifted to chess. What happened was that I read Stefan Zweig's *The Royal Game* (in my opinion the best story about chess ever written) and tried to drum up a game and couldn't. So I

[3] I would have liked to have asked her if her father had ever sung *"Deutschland über Alles"* and, if so, what that proved, but I was quite certain that she would then assault me and I managed to keep it down, thank goodness.

tried strategy. I gave *The Royal Game* to Ed James and said, "Would you like to read a good story?"

An hour later he came to me and said, "Would you like to play a game of chess?"

We played quite a few games, but, as usual, I was steadily beaten and my ardor finally cooled.

In participating in the round of pleasures, I remained prudent, of course, and when payday came around I was generally the only in the barracks who was not long out of cash. On March 31, for instance, various fellow soldiers owed me a total of $11—to be paid back, without interest, of course, on payday.

In fact, things went along so smoothly that on March 22, when the news arrived that President Truman had postponed the Bikini atom bomb blast for six weeks (hence six weeks longer to wait—I *knew* it, I *knew* it), my indignation and despair, though present, were distinctly less intense than they might have been.

5

We were all finally given temporary assignments to keep us busy until we shoved off for Bikini, and I, of course, was made clerk-typist.

That meant a certain discomfort, for I no longer wore fatigues or pulled KP, and when I came up during mess call for my beef and mashed potatoes, it meant that I might find another of the critically needed specialists standing behind the counter in fatigues and serving me. It was a near squeak, then, as to whether I got the mashed potatoes on my plate or on my uniform.

One of my duties as clerk-typist was to help make up the "morning report." In essence this was a daily account of the whereabouts and status of every individual in the company. Each person who went on furlough, or sick leave, or was AWOL, or who returned from same, had to be mentioned. Each person who was newly assigned to the company or newly detached had to be mentioned—and, as I recall, by full rank and serial number. Each promotion or demotion had to be mentioned. Finally, at the end, a double-entry summary had to be made of all the personnel, listing them downward by rank from five-star general to private and across in every category of presence or nonpresence. Totals had to be recorded both down and across, and the grand total of all the downward totals and of all the crossward totals had to come out the same—on pain of evisceration, I think.

The actual report was made out in pen and ink by a corporal who was an old hand at it.[4] When he was through with the report he would hand it to me to be typed up. That was by no means a sinecure. It had to be typed with no errors. Every mistake, even that of a single letter, had to be corrected and then initialed by the commanding officer, and the commanding officer objected to that because he could only occasionally remember his initials.

Furthermore, there was a strict system of abbreviations that prevailed. The word "for" was abbreviated "fr," the word "from" was abbreviated "fm," the word "today" was abbreviated "tody," and so on, in the interest of conciseness. Of course, if a word were not on the list of compulsory abbreviations, it was forbidden to abbreviate it. Thus if there were occasion to use the word "approximately," to use the abbreviation "approx" would necessitate redoing the entire report. The military mind remains unparalleled as a vehicle of creative stupidity.

I sometimes asked the corporal to let me do the morning report from scratch, just for the fun of it. He consistently refused for fear, I suspect, that I would take his job away from him. One morning, however, he came in with the statistics of the day and said, "Okay, Asimov, do it yourself this time."

I saw the reason for that at once. A whole batch of promotions had come through; each had to be mentioned individually, and the double-entry column had to be radically revised. (Ordinarily, the double entry for one day was very much like the one for the day before so that it offered little trouble.) Working through all this, plus the usual complement of more ordinary changes in status, took me over an hour. I was rather shamefaced when I brought it in, later than usual, to the commanding officer.

He held it upside down and considered it carefully. "Are you sure this is all right, Private?" he asked.

"Yes, sir," I said.

"Good!" I showed him where to sign his name and he carefully blocked out the letters, getting most of them right.[5]

I then handed it to the corporal who took it to the headquarters building where a bevy of WACs labored to produce a similar morning

[4] I remember him because he wrote a few pages of pornography that remain, to this day, the most skillful I have ever read and that I'm certain consisted of a personal reminiscence.
[5] My remarks impugning the intelligence of officers need not be accepted as literally true. It's just that while I was in the Army I swore a mighty vow that someday I would write a book impugning their intelligence, and vows are sacred, you know.

report that had to check with ours exactly, or a whole series of officers went into a whole series of tantrums.

The corporal walked in (I found this out later), tossed the morning report on the desk, and said, "There it is."

A WAC looked up round-eyed. "You're finished?"

All around her the floor was littered with morning-report blanks that hadn't worked out.

"Sure," said the corporal, nonchalantly, "nothing to it."

"Nothing *to* it? I'll bet your report is all wrong."

"Bet it isn't."

It took the WACs half a day to produce a report they could agree on and one in which the double entry checked, and when they were done, they found, to their unutterable chagrin, that it matched the corporal's report to the last digit—and until then, they had all had the serious suspicion that the corporal's brains could be switched with that of a Siamese cat to the serious harm of the cat.

Several days later, I was sent to the headquarters building on some trifling errand and announced my name. This at once made me an object of curiosity. At all offices possessing my records I invariably became known as "the 160," and all the girls flocked around to see if I had two heads.

One of them, struck by a horrible suspicion, suddenly asked, "Say, do you work for Corporal So-and-so?"

"You bet," I said, cheerfully.

"And did you make out the morning report on such-and-such a day?"

"The day with all the promotions? That's right."

"Well, no *wonder*," she said, in exasperation. "Listen, don't tell that bum you told us."

"Of course not."

I imagine they plotted some revenge, but if so, I never discovered its nature.

6

My typist duties made it possible for me to carry through a project that we seven specialists had long been brooding about. It seemed to us quite clear that we weren't doing anything of importance in connection with Operation Crossroads; that our inspection of the material exposed to the blast could be performed by any eighteen-year-old nonspecialist and that, in fact, the eighteen-year-olds and we were being assigned to the work without distinction among us. We were just being wasted on the project, to make various officers seem more important, and ought to be sent back to our original units—where we could apply for discharge.

The trouble was that we could not appeal on this basis to anyone in the military. We had to go through channels, starting with our immediate superior, who would, of course, quash it at once and give us much trouble in the process.

Nor could we write to Congress, since that was forbidden.

It occurred to me, then, that we could write to Dr. Bradley Dewey, who was head of the American Chemical Society. After all, the ACS was my professional society, and I was a member in good standing. The other specialists were also either chemists or chemical engineers.

If Dr. Dewey cared to take the matter further, that would be his responsibility. We would certainly be careful not to ask him to do anything. A copy would also be sent to Credo's wife, who knew a senator. If she happened to take it to him, that was not our fault either.

I typed up the letter carefully on April 1 (it didn't occur to me that it might be taken as an April Fool joke, or I would have dated it March 31.) It covered three pages and came, I should judge, to about thirteen hundred words. The composition was entirely mine, and I still have a copy of it, but it is too tedious to quote, except perhaps for the last paragraph:

"Perhaps this is a sample of a more general misuse of men thoughout the Army. If so, it should be investigated, for the overall good of America's scientific future."

Once it was done, there came the matter of signing it and, to my amazement, after having enthusiastically concurred in the writing of the letter, and having energetically approved my first draft, there came a general reluctance to sign. In particular, no one wanted to sign first, since each claimed that the first signer would be assumed to be the ringleader.

I said, "Well, then, since I'm the ringleader, I'll sign first. Who wants to be second?"

And they were *still* reluctant. So I said, "Then let's sign in alphabetical order. That still leaves me first and we can all say that the order of our names is merely alphabetical and has no other significance." And then they signed.

We then mailed off the letter and it was as though it had been dropped off into space. Nothing seemed to come of it.

7

On April 8, the specialists entered the barracks suddenly, with news for me. They had signed up for officers' training school. I had

been wondering where they were all day, and now I was both astonished and upset.

I told them that they were crazy; that they would be compelled to
sign up for two years if they did that, whereas, as privates, they could
strive continually for discharge.

Nonsense, they said, no one was getting discharged, and if they
had to stay in the Army, they might as well be officers and comfortable.
Besides, once they signed up they would get an instant furlough. If I
signed up, I could get back at once to see Gertrude.

I held off, growing angrier by the minute, calling them traitors and
renegades who had turned their back on the letter we had all sent off. I
refused, despite all their blandishments, to join them. Even though it
meant remaining behind in Operation Crossroads all alone, even
though it meant missing the chance for quick reunion with Gertrude, I
wouldn't sign up for officer training and wouldn't give up my drive for
discharge.

And when I made it clear that nothing they could say would alter
my opinion, they broke down and admitted it was a practical joke.
They were going to pay me back for not pulling KP by luring me into
attempting to sign up for officer training and making a fool of myself.

It took them quite a while to smooth my ruffled feathers, but I was
secretly enormously pleased with myself. I had held to my principles!

8

On April 4, I had received an unusual piece of mail—a package
that turned out to be a complimentary copy of *The Best of Science Fiction*, with "Blind Alley" included in it. Once again, a small memory of
older, happier days assailed me.

The pressures to which it gave rise built up within me. On April
10, I dug out the first draft of "Evidence," which I still had, but which
I had done nothing with for nearly two months. Since I was a clerk-
typist with nothing, at the moment, to type, I put the entire eight
thousand words into final copy on that day.

The next day I went to the post office in Honolulu and mailed it
off to Campbell—airmail, registered, return receipt requested—for
$1.70. I asked him, if he took the story, to send the check to Gertrude.

He did take it and he did send the check to Gertrude. The check
arrived on April 20 and I got word of it from her on April 29. What's
more, the story was paid for at the new high rate of a full $.02 a word,
so that the check came to $160.

9

On April 15, I attended a Passover Seder given at McKinley High School in Honolulu. There was a $2.00 charge for civilians, but it was free to servicemen. It was the first Seder I had attended since my father's, eighteen years before.

I enjoyed it tremendously. Heroically and steadily, I plowed through the endless supply of good things to eat. In addition, there was sweet port wine at each table into which all could dip, ad lib—and since that is by all odds my favorite form of liquor (when I can bring myself to drink any at all), I ad libbed quite a bit.

I was as high as a kite in no time, and by the time I made my way home, I sloshed as I moved.

I walked into the barracks compound singing Passover songs quite loudly and made considerable noise as I got into the barracks itself. Several of the boys, particularly Dylewski, woke up at once and demanded to know who it was. I was the only one absent and I didn't drink, so the obviously drunken swine who was staggering from one bed to the other couldn't be me.

"It's me," I called out happily. "Is that you, Stash?" (That was the diminutive of his first name, in Polish.)

"Asimov?" he said, wondering.

"Stash," I said, spreading my arms wide, "I love you."

Whereupon he jumped up tensely, threw himself into a posture of self-defense, and said, "You try to hug me and I knock you down."

I was helped into my cot and someone pulled some of my clothes off me and I lay giggling there all night. It was the only day in the Army in which I was truly happy. I guess that's why people drink.[6]

I had no reason to be proud of this experience of drunkenness. The others easily outstripped me. On April 27, the other specialists *all* got drunk for some reason or other. Upton, who had the bed next to mine, lay there hiccuping and slowly and repetitively protesting his love for me.

"Yes, Ed," I kept saying, soothingly, and then I recited for him, dramatically:

> The love of a man for his brother
> And the love of a child for its mother
> Are nothing at all compared to the love
> Of one drunken bum for another.

[6] I balanced the Passover celebration by spending Easter Sunday, the twenty-first, at a Lutheran Church with a couple of Protestant soldiers. I sang the hymns lustily.

Upton listened carefully and nodded and said, "That's right. That's right." Then he leaned over the side of the bed (the far side, thank goodness) threw up, and went to sleep.

10

On April 30, we left our barracks, in which I had stayed forty-six days, and moved onto the *Cortland*, a ship in the harbor. It would take us to Bikini.

I was sorry to leave the barracks, for I had spent a quite tolerable time there despite my separation from Gertrude. I was also sorry to leave the other specialists (after two months of close association), for they were distributed among other ships.

On that day, too, I completed my first half year in the Army and I was rather astonished I had survived it as well as I had. I hadn't even gotten into trouble with any of the officers except—nearly—once.

I was walking down the street near the barracks one morning, with my cap shoved back on my head, my hands in my pockets, whistling cheerfully—quite as though I were a teen-ager back in Brooklyn—and I passed a colonel.

The trouble was that I passed him without seeing him, as I used to pass the candy store's customers once.

"Soldier!" came the call.

I stiffened, stopped whistling, withdrew my hands from my pockets, adjusted my cap, and stepped up briskly. "Sir?" I said, saluting.

He returned the salute, "Do you know who I am?"

"I don't know your name, sir, but you're a colonel in the United States Army."

"Did you salute me when you passed me just now?"

"No, sir."

"Why not?"

"I was thinking of something, sir, and I didn't see you. I'm sorry, sir."

He asked me if I knew the reason for military courtesy and I was able to give him a reasoned exposition. He asked me to whom I was assigned and I told him. He asked me what I was doing, and I explained my position as critically needed specialist on Operation Crossroads.

"And your qualifications for that job?"

"Two degrees in chemistry from Columbia University, sir."

Up to that point, I was sure I was going to be reported and disciplined, but now he sighed. I guess the thought of a private with two degrees in chemistry broke his heart. He said, "I've been in the Army for thirty years, and I'll just never get used to these new ways."

He left me in discouragement and I waited till he was out of sight, then went my way.

11

Life on the ship was rather easygoing. I wangled myself a job as a typist and once again didn't pull duty. I spent most of my time reading and eating (the sailors fed themselves well) and watching movies. The high point, as I recall, came when I managed to liberate an entire frosted layer cake out of the kitchen, then sat in a secluded corner of the deck watching a movie while I ate the *entire* thing very slowly.

Then, on May 13, 1946, when I had been on the *Cortland* for two weeks, something very unexpected happened. I received a letter from Gertrude, telling me that her allotment had not arrived and that when she called to inquire, they told her that the allotment had been stopped because her husband (me!) had been discharged.

The allotment was $50 a month, and I didn't want it stopped. Worse, what if my application for discharge back in February had been approved and I had never been informed?

The next day I got off the ship, despite the protests of the officer in charge of us. (A stopped allotment is a serious thing, and I was able to outindignation him.) I then went from officer to officer, at each stop demanding that either Gertrude get her allotment if I were still in the Army, or that I be sent back home if I were not. I also hinted that I was in a peculiar position since my wife must believe that I was out of the Army and that nonappearance at home might be very suspicious from the marital standpoint.

I finally worked my way up to Colonel Jordan, who was in charge of all Army operations. He was a rather stout man, who impressed me as a rather good-natured, long suffering fellow.

He listened to the story, and said, "But how can you possibly have been discharged?"

"I don't know, sir, but that's what my wife was told. Here's her letter."

"You never applied for discharge, did you?"

"Yes, I did, sir. On February 11, I applied for a research discharge under Order 363."

He spread his arms. "Well, it's probably some mixup but it's against Crossroads policy to send anyone to Bikini who may be subject to discharge. I may have to take you off the project."

I returned to the ship and must have set a world record for holding my breath, for the *Cortland* was due to leave for Bikini three days later, on May 17.

The next day I went to see Colonel Jordan again, and it was official. I was taken off Operation Crossroads and was not to go to Bikini. I was, instead, to be sent back to Camp Lee.

I was delighted.

On the morning of May 16 (Gertrude's birthday), I was off the *Cortland* after a fifteen-day stay aboard, and I was officially off Operation Crossroads, too, after seventy-five days on it. I had accomplished it with just one day to spare.[7]

On May 17, the *Cortland* sailed, as did the other ships. The other six specialists were off to sea on the way to Bikini, and I remained behind on Oahu. In a way, I had betrayed them, but it was through no voluntary act of my own; it was the Army's act of stopping Gertrude's allotment that had brought it about. In my place, each one of them would have done what I did.

12

On the nineteenth, my orders came through, and I was sent back to the United States "by the first available water transportation." That meant six days at sea, but that was good enough. An airplane would have been much faster, but I decided I didn't want an airplane.

It was not until May 27, after I had been off the *Cortland* for seven days (and by now the specialists must be at Bikini), that I was finally moved. To my surprise, I was taken to an airport and told to get on a plane.

I tried to protest, pointing to my orders, but a sergeant said, "Private, don't give me a hard time. Get on that plane!" So I did. It's a lot harder to argue with sergeants than with colonels.

A little after midnight the plane took off, and Honolulu disappeared in the distance. I had been in Oahu for seventy-four days—2½ months.

It was not much of a plane. It was a large propeller-driven transport with its insides eviscerated so that it could carry as many men as possible. I tried to sleep stretched out on the floor, but that didn't work very well. When dawn came, we found ourselves flying over clouds equipped with little blue triangles here and there. It finally dawned on me that these were spaces between the clouds and I was seeing the Pacific Ocean.

---

[7] It may have been a lucky day indeed. Decades later it turned out that leukemia was substantially more common among people who had at one time observed atomic-bomb tests than among those who hadn't.

41

Discharge

1

At 5:00 P.M. local time on May 28, 1946, the plane touched down near San Francisco and I was back on continental United States soil after eighty days. That evening I called my father and heard his voice for the first time in nearly three months. I had failed in my attempt to get Gertrude, so I asked him to pass on the news of my return.

To my astonishment, he seemed displeased at my return. He wanted to know why I had been sent back.

I said, "The Army stopped Gertrude's allotment because they said I was discharged. They sent me back to look into the matter."

My father said, "It will look funny for the customers. They might think there was something wrong."

And I said, with more than a touch of impatience, "The hell with the customers. I'm not going to stay five thousand miles away from home just because they might think it's funny. If you think more of them than you do me, that's *your* problem."

I was furious with my father, but eventually I found out what was bothering him. A postwar letter from his brother Boris had informed him that his brother Samuel was an officer in the Red Army—possibly a major or a major general (it was difficult to figure out the meaning of the Russian word).

My father had passed on the news to me and I had mentioned it to my friends in Hawaii as an item of humor. My father thought that this might have activated Army suspicions of me.[1]

2

On May 30, 1946, I took the train East. I had an upper berth to myself this time. The next day I was back in Ogden, Utah, where I didn't bother to buy a postcard, or even get off the train. I was alone on this journey and I didn't trust my sense of direction. On June 1, in fact, when we stopped in Omaha, I recorded in my diary,

[1] I never heard any news of my Uncle Samuel again. I presume he's no longer alive, and I certainly have no intention of trying to obtain any information concerning him from Soviet authorities.

"I got off at Omaha to get a paper and a bar of chocolate and nearly didn't find my way back (which is the reason I don't get off usually)."

On June 2, the train arrived in Chicago, and there was a four-hour layover, during which I had to switch to another train. At the other station I called Gertrude and heard her voice for the first time in eighty-seven days. She still had not received her allotment—just a form letter saying it was being looked into.

The train from Chicago was a coach and I slept sitting up with the help of a pillow rented for fifteen cents. Later on the afternoon of Monday, June 3, I found myself at Fort Bragg, North Carolina. That, for some reason, was where my orders sent me.

It was my intention to get new orders cut to send me to Camp Lee, where I could find out about the discharge matter, but it turned out that I had a fifteen-day furlough time coming to me, plus three-day travel time. I decided to take that and postpone the fight for a while.

By 5:00 P.M. on June 4, I was on the train for New York, and by 10:30 A.M. on June 5, I was at Windsor Place, and at 1:00 P.M. Gertrude was there. It was exactly 101 days since I had last seen her. I worked it out to the hour in my diary—2,418 hours.

It might have been better. She was working on evening duty at the Henry Paper Box Company and I had to go there and sit while she did her work, which was not the romantic reunion I had been longing for during my over three months of exile. I recorded in my diary, however:

"In the night, I finally slept with her again. . . . It's too bad about the fellows at Bikini."

3

On Tuesday, June 11, I seized the opportunity to see Campbell for the first time in half a year, and took my father with me. It was the first time my father had ever met Campbell. Ted Sturgeon was there and we greeted each other gladly.

My father went off, then—he had to get back to the candy store—and Campbell and I lunched together. I had an idea for another positronic robot story to be called "Little Lost Robot," and I advanced it. I didn't think I would have a chance to write it until the discharge question was settled one way or the other, but I didn't like to see Campbell without advancing any ideas.

After that I went up to Columbia and saw Dawson for the first time in almost a year. I told him I was doing my best to get out of the Army and back into Columbia, and he was most enthusiastic (or, in his kindhearted way, he pretended to be). My next step was to register for a housing project that Columbia was planning to sponsor in Nyack. (After all, I would have to live somewhere.)

Gertrude and I went for *two* trips along the boardwalk to Coney Island—alone on June 13, and along with Roy Machlowitz and a friend of his on the fifteenth. Roy visited New York regularly and, almost as regularly, visited Gertrude or called her—which was good, because I could rely on him for news about her.

Roy sometimes expressed apologetic embarrassment at escaping the draft. He had a history of rheumatic fever from which he had recovered completely in everyone's eyes but those of the draft board. I brushed it off and finally put an end to his apologies by saying rather sharply that if his induction meant my discharge then I would push for his induction—but that since I stayed in the Army whether he was in or out, he might as well stay out.

On June 21, my furlough was in its last day and I got back on the train for Camp Lee—and on that same day, Gertrude got a letter reinstating her allotment. The whole thing had been a clerical error, and I was *not* out of the Army.

Actually, I didn't think I was, and I didn't complain. The error got me two weeks in New York with Gertrude and reassignment to Camp Lee, where I could push for discharge. Without the error, I would have been on Bikini with the other specialists for three weeks now and with considerable additional time to go.

I felt too relieved that this had not happened to feel properly guilty.

4

On June 22, 1946, I was back in Camp Lee, exactly sixteen weeks after I had left it. The next day I went to Petersburg to look up Gladys Credo. She was Robert Credo's wife; she was the one who knew the senator. She had gotten work at Petersburg to be with Bob while he was at Camp Lee and she had kept her job there while he was gone. I felt it was my duty to report to her on events (and to get her to tell me I hadn't done the wrong thing to get out of it when circumstances allowed me to).

She turned out to be a very attractive woman with whom it was a pleasure to talk. I told her about the fourteen weeks we specialists had shared together, and dredged up every story involving Bob that I could remember. The time passed pleasantly, and I saw her a few more times thereafter.

On June 24, I found out what had happened to my application for discharge. It had made its way to Washington and had been placed in suspended animation because I was being placed in an assignment that would utilize my research abilities "to the full." That referred, of course, to Operation Crossroads, which, in all the time I was assigned to it, made no use, not a scrap, of any research abilities of mine, and would not have done so if I had remained with it to the end.

My next step was to avoid being reassigned to something that would continue the suspended animation. I therefore went to Kriegman and asked him to have me assigned to his staff as typist. In that way I would be pinned to Camp Lee and could continue my moves. Kriegman pulled the necessary strings and once again I was off details as of June 27.

On June 30, the first of the two atom bombs was dropped at Bikini. I read about it in the newspapers and, in contrast, Camp Lee seemed rather tolerable to me.

I had a seventh furlough over the July 4 weekend, and on Sunday, July 7, I negotiated the trip from New York to Camp Lee for the seventh time.

5

On July 11, I finally had my discharge hearing. I went in with many a pat on the back and many a grinning remark that no one at Camp Lee had ever been discharged at his own request. At other camps, maybe, but never at Camp Lee, which was a real "chicken outfit."

The interview lasted fifteen minutes, during which I did my best to appear quiet and reserved. I explained the nature of my research at Columbia, why I had ceased doing research (there was no question but that at the Navy Yard I was helping the war effort), and how certain I was that I would go back to research the instant I was discharged.

They then asked me if I would not be able to work at the Army's scientific labs in Chicago, or in chemical warfare, and I did my best to point out that they wouldn't suit me as well as theoretical or "pure" research.

Finally, one of them asked me why I had not tried out for officers' candidate school. I suggested that my eyes would not meet the required standards, but he said he thought that objection could be met. Was there any other reason?

This question, I knew, was the jackpot, win or lose. If I expressed disdain for officer status, then I could stay in the Army for life, as far as they were concerned, and be a private every day of it. If I expressed enthusiasm for officer status, they would have me sign an application for officer training. Neither alternative was bearable and I had to find something that was neither disdain nor enthusiasm and I had to do it without perceptible pause.

I thought more rapidly than at any time since the case of Professor Thomas, 4½ years before. I said, more or less, this:

"If my eyes do not disqualify me, sirs, then I don't think that there is anything in my intelligence or in my educational background that could possibly disqualify me. However, as I am certain you all know, it takes far more than intelligence and education to make a good officer. It takes initiative, courage, and a stability of character, which, to my regret, I don't think I possess. It is embarrassing to have to admit it, but if I lied on the subject in order to become an officer, the Army would discover the lie quickly enough."

They didn't ask me anything more, and I was relieved. I didn't want to be an officer under any conditions and that in itself was a character trait that disqualified me, so that my statement was true enough. I had phrased it in such a way, however, as to leave them flattered to ecstasy.

I left, hoping for the best.

And that same day, simply because of the work I was doing for Kriegman, I was promoted to corporal, got my stripes, and had them sewn on. After eight months and ten days as a buck private, I had become a noncommissioned officer!

While I was in town having my corporal's stripes sewed on, I met Gladys Credo, who told me she was writing a letter to Bob, asking for a divorce.

I looked at her in horror. "Because of anything *I* said about him?"

"No, no," she replied. "I've been thinking of it for a long time."

6

I felt pretty good about my corporalcy. It meant a little more money, of course, but what was really important was that I was promoted. My incapacity to gain promotions, exhibited so forcefully at the Navy Yard, made my promotion a matter of distinction. I wrote to Gertrude about it and made sure that on the return address I wrote Corporal Isaac Asimov, with the first word underlined.

Then, the next day, July 12, my first full day as corporal, I was sent down to the post office to run an errand. I had been there before and had dealt with a young woman who had seemed both efficient and intelligent.

This time she was not at the desk but some male soldier was. He was talking to someone and paying no attention to me. I stood there, growing visibly more impatient, and when he turned to me at last I told him what I wanted in rather peremptory fashion.

"Can't be done," he said, lazily.

"Oh yeah?" I said. "Well, how about letting me speak to the WAC over there?"

He turned to call her and, for the first time, I noticed he wore a captain's bars. Such was my surprise at encountering an officer where I had thought I was speaking to a fellow corporal that I did precisely the wrong thing. I snapped to attention, saluted, and said, "Beg your pardon, sir."

It was virtual suicide. The captain who, until then, had treated me as a human being, if a totally unimportant one, now turned upon me with a snarl. I had shown fear and, as any other dog would have done, he raised his hackles and the corners of his lips at the scent of it.

"How long have you had those stripes, Corporal?"

"I sewed them on yesterday, sir."

"And they went to your head right away, didn't they?"

It rather took my breath away that even an officer could imagine that corporal's stripes would make *me* proud in themselves, but I just said, "I'm sorry, sir."

He then proceeded to chew me out in true captainly fashion. (Officers are given a six-week course on outchewing and a six-minute course on military strategy.)

I was certain that I would be broken to private after twenty-four hours as a corporal and I was even revolving methods of explaining this to Gertrude—but the captain wore himself out with the expulsion of sufficient steam and decided to take no further action.

7

If he *had* broken me it would have made very little difference, for on July 18, 1946, two months and five days after Gertrude's letter had initiated the whole thing, I got the news that my discharge was approved. My little speech, I suppose, had done the trick.

I began at once to prepare for shipping out to Fort Meade, the place that had been my home in my first week as a soldier.

While doing so, I attended the first wedding in my life on Saturday, July 20, and did so in almost civilian effervescence. I was warned that at the reception there would be a lot of gentle old women who would not appreciate my notions of humor and that I must be very quiet. I promised and, on the whole, behaved myself until the bride-to-be fanned herself and said that, really, now that the whole thing was soon to be over, she didn't see what the excitement was about.

"Really?" I said. "Wait till tonight."

And I was promptly dragged out as unfit for genteel company.

That night I was taken to the noncommissioned officers' club and encouraged to drink. I was only too glad to do so because I was feeling hilarious. I grew even more hilarious after a few drinks and came to be incapable of walking in any trustworthy fashion. I had to be escorted to the latrine twice (though I do believe I was still capable of unzipping on my own) and then had to be carefully put to bed, as on the night of the Seder three months before.

The next day I awakened with the first hangover in my life, and the humor of the thing eluded me. When I spent a social day with Lieutenant and Mrs. Kriegman, therefore, I stayed shudderingly away from any liquor.

8

Early on the morning of July 24, 1946, I was on the train to Fort Meade and left Camp Lee forever 8½ months after I had seen it for the first time. On that day the second atom bomb was exploded at Bikini, and my fellow specialists were still there. I still felt too good at my own fate to feel guilty about theirs.

Sometime later I received a letter from Ed James, dated June 28. He told me that the letter I had written on April 1 had slowly made its way from the ACS president to the desk of the Secretary of War, and back down again to the admiral in charge of the test.

From the letter, and from still later information I received, it seems that the remaining six specialists were called in and chewed out at the admiral level. They held fast, claimed that the letter had only gone to their professional organization, that they hadn't the slightest idea it would go elsewhere, and managed to put the blame on me. That was the intelligent thing to do since I wasn't there and couldn't be punished. Besides, most of the blame *did* belong to me.

There was some talk of court-martial but it couldn't possibly have stuck. In the end, although the letter did not get them off the Operation, it did (Ed told me) result in their getting barracks and better living conditions as a way of quieting them down. They were taken off KP, for instance, so it all did some good.

I *did* feel guilty at having been out from under when the refuse hit the fan.

9

By dinnertime I was at Fort Meade. I mailed my belongings ahead to Windsor Place, and at 4:30 P.M. on July 26, 1946 (my fourth wedding anniversary, as it happened), I was duly mustered out of the Army with an honorable discharge.

I had been in the Army for eight months and twenty-six days, just about one third of the two-year-hitch I originally assumed would be my lot, and for about one month of that time, all told, I was on furlough in New York. At no time had it *really* been bad. Homesickness and frustration were all I suffered, and if I could have avoided those, I might even have had a rather good time.

I took the train back to New York and called up Gertrude as soon as I got into the station. She said, "Go to a hotel."

I said, "What!"

Apparently she had had a small cyst removed from one of her lower eyelids and the operation had produced a black eye and she didn't want me seeing her like that.

What nonsense! I refused to go to any hotel unless she went with me, and by 11:30 P.M. I was with her. I had made my anniversary by half an hour, and that anniversary was the happiest one I spent with her.

On Sunday the twenty-eighth I took the train to Windsor Place. I was in civilian clothes again (hurrah) and at the station, and an Army major inadvertently stepped on my foot.

"Pardon me," he said, automatically.

I waved a lordly hand, "That's all right, bub," I said, and with that, I *knew* I was out of the Army.

PART V

Into and out of Manhattan

42

Dean Street

1

On the twenty-ninth, I went to Columbia and arranged for my return. There was no question but that my status there was perfectly regular, and in September 1946 I would register and begin research.

Meanwhile, the month of August had to be spent largely in apartment hunting, and that wasn't easy. Now that the war was over, everybody wanted an apartment, and during the war years, none had been built. They were very scarce and, in consequence, very expensive. The apartments that Columbia was building in Nyack had been slowed by labor problems, wouldn't be ready for quite a while and, when we went to look at them, we found that they were not at all suitable.

There didn't seem to be any problem with money, however. My Army pay, Gertrude's allotment, and twenty dollars a week that her father paid her for working at the Henry Paper Box Company had kept us both going through the Army interval, and the savings account was intact.

There was still more the Army could pay us. Each veteran could get a certain amount of money for his education under something called the "GI Bill of Rights," the exact amount depending on the length of his stay in uniform. It was my intention to refuse to sign up for it on the grounds that I had done my best to stay out of the Army and once in, had done my best to get out of the Army, and that therefore it wasn't just to take money from them.

Everyone else on both sides of the family thought this attitude was quixotic of me and I let myself be talked into it. The deciding push came from the thought that I didn't know how long it would take me to do my research and I didn't want to fail to get my doctorate simply because I ran out of money.

The Army money might make my finances last just those necessary extra months that might make all the difference and with that in mind I let expediency triumph over principle. I do that every once in a while, and I always hate it. I hated it this time.

At least I was spared the discomfort of finding my beloved New York changed. Changed it undoubtedly was, but I was protected from that by my nonvisual tendencies. The only thing that bothered me about my long absence in Philadelphia was that I had lost touch with the politics of New York City and New York State—and in some ways I never caught up again.

Perhaps worse was that the students in the chemistry department were a new generation and now, at last, I was among the oldest of the students instead of the youngest—an uncomfortable blow.

You can't go home again.

2

Apartment hunting was interrupted on August 15 with a trip to Philadelphia, of all places.

Henry Blugerman needed paperboard for his company, and paperboard, too, was caught up in general postwar shortages. He knew of a place in Philadelphia where it might be obtained, so Gertrude and I agreed to go there.

We did, and found the place, but Gertrude expended all her eloquence to no avail. There was no paperboard.

We then went down to the Navy Yard, which I now visited for the first time in 9½ months. It was Gertrude's very first visit.

With my usual caution, and my desire to keep all options open, I asked if I might have a leave of absence to complete my doctoral research. The notion in my mind was this: If, after obtaining my degree, I could not find a job, I might (if I chose to) return to the Navy Yard, at least for a while. That might be preferable to unemployment.

It could be done, I was told, provided I returned, temporarily, to the Navy Yard as an active employee. I drew the line at that. It was too intolerable a way of keeping that option open. I resigned once and for all, 4⅓ years after beginning work there.

We had dinner with Bernie Zitin, Leonard Meisel, and Roy Machlowitz at Shoyer's, Philadelphia's famous Jewish restaurant, which I had eaten at for the first time shortly before induction. Meisel then drove us to Wingate Hall, which we had left nearly a year before, in order to get information concerning some relative of the manager who managed apartments in New York.

Then we took the train back. It was the last whiff of our Philadelphia years.

3

On August 12, we had located a furnished 1½-room apartment, with a closet-kitchenette, that might do. It was distinctly smaller than our Philadelphia apartments and was nearly double the rent—$70 a month—but it was in New York, not in Philadelphia. In fact, it was on 213 Dean Street, which was within walking distance of the downtown Brooklyn shopping district. That was an undeniably good point.

We had to consider it, and the more we looked elsewhere at altogether impossible places, the more the Dean Street apartment looked reasonable to us.

By August 27, I was so certain that the Dean Street apartment was the best we were going to get that I went to considerable trouble to beat the landlord down to $50 a month by promising to pay him the entire $600 for the year, in advance. The money was paid over on the twenty-ninth and that brought our bank account down to $3,330. As I said in my diary on that date, rather gloomily, "We are now the proud possessors of a closet on the first floor of 213 Dean Street, Brooklyn."

4

Meanwhile, though, on August 20, I had picked up the September 1946 *Astounding*, which contained "Evidence."[1] Could I have imagined when I mailed off the story from Hawaii four months before that I'd be reading it in the magazine as a civilian?

On August 22, 1946, I received my Social Security number: 055-24-6410.

That same day I received a letter from Gerry Cohen. He was still at Aberdeen Proving Grounds and he was under the impression I was still at Operation Crossroads.

On August 30, Katherine Tarrant told me of a new anthology, *Adventure in Time and Space*, edited by Raymond J. Healy and J. Francis McComas. It was a large Modern Library giant put out by Random House and contained a number of the best pieces of the Golden Age of magazine science fiction.

One of the stories it contained was "Nightfall," the second of my stories to be anthologized. For it, Katherine said, I would get $66.50 (the check arrived on September 7). I now thought of that sum as representing six weeks' rent or one year's gas and electricity.

I bought a copy of the anthology—$3.01 with tax.

5

On September 4, 1946, we moved into 213 Dean Street. It was the first time we had an apartment of our own, however small, in almost exactly a year, and the first time ever in Greater New York.

[1] See *I, Robot*.

And on September 6, my letters to the various specialists began to return, marked "moved—address unknown." By now, apparently, Operation Crossroads had broken up. The original estimate of six months had been fair enough after all.

6

On September 9, I went to see Campbell and brought up "Little Lost Robot" for further discussion. I had made two false starts. Campbell pressed to have me try again, and we even discussed two more Foundation stories.

I went home full of eagerness and started "Little Lost Robot" a third time, on September 10. It was about a robot which, interpreting an order too literally, lost itself in a crowd of similar robots and had to be identified quickly or great danger would ensue.

This time I had no trouble and, working steadily, I finished it in five days, even though it was ten thousand words long and the longest of the robot stories to date. On September 16, I took it in to Campbell at 11:30 A.M., and at 2:30 P.M. I called him and found it was an acceptance at $.02 a word. On September 28, I received my check for $200. It was my first post-Army sale.

Something else followed almost at once. On September 14, I had received a telegram from a lawyer who said that his client (whom he did not identify) wanted to buy all rights to "Evidence." I went to see the lawyer on my way to Campbell on the sixteenth, and all I could get out of him was that his client wanted movie rights in particular and would pay $250 for it.

Campbell told me he thought $250 was fair for movie rights to a short story, but Gertrude suggested I ask $1,000. (Gertrude was nearer right, but neither she nor Campbell understood the situation any more than I did. I ought to have granted movie rights for a specific period, said rights to be renewed for more money at the end of the period. Selling all rights permanently for any sum was terrible and I was being cheated, but of course I didn't know that.)

I called the lawyer and asked for $1,000 and that I wouldn't discuss the matter any further unless I knew who his client was.

On September 20, the lawyer called again and said he was representing Orson Welles. I jumped for joy and let him have the movie rights for $250. Welles was a favorite of mine, both for his movies and, in those days, for a newspaper column he was writing.

I got *Astounding* to grant me the necessary rights on September 27, took them around to the lawyer, and collected my $250. I felt great, but the whole transaction was barren. The picture was never made, and from that day to this, Welles owns the movie, radio, and television rights to that story and I cannot sell it elsewhere. What a fool I was!

7

Professor Boyd of Boston University School of Medicine was in New York on September 18, at the home of a friend of his—Arthur Sard, a mathematics professor at Queens College. Boyd had been corresponding with me all through my stay in the Army and I was eager to meet him.

I made my way out to Queens and spent the day with him and the Sards from 2:00 P.M. to 10:00 P.M. This included an elaborate and rather formal dinner, for in my diary I remarked on the fact that the salad was mixed in a large wooden bowl, that the chicken was carved by Dr. Sard, and that there were lit candles on the table. I had never encountered such articles of sophistication before.

Boyd himself was forty-three at the time, a stocky fellow of about my height who (in my opinion) looked like H. G. Wells. We liked each other.

8

On Monday, September 23, 1946, I registered at Columbia again, just as though the 4½-year lapse had never been. I had left a young man of twenty-two; I came back nearly twenty-seven. Had I not been interrupted, I might conceivably have earned my doctorate at the age of twenty-four, which would have been more in accord with my child-prodigy status; but now that could never be. Tens of millions of people had suffered far worse than I did in the course of World War II—but when no one was looking, I sometimes mourned the four-year delay.

But at least I had done all my necessary coursework before I had left Columbia. Now it was only necessary to do research and nothing more.

On October 1, I was assigned a research room and started in from the beginning. I discovered, rather ruefully, that in the war years, Linus Pauling's theory of resonance had taken over organic chemistry completely so that I was virtually a beginner again and would have to learn the subject afresh.

I was asked to be lab assistant at a small salary, but I refused. I dared lose no further time from my research—and I didn't need the money.

I am ashamed to say I felt a small glow of mean triumph. When I had started research before leaving for the Navy Yard, I had asked to be a lab assistant because at that time I needed the money—and they had refused me. Well, now *I* refused *them*.

9

Now that I was in New York, bits of the past floated up. Gerry Cohen, my most reliable companion in basic training, showed up in our apartment on a visit on October 5. He was still in the Army and regaled us for three hours with erotic incidents from his recent past. They fascinated us but they might, of course, have been exaggerated.

Then, on the evening of October 12, we had dinner with Joe Goldberger and Lee, along with two friends of theirs (Goldberger had taken to calling himself Gould). It was very pleasant and the food was good though I commented on the high prices with some indignation in my diary. Veal cutlets for Gertrude and myself set us back $1.50 apiece.

On October 19, Gertrude and I visited Fred Pohl and his second wife at their apartment in Greenwich Village. I tasted caviar for the first time on that occasion. While there, a fellow Futurian, Dirk Wylie, and his wife, Roz, showed up. Wylie was not well and he died a few years later. Robert Lowndes, who had put on considerable weight, also dropped by. We weren't kids anymore, any of us.

And there was a science-fiction convention.

I hadn't attended any conventions since that first one in New York in 1939. It had set a fashion. Every year over the Labor Day weekend, a "world science-fiction convention" was held. The war years of 1942, 1943, and 1944 were skipped, but except for those, no year has been missed.

The convention is held in a different city every year, and frequently the cities are much too far away for me to get to, considering that I hate to travel. I had attended none of the world conventions since the first.

There were, however, also local conventions held in various cities each year. The oldest of these is the "Philcon," a convention held by fans in the Philadelphia area—and always in Philadelphia, of course.

Although Bob Heinlein and I had left Philadelphia after the war and returned to our native haunts, Sprague de Camp did not. He remained in the Philadelphia area and naturally became an important cog in Philadelphia science-fiction circles and in their convention activities.

Sprague invited me to the 1946 Philcon and, on October 27, I went down to Philadelphia. The difference between postwar and prewar was quite marked. My robot stories and the Foundation series had made me a science-fiction celebrity of the first rank, so that I signed endless autographs and was interviewed by a newspaper reporter for the first time.

As an indication of the passage of time, one of the young women I met there happened to be one of those I corresponded with in the prewar days. I was married, of course, but she had gone me one better. She had been married and divorced.

I then had dinner with the de Camps, whom I hadn't seen in over a year.

Then Ed James of Operation Crossroads, who had just gotten out of the Army, came to New York on October 29, and we got a special-delivery letter informing us of the fact on that very day. Dinner was about to be started, but we put everything back in cupboards and refrigerators and dashed out. We had a fancy dinner for four (Ed's wife was along with him).

After Ed returned from Crossroads, he and his wife stayed in Petersburg at Gladys Credo's old rooms and apparently the landlady told them lurid tales about Gladys *and me.*

I was horrified and said, "But I was never alone indoors with her, Ed. Either I saw her in the company of others, or I met her in the street and talked to her there."

Oh well. As Hamlet said, "Be thou as chaste as ice, as pure as snow, thou shalt not escape calumny."

And speaking of calumny, the rumors went around Crossroads that I had been taken off the project for any of a variety of reasons discreditable to myself.

10

Things disappear as well as reappear.

In Philadelphia, Gertrude had made a bust of me in clay. It was nearly life-size and it was an excellent likeness. People who visited us, knowing nothing about the bust, would see it and know at once it was of me.

I was very fond of it myself. After all, it both looked like me and was handsome, and that's a combination that's hard to beat.

But on the morning of October 7, 1946, Gertrude and I, while scuffling playfully, managed to knock it off the bookcase and it smashed into a hundred pieces. I still miss that bust.

Then, on October 10, Gertrude played with some mercury I had brought home for its amusement value. It is fun to play with, since it is so heavy and so nonwetting. Unfortunately, Gertrude did not remove her wedding ring while playing with it and mercury will not only wet gold, it also will mix with it readily. Her ring turned a silvery color.

I took the wedding ring to school the next day and tried driving off the mercury by heating it gently under vacuum. That merely turned it from a silvery color to a dull-gray one. I then tried to heat it more strongly in a Bunsen burner flame and the gold began to melt. (That was one of my more stupid feats since there were sound chemical reasons—I won't bore you with them—for anticipating just that.) I snatched the ring out of the flame but it was clearly ruined.

Eventually, John Blugerman removed the mercury, which was only in the gold surface, by drilling it off with a dental drill, but the ring wasn't really useful thereafter.

I missed that ring, too. It had been engraved with our initials and the wedding date.

11

For once I was getting along with a superior. Professor Dawson and I were soulmates.

This was not because I had ceased to be me. It was entirely because Dawson didn't mind my peculiarities. Indeed, he was amused by them.

For one thing, I was always running into him with excited ideas, or comments, or results. "Phenomenon-a-minute Asimov" he used to refer to me in speaking to others.

Sometimes the excitement arose over something not entirely creditable to myself.

One time, for instance, I reported to him that a sample of enzyme wasn't working no matter what I did. I was very gloomy about it for I couldn't understand what I had done wrong. And then I became aware of the fact that I was not using a 2-milliliter pipette, but a 0.2-milliliter one—one that had only one tenth the capacity of the former, though it had the same outward dimensions. Therefore I was always adding just one tenth the amount of enzyme I thought I was adding.

This was a terribly stupid mistake for a chemist to make. A good chemist should be able to tell the capacity of a pipette in the dark just by the feel of it.

Of course, I was far too excited to think about the stupidity of the matter and, therefore, to hide the fact so that no one would know how stupid I was. After all, I had solved the problem of the nonworking enzyme. I therefore rushed into Dawson's office (quite disregarding the fact that he was talking to someone) and said, "I've got the answer to the enzyme problem, Dr. Dawson. I was using a 0.2-milliliter pipette instead of a 2-milliliter pipette."

Another research professor might have kicked me out of the laboratory for aggravated stupidity in the first degree, but Professor Dawson chose to regard it as an example of honesty. In fact, he was quoted to me as using the term "absolute integrity" in reference to myself, and I didn't quite have the absolute integrity to tell him it was only stupidity.

As a matter of fact, Dawson had lots of opportunity to observe my stupidity/integrity. According to a system he had himself worked up, all students entered all experimental results each day in a notebook in which every page was backed by carbon paper and an identical copy page. At the end of each day, the carbons were handed to Dawson.[2]

I handed in my carbons dutifully each day, and every week Dawson and I would go over them together. Since I was always undeft enough to have some experiments that went stupidly awry, Dawson had many occasions to laugh.

It turned out, as a matter of fact, that he had saved a particular set of experimental results I had recorded in early 1942 before I left for the Navy Yard. I had conducted the experiment with such incredible lack of skill that my results came out all over the place. I made a mark for each observation on the graph paper, and they covered the paper in almost random fashion. It looked as though the paper had been hit by shotgun pellets, a point I incautiously mentioned, so that everyone called it "Asimov's shotgun curve" after I had drawn a curve of the proper shape cavalierly through the midst of the marks.

Every once in a while, then, when Dawson wanted to boast about me to someone, he would pull out that shotgun curve. Apparently, the logical thing for any student of normal intelligence to do was to record their observations on scrap paper *before* entering it in the book and then enter them only if they looked good—and it never occurred to me to do that. That was just compounded stupidity, again, but Dawson chose to consider it absolute integrity.

Of course, he knew very well that I was a hopeless mess in the laboratory. At one time he said to me, "Don't worry, Isaac. We've got plenty of hands and if you can't run the experiments we'll hire someone to run them for you. You just keep getting the ideas; that's what we need."

On the other hand, he could speak, frankly, too.

I once told him of my futile attempts to enter medical school, for

---

[2] The idea was, I think, that no student could then hocus the observations, though that notion didn't occur to me for years. I thought Dawson just wanted to look at the observations. Eventually, when it finally occurred to me that some people considered it conceivable that observations could be altered, I wrote a mystery novel about it.

he was now serving as the premedical adviser, and he said to me, "It's a good thing you didn't get in, Isaac."

"Oh? Why is that, Dr. Dawson?" I smirked, for I expected him to tell me what a great chemist I was and how the world of chemistry couldn't have endured the loss of me.

"Because you would have made a lousy doctor, Isaac."

Well, it was true.

I owe a great deal to Dawson and I am selfish enough to wish it were true that (as he keeps telling me in recent years) his greatest claim to fame now is the fact that he was my research professor. If it were true, it would be a pleasant way of returning, even if only inadequately, his faith in me and his kindness to me.

12

On November 1, 1946, I was aware that it was just one year since I had been inducted into the Army, and that it was better than three months since I had gotten out. It gave the day such a glow of relief.

And on November 5, Gertrude was able to vote as an American citizen for the first time. Thomas E. Dewey was running for governor of New York on the Republican ticket and we both voted against him, of course—but he won.

That election, in fact, put the notorious Eightieth Congress into office, the first Congress in a quarter of a century to be dominated (narrowly) by the Republican Party. Truman had proven so inept in the eyes of the country that there were strong cries for his resignation, even from Democrats.

Heinlein seemed to me to be an ultraliberal all through the days of the Navy Yard, and so had Leslyn. Now I got a letter from Heinlein saying that it was his idea that Truman appoint a leading Republican as Secretary of State and then resign. The Republican would succeed to the presidency and would run the country with a Republican Congress. This was the first indication to me that he had grown conservative.

I disapproved of this suggestion that the Constitution be subverted and that the United States be converted into a parliamentary democracy, but I did not choose to quarrel over it. I answered with a short letter of bare disagreement.

13

I had not entirely lost the knack of being rejected. Back in February 1942, Campbell had rejected "Victory Unintentional," and in the 4½ years since, I had written eleven stories and sold them all.

Now I heard that *Thrilling Wonder Stories* was trying to improve the quality of its stories and was willing to pay $.02 a word, matching *Astounding*'s rates. I raked through the barrel and found "Big Game," which I had originally written as a Probability Zero story five years before. It was only a thousand words long, but I rewrote it, lengthened it to three thousand words, and called it "The Hunted." I sent it to *Thrilling Wonder* on October 30, 1946, and on November 9, it was rejected. I was rather devastated. My name had not yet become magic. It couldn't carry everything.

But it was really a pre-1942 story. I consoled myself with that and continued working on a new Foundation story, which I called "Now You See It—"

I got the news that same rejection day, in a letter from Leslyn, that Bob Heinlein had sold a science-fiction story to *The Saturday Evening Post*. In the 1930s, *The Saturday Evening Post* had been the Mecca and Paradise of all writers. Any beginner automatically sent his first miserable little brainchild to the *Post*, and anyone who got in at any stage in his career had Made It.

The cachet still lingered in 1946 and it was good that Bob had gotten in.

To be sure, my first reaction had been of miserable envy—Bob could make the *Post* and I couldn't even make *Thrilling Wonder*. It didn't take much thought, however, for me to see that Bob had done us all a terrific favor and that there was reason to rejoice. Every science-fiction writer would find the world easier for him because Heinlein had made the field more respectable and, sooner or later, we would all profit as a result. Between Heinlein and the atom bomb, it became difficult to think of science fiction as childish and silly anymore, and there were great days ahead.

Heinlein no longer wrote for *Astounding*, however. I think he and Campbell must have come to a bitter parting of the ways over something. I don't know what it was. Campbell never volunteered information, and I didn't think it proper to ask.

14

I got a letter from Lieutenant Kriegman on December 2, except that he was Captain Kriegman now. He wanted Gertrude and me to visit him at his home in Newark. I was tempted, but the date of the visit coincided with my initiation into Phi Lambda Upsilon, the chemists' honor society.

I had the choice between looking back toward the horrible days of the Army or forward toward a possibly glowing chemical career, and I chose to look forward. It was a hard choice and it rather spoiled the initiation for me since Kriegman had been good to me. For some years after that, I got a card from Kriegman each Christmas with a letter written across it. I responded each time, urging him to write more often, but he never did.

15

By and large, in this second period of research at Columbia, I dealt with a new generation. The fellow students of 1939 to 1942 were all gone, and the fellow students of 1946 were unknown to me. There were occasional connections, though.

I met Ira Weill, for instance, who, except for red hair, looked very much like Lester Weill of Hilltop days. They were brothers and from Ira I learned that Lester was married and was at the University of Akron.

I made new friends, of course. One graduate student was a beautiful red-headed girl named Gerry, brilliant and full of drive. I admired her enormously, and not just for her beauty. We used to argue the matter of feminism in those days. She complained bitterly about the difficulties women encountered in entering scientific research.

I was sympathetic but, playing devil's advocate, I pointed out that there was the feeling that women, after doing their research and getting their degrees, would then get married, have children, and retire into domesticity—and they would have taken up the place that some man could have used to get his degrees and become a working scientist. (Naturally, I was thinking of Irene.)

Gerry argued this point strenuously and, when it seemed that justice was on her side, I gave up. She went on to get her Ph.D., then married a fellow researcher, had children, and retired into domesticity—at least for a while.

There was James Mann, who shared my research lab at the start. He resembled Tyrone Power in looks (in my eyes, anyway), was a very pleasant fellow and, after a while, joined the Unitarian Church. He was a nonobservant Jew and he urged me to find the same spiritual home, but I refused firmly. I intended to be a nonobservant everything.

16

Apparently our family had Americanized itself into birthday presents. At least on December 7, 1946, my mother bestowed upon me a wristwatch as an advance gift of that sort.

It pleased me at the time, and the remarkable thing, in my opinion, is that I still have it. It's been cleaned innumerable times and has been repaired on occasion, and its face is so dark the numbers are hard to read—but it still works, and I still use it on occasion.

17

On December 10, I got a letter from Gerry Cohen to the effect that he had been discharged and was a civilian again.

Each time someone I knew in the Army reported he was out, I felt that another link with that deplorable episode in my life had been cut. I was getting to feel that not only the Army, but also the Navy Yard had been a kind of extraneous intrusion upon my life. Those years began to seem, as they have seemed ever since, far less real to me than the years before 1942 and since 1946.

18

I feel that, as a matter of principle, I ought to record every piece of egregious Asimovian stupidity I can remember, if only to have it act as a partial canceling-out of the unjustified reputation I have for universal wisdom.

We received a gas bill for $6.50 toward the end of 1946, which was just twice as high as the gas bill anyone else in the apartment building got. We checked that, to make sure, and we were furious.

On December 11, I went to the offices of the gas company in downtown Brooklyn to demand reparation, restitution, and a groveling apology. I waited in line in the greatest indignation and when I finally got to the window, I slapped down the bill and said, angrily, "See here, we have never used enough gas to bring us up to the $2.00 minimum. We have no children. We both work. We cook perhaps four meals a week. How can we possibly get a bill for $6.50? I *demand* an explanation."

The man behind the counter looked at me mildly. "You really insist on an explanation?"

"Certainly. If you can think of one besides general incompetence."

"Fortunately," he said, "I can think of one. This is an electric bill."

You never saw so quiet and humble a retreat in your life.

19

Part of my duties as a research student was to prepare a seminar on my research. I had to explain the nature of the problem, then go on to explain what I was doing and why, what I hoped to accomplish, and so on. When I was done, I was expected to field searching questions from the floor.

Other people in the department were supposed to attend, and the idea was that no one was to become too ingrown, that each student should be exposed to all the other currents permeating the Columbia chemistry department.

That was the theory, but many people found seminars frustrating. Those who lectured on the problem seemed never to grasp the level of ignorance of those not working on it—or were afraid to show anything less than complete erudition. In five minutes, usually, the lecturer had left his audience behind and completed his presentation talking only to himself and his research professor.

I did not intend to do this in *my* seminar, which was slated for December 17. I lacked intellectual insecurity and I did not feel it necessary to be erudite. Besides, I had my fiction-writing experience, in which one has to assume the reader begins by knowing nothing of the story one is going to tell.

I prepared my talk meticulously, therefore, from first principles. I went into the seminar room some hours before the talk, and covered all the boards with equations and chemical formulas. One student, stumbling into the room as I was finishing, looked at the mass of hieroglyphics with dismay and said, "I'll never understand this."

I said, soothingly, "Nonsense. Just listen to everything I say and all will be as clear as a mountain pool."

What made me so sure of that, I don't know, but that's how it was. I gave the talk from the beginning and moved slowly along all the equations and formulas, without having to suffer the distraction and interruption of having to write them down as I talked.

In the end the audience seemed enthusiastic and Professor Dawson told someone (who promptly passed it on to me) that it was the clearest presentation he had ever heard. It happened to be the first time I ever presented a formal hour-long talk to an audience in my life.

20

My father turned fifty on December 21, and my father's birthday always meant Christmas and the end of the year.

The year 1946 had ended far better than it had begun, but it was not one of my more successful writing years. I had sold only two short stories (both in the positronic robot series) and nothing more. That was not surprising. Between the Army in the first part of the year and research in the second, there had been little writing time.

Even so, my two anthology sales and my sale to Orson Welles raised my total writing income for 1946 to $718. There was also my Army pay, Gertrude's Army allotment, her earnings at the Henry Paper Box Company, and the money I got from the GI Bill of Rights. It all came to between $2,000 and $3,000 and, with the writing earnings added, our bank account did not suffer that year.

21

On January 2, 1947, I was twenty-seven years old. It was a wonderful birthday, because I couldn't help comparing it with my twenty-sixth, which was spent in the Army. On the other hand, I was more than half as old as my father. I was suddenly aware that I was older by nearly four years than my father had been when I was born.

I was becoming distinctly mature.

I bought myself a postbirthday present—a slide rule. I had ordered one from the bookstore a long time before, but there was a postwar backlog of orders to fill and it wasn't till January 10 that mine came through. It was, according to my diary, "A Dietsgen decitrig duplex polyphase log-log slide rule" and it cost me $16. I still own it and it works as well as ever.

A hundred-page booklet of instructions came with it, and I read just enough of it to get the idea and then fiddled with the slide rule itself and learned how to work it. It was much more fun doing it for myself.

If Razran had only showed me how to multiply two by three on the slide rule back in 1936, I would have gained a decade.

My first use of the slide rule was to check some of the figures in Gertrude's bookkeeping in connection with the Henry Paper Box Company. It was an exciting procedure, marred only by the fact that every time my reading disagreed with her figures, it was my reading that was wrong.

22

Another connection with Army life was broken. Jerome Himelhoch, who had been part of Kriegman's group along with me in my last weeks in the Army, was himself out of the Army now. We visited him and his family on January 31. On the way there, I took Gertrude to my

Columbia research laboratory for the first time and proudly showed her the fancy equipment I was using.

23

I finally finished "Now You See It—" on February 2. It was twenty-five thousand words long, only half as long as "The Mule," but it still took me several months to complete.

Partly this was because I was *still* collecting my notes for the book on World War II I wanted to write. Looking back on it now, I grow impatient with myself. How ridiculous it was.

It finally came to an end some weeks later when I went over the notes. I found that I had taken as much as thirty-five thousand words from a single book and that I had in excess of two million words of notes altogether. I started indexing the notes toward the end of February, and that was the giveaway. It was clear that the indexing was an impossible job, and the whole project suddenly faded and died. I doubt that I ever wasted so much time on so futile a project in my life—but at least I learned how *not* to write a nonfiction book, so perhaps it wasn't all that futile after all.

On February 4, I visited Campbell and handed over "Now You See It—" While there, I picked up an advance copy of the March 1947 *Astounding*, which had "Little Lost Robot"[3] in it.

For the first time, however, Campbell was not completely satisfied with a Foundation story. We disagreed on the ending.

After all, I had grown a little weary of the Foundation and all its works. I had been working on it, on and off, for five years. I had written seven stories, totaling about 185,000 words. I felt it was time to end the thing and get on to something new. Therefore I rounded off "Now You See It—" in such a way as to make it a reasonable ending of the series.

Campbell would have none of it. After he read the story, he told me I could not use the ending as I had it. I had to make the story open-ended and continue the series. He was quite firm about it and I still wasn't in any position to brave Campbell's displeasure.

I rewrote "Now You See It—" according to instructions, the task taking me but a day, and brought it in again on the tenth. Campbell accepted the new version at once and on February 14, 1947, a check for $500 arrived. It came on the fifth anniversary of my blind date with Gertrude.

[3] See *I, Robot*.

24

The $500 made me feel prosperous indeed. The next day we bought a mink-dyed opossum fur coat for Gertrude for $200. It was our first real splurge and it made me feel like a "good provider."

My parents were feeling prosperous, too. At just about this time they were buying a second house close to the store, one that was at 1618 Tenth Avenue, for $9,500.

It was their deliberate intention to extend their real-estate holdings bit by bit until their rental receipts covered mortgage, maintenance, and taxes, with enough left over to make it possible for them to retire from the candy-store business.

25

I received a personal letter from Orson Welles on March 3, 1947, and I was delighted and impressed. He said he'd be in New York City soon and would like to meet me.

Alas, he never came; or if he came, he certainly never got in touch with me. That letter, added to the $250, was all I ever got for trifling away the electronic rights to "Evidence" forever.

I made a closer contact with another celebrity. Arnold Toynbee's *A Study of History*, which Sprague had admired so and to which he had introduced me, had roused the interest of *Time*, and Toynbee had become a world celebrity.

On March 10, 1947, Toynbee was lecturing at Bryn Mawr, near Philadelphia, and Sprague was enormously excited. He suggested I come to Philadelphia to hear Toynbee, and although my own infatuation with Toynbee had passed, I have always found it difficult to resist Sprague, whom I have always admired just this side of idolatry both as a person and as a writer.

I went to Philadelphia, therefore, and, in Sprague's company, listened to an hour lecture by Toynbee on contacts between civilizations. I found it fascinating, and afterward, when Sprague managed to make his way to Toynbee and to introduce me, I was delighted at the opportunity of shaking hands with the man.

Afterward, Sprague and a few others started a "Toynbeean Society" and I was made "temporary secretary." Nothing very much happened to the Society after that (that I knew of, at least), so I suppose it didn't get far.

26

Meanwhile, I was working steadily and successfully at my research, which consisted of making many, many "chronometric" measurements.

It worked thus: A certain quantity of enzyme was mixed with and allowed to work on a compound called catechol. While it was working, drops of the mixture were dribbled into a starch-iodide solution resting on an illuminated, milk-white sheet of glass. At a certain point in the enzyme reaction, enough quinone was produced from the catechol to turn the iodide into iodine, which reacts with the starch to form a black addition-compound. The first trace of a black fog against the illuminated background as a drop falls into the solution marks the end point.

The time between the start of the enzyme reaction and the end point is measured with a stopwatch. The important part of the research then lay in analyzing the time measurements and trying to build a picture of the enzyme-catechol interrelationships that would account for them.

I would stand there running test after test with my stopwatch in hand, making use of all sorts of different conditions and recording the time in every case. I once ran as many as 32 chronometrics in a single session, but I was told that Lloyd Roth could run 50 or 60. A fellow researcher, Frank Mallette,[4] claimed he had once done 120 in one day. How all this was possible, I couldn't imagine, but considering that I was my undeft self, I considered 32 sufficient.

One thing I found was that I could not duplicate the results of anyone before me. Thinking about it, I decided that it took time for the enzyme to mix with the catechol, so that the reaction didn't proceed at top speed from the beginning. I tried stirring the solution faster and faster, and sure enough, my results differed less from the ideal the faster I stirred. I therefore introduced a "mixing time" constant into the equation and everything worked perfectly. How the devil the preceding investigators had managed to get ideal results without taking mixing into account I was never able to figure out.

27

For three months, ever since I had sold "Now You See It—," I had been limping along with a story called "No Connection." This story

---

[4] It was Mallette who had been an assistant in the food analysis laboratory and who had, under instructions, given me difficult unknowns to "get rid" of me. I heard the story from him at about this time.

began as a result of a conversation Campbell and I had gotten into over my story "The Hunted." After *Thrilling Wonder* had rejected that story, I tried it on Campbell, who shook his head, and in the conversation that followed, free association seemed to give rise to the notion of a co-operative society of intelligent bears threatened by an aggressive society of intelligent chimpanzees.

I wasn't too enamored of the idea so that it went slowly, but I was determined to finish it. After all, it was neither a robot story nor a Foundation story, and with few exceptions, every story I had written in the past six years had been either one or the other. I was becoming anxious not to find myself in a Foundation/robot rut.

On May 20, I finally finished it, and took it in to Campbell on the twenty-sixth. It was 7,500 words long, and on May 31, I received a welcome check for $150.

In my conversation with Campbell on the twenty-sixth, however, something rather unusual came up. It came about this way:

In running my chronometric experiments, I put my enzyme solution into the vessel first and then quickly dumped the catechol solution into it. The enzyme reaction starts at once. First, of course, I had to prepare the catechol solution fresh, for it would undergo spontaneous changes that would make the experiment meaningless if it were allowed to stand around too long.

At the beginning of each day, therefore, I would prepare the catechol solution. I would weigh out a fixed quantity of solid catechol, which comes as white, very fluffy, needlelike crystals, and then I would dump it little by little into a beaker of distilled water.

Catechol, as it happens, is very readily soluble, especially when it exists as fluffy crystals that present a large surface to the water. The result is that as soon as the catechol touches the surface of the water it dissolves. It just seems to vanish without ever penetrating the water's skin.

As I watched it one morning[5] I thought idly: What if it dissolves just *before* it hits the water?

That, I thought at once, might make the basis for a science-fiction story.

But then I thought again. It would not be long now before I would have to write up my research observations in the form of a long and complicated dissertation. That dissertation would have to be written in a convoluted and stylized fashion or it would never pass.

I dreaded that. I had spent nine years now trying to learn to write clearly and well, and now I would have to write a dissertation tur-

[5] I did not record, in my diary, exactly which morning, but it could not have been long before May 26, 1947.

gidly and sloppily. It would be even worse than doing a Navy Yard specification, and I didn't know how I could bear it.

Well then, instead of writing a story about a compound that dissolved before it hit the water, why not write a mock dissertation about it? Why not deliberately write turgidly and sloppily and in this way draw the fangs of the monster?

I suggested such a thing to Campbell on that May 26, and he laughed and said, "Go try it."

On that same May 26 something else happened. *Thrilling Wonder*, despite its rejection of "The Hunted," still insisted it wanted *Astounding*-type stories from me, so before I visited Campbell that day, I had dropped in to see the editor of *Thrilling Wonder*. The editor was, at this time, Sam Merwin, Jr. (his father and namesake had been a well-known author and editor).

It was the first time we had met. Sam, a plump and friendly man, told me that not only did he want a story from me but also he wanted a 40,000-word lead novel for *Startling Stories*, the sister magazine of *Thrilling Wonder*. *Startling* featured such a lead novel in every issue, and good ones were hard to come by. I was enamored with the notion myself, since 40,000 words at $.02 a word came to $800, so I agreed to try.

I got to work on the story for Merwin on June 2. I called it "Grow Old with Me." This was supposed to be a quotation from Robert Browning's "Rabbi ben Ezra" and should have been "Grow Old Along with Me," but I remembered the line incorrectly and didn't bother checking.

It dealt with an old tailor who managed to get transferred into a future in which old people underwent euthanasia unless they could prove themselves useful to society. The problem was to work out a way in which an old tailor from the past could prove useful enough to a society of the future to be kept alive. I was so excited at the thought of $800 that I did ten pages that first day and five the day after.

Then, on June 5, unable to resist the other project, I began writing my mock dissertation, which I called, in true dissertation form, "The Endochronic Properties of Resublimated Thiotimoline." (I had intended a still longer title but it would have to fit into the *Astounding* Table of Contents and I would have to be realistic about it.) I finished it on June 8, complete with tables, graphs, and with references to nonexistent journals, and then took it in to Campbell.

I didn't hear from him immediately, but when I called him on June 20, he said he would take it. It was only 3,000 words long (the joke wouldn't carry for longer than that), but $60 was a pleasant sum for a couple of hours' work on each of four days, and I was delighted when the check arrived on August 15.

By July 1, I had some 12,000 words of first draft done on "Grow Old with Me," and I took it in to Merwin as proof I was working. To my not-altogether-pleased surprise, he asked to read it, and told me to come back in the afternoon. I did and he told me he had looked over it, liked it, and only hoped I could keep it up. I assured him I could.

28

On June 26, 1947, meanwhile, Stanley was graduated from Brooklyn Technical High School, a month before his eighteenth birthday. Gertrude and I held the fort in the candy store while the rest of the family attended the exercises.

Stanley planned to go to New York University and had gotten a $100-a-year scholarship there. My father shook his head and said that a $200-a-year scholarship was required. (Tuition fees had risen since my day.) There was still the possibility of a state scholarship, however.

When I learned of this, I promptly said that if the state scholarship didn't come through, I could make up the $100-a-year difference myself.

I made the offer eagerly. I was proud that my savings from the Navy Yard and the Army and that my earnings from my writings made it possible to offer $400 without its seriously affecting my solvency. My father, however, flatly refused my repeated offer.

29

In early July, we received letters from Bob Heinlein that pointedly did not mention Leslyn, and Gertrude said, at once, that they were splitting up.

I refused to believe it, but she was right, of course. A letter from Sprague confirmed it. I promptly wrote to Bob expressing sympathy over his marital problems, and he wrote back just as promptly saying he had no marital problems. I took it to mean that his marital problems had been solved by separation, so I said no more.

30

I took a course in the summer of 1947 on advanced organic theory. It was designed to help bring me up to date on the new theories that had taken over in my absence during the war. These represented the ap-

plication of quantum mechanics to organic chemistry, the use of electronic formulas and of the phenomenon of "resonance," which stabi-
lized certain chemical configurations and not others, the studies of
reaction intermediates, and the prediction of the course of chemical
change in the light of such things.

All these had made their appearance before the war, even as long
ago as in Linus Pauling's *The Nature of the Chemical Bond,* which was
first published in 1932. The notions had been penetrating the schools
only slowly, however, and had then suddenly saturated instruction during the war years—just in time for me to miss it.

It's not surprising, then, that I had a difficult time with it, as did
most of the class, and in the end I took a cowardly H (which simply
meant "attended" and involved neither mark nor credit), as did most
of the class.

In addition to taking the course, I spent the summer of 1947 making endless calculations concerning my chronometric observations. I
was trying to find the most satisfactory theories, the clearest explanations of what was happening—in short, the best possible way of arranging my forthcoming dissertation.

And I also spent it on "Grow Old with Me." On August 3, I began
to put the accumulated first draft into final copy. By August 27, I had
quite a bit of it in final copy and took it in to Merwin for an interim report, so to speak. Again, he wanted to read it. I called him the next day
and again found he liked it. He urged me to continue at full speed.

43

Windsor Place Again

1

On August 10, a working telephone was finally installed in our apartment, only eleven months after we had applied for one. It was the first telephone I had ever had that was entirely my own and that did not require that we put a coin into it.

Naturally, it was a wonderful toy to begin with, and we called up everyone we knew that took only a local call.

But there was no time for euphoria, for we were once more having apartment problems. Our year's rent carried us through August, and we now had to make up our minds whether to renew for another year.

It didn't really seem that we had much choice. We had tried, on and off, to find other apartments. We had, for instance, applied for an apartment in Stuyvesant Town, a huge complex being built on the East Side of Manhattan between Fourteenth Street and Twenty-third Street. The trouble was we had never heard anything from it. Nor had we heard from other applications we had made. It looked as though we would have to stay put.

But then, on August 8, my parents had a proposition for us. They owned the house they lived in, remember. They lived downstairs and the tenant lived upstairs. Soon after I had come out of the Army and was looking for an apartment, my parents wondered if I could move in with them, but there was no way they could kick out the tenants and, in any case, I didn't want them to. Living with my parents would offer problems enough without my having to feel guilty about where the previous tenants were living once we had turned them out.

But it now turned out that the tenants were moving out of their own accord. The apartment would be empty and ready for us, and it would be six rooms. How about it?

It put Gertrude and me in an almost unbearable bind. After a full year in a room and a half, six rooms seemed like such space, such palatial luxury. On the other hand, it meant living in the same house with my parents, and neither one of us wanted this. With the best will in the world, my parents would interfere with and restrict our freedom.

My parents then upped the ante by saying they would spend

$1,500 on renovating the tenants' apartment and move in themselves. They would then let us have the superior downstairs apartment—which would mean Gertrude would not have to climb stairs.

On August 21, we made our decision. We would move into my parents' house. It would be our fifth move since we married.

There would be difficulties, of course, quite apart from combining the roles of parents and landlord. For one thing, after five years in small apartments we had never accumulated any significant amount of furniture. We didn't even have a proper bed, since we had always had a Murphy bed, or had made use of a convertible couch. How would we fill six rooms?

In addition, my parents' apartment didn't have the usual amenities of modernity. For instance, a refrigerator did not come with it. We would have to buy one and, in fact, the moment we decided to move, we began shopping and, on August 29, bought a refrigerator for delivery on October 1. It cost us $225 and it was rather a revelation to me that the time had come when I could consider such purchases as possible. Nine years before a bill of $60 for the purpose of fixing my teeth had seemed so impossible that the only practical alternative seemed to have been to let my teeth rot.

On occasion we would drop in at my parents' and watch new flooring being put down in the apartment they were going to use, and new wall sockets; then we would go out and shop for a bed.

Such problems are not colossal. There are many worse things than having to take the trouble to buy items you can afford for a new living space far more spacious than your old and scarcely any the more expensive. It was, however, tedious. Neither Gertrude nor I enjoyed shopping, and I myself was trying to organize my research into an acceptable dissertation and was also trying to finish "Grow Old with Me," my most ambitious writing undertaking since "The Mule." I hated the time it took to shop and I hated the general dislocations of moving.

2

A welcome break came toward the end of the month of August.

It was time for the annual world science-fiction convention—the fifth. I had missed the second, third, and fourth, which were held in far-distant places such as Chicago and Denver. The fifth, however, was to be held in Philadelphia, and heaven knows I could reach that.

To be sure, the world science-fiction convention had become a multiday affair held over the Labor Day weekend. What with the question of moving and shopping filling our thoughts and our days, we could not go for the entire weekend, but we could manage one day—Saturday, August 30, 1947.

We took the 9:00 A.M. train to Philadelphia and visited Meisel to begin with. After a small lunch we went to the hotel where the convention was in progress. I greeted many of the people whom I already knew well—Campbell and de Camp, notably—to say nothing of newer friends such as George O. Smith and Sam Merwin.

George O. Smith, I remember, catching us alone, semi-amused us with a long disquisition on the advantages of masturbation over other forms of sexual activity.

I met Edward E. "Doc" Smith for the first time. From the late 1920s and through the 1930s right up to the rise of Heinlein, Doc Smith was the most towering figure in science fiction, thanks to the enormous scope of his novels. He was the first, in his story "The Skylark of Space," to deal with interstellar flight, as opposed to mere interplanetary ventures. He was a gray-haired, fatherly figure, fifty-seven at the time, and very popular, even though it was well recognized that he was no longer at the growing edge of the field.

There was also present Lloyd Eshbach, who was a science-fiction book publisher. He had a small publishing firm that put out limited editions of science-fiction favorites. The editions did not make very much money, but to have magazine science fiction in book form was an awe-inspiring thing. He told me he would like to publish the Foundation series in book form. I said I was perfectly willing—but nothing ever came of it.[1]

After dinner, Meisel and I went out to the de Camps and stayed the evening. Catherine was her usual endearingly voluble self, and managed to tell us that she had posed in the nude for Bob Heinlein (with Leslyn present, of course) and, when she described the pose, I suddenly remembered the pictures I had seen in Campbell's place 5½ years before.

I said, in energetic astonishment, "Was that *you*?"

"Why, yes," she said.

And Sprague, with his own gift for understatement, lifted his eyebrows and said mildly to Catherine, "My dear, you get an *F* for discretion."

Whenever I try to think of Sprague at his most characteristic, and

---

[1] I heard later that the convention voted for "favorite author" and I finished in eleventh place. Henry Kuttner was in first place.

his most lovable, it is that moment that comes back—the raised eyebrows and the look of mild rebuke.

3

Then we went home. We spent Labor Day (September 1) at the Bronx Zoo, with Roy Machlowitz. It was my first visit there and the first time I ever saw such animals as gibbons, hummingbirds, and a panda. The duck-bill platypus was the great attraction of the zoo at the time, but the building that housed them was closed by the time we got to it—so to this day I've never seen a platypus.

My mother's fifty-second birthday came on September 5, 1947, and when we visited her to commemorate the day, we found that she had discovered what everyone discovers when they undertake anything to do with building or renovation: The actual expense invariably outstrips the estimate. They had planned to spend $1,500 and it was costing $2,000.

I was uneasy about that, of course, since I felt that it was my duty as a son to offer to pick up the tab for anything over $1,500, but that was certainly not my duty as a tenant—and the incompatibility of the two roles bothered me.

The incompatibility became more acute when my parents became aware that we were planning to furnish the apartment rather skimpily, with a view to moving out eventually. After all, we couldn't possibly expect it to be our lifetime home—but that, apparently, was exactly what my parents thought it would be, or should be.

There were arguments between us on the matter (myself and my parents, that is, for Gertrude wisely did not interfere), and I was more than ever determined that though we would move in for the experience of space at last, we would move out when something better came along.

My attitude toward my mother's attempt to dictate our system of buying furniture was described as follows in my diary: "I was very, very peeved indeed because what the hell business is it of hers?"—which puts it in a nutshell.

4

I had to look toward the future in other ways, too. I was certain that sometime in 1948 I would complete my research, get my degree, and be out in the cold world. It meant I would need a job, for nothing in my nine years' career as a professional writer gave me any cause to suppose that I could ever support myself with my typewriter.

Until now I had always postponed the evil day of job-hunting by choosing to go on with further education (except for the emergency days of World War II, when the job came hunting me), but now surely that would have to come to an end. What to do?

One avenue opened up with the annual convention of the American Chemical Society, which was to be held in New York in 1947.

The chief activities at such conventions involved the presentation of papers, but in addition there was set up a kind of temporary and concentrated employment bureau. The convention offered prospective employers a dense gathering of young men and women about to leave school, so there was a clearinghouse where students could list their qualifications, and employers their needs. It was to be hoped that happy career marriages could be made by fitting one to the other.

On September 13, then, I registered for the convention, and the next day I registered at the employment clearinghouse. With my usual Asimovian flare for relying on lofty principles when that was not advisable, I added to the card on which I listed my vital statistics and my qualifications the totally unnecessary note: "Not interested in any work having any connection with the atomic bomb."

This was stupid, since no one was likely to offer me such work, and if anyone did, I could always have turned it down. As it was, I made myself seem like a trouble-making radical, and you can guess the result. Throughout the entire five days of the convention, I received not one call to an interview—not one. I drew a complete blank.

On September 15, however, as I was walking through the lobby of the hotel, I noticed approaching me from one side none other than Milton Silverman, one of my boon companions at Columbia before World War II, and from the other, Al Cooper, with whom I had studied for desperate hours prior to my second and successful try at the Qualifyings. We met in a three-point coalescence.

It made for an excited afternoon of being brought up to date. All three of us were now married, but Silverman and Cooper each had a child. Furthermore, each lived in Queens, each had a job, and each was dissatisfied with his job. I felt a little backward and embarrassed at still being in school.

I persuaded Silverman to get his wife, and Gertrude and I took them both to dinner and had them spend the evening at our apartment. The next day I spent with Cooper. He got one call for an interview.

Cooper was making $4,500 a year, which to me seemed beyond the dreams of avarice. Silverman, I speculated in my diary, "is probably getting even more." Then I wondered, "So why is Cooper so poor? He only has one suit, etc., etc."

The utter failure at the convention put me under a dank blanket

of apprehension concerning the future. I had for quite a while been totally absorbed in the gathering success of my research—the clear indication that I would have an interesting dissertation and therefore my degree. I couldn't help but view that as the climax of my education and
my life, almost as though I were envisaging a cartoon in which I stood
on a podium with light radiating from my head, stars going on and off,
and the caption reading, "Success!"

Except that that's not how life is. It goes on, and by the time I
had my degree, I must also have a job, and how was I going to get that?
Aside from the lack of interest at the convention, the fact was that the
job market had been declining steadily since the war, and as a Jew who
spoke with a Brooklyn accent and, as anyone could tell at a single
glance, lacked sophistication and poise, I was scarcely in the first rank
of candidates for any job.

5

There was the other side of my life—writing. After a summer's
solid work, I finished "Grow Old with Me" on September 22, 1947, and
it was forty-eight thousand words long. Only "The Mule" had been
longer, and not by much.

On the twenty-third, I took it in to Sam Merwin, who instantly
greeted me with the news that Leo Margulies, his boss, had decided
that the attempt to publish *Astounding*-type stories was a failure and
he now wanted blood-and-thunder *Amazing*-type stories.

I shrugged that off. After all, he had specifically ordered this story,
and on two separate occasions he had read portions, approved them,
and urged me to continue. Whatever the requirements for the future,
therefore, he was committed to this story, in my opinion. My chief fear
was that he was going to use the change in policy as a device to get me
to accept a lower word-rate. I told him quite firmly that $.02 a word
was the price agreed upon.

Then, on September 25, I registered at Columbia University and
began my thirteenth year as a student there. (Even during my years in
the Navy Yard and the Army, I was kept on the Columbia books as a
student in good standing.) Half my entire life, almost, had been spent
at Columbia.

Meanwhile, my parents moved upstairs into the renovated apartment, the downstairs apartment was cleaned up and readied for us, furniture began arriving from the various places at which we had ordered
it, and finally, on September 29, 1947, we moved into 192 Windsor
Place. Once again it was an easy job and a cheap one. It cost only
$9.00. We had been in Dean Street just about thirteen months.

The biggest pang was giving up the telephone. We had waited eleven months for it, but had had it only forty days. Now we would have to wait again. (Of course, we could always use my parents' phone in an emergency, but it was precisely that sort of entanglement I dreaded.)

6

On October 1, I called Merwin to find out what progress had been made in connection with "Grow Old with Me" and, to my horror, he told me it might be rejected. "Cross your fingers," he said. I felt more like crossing his head with a brick.

If that weren't enough to depress me, we had a feeling of letdown over the new apartment. It was large by our previous standard, of course, but it was also old-fashioned and gloomy. It was quite clear we would have to continue to search for new apartments and be prepared to move again.

About the only bright spot was school. On the morning of September 27, a Saturday, I met with Dawson, taking advantage of the fact that there were no classes that day so that we could talk in private and at leisure.

I spread out all the work I had done over the summer, the calculations, the equations, the theoretical explanations, and he seemed quite pleased.

We were not totally isolated, for the telephone rang while I was there and Dawson said, in part, "Oh *him!* He's one of my best students. He's going places, that boy is. He'll be finished about the middle of the year."

It was obvious he was speaking of me (actually, it was in connection with a possible job that, it turned out, I did not want). I discounted the compliments since he could scarcely say anything else with myself sitting right there. I was, however, delighted to know that he thought I would soon be completed.

On October 5, I started writing up my dissertation. It would be a long job, I knew, since there were bound to be places where it would seem to me I needed more data, and then I would have to locate those data and pray everything turned out right.

7

On October 15, after several fruitless calls to Merwin, I got him and he said that the story would need revision. I chased down to his office and asked for Leo Margulies, being unwilling any longer to deal with Merwin.

Out came Merwin, to my annoyance. He told me what revision would be needed and, in brief, it meant throwing away the story, writing a much worse one—and with no guarantee of a sale then, either.

For the first and only time in my life, I openly lost my temper with an editor. I snatched up the manuscript, said, "Go to hell," and stalked angrily out of the office.

It was wrong of me to do that. An editor is entirely within his rights to reject a story, even a story he has ordered. I was not, however, able to think clearly at the time. Twice I had brought in what I had written for his opinions and suggestions—something I had never done for Campbell—and twice he had encouraged me to go ahead.

Furthermore, I had spent the summer working on it and now I felt humiliated. For five years now, when I had worked on a story I would sell it, and Gertrude had come to take that for granted. This time I would have to come to her with a failure and a wasted writing-summer, and I hated that.

I never submitted anything to Merwin again and, for a considerable time, thought of him only with anger.

8

Gertrude had just passed her thirtieth birthday and we still had no children. Recognizing the danger of increasing age in connection with childbirth, we had ceased taking precautions for the past couple of years, but there had been no result.

One difficulty, of course, was that Gertrude's periods were irregular, so it was difficult to tell when she might be ovulating and even more difficult to tell if she had skipped a period.

Of course, I didn't take the attitude that only women could possibly be responsible for any delay in having children, so I had myself examined and I was told I had a low sperm count. Between that and Gertrude's irregularity we realized, by the time we had moved into Windsor Place, that the chances for conception were lower than normal. The doctors we saw uniformly assured us that the chances were *not* zero and that we merely had to be patient, but as the months passed, we lost heart and gradually came to face the fact that we were quite likely to remain childless.

9

As I progressed on my dissertation, I went over it with Dawson, who insisted on considering each sentence at length and deciding how it could be made more accurate.

It was a chore for me because I was used to writing quickly and to consider only my own judgment in such matters. However, I wasn't writing for an editor but for a committee of professors, and Professor Dawson knew better than I how to appease them. I therefore consistently followed his suggestions, although I moaned now and then.

The greatest difficulty arose over my use of the constant M. I had introduced it at the appropriate time to indicate how the well-known chronometric equation, which had appeared in a number of papers emerging from Professor Dawson's group, could be corrected and, by use of it, made more nearly a straight-line function.

After a while, Dawson put down his pen and said, "What is M?"

I was surprised. "Why, you know what it is, Dr. Dawson. It's mixing time."

"Why don't you say so?"

Now I was really surprised. "But Dr. Dawson, if I say so *now*, I kill the suspense." I couldn't believe that I had to explain this.

"Isaac," he said, "I hate to break the news to you, but you're not writing one of your science-fiction stories."

I was horrified. "You mean I have to define M?"

"The instant you first use it."

I did so, though I muttered something about "ruining the whole thing."

It really did spoil my fun and erased any pleasure I could have had in the dissertation. Nor did it really help. Once it was all done and under consideration, one professor was reported to have said, "It reads like a mystery story." And he didn't say it with approval.

10

Our application to Stuyvesant Town, which we had assumed to be dead, suddenly came to life. We had scarcely been in Windsor Place a month when a representative of the development came to investigate us and to ask the same questions we had answered at the time of our first application. Then he left. Nothing had really happened, but it was clear that there were possibilities.

My parents became aware of this and were, of course, furious that we would even dream of leaving.

I was rather bitter. Had this happened two months before, had we known that our chances at Stuyvesant Town still existed, we would surely have stayed in Dean Street and been spared parental complications.

The move from Dean Street had entailed another disappointment.

On November 8[2] I received a postcard from Fred Pohl concerning a new organization.

It seemed that the old Futurians had been revived in a new incarnation. It was called the "Hydra Club" now, precisely because like the old Hydra of the myths, there was a new head growing where the old had been cut off.

Pohl, in his card, invited me to a meeting. He and Lowndes would be there, as well as Lester del Rey and Theodore Sturgeon. Where the old Futurian Club had been a fan organization, the Hydra Club would be an organization of professional writers and editors. (It could have the same membership, however, since so many of the Futurians had graduated, by now, from fans to professionals.)

The only trouble was that the invitation was for the seventh, and there had been a delay because the card had gone to Dean Street first. I missed the meeting and was sorry. (Pohl announced, by the way, that he had been divorced a second time.)

I did attend a Phi Lambda Upsilon smoker on the fourteenth, however. Dawson played the piano and we all sang, with my own voice not the quietest, as you may well imagine.

11

My employment fiasco at the ACS convention two months before was a little eased when an industrial firm finally did ask to interview me through Columbia. I suspect they were not after me specifically, but were going through the list of Columbia soon-to-be graduates.

I spent forty-five minutes with a representative of Carbide and Carbon on November 19, but I wasn't stirred. Their research laboratories were in West Virginia, and I had no intention of going to West Virginia.

12

On November 21, 1947, I finally had a chance to attend a meeting of the Hydra Club.

It was held at the home of Judy Merril down in Greenwich Village and it was there I got to meet her for the first time. Judy was twenty-four at the time, a striking-looking girl, and a quick-witted one who was into women's lib decades ahead of her time. She was the kind of girl who, when her rear end was patted by a man, patted the rear end of the patter.

[2] On this day, an abdominal pain of Marcia's was diagnosed as appendicitis, and the appendix was removed before nightfall.

A number of the old Futurians were there, and there was also a young woman who told me she was a Lesbian. She was the first Lesbian I encountered with the knowledge that that was what she was. I was astonished to see that she looked just like an ordinary woman—I don't know what I expected she would look like.

The young woman may, of course, have been pulling my leg, for I suspect she could see from my reactions to what she said that I was not your cool and suave man-about-town. Her tales instantly became lurid as she described her bisexuality and her orgies and I sat there with my eyes like saucers.

13

On December 16, I got the January 1948 *Astounding*, which had "Now You See It—"[3] as the cover story. Since the writing of "The Mule," I had been turning out few stories and therefore publishing few. My writing career seemed to be creaking to a halt, and I somehow accepted that as a sign that my chemical career was picking up speed.

Unfortunately, my chemical career was not picking up speed in any visible way. Representatives of other industrial firms interviewed me after Carbide and Carbon had, but all of them, without exception, showed a monumental lack of interest. There was every sign that I might reach my degree with empty hands and become a supereducated member of the unemployed.

Industry, however, isn't the only possible source of work. There is also the academic world. I was told that Erwin Brand, a biochemist at Physicians and Surgeons, needed an assistant, so I went up to see him on December 18.

He was a little gnomelike creature, who spoke with machine-gun rapidity between puffs at a cigarette. He chain-smoked. Each cigarette burned down until what was left was virtually invisible between his fingers, and then it grew to full size miraculously. I never quite caught him replacing or lighting a cigarette. He talked without a break for the entire 2¼ hours I was with him.

He didn't exactly offer me the job and I didn't exactly ask for it. In fact, I had the queasy feeling it would be a desperate mistake to take a job with him. He was a prima donna and the trouble was that I was one, too, and there cannot be two on the same project. If I were going

[3] See *Second Foundation* (Gnome, 1953, later Doubleday), where it appears as Part I—"Search by the Mule."

to work for someone it would have to be for a gentle soul with infinite patience and a wide tolerance, like Dawson.

I did ask about the salary out of curiosity. I suggested $4,000 per year and he countered with $3,600. In Navy Yard terms, I was asking for a P3 and he was offering a P2—so that 2½ more years had passed and I still wasn't getting a promotion.

I came back to Columbia quite depressed and Dawson comforted me, telling me I wasn't to take that job and he would be sure to find me a better one. (Poor fellow. He couldn't invent a job where none existed, but then I didn't really expect him to find me one.)

14

Roy Machlowitz came to see us every time he was in New York, it seemed to me. He was in town for ten days over the Christmas season of 1947 and he called up to arrange a trip to some museum. The date set was December 26, 1947.

The forecast on Christmas night was for "light snow" the next day, and I was at once dubious. I don't believe "light snow" forecasts.

When I woke on the morning of the twenty-sixth, there was six inches down and it was still snowing. It was all I needed to see. I called up Roy and canceled the museum bit. Unbelievably, he argued with me. I was adamant. I know a major snowstorm when I see one, and neither Machlowitz nor the Weather Bureau could argue me out of it.

So we stayed home and, on and off, watched the snow pile up to a record one-day fall of *twenty-six inches!*[4] It stopped the city cold.

As I think back on it, I am amazed at how little it affected us. It was the Christmas season, so I didn't have to go in to school. There was no work that had to be done there anyway, and it was best for me to be at home working on my dissertation, which I had been doing for a couple of months now and which was going along swimmingly.

We had no automobile so we didn't have to worry about digging it out. We had no children so we didn't have to worry about milk supplies or anything like that. For that matter, we had plenty of canned food in the house and all was well.

It was, in fact, a rather pleasant day for us as we watched the blanket of snow come down, turning the city quiet and peaceful and clean and white. It was a day on which even the candy store could have been closed. I don't think that ever again was I in a position to watch a

[4] The Weather Bureau managed to stay two inches ahead of the fall all day long, promising an end that never seemed to come.

major snowstorm without having to be concerned and worried in a dozen different ways.

15

The year that ended in snow was a rather icy one from the standpoint of my writing career. I had sold three stories in 1947 as compared with two the year before, and one of my 1947 sales had been quite a long one. Nevertheless, there had been no anthology sales, no Orson Welles money (no "subsidiary sales," in short), and the disappointment of "Grow Old with Me." I ended the year with $710, just a hair under the 1946 mark.

16

I had entered Columbia University as a freshman at fifteen. I celebrated my twenty-eighth birthday on January 2, 1948, and I was still at Columbia.

Later that month—on the fifteenth, to be exact—I picked up a little gray female kitten, three months old. I hadn't had a cat since my single days and I wasn't sure how Gertrude would feel about it. I was delighted to discover that she was as fond of cats as I was.

I tried to call it "Smoky," but Gertrude called it "Putchikl," a kind of Yiddish distortion of "Pussy," and Putchikl it became.

It was a sweet and gentle little cat. We kept its box down in the cellar and it went down there when nature called. We kept it in the cellar (which connected directly with our apartment) when we wanted it out of the way, but if at any time we opened the door and called "Putchikl!" it came running upstairs with some of the sound effects of a team of galloping horses.

In the warm weather, we let it stay in the backyard sometimes, but it quickly learned how to open the window screen from the outside and make its way inside. This could be disconcerting, for when we had it outside overnight it would make its way in at dawn and get into bed with us.

If it merely cuddled down somewhere against our bodies that would have been all right. We wouldn't have minded. Sometimes, though, for some cat reason of its own, it would decide to gaze earnestly into our faces (usually Gertrude's) and wait for us to wake up. The effect of opening one's eyes blearily and finding the whole field of view from end to end filled with a cat's face is a startling one.

Since we fed Putchikl well, it never developed the need to behave as a predator. Once (on May 3, 1948, actually) a little mouse appeared in the kitchen and Gertrude, becoming aware of it, left in a hurry and closed the door. She consulted me, but I was a broken reed. I couldn't imagine what one did to get rid of a mouse, except, perhaps speak crossly to it.

Then Gertrude said, "Putchikl! Of course!" We opened the cellar door and Putchikl came bounding up in great delight. She was snatched up and shoved through the kitchen door, which we opened for the purpose, then closed behind her. We then both listened for the sound of shrieks and screams and tearing flesh and crunching bones. Nothing!

Finally, not knowing what could possibly have happened, we opened the kitchen door a crack and peeked in. There was the mouse sitting in the middle of the floor, clearly the unconcerned ruler of the room, and there, on a chair and looking very uneasy, was Putchikl.

Gertrude said, "Oh hell!," got a broom, and disposed of the mouse herself. She was very angry with Putchikl for the rest of the day.

44

Doctor of Philosophy

1

My dissertation was coming along slowly but steadily. I kept thinking of new ways of describing the manner in which the enzyme lost its activity as it worked, and every once in a while I had to run more tests under new conditions to test this facet or other.

It was the job situation that upset me and I grew more and more uneasy as the weeks passed.

Then, on January 20, 1948, a new opening arrived from a totally unexpected direction: Elderfield approached me. Elderfield!

For over eight years I had considered him the leading anti-Asimovian in the department, the one who above anyone else was convinced that I was not doctoral material. Yet without warning he offered me a postdoctoral position as his assistant.

It was the sort of job that had seemed possible with Brand, but Elderfield offered me $4,500 a year, more than I would have had the nerve to ask. I was to work forty hours a week, have two to three weeks' vacation, have technicians under me, and a good, solid problem.

Elderfield was working on antimalarials at the time. During World War II, malaria was a serious problem for soldiers in tropical climates. In fact, it was the most deadly disease in the world in that there were more people suffering and dying from malaria the world over than from any other serious ailment.

The chemical used to control malaria was quinine, but during the war, the Japanese controlled the main sources of quinine for a while and the Americans had to develop artificial antimalarials, synthetic chemicals that would do the work of quinine.

This had been done successfully, and Elderfield had worked on the problem. Now he was anxious to turn to the theoretical end—to find out *why* synthetic antimalarials worked and to use this knowledge to design an antimalarial that would work better than any other, and better than quinine, too.

I was tempted, even though I didn't know that I could get along with Elderfield, because the problem seemed interesting. I talked to Morris Kupchan who was running the problem and who was leaving, so that I would be replacing him—and he said the whole deal was excellent. He said there was absolutely nothing wrong with it in any way, provided I got along with Elderfield.

It was a relief. The degree was coming in just a few months and now, if I agreed to go in with Elderfield, it would not find me without a job. To be sure, it was not really a *job*—it was postdoctoral research, a position in which at best I could not stay many years and in which I was quite likely to stay only a single year. In a sense it would be as though once again I had opted for still more education while I postponed the real job crisis.

But I had to. And even a single year was one year in which I could continue trying.

I won't say it was satisfactory. Ever since 1939, when I had first failed to enter medical school, I had been improvising from year to year. Nine years had passed; it was 1948; I was twenty-eight years old; I was still improvising.

2

Fred Pohl was feeling the urge toward agenthood once again. He asked me where I stood as far as sales were concerned and I told him that for years I had been selling Campbell everything I wrote and had nothing outstanding—except "Grow Old with Me."

What was that? Fred wanted to know.

I explained and he offered to try to sell it for me. I had no great hopes. I had shown it to Campbell after *Thrilling Wonder* had turned it down, and Campbell said it might do as a complete-in-one-issue lead novel, but that in *Astounding* it would have to appear in two parts, and there was no natural break-point. He had other criticisms, too, which made me feel that even if there were a natural break-point, he wouldn't have taken it.

It turned out, though, that a young man named Martin Greenberg,[1] whom I had not yet met, was thinking of going into the science-fiction book-publishing business, and Fred thought he might be talked into doing "Grow Old with Me." There wouldn't be much money in it, but a book was rare in the science-fiction world and it would involve much prestige. It might lead to better things, and why allow a manuscript to do nothing but eat its head off in a drawer?

[1] Warning! Years later, I met and worked with *another* Martin Greenberg, one whose middle name is Harry. These are two different people and must not be confused. The one I refer to here does not have a middle name and I will generally refer to him as Marty. The other, later Martin Greenberg, when I refer to him, will be Marty the Other.

Me and Bill Boyd, 1947.

The "Cary Grant" picture of me, used on Pebble in the Sky *and other early Doubleday titles.*

doubleday
science
fiction

pebble
in the
sky

isaac
asimov

The jacket for Pebble in the Sky, 1950.

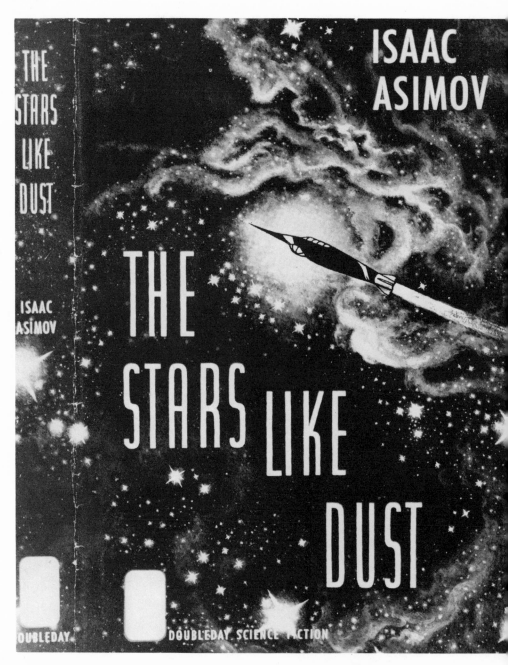

The jacket for The Stars Like Dust, *1951.*

At Hydracon, 1950. From left to right: Lester Del Rey, Evelyn Harrison, Harry Harrison, me, Judy Merril, Fred Pohl, Poul Anderson, Sprague de Camp, and P. Schuyler Miller.
PHOTO BY JAY K. KLEIN

Harry Stubbs (Hal Clement). PHOTO BY JAY K. KLEIN

Arthur C. Clarke. PHOTO BY JAY K. KLEIN

Harlan Ellison. PHOTO BY JAY K. KLEIN

John D. Clark. PHOTO BY JAY K. KLEIN

John Campbell and Evelyn Gold (of Galaxy) sharing a Hugo in Philadelphia in 1953. Gertrude is right in front of John. Willy Ley is on the extreme right with Mrs. Ley next to him.

I agreed with the logic and gave the manuscript to Fred. On January 31, Fred called to say that Greenberg wanted the manuscript. For a while, I really thought I was going to have a book, and I began to think I was lucky that Merwin had rejected it.

3

On February 1, Gertrude and I went to visit Milton Silverman and his wife at Forest Hills. It turned out that Silverman, after three years at a job, was making $5,000 a year, which made a starting salary of $4,500 with Elderfield seem pretty good.

What's more, Silverman didn't think I'd have gotten along with Brand, whom apparently he knew, and that relieved my feeling that perhaps I might have made the wrong decision in rejecting Brand (who had become more anxious to get me—perhaps because he found he was having trouble getting anyone else).

4

February 17, 1948, was the silver anniversary of the family's arrival in the United States.

Quite independently, it was also the day the March 1948 *Astounding* reached the stands. It contained "Endochronic Properties of Resublimated Thiotimoline."[2]

The previous June, when I had sold it to Campbell, I had feared it might come out not long before I was slated to be up for my doctorate and that it might be used to prove I lacked the proper gravity of character to make a good chemist. (It had, after all, been my effervescence and irreverence that had, at least in part, stood in my way as far as passing the Qualifyings and getting a promotion at the Navy Yard were concerned.)

So I asked Campbell to run the article under a pseudonym. I even picked the pseudonym, though I don't remember what it was. Campbell agreed, and that was that.

Now came February 17. Sharing my laboratory in those days were two other research students of Dawson. One was William Tarpley, a quiet, competent fellow who worked with a firm in New Jersey and who had been given time off to get his degree. The other was Morris Joselow, a large-faced, stoutish fellow.

It was Tarpley who introduced the subject that morning. He said,

[2] See *The Early Asimov.*

"Hey, that was a funny satire on chemistry by you in the new *Astounding,* Isaac."

I grinned foolishly and beamed with pride, as I always do on such occasions, and said, "Thanks."

And then after a goodish time, I suddenly remembered the pseudonym, and said, rather stiffly, "What makes you think the article was by me?"

Tarpley thought about it for a while and said, "Well, when I noticed your name on it, I thought, 'Gee, I'll bet he wrote it.'"

And Joselow said at once, "Don't tell me you put your own name on a satire on chemistry when your dissertation is coming up?"

Since that was precisely the thought that flashed through my mind, I went off and called Campbell.

Campbell remembered I had asked him to use a pseudonym, but he had an explanation for failing to do so. "I forgot," he said.

Perhaps Campbell forgot out of an instinctive feeling that forgetting was the proper thing to do. He had a number of infallible instincts.

For one thing, as I found out from Campbell a few weeks later, the article proved to be a howling success with the readers. He received a flood of letters from them and, as a matter of fact, interest in the article has never died down.[3]

Campbell said that some readers had even fallen for it and thought thiotimoline was a real compound. They flooded the New York Public Library (he said) demanding to see the journals I had quoted and were reluctant to believe the librarians who assured them there were no such journals.

Then, too, the thiotimoline article seemed to tickle the fancy of every chemist who happened to be a science-fiction fan. By word of mouth it spread to chemists who never read science fiction. I began to get requests to have it printed in obscure little periodicals put out by chemical associations. I got letters from chemists who clearly did not know I had ever written anything else.

The thiotimoline article was, in fact, the first thing I had ever written that made any mark at all outside the closed circle of science fictiondom—and I owed it to Campbell's forgetfulness.

But that still left me in trouble at home, and if I thought it would escape the eyes of the Columbia chemists, I was crazy. The very day after its appearance, Professor William von Doering, a young organic

---

[3] Indeed, inspired by the success, he tried in later years to have a gag article now and then, but they were rarely successful, unless I wrote them—even if I do say so myself.

chemist who was already making his mark in the world and who was himself the kind of eccentric who wore bow ties in a world of four-in-hands, stopped me in the hall to make humorous references to it. I also found out that another member of the department was a rabid science-fiction fan, so he couldn't possibly have missed it. And if two members knew, then there was no hope of secrecy—everyone would know.

I was sunk in misery and decided that I would never pass my Oral Examinations.

5

There was worse to come. For six months I had been fiddling proudly with a mechanism for the inactivation of the enzyme. I had postulated two kinds of inactivation, one being reversible and one not. By picking my reaction rates appropriately, I could neatly explain my observations.

Professor Dawson remained dubious about the mechanism but I kept pushing it with great self-confidence and was putting it into my dissertation.

Then, on March 1, 1948, while trying to disprove some alternate models suggested by Professor Dawson, I suddenly found myself disproving my own! As I said in my diary, "I found that out definitely at 4:00 P.M. and it was like a cold hand grabbing my heart and not letting go."

The props were knocked out from under my thesis. There was no way I could go through with that mechanism in the hope that nobody would notice, even if that would square with my peculiar sense of ethics, which it did not. It might have taken me six months to spot the fallacy, but Dawson, who was not an expert in kinetics, was uneasy with it from the start, and there would be bound to be someone on the committee who would see the error at a glance.

But if I abandoned the mechanism, I could not complete my dissertation, and I would not get my Ph.D. I would have to start all over again—perhaps even on another problem.

At 4:00 P.M. on March 1, 1948, then, I saw my Ph.D. go glimmering down the same path as "Grow Old with Me" had gone. Was this what it had all come to, all those years of child prodigiousness—just one coruscating, spectacular failure?

I had to do something. I couldn't see Dawson. He was in conference with another professor who had ripped up the dissertation of a fellow student. (That sort of thing *did* happen!)

So I went to the Henry Paper Box Company, where Gertrude was engaged in her usual stint, and insisted on going to the movies. This was in accordance with a theory of mine in which, under the pressure of panic, the thinking process goes into a circular rut from which it cannot emerge. The thing to do, then, is to distract one's self just enough to free the thinking and yet not distract one's self so much that thinking ceases altogether. The best way (for me) is to see a superficial movie that amuses the skin of my brain but not the muscle underneath.

We went to see Bob Hope in *Where There's Life*, which was perfect for the purpose. I emerged with a couple of alternate mechanisms that avoided the fallacy and that might, however, explain the observations.

By March 5, I finally got to see Dawson, explained the fallacy shamefacedly, and suggested the alternate mechanism, which I had bounced off Tarpley successfully and which was so much simpler that no fallacy could hide in it.

Dawson was, as usual, not surprised either at my stupidity or at the way I owned up to it, and was his usual encouraging self. He had me see some faculty members who specialized in such matters and I received a quick education from them.

I went back to writing the dissertation on the new basis, and the sense of panic subsided. In March, I saw Dawson nearly every other day and spent hours, it seemed to me, on single paragraphs. The deadline for turning in the dissertation in completed form was April 15, and I have never approached an income-tax deadline with the sense of desperately racing against time as I did that one.

6

As was predictable, I began complicating my new mechanism to make it seem more spectacular, but this time Dawson would allow me no display of erratic brilliance. Firmly, he drew me back to the original simplicity.

On March 21, we finished the dissertation, which reached the point where we were both as satisfied as we were likely to be. The next step was to produce the finished copy for distribution to the various professors who would make up the examination committee. That meant seven copies, typed as clearly and as error-free as possible. It meant a Table of Contents, a list of acknowledgments, neat tables, and diagrams carefully drawn and reproduced.

I began on the twenty-third, typing slowly and taking half an hour per page. It took all day to do fourteen pages. The next day I went to the School of Engineering and was taught how to use the equipment that would reproduce certain tracings I needed. (This was before the day of Xerox duplications.)

They also told me how much they would charge to do my diagrams for me in professional form. It came to as much as $40, and I was struck dumb. Professor Dawson said, "Do your own!"

Both Joselow and Tarpley had drafting equipment, and both brought theirs in. I learned how to use that, too, and, working as carefully as I could (considering my well-known lack of deftness), I made my own drawings.

I finished the dissertation, all seventy-four pages of it (enough length to make a good Foundation novelette, but with infinitely more sweating and less enjoyment) on April 3, and went over the whole thing, proofreading it with Stanley's help.[4]

On April 5, I had all the copies neatly bound and gave the original to Professor Dawson. At his suggestion, I then got tabs and placed them in each copy in such a manner that the interviewers could easily turn to any of the tables, figures, or appendices.

I still have several copies of the dissertation. The title is "The Kinetics of the Reaction Inactivation of Tyrosinase During Its Catalysis of the Aerobic Oxidation of Catechol," a far worse title than that of my thiotimoline satire.

What's more, I achieved a far more involuted and turgid academese than I had dared put into my satire. Here is a sentence taken at random from my dissertation: "It will be recalled that an analysis of the Chronometric Equation (see Section: The Q-t RELATIONSHIP) led to the conclusion that if the equation satisfactorily expressed the entire reaction course, the time required for half the original enzyme to be inactivated was independent of the initial enzyme concentration (see Equ. 8) and that the overall rate of enzyme inactivation was proportional to the 1.5 power of the concentration of active enzyme present in the system at any time (see Equ. 12)."

That's one sentence and it's enough. No need to risk coagulation of the brain by going any farther.

On April 6, my examining committee was chosen. There was Dawson himself, of course, together with Beaver, Dodson, Ralph S. Halford, and Charles G. King from the Chemistry Department. There was also David E. Green, a noted biochemist, from the Medical School, and Ryan from the Biology Department. The date of the examination was set for May 20, 1948, and I had six weeks to amuse myself by studying

---

[4] Stanley had managed to get the money to go to New York University, was finishing his freshman year, and was doing well.

desperately, by attempting to foretell the questions I would be asked, and by trying to find out from others what Doctor's Orals were like.

7

It was hard to believe during the month of March that anything at all existed outside the dissertation, but dimly I was aware of the great world outside. The Cold War was in full swing now and the Soviet Union was blockading West Berlin, so that we seemed almost at the edge of a shooting war again.

On April 9, in fact, a draft bill was offered that would subject those from eighteen to thirty to a new heightened draft, with a year of Army service required to gain deferment. Since I had had less than nine months of Army service and was still under thirty, a faint echo of the old feeling returned. The Army *again*? Had I outsmarted myself by too efficiently achieving a discharge?

It came to nothing, of course, but it reconciled me to civilian life, however hard I thought the dissertation period was.

My GI Bill of Rights benefits were running out but they would last just through that spring, and that should carry me through my Doctor's Orals. I was selfishly glad I had applied for the benefits against my principles, since they had paid all my educational expenses since my return to research.

What's more, it seemed that Gertrude was finally being replaced at the Henry Paper Box Company and that an accountancy student would come in three afternoons a week to do the bookkeeping.

It did mean that the family income was drying up. No more GI Bill of Rights, no more paycheck for Gertrude, and to top it off, I hadn't sold a single story so far in 1948. I hadn't even written one.

None of the leads into industrial jobs that I had followed during the winter were turning up anything, and the word was that Elderfield had failed to get some of the government grants he had applied for. I suddenly felt that even Elderfield's offer might not be secure.

It was fortunate that the upcoming Doctor's Orals filled my mind, or I would have been in a state of deep economic apprehension.

I did succeed in achieving a state of deep academic apprehension, however. On April 23, a fellow student working under Dawson, a woman named Irene Eiger, was up for her Orals, and all the students expecting Orals of their own came in for what we called the "death watch."

It wasn't just grisliness, you understand. The idea was to get her to tell us, in detail, all that happened. That would give the rest of us some idea of the climate of things, and we might then utilize the knowledge to prepare ourselves better for when it was our turn.

Unfortunately, Miss Eiger had a very rough time.

There are, generally, two types of responses to a Doctor's Orals. One is paralysis which, at its extreme, leaves you unable to answer any question, including "What is your name?" The other is hysteria, which at its extreme leads you to respond to "What is your name?" with a long, jolly peal of laughter.

Miss Eiger's response was, apparently, the former. Her dissertation was accepted, but she would have to repeat the Orals in September.

My heart sank. It seemed a bad omen for me, and I sought out Dawson for some much-needed commiseration, consolation, and fatherly patting. I finally found him walking down the main stairs. I went up to meet him.

"Dr. Dawson," I said, "Irene has just failed her Orals and . . ."

"Yes, I know," he said, walking briskly past me upon business of his own. "That's why I'm glad you're next. You'll show 'em."

It was nice he had faith in me, but I had no faith in myself.

My own dissertation had been approved for examination by six of the seven committeemen. Only Dodson remained to be heard from. Unless I got approval from him too, it meant that the dissertation would have to be revised to meet his objections, and that could mean a terrible delay. From day to day I agonized, trying to get Dodson to the point without offending him.

When Dodson finally came through, on April 26, it was with only "Qualified Approval." He wanted minor revisions. For one thing, he objected to my kinetics terminology, which incensed me at once, for I had carefully used the precise terminology used by Samuel Glasstone in his *Textbook of Physical Chemistry*. I saw Dodson on April 28, and it wasn't as bad as I had feared. He was perfectly pleasant and I was able to answer some of his objections, and I then introduced some minor revisions to satisfy the rest.

Dawson would not let me make the corrections in pen and ink, as I had assumed I would be able to. He insisted on retyping any page that had to be revised even by the omission of a single word. That meant six pages had to be retyped.

I accepted as a good omen the fact that on May 4, I was initiated into Sigma Xi, the scientists' honorary fraternity. I received a diploma and I attended a formal dinner at which Irving Langmuir spoke on rainmaking. He spoke to excellent effect for sixty minutes. Unfortunately, he went on to speak for thirty minutes more, and the audience grew restless. I learned from that that sixty minutes is the maximum length for any after-dinner speech.

8

I was still capable of losing sleep over matters not related to my dissertation. We were keeping Putchikl in the backyard regularly now, but expected her to come bounding happily to us whenever we called her. We also noticed that a big ugly tomcat was keeping company with her. We didn't like his looks at all and disapproved of the relationship, but Putchikl ignored our lectures and seemed to find him tolerable.

On the night of May 3–4, right after that incident with the mouse in the kitchen, Putchikl didn't come when we called her to say good night before going to bed. We stayed up and she still didn't come. Eventually we had to go to bed, but of course I didn't sleep.

At 6:30 A.M. I became aware that it was raining, and I went to the backyard window to try to call her again. There she was, looking cold and unhappy, on the windowsill, and there was the faithful old tom, keeping her company. She clearly deserved punishment for her nameless orgies, but I took her in to dry and warm her and patted the tom, who then proceeded to go to his home next door.

She then found a younger tom, a virile one who ravished her before my very eyes. I expected Putchikl to be embarrassed about this, but she seemed oblivious to the dictates of virtue and kept whining to be let out so that she might be ravished again.

9

The Doctor's Orals, I understood, were to begin with a speech by the candidate, outlining his dissertation and explaining it. Only after that did his questioning begin.

Unwilling to leave anything to chance, I wrote out a speech and memorized it. I recited it to Gertrude, who listened patiently. Then I recited it to Dawson, who listened to the thirty minutes' worth and said, "Cut it." By May 14, I had cut it down to twenty minutes and had to memorize the new version.

While I was doing this, the new state of Israel was founded, and the June 1948 *Astounding* came out with "No Connection."[5]

Most of the letter column in that issue was given over to thio-

[5] See *The Early Asimov*.

timoline, which made me uneasy. It was a bad time to remind the professors of the existence of the article.

10

On May 20, 1948, I got to school for my own death watch. The obsequies were to take place in Room 206 of the Low Library, a building and room with which I was unacquainted, so that I would not have the benefit of familiarity.

It began at 2:00 P.M. and after a lunch I had difficulty eating, I was ready. Or at least I was there.

It was clear that I was going to react in the second fashion: not paralysis, but hysteria. I was laughing as I went in.

I got up and gave my speech with only an occasional giggle, and then the questioning began.

It is no use asking me for the procedures in detail. I wrote nothing of it in my diary and I remember very little.

One fellow asked me how I knew the potassium iodide I used was indeed potassium iodide. My impulse was to answer truthfully that I never questioned it. It said "Potassium Iodide" on the label and that was enough for me.

Some dim instinct warned me that that was the wrong answer. I thought desperately and quickly and said, "Well sir, it dissolves as potassium iodide does, and yields iodine as potassium iodide does, and it gives me my end point as potassium iodide would, so it doesn't matter what it really is, does it?"

That was a good answer.

One fellow asked me how I knew that the enzyme I used was indeed derived from the mushroom species I said it was. I said that it came from mushrooms bought at the grocery store.

"So what?" said he.

"So *Agaricus campestris* is the only species sold in the grocery store."

"How can you be sure of that?"

Again I had to think rapidly. "If I had had any doubts, sir, I would have referred to a text on mushrooms."

"Whose?" he said.

I said, shrewdly, "Yours."

That was a bad answer. He hadn't written any such text.

At one point, I muffed questions I ought not to have muffed, as when I totally fumbled the difference between a hormone and a vitamin.

At another point when I didn't know the answer, I hesitantly guessed and Dawson, who sat opposite me at the other end of the long table, leaned back so that no one would see him (they were all looking at me, of course) and shook his head slightly from side to side.

Whereupon I said, despondently, "But I see that Dr. Dawson is shaking his head at me, so I guess I'm all wrong."

That was surely one time that Dawson had reason to disapprove of my "absolute integrity," for he turned a distinct pink and said, "You were not supposed to say that, Isaac," and everyone turned to him and made mock-serious comments about helping his student unethically.

No one was really unkind to me, however, and after an hour and twenty minutes, Professor Ralph S. Halford asked me the final question.

He said, "What can you tell us, Mr. Asimov, about the thermodynamic properties of the compound known as thiotimoline?"

For just an instant I was thunderstruck, and then the hysteria I had been fighting off all this time washed over me and I broke into peal after peal of helpless laughter and had to be led from the room.

I had reason to laugh. It didn't seem conceivable to me that they would tease me in that fashion if they had not by then decided to pass me. Apparently, thank goodness, they had read the thiotimoline article and had taken it in the spirit in which it was meant.

I was right. In five minutes they had come out and, as was traditional in the case of a pass, each held out his hand and said, "Congratulations, Dr. Asimov!"

I had made it. I was Isaac Asimov, Ph.D.

11

I called up Gertrude and my parents to inform them of this successful climax to my education. I then went out with Dawson, and with Joselow and Tarpley (who were waiting for me) to a nearby bar, where we all sat down and toasted my success.

I felt it was absolutely necessary to have a drink (as on the occasion of my Army discharge nearly two years before) but didn't know what to drink.

Dawson said, "What do you like, Isaac?"

I said, "I don't know. The kind of wine we drink at Passover, I guess."

"That's port wine," said Joselow, who was Jewish.

Whereupon Dawson ordered a Manhattan for me. I loved the Manhattan and ordered another. In fact, since Dawson made it clear that the sky was the limit, I ordered—and drank—five.

What Dawson didn't know was the effect alcohol had on me. By the time I was drinking my fifth, the Universe had turned into a pink haze and I could hear Dawson (dimly) say, "Let's get him back."

I walked back to Columbia, with Joselow and Tarpley on either side of me, holding me up, and Dawson (as usual, nattily dressed, and with his homburg at just the right jaunty angle) walking a full ten feet behind in an effort to make it clear he was not connected with the sordid spectacle just ahead.

Joselow and Tarpley got me back to the laboratories and, over my feeble protests, began to ladle dipper after dipper of black coffee into me. It took three hours and several visits to the bathroom (where I used my chronometric stopwatch to time the duration of the urination and then tried to announce the results when I emerged) before they felt I could be trusted on the subways.

I had a quick dinner with Joselow and his girlfriend and then I eventually got home to an anxious Gertrude.

I went to bed almost at once but, thanks to the coffee and the excitement of the day, there was no chance of sleeping. Gertrude told me the next morning that I lay in bed all night giggling every once in a while and saying, "*Doctor* Asimov."

I had gotten my degree twenty months after returning to research.

As it happened, John Blugerman was completing his dental-school stint and was ready to get his doctorate (of dental surgery) as well. Commencement day for both of us was June 1.

12

I had refused to attend commencement day when it was a question of getting my bachelor's or my master's degree. Obviously, the matter of my doctor's degree was something else. My father, particularly, wanted to attend.

I compromised. I was not going to put on a cap and gown. I was not going to go through the ritual. With eight thousand graduates of all sorts, where was the distinction? It would be enough to sit in the audience. I took Gertrude, and my father. Henry Blugerman met us there.

The academic procession lasted half an hour with candidates pouring in from four directions. I was thankful not to be part of it. It was bad enough sitting under the hot sun in the bleachers.

The ceremony itself was hard to endure but finally Columbia's president, Frank D. Fackenthal, worked his way through all the gradations of degrees and reached those who were getting the degree of Doctor of Philosophy in the sciences. A number of cap-and-gowned individuals arose and Fackenthal conferred the degree on them.

As he did so, I leaned over to my father and whispered, "A cloud from heaven is showering gold on them, Pappa, and it's showering gold on me, too, at this very minute, even though I'm not up there."

My father wasn't amused. He wanted me up there.

After commencement was over, I took Gertrude and the two fathers to Havemeyer Hall where, as luck would have it, Dawson was present. I introduced everyone and my father simply beamed. One of his reasons for coming to the United States was to insure a better life for his children, and he had labored toward that end all those years in the candy store. Now his firstborn had worked his way up to the very highest academic degree.

After my father and Henry left, I went to University Hall to pick up my diploma. It was a small and unimpressive thing, written in English. It was, however, the only one of my diplomas that I saved. I framed it, put it up on the wall, transferred it through all my shifts of abode and, at the present moment, it is still on my wall.

The only sour note of the day was that the Columbia Appointments Office had issued a handout to the newspapers saying that the *average* Ph.D. salary, fresh after graduation, was $5,400 a year. Since I was only going to get $4,500 from Elderfield, it was clear that I was considerably below par.

45

Stuyvesant Town

1

The next day, June 3, 1948, I officially started my postdoctoral stint with Elderfield.

Tarpley told me, however, that there was an opening at Schering Corporation (where he worked) for a protein chemist. An industry could scarcely pay as little for a Ph.D. as an academic would, and since I was rueful of my below-average income, I agreed to go to Schering for an interview. I tried not to think what would happen if they offered me a job at a high salary and I had to go back and tell Elderfield, on my very first day on the job, that I was quitting.

I went to Newark and took a streetcar to Orange Street, following the directions Tarpley gave me. He neglected to tell me that there were various Orange streets and that I had better specify the Orange Street in a particular town. I didn't. I just asked to be left off at Orange Street, was deposited in the wrong one, was unable to find Schering, and came back in great confusion.

I had accomplished nothing and Tarpley was furious with me. I tried again on June 7, made it that time, was interviewed, gathered that the salary was to be no better than Elderfield's in any case, and dropped the matter rather thankfully. I would not be tempted into the shame of breaking my word; I would stick with Elderfield for at least a year.

2

Now that I was through with my doctoral effort, I felt it possible to begin new things. For one thing, I bought a copy of Glasstone's *Textbook of Physical Chemistry*, which I referred to earlier. It was the first scientific book I ever bought of my own volition and not because it was a class requirement.

It served as the nucleus of my personal library of science which, as the years passed, was to grow larger and larger and more and more important to me.

Second, it was time, at last, to begin a new science-fiction story. It was now a full year since I had made my last sale—the thiotimoline piece. Since then, I had written only "Grow Old with Me," which, of course, had been a fiasco. On June 3, 1948, therefore, I began "The Red Queen's Race," a tale involving a time-travel paradox. It featured a tough-guy detective as hero—quite unusual for me.

I was pushed into it, perhaps, because once "No Connection" appeared, I had no stories in press—not one—nothing that was slated to appear. That made me feel my science-fiction career was over, and I couldn't bear that.

Meanwhile, I had the usual share of mishaps in daily life.

On June 10, Gertrude went off shopping and left me my dinner of meatballs and potatoes in a delicious sauce. I loved it and ate it with the greatest pleasure, but did think that the portion was rather large. Even though I was used to large portions (for both Gertrude and I were brought up in the Jewish tradition of eat-eat-eat), this was a little too much so.

You guessed it: Gertrude had neglected to say that the dinner was for herself as well as for me, and I had eaten the whole thing, her half and mine together.

Then the next day, Sprague de Camp was in New York and now that we had a larger apartment, we could invite him to have dinner with us and sleep over. He did, and we fixed up the couch for him.

The next morning he could hardly breathe or move. It was in that fashion that he discovered we had a cat—which we had never thought to mention. It was in that fashion, too, that we discovered he had a virulent case of cat allergy—which he had never thought to mention.

As for work with Elderfield, it chugged along. The great novelty was that I had a technician working for me, a very attractive and intelligent girl named Bella, who was married to Jerome Berson, who was, in turn, working for his Ph.D. in the department.

I had difficulty learning how to leave the work to her, but it was better when I did. She could work in the lab more efficiently and intelligently than I could.

One important aspect of the work was the necessity to freeze-dry material—that is, one freezes the substance and draws the water off by means of a vacuum. To keep the material frozen with a minimum expenditure of energy, the container with the frozen material should be placed in an insulated box. To buy an insulated box would cost $108, so I set about designing and building my own. I did it, too, with the help of another technician named Teddy. The materials and man-hours invested proved to come to many times $108, but I have always found it difficult to persuade people that it is easier to let professionals do the work and buy the result. I didn't even try to argue the point with Elderfield.

3

On June 26, Gertrude and I visited the Himelhochs. The visit was uneventful but we were driven back only as far as Seventy-second Street and Broadway. According to my diary, "from there we walked to Forty-second Street and Sixth Avenue via the Park side and Times Square. That was awfully pleasant—it being 2:00 A.M. and nice and mild."

The thought of walking from Seventy-second and Broadway to Forty-second and Sixth (where we got the subway home, you see) by way of Central Park West and Times Square at 2:00 A.M. *today* would strike me dumb with terror.

4

On June 30, 1948, we heard from Stuyvesant Town. They wanted us to come in for an interview immediately after the Independence Day weekend. On July 6, Gertrude went there, the round trip costing $.20. (The subway fare had gone up to $.10 on July 1, doubling the long-time traditional nickel fare, and I thought enough of that to enter it indignantly into my diary.)

It was clear that the Stuyvesant Town people were ready to give us an apartment, but Gertrude did not like to take the responsibility herself, so I went there with her the next day and we agreed to take Apartment 9-C on 273 First Avenue. This was at East Eighteenth Street.

The rent was going to be $65 a month. It was the highest rent we had ever paid, but then I had never been making $4,500 a year before, either.

To us, it was a clear-cut case of an improvement. It was a modern apartment, new and clean, with a modern (if small) kitchen and a modern bathroom. It was only three rooms and there was neither cellar nor backyard, but then it was nine floors up, there was plenty of light and air, and there were a whole group of apartment houses in which we might find friends.

To my parents, of course, it was a horrible blow. They felt hurt, naturally, at my not wanting to live with them—but the fact was that I didn't. The apartment we were living in was dreary and the neighborhood was decaying and, frankly, living near the candy store was depressing. It reminded me of a life I thought I had left, and I felt as though I had regressed badly now that I had returned to it.

It would mean no financial suffering for my parents. In fact, they told us, rather defiantly, that they already had a prospective new set of tenants who would be willing to pay $90 a month. It proved necessary, in fact, to plead with my father (who was angrier than my mother was) not to make definite arrangements about the apartment before July 20. That was the day we were to sign the lease and, in my usual hunger to keep all options open, I didn't want to find myself unable to back out if I wanted to.

My father agreed reluctantly, but it was quite a while before he and I were on a friendly basis again.

Despite all this, I finally managed to finish "The Red Queen's Race" on July 11, and I mailed it to Campbell the next day. I did not take it in since some months before, Street & Smith had moved its operations to Elizabeth, New Jersey, and Campbell had gone there. The move was better for him since he lived in New Jersey, not far away, but it tended to reduce the number of my visits.

On July 16, I received a check from him for $190. That was rather better than $.025 a word, since the story was only seven thousand words long. It was the first sale I had made to him—or to anyone, for that matter—in thirteen months. It was also the only story I wrote and sold while I lived at 192 Windsor Place.

On that same July 16, we gave away Putchikl, who was not well and whom we'd be unable to take with us when we moved. Gertrude wept bitterly for days.

Also on that same day, I met Lloyd Roth briefly at lunch. He was passing through New York. He had turned completely gray and a third child was on the way.

5

On July 20, 1948, we signed the lease at Stuyvesant Town, and on July 29, we moved. We had stayed at 192 Windsor Place only ten months. It was our sixth move since marriage and this time the moving cost $45.

John Blugerman helped us move, which made it bearable and, at the end of the day, all three of us had dinner at the Kavkaz, a Russian restaurant in the neighborhood. John and I had shishkebab, but Gertrude ordered beef stroganoff, which was described as consisting of chunks of beef in a sour cream sauce.

The thought of beef in a sour cream sauce seemed stomach-turning to me, and when it arrived, with the sauce looking oddly gray, I made a face. Gertrude, however, talked me into trying one mouthful and I was an instant convert.

When I showered and turned in that night, it occurred to me that in all my New York years, I had lived only in Brooklyn. That was true for Gertrude, too. Now, for the first time in our lives, we were Manhattanites. It was a belated way of celebrating our sixth wedding anniversary, which had passed almost unnoticed on the twenty-sixth as we were beginning our packing.

In all the years I lived in Brooklyn as a youngster, I had known nothing of the glamor of Manhattan. It was only a name on the map to me and I knew it was smaller than Brooklyn. (I was very much a Brooklyn patriot.)

Nor did trips to Manhattan enlighten me as to its special characteristics. On the rare occasions that the family went to Radio City Music Hall, or when I commuted to Columbia, or visited Campbell's office, it was by subway and I saw none of it except for whatever track I followed from a subway station to my destination. (And it was characteristic of me that I never looked to the right or to the left.)

It was only when I moved to Stuyvesant Town and began to live in Manhattan that I became aware of its unusual characteristics, its skyscrapers and canyons, its stores and restaurants, and, above all, its incredible intellectual ferment.

Even allowing for this, though, the new apartment wasn't a total joy. Stuyvesant Town was still being built, so that there was the noise of construction through the day. Worse than that, there were puddles and standing water, which bred mosquitoes, and the fancy windows needed special screens, which had not yet been installed. Consequently, there was a mosquito plague such as I have never lived through before or since, and mosquito repellents didn't seem to help. One evening, I managed to stalk and kill ten mosquitoes on the wall and ceiling in twenty minutes.

6

One of the factors that made the first month in Stuyvesant Town bearable was that we were looking forward to going off on vacation. We hadn't had one since the disastrous Hilltop Lodge venture of 1944. In 1945, the draft situation made it impossible. In 1946 I was in the Army. In 1947 I was working on research and "Grow Old with Me."

In 1948, we were determined to go, and Gertrude picked out a likely spot from advertisements. It was a place called Chester's Zunbarg in the Catskills.

On August 15, in beautiful weather, we left for the place, and as soon as we had arrived it seemed we had made the right choice. We got there at 2:00 P.M., just as Sunday midday dinner was concluding, but we were quickly served a steak apiece. Later, after we had unpacked Gertrude went for a swim (she could swim like a fish and dance like a sylph, which made it hard for her, since I could neither swim nor dance).

The people we met were pleasant indeed, especially a nice couple at our table, Jack and Ida Saltzman, who lived in Seagate at the western tip of Coney Island. What's more, the entertainers included one Bernie Hearn, who had amused and pleased us at Allaben Acres in 1942, a connection that was pleasantly nostalgic for me.

We spoke to him afterward quite enthusiastically and described the earlier period of pleasure he had given us. He looked pained and it occurred to me that it might bother him that after six years, his role in show business was still confined to the borscht circuit. I sympathized rather achingly when I thought of all the years that had passed leaving me *still* at Columbia.

The Saltzmans left on Tuesday morning, but in came Ruth and Isaiah Frank, with whom we grew friendly at once. Isaiah (the only person I ever met who bore the name) worked at the State Department, which was impressive.

Then, too, we met Jack and Shirley Segal (he was tall and a little stout, and she looked rather like Mazie back in Decatur Street). They were going to be moving into Stuyvesant Town soon. We fell on each other's neck, of course.

Also with us was a young woman named Edith, rather small and with a large nose, but quite attractive. She could speak Yiddish even more fluently than I could. I called her "Mammalooshen" (mother tongue), a term often used to mean Yiddish, and we amused ourselves by swapping jokes in Yiddish.

Gertrude joined the arts and crafts group and made a copper pin with a G on it. At the last minute I suggested a slightly asymmetric design that would cause the pin to seem to lean along with the G. I was instantly considered by the arts and crafts teacher to have an artistic talent, which was ludicrously wrong, of course. In any case, it was a success, and Gertrude wore the pin for years afterward.

We square danced, took tango lessons, and played Ping-Pong and charades. We had a good group for the last—the kind that could quickly work out "neutron-induced uranium fission."

I shone when we quickly discovered that out of a nine-word phrase the second word was "the" and the fourth word "river." I made the necessary intuitive leap and said, "And even the weariest river winds somewhere safe to sea," and created quite a stir in doing so.

On the last day, I learned the words and tune to all four verses of "Venezuela," which is one of my favorites to this day. Add to this the fact that the food was good, copious, and frequent, even to regular midnight snacks, and I think it must rank the best resort vacation we ever had. I have always regretted that we only stayed a week.

We got back to Stuyvesant Town on August 22 to find that John Blugerman had been there the day before to bring in the mail and to check that everything was all right. (We had given him the keys for that purpose.)

He also left a note in which he rather hilariously paid tribute to my intelligence. It seemed that I had carefully guarded the apartment against burglary by putting our radio and typewriter in an unlocked closet, and doing other things of equal subtlety. I had made a careful list on a piece of paper of all the shrewd things I was going to do: "Place radio in hall closet. Place typewriter in linen closet under sheets." Then I had forgetfully left that piece of paper on the desk in plain view.

Fortunately, no burglar had entered to take advantage of the kind help I had offered him.

7

The weather had been beautiful at Chester's Zunbarg, with only one cloudy day. It was rather less than beautiful in New York. On August 25, a heat wave of nearly record proportions began. The average temperature, day and *night*, remained above 90 for three straight days, with highs of 98, 101, and 98, respectively.

Those were the days before everybody and his dog had air conditioning and before apartment houses were built with central air conditioning as a matter of course. In any case, Stuyvesant Town wasn't air conditioned. That, compounded with the mosquito problem, enabled us, involuntarily, to test how long the human body could exist without sleep.

For relief, we went to the nearby movie house, the RKO Jefferson, and stayed there as long as we could. On Saturday, August 28, we spent five hours there, seeing one show that included two features, a Movietone news, a travelogue, three cartoons, and five vaudeville features. Everything was wonderful, everything was marvelous—as long as the temperature was 70.

The program, fortunately, changed that night, so the next day we were back for five more hours without having to repeat.

Jack and Shirley Segal, whom we had met at Chester's Zunbarg, moved into Stuyvesant Town at the start of the heat wave and in the months afterward we were close friends, visiting back and forth constantly. Another couple from Chester's Zunbarg also lived in Stuyvesant Town, and we often made a sixsome. In no place in which we had ever lived before had there been such offhand social contacts, and that began to make up for the heat and mosquitoes.

Of course, the heat passed eventually and as construction proceeded, the mosquitoes passed, too, and even the worst of the noise.

By September 1, I had settled down sufficiently to begin a new science-fiction story, "Mother Earth."

8

We did some visiting outside Stuyvesant Town, too. On September 2, Gertrude and I visited my parents back on Windsor Place and tried to make friends again. It was difficult. My father stubbornly remained aloof.

On the fourth, we visited the Saltzmans, whom we had met in Chester's Zunbarg. We managed to find the Saltzmans' place at Seagate only with difficulty (stopping in briefly at the Blugermans' first) but managed to be the first to arrive anyway. My inability to force myself to be late has universally annoyed those who come with me and those whom I visit. My own attitude is that *someone* has to be first and if *we* come first we can make up for it by being the first to leave—and that if a hostess says six-thirty, she should be ready at six-thirty.

All this closely reasoned logic has never impressed anyone, but in this case at least, it was just as well we arrived early. The Saltzmans had a television set and they allowed us to watch it for half an hour before the remaining guests started to dribble in. It was the first time we had ever seen television. We were fascinated, of course. It seemed a way of watching something very like a perpetual movie and doing it at will and without charge.

I often said, in the days when we went to the movies two or three times a week, and had just finished sitting with a crowd of talkers, rustlers, smellers, and in-the-wayers, that the only civilized way of watching a movie was in one's own home—and here we had something that seemed to be my ideal come true, although with commercials. That first time I watched television, even the commericals seemed fascinating.

When the rest of the party arrived, the talk turned to politics. It was a presidential election year. Truman was running for election in his own right and opposing him was Dewey, who had failed against

Roosevelt in 1944. The southern conservatives were running Strom
Thurmond on what was popularly called a "Dixiecrat" ticket. Also in
the field was Henry A. Wallace, who had been Roosevelt's Vice-
President from 1941 to 1945 and who tried to rally the New Dealers.

Everyone at this particular party was pro-Wallace and that was
when I decided to vote for Wallace, too. I was convinced that Truman
couldn't win and that Dewey would be the next President. All the
newspapers said so; all the pollsters said so; and, frankly, my own estimate of the situation said so. I might as well, then, cast a protest vote
for Wallace.

9

My postdoctoral work was going on unimpressively. I was running
tests of all kinds on antimalarials, making observations, preparing
graphs, trying to find out what happened to it in living tissue in order
to decide whether it was changed into some intermediate form that was
itself more active. Then, perhaps, the intermediate could be isolated,
analyzed, synthesized, and used directly.

The trouble was that I didn't see anything coming out of my
efforts. I was constantly terrified that Elderfield would say so and kick
me out—not that I was afraid either of him or of being kicked out in
themselves—but the specter of unemployment was a very fearful one
for anyone who had spent his second decade of life in the Great
Depression.

On September 7, however, the Segals dropped in and Jack asked
me what kind of work I was doing. They knew I was doing chemical
research at Columbia but knew no details. My mind was full of it at
the time so I explained the importance of antimalarials, the nature of
quinine, atabrine, and quinacrine, using my hands and fingers to represent chemical formulas. I explained that what we wanted to know was
what happened to these substances in the human body to see if these
were changed into the real antimalarial and what that might be.

They listened in apparent absorption, and, at the end, Jack said to
me, "You're a very good explainer. I wouldn't have thought anyone
could have made that clear to me."

I laughed, and was pleased, and we went on to other things, and
eventually the Segals went home.

The effect on me, however, was similar to the one that had followed young Emmanuel Bershadsky's praise of *The Greenville Chums
at College*. I had on that earlier occasion begun to think of myself as a

writer; now, as a result of Jack's remark, I began to think of myself as an explainer. I never forgot, and the desire to explain began to grow on me from that day.

What's more, I stopped worrying about Elderfield and his opinion of me. I decided I was good at my work.

Thank you, Jack Segal, wherever you are.

10

On September 24, we actually had a phone installed. For the first time since that forty-day period in Dean Street a little over a year before, we could call and receive calls at will.

The very first call we got on our new telephone was a wrong number. We thought that was amusing but it didn't seem so after a while. The French Hospital had a similar number differing only by the inversion of the first two letters. It was a natural error to dial us instead of the hospital.

The hospital received hundreds of calls each day, and of these calls, one out of ten, perhaps (from those with the dimmest minds, of course), would reverse the letters. Up to a dozen times a day, then, the telephone would ring, and some semiliterate voice would say, "French Hospital?"

Each person called us only once, of course, and we would then tell them they had dialed wrong and sometimes they would express regret. (Mostly they would hang up with a bang as though it were our fault they had lost a dime.) To us, though, it seemed as though it were the same person calling us over and over again, stupidly oblivious to his continuing mistake.

I used to have daydreams in which someone would call and say "French Hospital?" and I would say, suavely, "Whom would you like to speak to?" and they would say, "Jane Doe," and I would say, "I'm sorry, but she passed away last night in great agony," and hang up.

Naturally, I never said anything of the sort and wouldn't have said it in reality for anything—but it was a satisfactory daydream.

11

The Orson Welles disappointment (I had long ago given up hope of "Evidence" ever being turned into a movie) had an odd offshoot. On September 28, 1948, I received a letter asking for permission to use "Victory Unintentional" in an anthology that would bear Welles' name as editor. He offered $75 and I accepted.

This was the story Campbell had characterized as "butyl mercaptan" six years before. It had only netted me $70 when I had first sold it and so this, my third anthologization, was the first that brought me more money for the anthology than for the original sale.

12

The first indication, in my diary, of my growing hatred for the smell of tobacco came on October 7. We went to the movies with the Segals and my diary states: "We sat in the balcony because the Segals wanted to sit there (so they could smoke, I suppose) and, as a result, we couldn't hear well and were choked with tobacco." I was sufficiently indignant at this to add, "I'm averse to going with them anymore."

Gertrude smoked, of course, and I disliked that more and more.

13

October 12, 1948, was a university holiday because General Dwight D. Eisenhower was being inducted as university president. Eventually he received a telephone extension number that was exactly like mine but for an inversion of numerals.

Thinking of the troubles we had with the inversion of our home telephone number, I kept expecting to get calls intended for Eisenhower. I even had daydreams of having someone call me and say, "Hello, Ike?" (I'd know it wasn't for me, but for Eisenhower, who affected that irrelevant nickname, while I allow very few people to call me that.) I would then lean back and say, cozily, "Yes?" and see what happened. However, no one ever made the mistake.

After Eisenhower had been in office a couple of months, he sent out a form letter to all the alumni. I was an alumnus so I received one. On impulse, I replied to him. Before too long I received a two-paragraph letter from him, dated February 11, 1949, which was polite and personal (it quoted a passage from my letter, so it had to be a direct answer) and which was, as nearly as I can tell, signed by him in person.

It was even better than the letter from Orson Welles, and I still own it.

I did not attend any of the ceremonies on October 12, however, but seized the chance of getting out to Elizabeth, New Jersey, where Campbell was now located, in order to see him. I had completed "Mother Earth" two days before, doing its fifteen thousand words in just under six weeks, and I wanted to submit it to him. (After asking for a small change in the end, the next day, he took it, and the story earned me $375.)

Campbell was more interested in the Foundation series, however. He had been sending me several letters while I was working on "Mother Earth," asking me to finish it and start another Foundation tale. During our session on the twelfth, we discussed my idea on this and I finally persuaded him to let me reveal the whereabouts of the Second Foundation. He did so on condition I make the story fifty thousand words long so that he could run it as a serial. (I suppose he suspected, from my attitude, that the new story would be the last of the Foundation series, and he wanted to end it on a high note.) I agreed to call it "—And Now You Don't" to tie in with the title of the previous Foundation story, which I had completed 1¾ years before.

I began "—And Now You Don't" on October 16, and from the very start I knew I would have trouble.

You see, each Foundation story assumes, as a background, all the previous stories, but I couldn't assume that every reader had read and remembered all the rest. Therefore each story had to manage to explain everything that had happened before, and as the series grew longer and more complex, this became more difficult. "—And Now You Don't" began with a teen-age girl reciting the previous events as part of a school assignment. I managed to work it in, but I decided it would have to be the last time.

My positronic robot series was completely different. Each story was independent, and knowledge of any of the previous stories was generally not required. It could go on forever.

14

On October 21, 1948, I committed another one of my grosser stupidities. Sprague de Camp had come to New York to attend a meeting of the Authors Club. He was a great joiner and he suggested I attend as his guest. The meeting was for 7:00 P.M.

I am an early dinner eater, never eating later than six and sometimes eating as early as five. Since I tend to assume (as everyone does) that my personal idiosyncrasies are cosmic laws followed by all people, I presumed that the gathering was an after-dinner meeting.

Unfortunately, work kept me rather later than I expected that day and I fretted, rather petulantly, at not having enough time to eat in proper leisurely fashion before going to the meeting. I bolted dinner and arrived at the meeting in time—to find everything spread out for dinner.

Since I couldn't quite bring myself to admit to Sprague that I had already eaten dinner, I ate another dinner but, for the first time in my life, I ate slowly and abstemiously.

Catherine de Camp was there. I hadn't seen her in over a year and she was now forty-one, but she still looked as young and as beautiful as ever. This was a recurrent pattern. I wouldn't see her for some time and then would encounter her with the advance apprehension that I would view the ruins of a once-lovely woman—and she would always look as though time had stopped still.

15

I finally got the printed copies of my dissertation (prepared at huge expense by a professional printer) on October 27, 1948. I handed out copies to those members of the faculty who had examined me, gave a number to Dawson and seventy-five copies to Columbia University, which undoubtedly still has a number of them in its files along with all the other dissertations by all the other students.

I have a copy myself, which I have had specially bound.

16

November 2, 1948, was election day. It was Gertrude's first chance to vote for President and we went to the polls together. I'm not sure who Gertrude voted for, but I followed the determination I had come to at the Saltzmans' and voted for Wallace.

That night I listened to the election returns only to find out how many votes Wallace had received. Before the returns began coming in, I noted in my diary that Dewey was a sure victor.

If I didn't have a diary, it would be so easy to make use of a sincere (but flexible) memory to recall that I had had a great many very perceptive premonitions—that I had felt Truman would win—that I had said so—that I had insisted in the face of a huge horde of scoffers that he would win.

Not so. I have a diary and it says that I was convinced Dewey would win. If I had thought Truman had had a chance I would certainly have voted for him rather than have thrown away my vote.

Nor was it easy to convince myself of what was happening once the votes started coming in. At 8:40 P.M., I noted in my diary, "The Truman debacle has not yet begun. He's leading 740,627 to 627,669—but it won't be long, I guess."

After that, every few minutes I would write "*Still* Truman" in clear surprise. Even at 2:30 A.M., when I finally decided to go to bed, I couldn't believe Truman would win. I felt that the four states taken by Thurmond would throw the election into the House of Representatives.

The next morning I woke to find Truman had won in the most thrilling upset in American political history. For a while, he was popular as the feisty little guy who had had faith in himself when everyone else had given up, but that didn't last. He was quickly once again an unpopular President—with me, as well as with everyone else.

17

My parents visited the Stuyvesant Town apartment on November 7. They refrained from ecstasies, but neither were they nasty. It was a reconciliation of sorts, but there were renewed recriminations from my mother when she found I had dedicated the printed dissertation to Gertrude rather than to her. I thought that was totally unreasonable.

In those days I was learning to like Chinese food. I had eaten in Chinese restaurants frequently, but had known only of chop suey and chow mein. Then one day I started ordering such items as shrimps in lobster sauce or sweet and sour pork, and I never ordered either chop suey or chow mein again.

It was on November 14, at a dinner with the Segals, for instance, that I tasted egg rolls for the first time. This is very odd. Considering my fondness for Chinese food today, I would have sworn—barring the evidence of the diary—that I had been weaned on egg rolls.

18

During October, I wrote a report for Elderfield describing what evidence I had gathered concerning the existence of the intermediate in the body and its possible nature. Elderfield seemed satisfied with it and confident he could use it to get a renewal of his grant.[1]

Elderfield was so confident of the renewal that on November 26 he asked me how I would like to stay on for a second year at an increase in salary. I managed to avoid answering. I felt increasingly that it was time I had something more permanent; I couldn't go on from year to year

[1] Ever since World War II, scientific research had become increasingly dependent on government grants, and professors came increasingly to be more interested in that which would elicit grant money than in that which would increase human knowledge—which I found depressing. What's more, grant money was increasingly used to subsidize students going for their Ph.D. I might conceivably have been the last Ph.D. student to get through without one cent of grant money.

like this, and even Elderfield said flatly that a second year was all he
could manage. I found out later that he was putting me down for
$4,800 for the next year. Bella, my assistant, was down for $3,000.

19

On November 30, 1948, a fellow student, Burnett Pitt, received his
Ph.D. We were friends, but rather cool ones. He was short, dark, sardonic, and rather close-mouthed. I didn't think he liked me, though
that may just have been my misinterpretation of his way of talking.

20

During World War II I had loved the comic strip "Barnaby" and
was devastated when the cartoonist Crockett Johnson grew tired of it
and stopped. Johnson had all kinds of clever touches that amused us
all. When Atlas the Mental Giant couldn't remember O'Malley's name
until he worked out a determinant on the slide rule he always carried
with him, Meisel informed us delightedly that when the determinant
was worked out, the answer was really O'Malley.

I didn't think I would ever enjoy a comic strip as much as I had
that one, but in 1948, Walt Kelly came out with "Pogo" and it was a
case of love at first sight. I actually began to cut out the strips, paste
them in a book, and save them. Later on, of course, Pogo books came
out with the individual strips collected and I no longer had to save my
own. I just bought the books. ("Barnaby" strips had come out in two
books of their own, which I bought and still possess.)

21

On December 4, 1948, there was a very pleasant Hydra Club meeting at Fletcher Pratt's place. He had started with three marmosets and
now had fifteen and the place smelled terrible as a result. He offered us
a marmoset, but though it looked very cute (not very different from
Fletcher, in fact) we refused with a shudder.

Fred Pohl was there. He had now married for a third time—to
Judy Merril.

Also present was Fredric Brown, a short, thin fellow who looked
like a bookkeeper but who wrote excellent science-fiction short-shorts
and amazingly good tough-guy detective novels. His book *Screaming
Mimi* is a classic and my personal favorite of the things he wrote. He
was a chess buff and wanted badly to play me, even though I told him

it was almost impossible for me to win a game against anyone. I had visited his apartment one time not long thereafter and he beat me rapidly in two games.

He talked as he played, however (perhaps without knowing it), and constantly reasoned out what he thought I was doing. I caught on and started doing what he thought I was doing, and in the third game I managed to elicit a draw.

Pauline Bloom was also at that Hydra Club session. She was the person who had invited me to join the Brooklyn Authors Club seven years before and through whom, therefore, I had indirectly met Gertrude.

As for remarriages, we got a Christmas card from Bob Heinlein later in the month. It was signed Bob and Ginny. It seems he had married Virginia Gershtenfeld, who had been at the Navy Yard with us as a WAVE.

The January 1949 *Astounding* appeared with "The Red Queen's Race"[2] included.

22

The year 1948 was still another poor writing year. I had sold two stories and had had one anthologization sale, and my total earnings from writing came to $640. From 1944 on, each year had seen me earn less from writing than the year before.

Of course, 1948 was better than 1947 in that I had a paying job. I had earned $2,625 working for Elderfield in 1948 so that my total income was roughly $3,300. It was about my Navy Yard income, which certainly represented no progress in four years, considering that prices had gone higher in the aftermath of the war.

23

On January 2, 1949, I celebrated my twenty-ninth birthday, which I found rather upsetting on two counts. It was, for one thing, the last year of my twenties and there was the unavoidable thought that in one year I would be *thirty*. That was no age, surely, for a child prodigy like myself. In fact, so drearily was I aware of my advanced state of chronological decay that, for the first time, the thought of an autobiography occurred to me.

Second, despite my advanced age I had not yet settled down and

[2] See *The Early Asimov*.

found my life's work. For the fifth time in a row I had celebrated my birthday in a new dwelling place and in each case the place was clearly a temporary one. How long would that continue?

And despite Elderfield's offer of a second year, I felt no great security in my job. Elderfield was capable of fearsome acts on impulse. He had a graduate student named Chapin Smith who had been working on various problems of synthetic organic chemistry for three years without much success.

I had been working with him closely for some months and found him a thoughtful, intelligent fellow, but on January 6, 1949, he returned from a Christmas vacation and was greeted, quite suddenly and without warning, by the news that Elderfield was pitching him out on his ear.

Nor could I find any security in my writing. As I said, 1948 had been a disappointing year and though I was working on "—And Now You Don't," which had the potential of earning me a large check, I disliked it intensely and found working on it very difficult.

There was one minor note of success. My story "No Connection" had been picked up for anthologization in a collection to be called *The Best Science Fiction Stories: 1949*, and edited by Everett F. Bleiler and T. E. Dikty. It was the first time anyone ever planned a regular annual series of anthologies to include the best of the year. That brought in $35.

As for books of my own, that seemed an utter will-o'-the-wisp. Although I had been told that Martin Greenberg would do "Grow Old with Me," the manuscript was back again. He had founded Gnome Press, but somehow nothing happened—at least not with me. At one point I seem to recall meeting him and discussing some changes, but it was all very lukewarm.

Fred Pohl told me that Doubleday was thinking of putting out a line of science-fiction books and he wondered whether they might be interested in "The Mule." I didn't mind having him check the matter and I gave him copies of *Astounding* that contained the story. Unfortunately, that came to nothing also.

I was at one of my low points as 1949 opened and it was clear that I had better start intensifying my search for a regular job. I could postpone it no longer.

46

Job Hunting

1

It was at this crucial moment of uncertainty that I received a phone call from Bill Boyd of Boston University School of Medicine on January 12, 1949. He was in town to give a talk on blood groups (his specialty) at the New York Academy of Medicine.

He had also written me a letter, which arrived after his phone call. In it, he told me he had been promoted to full professor of immunochemistry and that he was under the impression that the Medical School would want a replacement for him in the Biochemistry Department. He had mentioned my name in that connection, so how would I like to be assistant or associate professor?

I attended the lecture on the thirteenth with my head in a whirl.[1] I had never really thought of an academic position. I had always assumed I would get some job with an industrial firm and work as I had in the Navy Yard, only much more responsibly. But a professorship!

On the other hand, it would be in Boston. Philadelphia was a hundred miles from New York and I had found the distance upsetting. Boston was two hundred miles away.

I met Bill's wife, Lyle Boyd (a gentle and sweet, quiet-spoken woman) on this occasion and the next day, Gertrude and I had dinner with the Boyds and the Sards. After dinner, we went to a jam session at which very loud music was played and which I *hated*. It was as though I had suddenly been thrust into a new and untried world as a warning of what would come if I took an out-of-town job.

Then on January 20, I got another letter from Boyd that seemed to deflate everything. It was not a professorship at all that would be offered but only an instructorship (a status that lacks the august title). The offer was for a year only with no guarantee of a continuation or advancement (although, of course, both would be in the cards if I gave satisfaction), and the salary was $4,500. It seemed little, if at all, better than what I had with Elderfield, and I wasn't going to move to Boston for that. I turned it down out of hand.

Bill gave a very good lecture and was dressed in a tuxedo. I think it was the first time I had ever seen anyone in a tuxedo.

The next day, I told Elderfield I had turned down the instructorship and he approved. He made it quite clear, without actually saying so, that he would take better care of me than that and expressed approval of a new report on my work.

Then, on January 26, Elderfield went to Washington to make final arrangements on the grants for next year and returned in what seemed to be a state of excitement. He told me that the portion of the research in which I was working had been turned down and that I was through. Perhaps because he felt guilty about it since he had done nothing but praise my work, he told me I could stay on till June 30.

I had five months in which to find a job, and I was back exactly where I had been at the American Chemical Society convention in 1947 and with somewhat less time in which to find salvation.

At once I began pulling what strings I possessed to see if some jobs would open up. I had Dawson send letters to places where his opinion was of some use. I tried to contact other faculty members with whom my relations were pleasant.

Then, following my usual tactics of trying to keep every option open, I even did my best to keep Boston warm. On the twenty-eighth, I received a letter from Professor Burnham S. Walker, Boyd's boss and the department head. He had read the copy of my dissertation I had given Boyd, and he was "particularly impressed" with it. I promptly sent off a pleasant reply, trying to indicate that I didn't consider the job offer dead.

2

One of my "strings" was a young man who lived near my father's store. He worked at Charles Pfizer's, a chemical firm in Brooklyn. It was a prosperous firm that did a good deal of work in enzymes and allied fields. The site was right and I was eager. My friend made an appointment with me for February 4.

I arrived at Pfizer's at 9:50 A.M. for a 10:00 A.M. appointment, and it quickly appeared that they really didn't want me. In fact, they didn't even want to see me. Why they had made the appointment I don't know, but as time passed, it seemed to me that they hoped I would grow tired of waiting and go home.

I wasn't going to make it that easy for them. I dug in my heels and prepared to wait all day. What I thought I would prove by that, I don't know, but I couldn't bear to leave and have them carry the field by default. My acquaintance, greatly embarrassed, came down to wait with me at 11:00 A.M. and then took me to the company cafeteria to have lunch. It appeared that everyone had their own private linen napkin kept in their napkin ring for them and used for a period of time so that each had his own comfortable food-stains on it. I was told that people were assigned seats and that these were shifted now and then to make sure everyone met everyone.

I smiled and said, "It seems like a very comfortable prison," and my acquaintance looked unhappy.

A person came down to interview me at 2:00 P.M. He was bald, had red-rimmed eyes, and while not actually drooling, spoke moistly. I disliked him intensely on sight.

He did not apologize for the delay and began by explaining he had no place for me, since bacteriology was required, which I did not have, and since times were getting harder. Why he couldn't have told me this at 10:00 A.M., or why he consented to an appointment at all, I don't know.

I gave him a copy of my dissertation the instant he appeared and some days later he sent it back in the mail, referring to it as "your little brochure" as though he didn't know a doctoral dissertation when he saw one.

I have never forgotten and never will forget Charles Pfizer's. I have since, on occasion, received letters from people at Pfizer's asking for my co-operation in one way or another. As long as the request is on official company stationery, I simply do not answer. It's childish of me, of course, but there's no way in which I can guarantee never being childish.

3

Looking back on it, I think that incident on February 4, 1949, represented the low point of my career, with both chemistry and writing seeming to be at the nadir.

The very next day I met the future and, of course, didn't know it.

At a meeting of the Hydra Club on February 5, I met the editor in charge of Doubleday's new science-fiction program. He was Walter I. Bradbury, an intelligent and kindly man who, in my eyes, looked exactly like the British actor Leo Genn. He was, at that time, thirty-four years old.

He told me he had read "The Mule" and had liked it, but that everything must go through an editorial committee (as is indeed true at Doubleday, even for this book).

As always in such cases, I labored to keep my hopes low, for I dread disappointment. I was right to do so in this case, for nothing came of it and I heard of the rejection of "The Mule" on the thirteenth. Nevertheless, Bradbury was still the future for me.[2]

4

The following weeks were spent almost exclusively on job hunting, as I haunted employment agencies and continued to have everyone I know tell me about any place at all in which they might have pull.

For a while, the most hopeful line seemed to be through a fellow student at Columbia, Allan Gray. His father was research director at Wallerstein's, a firm that did research on beer and was particularly interested in the kind of enzymes in yeast, for instance. He promised to mention my name to his father.

I thought beer was a devil of a thing for me to become involved in, but I imagined I would be doing chemical work that might have theoretical interest outside the world of beer—and the firm was in New York —so I said I was interested.

I went to Wallerstein's on February 23. It was on Madison Avenue in the lower thirties and to my great relief, it did *not* smell of beer. Allan Gray's father was pleasant and decent, quite the reverse of the egregious man at Pfizer, and I liked the laboratory.

I actually thought I had a good chance here but I did not allow that estimate to slow me in my frenetic search.

Dawson, for instance, offered to write a letter to Johns Hopkins where a friend of his was looking for staff members. I wrote a letter and even got Elderfield to write one backing me up.

5

On February 25, 1949, three things happened.

First, a letter from Johns Hopkins was sent to Dawson asking him to send me down to Baltimore for an interview.

Second, a letter had arrived from Boston University asking me to come up to Boston for an interview.

Third, Fred Pohl, not giving up his new urge to be an agent, suggested I let him try "Grow Old with Me" on Doubleday. By now, remembering rejections by Merwin, Campbell, and Greenberg, I had grown thoroughly convinced it was an inevitable loser.

"No, Fred," I said, "it stinks."

[2] As a side issue, I now weighed 190 pounds, having gained 36 pounds in my 6½ years of marriage.

"Who cares about *your* opinion?" said Fred. "Let's see what Doubleday thinks."

So I thought: Well, what harm? I promised I'd get the manuscript over to him sometime.

I made an appointment for March 4 at Johns Hopkins and for March 10 at Boston University. In an effort to make myself look respectable (and remembering the dapper appearance Dawson always had) I bought myself a homburg hat for six dollars. It was the first hat I had owned in many years. How a homburg hat could possibly help me when I was always interviewed indoors and would have to take my hat off the moment I passed the door I can't possibly imagine. As it turned out, I almost never wore the hat and I've never bought another.

On March 4, I took the 6:30 A.M. train to Baltimore, fortified by the knowledge that Al Nason, a Columbia student in the Botany Department, had been interviewed at Johns Hopkins two weeks before and had gotten an offer of $4,200 plus moving expenses. The salary was disappointingly low to me, but he was offered the title of assistant professor.

At Johns Hopkins I met Professor William D. McElroy (who reminded me of Elderfield a bit in appearance and manner). McElroy was as pleasant as could be and told me that the post would be an assistant professorship and would carry $4,500 as a salary. (Nason was not yet a Ph.D., hence the lower offer to him.) It was clear, however that McElroy didn't want me. He admitted that he needed someone with more experience in trace metals than I had, and that he had already accepted as many men as he could take so that he could only make me an offer if someone turned him down—which he didn't think was likely.

I crossed off Johns Hopkins.

6

There was life in areas outside job hunting. I was turning my dissertation into a much briefer paper, suitable for appearance in some chemical journal—if they were willing to accept it. This meant periodic sessions with Dawson, as in the previous year, and I was slowly finishing it.

I was also drawing toward the end of "—And Now You Don't."

Then, too, I received a request, at about this time, for a story for a new science-fiction anthology. Oddly enough, I was asked to pick the story myself and to give a reason for my choice. There was only one catch: I must not pick a story from *Astounding* because they could not clear permissions from that magazine. That put me in a bind, since my best stories had all appeared in *Astounding*.

I chose "Robot AL-76 Goes Astray" and in giving my reason for the choice carefully refrained from saying it was any good (which it wasn't). I simply said it was my humorous robot story and I had picked it for its lightheartedness.

I made my Introduction lighthearted, too. In fact, as I reread that Introduction now, I see in it a considerable bit of that style that was to become common for me at later times—a mixture of self-denigration and self-esteem in equal quantities. I said at one point:

"In a sense, it's a self-satire. Of course, it's a great day for an author when he becomes important enough to be satirized, and if I waited for a spontaneous gesture on the part of others, I could wait decades—centuries, if I lived long enough."

It earned me $30, but when the anthology finally appeared, later in the year, it turned out to be money ill-got. It was entitled *My Best Science-fiction Story*, the subtitle being *As Selected by 25 Outstanding Authors*. I didn't mind being an outstanding author but, my goodness, "Robot AL-76 Goes Astray" was *not* my best science-fiction story and I never said it was. I chafed quite a bit at that.

7

I received a nice letter from Lyle Boyd, inviting me to dinner on February 9, so I took the *Yankee Clipper* from Grand Central Station at 1:00 P.M. and had an excellent dinner with the Boyds, meeting their twelve-year-old daughter, Sylvia, for the first time.

They put me up overnight and I remember having considerable trouble sleeping (as almost always in a strange bed). Since they had shelves of books in the room assigned me, as in all the other rooms, I searched them and found *Lady Chatterley's Lover*, which I had often heard of but had never read. I read some of it, but it was definitely not a soporific.

On the morning of the tenth, Bill drove me to Boston University School of Medicine. It was in a slum section of Boston and right across the street from Boston City Hospital. I met Professor Walker for the first time. He was forty-seven years old, very taciturn and unsmiling but with a quiet sense of humor that was unmistakable.

The ante had gone up. I was still only being offered an instructorship, but the salary was going to be $5,000, and a one-month vacation with pay was to be included.

I was introduced to Dr. Henry M. Lemon, who was heading the project in which I was to be employed and who controlled the grant money out of which I was to be paid. He was round-faced and grave, obviously completely absorbed by the work he was doing, which dealt with the enzyme content of human cancer tissue and how it could be distinguished from the enzyme content of normal human tissue (with obvious implications as to diagnosis).

It was clear, however, that his gravity, unlike Dr. Walker's, held behind it no sense of humor at all. That bothered me, since I had long learned that no one could long endure me who didn't have one.

I also met Dr. Matthew Derow, a bacteriologist, who was pleasant, jovial, and very talkative. Little he said was ever in a serious vein, but that sort of thing always suited me.

Walker told me I would be expected to help teach the Medical School freshmen and asked if I could teach biochemistry.

"Certainly," I said.

Since he didn't ask me if I had ever taken any course in biochemistry, or if I knew anything about biochemistry, I felt it would be impolite to force upon him the information that the answer to both those possible questions was "No." The course wouldn't start till February and by then I should know enough to get along.

I asked him to send me a letter formally offering me the position and then I went home wondering if I ought to accept it.

8

Back in New York, everyone at Columbia told me to jump at the offer, and if the school had been located in New York I would have.

I love New York. I had never felt at home in Philadelphia and I don't know that I would ever feel at home in Boston. And yet I didn't love New York to the point of wanting to starve in it.

I attended to my other affairs while trying to come to a decision. For instance, I had to get the manuscript of "Grow Old with Me" over to Fred Pohl.

I walked over to his apartment on March 11 and found he wasn't in. (After a lifetime without a phone, I couldn't seem to get the hang of the notion that one calls a person first, to see if he's in and willing to receive, before one walks over.)

What I did next is hard for me to believe, even though my diary says I did it, and I *remember* I did it These days, when I deliver a manuscript, I take it to the editor personally, and don't let go of it till I see that the editor has a good grip on it. Furthermore, I make him or her swear on the River Styx that he or she won't lose it. If the editor were too far for a personal trip, I would send the manuscript by registered mail, return receipt requested, and threaten the entire post office with instant thermonuclear annihilation if anything went wrong.

In this case, though, on March 11, 1949, I was so utterly uninterested in "Grow Old with Me" that when Judy Merril's eight-year-old daughter, Merril, answered the door and said, in her childish treble, that neither her stepfather nor her mother was home, I thrust my manuscript at the eight-year-old infant, said, "Here—give this to your old man when you see him," and marched off.

9

I finally got my own citizenship papers. That didn't make me any more a citizen or any less a citizen than before. I had been a citizen ever since 1928. With my own papers, however, I didn't have to get my father's every time I had to prove citizenship. Still, any future biographer will run the risk of thinking I did not become a citizen till 1949 if he is careless with the documentary evidence.

Even after all the data had been gone into at the appropriate government office, it was not enough. They asked to see my mother. On March 30, my mother and I went to the office for the purpose. My mother got dressed to the brim, including a fetching black hat with a veil suspended from it and dangling in front of her face.

At the subway station, while waiting for the train, she walked over to a peanut vending machine (which they had at the stations in those days) and put in a penny (which was all they asked for in those days). Out came a penny's worth of peanuts, which she tossed dexterously toward her mouth. The next thing I saw was my mother fighting away in front of her face as though she were defending herself from a swarm of bees. I went rushing over, but it turned out that in tossing the peanuts into her mouth, she had forgotten she was wearing a veil.

At the offices, she was closeted with the official privately, and when I entered finally and asked what it was all about, he wouldn't tell me. After we left, I asked my mother, and she said that because of the inadequacy of the documentation of her marriage, she had to testify that I was not of illegitimate birth.

I laughed, not so much over the suspicion, but over the embarrassment of the official, who could not bring himself to mention it to me (for fear I suppose, that I would go into a rage and knock him down).

10

I then took my mother home and went on to Elizabeth, for I had finished "—And Now You Don't" the day before, at last. While there we discussed another positronic robot story, to be called "The Evitable Conflict."

On March 31, Campbell took "—And Now You Don't," and a check for $1,000 came on April 5. It was the most I had ever gotten for a single piece of writing, and was, in fact, the largest check I had ever seen.

The story was, however, the last of the Foundation series, which I had been working on now, on and off, for 7½ years and which included eight stories that had earned me a total of just over $3,600.

I had gone through too much trauma on "—And Now You Don't" to continue the series. I had spent too much time, far too much, on working out twists in the plot that would fit what had gone before. I think that by this time even Campbell realized that I had had enough, though I'm sure that if he could have had his way, he would have had me work on the Foundation forever, since there was no question that the stories were crowd pleasers.

11

Even more exciting, in a way, was the news that Fred Pohl brought to me. Doubleday had considered "Grow Old with Me" and was willing to publish it as a *book*, provided I rewrote it and lengthened it from its 40,000 words to the full novel-length 70,000.

They were willing to pay me an option on it of $150, and I would be able to keep this option, even if my revision and lengthening proved unsuitable. What's more, if they liked the revision, they would pay me another $350 and then publish it as a book and pay me a royalty of 10 per cent of the royalties on all sales up to 5,000 and 12½ per cent thereafter. Since the book would be priced at $2.50, that meant a whole silver quarter for every copy sold, and if more than 5,000 were sold, then $.3125 on every copy afterward.

This was a magnificent prospect, but I had grown cynical where "Grow Old with Me" was concerned. Somehow, I thought, it would manage to be rejected.

Well, I would take the option, so that the story would have earned *something*. I would then make the revision and we would see.

On March 31, Pohl handed me a check for $135. He kept $15 as agent's fee on the option. He was my agent once again, as he had been nine years before.

12

Finally, on April 4, I received a formal notification from Dean James Faulkner that I had been appointed an instructor in biochemistry at Boston University School of Medicine as of May 1, 1949.

Well, what could I do? I had been looking for a job madly for two months, and this was the only one that turned up and, except for the fact that it was in Boston, it was a satisfactory one. On April 5, I accepted officially and that meant farewell to Stuyvesant Town and, far worse, farewell to New York.

Once I had sent in my acceptance, Mr. Gray of Wallerstein was ready to offer me a job, but it was too late. The die was cast.

13

In making this decision, I completely ignored the potential earning power of my writing. Looking back on it now it might seem amazing that I did so, but *at that time* it would have been madness to do anything else.

Let me recapitulate.

Since the first moment I had stepped into Campbell's office on June 21, 1938, nearly eleven years had passed. In that interval of time I had written only science fiction, and I had reached the top of the tree. Campbell *was* the top of the tree.

I had written sixty stories in that eleven-year interval and had sold and been paid for forty-nine of them (fifty if you want to count the option of "Grow Old with Me"). Of these sales, twenty-eight had been to Campbell. In the past seven years, I had written eighteen stories and had sold seventeen of them to Campbell. (The exception was, of course, "Grow Old with Me.")

There was no place else for me to go. Heinlein had moved on to the slicks, but I knew I couldn't (or I thought I knew I couldn't).

Well, was it enough? Could I support myself writing?

No!

During my eleven years as a professional science-fiction writer who for seven years had been at the top of the tree, I had made a total of $7,593, or just about $700 a year. To be sure, I hadn't been a full-time writer at all, but my best year, 1944, had only brought in $1,100, and as a full-time writer I would do well to double that, and $2,200 a year would not support me.

In fact, could I even double the rate at which I earned money if I spent full time at the typewriter? It wasn't writing time that was the bottleneck. You might remain at a typewriter hour after hour after hour, yet produce very little. What one needs is *thinking* time, and that can't be rushed. You have to think up your plots and your complications and your resolutions, so that most of your time is going to be spent thinking and not typing.

My very success with Campbell made it difficult, in a way, for me to take my writing career seriously. Might it not be that I was a one-editor writer? Perhaps I could only please Campbell and no one else. Worse yet, I always discussed my stories with Campbell, so there was a question in my mind as to how much of the success of my stories was mine and how much Campbell's.

The one story I had written in recent years that did not involve any discussions at all with Campbell had been "Grow Old with Me," and look at what had happened there.

What would happen to me, then, if something happened to Campbell? If he quit or were fired or died? Might it not be possible that I would then find suddenly that I was no writer at all?

Something like that almost happened on April 9, in fact. On that day I happened to call my mother to pass the time of day and was told that my father had heard on the radio that Street & Smith had suspended all its pulp magazines. For a short time, in my mind, *Astounding* was gone, Campbell was gone, and I wasn't a writer anymore.

Then I got the New York *Times* and found that Street & Smith had indeed suspended all its pulps, but that there had been one exception: *Astounding* would still continue to be published!

Still, the escape was a narrow one, and despite my recent sale of "—And Now You Don't" and the huge check it had brought in, I felt completely insecure as far as my writing career was concerned. There was no way I could see myself making a living at the typewriter in any way or under any circumstances—so I accepted the job at the Medical School.

14

And yet if Campbell represented a dead end to me, was there any way of branching out? If I couldn't follow Heinlein into the slicks, was there anyplace else I could forge a path for myself?

On March 21, 1949, I had attended a lecture given by Linus

Pauling. It was the best lecture I had ever heard. Even Gertrude, who was present, and who did not understand a word, enjoyed it. It was possible, then, to make science attractive to anyone.

Inspired by Pauling's speech, and remembering Jack Segal's remark months before about what a good explainer I was, I decided to write a piece of nonfiction. I called it "Detective Story for Non-chemists" (a title based on Tarpley's remark, once, that a good chemist had to have a detective instinct). It dealt with the manner in which chemists had worked out the chemical structure of the molecule of biotin, one of the B vitamins.

I finished it on April 3 and sent it to Campbell, for *Astounding* regularly published a nonfiction piece or two every issue. My thiotimoline article had been published under that heading, for instance. Campbell returned "Detective Story for Non-chemists" at once, however. It was far too straight, far too detailed, far too dull. I did not, however, forget it, or my general desire to write nonfiction.

On April 6, I began the revision of "Grow Old with Me." I note that in my diary of that day I had finally learned the correct quotation and called it "Grow Old Along with Me." That was the title I used thereafter and it cheered me to do so. I think I felt a sneaking suspicion that changing the title would break the jinx.

I worked on the story every day, and the revision and lengthening went rapidly.

And on April 14, the short version of my dissertation was completed and I was ready to send it off to the *Journal of the American Chemical Society,* which was the *Astounding* of the chemical journals.

47

Boston

1

On April 20, I went to Boston to look into the matter of housing—obviously the first hurdle to get over. Again I stayed at the Boyds' and that evening I met Fred Whipple, a Harvard astronomer, and his wife, Babbie. Fred was tall, slim, good-humored, and forty-two years old; Babbie was short, smiling, and pretty.

That evening, Bill broke the rather shocking news to me that he was planning to go to Cairo, Egypt, to take a civil-service position as a P7. It caught me by surprise and my spirits fell sharply. Bill was the only person in Boston I could count as a friend. With him gone I would be a stranger in a strange land. I might not have accepted the job if I had not had the comfortable feeling of at least one known quantity I could cling to.

Bill, perhaps sensing my distress, offered to take me along as a P6, but I wouldn't return to civil service even in New York, let alone in Cairo, so I refused. I returned by train on the night of April 21–22, stayed awake all night, and came home in complete panic. I didn't want to leave New York. I was afraid of the new and frightening city that Boston had suddenly become when I discovered Bill would not be there.

On returning home, I found that the May 1949 *Astounding* had come, with "Mother Earth"[1] in it, but that was scarcely compensation.

2

Sunday, May 8, 1949, was Mother's Day. It seemed inappropriate that I should wake at 5:00 A.M. with an acute and continuous abdominal cramp. I could not lie down or sit or stand. I could only walk back and forth, doubled up and groaning.

After twenty minutes of this, we were on the point of calling a doctor, since both Gertrude and I were suspecting acute appendicitis, when the pain started easing up, then went away. It left me with a feeling of relief and, almost, euphoria, for there is nothing like the absence of pain, after pain.

[1] See *The Early Asimov*.

It did not recur, and so we did not take up the matter with a doctor. Gertrude and I both still lived with the notion that one didn't see a doctor if one didn't have to.

It was too bad. Had I known what was wrong, I might have been spared future discomfort.

3

On May 10, I gave my first lecture for a general audience. It was for Pauline Bloom, of the old Brooklyn Authors Club. She had a writing class and wanted me to talk on science fiction and fantasy. The audience consisted of about thirty people, mostly middle-aged women, and I doubt that any of them knew anything at all about science fiction or fantasy. My diary states, "I did very nicely" but gives no details and I remember nothing about it.

But it was another quiet beginning for a facet of my life.

4

On May 12, I went to Boston for a third time and, for the first time, Gertrude accompanied me. We tried to find living quarters, but returned on the fifteenth, having spent $76 and gained nothing.

But then, on May 17, we received a letter from Lemon, who told us that a two-room apartment, with kitchenette and bath, completely furnished, and redecorated only half a year before, would be available half a block from the school from June 1 to September 1 at $60 a month. I sent off an acceptance, sight unseen. How bad could it be after all? Certainly the location was convenient, and we would have three months to find something better.

May 20 was the anniversary of my successful Doctor's Orals, and "a lot of good it's done me" was the gloomy comment in my diary. The next day, however, I completed the revision of "Grow Old Along with Me." It had taken me 6½ weeks. On May 22, Pohl dropped around to pick up the new manuscript and deliver it to Doubleday.

5

On May 29, 1949, Bradbury called and got Gertrude on the phone. He told her that Doubleday was taking the revised "Grow Old Along with Me" and it would be out as a book the next January. Gertrude called me with the news, for I was at Windsor Place at the time.

I was delighted. It seemed a happy send-off.

But it was difficult to be altogether happy. I was leaving Columbia at last nearly fourteen years after I had first entered it, and although I had longed often enough to be through with it, now that I was really going to leave, it was hard to forget that I had spent half my life associated with it. Then, too, I was leaving New York City for the second time, nearly three years after having gotten out of the Army and returned, and this time it was not "for the duration"; it might be for all my life.

I remember I met old Professor Thomas on the Columbia campus on Friday, May 27, my last full day on campus. He was getting on in years now and walked with a cane.

I said to him, "Well, Professor Thomas, I'm leaving Columbia today after fourteen years."

I thought that the least he could do would be to break into tears, but he only banged his cane against the brick walk and said, "About time! About time!" turned, and tramped off.

Morris Kupchan, my predecessor on Elderfield's projects, was working in Boston now. He drove us to Boston on May 31, and there we saw what we had sublet at 42 Worcester Square in Boston. It was unbelievably horrible. The furniture was old and unpleasant; the shower was a tin stall, where, we found, the water was bound to turn cold or hot depending on which taps were being opened or closed elsewhere in the building. There was no refrigerator and we would have to eat out. (There was the school cafeteria, fortunately, which was cheap, but had no other merit.)

It was our seventh move since marriage, and it was clear that our very first order of business would be to arrange an eighth move.

6

On June 1, 1949, I showed up at the Medical School and spent my first day at the job. It wasn't encouraging. I discovered that Bill Boyd, a full professor, was making $6,000. I seemed, financially, to be already near the top for an academic job. I doubted if I would ever make, even in a good writing year, as much as $10,000.

Oh well—so I would never be rich. My salary would do for a childless couple, especially since my savings had been slowly accumulating as a result of cautious and frugal living in the past and now stood at $6,200.

If, that is, the job continued. The trouble was it lacked security. My salary did not come out of Boston University funds. It was out of funds from government grants obtained by Lemon, and each year those grants would have to be renewed or I would face the sudden kickout, as had been the case with Elderfield earlier in the year.

Gertrude was very aware of this and downcast over it. I tried to assure her that the grants would surely be renewed, but she said, "It will always be a matter of tension while we wait," and of course, that was true.

But we had to carry on, and apartment hunting was the order of the day. A solid week's search netted us something in Somerville, the town just north of Cambridge, which, in turn, was just across the Charles River, to the north of Boston.

It was in a pleasant neighborhood, on a busline that would take me to the elevated that would in turn take me to the school. (This was important, for we had no car and had to depend on mass transportation.) It was also near a shopping center and had a roomy and pleasant kitchen. The other three rooms were small and it was in an attic, two flights up. We beat the rent down from $85 a month to $75, and then put down a $10 deposit. We paid the first month's rent on June 20, and here we were with an apartment at 762 Broadway in Somerville, while still paying rent at Stuyvesant Town.

The pain of double rent was soothed a bit by the fact that on the same day I got the balance of the advance of "Grow Old Along with Me"—$315 after Pohl had taken his share.

Walter Bradbury, by the way, wrote to ask me for a different title for the book, since *Grow Old Along with Me* did not sound like science fiction, and, indeed, carried romantic implications. He was quite right. On the twenty-fifth, I decided to change the title to *Pebble in the Sky*.

7

We got a welcome break over the Fourth of July weekend, when the Boyds, who had not yet left for Egypt, took us out to their summer place in New Hampshire. It was in beautiful countryside, 3½ hours northwest of Boston, and far away from everything. There was a sense of complete isolation (no neighbors in sight, no telephone) that made all trouble seem to disappear. The Boyds said that they considered it their true home.

They called it "Kasr ed-Dam," which was Arabic for "House of Blood." There was nothing ghoulish about that. It was just that blood groups were Bill's specialty and that both he and Lyle had traveled much in the Middle East and had studied the blood groups of mummies, for instance.

The one difficulty as far as we were concerned was that the house was so isolated that it had neither electricity nor plumbing. In the twilight, kerosene lamps were lit. The light was unsatisfactory, though we could play bridge by it. On the other hand, we couldn't really drain the kerosene reserves by keeping them burning very long, which meant going to bed unusually early even though it was near the summer solstice and the day stayed fairly bright till past 8:00 P.M.

The absence of plumbing was worse. There was an outhouse, which could be reached by going through the woodshed. I objected seriously to the smell and to the flies, but over a four-day period there was no way in which I could avoid resorting to it a number of times.

The first morning I wandered vaguely about looking for a shower, and it slowly dawned on me that there wasn't one. I put the problem to the Boyds, who seemed a little surprised that it should concern me. I had to settle for sponging myself with lukewarm water in the woodshed, which was better than nothing but which left me unsatisfied.

Even considering the lack of these creature comforts, we had a wonderful time, however, and we loved Bill and Lyle. It made it all the worse to go back to the nitty-gritty of life and to think that they would be leaving soon for Egypt.

I talked to him about that in among the four-day glut of conversation in which we all wallowed delightedly. Drawing from my experience at the Navy Yard, I drew a dark picture of what he would find civil service to be. As a matter of fact, I made it rather worse than it was because I hoped he would change his mind. He didn't; he was determined to go.

Over the years, I discovered that Bill was a disappointed man. He had been an undergraduate at Harvard, and he longed to be on the Harvard faculty. His best friends (Whipple, for instance) were on the Harvard faculty and he held to them tightly as though he hoped this would make him one, too, vicariously.

Although he was world famous as a blood immunochemist, it bothered him to be at Boston University. During the war, he had switched to Harvard to work on some blood-fractionation project but had not gotten along with the head of that project (an overbearing tyrant, from all accounts), and Bill had had to come back to Boston University, something he apparently considered a defeat.

Now he was leaving again in search of greatness, and nothing I said was going to keep him home.

8

The movers picked up our furniture in Stuyvesant Town on July 20 and it was good-bye to Manhattan, exactly one year after we had signed the lease and become Manhattanites. We moved the furniture into the Somerville apartment on July 22, and four days later we celebrated our seventh wedding anniversary.

But if it was off with the old, it was also on with the new. On July 27, I met Harry Stubbs for the first time. He wrote science fiction under the name of Hal Clement, and then and ever has proved a wonderful person—quiet and kind. I've never known him to lose his temper or to say an ungentle word.

On July 29, we left the sublet after a two-month stay and completed our eighth move. It cost us just $100. Naturally, it was once again a super heat wave, with temperatures topping 95 day after day.

But then, at least we had a telephone installed at once—our third. From that day to this I have never been without a phone.

In Boston, I felt as much an exile at first as I had felt in Philadelphia. Boston, however, was a livelier city than Philadelphia had been, and my surroundings were academic rather than bureaucratic, which meant they were more stimulating.

As time went on, I rapidly grew to like Boston and New England generally. I found a liberal newspaper, the Boston *Globe*, and I discovered there was no shortage of eating places or science-fiction fans. Eventually, when mobility increased, I discovered that the New England countryside was delightful.

PART
VI

*Two Careers, but
Where Next?*

48

Somerville

1

The Somerville apartment was about six miles north of the Medical School, but the commuting didn't bother me, even though it meant both bus and elevated. A New Yorker is used to that.

What was really bad was the heat. The house was poorly insulated and the apartment was, literally, a converted attic. It grew *hot* on hot days, really hot, and was up to ten degrees warmer than it was in the shade under a tree, for instance. You can imagine what it was like on August 10, when the temperature in the shade hit 101.

What's more, there was no shower, and we had to take baths. After a while, though, I discovered this was no great sacrifice. I found that a warm bath in the morning, or a cool bath in the evening, was wonderfully relaxing, and I enjoyed reading while soaking. The problem then became one of not soaking the book if I dozed off, or of dipping my nostrils below the water level and waking up strangling.

But then, Somerville was an improvement on Worcester Square, and summer was half over by the time we got in.

What's more, we could at least miss some of what was left of the summer by going off to some resort. Again working through advertisements, we chose a place called "Birchtoft" in Jaffrey, New Hampshire, about sixty miles northwest of Boston. It was the first time we ever planned a *two*-week vacation.

Life went on, too. On August 4, after a couple of days of relative coolness, I managed to start the new robot story, "The Evitable Conflict," in which I pictured a world run by intelligent computers cooperating subtly enough to leave humanity with the illusion that it was still in charge.

On August 15, I got a new kind of acceptance: The *Journal of the American Chemical Society* was going to run my paper.

2

On the nineteenth we took the bus to Jaffrey, and our first impression of Birchtoft was as woeful as our first impression of Hilltop Lodge had been back in 1943. Our temporary quarters were horrible, and the food was poor and rather flatly American. There was bacon at breakfast and none of the Jewish delicacies we had had at Chester's Zunbarg—which we missed unbearably the first few days. What's more, the lake was ten minutes distant through the woods.

On the first day, however, one of the guests, seeing that we were clearly unhappy, spoke consolingly and assured us the place would grow on us—and indeed the place did seem to improve with time. We got better quarters, the food wasn't so bad after all, and the walk through the woods to the lake was actually pleasant.

The master of ceremonies was Leonard Cibley, who was a student at the Medical School (the world is always a surprisingly small one), and he was excellent at dialect jokes. I envied him exceedingly. I tell jokes very well myself, but can only handle the Yiddish dialect.

The weather was variable. The first few days were actually cold, and a fire had to be built in the sitting room. Considering that it was one of Boston's hottest summers, it seemed ironic that, after our superheated Somerville attic, we were to be sitting there shivering but there was a welcome novelty to it also. There were other days, however, when the temperatures went into the nineties.

We met Morris and Lillian Cohen, who were a particularly pleasant couple; he short and bald, she short and blond, both highly articulate. They were celebrating their sixteenth wedding anniversary. We grew friendly with them when I noticed Maury (as we eventually came to call him) carrying a copy of the current *Astounding*.

He didn't know who I was, since it was customary at resorts to use first names only, as another way of shutting out the real world, and I felt it safe and unembarrassing to ask if he had read any of the stories of the Foundation series.

"Oh yes," he said. "They are very good, and the author is your namesake. He's Isaac, also."

"His last name," I said, "is also a namesake of mine. For my last name is Asimov, just as his is."

After that we were inseparable.

We left Birchtoft on September 2. The two weeks cost us, all told —special expenses, tips, and everything—$250, and we felt it was well worth it. We were getting a little less cramped about money.

3

The science-fiction book-publishing business was catching. If Doubleday began, could the other publishers be far behind?

On September 6, 1949, I got a letter from Little, Brown, one of the two large publishing firms based in Boston. (The other was Houghton-Mifflin.) They wanted to know if I had a science-fiction book for them.

I called up all atremble and a young woman, Jane Lawson, invited me to lunch on the eighth to discuss the matter. It was the first time I had occasion to deal with a woman editor. Considering my bringing up in the male world of early magazine science fiction, I wouldn't have thought such a thing could exist.

She took me to Locke-Ober's, Boston's most prestigious restaurant, which I visited for the first time. She insisted that I have a fancy meal, and I didn't have the nerve to cross her—she was an editor, after all.

Since she ordered a whiskey sour, so did I, and since she ordered a shrimp cocktail, so did I. Then she had swordfish (which I had tasted for the first time some weeks before—Boston is famous for its seafood) but *insisted* I order the more expensive lobster. I did, and struggled with it, for I may have had lobster before (I don't remember) but I was certainly not at the stage where I could handle it easily. And then apple pie à la mode and coffee.

I didn't enjoy a bite of it because I knew that the bill would come to about ten dollars (it did) and that was going to put a fearful drain on my pocket money. It was even conceivable I might suffer the incredible humiliation of having the bill come to more money than I had with me.

Then, when the meal was over and the waiter arrived with the bill, he simply handed it to Miss Lawson, who, to my astonishment, quietly and efficiently paid it. It had just never occurred to me that a woman could pay a restaurant bill.[1]

During the lunch I tried to tout my Foundation series, and later on, I brought her all the manuscripts. Alas, she didn't want them, and after reading them, handed them back.

4

There was still Doubleday. I went to New York on September 14 and gave the manuscripts of the Foundation series to Bradbury (I was beginning to call him Brad, as all who knew him did). He, too, decided

[1] Looking back on it, I realize, of course, that Miss Lawson was a steady customer whom the waiter knew and that she frequently had a male writer as her guest so that it was quite routine for her to take the bill. Nor was it she who paid, but Little, Brown. This was something it was hard for me to grow accustomed to, since I have never been on an expense account. Once, when I was having lunch with Campbell, I tried to reach for the check and he placed his large hand on mine, pinning it to the table, and said, "Never argue with a giant corporation, Isaac." I've tried to remember that.

he didn't want to do them. What he did want to have me do, however, was to come up with an idea for a novel by November, and if he liked the idea he would arrange for a contract and pay me money in advance.

I gave him a picture that had been taken of Gertrude and me just before I had gone off into the Army. Doubleday used only the half that was myself, of course, and planned to put it on the book jacket of *Pebble in the Sky*, which was now scheduled for publication on the following January 19.

It was an incredibly handsome photograph of myself, without glasses, at twenty-five, and it is still there on several early books. I would have liked to use it permanently; I would like to use it even now. However, I started getting very friendly letters from young women who happened to read those early books, and Gertrude warned me that if any of them dropped around to see me and found out what I really looked like they would rend me limb from limb. I decided she was right so that the photographs on my books have been aging at more or less the rate I have been.

On September 16, 1949, I visited Campbell and spent three hours with him.

"—And Now You Don't," he told me, was going to run as a three-part serial (my first three-parter), with the first part appearing in the November 1949 issue. It was during that visit that I first heard "of Hubbard's dabblings in amateur psychiatry" (as I put it in my diary).

This was going to develop into "dianetics," out of which Hubbard was to make his fortune and gain his godhead. Campbell was unabashedly enthusiastic about it, and this marked his first dip into the kind of mysticism that was to consume him for the rest of his life. As I listened to Campbell describe what was to become dianetics, I sat there, cold and untouched.

5

Once the summer heat was over, the Somerville apartment became quite bearable. We had an active social life not only with the New York people who had come to Boston for jobs, but also with some of the people we had met at Birchtoft. Then too, I attended seminars with ambition and energy, not only at the Medical School, but also at Harvard and MIT. I was doing my best to get the feeling of being part of the academic life, and I was trying to take it for granted that my salary would be continued for year after year.

Boston University Medical School was an old institution. Its three buildings were ancient and the laboratories were less impressive than those of Columbia, let alone the Navy Yard. Its drabness seemed suitable for the South End, a very rundown section of Boston.

The main campus of Boston University, on Commonwealth Avenue in the Back Bay, was much more modern and impressive, but the Medical School's location, poor as it was in a material sense, was between Boston City Hospital and Massachusetts Memorial Hospital, and that was good for clinical training.

As for myself, since I was not visual, I got used to the drabness quickly and got to work on my research project, in which I intended to deal with the structure of nucleic acids. Among other things, I set about trying to make use of paper chromatography as a tool. This was a way of separating the components of a complex mixture by having them travel at different speeds along porous paper. In this way I hoped to determine the percentage of different bases in nucleic acids taken from normal and cancerous tissue and, perhaps, get an inkling of the basic chemical change that brought on cancer.

In hindsight, I am quite convinced that this line of attack would not have given me any useful information on the cancer problem, but I might have come up with something interesting in other directions if the course of events had allowed me to continue my research long enough. Who knows?

In October, meanwhile, I tackled "The Evitable Conflict" in earnest and finished it in four weeks. I mailed it to Campbell on October 31, and on November 7, I received a check for $180. If we don't count "Grow Old Along with Me," then "The Evitable Conflict" was the eighteenth story in a row that I had written with only Campbell in mind and that Campbell had taken.

Meanwhile, on October 25, I received the galley proofs of *Pebble in the Sky*. It was the first time I had ever received galley proofs, and I handled them almost reverently and went over them with painstaking slowness. It took me a whole week to do the proofing.

Gertrude and I were picked up by Kupchan on November 4 and driven to New York (or to the Bronx at least, and we went the rest of the way to the Blugermans' by subway). I brought the precious proofs with me and made a date to see Bradbury on Sunday afternoon.

There was no reason for him to interrupt his weekend to see me on a Sunday afternoon, but he wanted to make sure I had done the proofreading well. Brad was another one of the list of people in my life who have been moved by my lack of sophistication and by my air of eager incompetence to take a lot of trouble over me and to protect me.

There's no need to mention Campbell and Dawson as two other examples.

On Sunday, the sixth, then, I visited my parents and showed them the galley proofs to their great satisfaction and then went on to Brad's place. He lived in Peter Cooper Village at that time, a development right next to Stuyvesant Town, with larger apartments at higher rents. I met his wife and his young daughter and then we sat down over the proofs.

He went over them, as Dawson used to go over my dissertation, checking what I had done and showing me how to do it better. Eventually he was satisfied and said I seemed to have done a careful job.

I was gratified and said, "Yes, it's amazing what you find when you see things in cold print. There was a place there, for instance, where I had my characters 'say icily,' and 'say frostily,' and 'say frigidly' about twenty times in two pages. I cut out all those adverbs."

"Good," said Brad. "It's always strongest if you just say 'he said' and use adverbs only as a last resort."

"Right," I said. "Goodness! The way it was, *The New Yorker* would have listed them all in their 'infatuated-with-the-sound-of-his-own-words' department."

Brad looked at me with a wild surmise and said, "Where are the passages you're speaking of?"

I showed them to him and he went through them and put back all the adverbs. It didn't do any good—*The New Yorker* never picked it up.

While there, I outlined the plot of a new novel, and he told me to go ahead. He wanted the first two chapters and an outline before writing a contract.

6

I found things going well when I returned to Boston. On November 9, there came news that Lemon had already obtained a renewal of his grant, so I was assured of a salary for a second year. Things seemed to be going far better than they had under Elderfield.

Besides which, I now made the discovery that books, unlike magazine stories, made money by themselves while the authors slept or dallied or twiddled their fingers. That same day I got a telegram from Fred Pohl to the effect that Unicorn Press, a small book club specializing in mysteries, had taken *Pebble in the Sky* for an advance of $1,000. Such earnings were split half and half between publisher and author, with Fred taking his agent's 10 per cent of my half, but that still meant $450 for me eventually when it came to statement time.[2] Well, goodness, that was half a year's rent and I hadn't had to do any work for it at all.

This was the kind of inspiration to get me right to work by November 15 on the summary of a new novel, *The Stars, like Dust—.* I started the novel itself on the twentieth.

This is not to say that this new variety of writing success didn't bring some problems in its wake. At about this time, I received a copy of the book jacket for the forthcoming *Pebble in the Sky.* I was delighted, especially with my own handsome dream-prince of a photograph.

The back cover, in addition to the photo, had a biographical sketch, and the last sentence was, "Dr. Asimov lives in Boston, where he is engaged in cancer research at Boston University School of Medicine."

It had never occurred to me that the Medical School might be mentioned and now I wondered if the school might be offended by this. It was too late to change the jacket and I was not of a mind to hang by my thumbs and wait for an explosion. I thought I would have to confront the issue now and I already knew that I could not give up my writing. If it came to a choice . . .

I asked for an appointment with Dean Faulkner, and when I kept that appointment, I put it to him frankly. I was a science-fiction writer, I said, had been for years, and the people who hired me knew this was so at the time they hired me.

My first book was coming out in a month or two, under my own name, of course, and my association with the medical school was mentioned on the back cover. I hadn't known it would be, but there it was. Did he want my resignation?

The dean considered thoughtfully (he was a true Boston Brahmin with a long face and an easy smile) and said, "Is it a good book?"

Cautiously, I said, "The publishers think so."

He said, "In that case the medical school will be glad to be identified with it."

That took care of that.

7

Bill Boyd had gone to Egypt at the beginning of September, and I heard from him with fair regularity. He was ecstatic at first but by No-

[2] Book publishers pay accumulated earnings twice a year—February and August in Doubleday's case.

vember there was a more sober air to his letters, and he now said that he would definitely be back when his two-year hitch was up.

Roy Machlowitz showed up in Boston on November 25—a breath of the long-dead days in Philadelphia. He was married now and his wife came with him. We had lunch together, visited the glass flowers at the Harvard Museum (which I secretly thought overrated), fed them a swordfish dinner, and all went well.

Talking about dinner, during those early months in Boston, the Boyds and the Whipples introduced me to a club called "The Decadents." The purpose of the club was to meet once a month for some fancy ethnic meal, with each month someone else serving as host. One month, for instance, we went to a restaurant for a Syrian meal. It was my first experience of the Middle Eastern cuisine, and I loved it.

On December 10, a few days after Babbie Whipple had given birth to a baby girl, we all went to a Chinese restaurant, where the Chinese consul and his wife did the ordering and ate with us. We had dishes we had never had before and were never to have again. All I could say in my diary was "Two soups, five main courses, all new, all delicious, all indescribable." It was the best Chinese dinner I have ever had.

8

On December 20, I completed the outline of *The Stars, like Dust*— along with the first two chapters written out in full, exactly as Bradbury had asked me to do. It was all ready to be taken to New York.

On the twenty-third Kupchan drove us to New York for Christmas-New Year's, and the next day we had an old-fashioned feast at the Blugermans'. Mary had prepared nothing less than a twenty-six-pound turkey. The five of us managed to finish nearly half of it at dinner.

On Christmas Day it was my parents' turn, and after visiting them I delivered the chapters and outline to Bradbury.

9

In those days, Gertrude and I were going through a fit of playing charades. We engaged in it at every opportunity and, of course, it was bound to give rise to occasional frustrations that were murderous at the time and funny afterward.

Sometimes the frustrations were deliberately arranged. After all, as one played charades and grew more expert, one developed a set of signals that turned it into almost a deaf-and-dumb language so that no phrase remained unpenetrated long. To cure dullness, there was occasionally a conspiracy to arrange to have a relative newcomer deliver a phrase we all knew but deliberately misguessed. No matter what he or she signaled, all the rats in the audience assiduously suggested synonyms and never landed on the right spot. It was fun to watch the demonstrator slowly curdle and disintegrate, but we could never go too far, for either one of us would start laughing or we would fear a real stroke. We would confess and there would be a furious demonstrator who would take hours to recede from his or her high fever.

It was more dangerous to really strike an insoluble syllable, through impenetrable stupidity, for then there would be no end, short of absolute irreversible insanity.

I once had to demonstrate Hamlet's heartfelt cry, "What's Hecuba to him, or he to Hecuba?" and got all the short words across in short order, assuming they would all know "Hecuba" as soon as they got the rest. Unfortunately, the audience consisted of illiterate chemists and I had to get "Hecuba" across to them.

I divided it into three syllables and got the first two across so that now they had, "What's Hecu— to him, or he to Hecu —" and there it stuck. Nothing I could do could get across a "buh," although I would have sworn a child of three who had never heard any language but Montenegrin would have known the entire phrase by then. Finally, I screamed incoherently and left the room. I wasn't really mad. I came back after a few hours.

My sharpest memory, though, is trying to get the word "one" across to a particular person. I held up my forefinger confidently and she said, "First word!" as a matter of course, because that is the recognized sign for the first word of a phrase. I shook my head vigorously, and held up first the forefinger, then the middle finger, too, and finally the ring finger as well, indicating each stage in exaggerated fashion, and she said, "One, two, three." I nodded with fatuous glee and held up one finger, signifying the first of these three words, and she said, "First word."

My eyes grew bloodshot. I went through the same ritual. She said, "One, two, three," at which I pointed to the first finger and slowly curled down the other two. She said, "First word."

I was jumping up and down in frenzy, unable to get out of the routine I had chosen for myself. I indicated one finger, two fingers, three fingers, then shook the first finger under her nose; I did it over and over and over, and finally left the finger there while performing an *entrechat* and split to emphasize it completely.

Finally, a look of dawning comprehension permeated her entire being and she said, "Finger!!!!!"

I don't know what happened after that. Everything went black and the next thing I knew it was morning.

10

I visited Columbia on December 27, 1949. Dawson had had a bad time with his ulcer and it was his first day back at work. Gerry Krueger, the beautiful redhead who had argued feminism with me, had just gotten her doctorate.

The next day I had lunch with two gentlemen from Unicorn Press, who had taken *Pebble in the Sky*. One was Hans Stefan Santesson, fat, bottom-heavy, and very soft-spoken with the trace of a Swedish accent. The other was Clayton Rawson, tall and long-faced.

Present also was Martin Greenberg, roughly my age and with a Brooklyn accent like mine, but with a mustache added. He had missed out on *Pebble in the Sky*, he admitted, but he was anxious to do a collection of my robot stories. I was eager to have him do it, since Bradbury had told me he was interested only in novels and not in short-story collections.

On December 29, I had lunch with Bradbury. He had a preliminary copy of *Pebble in the Sky* with him and gave it to me, smiling his delight at my reaction.

My first book!

I held it in my hand as an actual existing entity four days before my thirtieth birthday, although it was not to be published officially for over three weeks.

Brad was less than encouraging, however, concerning my new novel, *The Stars, like Dust—*. No contract. He would give me an option for $250 to keep me working, but he would have to see six or seven chapters now before a contract would be possible, and the six or seven would not include the first two chapters—which he was throwing out.

I had apparently committed the customary sin of the sophomore novel. The first novel was fine since I was writing as a novice and had no reputation to uphold. Once it was accepted, however, I was a "novelist" and had to write the second novel while keeping that reputation secure, which meant I had to write deeply and poetically and wittily and so on.

Bradbury got my error across to me very easily.

He said, "Do you know how Hemingway says, 'The sun rose the next morning.'?"

I had never read Hemingway, but I had heard of him, of course. I said, "No. How does he say it?"

He says, 'The sun rose the next morning.'"

I got it. From that day to this, I labored to make my style a spare one. I eschewed all ornamentation for its own sake, and if ever my style seems to depart from the starkly straightforward and simple, it is only to achieve humor.

11

On December 30, I was at the most crowded and successful Hydra Club meeting I ever attended. Almost everyone I knew was there, from friends as old as Fred Pohl to those as new as Hans Stefan Santesson.

Marty Greenberg was there and carried through on his promise. He had with him a contract, which I signed, and that meant that Gnome Press would do a collection of my robot stories. There I was, with my first book not yet officially published and with a second under contract and a third under option.

John Clark was there with his wife, Mildred, who was a formidable woman, large, rather plump. Clark's friends apparently did not like her. In order to see him without her, Fletcher Pratt had the idea of starting a stag organization, whose only function was to have monthly dinners to which Clark could be invited *sans* wife. It was to be called "The Trapdoor Spiders," since the notion was that the husbands would get into a hole and pull the trapdoor shut behind them as protection from Mrs. Clark.

The organization had already been in existence for some five years and was still flourishing.

Bradbury was there and already had a review clipping from *The Retail Bookseller* that praised *Pebble in the Sky*.

Harry Schwartz was there. He was a fellow Boys High student who had been in the class before me, and he was eventually to become a well-known writer for the New York *Times* in the field of economics and medicine. I remembered him only vaguely, but he remembered me quite well and seemed astonished that I had achieved anything but a ticket to the looney bin. I guess he didn't take the trouble to get past my effervescence.

Sam Merwin and Leo Margulies were there, and though Sam had laryngitis, he managed to apologize over what had happened to "Grow Old with Me" 2½ years before. I could now afford to shrug it off. Doubleday had found it more valuable because it had not been published and they might not have taken it if it had been. Since I wouldn't trade ten magazine appearances for that book, I now realized that Merwin had, all unwittingly, done me an enormous favor by rejecting it.

12

On the night of December 31, 1949, as though to cap the pleasant events of the past few days, I had the best New Year's Eve party I had ever had. It was at Rosalind Wylie's. She was Dirk Wylie's wife and had been a Futurian in her own right.

Roz was quite obese at that time (though pleasant, active and unself-conscious) and had a sister and a mother who were even fatter. She had a younger sister, however, who was thin and attractive, and Roz said she was formed out of the scraps left over from the other women of the family.

There were enormous quantities of food and I ate everything. I felt so hilarious over *Pebble in the Sky*[3] and the forthcoming robot story collection and *The Stars, like Dust*— that I had five whiskeys in a daredevil mood, with predictable results. I got high—and I mean stratospheric.

Gertrude, who was as much a teetotaler as I was, also gave in to the temptation, and in the end, Fred Pohl had to drive us home and see that we managed to get safely through the Blugerman door.

It was in this way that 1949 came to an end. It had seen me finish the Elderfield interlude, finish at last with Columbia, leave New York, and go to Boston.

Most of all, it had seen my writing suddenly revive and bound to a new height. I had sold a short story, a serial, and a book. I had had two stories anthologized and I had options on two more books. My total writing earnings for the year[4] came to $1,695, which finally surpassed the previous record year of 1944—and by half again as much.

What's more, my earnings as a chemist, from Elderfield and from the Medical School, came to $4,800, so that my total income for the year 1949 came to just under $6,500. I was satisfied. That was twice the income of my Navy Yard days, and it represented an advance even if

---

[3] I had obtained a copy for my parents, which I had autographed, and I could see that my father felt that I had fulfilled all his hopes at last. I think it was then he finally forgave me my failure to get into medical school ten years before. And after all, I *was* in medical school, wasn't I? And as a faculty member!

[4] Up to this point I have carefully listed every check I received, but from here on it it would be far too complicated to do so. I will mention important ones if they play a role in my life, but otherwise not. I will, however, continue to give my annual income, since its ups and downs influenced the course of events.

one allowed for inflation. With books in the works I hoped to do still better in the coming year.

13

On January 2, 1950, I celebrated my thirtieth birthday after returning to Somerville that day. Once again I had a birthday in a new place.

Since this was a particularly significant birthday (I was *thirty*), I took the trouble to summarize my writing production in my diary. I had published forty-four stories in the magazines, of which six had been reprinted in anthologies (four hard-cover, two soft-cover). One more magazine story, "The Evitable Conflict," was in press, and two more of my already published stories were to be anthologized shortly. And, of course, there was my one book about to be published, and two more in preparation.

It wasn't bad for a hobby, but I still didn't dream it could be my profession.

As for my instructorship, which I then considered my *real* profession, the halcyon days of the first half year of the Medical School were drawing to a close.

The biochemistry course was given to the freshman class in the second semester. In the first semester, the class took anatomy chiefly, and while that first semester endured, the biochemistry professors could engage in research and in all sorts of ancillary activities—and that's what I had been doing since I arrived.

The last week in January, however, meant the beginning of the teaching semester, and I had never done any teaching. There came a time when Dr. Walker called a meeting of the department and divided the lectures among the various faculty members. I was awarded eleven of them, concentrating on the more chemical. My first lecture was scheduled for February 7, and it was to deal with simple lipids. (To this day, I can't hear the phrase "simple lipids" without being instantly back—in imagination—in the Somerville apartment, wondering how I would make out.)

14

By January 15, 1950, the option on *The Stars, like Dust*— was formalized and I started the novel a second time.

I still had my outline. I had never tried to write any story, however long, with an outline. None of my Foundation stories had been outlined, though both "The Mule" and "—And Now You Don't" had been fearfully complex. Nor had I outlined *Pebble in the Sky.*

I found out quickly enough that my instinct was correct. I could not follow the outline. The story evolved as it rolled out of the typewriter and moved in its own direction, quite outside my control. For a while, I kept trying to drag the story back on the rails and then I gave up and threw the outline away.

I have never used an outline again for anything. In fact, I think it was my attempt to use an outline that is one of the reasons *The Stars, like Dust—* is the least favorite, to me, of my novels.

I had a completely false idea, by the way, of what reviews were like. On January 19, when *Pebble in the Sky* was officially published, I bought up all available New York and Boston papers, thinking that each would carry a review.

Then I thought there was some delay, and each day I would record my disappointment that nothing had appeared. However, Brad told me Doubleday got reviews from all over the country and he would save those that showed up for *Pebble in the Sky* and let me see them when I was next in New York.

Just to make sure, I signed up with a clipping service.

15

The Campbell era of science fiction ended with the decade of the 1940s.

From 1938, when Campbell had first become editor of *Astounding,* through 1949, a period of twelve years which, by the purest coincidence, covered that portion of my writing career that preceded my first book, *Astounding* was the only science-fiction magazine that counted. Other magazines were all fringe operations designed to publish stories that Campbell found not good enough or that authors knew in advance he would not even look at.

But then, with the new decade of the 1950s, new magazines appeared that were to rival *Astounding.* Campbell continued to be important but he would no longer be a lonely giant. He would have competitors.

The first of these new magazines was *The Magazine of Fantasy and Science Fiction* (usually referred to as *F & SF*), edited by Anthony Boucher and J. Francis McComas. It began as a quarterly, and I picked up my first copy on January 24, 1950.

There were signs of inflation. The science-fiction magazines, which used to be twenty cents an issue or less, had by now advanced to twenty-five cents, and *F & SF* was thirty-five cents.

16

On January 29, the New York *Times* finally reviewed *Pebble in the Sky*, a review that ended with, "Mr. Asimov is an old hand at this sort of thing and this novel makes for fine reading." I was satisfied, especially since both Sprague and Bob Heinlein wrote to tell me how much they liked the book.

17

The next day the teaching semester started and I was sick—a cold had developed into laryngitis. I went around for a week, practicing the phrase, "Today we take up simple lipids" to check on how my voice was progressing, till Gertrude said that she had never grown so tired of a particular sentence in her whole life.

Even before I gave my lecture, of course, I had to carry my weight in the biochemistry laboratory. The first session of the lab was held on January 31, 1950, and I stood there in my white lab coat feeling very superior and professorial with all the students deferentially calling me "Doctor."

Then one student came over and with no trace of wise-guyishness at all, said, "Pardon me, Dr. Asimov, are you a Ph.D. or a real doctor?"

It put me in my place. A Ph.D. is the highest academic degree there is, and is awarded only for original research. An M.D., on the contrary, is given out on satisfactory completion of schoolwork and is, academically, of no greater value than a Bachelor of Arts. Nevertheless, in a medical school, those with no more than a Ph.D. are second-class citizens. I knew that, but the student's question brought it home, and the value of my academic career in my own eyes, at least as long as I was in the Medical School, declined.

Then, on February 7, I gave my first lecture—on simple lipids—and survived.

Dr. Walker was surer of my talents in this direction than I was. He had been invited to give a talk at Bates College in Lewiston, Maine. He couldn't go, but suggested they invite me, telling them I was "an interesting speaker" and "quite a colorful character." I was invited for the fourteenth.

So it was that on February 14, 1950, I took the train to Lewiston. It was the first time I had ever made a trip for the purpose of giving a talk, but like all my talks thus far (except the one to Pauline Bloom's group the preceding May) it was to an academic audience. And as in the case of all my talks, without exception, thus far, it was without fee.

I was met at the station, taken to Lewiston's best hotel, and fed a turkey dinner before the talk. I spoke to perhaps sixty people, and they sufficed to fill the room. I don't remember what I talked about and I didn't note it in my diary, but I did speak extemporaneously, something I have done ever since. I did say in my diary that the talk "met with roaring approval. Applause! Laughter! I laid them in the aisles."

I'm sure I did. I always have since (well, nearly always). Talking that successfully, off-the-cuff, to an audience of strangers, cured me of my panic at lecturing.

Thus, on February 12, just before the Bates lecture, I had gone to Walker with a certain worry.

"Dr. Walker," I said, "last night I dreamed I got up before the class to give my lecture and I couldn't think of a thing to say. Do you think there's something ominous in that?"

"I think there's something normal in that," he said. "We all have dreams like that. Wait till you dream that you not only can't think of a thing to say but that you're standing there naked."

After the Bates College talk, however, I no longer had dreams like that.

18

A more unusual event took place on February 5, 1950. In the company of three minor show-business people (one of whom had once corresponded with me), Gertrude and I went to the New College Inn, something that would now be referred to as a gay nightclub.

The entertainment was by men who were heavily made up, or in women's clothes, or both. It was very good and the men were very pretty. "Good heavens," I muttered to Gertrude, "I could almost believe I married the wrong sex."

Once was enough, however. My curiosity was sated. I have nothing against gays—may they live long and prosper; but I have never sought out such entertainment again.

19

Reviews of *Pebble in the Sky* kept trickling in, and by and large they were favorable. Roy Machlowitz wrote a long letter in which he pointed out numerous weaknesses in the book, and his wife, Eleanor, added a letter in which she mentioned weaknesses he had missed.

I found out at once that I was not one of those authors who welcomed "constructive criticism." I replied with a letter that clearly revealed, I am afraid, that I was not in the least grateful for the help they were giving me, and our friendship trickled to an end.

The Machlowitz letter came just as I was sending the first third of *The Stars, like Dust*— to Brad, and I didn't like having my confidence shaken in this way.

20

One of my Boston friends—a Gentile—dropped around on February 21, 1950.[5] He was apparently in a spot of financial trouble and needed $200.

Well aware that one routinely asks twice as much as one needs, expecting it to be cut in half, I pulled out my checkbook and offered him one hundred. He accepted gladly.

He paid it back a month later, and in full, and said, "You know, I went to all my Christian friends and they all turned me down. I went to you last because you were Jewish and I didn't think you would lend me the money—and you lent me the money at once."

"Gee," I said dryly, "and without interest, too. I guess I forgot I was Jewish."

Perhaps he had learned something.

21

I was reviewing books on occasion for the New York *Compass*, a short-lived liberal paper that I read assiduously. The novelty of reviewing made it enjoyable at first, but it quickly palled on me. It occurred to me that if I didn't like adverse criticism of my writings, however mild that criticism might be, others might not either. And if I couldn't take it, I shouldn't hand it out.

Another source of disillusion arose in connection with Immanuel Velikovsky's *Worlds in Collision*, which was published that spring. Harper's ran excerpts and touted it tremendously, and I was fooled into thinking that it was an important book.

I got a copy, read it, and found it, although interesting, nothing

---

[5] Yes, I remember his name but if a story reflects unfavorably on a friend, I hope you don't mind if I omit his name as a general rule. The fact of his Gentility is crucial, however, so I mention it.

but a fairy tale and rather a foolish one. I asked the *Compass* if I might review it, and in this case I had no compunctions about a bad review. I didn't complain about the writing, merely about the content, and I thought it was important to explain that the book was astronomical gibberish and of no value whatever.

I wrote the review and the *Compass* refused to publish it because its publisher apparently disapproved of its contents. I did not appreciate that sort of censorship and I did nothing more for the *Compass*.

22

On March 1, 1950, I had another academic disillusionment. One of the three instructors in the department received a promotion to assistant professor and it was not I, although I had been the first of the three to be hired. The young man promoted was an M.D., however, and that pointed out a practical disadvantage of my second-class status.

It depressed me and, to add to the depression, I was hearing nothing from Brad on *The Stars, like Dust—*.

The only thing to do was to begin putting my robot stories into shape for Marty, making minor adjustments to remove internal inconsistencies.

I decided to include all eight robot stories that Campbell had published over a nine-year period, from "Reason" in 1941 to "The Evitable Conflict," which was soon to appear. Then, too, as a first story, I would include "Robbie," which Campbell had rejected but which Pohl had published in *Super Science* as "Strange Playfellow." These were quite enough, with some added introductory material, to make up a 70,000-word book, so that there was no need to include "Robot AL-76 Goes Astray" or "Victory Unintentional," which I thought were inferior.

I called the collection *Mind and Iron*.

23

On March 8, my first scientific publication appeared. The February 1950 issue of the *Journal of the American Chemical Society* contained, on page 820, a nine-page paper entitled "On the Reaction Inactivation of Tyrosinase During the Aerobic Oxidation of Catechol" by Isaac Asimov and Charles R. Dawson. It was, of course, the short version of my dissertation.

It was not only my first scientific publication, it also was my longest and my best.

Over the next three years I was to publish six papers on research work done in my Boston University laboratory. All of them were in collaboration with others who did the actual work, though I did the supervision and the actual writing. All those papers were unimportant and I enjoyed none of them. After 1953, I never again published a scientific paper involving research.

The trouble was that I hated writing research papers. Even while I still thought of myself as a researcher, I scorned and detested the writing end of it. Writing a research paper is a tedious and stylized job. You cannot write as you wish; you cannot use English; you cannot have fun.

It was even worse than being back in the Navy Yard making certain that no paragraph in a report was anything but a repetition of a paragraph in some earlier Navy Yard report.

Preparing my dissertation with Dawson had been an unsettling experience, but I found that writing papers on my own was no better. Such papers had to pass the eagle eyes of Walker and Lemon and then, on being submitted to a journal, had to undergo the dour glances of nameless reviewers. In the end, nothing got through but well-chewed cud.

I might not have minded, but I felt myself to be a writer, and I hated having my name on such limp and bedraggled material.

24

On March 13, Brad called me. He was rejecting the new version of *The Stars, like Dust—*. It was still too overwritten and I would have to try again. He was sending the copy back, copiously red-penciled. After the glorious beginning of the year, it looked as though I were roller-coasting downward again.

On that same day, however, Fred Pohl wrote me concerning "Little Man on the Subway," the story we had collaborated on ten years before. It was to appear in a little semipro magazine called *Fantasy Book*. It was a short-lived magazine that only put out about nine copies, but "Little Man on the Subway" appeared in the sixth and eventually I got a copy of that magazine and there was the story in it, and in the lead position, too.[6]

The longest story in that issue was "Scanners Live in Vain" by an unknown called Cordwainer Smith. I read it and thought it very unusual but very depressing. It turned out that in later years it was consid-

[6] See *The Early Asimov*.

ered a classic, and Smith (a pseudonym) went on to become what was almost a cult object.

The payment for "Little Man on the Subway" was $10, of which I only got half, of course. It was the first time I had a science-fiction story appear in any magazine but *Astounding* in eight years.

Fred then sent me word that he had also sold the other story on which we had co-operated, "Legal Rites." This one went to *Weird Tales*, and the payment was $40 for each of us.

But then I also had the manuscript of *The Stars, like Dust*— from Brad, and it was torn apart. Fred's news was an upward ripple in a downward avalanche, and the two collaboration sales couldn't even begin to compensate for the double failure of my new novel. As I said in my diary, "I feel like a fired science-fiction writer."

At least I had gone over my robot stories, made the necessary corrections in the printed versions, and left them for Gertrude to type up.

And on April 1, 1950, I started *The Stars, like Dust*— for the third time, from scratch.

25

On April 6, I received the news from Sprague de Camp that Campbell and his wife had separated and that Doña had moved in with George O. Smith.[7] Apparently, Campbell's overwhelming involvement with dianetics had been the last straw for Doña.

That same day Kupchan drove to New York, and on April 7 I went in to see Brad with Chapter 1 of the third version of *The Stars, like Dust*—. He said he liked it, but I suppressed my enthusiasm. It was only the first chapter.

On the ninth, I went to Philadelphia to attend an American Chemical Society meeting, and there I met with the de Camps. The next day I visited the Navy Yard for the first time in four years, but already there had been enough changes in personnel to make the place strange to me. I never went back again.

On the thirteenth, Sprague and I went over the new May 1950, *Astounding*, which, with great fanfare, ran L. Ron Hubbard's 16,000-word article "Dianetics."

Apparently, Hubbard was maintaining that all human beings had their thinking mechanisms distorted by impressions received in the fetal stage. The fetus could hear, be aware, and misunderstand all that

---

[7] There was always the tendency, somehow, for marital musical chairs in the science-fiction fraternity. Dick Wilson, for instance, had married Fred Pohl's first wife.

took place, and these misunderstandings produced all the wronghead-edness that plagued the human species. If each individual could be taken back, mentally, to the fetal stage by having "auditors" question them, and if all these misinterpreted impressions were erased, that individual would become "clear" and a very superior human being.

Neither Sprague nor I were in the least impressed. I considered it gibberish.

Then back to New York, and on April 14, I visited Campbell. He would talk of nothing but dianetics. I didn't argue much; I just remained impervious and said I didn't believe it. Finally Campbell said, half in anger and half in jest, "Damn it, Asimov, you have a built-in doubter."

"Thank goodness I do, Mr. Campbell," said I.

26

I was back in Boston on April 16, and marked my first test papers. I quickly realized that although I didn't mind giving lectures, I hated giving tests and I loathed marking them. I couldn't stand being responsible for low marks.

Where the questions required short factual answers, the necessity of placing crosses next to some was absolute and not a matter of judgment. I was then spared the feeling of guilt. Questions requiring essay answers, however, were just too much for me, so after my first experience, I always avoided essay questions when I could.

On April 17, I got a letter from Bill Boyd. His job had folded and he would be back at the Medical School in September.

27

Occasionally, we would watch television at a friend's home. Even before we had come to Boston, we had watched Milton Berle on two occasions at the Saltzmans. I had not been impressed. My fascination with television on the occasion of my first sight of it had not survived the repetition.

But then on April 22, 1950, we visited the Whipples and, for the first time, we saw Sid Caesar and Imogene Coca in "Your Show of Shows." That was different. To have entertainment like that in your home was a delight. I felt my snobbish antitelevision attitude evaporate, and we began, from that point onward, considering the possibility of getting one for ourselves.

49

Beyond Campbell

1

For twelve years, nearly, Campbell had been the center of my literary existence. He had nurtured me, protected me, fostered me, and made me what I was, and there is no way in which I can ever be sufficiently grateful to him.

By 1950, however, I had grown beyond him.

In part, it was because he had taken a wrong turning. He had moved into dianetics and from there into a series of other follies, and there was no way in which I could follow him. Furthermore, he could not separate his personal views from the magazine, but strove to incorporate those views into the stories he elicited from the authors, and many authors were only too delighted to comply and to "press Campbell's buttons." I could not do it any more than I could comply with his penchant for human superiority over extraterrestrials in earlier years.

Second, there were new markets opening up, and I wanted to branch out. I did not want to be a one-editor author. Moving into the book field and being associated with Brad and Doubleday was a major step for me, and on April 28, 1950, something else opened up.

On that day, I got a letter from Horace L. Gold. I had met him once or twice before the war, and a story, "None but Lucifer," by him and Sprague de Camp in collaboration was one of the most powerful lead novels in the old *Unknown*. His solo short story, "Trouble with Water," also in *Unknown*, was likewise unforgettable.

Now, it seemed, Horace was starting a magazine of his own, and he was writing to ask me for some stories.

I responded politely and suggested an idea for a story I called "Darwinian Poolroom." I was deep in the third attempt of *The Stars, like Dust*—, which seemed to have been occupying me forever, and I welcomed the thought of a break.

By May 7, I had once again finished a third of the book, in its third version, and the next day I mailed off one copy to Fred and one copy to Brad. Nothing to do but wait again.

Meanwhile, I could do other writing, and though Horace had been less than enthusiastic about my idea, that didn't bother me. If he didn't want it, someone else might. It was only twenty-five hundred words long and took me only a couple of days to write.

I made use of the same device I had used in "Super-Neutron" and in "Day of the Hunters," one in which the story is told in the form of a conversation among congenial spirits. I sent it off to Horace and waited to hear.

I needed some good news, for the weather was warming again, and the attic apartment in Somerville was warming even faster. We dreaded another summer there—and a full one this time. Even a visit to the MIT science-fiction society on May 12, my first contact with Boston fandom, did nothing to cheer me up.

2

We seized the occasion of Mother's Day on May 14 to call our respective families, and there was news on both sides. Stanley, who was finishing his junior year at New York University, had been working on its newspaper steadily and had been elected co-editor-in-chief for the next year.

And as for Henry Blugerman, he was selling the Henry Paper Box Company. He had owned it five years and it had been a hellish time, for it had been marginal at best during the entire period.

For me, though, the important news came the next day, when I got a telegram from Brad to the effect that he liked the third version of *The Stars, like Dust*— and this time I was to complete the novel. There was no talk of contract; that would take place with Fred, who was now in business as the Dirk Wylie Literary Agency. (Dirk Wylie, with whom he had started it, was now dead, and Rosalind was a widow.) Fred wrote quickly and told me that *The Stars, like Dust*— would involve a $750 advance, half again as much as that which *Pebble in the Sky* had commanded.

In addition to that, he was peddling a short story of mine that I called "Flesh and Metal." It was an attempt on my part to write a robot story that would sell to the slick magazines à la Heinlein. It had a handsome robot in it, a smitten housewife, and a tables-turned Cinderella bit. I thought it couldn't miss.

It had, however been circulating all through 1949 and early 1950 and had been missing every time.

Finally, *Amazing* decided to turn classy and publish very literary material by paying $.05 a word—an absolutely unprecedented fee. Fred managed to place "Flesh and Metal" with them and got $250 for merely 5,000 words. And Gold eventually accepted "Darwinian Poolroom."

To top it off, Gertrude had completed the typing up of the robot collection by May 18. It was a beautiful job and well done. She had worked long and hard.

3

But what about a different apartment? What about one that was not a steambox in the summer?

The trouble was that we were confined to the public transportation lines and decent apartments were invariably nowhere near those lines. The alternative was to buy a car, but neither Gertrude nor I could drive one; and I, for one, was afraid to drive one.

Gertrude was less afraid, and on May 16, 1950, her birthday, she celebrated by taking her first driving lesson. I was rather awed by her courage and I suggested that if she learned how to drive, we could get a car and she could chauffeur me when necessary.

The lessons continued through the month, by the end of which I had completed my first year at the Medical School. The Medical School wasn't bad, all told. It was infinitely more congenial than the Navy Yard had been, and Boston in peace was more colorful and pleasant than Philadelphia in wartime had been. I was not unhappy.

And *The Stars, like Dust*— was now racing ahead. I was at it every day and it was giving me no trouble.

On May 31, 1950, I celebrated the completion of my first year at the Medical School by being on a local radio talk show. I listened to a tape of myself the next day and was horrified to find that I sounded exactly like Stanley. Everyone, at my urgent questioning, assured me that that was exactly how I sounded. Apparently, my voice, sounding in my own ears through the bone cavities of my skull, sounds much deeper and resonant than it sounds to others.

4

Bill Boyd was back on June 2, 1950. He had not even waited till September. It had, apparently, been a very disillusioning experience, but I think he was humiliated at having once more to come back to the Medical School.

He said to me, "Do you remember, Isaac, when you outlined to me all the unpleasant things that happened at a civil-service job?"

I nodded guiltily. It had only been eleven months ago. I well remembered that time when I hoped I would talk him out of going.

He said, "I wish I had listened to you. Everything you said would happen *did* happen, and even worse than you said it would."

On that same day I attended the Medical School graduation ceremonies. It was a senior class that I hadn't taught, of course, so I knew no one; and even if I had, I would have found it boring. I avoided graduation ceremonies thereafter.

5

Gertrude finished her driving lessons on June 6, 1950, but her teacher wasn't sure she would be able to pass the test, and Gertrude felt rather disappointed over that. Fortunately, we were slated to go to New York the next day, so there would be time to think it through and decide whether to take more lessons.

On June 8 I visited Fred, got my advance for *The Stars, like Dust—*, and handed over additional chapters. I also gave him the manuscript of the robot story collection. Martin Greenberg had rejected my notion of calling it *Mind and Iron* and suggested it be called *I, Robot*.

"Impossible, Marty," I said. "Eando Binder wrote a short story called 'I, Robot' back in 1938."

To which Marty answered, with unassailable logic, "F— Eando Binder."

So *I, Robot* it was.[1] There is no question that Marty's title was far better than mine and probably helped sell the book.

After that, I went on to see Horace Gold who, as it happened, lived in Stuyvesant Town, so that the visit was an exercise in nostalgia for me.

Gold turned out to be a handsome, talkative fellow who was even balder than my father. (I once casually combed my hair at his mirror and, viewing the process with disfavor, he said, "Do I flex my muscles in *your* presence?)

His wife, Evelyn, looked rather like Gypsy Rose Lee in my eyes, and seemed quite extroverted.

Horace and I discussed future stories, when suddenly he said, "Pardon me," got up, and left the room. I assumed he had gone to the bath-

---

[1] Years later, some television show put Eando Binder's "I, Robot" on the air, using his title. Many people watched, thinking they were going to see one of my stories, and quite a few of them wrote indignant letters to me about some joker using my title. I had to write to each of them and explain carefully that it was I who was the joker and that Binder was there first.

room, and I was waiting patiently when Evelyn came to me and said, "I think you'll have to leave now."

I rose in alarm. "Have I done something?"

"No," she said, "he's not well."

It turned out that, partly as a result of his war experiences, he could not go out in the open and was confined by his own fears to his apartment. Nor could he speak for long to people he didn't know.

I was horrified, expressed my sorrow, and turned to leave. As I reached the door, the telephone rang, and Evelyn answered.

"It's for you," she said, and I turned back from the already opened door.

"Who knows I'm here?" I said in astonishment, but it was Horace calling from the bedroom by means of his second phone. So I remained and sat in the living room, talking to Horace in the bedroom for about an hour.

This was a pattern. Once Horace was on the phone, he wouldn't get off; it was the only way he could relate to other people without panic. It was all right at first, but there came a time when I dreaded a phone call from him and would invent all kinds of emergencies to get off.

The next day, June 9, I visited Columbia. Tarpley had been mugged just two nights before, just off the Columbia campus. (The city was becoming steadily more dangerous.) His wallet had been taken and he had been sufficiently banged up to require stitches. He was going to be getting his Ph.D. in October.

As for Elderfield's group, they had isolated the intermediate compound whose existence I had pinpointed and told me it was four times as effective as plasmochin—so I had done some good.

Brad called me to tell me he liked the additional chapters of *The Stars, like Dust*—, and I felt expansive enough to take all the Blugermans to a shore dinner at Lundi's, where we wreaked havoc on the lobster, chicken, and steamed clams. The whole bill came to $24, but I had come a long way since $10 had scared me silly at Locke-Ober's.

And on June 11, we were back in Somerville.

6

In Somerville, Gertrude was still uncertain as to her next step with regard to the driving lessons. I suggested that she take it easy for a while and that I would take driving lessons. That would give us two chances, and if either of us made it, we could get a car. Then, too, she could wait till after I had taken my test, pass or fail, before she would have to decide whether to take the test herself or to take additional lessons. In all this I put on a show of confidence I did not feel.

On June 12, then, I took my first driving lesson and, as it happened, one of the first-year medical students, whom I had just finished teaching biochemistry, was making some odd change by teaching at a driving school and he was to teach me. This meant I could rely on patience and intelligence, and it eased my fears.

He got me in the car and showed me how to turn on the engine after making sure the car was in neutral. Then he had me step on the clutch and put the car in reverse. Then he told me to let the clutch come up slowly and just let the car move a few feet and then step on the brake.

I did as he said and as the car began to move, a very peculiar and utterly unforeseen thing happened to me: I found that I loved the sensation; that I felt in control. The next day, I was actually driving, shifting gears, and turning corners. I continued to love it. By the third day, I was determined to buy a car as soon as possible.

Why that should be I don't know, but I have loved to drive ever since. It is the only way in which I really enjoy getting from here to there (aside from walking).

On June 17, we were shopping for a car and looking at Plymouths. Then we went to Durgin-Park for a farewell dinner with the Bersons, who had, by a pleasant coincidence, also spent 1949–50 in Boston. Now, however, Jerry Berson was getting a job at the University of Southern California, and he and Bella would be leaving soon. That was the worst of making friends in the academic world—all its members were peripatetic.

Also present were Roger and Carolyn Newman, who were friends of the Bersons originally, and with whom we had often hobnobbed that first year in Boston. Roger was leaving, too, for Cal Tech. I remember Roger best for a lesson he taught me, perhaps inadvertently.

My clipping service had been sending me all kinds of reviews of *Pebble in the Sky*, and I had bought a scrapbook and had been carefully pasting them up. On June 24, when the Newmans and Bersons were visiting our attic apartment, I brought out the book and went over the reviews very pridefully for them.

During the course of that, I heard Roger say in a very low voice, to himself rather than to anyone else, "The old lady shows her medals." (That was, of course, the name of a play by James M. Barrie.)

I pretended I hadn't heard, closed the book as soon as I decently could, and put it away.

From that day on, I have never showed my reviews to anyone nor, as far as is humanly possible, done anything that could be construed as showing my medals.[2] Thank you, Roger Newman, wherever you are.

[2] Of course, you might construe this autobiography as a case of showing my medals, but I'm doing my level best to show my boobie prizes as well.

7

On June 19, we put down a deposit of $25 on a new Plymouth that would cost us $1,650 altogether. I wasn't satisfied with just the driving lessons, either. I invited my fellow instructor, Fabian Lionetti (a quiet fellow with a permanently furrowed forehead and a somewhat hesitant manner of speaking), to dinner, after which he took me for a long drive in his car, describing what he was doing and why, and giving me numerous practical lessons on car maintenance and car expense. It was a little frightening, but I was unshaken. I had to have a car.

8

On June 23, I received the September 1950 issue of *Weird Tales*, with "Legal Rites"[3] as the lead story and on the cover. *Weird Tales* was a fantasy magazine, not science fiction, and it had made its first appearance even before *Amazing* had. *Weird Tales* had had a colorful history, but it had been going downhill for a long time and had not much longer to live. This was the only time I ever appeared in it and I am rather glad, for sentimental reasons, that I managed to make it before the magazine died.

9

On June 25, 1950, North Korean forces invaded South Korea, the United States sent troops into Korea, and the Korean War had begun. I feared a repetition of all the miseries of World War II, but the Korean War was a minor squabble in comparison, and since I was over thirty by now, there was never any question of my being drafted.

Stanley was the one in danger now, for he would be twenty-one in a month and was just the right age. However, his eyes were worse than mine, and when he underwent his physical examination, they were listed as 20/600, which made him a 4F.

10

We went to New York on June 30 to attend a science-fiction conference. I showed up at 3:00 P.M. on July 1, just eleven years after the first convention I attended, but this time, of course, I was a big wheel.

[3] See *The Early Asimov*.

Among those whom I now met for the first time were Poul Anderson, another one of Campbell's discoveries, whose first story was "Tomorrow's Children" in the March 1947 *Astounding*; Jerome Bixby (then editor of *Planet Stories*); and Bea Mahaffey (the editor of a new magazine, *Other Worlds*). Bea was a science-fiction editor who was not only a woman but also a young and beautiful woman at that.

The next day was the big day of the conference, with many speakers. It was my turn at 4:10 P.M. I spoke to an audience of 150, the largest I had ever had. Gertrude was brought in (rather against her will) by Roz Wylie. Gertrude sat in the last row, in agony over my possible embarrassment, just as on our honeymoon when she had sat in the balcony while I was competing in the quiz. After I had spoken for a while, I noticed she had changed seats and was now in the front row; she had apparently stopped worrying.

She had reason not to worry, I gave a very successful talk, without notes and without preparation of any kind. It was clear to me that I loved talking in general and that I loved the laughter and applause.

In the euphoria that followed the talk, I let Brad buy me a drink. I also let Fred buy me a drink. Then it was Brad's turn. Well, you're ahead of me. By banquet time I was drunk.

After I had gotten distinctly drunk, I saw Sprague de Camp in the distance, felt overwhelmed with love, called out "Sprague," and ran for him. He looked horrified and left in a hurry. I think he was afraid I would hug him or something, and he may have been right.

At the banquet, while I maintained an uneasy silence and tried to sober up, someone said, "Oh they're taking a picture of us" and so they were, one of those panoramic banquet views.

"Where?" said I, swinging around in my chair and looking at the camera with a vague, drunken stare and the camera snapped. When the picture was developed, there was our table (in the background, fortunately) and there was I, clearly drunk, though too small to notice unless pointed out.[4]

The best part of the day to me, though, was listening to Lester del Rey's speech in which he lambasted dianetics very rationally and without stint. Campbell was not in the audience, I noted.

Horace Gold called me the next day and talked me into promising to do another story for him. On the train back, on July 4, I started one that I called "Potent Stuff," using nothing more than pen and ink.

[4] A year later, *Life* did an article on science fiction in which this banquet picture was featured. How embarrassing that the only time my face ever appeared in *Life* it was a drunken face.

11

On July 6, I had my last driving lesson, and on July 7, I took my driving test. I thought I did very well, but the testers are in a position that appeals to all the latent sadism in one. The people taking the test are invariably frightened, tense, and pitifully anxious to please. Naturally, any person with talents sufficiently small to make it necessary for him to make a living testing drivers can't resist that.

I drove about quite a bit, following all orders and making no mistakes that I could see except for beginning to drive into a one-way street the wrong way when the tester deliberately ordered me to do so. He stopped me, of course, and told me roughly that I shouldn't follow illegal orders. He was quite right in that.

At the end, he asked me the ethnic nature of my name, and I said, "Russian." "Were you born there?" he wanted to know, and I said, "Yes," wondering if he were going to have the nerve to refuse me a license on that ground. After all, the North Koreans were still advancing quite rapidly into South Korea and it was doubtful, as yet, if the American forces pouring into the country could stop them. If the Soviets chose to join the North Koreans, World War III was around the corner.

But the tester just said, "Well, I hope the Russians drive tanks the way you drive this automobile."

So I managed a smile that served to convince the idiot I was congratulating him on the subtlety and sophistication of his sense of humor, and he passed me.

I had my first driver's license!

It meant that Gertrude could relax. Since I had a license, and since I liked to drive, I could drive for both until she felt like taking lessons again.

What I didn't have, though, was a car. I was still waiting for it to arrive at the dealers from whom we were purchasing it, and the dealer was talking dolefully about delays because of the war in Korea.

While waiting, I mailed off "Potent Stuff" to Horace Gold, and Gertrude finally decided where we would go for a vacation that year. It would be to Camp Annisquam, on the seashore, this time—at Cape Ann in Massachusetts, to be specific. Two weeks again and this time it would be in the shank of the season—last week of July and first week of August.

We began packing on July 22 (our first anniversary in the Somerville apartment), and on that day my very first Doubleday statement and royalty check arrived. Such statements have been a semi-annual feature of my life ever since.

12

The two weeks at Annisquam were highly successful. We met nice people, saw pleasant shows, took various ocean and land trips to Gloucester, Rockport, Marblehead, Wingershaek Beach, and so on.

What I remember most clearly, though, was my co-operation with the waiters who were trying to write parodies of the songs in popular musicals; parodies that would have local significance.

They were having trouble, and knowing me to be a writer, they asked my advice. I looked over what they had done and said, "No, no, you've got to match the original lyrics, syllable by syllable, stress by stress, and rhyme by rhyme, or the music won't fit and the whole thing won't sound clever. For heaven's sake, don't try to improve on Cole Porter."

"What do you mean?" they asked humbly.

"I'll show you," I said. "You're working with *Kiss Me, Kate,* so let's start with *'Wunderbar.'*"

After a while, I wrote:

> Annisquam, Annisquam
> We've taken ocean trips
> But when the sea ain't calm
> Take the train to Annisquam.

"Sing it!" I said.

They did and they were delighted with the way in which the syllables slid into the music.

They insisted I go on to the other songs and contented themselves with observation. I worked away matching syllables and keeping all the internal rhymes. I said, for instance, "Such tender slips make slender tips increase," and "Could she fill with prattle still the cattle boat to Salem," and, "We broke all the laws upon the shores of Wingershaek."

Then I had to attend all the rehearsals to make sure that they sang the songs correctly, and I took the lead baritone part myself. What it amounted to was that I spent a major part of the vacation indoors working.

Gertrude pointed out the folly of paying premium vacation rates and then spending the time working for the management.

I tried to explain to her that the shoe was on the other foot; that I was enjoying myself and that I would have been dreadfully unhappy if

I had not been permitted to do this. I would rather have written the parodies than do any of the vacation things that everyone else was doing. (When it was all over, the owners of the resort gave me a twenty-dollar rebate for my help, but I just turned it over to the waiters.)

On July 26, Gertrude and I celebrated our eighth anniversary, and since we had made no secret that it was coming, the Annisquam management brought out a cake. Someone yelled "Speech!" and everyone was thunderstruck and perhaps a little chagrined when I promptly got up and made one. Apparently, it was customary to shout "Speech!" and equally customary for the honored couple to be entirely too bashful to oblige.

13

By the time we got back to Boston, the situation in Korea was at its lowest ebb. The Americans had been forced into the southeastern corner of the country, around the port of Pusan.

What selfishly struck me as more important, however, was that the dealer had my car. I spent all of August 7 having them put in various accessories that I wanted and signing up for insurance. On August 8, 1950, at the age of thirty, I owned my first car.

Combine that with the fact that writing earnings kept pouring in, and I was a happy man. My share of the Unicorn Mystery publication of *Pebble in the Sky* came in, together with news of further anthologizations of this story and that. There was also a report of the sale of second serial rights to *Pebble in the Sky*. (I didn't even know what that meant till it was explained to me. It turned out to mean magazine publication after the book appearance. First serial rights involves magazine publication *before* book appearance.)

On Wednesday, August 9, I drove my car to work for the first time and hardly got lost, just a little bit on the way back. On Friday, I tanked up with gasoline for the first time. It cost nearly 27 cents a gallon, and I was appalled at the expense. I was also aware, for the first time, of the dreadful conditions of the streets. Every bang and rattle the potholes imposed on my car were so many stabs to my vitals.

The real test came on August 12, when, at the Boyds' invitation, we drove to their summer place. It took us 4¼ hours to get there, driving very slowly, and 3½ hours to get back, driving more quickly. We traveled 176 miles round-trip to stay with the Boyds about three hours, but we weren't there to visit but to have me practice driving, and that practice I had. Despite all my driving lessons, it was only when I returned from the Boyds that I felt I could drive.[5]

After that, I returned the car to the dealer to hold it for me for the rest of the month because I was going to the Breadloaf Writers Conference and didn't yet dare to drive there.

14

The Breadloaf Writers Conference was held in conjunction with Middlebury College, in Middlebury, Vermont. It was the oldest and most prestigious of the writers' conferences and was held every year in the last half of August.

It was run at that time by Theodore Morrison of Harvard, but among the important men of the faculty was Fletcher Pratt, and it was he who had urged me to attend.

I arrived in Breadloaf on August 16, 1950, without Gertrude, who chose to go to New York and stay with her parents. Pratt was there, of course. Also William Sloane, a publisher who had authored two well-thought-of science-fiction novels, and Catherine Drinker Bowen, a popular historian.

Present in addition was John Ciardi, tall, slim, with a shock of dark hair and an incredibly majestic nose that would have made it possible for him play Cyrano without makeup. He had a beautiful bass voice that was delightful to listen to. He was a poet and when he lectured on poetry there was no use in his trying to distinguish between good poetry and bad poetry. When *he* read poetry, it all sounded good.

The bookstore contained copies of books by the various faculty members, and that meant it contained copies of *Pebble in the Sky*.

It was at Breadloaf, I think (though just possibly at Annisquam, three weeks earlier), that someone came to me, shook my hand vigorously, and said, "Congratulations."

"On what?" I said.

"On keeping your name. It takes courage to insist on being called 'Isaac.'"

"Not at all," I said, offended. "I *like* the name."

And every time after that, this man who loved my bravery called me nothing but "Zack," a nickname I despised.

While at Breadloaf, I got a call from Fred Pohl, who told me that

[5] By then the Americans were on the offensive in Korea and it was clear we were not going to suffer the humiliation of being pushed into the sea.

Horace Gold had seen what there was of *The Stars, like Dust*— and wanted to serialize it in his magazine, which he was calling *Galaxy Science Fiction*. He assured me that Brad would approve (but I worried about Campbell—and then decided not to, since *Astounding* was filled with dianetics for issue after issue at this time).

The only catch was that Horace wanted me to introduce a new element of suspense. Everyone would have to be looking for a mysterious document, which would turn out at the very end to be a copy of the United States Constitution.

I objected very strongly to that, saying it was corny and downright unbelievable. No one could suppose that an instrument of government suitable for a primitive nation forming a small part of a single world would be suitable for a stellar federation. Fred soothed me and said that I could explain that the document was merely an inspiration. It would satisfy Horace and I could take it out for book publication.

So I agreed, but when I told Brad, apologetically, that I would have to add this for Horace's sake, he said, "That sounds great. We'll keep it in the book version, too." And he did, which is the chief reason why *The Stars, like Dust*— is my least favorite novel.

The faculty at Breadloaf recognized my established-writer status and didn't lump me together with the other students. Bill Sloane, without warning, called me to speak on the nonhuman heroes of science fiction and I gave a one-minute impromptu speech that went over well.

Then, on August 26, I helped out in the session that was designed to teach interviewing by allowing myself to serve as the subject of an interview. I was told by the faculty to answer briefly, and to interpret questions narrowly and literally, so that the students would learn how to ask questions properly.

One student, a dentist in real life (as I recall), after it had been established that I did quite a bit of writing, asked how much money I made in this way.

I hesitated, and then said, "About as much as I make at my job as an instructor."

He laughed and said, with what I took as a sneer, "That's all?"

I would have answered angrily, but Pratt intervened, and scolded him for his impoliteness to someone who was trying to be of service to them.

There were still three days to go, but one of the students was driving back to Boston that day and invited me to come with him, and on impulse, I went. The dentist's remark was the deciding factor, I think.

15

At about this time, Heinlein forged another advance, for both himself and for the science-fiction world in general. He was science adviser to *Destination: Moon*, the first intelligent science-fiction movie made.

I went to see it, with considerable excitement, after I got back from Breadloaf. I was willing to overlook the Cold War jingoism at the start, and some minor unlikelinesses such as a lunar surface that seemed to be composed of dried-out sediment.

What bothered me and, indeed, ruined the picture for me, was that an amateur actor, whom I had never seen before and have never seen since, was hired to portray a comic stowaway from Brooklyn. Aside from the fact that the comic Brooklynite was a weary cliché and that Heinlein, remembering me, might have avoided it, there might at least have been some attempt to get a Brooklynite to do it. There must, after all, be thousands of transplanted Brooklynites in Los Angeles. Instead, the character chosen to play the part could *not* duplicate the Brooklyn accent. It was painful to listen to what he *thought* was a Brooklyn accent.

16

On August 28, I got my car back and had a sudden inspiration. Why not take advantage of my mobility to have a pleasant lunch?

I was accustomed to eating lunch at the local Howard Johnson's, which was good enough for the peasantry, but surely now that I had a car, I could drive downtown and have a leisurely lunch at some fine restaurant.

Into town I drove and learned the hard way about parking spots and their nonexistence, about downtown lunch-hour traffic and their nonmobility, about one-way streets and their nonpredictability. It took me nearly an hour to get back and then I parked the car at Howard Johnson's, trembling so hard I could hardly hold the wheel—and when I calmed down, I ate there. It was a valuable lesson.

17

On August 29, 1950, I *drove* to New York for the first time. It took me seven hours, counting time for getting gasoline and having my oil changed, but I did it without getting lost and without accident.

Once in New York, I gave more of *The Stars, like Dust*— to Brad and promised him the last three chapters within two weeks.

On the thirty-first, I celebrated my new mobility by driving Gertrude to Campbell's in Elizabeth and having lunch with him there. Hubert Rogers, the illustrator, was with us and he amused me enormously by telling Campbell calmly that he thought Hubbard was a faker and that dianetics was nonsense. I kept my mouth shut, since Rogers clearly needed no help.

Then I drove Gertrude to Windsor Place, parked the car there, went into Manhattan, came back, got the car, and drove to the Blugermans'. Who would have thought, a quarter year before, that I would be driving everywhere like this?

One of the things we did in Manhattan was to visit Gold. He gave us a copy of the October 1950 *Galaxy*, the first issue, which contained "Darwinian Poolroom."[6] When I read the issue I had to agree, with some awe, that Horace had put together just about the best issue of any science-fiction magazine I had ever seen. My own story was the weakest thing in it.

Horace kept it up, too. From the first issue, *Galaxy* was in a tie with *Astounding* for the title of best magazine, in the eyes of most fans. Many of them (even I, myself) felt that *Galaxy* had a bit the better of it.

Much less important was the fact that the November 1950 *Future Fiction* contained "Day of the Hunters."[7]

Henry Blugerman had a job again, as superintendent at a paperbox firm, and we visited him at his place of business on September 1. That was the sort of job he had before his ill-starred venture into entrepreneurship, and words cannot describe how relieved I was that he was back where he belonged.

I got a new typewriter at last while in New York. It was another Smith-Corona portable and replaced the old one that my father had gotten for me twelve years before. I carefully kept the old one as a fall-back, however, following my usual procedure of keeping all my options open.

On September 3, I drove to Newark, where I gave a talk at Sam Moskowitz's science-fiction group there. After dinner, I drove back to Brooklyn at night. It was the first night driving I had done and, as I said in my diary, "Snow and ice are all I have not yet experienced." But then, I was in no hurry for those.

On September 5, 1950 (my mother's fifty-fifth birthday), I drove

[6] See *Buy Jupiter and Other Stories* (Doubleday, 1973).
[7] See *Buy Jupiter and Other Stories*.

Gertrude and myself back to Boston. It took me only six hours that time, and at one point I actually hit a speed of eighty miles an hour.

By September 8, I had a note from Brad to the effect that the new chapters were very good, that I was constantly improving, and that Doubleday wanted to stick with me.

Good! For I wanted to stick with them!

I finally finished the last word of *The Stars like Dust*— on September 17 and mailed it off on the eighteenth. It had been much harder to write than *Pebble in the Sky* but it was done and "in press," as I now learned to say.

18

Meanwhile, a new and completely different project had been begun, quite unexpectedly.

Ever since Bill had come back from Egypt he had been aching for some project he could throw himself into that would wipe out, in his own mind, the fiasco of the Egyptian venture. He had done a very highy regarded text in immunochemistry and had revised it into an equally good new edition. Now it occurred to him to do a general text of biochemistry for medical students. On September 12, 1950, he suggested this to me, and asked if I would be willing to help and make it "Boyd and Asimov."

The suggestion intrigued and delighted me. I had an instant vision of having a complex, authoritative, and large textbook lined up on the shelf along with my science-fiction novels, thus lending myself new prestige as a double-threat man, both fiction and nonfiction.

Besides, it was something new and therefore something interesting. There was only one catch: Bill was a full professor and his time was his own. I, however, had Dr. Walker as my academic employer and Dr. Lemon as my research employer, and they might not be willing to have me spend my time on a textbook. Boyd suggested we ask Walker directly, and the next day we did.

His reaction took us by surprise. He did more than give me permission. He joined the project and it became "Walker, Boyd, and Asimov." I don't know that Boyd was very pleased to have his seniority bumped like that, but Dr. Walker was a very good biochemist and his collaboration was bound to help the book. Besides, if Dr. Walker was part of the project I didn't see that Dr. Lemon could object.

Walker got to work at once. That very night we were invited to his house to help compose a letter to Williams & Wilkins, the textbook publisher whom Walker thought would be best for the purpose. It was on that occasion that I met Mrs. Walker, whom I describe in my diary as "a tough and talkative woman," which is exactly right. I then added a calm, "We drove, of course."

We made up a list of chapters, assigned one third to each of us and, by September 20, a Williams & Wilkins representative, Dick Hoover, was over to see us. We were in business.[8]

19

Henry Lemon, intent on improving my technical background, signed me up for a week's course in New York on electrophoresis, a technique for separating complex protein molecules in blood and else-where—and for purifying proteins such as enzymes.

I was not at all enthusiastic about this because I had long come to the conclusion that nothing was ever going to make a good lab techni-cian out of me, but there was no way I could tell him that.

On Sunday, September 24, 1950, I drove to New York, and the next day I began the course. There were two lectures each day, one from ten in the morning to noon, and the other seven to ten in the eve-ning. The afternoons were our own. That first day of the course, for in-stance, I filled in with lunch with Brad, and then with visits to Fred and to Horace.

The next day I saw Stanley and visited him the day after at the *Compass*, where he was doing some work to gain experience in the reporting profession.

On the twenty-seventh, I met Sidney Cohen for the first time in eight years, the first time since my day on the roller coaster with Ger-trude. He himself was still a bachelor, though his younger brother and sister were each married. He was practicing neurology and psycho-therapy and had not changed in appearance at all. It was a great pleas-ure to see him.

I was at a Hydra Club party the next day and Fletcher Pratt was insistent that I return to Breadloaf the next year and bring Gertrude with me so that I would not be tempted to return prematurely. He hinted at semistaff status, which would mean I would not have to pay full tuition. I was tempted.

On October 1, we drove back to Boston after a sleepless night, so that I discovered how difficult and dangerous it becomes to drive when your eyes keep wanting to close.

I didn't get much out of the electrophoresis course, by the way.

---

[8] It was at about this time, after over a month of stalemate in Korea, that the Americans finally broke through by a brilliant landing at Inchon, Seoul's port. With the Americans in their rear, the North Koreans had to retreat pell-mell and their gamble was lost.

20

On returning, I found a letter from one Gotthard Guenther, who was lecturing on science fiction at the Cambridge Center of Arts. The first lecture was on October 3, and I decided to attend.

I took a seat well in the back without making myself known, and I had not yet reached the stage where I could be recognized offhand. I could therefore listen in welcome anonymity.

Guenther, it turned out, was a German—a Prussian, in fact—and spoke with a thick German accent. He was, however, by no stretch of the imagination a Nazi, but was indeed a kindly and sweet gentleman, and utterly other-worldly.

Yet he still had a peculiarly Teutonic notion of the mystical value of soil. He felt that civilization was a product of the Old World and could not flourish indigenously in the New. (When someone raised the question of the Incas and the Mayas, he dismissed them with a wave of the hand.)

Therefore, he maintained, when Old World civilization was transplanted to the New World, a distortion was introduced and one of the ways in which this distortion was evidenced was by the peculiar American invention of science fiction, which was not to be confused with earlier European ventures in the field (Jules Verne, for instance). American science fiction turned Old World values upside down.

Take, for instance, he said, the story "Nightfall" by Isaac Asimov. (At this point, I shrank lower in my seat.) It dealt with stars as instruments of madness, whereas in all Old World views of the universe, the stars were seen as gentle, benign, and friendly.

He continued to describe the manner in which "Nightfall" reversed or distorted common views and, in general, built up an interpretation of the story that had me gasping.

When the lecture was over, members of the audience flocked around him, and I waited patiently. When I was the only one left, I said, "Dr. Guenther, your analysis of 'Nightfall' is all wrong."

"Well, that is a matter of opinion," said Dr. Guenther, smiling gently.

"No, it is not," I said, forcefully. "I am *certain* you are wrong. Nothing of what you said was in the author's mind."

"And how can you know that?"

That was when I let the guillotine blade fall. "Because, Dr. Guenther, I am the author."

His face lit up, "You are Isaac Asimov?"

"Yes, sir."

"How pleased I am to meet you." Then he said, "But tell me, what makes you think, just because you are the author of 'Nightfall,' that you have the slightest inkling of what is in it?"

And of course I couldn't answer that question because it suddenly became clear to me that there might well be more in a story than an author was aware of.

Dr. Guenther and I became good friends after that, and on October 17 I gave a guest lecture to his class.[9]

21

I was already working on my share of the textbook, which we finally decided to call *Biochemistry and Human Metabolism*. My first job was Chapter 2, which was "Protein Structure." I worked away busily and discovered I enjoyed writing nonfiction but, alas, I had the same trouble I had with my dissertation. Writing became a committee affair.

After each chapter was done (and that meant endless looking up of references in the library, listing the important ones, constructing formulas, and so on), Walker, Boyd and I would go over the thing, word by word. It was even worse than my experience with Dawson.

For one thing, Walker and I were antithetical in style. I wanted to be chatty, colloquial, and dramatic; Walker wanted to be terse, formal, and cold. More often than not, Boyd sided with Walker, and it was not long before it seemed to me the textbook was more trouble than it was worth.

Having entered into it, however, I could not drop it, and I spent many months in the library, at the typewriter, and in conference. As much as possible, however, I did the work in school and left evenings and weekends free for my science fiction.

22

I couldn't very well forget my science fiction, for it was doing well. On October 17, I got my copy of the November 1950 *Galaxy*, the second issue, and it had "Potent Stuff" in it. Horace had changed the title to the totally unimpressive "Misbegotten Missionary." It kept that title through various anthologizations, but when the time came for it to be

[9] By then, American troops had reoccupied all of South Korea and had begun an invasion of North Korea under the gung-ho leadership of General Douglas MacArthur.

included in one of my collections, I changed the title to "Green Patches."[10]

On the nineteenth, I received the galley proofs of *I, Robot,* and on the twenty-fourth, the galley proofs of *The Stars, like Dust—*. This time there was no week spent on the loving caressing of the words. I adopted the principle I have used ever since. I got to it at once, went through it at a gallop that evening, and mailed it back the next day.

Then, too, I was writing a new short story. I had to. I felt guilty about having given *The Stars, like Dust—* and two short stories to Horace Gold. I had to balance it with something for Campbell.

On the weekend of October 14–15, 1950, I began a story called "Breeds There a Man?" and worked on it madly. It took me just two weeks to finish it, though it was 12,000 words long. I sent it to Campbell and he bought it without trouble. My conscience was at rest, especially since I thought it was a particularly good story. It was set in the near future and dealt with current problems—the need to work up a defense against the atom bomb—which is something I don't usually do. To be sure, I had an offbeat angle to it, with humanity representing an experimental culture being developed by intelligences (unspecified) somewhere off in space—a little like my thesis in "Death Sentence."

23

Toward the end of October, Gertrude had an idea. She enjoyed typing up *I, Robot* for me and it had made her feel more part of my work.

Since we couldn't have children (and by now, all efforts failing, we had both resigned ourselves to our status as a childless couple), why not arrange a life based on that?

Why shouldn't I get a dictating machine and dictate my stories? That might prove easier and faster than typing them. Then Gertrude would type them up. We would be a team.

I was fascinated by that. I looked into the matter and found that for $400 I could get an Audograph machine on which I could dictate stories onto small, thin, plastic records, which could then be replayed with a foot-pedal device for starting and stopping, so that, through an earphone, a typist could hear a phrase at a time.

I discussed the matter with an Audograph representative and found I could get such a machine within six weeks. What's more, he agreed to let me have a thirty-day trial before requesting me to pay. (I

[10] See *Nightfall and Other Stories* (Doubleday, 1969).

explained there was no way of knowing if I could dictate a story without trying to do so first.)

On November 9, I got my Audograph, dictated a letter, and Gertrude transcribed it. It went very well. On the eleventh, I got to work in earnest and began dictating the first scene of a new story called "Hostess" into the Audograph. In 2½ weeks, I had it finished and transcribed—12,000 words. What's more, it read just as though I had written it in the usual manner. We were a good team and we were both delighted.

24

While the story was being written, however, something very frightening took place.

On November 21, 1950, right after the morning rituals of elimination, bathing, and shaving, I was struck with acute abdominal cramps that I recognized at once as being similar to that which hit me in Stuyvesant Town two years before. The difference was that then it lasted for twenty minutes and now it went on and on—and on—

I endured the agony for two hours before breaking down sufficiently to send a frightened Gertrude across the street to fetch a Dr. Adler, whose nameplate we saw in his window. Fortunately he was in and fortunately he ran over.

I thought it was appendicitis, of course, but he asked questions about the location and made the correct diagnosis. I had a kidney stone and what I was suffering from was "renal colic." No doubt I'd had one two years before and passed it.[11]

Dr. Adler said that the pain would pass but that I would need X rays to locate the stone. He offered me morphine to ease the pain, but I refused, having an antipathy to addictive drugs. He left and after fifteen minutes more I could not bear the martyrdom and, in an agony of shame, sent Gertrude across the street to ask for the morphine.

Back came the doctor. He had called an ambulance and off I went to a small local hospital. It was the first time in my life (and the only time so far) that I was in an ambulance, and the first time I was in a hospital as a patient.

There they gave me a hefty shot of morphine, and in a little while the pain left. More than the pain left. All my troubles, all my concerns,

[11] Had I reported the pain to a competent doctor two years before, and had it been diagnosed, I could have taken appropriate preventive measures—making certain I drank two quarts of water a day—and would then probably have prevented the much greater agony now.

all my worries left. I lay there, I remember, facing the wall, in complete peace. It wasn't euphoria; it was better than euphoria; it was quiet, calm nirvana. I didn't feel bored. I didn't have to think. I just lay there at rest. Neither before nor since have I ever felt so free of all the endless indignities of life.

Gertrude sat at the bedside and I, with my back to her, felt her holding my hand. I don't know how much time passed, but a nurse came in and asked Gertrude if she would care to eat and assured her I would be all right. Gertrude left. I did not know this at the time; Gertrude told me of it afterward. All I know was that after a while, I was conscious that Gertrude was not holding my hand. I wondered if she were still there, but it seemed too much trouble to turn around. I felt only the smallest, most distant pang of regret at the thought that she might not be there, and then I let that go, too.

The memory of that one time under morphine convinces me that I will have to be under equivalent pain before I ever accept another shot. That feeling of ultimate peace, if experienced just a few times, would have an attraction I couldn't resist and I would be an addict. Fortunately, I have never had to accept another shot.

By dinnertime I was myself, sufficiently myself to be apprehensive that the pain would return, but it did not. While I was sedated, the kidney stone stopped doing whatever it had been doing to cause the pain.

They fed me, to my great satisfaction. I am very fortunate that I like food, for though people complain bitterly about banquet food and hospital food, for instance, I find them good. (There's always the memory of the Navy Yard cafeteria, of course, but that was exceptional.)

Then, just before I was expected to fall asleep, they brought me another glass of orange juice. It looked a little oily but I just said, "More orange juice! Good!" and took a swig.

Now, there are some tastes you never forget. What there was in that orange juice I had taken only once before, when I was a boy of no more than eight—but I remembered it at once.

"Castor oil!" I said, aghast.

"Finish it," said the nurse, austerely.

I finished it. That night, I did not sleep.

I have never had any need for laxatives. I am always perfectly regular. Therefore, to dope me with a good, strong one created havoc. I was up all night emptying. I think my alimentary canal must have sent out for extras.

The next day they injected into one of my veins an iodine-containing compound that was opaque to X rays, waited till it was being eliminated through the urinary tract, took the necessary X rays, and located the kidney stone. It was partway down the left ureter.

They told me that I might pass it if I drank a lot of water constantly and never let myself get dehydrated. Not only would that help pass the stone but also it would keep me from forming others.

(When I was told all this, I suddenly remembered that once my father had told me that a doctor had said he had "sand in the urine." These were probably crystals, tiny stones. The tendency to stone formation was undoubtedly inherited.)

They sent me home and told me that if I didn't pass the stone in two weeks to come back and they would probe for it.

Well! I didn't intend to do that unless forced into it, so I spent the next few weeks drinking water. As I said bitterly on numerous occasions afterward: Other people drink when they're thirsty; I drink when I pass the sink.

It meant frequent visits to the bathroom, all the more so since the urinary tract was irritated, especially when the stone worked itself lower and began to push the button that signaled "You've got to go." (It also meant that, to this day, if I ever sleep through the night without having to get up at least once to visit the bathroom, it means I haven't been drinking enough water and am in danger.)

Since I was told to catch the stone for analysis if I could, I had to urinate into a jar (when this was possible) and inspect it to see if I had caught anything. In this fashion, weeks went by. Sometimes I was in dull low-back pain, sometimes I was uncomfortable, but there was no agony such as that on the first day.[12]

[12] While I was in the hospital, American troops had reached the Chinese border, and virtually all of North Korea was under American control. The war looked over to me and it did to MacArthur, too, for he promised the soldiers they'd be home by Christmas. Unfortunately, on November 28, Chinese troops poured across the border and caught the overconfident Americans by surprise and sent them into headlong retreat.

50

Pregnancy

1

On November 29, 1950, I received a letter from Sprague de Camp. Catherine was pregnant again. She was forty-three years old at the time.

I sighed. In my more despondent moments over the problem of children, it seemed to me that everyone could have them, and did have them, except us.

Concerning my literary children, however, there was no problem. We drove to New York on December 1, and the next day I went to Greenberg's office and found him and his partner, David Kyle, placing covers on a number of copies of *I, Robot*.

My second book!

I autographed a number of the books for Greenberg's use and then went to a bookshop where an "autographing party" was held. It was my first such affair and it was not exactly an exuberant success. About ten people bought books and I autographed them.

On December 3, Gertrude and I went to Newark to attend Moskowitz's group, the Eastern Science Fiction Association. Ted Sturgeon was the speaker and talked about his story in the next issue of *Galaxy*. I was transfixed with horror. One of the gimmicks in his story was precisely mine in "Hostess." What's more, he had Derek and Verna as male and female characters, and I had Drake and Vera.

I felt this was going to make it impossible for Horace Gold to use "Hostess." It nearly did. After he read it, he told me I would have to make changes to reduce the similarity, and he said it regretfully for he thought mine was the better story. I objected that the changes he asked for would kill the point of the story, but he insisted.

2

On the way back to Somerville on December 4, Gertrude, who had become so involved in my stories that she wanted to know as much as she could, asked me where I got my ideas.

"Anywhere," I said. "I could write a story about a trip from Boston to New York, for instance."

I thought about it for a while, told her the plot that occurred to me, and the next evening began to write a story I called "What if—?" It was actually an *Unknown* story, a tale of alternate time-paths revealed by a supernatural figure, but I did my best to make it sound science-fictiony. I completed it in two weeks.[1]

3

On December 12, I ate my first pizza and found it delightful.

At about that time, too, *The Stars, like Dust*— began running as a three-part serial in *Galaxy*, under the absolutely silly title of "Tyrann." (Gold was a good editor, but his taste in titles was execrable.) The first part made the cover in the January 1951 *Galaxy*.

4

I completed my education in driving now by finding ample opportunity to make my way through ice and snow. On December 15, when I was approaching a friend's home far out in the suburbs, I found myself caught on icy roads. I made it, but it was a frightening experience.

Then, on December 26, I found that I had to get back from school in falling snow and a thick layer on the ground. I was very uneasy about it. Mrs. Walker, who worked at the school, teaching chemistry to student nurses, volunteered to come with me. This was courage above and beyond the call of duty on her part. I got home safely, but the added security of having her in the car to advise and help if that were necessary was, I'm sure, what made it possible.

And meanwhile, I had begun a new novel, *The Currents of Space*.

5

Gertrude was having trouble with her period. She was usually irregular and one couldn't predict when it would come. Once she was within a week of one, however, she could tell unfailingly that one was on the way.

In the beginning of December, one was on the way, and we both waited patiently, and it didn't come. She remained premenstrual for weeks and both of us grew impatient and concerned.

On December 28, we drove to New York, and the next day I saw

---

[1] By now the Americans had evacuated North Korea. We had not suffered such a defeat by a foreign enemy since the British took Washington in 1814—and it was MacArthur who suffered it.

Brad and told him about *The Currents of Space*. It was to be a complicated story of interstellar intrigue and racism. He approved.

Then to Gold's, where I rewrote "Hostess" on the spot, and he
took it at $.03 a word. After that, I sat back and unloaded some of my
troubles, not the least of which was my concern over Gertrude's condition. "Her period won't come," I said. "She's been on the verge all
month and nothing happens."

And Evelyn Gold, who had a son, said, "For goodness' sake, Isaac,
she's pregnant."

I laughed and said, "Don't be silly."

I stopped off to see Campbell the next day, and he agreed to
match Galaxy's $.03 a word. He also told me that I "was one of the
greatest science-fiction writers in the world." That meant much to me
coming from Campbell. He didn't flatter.

And if so, he had made me that. He had brought me a long way in
13½ years.

6

And so 1950 came to an end. It was the first year since 1944 in
which we did not move once in the entire year.

In it, I had published two books. Because the question often arises
these days as to the number of books I have published and because I
am frequently asked to list them all (which I cannot do very easily), I
will list them in this book year by year. To list them in this fashion will
mean, furthermore, that I won't have to deal with each of them separately as they came up, if there is no real significance in doing so. For
1950, then, we have:

1. *Pebble in the Sky* (Doubleday)
2. *I, Robot* (Gnome)

Financially, 1950 was an utter surprise. There was no way I would
have predicted it, but everything seemed to move in my favor. The stories I wrote were longer and were sold for higher rates. When Horace
took *The Stars, like Dust*— for serialization, that alone brought in
nearly as much money as I had made in all of 1949. Add to that the advance from Doubleday on that same book, and the royalties they paid
me on *Pebble in the Sky*. There were other sales at rates of up to $.03
a word, and apparently an ever-increasing market in anthologizations.
By mid-July of 1950, I had matched my 1949 record, and by the end of
the year, my earnings had just topped the $4,700 mark.

It was nearly three times the previous record of 1949, over half of what I made in all the years of writing before 1950, more than I made as an annual income from Elderfield, and almost as much as the $5,000 stipend I earned at Boston University. And all this from a spare-time activity.

For the *first* time, the thought flickered across my mind that I might conceivably make a living as a writer if I chose to.

In a way it was exceedingly fortunate that this had happened when it did and not two years sooner. Had I reason to think the thought at the end of 1948, rather than at the end of 1950, I would never have been persuaded to move to Boston in search of a livelihood. I would have been content to remain in New York and take a job there, if anywhere.

And that would have been bad, I think. My academic position at Boston University School of Medicine was valuable to me; the prestige it brought was useful; the background it supplied for writing other than science fiction was indispensable. No, my literary poverty lasted just exactly long enough. It served to deposit me in the Medical School, and then it rose sharply so that I would not be stranded there for life.

7

With all that, I was ready for a hilarious New Year's Eve party and, as the year before, we celebrated at Roz Wylie's house.

It differed from the previous year's celebration in two ways. First, I didn't drink. This year I was driving, and that meant no funny stuff. Second, there was kissing going on. (There may have been more than that, for all I know, but I was aware only of kissing.)

I took part in the kissing, too, for the one thing I particularly remember about that evening was kissing Evelyn Harrison, the pretty wife of Harry Harrison (who was then just beginning what was to become a career as a science-fiction writer of the first rank). Rather without my intending it, it became a passionate kiss—something I didn't indulge in outside the marital bond. It lasted quite a while by the time we pulled apart.

It was a little frightening to find myself reacting so, but rather pleasing to find I was inducing a woman to react so.

It was a pleasant thought for the next morning. That, and the fact that my writing earnings were very nearly equal to my instructor's salary so that I hadn't really lied to the dentist at Breadloaf four months before. That, and the subsidiary thought that my *total* income for 1950 was very nearly $10,000, a figure I had always thought of as the dream income representing the absolute limit of which I was capable.

8

But I couldn't linger over the past, for we were, as always, moving into the future at the same relentless, unvarying pace as always.

Though I had laughed heartily at Evelyn Gold's suggestion that Gertrude was pregnant, I didn't forget it. I put it to Gertrude on January 2, 1951, while we were driving to Boston. (That was one way of celebrating my thirty-first birthday.)

She admitted she thought she might be, but had been reluctant to speak of it for fear of seeming foolish. Figuring backward, she thought she might have become pregnant on December 1 or slightly before— shortly after the kidney-stone incident.

The next day we consulted Adler, and he told us how one went about arranging for a pregnancy test. On the fourth I rushed a urine sample downtown and on the fifth the results came in. Gertrude was indeed pregnant! When I had received news of Catherine's second pregnancy and had sighed over our own inability to do the same, Gertrude was about to be under way.

The fact of the pregnancy did not stop our scheme of dictate-and-transcribe. I had been asked by Raymond J. Healy (one of the co-editors of *Adventures in Time and Space*) to collaborate on a new idea of his, an anthology of *original* science-fiction stories, for which he would pay competitive rates. It seemed interesting and on January 6, while I still had stars in my eyes over the pregnancy, I began "In a Good Cause—," an ironic story in which the carefully developed villain turns out to be the hero in the end. It was very Campbellesque and rather against my own philosophy, but a story sometimes takes the bit in its own teeth.

There were, then, three stories dictated by me and transcribed by Gertrude: "Hostess," "What if—?," and "In a Good Cause—." I considered all of them good stories, quite comparable with those I typed, and all three were successful. Healy took "In a Good Cause—," and "What if—?" was sold later on.[2]

One thing the pregnancy initiated was a rise in the intensity of our search for a new apartment. We already knew that we didn't want to stay another summer in the attic, but with the baby scheduled for Au-

[2] And meanwhile, American troops were retreating in South Korea again, and Seoul and Inchon were lost for a second time.

gust, the matter became something of utter urgency. There was no way I could allow Gertrude to go through an attic summer while in the last stages of pregnancy.

By January 9, we were looking at new places and undergoing the usual uncertainties and heartaches of trying to make some decision.

9

No doubt the trotting around after apartments and the anxieties arising therefore made things very difficult for Gertrude. On January 28, she began staining, and, in an agony of apprehension over a possible miscarriage, I rushed her to the Massachusetts Memorial Hospital (the one associated with the Medical School), where Anthony Elia, her obstetrician (and head of the Obstetrics Department at the Medical School), seemed unworried.

But I was worried. Gertrude stayed in the hospital two days, and I kept rushing over only when I could for, of course, the biochemistry class (my second) started on the twenty-ninth, and whatever happened to Gertrude, the show must go on.

My distraught alarm was such that on the obstetric floor the joke went around, "Gertrude did not have a miscarriage, but Isaac had five." Such delightful humor!

At any rate, they wouldn't keep her any longer and swore to me that she would not have a miscarriage, so I brought her home on January 30.

After that scare, we felt we had to take it easy, and the dictate-and-transcribe routine stopped and never restarted. Too bad! We had something good going there.

The thing I remember most about that three-month period of dictate-and-transcribe was Gertrude coming in with one of the thin blue-green records and saying, "I can't transcribe this."

"Why not?" I said.

"Well, listen to it."

I listened. It was a scene in which two characters were arguing and the argument grew steadily more heated. And as it grew more heated, so did my voice, until, at the peak, I was not dictating but snarling incoherently.

I had to repeat the entire passage, making an effort to remain cool. I had never realized up to then how closely I mimicked the emotions of my characters.

10

All through this period—indeed, ever since the kidney-stone episode ten weeks before—I had been living with dull pains and uncomfortable urination, and had steadfastly refused any thought of going to the hospital and being probed or catheterized.

Finally, on January 31, 1951, I felt the kind of pain that I could associate with only one thing. I grasped for the jar, which I was too lazy to use all the time, and urinated into it. The pain was like a hot spear being shoved through the urethra from the inside out. After I stopped hopping about and groaning I looked at the jar and there was the stone. It was a little over a quarter inch long and about an eighth of an inch wide, yellow-brown in color, and very jagged.

I took it in to school. Dr. Walker said he had never seem so large a kidney stone passed (news I greeted without enthusiasm, since I saw no benefit to setting a world record in this regard). Dr. Derow analyzed it and said it was calcium oxalate dihydrate. This was good in one respect: It was a slow-growing variety of stone and was not likely to grow too large to be passed. It was bad in another respect: It was a jagged variety of stone and the most painful of the different kinds.[3]

11

By this time, my expertise had reached the point where writing was virtually painless. On February 4, 1951, I began a story called "Nobody Here but—" and, without visible effort, I finished its 5,000 words in two days.

I was hoping I might place it in some slick magazine. This was not an entirely new ambition of mine. It antedated even Heinlein's appearance in *The Saturday Evening Post*. When we were living in Wingate Hall, I had written a "mainstream" romantic short story I had intended for *Collier's* but had never managed to sell anywhere.

"Flesh and Metal" was science fiction, but it had an element of romance, and I had vainly tried to sell it to the slicks before it went to *Amazing*. And now "Nobody Here but—" was submitted to the slicks, but uselessly.

On February 8, I received a request from a magazine that was not a pulp. It was *The Writer*, which, as its name implies, is an instructional

[3] And by now the American retreat in Korea had come to an end and we were beginning to jab northward again.

and inspirational magazine for beginning writers, and which then paid $10 an article. What's more, it didn't want a story, but a nonfiction piece, only 2,000 words long, on science fiction.

I obliged and took the article in on February 23, since *The Writer* had its offices in downtown Boston. That gave me the occasion to meet Abe Burack, the editor, loud-voiced, aggressive, very opinionated, full of advice on anything and everything—and very kindhearted.

He took my article, which I called "Other Worlds to Conquer." It was the first nonfiction piece I ever did for a paying market—though not a very-much-paying market.

Meanwhile, Greenberg, having done *I, Robot*, offered to do the various stories of the Foundation series in three volumes. I was more than willing. I was delighted. Little, Brown and Doubleday had turned them down[4] but, in my opinion, they deserved hard-cover publication just the same. They were the most ambitious stories I had ever done and the best received by the readers.

By February 28, 1951, Marty sent Fred the first $100 installment of the advance for the first book, and Fred sent me my $90 cut. The first volume was to contain: "Foundation," "Bridle and Saddle," "Wedge," and "The Big and the Little." The second book would contain "Dead Hand" and "The Mule." The third book would contain "Now you See It—" and "—And Now You Don't."

The second and third books would be 75,000 words apiece, which was fine. The first book, however, would be just under 60,000 words, which was a little short.

Marty wasn't fazed. It seemed to him that, in any case, the series started too abruptly. He urged me to write a short introductory section that would serve as an easier beginning for the whole series.

It was a good idea. I wrote an opening section called "The Psychohistorians," which was over 10,000 words long and which filled out the first book. Since it was written in March 1951, the very first section of the first of the three books was the last part of the series to be written—and it gave me the opportunity to introduce Hari Seldon in life.[5]

12

At work I was growing grumpy. The fact that Gertrude had a child nearly halfway to birth strengthened my feeling that I needed more out

---

[4] The more fools, they.

[5] In that month, too, the Americans recaptured Seoul, and more or less reached the Thirty-eighth Parallel, which was the dividing line when the war had started nine months before. From then on the war settled down into a stalemate.

of the job—a better title—a higher salary. The fact that we were still looking for apartments in a pretty steady way and were having no luck whatever disillusioned me with Boston. That and the knowledge that my writing was doing well made me the readier to consider giving up the job if I could not have my way.

I began, therefore, to put the pressure on Dr. Walker for an assistant professorship. Dr. Walker said he was willing and that I deserved it. However, Fabian Lionetti had been hired only a month after me and he did not want to promote just one of us; he wanted to promote both, and until his budget was in a position to let him do so, he wouldn't promote either.

I chafed considerably at this.

I also chafed at working under Henry Lemon. I found his solemnity wearisome and I could not share his perpetual concern about grants. I wanted my salary to come out of the school's pocket so that I wouldn't have to worry about grants.

Lemon was also keen on publicity, which was a matter of lesser importance to me. On March 20, 1951, for instance, he came into my lab to tell me that a Boston *Globe* reporter would be around to interview us in connection with the opening of the annual cancer drive, and I said, "I'm afraid I'm leaving for New York tomorrow, Dr. Lemon."

He was clearly angry, but I went anyway.

Lemon was a social conservative, and I wasn't. I came in one hot summer day, for instance, in my usual summer attire—that is, sport shirt and slacks. He drew me to one side and told me that it would look better for a faculty man to wear a tie and jacket. I told him I didn't plan to wear a tie and jacket in hot weather unless and until they air-conditioned the building—and I stuck to my costume.

To him, my writing science fiction was like my wearing a sport shirt. It wasn't done, and it bothered him. In fact, he began worrying that his grants might suffer if the science referees in Washington began to realize that his right-hand man wrote science fiction.

All in all, I grew restless at the realization that my salary rested in the hands of a man who disapproved of me. More and more it became one of my ambitions to get rid of Lemon as the source of my income— and I suspect it came to be one of Lemon's ambitions, more and more, to get rid of me altogether.

13

I did go to New York on March 21, 1951, and the next day I had lunch with Howard Browne, who was now editing *Amazing*. He was a large, jovial fellow who had had the intention of making it a quality magazine and had bought stories at $.05 a word for that purpose, including my "Flesh and Metal," until the publishers had pulled the rug out from under him by flinching at the thought of putting out all the money that would be required.

So "Flesh and Metal" came out in the April 1951 Amazing, which looked much as that magazine always had. However, Browne had changed the title to "Satisfaction Guaranteed,"[6] a change that was much for the better.

The next day I had lunch with Bradbury and Pohl, and a new project came up. Television was here to stay; that was clear.[7] Why not take advantage of it, then? Radio had its successful long-running series, "The Lone Ranger," so why not a "Space Ranger" modeled very closely upon that? If I were to write a juvenile science-fiction novel featuring a Space Ranger, we could get a long-term television series out of it that would coin millions for all concerned—including the author, the agent, and the publisher of the novel on which it was based.

This, of course, assumed that television would be like radio, full of fixed, long-running series. None of us dreamed that for some reason, perhaps because the addition of the sense of vision enormously hastened a sense of satiation, television series would very rarely last more than two or three years. We also didn't know that a juvenile television series to be called "Rocky Jones: Space Ranger" was already in the works.

None of these things bothered me. I had no more future vision than anyone else. I assumed, too, that the series would be indefinite in duration and would make millions. What bothered me, though, was that all the television I had seen (except for Sid Caesar and Imogene Coca) was uniformly awful. What good would millions of dollars do me if I were ashamed of its source?

I explained this and Brad at once said, "Use a pseudonym."

That was a relief. I agreed to write a pseudonymous novel.

14

There was a Hydra Club meeting the next day. I met Fritz Leiber there for the first time—tall, handsome; in fact, with almost theatrical good looks. Harry Harrison and Evelyn (whom I had kissed last New Year's Eve) had split up, but not as a result of the kiss, as I had fearfully thought for a moment. Apparently, she had grown interested in Lester del Rey.

[6] See Earth Is Room Enough (Doubleday, 1957).
[7] The Blugermans had a television set now, and when we were staying at their apartment, we watched it as much as we could.

51

Waltham

1

After we got back from New York, things began looking up. The obstetrician finally detected signs of life, and for that matter, so did Gertrude.

Then, on March 28, 1951, we finally found the apartment we were looking for. It was in Waltham, about nine miles due west of the Medical School and near a public transportation line, though not a fearfully convenient one. (Still, we now had a car.)

It was a four-room apartment, with two bedrooms—one of which I could use as a study until we had to convert it into a nursery. It had a beautiful kitchen, a pleasant hall, adequate closet space, and most of all, it was the top floor of a two-story house so that it had four-way ventilation—even a small veranda. The rent was $100 a month, which we could swing on my school salary alone, and with the writing earnings added, there would be no trouble.

Two days later we closed the deal, and for once I was certain we were doing the right thing.

At least I knew we were right as far as the apartment was concerned. I wasn't at all sure I should stay on the job. It would have been nice to get some commitment of advancement before I took a new and more expensive apartment, but the developing fetus wouldn't wait, so neither could I.

On March 30, I mentioned the possibility of a raise in pay to Lemon and he looked at me blankly as though he had never heard the phrase before and wondered what it meant.

On April 5, I sought a conference with Dr. Walker (who had been away from school for some time because his mother-in-law had died) and, for the first time, explained that I wanted to be a full member of the faculty with my salary coming from school funds and not from Dr. Lemon's grant. After that, more or less by coincidence, Lemon saw Walker and explained how unsatisfactory *I* was. Of course, the news of that got to me and raised my anger several notches.

On April 9, Walker and Lemon had a conference with Dean Faulkner and it was decided that I would *not* get a professorship, though I *would* get a raise.

I was dissatisfied with that and decided that if I could not alter their minds, I would quit. I had put down my deposit on the Waltham apartment, but that didn't bother me. Unemployment would not mean starvation. Thanks to our careful saving ways, we now had nearly $10,000 in the bank, and I was convinced my writing could carry me for quite a while.

After all, my third book, *The Stars, like Dust—*, had been published, and my fourth book, *Foundation*, on which Gertrude was busily working, would be out in the fall. Two more books based on the Foundation series were also slated for publication. What was most important was that on April 4, Brad called me to tell me that on the basis of what he had seen of my new novel, *The Currents of Space*, he was sending me a full contract. He was now sufficiently confident in my ability to be able to skip the "option" stage.

With all that, the specter of unemployment was no longer a terrifying one. The days of 1947 through 1949 were gone and, I strongly suspected, were never going to return.

Besides, I had another trump card. There was the textbook, on which we were making great progress. I was carrying my full share of the load and I had the feeling that Walker would not lightly let me resign, since I intended to make it quite clear, if push came to shove, that I would not contribute further to the book if I did, and would withdraw what I had already written.

By mid-April, I could feel occasional thumpings when I placed my hand on the maternal abdomen. And as for the other variety of children, the May 1951 *Galaxy* appeared with "Hostess."[1]

2

I was also engaged, at this time, in doing what I could to further Stanley's career. He would be graduating from New York University in a few months and he had determined on a journalism career. I consulted Dawson on the possibility of helping Stanley get into Columbia School of Journalism. Dawson met Stanley and called me on April 6 to tell me that it had been very pleasant meeting "another Asimov" and that he would do what he could.

Stanley *did* go to Columbia School of Journalism the following September and, though to this day I tease him by telling him I got him

[1] See *Nightfall and Other Stories*, in which I restored the story to its original version. To be sure, Horace had changed my heroine's name, Vera, to Rose, because Vera was the name of the publisher of the magazine. I thought that a silly delicacy, but let that change stand.

in, there is no question but that he did it on his own qualifications and would have done it just as easily if I had not existed.[2]

3

On May 1, 1951, we underwent our ninth move as a married couple in almost nine years of marriage. We moved out of the attic apartment after having lived there 1¾ years, a longer period than in any place since Wingate Hall. Our new address was 265 Lowell Street, in Waltham.

A new refrigerator, which we had bought for $270 ten days before, was there waiting for us, and two days after we moved in, a telephone was installed. It was not a dial phone so that we had to dicker with an operator—the one and only time this has happened to me. It was a party line and we shared the phone with another customer.

The irritations of a party line almost negated the value of a telephone. There were the telephone rings that disturbed you but were for the other guy. There were the telephone calls that could not be made because the other party was engaged in an interminable conversation. There were the important calls you were making that were interrupted by the other person's trivial needs. Bah!

But there was nothing we could do about it except to go about our business. By May 7, Gertrude and I, between us, had copied over the early Foundation stories, smoothed out the transitions, and made some minor changes. The manuscript was ready to be handed to Marty on our next trip to New York.

4

As the year heated up, we found that the Waltham apartment was not exactly a cool one, either. It was on the top floor, after all. It was, however, an improvement on Somerville. On May 15, the temperature in the open shade went to 89. In Somerville that would have meant an inside temperature of near 100. In the new apartment, the temperature was only 83. The next day (Gertrude's birthday) it was 91 outside and 85 indoors.

There was also the advantage of the veranda, which had a waist-

---

[2] On April 11, President Truman fired General MacArthur. At the time this made Truman a villain to almost the entire country, though it made him a hero to me, but there is no question that the hindsight of history is on my side and would agree that MacArthur's insubordination was a danger to the country and could not be endured.

high wall and a roof, but was not screened. Gertrude could, and did, make up a cot there, and on hot nights she would sleep there while I slept indoors.

5

The June 1951 *Astounding* arrived and had "Breeds There a Man?"[3] in it. I was very pleased. It had been exactly one year since I had last had a story in *Astounding,* and in that interval, I had had two shorts, a novelette, and a three-part serial in *Galaxy.* Six of the first eight issues of this new magazine had had something by me in it, and I felt like a traitor. With "Breeds There a Man?" I felt better, and I made up my mind to offer *"The Currents of Space"* to Campbell for serialization.

It was about now, too, that *Life* came out with an article on science fiction and ran the banquet photograph of the July 1950 convention at which Brad and Fred had lured me into drinking. I got a copy at work and there I was, far in the background and not very recognizable, but clearly drunk.

Gertrude sat next to me, much more nearly in focus, smiling and looking very pretty indeed, though unfortunately only half her face showed. I called her on the phone and said, "Gertrude, your picture is in *Life* magazine."

I expected disbelief but she just said, with mild puzzlement, "I didn't give them a picture." She didn't even ask *why* she was in.

6

On May 21, 1951, my raise finally came through, retroactive to April 1. I would be paid now at the rate of $5,500.

It gave me no satisfaction at all. It was humiliating to have made such a fuss and to have had to go through conferences and pleadings and threats for so little. One good novelette could bring in more than the annual increase and I would have been thanked for it by the editor, praised for it by the readers, and paid additionally for it by anthologists.

Besides which, there was usually only a small plum in the department budget to divide (if any), and if I got $500 extra a year, someone else in the department, without my ability to make money on the side, might not get it. It seemed improper for me to scrabble for these small sums when I needed it less than the next guy.

[3] See *Nightfall and Other Stories.*

As a result, I specifically denied any interest in pay increases from this time onward. Any that I received henceforward came without any move toward it on my part. What I was after was a change in the source of the money, and a promotion in title.

Nevertheless, I let the increase in salary mollify me to the extent of preventing an instant resignation. I needed some face-saving device to prevent it, for we had just moved into the new apartment and the baby was due soon. However little I feared unemployment I didn't want to have Gertrude facing it at this point. She had enough difficulty without it.

7

On May 25, we drove to New York again. The next day I handed the manuscript of *Foundation* to Greenberg and a new novelette, "Greater Love," to Gold.

Horace read the story then and there and demanded some changes. I argued about them and gave in on some but held out stubbornly on others. I spent the next day rewriting at the Blugermans' and handed in the revised story on Monday.

That Monday, the twenty-eighth, I spent four hours with Campbell, who was apparently working in New York again, at least part-time. He told me he was doing an anthology of stories from *Astounding* and that he wanted to include "Nightfall." I didn't mind getting the money, but I felt it necessary to remind him that it had already been anthologized.

He said, "That doesn't matter."

It was the first time I realized a story could be anthologized more than once.[4]

Campbell also told me that he had broken with Hubbard and was out of the dianetics movement. That didn't surprise me, really. I knew Campbell and I knew Hubbard, and no movement can have two Messiahs.

I also gave him a little gag-story called "Shah Guido G.," which carefully built up 3,000 words of plot to end on a silly play on words. These days that sort of thing has become rather commonplace in science fiction, at least in submitted manuscripts, if not in accepted ones, but in 1951 it was a daring venture on my part.

[4] It's lucky it can be. To date, "Nightfall" has been anthologized fifteen times that I know of, with more to come, and it has made me considerably more money through anthologizations than it did in the case of the original sale. And "Nightfall" doesn't hold the record for me in anthologizations, either.

The next day, Gertrude and I had lunch with Brad. The Space Ranger television show was still up in the air, but Brad was ready to have a contract prepared for the juvenile novel.

May 30 (Memorial Day) I spent at the Blugermans' writing a story called "The Monkey's Fingers," which dealt humorously with a writer and an editor having an argument such as I, myself, had just had with Horace over "Greater Love." In fact, it dealt with the same argument. I had a monkey-brain computer decide the issue.

On the thirty-first, I discovered Campbell had rejected "Shah Guido G.," which depressed me, for it was the first short story of mine that he had rejected in nine years—but it deserved rejection, I guess.

Horace, however, accepted the revised "Greater Love" but demanded a new name. In the end, he used "C-Chute," which I thought uninspired—but good enough.

It wasn't till June 6 that we drove back to Waltham. It was amazing the freedom the car gave us. We could come and go as we pleased depending neither on the goodwill of others nor on the schedules of trains and buses.

8

On June 7, 1951, I received a letter from R. R. Winterbotham, the first in about nine years. It was as friendly as ever but there was a business angle to it. He was now editor of a syndicated newspaper page for boys and girls and he wanted an eight-hundred-word short-short for young readers.

I thought about it and decided to write a little story about school. What could interest children more? It would be about a school of the future, by way of teaching machines, with children longing for the good old days when there were old-fashioned schools that children loved. I thought the kids would get a bang out of the irony.

I called the story "The Fun They Had," wrote it at a sitting, and sent it to Winterbotham, who sent me an enthusiastic ten dollars for it in August. It wasn't much, of course, only a penny a word for a thousand words. Fred Pohl didn't have anything to do with it, but he was my agent so I sent him his dollar.

The next time he saw me, he lectured me. I should not have done it for a penny a word. I offered the feeble excuse that Winterbotham was a friend and that by the Code of the Woosters, you don't let a pal down. He told me there was no room for friendship in this business, and since I had no arguments to offer, I just listened meekly.

Still, I knew that if I were faced with the same situation a second time, I would sin again. I felt a little impatient with agents. It seemed to me that if ever Fred Pohl stopped wanting to be my agent, I wouldn't accept any other agent ever. Then, if I felt like obliging a friend, I could.[5]

9

Other projects were moving ahead, too. On June 10, I began the Space Ranger novel. I wanted a science-fiction-sounding last name for my hero, and that was Starr. We had already decided to name our baby (if a boy) David, so I called my hero David Starr, and the book became *David Starr: Space Ranger*.

I needed a pseudonym. I wanted one that was short and colorless so that it would not compete with my own name. At about that time, I read that the suspense-story writer, Cornell Woolrich (whom I admired), faced with the necessity of choosing a pseudonym, decided to use a nationality as the last name and selected William Irish. At once, I selected Paul French,[6] and he became the author of *David Starr: Space Ranger*.

10

We were still working on the textbook, Walker, Boyd, and I, and I continued to fret over being interfered with by two co-authors.

Whenever I was outvoted on some phrase, or on some method of literary attack on a problem that was near my heart, I would mutter that I would write a biochemistry book of my own someday—and for the general public, not for medical students. Then it would be the way I wanted it and not the way anyone else did.

Bill Boyd took me seriously. In 1950, he had published with Little, Brown a popular book on genetics that was called *Genetics and the*

[5] As it was, things didn't turn out so badly. "The Fun They Had" turned out to be an extremely popular story, and so far I have counted twenty-four anthologizations, with more in the works and no signs of it ever stopping. It has also appeared in science-fiction magazines, in my own collections, in foreign languages, and so on. It has probably earned me several thousand dollars so far—which is too bad in a way. It takes the gloss of nobility off what would otherwise have been an unselfish desire to help a friend.

[6] In time to come there were always some people who knew nothing about either me or science fiction who gathered the impression that I used Paul French as my pseudonym for all my science fiction because I was ashamed to put my real name to it. That irritated me beyond measure. I never used Paul French for any of my writing but the Space Ranger stories, and as soon as I could, I put those stories under my real name.

Races of Man, and it was doing well. His editor there was Angus Cameron, and it seemed to Bill that Cameron might be interested in having me do a popular book on biochemistry. Through his good offices, therefore, I made a luncheon date with Cameron for June 15 at Locke-Ober's.

There was a pleasant symmetry to this. Bill had long been a science-fiction fan—indeed that was how he came to know me and how I came to get the job at the Medical School. Knowing me personally had activated the urges he had had to write science fiction, and at about this time, he and Lyle together began to turn out stories in collaboration. They wrote under the name Boyd Ellanby (L. and B.), and I gave them strong moral support. They eventually published a dozen stories or more during the next half-dozen years, and now Bill was helping me in the direction of nonfiction.

My lunch with Cameron was an interesting one and it sounded hopeful at the time. Unfortunately, I wanted a book in which I would progress from the simple to the complex, and he wanted to move from the familiar to the unfamiliar, and I simply wasn't going to do any book unless I could do it my way. My desire to write a popular biochemistry was forced to hang fire, therefore—but I didn't forget about it.

11

In any case, the forthcoming baby was taking up more of my time. In June, Catherine de Camp had her second child, another boy; Babbie Whipple had her second child, another girl. Now I could react with camaraderie instead of wistful sadness.

Gertrude and I took classes for would-be parents and practiced diapering and holding dolls, and we listened to lectures on formulas.

What's more, we were buying baby carriages, Bathinettes, cribs, and so on. Gertrude, who was in her seventh month, was looking very pregnant indeed.

12

On June 17, I listened to a dramatization of *Pebble in the Sky* on a radio program called "Dimension X." It was the first time anything I had written had ever been put on an electronic medium, and I was absorbed. The radio writer was the young but able Ernest Kinoy. It was only a half-hour show, so it was an enormously altered version. It even had a catastrophic ending rather than my happy one, but I liked it; it was well done.

There was only one little catch: My name was not mentioned on the program at any point, and I was indignant.

I called Campbell who was, I understood, technical adviser to the program. He told me he was no longer connected with it. I called Brad but he wasn't home (it was a Sunday). I called Fred Pohl and he was quite short with me and told me to act my age. *That* one confused me, since agents were supposed to be more understanding than that. I found out from him later (in a letter of apology) that at the time I had called he was having a terrific fight with Judy Merril as his third marriage was breaking up.

I wrote letters all around and in the end Brad was able to make the "Dimension X" people apologize and mention my name on the next week's program, but that wasn't the same, especially since they mispronounced it.

Oh well, the galleys of *Foundation* arrived on June 23, and that gave me something else to think about.

Then too, Fred told me he had sold "Shah Guido G" to *Marvel*, which had once published several issues before the war and was now being revived.

As it happened, magazine science fiction was on the eve of its biggest boom. The success of *Fantasy and Science Fiction* and of *Galaxy* was producing a horde of imitators. It became impossible for me to fail to sell a story to someone, even if the story were rather less than average in quality.[7]

13

In July, we put in some concentrated work on the textbook, working mostly at Boyd's house. Our ninth wedding anniversary, on July 26, 1951, was therefore rather a pleasant one, for Walker, Bill, and Lyle Boyd, and Gertrude and I all went out to dinner.

As for *David Starr: Space Ranger*, I worked on that almost every moment I wasn't working on the textbook. It went quickly, and on July 29, it was done. I sent a copy to Brad and another to Fred the next day.

14

Sometime toward the end of August was baby day, and we were rather desperate to have some sort of vacation before that came. We were afraid to get away from the city for too long a period in case of

[7] By now, the Korean War was a year old and, with the failure of MacArthur's bid for victory, extremely unpopular. Truce negotiations were under way.

emergency, but we managed to go to New York over the July 14–17 weekend.

We seized at any nondistant, nonlong trip we could make. There was an annual picnic at Dean Faulkner's estate, for instance, and we went to that. The estate was very close to a summer resort, and I managed to eat three lobsters.

Then on August 4, we made a motor trip to Rockport, which was not very far from Camp Annisquam. Rockport is a quaint old fishing village, carefully designed as a tourist trap, but we liked wandering through its stores, even though we rarely bought anything. We repeated the trip periodically in later times.

15

It's not surprising that friends of mine tried to write science-fiction stories. If I could do it, after all, surely anyone could.

It was pleasant that some of them succeeded. The Boyds were a case in point. Another was Armin Deutsch, then a Harvard astronomer and one of the Decadents. He called me up one day and said he was writing a science-fiction story. Could he read me the beginning?

"Go ahead," I said, in resignation.

He read a few paragraphs and I grew excited. "Let me see the rest," I said. "It sounds good."

The next time we met he gave me the manuscript. I read it, and said, "Send it to Campbell. He'll take it."

He sent it and Campbell took it. It appeared in the December 1950 *Astounding* and was called "A Subway Named Möbius." It was a delightful satire on the Boston subway system and was just a crackerjack story. Deutsch never wrote another story, as far as I know.[8]

Then, too, I had a friend named Jesse Charney, whom I met through Roy Machlowitz. Charney was a chemist at Sharp & Dohme and visited me on August 9, bringing me the news that Roy had quit the Navy Yard and was now working at Sharp & Dohme also.

Charney was a fat man, but enormously bright, and he wrote a story that he showed me. Again, I grew excited and advised instant submission. Campbell took that story, too, and it appeared in the May 1951 *Astounding* under the title "Success Story." Charney used the pseudonym Julian Chain. He published three more stories and then he quit, too, and that was all.

[8] He was a tall, thin fellow with a peculiar congenital disorder in which cholesterol accumulated in the joints of his extremities. It probably accumulated elsewhere and killed him; he died fairly young.

52

David

1

On August 19, 1951, Gertrude was in her third day of intermittent cramps, and I was growing increasingly nervous. Gertrude pooh-poohed it, but by nightfall I was frantic. I began to argue in favor of taking her to the hospital, but she was afraid of going there, finding it was a false alarm, having to return, and then going a second time a few days later.

I kept saying distractedly, "But I don't know how to deliver a baby."

By midnight, the cramps were pretty regular and I think she got to thinking of what might happen if I were forced to *try* to deliver a baby. She knew perfectly well how undeft I was at lab work.

She consented to have me take her, therefore, and I got dressed as any husband would under such circumstances—in a screaming panic. (What if the car didn't start? What if I were so nervous I had an accident?) Then I was ready at last, complete with a packed suitcase, but where was Gertrude?

"Gertrude!" I called in distraction. "Gertrude!"

My God, the shower was going.

"What are you doing taking a shower, Gertrude?"

It seemed she wanted to be sweet and clean for the medical people.

"Who *cares*? It's their job. You think everyone comes in powdered and scented?"

But she wouldn't listen. We didn't get to the hospital till 3:00 A.M. Gertrude, who had settled down the instant she was in the car, decided the baby wasn't on the way and she grew discontented over my panic having forced her to the hospital. "Why do you have this tendency to panic, Isaac?" she asked.

I *was* feeling rather stupid, but at least it meant I could drive slowly and avoid accidents. When I pulled up at the curb at Massachusetts Memorial Hospital, a block from the Medical School, I hopped out of the car and ran around to the other door to help her out. I found her momentarily unable to move—the cramps had started again and they were lulus. Thank goodness we were there.

I checked her in and then came the wait. A first pregnancy often involves a long labor, and by dinnertime, fifteen hours after I had taken her to the hospital, she was still in the labor room.

I kept walking up and down, leaving for the Medical School, coming back, walking up and down. Theoretically, I should only have been there in the visiting hours, but I wore my white lab coat and everyone in a hospital is conditioned to question no one in a white lab coat.

Finally, at 7:45 P.M. on August 20, 1951, right in the middle of visiting hours, of course, Dr. Elia came striding out into the hall with his face mask dangling about his neck, a huge smile on his face, his right hand thrust out.

"Congratulations, Isaac, it's a boy," he said, and the visitors standing about broke into a spontaneous cheer.

David Asimov had appeared in the world.

He was a little baby, even though he was full term. He was only five pounds, four onces, and since forceps had had to be used, his head was misshapen.

Everyone told me not to worry—that this was a common state of affairs and that David's head would round itself out nicely. Eventually, it did.

2

We weren't exactly young parents, I was thirty-one, Gertrude was thirty-three. We had been married just over nine years and had given up hope. So when we sent out announcement cards, I scrawled over some of them "They laughed when we sat down to play . . ." That got a grin out of those who, like myself, were old enough to remember the famous old advertisement for a correspondence course on how to play the piano.

David was considered premature because of his weight and it wasn't till he was four days old that he was taken out of the incubator and put into Gertrude's arms, and because he seemed too small to have enough suction for breast feeding, he became a bottle baby.

On the twenty-fifth, the Blugermans arrived, and I took them to the hospital to see their first grandchild.

On August 27, Gertrude left the hospital and came home, but they held onto David one more day. On the twenty-eighth we went in and brought him home. It was a terribly frightening thing to have the responsibility for a tiny scrap of life—much more frightening than trying to take care of a kitten.

We had hired a practical nurse to sleep in and take care of David for a while, till Gertrude really got on her feet and learned the ropes. It was a disaster! A more incompetent and unpleasant practical nurse I couldn't imagine.

Yet maybe that was a good thing. We were so anxious to get rid of her that when she was gone and we were left alone with David we were too busy feeling good about her being gone to feel scared about being left alone with a baby. By the end of the month, David weighed five pounds, eight ounces.

During that interval the November 1951 *Marvel* appeared with "Shah Guido G."[1] in it. It was the first of my stories to appear in the days of my fatherhood.

3

On September 3, I got a call from Fred. He was buying out Roz Wylie and assuming sole control of the Dirk Wylie Literary Agency, but that meant he needed money. Could he borrow some?

That put me in a bind. With a newborn baby, I suddenly felt shakier economically than I had as a childless person. So I asked, "Has my Doubleday royalty check come in yet?"

Yes, it had, and it amounted to $443.

"Very well, then," I said. "Hold onto that till you can afford to pay it to me."

That set a pattern that was to continue for two years. Fred was chronically hard up. One of the reasons was that he was paying new and struggling writers out of his own funds to keep them going, whenever he was certain their stories would eventually sell, or when their stories had sold but the buyers were slow in paying.

This meant, of course, that he had to hold off on the money of those who, like myself, could afford to wait. He was chronically in debt to me, therefore, from this point on, but I didn't worry. For one thing, I always knew exactly how much he owed me, and his payments, though late, did come. For another, I owed him so much in a non-financial way that I could scarcely complain.

4

On September 4, advance copies of *Foundation* arrived, and other things were moving, too. The textbook, for instance, was in its last stages, and soon we would have a completed manuscript.

On September 21, Gotthard Guenther (who had once developed his odd theory of the significance of "Nightfall") called to tell me that

[1] See *Buy Jupiter and Other Stories.*

his German publisher wanted to put out a German edition of *I, Robot*. This was eventually done. It appeared as *Ich, der Robot*, and it was the first time anything I had written appeared in a foreign language (or at least it was the first foreign translation I saw).

5

The first problem with David, other than the day-to-day feeding, diapering, washing, and weighing, was the matter of circumcision.

Gertrude and I took it as a matter of course that there would be no religious ritual involved and we were certainly not going to try to have the ceremony performed on the traditional eighth day, when he was entirely too small and fragile.

On the other hand, I didn't want to let circumcision go altogether. It was a hygienic move, I believed (though I might have been the readier to believe it out of a lingering superstition), and I didn't want to seem to be *denying* that David was Jewish.

I compromised by having him circumcised by his pediatrician, who happened to be named John J. Ryan. You couldn't ask for a more Gentile circumcision than that. The operation took place on September 22, 1951, when David was thirty-three days old.

6

Bill Boyd pulled an unexpected surprise on me on October 1, 1951. He was hiring Bernie Pitt as an assistant. Bernie had been at Columbia with me in 1948 and I remembered him well.

Bill knew Bernie was a classmate of mine since Bernie had told him so. Bill therefore asked me what I thought of him. This put me in a bind. Bernie was very bright, but I remembered his sardonic sense of humor and I was convinced he would not find Bill's bumbling peculiarities as endearing as I did. Nor did I think Bill would find Bernie's occasional bitterness pleasant.

That, however, was just my opinion, and I couldn't spoil another man's job opportunity. I just said, "Well, he's got a pronounced personality, Bill. You'll have to get used to it, the way you got used to mine."

"I'm sure there will be no problem," he said.

I could just smile doubtfully.

What didn't help my self-love was that Bill's grant enabled him to pay out a sizable sum to Bernie and that Bill lacked the discretion to keep quiet about it. He proudly announced he was going to pay Bernie

$7,000—which made my $5,500 after over two years on the job look pretty sick.

To be sure, Bernie would simply be an assistant to Bill and would carry no faculty status. In view of the fact that I was only an instructor, that wasn't enough. Once again, I put pressure on Walker for a promotion in title. I said nothing about money.

7

The October 1951 *Galaxy* appeared, containing "C-Chute,"[2] and a couple of hard-cover anthologies came out with stories of mine in them: "Death Sentence" and "The Red Queen's Race." They were the ninth and tenth hard-cover anthologies to contain stories of mine, and I was becoming used to it, even unmoved by it.

On October 23, 1951, we were finally finished with the manuscript of *Biochemistry and Human Metabolism* after just over a year of fairly hard and unremitting labor. I judged its length to be something over 300,000 words, of which I had written a third. On that day, we sent it off to Williams & Wilkins by Air Express.

On October 29, I had the galleys to *David Starr: Space Ranger* and I had finished a 10,000-word novelette called "Youth," which only took me ten days. About the only bad news about writing that month was the return of the first third of *The Currents of Space* from Brad. He found me overwriting in spots again and wanted certain changes.

Meanwhile, I had heard from Scott Feldman again, the friend of my bachelor days. A surprising sea change had overtaken him. His kindness to Wodehouse in wartime internment was not forgotten by that gentleman.

After the war, Wodehouse came to the United States and never returned to Great Britain (although the bitterness against him died down and he was eventually knighted by Elizabeth II). In the United States, he offered, in gratitude, to let Scott serve as his agent. Scott eventually changed his last name to Meredith and, beginning with Wodehouse, founded what is perhaps the most successful literary agency in the United States.

Now Scott wrote me. Apparently he was of the opinion that Fred Pohl's literary agency was on the point of failure and he suggested that I become a client of the Scott Meredith agency.

It might well have been to my financial benefit to do so, but there was no way I could let Fred down just because he was having a hard

[2] See *Nightfall and Other Stories.*

time. Besides, if Fred left the agency business I intended to have no
agent at all thereafter. I replied politely to Scott and refused.

8

David filled our lives. We watched eagerly for all signs of development. On October 7, when he was forty-eight days old, he smiled for
the first time, and had been able to follow our moving fingers with his
eyes some days before that. On October 11, he consumed his first solid
food.

The one disturbing development was that he was getting strange
patches on his skin which, on October 20, were finally interpreted by
Dr. Ryan as an allergy to milk. He assured us it would pass but that, for
a while, David would have to switch to soybean extract, which would
supply all necessary nutrition and which was nonallergenic. By now he
was two months old and weighed nearly ten pounds.

By the twenty-ninth, after nine days on the soybean regimen, the
patches on the skin were about gone, which demonstrated the cor-
rectness of Ryan's diagnosis.

I had a small dental problem of my own. The removable bridge
that replaced my one missing tooth was beginning to affect its neighbors. In October, then, my dentist (a meticulous worker who drove me
mad, however, by lecturing me in an ultrarightist manner while I was
helpless in the dentist's chair) outfitted me with a permanent bridge.[3]

9

Now that David was with us, it was difficult to go out together;
nay, impossible. We took to going to the movies separately, and on October 30, when I had to go to New York, I went alone, and Gertrude
remained behind with David.

On arriving in New York, I went straight to Fred Pohl's to find
out if he was indeed, as Scott had implied, about to fail. Mary Byers
was working for him now and I saw her for the first time since that episode, 12½ years before, when I had introduced her to the Futurians.
She was Mary Kornbluth now, was pregnant with twins, and was looking rather tired.

Fred admitted things were in a bad way. He was getting a divorce
from Judy, was desperately trying to stay afloat, and asked me to have
patience. Well, what could I do? I had patience.

[3] Permanent, indeed. It's still with me today, as staunch as ever, and has never given
me any trouble.

The next day I visited Brad, handed in the corrected galleys of *David Starr: Space Ranger*, and listened with a grin as he told me of how well *Pebble in the Sky* was doing. I also visited Scott Meredith, seeing him for the first time in nine years. He had put on weight, had taken off his mustache, was married, had a two-year-old son, and lived in Forest Hills.

On November 1, I saw Campbell, gave him "Youth," then drove back to Waltham. To my delight, David seemed to have thriven in my absence, and Gertrude had been able to take care of him without too much trouble.

That night, however, I felt the now-familiar pains of a kidney stone. My regimen of drinking water paid off, however. The pains were not nearly so bad as they had been a year before. I increased my water intake further, and after six days of intermittent discomfort, passed the stone. It was a tiny thing compared to the earlier one.

10

Fred Pohl visited us on November 10. It was a surprise visit; I hadn't expected him. It gave him a chance to admire David, however.

He brought some bad news: Campbell had rejected "Youth." (Later on, Gold was to reject it, too.) Fred spent some time telling me that I ought to write nonfiction articles. That, he said, was where the money was. He impressed me and I did not forget, but at the time, I was not ready.

11

On November 15, we drove to New York *with David*. He was nearly three months old now and it was on this occasion that my mother and father saw their first grandchild for the first time.

Among those whom I saw on my rounds on this occasion was Howard Browne, who was once again trying to start a high-class science-fiction magazine and who wanted stories badly.

When I got back to Boston, I started a story named "Button, Button" intended for Browne. Once again, I was attempting a humorous story, and once again, as in the case of "The Monkey's Finger," I overdid it badly. Those days, though, I could finish a story in four days, so the time investment wasn't overpowering.

On November 25, we moved David's crib out of the bedroom and set it up in the fourth room that I had been using as my workroom. After fourteen weeks, he had a room of his own—and I didn't. For half a year I had had a room to work in all to myself but now I had to move my typewriter, desk, and chair into the bedroom.

12

The layman's-biochemistry project suddenly got a new lease on life. I had written two different sample chapters in my attempt to please Angus Cameron of Little, Brown. He had persisted in not being pleased. But now he had left Little, Brown, and Jane Lawson seemed more interested. By December 2, I was writing a third attempt at a sample, and this time I just kept on going. Toward the end of the month, I had 33,000 words done, and Little, Brown finally decided to sign me up. I was delighted.

Less delightful was the fact that Howard Browne sent back "Button, Button." I seemed to have fallen out of luck with my shorter pieces. Was I being seduced by my novels into an inability to work at the lesser lengths?

I tried again for him, writing a 2,500-word story, a rather bitter one called "King Lear IV, 1, 36." This was a reference to Gloucester's famous remark, "As flies to wanton boys are we to th' gods./They kill us for their sport."

13

The Fred Pohl situation affected others. After all, there were other writers who were his clients, and not all were as patient as I was. I received a letter on December 11 from Clifford Simak, the first in ten years, asking about Fred's position. I answered as circumspectly as I could. I didn't want to lose Fred a client and I didn't want to allow Cliff to lose money, and I tried to tread a tightrope.

14

As far as the Medical School was concerned, I was turning grim, indeed. Since Walker remained adamant in his refusal to grant me a promotion, I began to look for another job.

I heard of an opening at the Veteran Administration Hospital in Bedford, about nine miles north of Waltham, and followed it up. On December 12, I secured an interview with a Dr. Hoffman. I spent 2½ hours with him and was shown around the hospital.

The job carried a P4 status, which involved a yearly salary of $5,940. It had its attractions, but it was civil service, and I didn't really intend ever to subject myself to that again. Besides, it wasn't money I wanted, it was a title.

Nevertheless, after thinking about the matter over the weekend, I felt that I had to put the matter to Walker squarely. On Monday, December 17, I told him that I had an offer and that unless I got my professorship, I would take it.

On December 20, Walker told me that he had spoken to Dean Faulkner who had, in turn, agreed to recommend me for an assistant professorship and to have my salary gradually taken over by the school, thus moving me out from under Lemon.

I presume Walker had had an embarrassing session putting pressure on the dean, for he seemed annoyed with me and told me that he wouldn't advise me to try "these tactics" again as they "might backfire." I answered, quite coolly, that I had been quite prepared for a backfire *this* time and, indeed, had expected one.

So I ended the year of 1951 as an assistant professor of biochemistry at last after 2½ years as an instructor. For the first time, I could call myself Professor Asimov.

15

On December 28, I drove to New York by myself. The next day I saw Pohl and he gave me a check for $884.67, clearing up his entire indebtedness of the moment. On December 30, I met Harry Stubbs in midtown Manhattan and drove him back to Boston with me. It was now I who was giving rides to other people.

David ended the year weighing fifteen pounds and, as nearly as we could tell, making normal progress.

As for myself, for the second year in a row I had published two books:[4]

3. *The Stars, like Dust*— (Doubleday)
4. *Foundation* (Gnome)

My writing earnings for 1951 were, however, a disappointment. I ended the year with a literary income of $3,625. It was only three quarters what I had made in 1950. It was better than my earnings in any other year by far, of course, but one is quickly spoiled.

My school income had gone up a bit, to $5,350, but that was not enough to make up for it. The total came to just under $9,000.

[4] In listing the books year by year, I will number them so as to give a running total of all of them. Those who question me about my books never ask how many I have published "this year"; they always want to know the overall total.

There were explanations, of course. The time I had spent on the textbook and on the layman's biochemistry book had been enormous and had brought me in nothing. Nevertheless, I felt a little shaken in my belief that I could support myself by my writing if I had to.

16

As invariably happened, the new year brought my birthday, my first as a father, and on January 2, 1952, I was thirty-two years old.

Events are no respecters of birthdays. On January 4, I heard from Howard Browne. He rejected "King Lear IV, I, 36" but, rather to my surprise, told me he was accepting "What if—," the story I had written in response to Gertrude's question about where I got my ideas.

Then, on January 9, the galleys of *Biochemistry and Human Metabolism* began to come in in three copies plus a master.

What we did was this: Each of us—Walker, Boyd, and I—searched our own copies for mistakes. We then foregathered. The author of that chapter would list the corrections and they would be entered in the master. Each of the other two would then add any other corrections he had found. Invariably, no one of us caught all the errors. Always, No. 2 could add to what No. 1 could find, and then No. 3 would come along with something both the others had missed. And on a surprising number of occasions, there were mistakes none of us found.

The publisher's proofreader himself searched for mistakes and would point out inconsistencies in capitalization, hyphenation, and so on. It was a dreadful chore to try to decide on consistency, especially when the three of us never agreed. Finally Bill Boyd said, "According to Emerson, 'A foolish consistency is the hobgoblin of little minds.'"

After that whenever we came to a trivial inconsistency, we would chorus "Emerson!" and let it stand.

The official notification that I was Assistant Professor having come on January 22, that was entered in place of "Instructor" on the title page of the textbook. That gave me enormous satisfaction.

17

On January 15, I got my advance copy of *David Starr: Space Ranger*. It was my first book written under a pseudonym.

In addition, I was working steadily on *The Currents of Space* and on the biochemistry book for Little, Brown. I was also organizing my Foundation stories, "Dead Hand," and "The Mule" to make up the second book of the series, *Foundation and Empire*.

18

David was five months old on January 20 and was able to sit up for brief periods.

On the twenty-fourth, though, he managed to get a small dumbbell-shaped rattle stuck in his mouth. We tried to remove it, grew panicky, used too much force, and scraped his gums. They bled and were undoubtedly sore for the next couple of days so that he wouldn't take his bottle.

It seemed to us, in fact, that from then on he was a poor feeder. The pediatrician kept saying, "If he doesn't want to eat, don't force him. He'll eat when he's hungry."

We could never believe that, though. We always feared that he was going to starve and we consistently kept trying to feed him against his will. This created a negative behavior pattern in David and we spent an inordinate amount of time trying to outsmart him and failing. We had a tendency, every once in a while, to trace it all back to the rattle incident.

19

Since David had been born, our moviegoing had dropped very nearly to nothing, which was difficult for us since we were confirmed movie addicts.

I can't say my taste in movies testified to any deeply intellectual instincts, by the way. I liked adventure movies and would see, with pleasure, almost anything with swordplay or with a chase sequence. And I liked comedy, the more slapstick the better, and musical comedies, too. Errol Flynn and Danny Kaye were surefire where I was concerned, and my all-time favorites were Fred Astaire and Ginger Rogers.

Oddly enough, or not so oddly perhaps, I didn't like what were called "science fiction" movies, with rare exceptions, such as *The Shape of Things to Come*.

For the most part, science-fiction movies seemed to be innocent of science and, for that matter, of acting, and I found them acutely embarrassing. *The Thing*, for example, was unbearably bad, and I was disgusted at the fact that it was made, and ruined, from Campbell's classic story "Who Goes There?"

The pressure to do something about the loss of moviegoing grew, and by the beginning of February, we were shopping for a television set. It took us a while to decide among alternatives, by on February 28,

1952, our television set came into the apartment. For four years we had watched television intermittently in the houses of other people, and now we had one in our own.

The immediate results were predictable. To begin with, we had a tendency to watch it day and night just to see people move and voices sound even when everything we saw was so miserable as to be almost emetic in its quality.

Then, where those programs we really wanted to watch were concerned we would not allow any interference and we would wait in fear that the set might choose that moment to break down. (The set did break down frequently, as all sets did in the pretransistor days, and we practically had a live-in TV repairman.)

The chief program that had us nailed to our chairs was, of course, "Your Show of Shows" with Sid Caesar and Imogene Coca, which I saw on my own set for the first time on March 1, 1952.

I would not allow anything to get in the way of my watching that show, and when the Whipples invited us to dinner for the night of Saturday the seventh, I was adamant in refusing, despite all their blandishments. I think I nearly lost their friendship over that incident.

53

Writing vs. Research

1

I was losing interest in research. This is odd, looking back on it. I had spent the entire decade of the 1940s pushing eagerly for permission to do research when I was at Columbia, then waiting longingly for the time when I could return to research when I was at the Navy Yard and in the Army, then doing research with dedicated fascination when I was back at Columbia.

I had thought of myself as a research chemist (or, later, biochemist) for a dozen years. To be sure, I was a writer also, but that was my avocation, not my profession. Writing was a spare-time activity, a sideline, something to make a little extra cash with and to gain a little extra importance with.

As long as I wrote only science fiction, that remained my way of thinking, for it would have been entirely unethical to write science fiction on school time, so I never did—and as long as my writing was for evenings, weekends, and holidays only, it had to remain a sideline.

It was the textbook that began the change. That was a scholarly work. It could be written on school time and, to a large extent, was. The reference work involved was done entirely on school time.

I discovered I preferred to work on the textbook than to do research. Consequently, I allowed it to invade my research time more and more.

To be sure, as a faculty member, I didn't expect to sully my own hands with laboratory equipment—all the more so since I was so unskillful at it. I did, however, interest myself in the work done by the various graduate students and assistants. I supervised, made suggestions, and, of course, worked on the papers. I did papers with Rose M. Reguera, Charles A. Fish, M. Moira Davison, and Morton K. Schwartz, all of them bright and hard-working—and yet it took more and more effort to do all this.

I found the feeling of being a research chemist (or biochemist) fading away. I had worked so hard for it, I had achieved a doctorate and even, finally, professorial status, and now, suddenly, it was leaving me—because I had found something else, something I had been doing for years before I started my research, yet which till 1952, I had never clearly thought of as my life's work.

I was beginning to think of myself as a writer and that was crucial.

The slow, uncertain, and devious route of research was bound to bother research workers who discovered they were failing to produce exciting and name-making results—and if you haven't made it by thirty-five, you're not likely to make it thereafter. It seemed to me that many unsuccessful researchers sought to find ways out in textbook writing, administration, or empire building. (After World War II, with government money being poured into grants, empire building—the piling of grant upon grant to pay for huge research programs in which others did the work—became attractive to many.)

I myself had no aptitude for administration and even less for empire building. My venture into textbook writing did not seem hopeful. I had, however, an outlet not available to most—commercial writing.

As research steadily lost its glamor for me, writing grew steadily more attractive. And as writing grew steadily more attractive, research steadily lost its glamor. Either tendency reinforced the other in a spiral that made me, with each month that passed, more of a writer and less of a researcher.

It was no wonder, then, that once we were through with the writing of the textbook, I did not go back to a fuller concern for research. I did not even want to. There was still work to be done with the textbook, and if that failed I had other projects that could be done on school time. There was the biochemistry-for-the-layman book I was doing for Little, Brown. It might be for the layman, but it was still a scholarly book, and I still felt it ethical to do it on school time, leaving my nonschool time for fiction.

The formal signing of the contract with Little, Brown came on February 7, 1952. Almost immediately afterward they sent me a $250 advance and I decided to call the book *The Puzzle of Life*. I felt myself finally to be in the business of writing nonfiction by myself.

2

Fiction remained alive, too. Unexpectedly, *Fantasy and Science Fiction* accepted "King Lear VI, 1, 36" and I was delighted. I had been reading *F & SF* since its inception and I had felt that its level of writing was distinctly above my own capacities. Its stories were more "literary" than mine ever were.

I had once thought the same of *Unknown,* and just as I had then longed to sell to *Unknown,* I now longed to sell to *F & SF*—and feared I never would.

But I *had,* and all Tony Boucher asked me to do was to change the title. Nowadays, offbeat titles are very common, but in those days they weren't. I changed the title to "Flies" and, actually, I thought it an im-improvement.

3

We finished work on the galleys of *Biochemistry and Human Metabolism* on February 20, 1952. On March 10, the page proofs started coming in and that meant indexing.

We decided that each one of us would index our own chapters. I had never indexed anything before, but I had a vague idea as to how it should be done. My philosophy was that any reader, using the index, should be able to find every mention of every topic of biochemical interest. I made an enormous pile of index cards for Chapter 2, "Protein Structure," for instance, with every amino acid listed every last time its name appeared.

I was dissatisfied with Walker's and Boyd's more cavalier attitude toward indexing, so there was another fault I managed to find with collaboration.

In the end all the cards had to be alphabetized, condensed, and the whole typed up neatly. That job fell to me because I wanted it and the others did not. It was incredibly time-consuming and nit-picking, but fortunately I enjoyed the process. On April 14, 1952, the index was completed and mailed off.

4

There is no stage in writing, however, at which failure cannot strike. All that negotiating with Little, Brown regarding *The Puzzle of Life*—all that writing of outlines and samples—even the contract-signing and advance—all came to nothing. When I turned in the book at last, they considered it and, on March 21, 1952, told me it was no go. They would not do it.

That was twice Little, Brown refused me. Three years before they had turned down the Foundation series, and now they turned down my effort to write a popular-biochemistry book.

On the other hand, I finished *The Currents of Space* at last on

March 30, after about a year and a quarter of work, and I confidently expected no failures there.

David was also making satisfactory progress. He was eating mashed meat now, thus becoming a carnivorous creature. (He objected to it a little at first.)

5

Volume 15 of *Cold Spring Harbor Symposia on Quantitative Biology* was an issue that had been devoted to the "Origin and Evolution of Man." A scholarly journal, *Evolution*, asked me to review that volume of the *CSH Symposia*, and I did so. It was 5,000 words long, an intricate and, if I say so myself, well-thought-out review, and it appeared in the March 1952 *Evolution*.

My copy of that issue reached me, and shortly after Lemon happened by, even as I was looking over my review with considerable satisfaction.

I showed it to him, feeling he might as well see I could do scholarly work independently of him. He glanced at it and said, "Why don't you put this effort into your research?"

I said angrily, "I did this on my own time."

And he said, "A research worker doesn't have his own time."

It was clear then, if it had not been abundantly clear before, that he and I were not on the same wavelength. It was probably at that moment that I came to the conscious decision that I was no longer a research chemist and that I would never again be one. If either Lemon, or the school itself, ever tried to make me become one, they would find they couldn't.

Let me make it clear that I was turning against research and not against teaching. I loved teaching, and the textbook was a form of teaching. I particularly loved lecturing

There could be no question but that my teaching was satisfactory. I had improved steadily in the organization, drama, and interest in my lecture presentations. (This would seem to be my own estimate of the situation, but I know the students agreed with me.)

On April 15, 1952, I gave my final lecture of the third teaching semester in which I had been involved. It was "Heat and Work," and somewhere in the middle, I delivered a ringing sentence on the concept of the "heat death" of the Universe, and there followed a wild and enthusiastic peal of applause that did not allow me to continue for quite a while.

A story reached me once that on another floor, a member of the Physiology Department said, "What's that?" at the sound of distant laughter and applause.

Another member said, "Probably Asimov lecturing."

And it was.

There's no question about it in my mind, and I'm willing to say it without hesitation, that I was the best lecturer in the school, and at no time ever did I skimp my teaching duties in favor of my writing.

My talent for lecturing was not something I hid under a bushel, and with much of the faculty (not all) this did not tend to make me a beloved comrade. What with my general eccentricity and self-assertiveness, and with my refusal to take part in academic social functions, I remained rather isolated except for a few chosen associates, of whom Boyd and Walker were the chief.

My relations with the students, on the other hand, were easy and informal, and on only the rarest of occasions was I forced to play the heavy professorial role. In fact, I was more or less under a continual strain to keep those easy relations from degenerating into outright camaraderie and, in particular, to keep from slipping into my usual suavity with the female students. *That* might have given rise to charges of favoritism. (On at least one occasion a male student grumbled that I was easier on the pretty females, something I would have hotly refuted had I not had the uncomfortable feeling he was probably right.)

And no matter how I tried to limit my natural tendency to be amiable, I felt there was considerable disapproval, on the part of stiffer members of the faculty, of my habit of informality. Perhaps they felt I was currying favor with the students—though to what end I might be doing so, I can't imagine. After all, popularity with the students didn't bring one promotions; rather the reverse.

6

All three of us drove to New York on April 16, and the next day I went to Fred's offices and found that Campbell had taken *The Currents of Space* for serialization. At $.03 a word, 70,000 words came to $2,100, or allowing for Fred's cut, $1,890. It was the largest single check I had ever received and a far cry from my first check for $64. That one check, in fact, was more money than I had ever made in any single year prior to 1950. That check meant that by the end of April 1952, I had already earned more money writing than in the entire year of 1951, and there seemed no doubt I would surpass 1950 and have a new record year.

Brad liked *The Currents of Space,* too; he thought it the best yet. He wanted another juvenile about David Starr, in addition. He admitted that there was no television series after all, but saw nothing wrong in my having a series of juvenile novels.

On April 19, I visited Horace Gold who, on hearing that *The Currents of Space* was going to Campbell, wanted the next novel to come to him. He suggested a robot novel and I demurred. I had only written robot short stories and didn't know if I could carry a whole novel based on the robot idea.

"Sure you can," he said. "How about an overpopulated world in which robots are taking over human jobs?"

"Too depressing," I said. "I'm not sure I want to handle a heavy sociological story."

"Do it your way. You like mysteries. Put a murder in such a world and have a detective solve it with a robot partner. If the detective doesn't solve it, the robot will replace him."

That was the germ of a new novel I called *The Caves of Steel.*

When I wrote it, I did my best to ignore this business of robots replacing human beings. That was typically Gold and not at all Asimov —but Horace kept pushing, and in the end, some of it was forced in, though not nearly as much as Horace wanted.

What pleased me most about *The Caves of Steel* when I came to write it was that it was a pure murder mystery set against a science-fiction background. As far as I was concerned it was a perfect fusion of the two genre, and the first such perfect fusion. A number of people agree with me in this.

And on April 28, 1952, David's first tooth, the lower left front incisor, made its appearance through the gum.

7

Of all the people in Breadloaf, I remembered John Ciardi most clearly. It had been my intention to return in 1951—I had half promised Fletcher Pratt I would—but during the last half of August, when the Breadloaf Writers Conference was always held, David was being born and I certainly couldn't leave then. So I had missed seeing John a second time.

However, he lived in a Boston suburb and was in publishing in a small way, having joined a publishing house called Twayne Press. He wanted stories for an anthology and I went to see him on April 30, and saw his brand-new, six-week-old daughter. Ciardi's wife, Judith, felt it was feeding time for the youngster, who was a breast baby. So she pulled out a breast and handed it to the kid. Judith was always an entirely extroverted, unself-conscious, delightful person and this was quite in character—but I didn't know where to look.

I didn't sell John a story to anthologize but I initiated a friendship that was permanent.

8

My story "Youth"[1] appeared in the May 1952 issue of *Space Science Fiction*. It was the first issue of that magazine—one of the many that suddenly weighed down the magazine stands. Few of them lasted long. *Space* lasted only eight issues.

It wasn't a bad magazine. It couldn't be bad, since Lester del Rey was editing it. Lester had difficulties with the publisher, however, and even he couldn't overcome that handicap.

9

Copies of *Biochemistry and Human Metabolism* arrived on May 24, 1952. It was my first nonfiction book, and I was terribly proud. I remember that Matthew Derow picked it up, opened it at random, and said instantly, "You've got a wrong formula here."

"Go on," I said in disbelief, assuming he was kidding, for Walker, Boyd and I had spent endless hours checking over every formula for accuracy. He showed me and, for goodness' sake, he was right.

We used the book as a text for the next teaching semester (my fourth) and offered trivial bonuses to any student who found a typographical error. On the one hand, it helped insure careful reading; on the other, we would find errors that we could correct in future printings.

It worked entirely too well. After our careful triple proofreading, the students found so many errors that even at a dime a throw (and a quarter for a mistake in a formula) it seemed to represent a serious financial drain. Unbelievable!

In the Waltham apartment, meanwhile, there were two built-in bookcases on either side of the fireplace. They were very small bookcases, but I guess the architects and designers didn't read—just as I didn't use the fireplace.

We did use the bookcases, though. On the top shelf at the right side I placed a copy of each of my books in chronological order, and it

[1] See *The Martian Way and Other Stories* (Doubleday, 1955).

gave me a certain austere pleasure to place *Biochemistry and Human Metabolism* in its correct place, immediately behind my juvenile. I showed the textbook no favoritism.

While the book was in preparation, Dick Hoover of Williams & Wilkins was very optimistic about it, but the fact is that the textbook was a distressing failure. For one thing, just about the time it came out, two other new biochemistry texts appeared—West and Todd's *Textbook of Biochemistry* and White, Handler, Smith, and Stetten's *Principles of Biochemistry*. Each was longer and better than ours. And even if the two competitors had not appeared on the scene, ours just wasn't good enough.

10

The year 1952 saw McCarthyism at its peak in the United States. At no time did it affect me directly in any way, but the spectacle sickened me. My liberal friends and I denounced Senator Joseph R. McCarthy to each other and if we were representative samples of American public opinion he wouldn't have lasted five minutes. The fact is we weren't. The average American was all for McCarthy and his simple-minded and destructive "patriotism."

I remembered what Ted Sturgeon had once said at a convention— that science fiction was the last bastion of freedom of speech. The censor minds did not read science fiction, could not understand science fiction, and would not know what to suppress if they did read it. If censorship ever got so sophisticated that even science fiction fell prey to it, then all was over. Every vestige of democracy would be gone.

So I set about giving my opinion of McCarthyism in a science-fiction story. I called it "A Piece of Ocean" at first, then changed the name to "The Martian Way." It dealt with Martian colonists with a problem, who were victimized out of a solution by a McCarthy-style politician and who were in this way forced to find a still better solution. I finished it on June 10. I did the 18,000 words in four weeks.

In this story, by the way, I described a "space walk" in euphoric terms, over a decade before space walks actually took place and apparently *did* induce euphoria.

11

As it turned out, my 1951 income tax was the last one I was ever to make out entirely by myself. It was clear that my 1952 income was going to be large enough to make it advisable to get professional help.

Maury Cohen (whom we had met in Birchtoft) recommended the firm of Gorsey and Woll to me. I went there and Sam Gorsey worked out my estimated income tax for 1952 for me. In later years, his junior partner, Saul Woll, a very sharp and quick-spoken individual, worked on them for me.

Once, I remember, I said to Saul, "Listen, are you sure I am taking off as many deductions as I might be? Are there any clever devices you can use that I know nothing of?"

Saul looked at me over his glasses and said, "Isaac, when you hire me, I make use of the cleverest device of all."

"What's that?" I said.

"I keep you out of jail," he said.

And I reached out and shook his hand. "That," I said, "is a good enough device for me. Keep on using it."

12

On June 14, Horace Gold called me. He wanted "The Martian Way" but he also wanted a complete revision.

Horace was becoming crankier as time went on, and I couldn't help notice the differences in the way the Big Three editors in science-fiction—John Campbell, Horace Gold, and Tony Boucher—handled their rejections.

Campbell, as always, wrote letters that were verbose, difficult, and impersonal. He based his requests for revisions on content. Tony was always friendly and laudatory and based his requests for revisions on style. Horace, however, was becoming increasingly personal and vilifying in his rejections.[2]

I had no trouble dealing with Campbell and Tony and generally went along with their requests if I possibly could. With Horace, however, I tended to become balky, and the crankier he grew, the balkier I got.

I remembered with annoyance the forced insertion of the U. S. Constitution in *The Stars, like Dust—*, the forced emasculation of the ending of "Hostess," and the long argument over "C-Chute." I refused a complete rewrite of "The Martian Way" and complained about it to Fred Pohl. I told Fred that, as my agent, he would have to protect me from Horace's harassment.

[2] Horace once said to me, concerning one of my submissions, "This story is meretricious." "It's what?" said I. "Meretricious," he said, proud of the word (the meaning of which I knew perfectly well). "And a Happy New Year to you," I said. Would you believe that he got annoyed?

Fred interposed, and the request for revision was reduced to a single point. There were only male characters in the story, and Horace wanted a female.

He was right, in a sense. I was discussing a pioneer society, but surely it contained women. I, on the other hand, was willing to accept them for granted. They were not an essential part of the plot and I feared having to create a romance in a story where, as I saw it, there was no room for one.

Finally, Horace said, "Just put in a woman. Any woman. Then I'll take the story."

That gave me a wicked idea and I promptly agreed. I rewrote the story, and gave one of the characters a rather shrewish and scolding wife. That was not what Horace had in mind ("Oh what a woman!" he muttered), but he stuck to his word and took the story.

And even as I began my revision of "The Martian Way," I also began work on the second edition of *Biochemistry and Human Metabolism*. This promised to be a perennial job, like painting a huge suspension bridge—as soon as you've finished, you begin all over again because the end at which you began the paint job needs another one by now.

Of course, we did not yet realize that the book was a failure, and if we had, we would have nourished the feeble hope that in revising it we could do away with its weaknesses and make it a success.

13

John Blugerman came visiting on June 21. He had been in the Army twice. After he completed dental school, he had to return to the Army, but this time as an officer, and he was stationed in a peaceful Europe, so it wasn't what it might have been.

He had been abroad for fifteen months and we hadn't seen him for a year and a half, but he hadn't changed; he was as slim and as handsome as ever. He saw his nephew, David, for the first time.

I took the opportunity of John's presence to go to New York on the twenty-third, knowing that there would be someone at home to keep Gertrude company and to help with David.

I visited Gold on the evening of the twenty-third (handing him the revised "The Martian Way"), and Judy Merril, now divorced from Fred, was there, too.

I moaned about having to go way out to Brighton Beach to stay at the Blugermans', since the subway trip took better than an hour. Judy pointed out that she had the use of an apartment in Manhattan and said I was welcome to the use of it along with her. I smiled uncertainly since I didn't know exactly what this would entail, and some possibilities frightened me.

I left shortly thereafter without further complaint about the subway ride, but when I got out into the street I found that Judy was right behind me. As we walked to the subway station at the corner, she renewed the invitation.

I said, in a nervous attempt at gallantry, "Of course, Judy, if I'm to spend the night with you, as a husband might do, I would expect a husband's privileges." (I guess I thought that Judy would laugh and refuse and I could go on to Brighton Beach on the *macho* plea that it was all or nothing.)

But Judy said, "Of course."

And I dashed down the subway steps.

This is not the kind of story I would tell, except that Judy herself told it, far and wide, with heaven only knows what interpolations, and I became the object of a certain gentle ridicule, for everyone knew my penchant for making gallant suggestions to the ladies. It was, I think, this story, as told by Judy, that produced the general feeling expressed to me by many a nubile young woman: "Oh listen, Isaac, if I said 'Yes,' you'd go right through that wall to get away."[3]

There is a sequel to the story. By the time I got back to the Blugerman apartment, I was in a deep state of worry. Everyone at the Golds' must have seen Judy leave immediately after me and they must all have come to the same conclusion. It was conceivable that the story, distorted and made worse (if that were possible), would reach Gertrude's ears and cause me infinite trouble.

Once I was at the Blugermans' therefore, I called Horace.

"Horace," I said, "I'm at my mother-in-law's."

[3] Note from Judith Merril: The whole point to this incident is contained in Isaac's understated phrase, "making gallant suggestions to the ladies." The fact is that Isaac (who was at that time a spectacularly uxorious and virtuous husband) apparently felt obliged to leer, ogle, pat, and proposition as an act of sociability. When it went, occasionally, beyond purely social enjoyability, there seemed no way to clue him in.

Let me pause to make clear that I am neither impugning Isaac's desirability nor claiming any extraordinary maidenliness for myself. Unattached as I then was, had I for a moment believed in the seriousness of his intent, I might well have been agreeable. As it was, however, I felt certain I would not be called upon to make any decisions about my own seriousness, when I carefully and with malice aforehand created this situation.

A parallel incident that occurred about the same time at a Hydra Club party at the Lotos Club seems to have escaped the famous Asimov memory. [No, it hasn't. I.A.] Asimov was known in those days, to various women, as "the man with a hundred hands." On this occasion, the third or fourth time his hand patted my rear end, I reached out to clutch his crotch. *He never manhandled me in vain again.*

"I don't care where you are," said Horace. "You're a grown man. You can be anywhere you want to be."

"No. I'm really at my mother-in-law's. Mary," I called, "come here and say hello to Mr. Gold."

Mary, completely mystified as to what was going on, said, "Hello" into the phone and then said to me, predictably, "What's going on?"

"Did you hear that, Horace?" I asked, urgently.

And he said, cozily, "I told you, Isaac, I don't care where you are. Judy doesn't have to change her voice." And he hung up and left me frustrated.

(Of course, my worries were needless. In the first place, I was completely innocent. And even if I were not, it was silly of me to think that anyone in science fiction would take note of any amorous event, however illicit. The thing was too common to do anything but yawn over.)

On the twenty-fourth, I visited Brad and Marty Greenberg, and from the figures they gave me, it seemed that my five novels had already sold some 30,000 copies in hard-cover, with *Pebble in the Sky*, which had now been on sale for a year and a half, having sold some 13,000 copies.

While in New York, I gave copies of the textbook to my parents and to the Blugermans.[4]

I returned to Boston in time to catch the peak of a heat wave, with the temperature topping 100 on June 26. John left on the morning of the thirtieth.

14

My relations with Doubleday had become easygoing indeed. No more outlines, no more options, no more let-me-see-a-piece. I had merely to say I would do a new Space Ranger juvenile and that was enough. By July 5, 1952, Doubleday informed me that a contract and an advance were on the way.

I needed a new name for my hero, though. Starr was all right, but David was pedestrian. I couldn't change it but I could give him a nickname—and one seemed such a natural that it occurred to me at once and I never sought another. The second book was entitled, therefore, *Lucky Starr and the Pirates of the Asteroids*.

---

[4] I did this routinely with every book I ever published. Almost the first thing I did when the author's copies came in was to mail one off to the Asimovs and one to the Blugermans. Each household gradually accumulated a fine library of Isaac Asimov books that threatened to push them out of house and home. Any suggestion that I stop overloading them, however, was met with instant indignation, and I could never stop.

15

The year 1952, was, of course, a presidential election year, and it seemed to be a sure Republican year. This time, unlike 1948, there could be no mistake. For one thing, Truman was so unpopular that it was difficult to see how he could fail to be an albatross, dragging any Democratic candidate down to defeat. For another, it looked as though Eisenhower would be the Republican candidate, and, if so, he would be undefeatable. I hoped earnestly that the Republican Party regulars, who tried valiantly to commit electoral suicide, would put through Robert Taft as the nominee, but they didn't manage.

What I remember most clearly about the Republican convention was MacArthur's keynote speech. He had become the deified leader of America's conservatives after he had been justly fired by Truman, and there was some hope that he would stampede the convention into nominating him by a pyrotechnic display of eloquence. The speech, however, fell so incredibly flat that I said to Gertrude (as recorded in my diary), "He is stepping off the podium into oblivion," and I proved to be right.

The Democrats nominated Adlai Stevenson of Illinois, who was only a name to me. Once I heard him speak, I became very enthusiastic, but that didn't blind me to the hopelessness of the cause.

It was the first time, by the way, that I watched conventions on television. It was incredibly dull, but the novelty of it kept me glued to the set through agonies of boredom.

16

Henry Blugerman arrived on a visit on July 7 and John, again, on the twelfth. It was Gertrude's idea that Henry, John, and I could all go to Annisquam for a week. She was particularly anxious that Henry get the chance of a vacation in this way. She did try to make arrangements to have a cottage for herself and David, but in the end she felt it would entail more trouble than it was worth, so we all went without her on Saturday, July 12, 1952.

The first night there I heard the Annisquam staff do my version of *Kiss Me, Kate*. It sounded great.

We were put in a room for three, which was something less than wonderful. Henry, it seemed, snored. Now, this is a common complaint, and I am told that I snore, too (though John didn't). Henry's snores were, however, stentorian, and I do not remember sleeping at all during the entire week we spent in the room.

Henry and John made full use of the ocean, since both could swim with great facility. I just sat on a shady part of the beach, reading.

Annisquam was not crowded that week and there was a particular shortage of young men. This should have put John at a premium, but he was not a gregarious, effervescent person, as I am, and the young girls seemed frightened of him.

They were not frightened of me. In fact, they found that if they sat around me, I would tell them jokes, sing songs, and make ribald remarks, so that after a while they were laughing and would forget there was a shortage of single men about.

I remember I entertained one young woman (rather plain) with a well-thought-out explanation of why it did not matter whether a woman was plain, why other things were much more important—intelligence, personality, warmth, and so on and so on and so on. And just as I thought I had made my point and nailed it down, she suddenly said, wryly, "But your wife is beautiful. Right?"

I said, "Right," and the argument was ruined.

The high point came on the evening of July 15, after dinner, when I suggested a walk to the highway where there was some sort of ice-cream parlor. I offered to stand any young woman willing to accompany me sundaes, sodas, or whatever they wanted, and with no limit to the numbers. Five of them came along.

They were all in their early twenties, all single, all reasonably pleasant in appearance. We all walked slowly, with myself between two girls with an arm about the waist of each—and changing girls periodically, so that none would feel neglected. It seemed to me that I was at my best, my most amusing and charming, and the sound of soprano laughter frightened the birds for miles around.

We reached the ice-cream parlor finally and I said, "All right, girls, anything you want."

The man behind the counter looked at them and then at me (who was, after all, fat and quite ordinary-looking) and said, "All these girls with you?"

"That's right," I said.

He said, "Can you take care of all of them?"

And I said loftily, "Do any of them look unhappy?"

And indeed, they didn't. I loved the look of awe and respect that shone in his eyes.

We finally got home on July 19 and the two Blugermans went on to New York. Gertrude had managed the city heat in our absence by sleeping on the porch nights. It was the equivalent of an air-conditioned room, and, since the landlord had now put screens around it, it was mosquito-free as well.

David had gotten through the week with no trouble also. In my absence he was weaned—or he weaned himself. In any case, he now rejected the bottle and preferred to slobber messily with a glass.

17

On July 23, 1952, we read in the paper that Laurence Oncley had died. He was a biochemist at Harvard whom we had met through Bill Boyd. Oncley was a tall and large man, soft-voiced and pleasant, and Gertrude and I liked him. The news was shocking. He had had leukemia for fourteen months, the news report said, and we marveled at how he had managed to hold up, remain cheerful, never let on. It was absolutely inspirational and we mourned his passing.

Then when we visited the Boyds sometime later, Larry Oncley walked in. Gertrude and I went to pieces. You don't come across three-dimensional ghosts often. What happened was, of course, that Larry was Laurence Oncley, Jr., and the obituary had referred to Laurence Oncley, Sr.

18

At about this time I was making out a will for the first time. Until now it was just a matter of leaving everything to Gertrude. With a child, I would also have to provide for him in case Gertrude and I died in a common disaster, so I felt I could put it off no more. For the same reason, I took out my first batch of life insurance.

That made me aware of my steadily increasing weight. On June 30, 1952, I weighed just 200 pounds stripped—some 55 pounds more than I weighed when I was married, and 30 pounds more than when I entered the Army.

I decided to go on a diet and even consulted a doctor about it. The doctor was Robert Cataldo (we had, after all, moved away from Dr. Adler), a small man, with a head shaved to mere stubble, and who spoke in an ingratiating whisper. Dr. Cataldo drove me slowly crazy by going through his usual routine of informing his patient on the facts concerning diet. Considering that I had written the "Lipids and Obesity" chapter in the textbook, there was nothing he could possibly tell me that I didn't know.

I did lose a few pounds as a result, but as is common in such cases, it didn't stay off.

19

On August 4, Fred wrote to tell me that Tony Boucher had rejected a story of mine called "The Deep," which I had written as a deliberate test as to whether you could do *anything* in science fiction. In this story, I invented a society in which mother love was considered obscene. Fortunately, Horace had taken it, and at a new high rate of $.04 a word.

In addition, Fred had sold "Button, Button" to *Thrilling Wonder* at $.015 a word. (That was more like the old days.)

At about that time, too, I got Howard Browne's new magazine *Fantastic*. It did indeed look very classy and he had obviously gotten the publishers of *Amazing* to take a chance on quality. That first issue —Summer 1952—had my story "What if—?"[5] in it.

Unfortunately, the magazine didn't last. It went five issues and was then combined with *Fantastic Adventures*. Too bad.

Finally, I received my first copies of *Foundation and Empire*.

20

On August 8, 1952, I had owned my car for two years and had just paid the final installment. It was mine outright now, and I had eighteen thousand miles on it.

As for David, he now had six teeth, was thirty inches tall, and weighed twenty-one pounds. On August 9, we took the giant step of hiring a baby-sitter to stay with him while we went off visiting. We came back to find David perfectly safe and happy.

21

I finally got a copy of *Ich, der Robot*, and even before that, Gotthard Guenther arrived on August 11 with a German-language anthology called *Verwindung von Raum and Zeit* (*Transcendence of Space and Time*). The second story it contained was "*Einbruch der Nacht*" ("Nightfall").

In *Ich, der Robot* I couldn't help but notice that all my characters spoke perfect German even though they were named Michael Dono-

[5] See *Nightfall and Other Stories*.

van, Gregory Powell, Susan Calvin, and so on. I asked Gotthard why they didn't translate the names, too, and have a Max Donnerheit, a Gustav Pommern, and a Sieglinde Kaspar.

He said, "Oh no. In Germany, we consider science fiction an American literary form and it wouldn't sound right without American names."

I saw his point. If you were going to write a sword-play historical romance, Monsieur du Vallon de Bracieux de Pierrefonds sounds much better than Mr. Joe Green.

22

Gertrude had her turn at a sort of vacation over the weekend of August 16–17. She went off on an auto trip with two girls whom we had met at Birchtoft two years before. They went to Annisquam for the Saturday and Sunday, and they, too, saw and heard the staff do my version of *Kiss Me, Kate*.

She told me, after she returned, that they had sat in front of two middle-aged women, one of whom excitedly said to the other at the conclusion of the show, "Wasn't it wonderful?"

And the second one said, "The music isn't so much, but the words were great!"

(Were you listening, Cole?)

After Gertrude returned, Sam Merwin called. He was in Concord, Massachusetts, temporarily, and wanted to see me. I visited him on August 19 and spent two hours with him. He apologized again for not taking "Grow Old with Me," and I waved it away.

And the next day, David celebrated his first birthday.

23

I might have gone to the Breadloaf Writers Conference this year, but I had spent a week at Annisquam, and enough was enough.

Besides, I *had* to spend the last week in August at a Gordon Research Conference. There are weeks and weeks of this in New Hampshire every summer, each week devoted to a different subject. The reason I *had* to attend was that this week's session was devoted to cancer, and Henry Lemon was going to talk there. I drove to New Hampshire on August 25, 1952, and was assigned to a room with Pat McGrady, a science writer.

He warned me of his snoring. "Wake me up if I snore," he said.

Well, he *snored*. He and Henry could have snored a duet that would have drowned out Krakatoa. And I *did* wake him—ten times a night. He would mutter, open his eyes, and look dazed. However, I could never manage to fall asleep in the twenty seconds before he started snoring again.

The only other thing I remember about the trip was sitting in one of the lounges trying to relax, when a gentleman sat down next to me, pulled out his pipe, and started to light up.

Noting the look of disfavor in my eye, he said, "You don't smoke?"

"No," I said, crisply.

"Well, if you don't smoke a pipe, you don't know what you're missing."

"Sure, I do," said I. "Cancer of the lip."

And since this *was* a cancer conference, there was a general roar of laughter, and the pipe smoker looked so discomfited it did my heart good.

24

David had taken his first tottering steps on his birthday, and by the end of the month he could stand quite well and walk quite a distance before flopping down. We took him to Norumbega Park on August 31. It was two miles away, about six minutes by car, and it was a children's Mecca, with rides and games of all kinds.

David was too young for it then, but we took him periodically and he came to love it. Things change in only one direction, however, it would seem. We watched Norumbega Park gradually deteriorate (as Coney Island did) till we no longer wanted to go there.

25

On September 11, the three of us went to New York in order to help celebrate *Galaxy's* second anniversary. When we got there, the Blugermans greeted us with the traditional roast-chicken dinner with noodle pudding.

The next day we attended the *Galaxy* birthday party and there were terrific *hors d'oeuvres*, hot and cold, and in vast quantity. Afterward, a bunch of us ate at an Indian restaurant.

I had lost some thirteen pounds since going on a diet—but most of it went right back again on that trip.

I met Alfred Bester for the first time at that party, which was memorialized in the October 1952 issue of *Galaxy*. The cover painting of that issue included a number of the people at the party (including

Horace, though he couldn't attend since he couldn't leave his apartment). My face was included, but it had me holding a cocktail which, of course, I didn't do at that party.

The next day, Stanley visited us at the Blugermans', and he and I and John and Gertrude all went out on the traditional stroll along the boardwalk to Coney Island. Stanley, who is absolutely unflappable, went on the Ferris wheel with Gertrude. Nothing could have gotten *me* on it.

(Stanley was twenty-two at the time, the same age at which I had flunked the roller-coaster test with Gertrude. It was at about this time that he began his life's work. He joined the Long Island *Newsday* as a reporter and then proceeded to move up onto the editorial staff. Then, over the years to come, a steady gradation of promotions brought him to more and more responsible positions on the newspaper.)

On September 15, I collected some sales data. Howard Browne's *Fantastic* had taken another story of mine—"Sally"—about intelligent automobiles. (That story is one of my favorites.) Campbell was taking a second thiotimoline article I had written for him, "The Micro-psychiatric Applications of Thiotimoline" (how things had changed in the four years since the first one had appeared!), and *Thrilling Wonder* was taking "The Monkey's Finger."

The October 1952 *Astounding* contained the first part of *The Currents of Space*, with two more to follow. It was the third serial of mine that Campbell had published. When I had been in his office on the September trip, I had admired a painting there and asked which story it illustrated. Campbell laughed and said, "Yours," and now there it was, on the cover of the magazine.

I eventually bought the original for $25 plus postage. I framed it and it is still in my office today.

The November 1952 *Galaxy* included "The Martian Way,"[6] which got the cover—with my name misspelled.

Somehow I thought that the story would elicit a mass of mail denouncing my own portrayal of McCarthyism, or supporting it, but I got nothing either one way or the other. It may be that my satire of McCarthy was so subtle that everyone missed it.

26

On September 23, 1952, I listened to Richard M. Nixon give his "Checkers" speech, the one in which he denied (for the first time, but not the last) that he was a crook. I had disliked him intensely for his

[6] See *The Martian Way and Other Stories.*

campaign tactics against Helen Gahagan Douglas, and for his active role in the McCarthy-like tactics of the House Un-American Activities Committee. In the Alger Hiss affair, I was convinced that Hiss was innocent and that Whittaker Chambers was a liar who was conniving with Nixon.

Now as I listened to Nixon give his patently dishonest speech, I felt a hatred for him growing that was never thereafter to diminish. I felt him to be an utter hypocrite with an instinct for personal aggrandizement at all costs. I went around saying, bitterly, "If the Soviet Union should conquer the United States tomorrow and should need a Quisling to rule us in their interest, Nixon would be their man."

I still believe that.

What made it worse, of course, was that I was quite convinced that the American public would fall for the speech—and it did.

27

More and more I was trying to establish myself as an independent entity at the Medical School. I managed to get a small grant from the Atomic Energy Commission with myself as principal investigator. That meant that I myself had money to spend.

I could hire Howard Bensusan to work for me now. Bensusan was a victim of polio and had to maneuver about on crutches, but he was cheerful, driving, and bright.

I also began to give a small course of my own for graduate students —one on protein structure.

At home, Gertrude began talking of buying a house. The thought frightened me, for I felt I would be lost with lawns and gardens to take care of and with no landlord to turn to if something went wrong.

Nevertheless, Gertrude was right. We could afford a house now and we should have one for David's sake if not our own. We began a desultory search, but if looking for an apartment and working up the nerve to make a decision was hard, looking for and making a decision concerning houses was infinitely harder.

Everything we saw was either obviously too expensive or obviously not good enough.

28

The Puzzle of Life was showing unexpected signs of life again. Macmillan asked me for a book, and when I told them about my popular biochemistry, they invited me to show them a sample. I decided to do a new version of the first chapter, doing it entirely my way and not as modified by Little, Brown pressure.

I finished *Lucky Starr and the Pirates of the Asteroids* on October 24, and took it in to Brad on October 28, when we three were in New York again.

I spent the evening with Horace, talking about the new robot novel, *The Caves of Steel*, for which Brad had agreed to let me have a contract.

On October 31, I visited my parents. They were buying *another* apartment house, which would make three houses that they owned, and they were trying to sell the candy store.

29

On November 4, 1952, the presidential election took place. Gertrude and I each voted for Stevenson, but it was a lost cause. At 5:45 P.M. I wrote in my diary, "Now I sit down and start listening to the Eisenhower landslide." Actually, I started viewing it, since, for the first time, I was watching an election on television.

By 8:25 P.M. it was all over and I watched only intermittently thereafter. It was no fun anyway. A computer, "Univac," was computing the results on the basis of initial returns and robbed the election of any suspense there might have been.

Univac is an acronym for "Universal Automatic Computer" but I somehow got it into my head, without thinking, that it meant "univac," or "one vacuum tube." From then on, I wrote a series of stories featuring a giant computer I called "Multivac."

The one thing I remember most clearly about that disastrous evening was one of the local races. A Massachusetts Representative, a Democrat, had bucked the landslide and had beaten Henry Cabot Lodge for a seat in the United States Senate. The television set showed him, slim, young, and attractive, thanking his campaign workers with so much charm and grace that I was deeply moved. It was about the only good news that evening, and I said to Gertrude, "What a pity he's Catholic! If he were Protestant he would be the next President of the United States!"

I spoke more prophetically than I knew, for the new Senator was John Fitzgerald Kennedy and he would indeed be the next President of the United States, even though he was a Catholic. Of course, I didn't think to tape-record my remark or to write it down, seal it in an envelope, and put it in a safe. Eight years later, when I reminded Gertrude that I had predicted it, she couldn't remember I had made the remark. And she was my only witness.

54

Out from Under

1

On November 8, 1952, I visited Norbert Wiener at his home. I can't find in my diary any indication of how I came to be invited there, and my memory fails me as well. It seems to me that it must have been through his daughter, Margaret (Peggy) Wiener, who was a graduate student in biochemistry at Boston University.

Norbert Wiener was a great mathematician and cyberneticist, certainly the greatest mathematician I have ever come to know personally. He reminded me of Bill Boyd in exaggeration. Norbert was much more brilliant, of course, but also much more peculiar in all the directions in which Bill was peculiar—bumbling, absent-minded, eagerly proud of his accomplishments. Like Bill, of course, he was lovable.

Norbert was humorous-looking—not ugly, but humorous-looking. There was the impulse to smile when you looked at him. He had a rounded abdomen like Santa Claus, a large head with a leonine head of hair, a bulbous nose on which spectacles were precariously perched, and exophthalmic eyes that gave the impression of seeing only vaguely and without detail.

2

Doubleday was in reasonable raptures over *Lucky Starr and the Pirates of the Asteroids,* and Macmillan showed a very cautious interest in my new first chapter of *The Puzzle of Life.* I began writing additional chapters to the latter and changed the name to avoid a too-philosophical interpretation of the subject of the book. I now called it *The Chemistry of Life.*

I also finished "The Pause," a short story involving a theme I had used before—the Earth under the control of much more advanced outsiders—and sent it off to Fred Pohl on November 13. I intended it for an anthology of original stories that he was editing.

3

On November 17, 1952, my mother called me. They had sold the candy store at Windsor Place, which they had possessed for one month short of sixteen years. I had helped them run it the first six years, and Stanley had helped the last ten.

What's more, they were not buying a new one; they were retiring!

For twenty-six years altogether, they had labored in four different candy stores (five, if we count the brief stay in the Church Avenue store), and now it was all over. They were out from under the incubus that had kept them buried alive almost since they had come to the United States and that had distorted my own childhood.

It was time enough. My father was about to turn fifty-six, my mother had just turned fifty-seven, and they could count on $50 a week earnings (after taxes and maintenance) from their houses. Nor were their children any longer a drain on them. All three had jobs and could support themselves and I, at least, could pitch in and help if the old folks got into trouble—which they never did.

It was a queer feeling. I could just barely remember the days before the candy store, and if you discount those dim flashes of Van Siclen Avenue, all my life centered about a candy store till just before I was married, and even afterward I could never think of my parents without one. And now it was gone.

The whole candy-store interlude had lasted only a quarter of a century. I could have sworn it was eternal.

4

The final installment of *The Currents of Space*, in the December 1952 *Astounding*, reached the newsstands on November 19, and only ten days later, on the twenty-ninth, I got my first copies of the book.

As a faint echo, the December 1952 *Galaxy* contained "The Deep,"[1] and the February 1953 *Startling* had "The Monkey's Fingers."[2]

Then too, though Fred had said he liked "The Pause," it was apparently vetoed by the publishers. However, some days later, on December 2, he said he would take "Nobody Here but—" instead. I couldn't complain. The second was the better story, in my own opinion.

On the same day on which I received the book version of *The Currents of Space*, I finally began the new novel, *The Caves of Steel*. I also began putting together "Now You See It—" and "—And Now You Don't," at Marty Greenberg's suggestion, to prepare the final volume of the Foundation series, *Second Foundation*.

Not so pleasant as all this was the fact that on December 4, *Planet* had put out a magazine called *Tops in Science Fiction*, which reprinted "Black Friar of the Flame."

[1] See *The Martian Way and Other Stories*.
[2] See *Buy Jupiter and Other Stories*.

I was annoyed for two reasons. In the first place, they didn't ask my permission, and if they had, I would have forbidden it, since it was not a good story and would reflect poorly on my reputation of the 1950s. Second, since they did reprint it, they might have paid me, but they didn't.

Unfortunately, they were quite within their rights in doing this, since they owned all rights to the story and could reprint without additional payment at any time. Other magazines did it, too, and often with my poorest stories. The January 1951 *Super Science*, for instance, reprinted "Victory Unintentional." And early in 1953, *Thrilling Wonder* put out *Wonder Story Annual*, which reprinted "Christmas on Ganymede."

On balance, though, when the Thanksgiving season came about I had numerous reasons to give thanks, and it was fitting that Gertrude got a ten-pound turkey with which to celebrate a traditional Thanksgiving all by ourselves (plus David) for the first time.

It turned out very well indeed, and Gertrude managed it just as well as ever her mother did. I told Gertrude so, too.

5

On December 27, 1952, I took the train to New York. (It seemed sensible not to take the car when there might be snow.)

The next day was rather unusual. In the first place, after I had lunched at my parents', we all got into a car.

The first unusual point was that my parents were going somewhere together with both their sons. It was a new life for them now that the candy store was gone. They were going to the movies together, to the library, to museums. They ate dinner out with Stanley and me.

Second, it was Stanley's car we got into. He was twenty-three years old, could drive, and had a car of his own. I hadn't managed this until I had reached the age of thirty. But then, nine years made a difference. The society he lived in at twenty-three in the year 1952 was far different from the society I lived in at twenty-three in the year 1943.

The third and most unusual point, however, was that Stanley was driving us to Nyack so that we could visit Uncle Joe and Aunt Pauline. I had not seen them for over fourteen years. After some conversation, we drove them to some point in the Bronx where they could catch the train to Mount Vernon.

That is all I said in my diary and I remember hardly anything else on my own. Uncle Joe was very talkative, I remember, and rather querulous. He had been to Israel and he hadn't liked the treatment he got there. I don't recall his showing any interest in either myself or Stanley.

After Uncle Joe and Aunt Pauline got out of the car, I said, "Oh heck, I forgot to ask them about Cousin Martin."

"It's a good thing you didn't," said my mother, censoriously. "He's dead."

I was stunned into silence and my parents didn't say another word about it. Such was their marked reluctance to speak about it that I never got around to asking what happened, either then, or ever. When I thought of it, my parents weren't around to answer my questions; when they were around, I never thought of it.

Stanley never found out either. I asked him recently and he didn't know. Marcia doesn't know, either.

Nor, after that day, did I ever see Uncle Joe or Aunt Pauline again. I presume they are dead by now, but if they are I do not know when they died or under what circumstances.

6

The year 1952 drew to a close and during its course I had published no less than four books, as many as I had in 1950 and 1951 put together. They were:

5. *David Starr: Space Ranger* (Doubleday)
6. *Foundation and Empire* (Gnome)
7. *The Currents of Space* (Doubleday)
8. *Biochemistry and Human Metabolism* (Williams & Wilkins)

Biochemistry and Human Metabolism was a collaboration, of course, but even one third of that book was longer (and certainly harder work) than any of the other seven books on the list, so I had no compunction in listing it as among "my" books. And, of course, the fact that *David Starr: Space Ranger* was under a pseudonym made no difference as far as I was concerned.

As for my writing earnings, the figure for 1952 reached an astonishing $8,550, nearly twice as much as the previous record year of 1950, and more than I had earned in all the years, put together, prior to the publication of *Pebble in the Sky*.

What was more important was that it was half again my school earnings of $5,500. (I couldn't help but feel a distinct triumph over that stupid dentist at Breadloaf. Amazing how small irritations linger even after large misfortunes fade.)

Just as my parents were now out from under, so also was I. I was out from under any feeling of financial dependence on my school position. I worried no further about how much they were paying me, and I could concentrate on more basic demands without worrying about being fired (and the main demand, of course, was to get out from under Lemon).

Furthermore, with a total income of over $14,000 for the year 1952, I got out from under the specter of economic insecurity. I wasn't certain that life could go on without catastrophe—who could be?—but barring acts of God, there seemed no reason that my literary output and earnings could not continue at this high level and between that and my savings, which had now reached $16,000, I would certainly never be in want and I would always be able to support my wife and child.

It was a good feeling—and none too soon, since I was about to turn thirty-three.

7

We spent New Year's Eve 1952–53 at the house of our friends Harold and Zelda Goodglass, making our way there through a sleet-storm. (I remember very few decent New Year's Eves, when it came to driving.)

What I remember best about that particular New Year's Eve party was that one guest, a rather loud, opinionated fellow to whom I took an instant dislike (since I'm a rather loud, opinionated fellow myself), began to lecture me on science fiction.

He was a recent convert and didn't really know much on the subject, but apparently he was overwhelmed at the imaginative character of it. He said to me, "Do you understand how much imagination you have to have to write science fiction? Can you grasp"—here he tapped his head as though urging me to think it through—"how creatively you have to think? Why, in order to write science fiction . . ."

He went on and on. I kept a polite look of interest on my face, saying "My, my," and "Really," every once in a while, and my host and hostess had a hard job to maintain their composure. The others there didn't know me—except Gertrude, of course, and she was in the kitchen and had been since the fellow had started talking on the subject.

She came out as he was at the peak of his peroration, listened a few moments in puzzlement, and said, "Why are you saying all this? My husband is Isaac Asimov."

And then I laughed. I couldn't help it.

The fellow was furious, naturally. He never said another word to me for the duration and he probably stopped reading science fiction after that.

8

January 2, 1953, saw me thirty-three years old, and I had a pleasant birthday present. Fred sent along a Doubleday contract for *The Caves of Steel*, a contract which called for a $1,000 advance.

Still, if Doubleday's stock was going up with me, Campbell's was going down. Now that he had broken with dianetics, he grew increasingly interested in parapsychology or, as it is also called, psionics, or, simply, psi. Increasingly, the stories in *Astounding* involved telepathy, precognition, and other wild talents.

It bothered me that Campbell's predilections should be so reflected in the magazine. It bothered me that I should see so many of his editorial comments so quickly translated into stories by over-cooperative authors. What's more, Campbell's editorials, which had grown to be four thousand to six thousand words long in each issue, began to infuriate me with their ultraconservative and antiscientific standpoint.

I was having a stronger and stronger impulse to stay away from him, but the ties of love, and the memory of all he had done for me, kept me from ever breaking with him. On my visit to New York toward the end of 1952, Campbell talked to me about a story idea he was thinking of. It was about someone who could levitate (a wild talent, see) but could not get anyone to believe him. Campbell wanted to call it "Upsy-daisy."

I hesitated, decided I could do it my way, and wrote it during the first half of January. I called it "Belief." I mailed it off to Campbell on January 12 and when I hadn't heard from him in ten days, I called and found there was a three-page letter on its way to me. As might have been predicted, I didn't have *enough* psi in the story; I had made it too rational.

I changed it as much as I could bring myself to, but not as much as Campbell would have liked and, in the end, he took it.

While I was waiting to hear from Campbell, I wrote another fantasy intended for Howard Browne's high-rate-paying magazine. I called it "Kid Stuff" and had it finished on January 25.

9

My interest in writing nonfiction was increasing. The writing of the textbook had inspired my thinking on various interesting subjects of trivial importance. For instance, how much of the various radioactive isotopes had disappeared in the course of the Earth's existence? It was simple to calculate, but it was the sort of thing people didn't do, since it wasn't important enough.

However, *The Journal of Chemical Education*, which was intended for chemistry students and their teachers, did sometimes print articles of this sort. Why not try them then?

I wrote an article called "Naturally Occurring Radioisotopes," and on January 23 mailed it off to the *JCE*. It was a very short article and the *JCE* took it and ran it in their August 1953 issue. It filled only one of their pages.

It wasn't much of an achievement and it didn't involve any research work. However, it appeared in a learned journal so it counted as a "paper" and I welcomed "papers" of any kind, however brief, nonresearch, and trivial they might be. After all, it was clear to me by then that I would publish very few research papers, and probably no research papers of importance. I made up my mind, therefore, to do more short pieces for the *JCE*.

10

Science fiction was becoming important enough to have books written *about* it. One of the first of these was Sprague de Camp's *Science Fiction Handbook*, slated to be published in 1953 by Hermitage House. Sprague sent me the manuscript on January 27, 1953, and of course it was a marvelous book. It contained an excellent short history of science fiction and had much to say about the current writers in the field, all of whom were described in Sprague's gentle and courteous style.

He included a brief biography of me, which contained no mistakes, and in it he had this to say: "Asimov is a stoutish, youngish-looking man with wavy brown hair, blue eyes, and a bouncing, jovial, effervescent manner, much esteemed among his friends for his generous warm-hearted nature. Extremely sociable, articulate, and witty, he is a perfect toastmaster."

Well, I could argue with that, but I certainly don't intend to. I'm convinced that Sprague's insistence on my "generous warm-hearted nature" dates back to the time I let him use my badge at the Navy Yard.

He also said, "Asimov writes a brisk, smooth, straightforward style with keen logic and human understanding." I don't intend to quarrel with that, either.

Later in the book he said, "Simak's stories may be compared with

Asimov's," which is perceptive of Sprague, since I consciously tried to imitate Cliff's style.

The sudden interest in science fiction in book form did not involve only myself, of course. Sprague too, was putting out hard-cover novels and collections as I was. One of them was *The Continent Makers*, a collection of Sprague's short stories published by Twayne Press (with which Ciardi was connected) in 1953. My copy arrived on February 2, 1953. Sprague had asked me to write an Introduction for it and I did. I called it "In re Sprague" and I was at least as complimentary to him as he was to me. We always had a real love feast going—but then we each meant it.

"In re Sprague" was the first Introduction I ever wrote to someone else's book[3] and it received no credit—my name was neither on the book jacket nor on the title page. This was silly of the publishers. Either my name was worth something and should have been advertised to help sell the book, or it wasn't and they shouldn't have bothered with the Introduction. This sort of thing never happened again.

11

My father's retirement didn't remain absolute. After a couple of months with nothing to do, he got himself a part-time job at a brokerage firm in Wall Street, sorting mail, handling supplies, and so on.

"Part-time?" I said.

"Yes," he said. "It's only forty hours a week."

Well, to an ex-candy-store keeper, that's part-time.

My father held onto the job for quite a while, though I always wondered how he managed to avoid being fired. Not a pencil or a paper clip moved, I was given to understand, without his permission, and I could imagine he needed closely reasoned excuses before he released anything.

Eventually, he learned to type up material, turning out perfect copy, provided (1) there was no hurry, and (2) the material handed him had no mistakes in spelling or punctuation. If there were such mistakes he carefully duplicated them.

12

Browne rejected "Kid Stuff," but Horace Gold took it for a new fantasy sister-magazine of *Galaxy*, which he called *Beyond*.

---

[3] It wasn't the last. Indeed, I have by now written so many that I honestly think it is possible that if all of them were counted it might turn out I have written more introductions to other people's books than anyone else in history.

New magazines continued to pop up. Even Hugo Gernsback put out a new magazine called *Science Fiction Plus* in February 1953. It was in the old large size, as though it were still the 1920s, and the stories read as though they were still in the 1920s, too. Sam Moskowitz did the real editing and it only lasted seven issues.

That's no disgrace, however. *Beyond* was a good magazine and it only lasted ten issues.

13

By the beginning of 1953, I had been an assistant professor for a year, but I was becoming impatient again. No move had been made to get me out from under Lemon. Part of my salary was still coming from Lemon's grant, and I could stand it no more.

Pretty soon, Lemon would be negotiating another renewal of his grant, and I was through. I told Walker on February 18, 1953, that I was not going to allow my name to go on it. The school would have to find my salary or this would be my last year on the job. (With the coming of the new year of 1953, by the way, I had been working longer at the Medical School than I had at the Navy Yard.)

Again, Walker went to see Dean Faulkner, and this time Walker emerged with the news that I would be on full school salary as of July 1, *but* the final thousand would have to be covered by my taking over a course in chemistry given to student nurses. It was a course that used to be given by Mrs. Walker, but she had to stay home more and more with an ailing father.

I thought I would rather take the salary cut and be given three months off instead of one month, but Walker wouldn't hear of that. He needed someone to replace his wife in that course.

So I agreed, with considerable foreboding, and told myself that it was worth it to get out from under a yearly renewable grant.

14

"Sally"[4] appeared in the May–June 1953 *Fantastic*, an advance copy of which reached me on February 26. *Fantastic* was still looking expensive and beautiful.

In the June 1953 *F & SF*, "Flies"[5] appeared, and a few months later, "Kid Stuff"[6] appeared in the September 1953 *Beyond*, the second issue of that magazine.

[4] See *Nightfall and Other Stories*.
[5] See *Nightfall and Other Stories*.
[6] See *Earth Is Room Enough* (Doubleday, 1957).

15

David was 1½ years old on February 20, 1953. He didn't talk much but he understood everything we said and he had a will of his own. When I took him out in order to have him walk under his own steam, it always ended in my having to carry him, for never, under his own steam, would he walk home. Nor, if he sensed that I would find it convenient for him to walk left, would he walk in any other direction but right.

By the time he was nineteen months old, he grew interested in television and learned to manipulate the controls. He was fascinated by the knobs that caused the picture to roll or to tear (or both, for that matter). He quickly learned, however, that this caused alarm and despondency in the breast of his parents, who then removed him from contact with the set. As a result, he sometimes quickly readjusted the set to produce a perfect picture when he heard loud cries of anguish in his rear.

16

The three of us visited New York on May 21, 1953, in order that I might attend a local New York science-fiction convention the next day. I met Robert Sheckley and A. J. Budrys for the first time on this occasion.

Fred Pohl was more and more closely involved with Ballantine Books at this time. This was a firm that was under the egis of Ian and Betty Ballantine, an extraordinarily attractive, clever, and inventive couple who had great plans indeed. Their intention was to publish books simultaneously in hard- and soft-cover under such conditions that the writer would make far more money than under the older systems.

Fred told me he was going to have all his writers work with Ballantine Books and urged me to agree to do so.

I said, miserably, "But I can't, Fred. Doubleday is doing my books, and I can't leave them."

Fred thought I could, since I would make far more money with Ballantine.

I thought about it some more and said, with a kind of wan hope, "Well, if Doubleday rejects a book or if it cheats me somehow, I can make the change. But how can I do it if they don't give me cause?"

"If they don't pay you enough money, then that's cause," said Fred.

I remember sitting there in his office quite a while, thinking about that. It would be great to make a lot of money with my writing, and I would feel silly if all the other writers went on to make a lot of money and left me behind.[7]

But then I thought of Brad taking my first book, and going over the galleys with me, and working with me to cure me of overwriting, and of being always kind and helpful, and I had to picture myself saying, "Sorry, Brad, you've been outbid."

So I finally said, "I can't do it, Fred. I'm sorry."

I left, more miserable than you could imagine, for I knew that from a business standpoint I had done the wrong thing.

And yet—though Ballantine Books flourished, it never quite fulfilled that initial hope of making all its writers rich. Doubleday, on the other hand, stayed with me and continued to help me and be kind to me, and do for me every bit, and more, of what I had imagined Ballantine might do for me, and so I had turned out to have made a very clever business decision after all.

I wish I could say it had been because I was an incredibly clever businessman, blessed with an unexampled gift of foresight—but it was nothing of the sort. I made my decision on the perfectly silly emotional ground that Doubleday had been good to me and that I must not return evil for good.

17

I was getting ready for a longer trip, the longest I had made since I was in the Army and the longest I had ever made voluntarily up to that point. The fact was that I had to go to Chicago. The American Chemical Society was meeting there, and months before, Lemon had felt I ought to give a paper there. If that were all, I wouldn't have gone, but it seemed to me, quite independently, that I should.

Giving papers at conventions is an important part of the research scientist's life. It is there that you meet important men in the field; it is there that you impress them (if you do well) and gain important contacts that might help in improving your career. Although I had put research behind me, I felt I ought to do it once at any rate—so I agreed to go.

I didn't look forward to it, though. It didn't even occur to me to go by plane, and that meant it would be an 18-hour trip by train. Nor would there be any specialists accompanying me to play bridge with me.

[7] I felt rather like that day on Hawaii when I thought all the other specialists were opting for officerhood.

I took the train on Sunday, April 5, and at once found out it wasn't as bad as I had feared. There were no upper and lower bunks, as there had been seven years before on that long cross-country trip. Instead, I had a roomette for the first time, and I had never even heard of a roomette till then.

To those who have never been in one it is precisely the dimensions of a double bed, since when the bed is lowered it fills the entire room. When it is raised there is a seat, a sink, and a toilet seat in it, as well as a small closet and a rack. I had complete privacy and I emerged only to make my way to the dining car and eat. It was a novelty and I enjoyed it.

The first evening in Chicago, I had dinner with Dick Hoover of Williams & Wilkins, who had seen the first edition of our textbook through its birthpangs and was now to supervise the second edition. Since I was being effervescent, he enjoyed himself and confided in me that the average professor made a deadly dinner companion.

This was a dangerous confession, for when he ordered dark German beer for each of us, I hated to show him what a deadly dinner companion I was by explaining to him that I didn't drink beer.

It arrived in giant steins about the size of a fire bucket each. I sniffed at mine, and though it was dark enough to be a cola drink, it smelled like beer.

"Drink up," said Dick, cheerfully, and went glug-glug-glug.

And I went glug-cough-cough-glug-wheeze . . .

"What's the matter?" he said.

"I'm not used to it," I said, my eyes watering, and tried again.

I managed to get it all down and then Dick somehow got the notion that I was drunk.

"On one stein of beer, too," he kept saying.

I kept saying, "I'm all right. Ain't nothing wrong with me, Dick."

But I must have been doing *something* wrong, for he insisted I was drunk. He kept shaking his head and I think he decided that some professors might be deadly, but at least they could carry more than a stein of beer.

Fortunately, he saw me back to my room safely.

On the morning of Tuesday, April 7, I gave my talk on the research we had been doing at the Medical School, to the usual apathetic audience of chemists. Unfortunately, there was no way of remembering that I was a chemist, and though I had my speech written out, I forgot to look at it, except occasionally for exact numerical values. What's more, I forgot I was supposed to be serious and managed to get a few titters out of an audience that ordinarily felt they had done all they needed to do for a speaker by not actually snoring. I remember only one of the titter provokers. I said, "The rat was then sacrificed." I paused and added thoughtfully, "Actually, the rat was killed, but chemists are religious people, and 'sacrificed' sounds more theological."

It was easy for me to talk. The rat may have been either sacrificed or killed, but either way I was not there at the time. In fact, when animals were brought into the laboratory for any purpose whatsoever, I instantly left.

I recognized the importance of animal experimentation and I have written in its defense, but those experiments will not be conducted by me or in my presence. I'm sorry, but I have never forgotten that cat I killed at Seth Low, and that is sin enough to weigh down my soul.

For that matter, my stay at the Medical School had been pure in another way as well. Early in my career there it was necessary for me to say something to, or learn something from (I forget the details completely) a member of the Anatomy Department. I went down to the anatomy lab for the purpose, and while waiting there I relaxed by leaning against a flat table on which a life-size wax figure rested.

Slowly, by the diffusion inward of I don't know what enlightenment, I began to realize what an anatomy laboratory was, and what the wax figure was. It was a cadaver—a dead human being.

I didn't disgrace myself. I didn't start back or turn sick. I merely continued to wait, with my eyes fixed firmly on the floor, completed my errand, and left. I never went back into the anatomy lab in all the time I was at the Medical School. I never saw another cadaver.

And to think I had tried to get into medical school as a student fifteen years before! I daresay I would have grown accustomed to dissection and learned to eat my lunch in the presence of human fragments, as I had once learned to do in the presence of cat fragments—but I'm glad I never had to learn to violate my own personal set of instincts.

18

On the afternoon of April 7, I called Bea Mahaffey, who was editor of *Universe Science Fiction*, and whose office was in Evanston, just to the north of Chicago. It seemed to me that I had to balance the deadliness of a scientific convention with some science-fictional lightheartedness (and Bea was pretty enough to make me feel very lighthearted indeed).

She asked me to write a story for her, and in a fit of expansiveness,

I asked her to bring me a typewriter, never dreaming she would take my grandiloquence seriously—but she brought me a typewriter.

I wasn't man enough to admit I had been boasting, not to a girl as pretty as Bea, so there was nothing to do but sit down and type out a story on the spur. Since the attempted climbing of Mount Everest was much in the news in those days, it occurred to me to explain the repeated failures by postulating the Abominable Snowmen to be Martians. It was a short, reasonably clever story, about 1,300 words long.

Bea read it as it came out of the typewriter, and bought it on the spot—with the provision that her co-editor, Raymond J. Palmer, approve. As it happened, he did, and I eventually received $39 for the story. (Palmer was the man who had sent me my first professional writing payment 14½ years before, and I would have loved to have met him, but he was away somewhere on that day. That is the closest I ever got to meeting him—but, sentiment aside, it was better to meet Bea.)

"Everest" represents the fastest sale I ever made. It was sold one hour after I had put the paper in the typewriter to begin. It was the first time I had ever sold a first draft.

Bea and I went out for dinner together, and I really exerted myself to impress her with my debonaire manner. (She wasn't going to find me one of Dick Hoover's deadly professors.) Indeed, so successful was I at being lively and witty and effervescent that the middle-aged waitress leaned toward me to whisper that she wished her son-in-law was as interesting as I was. Unfortunately, I was aiming at Bea Mahaffey, who remained relatively unmoved, perhaps because she had no son-in-law.

We went to the movies afterward and then I took her home. I can't honestly say I had anything wicked in mind, though I'd like to believe I was prepared for the worst. The worst proved to be, however, a shake of the hand and a friendly good-bye, and then she disappeared into her apartment house and I turned back to get the streetcar to my hotel.

The next day I took the train and was home on April 9. The roomette had lost the charm of novelty on the return voyage, and I found its supercompactness a little wearying.

19

My casually confident visit to *Universe* was evidence enough that I had come light-years from the time I had first crept, pallid and frightened, into Campbell's office fourteen years before. I was now well enough known so that I could walk into the office of any science-fiction editor, even one I had never met before, and expect to be treated as a celebrity.

It was not that I demanded or even wanted deference. I just wanted my eccentricities overlooked. I wanted to be able to come swirling in, talking as I came, making jokes, hugging all the young ladies— and not be thrown out.

Of course, there wasn't much room for me to spread myself at the offices of magazine editors. Those were small and cramped and often there wasn't even a secretary. It was different at a book publisher's, particularly a large one.

Doubleday was, of course, a large one, and already by 1952, my small peculiarities were becoming known and allowed for. It was taken for granted that things would be noisy when I was around, and any young woman I overlooked in my all-embracing suavity was liable to be offended.

Doubleday's offices, at each of the four different midtown buildings they occupied since I have known them, usually occupied several floors, each floor a rabbit warren of offices that are not particularly built for privacy. Secretaries usually sit out in the corridors and if the editors have offices, these have doors that are, characteristically, always open.

This meant that when I came in, my voice rebounded off distant walls and it was not merely my own immediate editor and secretary who knew of my presence.

My attitude toward young women amused everyone generally, I think, and the amusement was intensified, I think, by the general impression (frequently expressed out loud) that I was harmless. I even suspect that new girls were warned of my feckless lechery in advance so that they wouldn't run screaming or, worse yet, bop me on the nose. At least none of them ever did either. Mostly they just kissed back.

What struck me most forcibly about any editor's office, by the way (once I got my eyes off the young women), were the books. Every office consists largely of bookshelves.

But, then, that is what editors do—read. They read books and manuscripts and galleys and letters. They read not so much at work, where they are distracted by phone calls, conferences, and visits from loudmouthed cheerful authors such as myself, and snarling, complaining authors such as everyone else, but at home, where, apparently, they read till they fall asleep, face-down, on a manuscript, to begin again when they wake up bleary-eyed.

Why they do it, I don't know. I have never known an editor, from

Campbell on, who didn't fill his or her life with 176 hours a week of work—and who wasn't underpaid.

But there are compensations. When my present Doubleday editor, Cathleen Jordan, a mere slip of a girl, frowns—I tremble. That must be a delightful feeling of power that they have.

55

Science Fiction at Its Peak

1

I was very proud of the stories I was writing now. It seemed to me that they were much more deftly written than my stories of the 1940s. I think so to this day.

It seems to me that most people associate me with the 1940s and think of the positronic robot stories, the Foundation series, and, of course, "Nightfall," as the stories of my peak period. I think they're all wrong. I think my peak period came later—in 1953 and the years imdiately following.

By now, after all, the pulpishness in my writing had completely disappeared. That had been taking place all along, through the 1940s, but between what Walter Bradbury taught me and what I had learned at Breadloaf, the change accelerated under my own deliberate prodding.

My writing became ever more direct and spare, and I think it was *The Caves of Steel* that lifted me a notch higher in my own estimation. I used it as a model for myself thereafter, and it was to be decades before I surpassed that book in my own eyes.

Yet even as *The Caves of Steel* was raising my science fiction to a new level of expertise, something new was beginning.

A certain publisher, Henry Schuman, was interested in putting out a line of science books for teen-agers. For this purpose, he visited Bill Boyd in order to induce him to produce a teen-age version of his book *Genetics and the Races of Man*.

Bill felt entirely too busy at the moment to oblige, but once again he turned a nonfiction editor in my direction, as two years before he had done in the case of Angus Cameron of Little, Brown.

On the evening of April 14, 1953, therefore, I visited the Boyds in order to meet Schuman and talk to him.

I was perhaps not as eager to do nonfiction as I had been. After initial interest, Little, Brown had turned down *The Puzzle of Life*, and after initial interest, Macmillan had turned down *The Chemistry of Life*. What's more, it was clear by now that the textbook *Biochemistry and Human Metabolism* was neither a critical nor a financial success. The second edition would be a clear improvement scientifically, but I had no illusions that that would do anything to improve its earning power.

Besides which, science fiction was going like a house afire, and I was deeply involved with *The Caves of Steel*.

Nevertheless, Schuman was talking not of textbooks, not of books for the general public even, but of books for teen-agers. That was a new wrinkle. I agreed to give it serious thought, but I kept my enthusiasm low. I was not in the market for more fiascos—yet I thought about it.

2

I was more impressed with something else that happened at about this time. On April 22, 1953, as a gesture of friendliness, I took a young woman whom I had met at the school to lunch at Howard Johnson's. She brought a girlfriend along and, as is common for me, I flirted outrageously.

Generally, women do not take me seriously in this respect, and I tended to rely on that. The girlfriend, however, whom I was meeting now for the first time, returned innuendo for innuendo in the coolest possible manner and left me uncertain as to what to do.

Eventually lunch was over, and since I had agreed, to begin with, to drive the young woman I knew to her next appointment, I did so. Her friend accompanied us and then asked if I would drive her home to her place in Cambridge, and it would have been ungallant of me to refuse. When I got there, she invited me up to her apartment, and again it would have been ungallant of me to refuse.

What it amounts to is that she then seduced me.

Don't get me wrong. She didn't use force, or even much in the way of persuasion. Nor did I object or scream or fight.

However, I was *scared*, and even though I was alone with a woman in her own apartment, a woman who was plainly intent on sex, there wasn't a chance in the world that I would have made the first move. But I didn't have to. *She* did and I just followed along, with my teeth more or less chattering, and not out of passion.

I was just about a third of a century old and it was the first time I had ever indulged in illicit sex, either premarital or extramarital.

It left me riddled with guilt and yet, in an odd way, triumphant. I had never really felt myself to be "good in bed." I had known for years that I was not deft in the laboratory and I felt that sex was a kind of laboratory exercise that I was equally undeft at. I had no reason to think otherwise till then. This young lady, however, had apparently had a good time and was kind enough to say so.

For the first time I thought, "Hey . . ."

Now you might think that, having learned this, I instantly plunged into a maelstrom of sex.

Not so. I don't say I wouldn't have liked to, but the fact is that I didn't. I still felt guilty, and so I remained much as I had been before. The proof of it is that my writing continued at the same prodigious rate as before. Anyone who considers my output can see that I must spend virtually (and virtuously) all my time at the typewriter.

Nevertheless, not quite entirely. There were times, once in a rare while, when the occasion offered itself, when a woman would make it clear that it was all right with her, and then, if it seemed all right with me, too, I would allow the matter to work itself out to its logical conclusion.

I have no intention of recounting all the cases and times in clinical detail. My autobiography is not a peep show, but I must tell you enough to account for the way I am, it seems to me, and it is important that in the end, I was satisfied that I *was* good in bed. Independent evidence all seemed to point in the same direction, with no significant word or action to the contrary.

And, as it happens, though sex has nothing to do with writing or lecturing or any other cerebral occupation, so tightly is sexual achievement tied in with self-esteem that once I gathered I was good in bed, I was automatically far more self-assured in every other respect, and I believe this contributed to the mid-1950s as my peak period in science fiction.

3

I finished *The Caves of Steel* on May 24, 1953, and I was enormously pleased with it. Fred Pohl was pleased with it. Horace Gold was pleased with it. Horace was never so pleased, however, that he didn't want changes, and he called me up *collect* to tell me so in a seventeen-minute conversation. Nevertheless, he was going to pay me at the rate of $.04 a word, which meant $2,520 after Fred took his percentage.

At just about this time, too, advance copies of *Second Foundation* arrived, and now the entire Foundation series was in book form.

I was grateful to Marty Greenberg for putting out the Foundation series as well as *I, Robot* when no one else seemed interested in doing it —and on the whole he had produced attractive volumes.

It was quite clear by now, however, after three years of doing business with him, that he was extremely slow in paying even the smallest sums and that he did not produce the kind of statements that the contracts called for. I never knew how many copies of my books he sold so that I could at least know how much in debt to me he was. The situation looked worse when I compared it with the efficient and businesslike way in which Doubleday produced all statements in full detail, and all checks with prompt readiness.

My gratitude to Marty meant that I remained friends with him despite his laggardness in payment and bookkeeping and that I did not unreasonably dun him for money or grow unreasonably annoyed when he came up with one more ingeniously innocent reason for not being able to pay till month after next. My gratitude was not sufficient, however, to induce me to give him any more books. *Second Foundation* was the fourth and last book of mine to appear under the Gnome Press imprint.

Marty was annoyed at this at lunch, once, when it became clear he wasn't getting any more books from me, he said, rather violently, that it was a clear understanding between us that I was to alternate books between himself and Doubleday.

There was no such understanding at all, of course, though that was the way it had happened for four years, but I didn't argue the point. I simply said, "Where are the statements for the four books you now have?" and Marty changed the subject and never brought it up again.

4

On May 25, 1953, I fell prey to the social conformity of the 1950s and got myself a short haircut. It was not a crew cut, such as Lemon wore, but it was short enough (like Walker's) not to require combing.

The not-combing bit was a great relief, for even today I am no better at combing than I had been at Seth Low. I did not, however, like my short-hair appearance. I let my hair grow back to its usual length and never cut it short again.

On May 30, Edmund Hillary of New Zealand and Tenzing Norkay of Nepal climbed Mount Everest and stood on its topmost point, without reporting either Abominable Snowmen or Martians. This, as I noted in my diary, completely ruined my short story "Everest," which I had written for Bea Mahaffey two months before.

5

Paperback interest was finally coming into existence in connection with my books.

There had been a bid on *Pebble in the Sky* a couple of years before and, for a time, I thought there was a paperback sale. Then, however, *Pebble in the Sky* appeared in second-serial form in the Winter 1950 issue of *Two Complete Science-Adventure Books,* a magazine published by the *Planet* people, which featured two long stories in every issue and which lasted eleven issues. (The one in which *Pebble in the Sky* appeared was the first issue.)

The magazine was not a very successful one and it didn't reach a huge audience, but it cost twenty-five cents, and there was no question but that it tapped the very audience that could be expected to buy a twenty-five-cent paperback. The paperback people who were going to do *Pebble in the Sky* therefore withdrew, and rightly so.

Bradbury told me about it, quite frankly, and said it was a miscalculation on Doubleday's part, and I said, "Oh well, we'll do better next time."

I suppose Brad was pleased that I took it philosophically, for when he had a chance to return tit for tat, he did.

Fred Pohl had introduced me to Truman (Mac) Talley in the spring of 1953. Mac was then an editor at New American Library (commonly known as NAL), and he was interested in science fiction.

Fred told me, in fact, that he would like to take an advance look at *The Caves of Steel.* I was only too eager to show it to him and to try to increase his interest in my novels. I thought I might be able to go to Brad and tell him, proudly, how cleverly I had arranged for paperback rights to my novels.

To be sure, Doubleday controlled the paperback rights and only Doubleday could sign a contract with a paperback house, but that seemed to me to be only a detail.

Gertrude, David, and I went to New York on June 6, 1953, so that I could take in the various copies of *The Caves of Steel.* On June 8, I delivered a carbon to Mac, who promised me faithfully to give it back the next day at lunch.

I had lunch with Mac on the ninth and he did give it back. He was a pleasant person, good-humored and quick of understanding, with prominent eyes and the gift of gab, of moderate height and well dressed.

At this lunch, he looked even pleasanter than he ordinarily did, for he praised *The Caves of Steel* to the skies. He said that they couldn't use it for at least a year and a half, of course, since NAL would have to wait for publication first and then for an additional year. In the meantime, though, he wanted to do *The Currents of Space,* and he would be glad to let me have a $2,000 advance for its use.

I did my best to play it cool and not let him see how exciting that was—$2,000 for doing nothing. To be sure, Doubleday would take $1,000 and Fred $100, but that would still leave me $900.

I said, "You understand, Mac, that Doubleday controls the rights and that you'll have to talk to them." Then I added, fatuously, "But I'll explain that I want you to have it and I'm sure that will settle that."

That afternoon, I called Walter Bradbury and could scarcely contain my excitement. "Brad," I said, "Mac Talley of NAL has offered me a $2,000 advance for paperback rights to *The Currents of Space*, so grab it fast."

There was silence at the other end of the phone, and just as I was beginning to wonder if Brad had fainted with joy, he said, "Isaac, Bantam Books has just offered a $3,000 advance for *The Currents of Space*."

Now it was my turn to be silent. Finally I said, "What do we do?"

Brad said, "Did you commit yourself to Mac Talley, Isaac?"

"Yes, Brad, I'm afraid I did."

"In that case, we'll just have to give it to NAL."

I said urgently, "Listen, Brad. Doubleday would have gotten $1,500 of the $3,000; so take that much out of the $2,000 and let me have $500 for my share."

"No," he said, "we'll split the loss equally. That will make up for our mistake regarding the paperback rights on *Pebble in the Sky*. But one thing, Isaac."

"Yes, Brad?"

"Leave the business deals to us, will you?"

"Yes, Brad," I said, humbly—and I always have since then.

The incident meant a great deal to me. Doubleday had accepted a loss of $500 rather than cause me to seem to break my word.

My word means a great deal to me and I was in a sweat of gladness that I hadn't allowed myself to be lured away from Doubleday, for I didn't know if I could possibly get this kind of treatment elsewhere; and I was incredibly relieved that I had never let myself tell a man capable of such consideration that I was leaving him because I might get more money elsewhere.

I was also glad I had never told him that I had been tempted and had refused, because now I didn't have to feel that Brad's action was a reward. He did it simply because he was a decent person.

6

At a Hydra Club meeting on June 10, I met Arthur C. Clarke and Groff Conklin for the first time.

7

Now that *The Caves of Steel* was finished, I could consider Henry Schuman's proposition seriously. On June 12, I had dinner with him and he introduced me to a Dr. Washton, who was his science adviser.

We decided that I was to do a book on enzymes, hormones, and vitamins, the crucial chemicals of life. This meant the book would have less scope than the popular biochemistry books I had been trying to write for two years, but that was probably a good thing. I had been biting off too much. What's more, the book Schuman was proposing was to be only thirty thousand words long, less than half the length of a novel and even less than the length of a Lucky Starr juvenile.

Dr. Washton also gave me a short lecture on how to write for the early teen-age audience. He told me, for instance, that no sentence must be longer than twenty-five words.[1]

Meanwhile, there was another sort of nonfiction book in the air. Walker was pleased with the way we had worked together on the biochemistry text, and since he had hooked me into doing a course for student nurses, he suggested that we do a chemistry text for student nurses together.

I was not anxious to do this, for I was *not* pleased with the way we had worked together on the text, and I had many other books to do, which Walker had not. Nevertheless, I did not like to turn him down flatly.

I compromised by agreeing, without undue enthusiasm, and then leaving it entirely up to Walker to find a publisher. If he failed as I thought he might, I would be off the hook.

As I suspected, Williams & Wilkins turned down the proposal, but Walker then got in touch with McGraw-Hill. On June 25, McGraw-Hill wrote to ask for an outline, and I noted in my diary, rather callously, "Well, that's Walker's worry." I did not intend to move a finger to get the project off the ground.

8

My science fiction continued to go well. I had a contract for a third Lucky Starr book, and something new had come up.

---

[1] I followed instructions very carefully in this book, with the result I didn't like it very well when it was completed. It was the only book in which I accepted supervision of this kind. Afterward, I put the lecture out of my mind and just let the words flow naturally. Things went much better that way.

Twayne Press had the idea of producing what they called "Twayne Triplets." The plan was to have someone knowledgeable in science invent a planet with a particular astronomical or chemical situation, after which three different authors would write three different stories all based on that planet as background.

One of the backgrounds involved two stars and a planet at the apices of an equilateral triangle—which would be a stable "Trojan situation." There would then be a planet with two suns, each a different color, plus a few other items of interest. I could carry it from there, and two other authors, Poul Anderson and, I believe, Virginia Blish, were to do the other two stories of the Triplet. When all three were done we would have a book out of it.

I thought about it and found a flaw. I knew that I could write to order, but what about Poul and Virginia? What if they couldn't get around to it? What if they got stuck in the middle and never finished? The book would, in that case, never be done.

I said, "Is it all right if I sell first serial rights and have it appear in a magazine first?"

"Yes," I was told.

So I did just that. I talked it over with Campbell on my mid-June visit to New York and then spent the rest of the month working on the story (which Campbell suggested I call "Sucker Bait").

My caution paid off. Poul Anderson wrote his story (and eventually also sold it to Campbell), but I don't think Virginia got around to writing hers—and Twayne Press folded anyway. By then it didn't matter. I sold it to Campbell, who paid me $1,000 for its 25,000 words.

9

With July 1, my school salary went to $6,000 per year, but $1,000 was still slated to come from the student-nurse course. That was not good, since if the nurse-teaching turned sour, I might find myself back at $5,000, where I had started over four years before.

The money was not vital, but the insult involved in a salary cutback was. I made up my mind that if that was threatened, I would resign.

10

But why worry? It was time for vacation. This year, Gertrude determined that it would be Henry and she and I who would take a week off, while Mary would stay with David.

I was not sure this would work. David was now two months short of being two years old—very active and very strong-willed—and Mary might not be able to handle him.

Mary expressed her willingness, however, and Gertrude hadn't been away from David for nearly two years, so we chanced it.

We went to a resort named "Merriewoode" this time. It was on an island and there was a pleasant sense of isolation in knowing that people could only arrive, or leave, on a boat.

It was extremely quiet and we called back home frequently to make sure that David and Mary were all right. (They were.) About the only thing I can remember about the vacation otherwise is that we learned to play Scrabble in the course of it, and were hooked. Once we got back we bought a set and played endlessly.

11

When we got back on July 13, I invented my first limerick. A friend suggested a first line, which went "A priest with a prick of obsidian," and dared me to complete it.

After considerable thought, I said:

> "A priest with a prick of obsidian
> Was a foe to the hosts of all Midian.
> Instead of immersion
> Within a young virgin
> 'Twas used as a bookmark in Gideon."

I explained that the "hosts of Midian" was a biblical synonym for evil and that "Gideon" was a reference to the Gideon Bible, but no one thought much of it. However, when I challenged anyone present to do better, no one could.

On that same day, I began work on the book for Henry Schuman. I called it *The Chemicals of Life,* and even though it was a book intended for teen-agers, I felt it to be a scholarly book, and I did some of the work at school.

12

On July 18, I received a letter from Fred Pohl. He had given up the fight to keep going and was ending his agency. Suddenly I was without an agent again after he had represented me for 4¼ years.

My feelings were mixed. I was sorry that he had failed, but I was eager to represent myself. As he had for most of the time he represented me, Fred had some money of mine he had held back. Eventually he paid me, but for the final $1,000, I traded him my contracts. He controlled the contracts for my first seven science-fiction books and I would have had to pay him 10 per cent of any further earnings I made on those sales that had taken place while he was my agent. I didn't expect that Fred's cut on what was still to come would amount to $1,000, but it was worth it to me never to have to go through the bookkeeping.

I have never had a literary agent since, and to be honest I have never wanted one.

13

July 26, 1953, was not only our eleventh wedding anniversary, it was also the eleventh wedding anniversary of Bernie and Ruth Pitt, who were now as well ensconced in the department as we were. We joined forces and celebrated the combined anniversary at a steak house in Framingham.

What we did not know was that on that very day someone named Fidel Castro attempted a coup in Cuba and failed to overthrow the dictator, Batista. Castro began a guerrilla movement, however, which he called "the Twenty-sixth of July Movement" and he kept it going in eastern mountains until it was successful.

Also on that day, a truce was finally signed in Korea, ending the Korean War, in stalemate, after three years and a month.

14

Scott Meredith wrote me a letter as soon as he heard of Fred's failure and offered to take me on, but for the second time I refused politely. Forry Ackerman also wrote to make a similar offer, and I refused that, too.

I think everyone waited for me to get either tired or disillusioned with representing myself, but they had a long wait. I never got either tired or disillusioned.

Fortunately, the passing of Fred's agency in no way affected the even tenor of my writing, and we celebrated David's second birthday on August 20 pleasantly and calmly.

15

The eleventh World Science Fiction Convention was being held in Philadelphia over the Labor Day weekend, and on Thursday, September 3, 1953, we went to New York, where we left David, then on to Philadelphia on the fourth. The convention was beginning and I met Randall Garrett, James Gunn, and Philip Farmer, three new authors I had not met before.

Garrett was an incredibly intelligent fellow who bubbled over constantly. It was as though his tap had been turned full-on and nailed there. Mine seemed to be turned on also, I admit, but I could always shut down if I had to. He, apparently, could not. When I turned it on, too, though, the pair of us were incredibly loud.

Gunn was a quiet, youthful, and handsome fellow, while Farmer was equally quiet, not quite so youthful, and not quite so handsome.

At that same convention I met another personage, not a professional author yet, but destined to become one, and a more colorful one, perhaps, than anyone else in science fiction, even myself. He was just a boy then, perhaps no more than eighteen.

He was a little fellow. He insists he is five feet, five inches tall, but that is, I think, by a specially designed ruler. He is five feet, two inches tall by the internationally accepted yardstick. Either way he had sharp features and the livest eyes I ever saw, filled with an explosive concentration of intelligence.

Those live eyes were now focused on me with something that I can only describe as worship.

He said, "Are you Isaac Asimov?" And in his voice was awe and wonder and amazement.

I was rather pleased, but I struggled hard to retain a modest demeanor. "Yes, I am," I said.

"You're not kidding? You're *really* Isaac Asimov?" The words have not yet been invented that would describe the ardor and reverence with which his tongue caressed the syllables of my name.

I felt as though the least I could do would be to rest my hand upon his head and bless him, but I controlled myself. "Yes, I am," I said, and by now my smile was a fatuous thing, nauseating to behold. "*Really*, I am."

"Well, I think you're . . ." he began, still in the same tone of voice, and for a split second he paused, while I listened and everyone within earshot held his breath. The youngster's face shifted in that split second into an expression of utter contempt and he finished the sentence with supreme indifference "—a *nothing!*"

The effect, for me, was that of tumbling over a cliff I had not known was there, and landing flat on my back. I could only blink foolishly while everyone present roared with laughter.

The youngster was Harlan Ellison,[2] you see, and I had never met him before and didn't know his utter irreverence. But everyone else there knew him and they had waited for innocent me to be neatly poniarded—and I had been. Someone might have warned me, but no one did.

It was all good clean fun, and ever since then Harlan and I have loved each other deeply and truly, but he can't ever come near me without my breaking out into a rash of small-jokes, and he is equally prone to fat-jokes.

The fan world tends to think there's a deadly feud between us, but they're quite wrong. It's just our way of honing our wise-guyishness against each other's sensibilities.[3]

On the evening of the fifth, Sprague, John Clark, and I went out to a local radio station where a local talk-show host interviewed us. We were made to order for him, for he thought it the funniest thing in the world that science-fiction people were having a convention. ("What do you do, wear beanies?")

Sprague answered very patiently, for he is the soul of dignity and forbearance, but I chafed a bit. Finally, when it was my turn again, the host said to me, "Say, I have a question for you: Suppose you are on Pluto and you're wearing those funny space helmets. How do you kiss?"

"You don't," I said, glowering at him. "You carry on a Plutonic love affair."

The studio audience broke up and it was the host's turn to glower. Apparently guests are not supposed to take the play away from the host. He didn't speak to me again.

I was toastmaster at the banquet on September 6, and did well. It was my first stint as toastmaster, but not my last.

16

I finished *The Chemicals of Life* on September 15, 1953. It had taken me only nine weeks despite the interruption of the convention and the confusion following the end of the agency.

I made an important discovery: It was easier and faster writing nonfiction than fiction. I had thought so when I wrote the textbook, but the long and tedious sessions with Walker and Boyd had obscured the discovery.

[2] Harlan insists he said, "You aren't so much," but I think well of my memory and I'll stand by my version.
[3] Lester del Rey and I are a lot like that, too.

In fact, I was sorry I had finished the book, and I was therefore intent on writing another one of the sort—but not right away, for the second edition of the textbook was in high gear.

Till now I had been collecting new chemical findings that would require revision and expansion of the text, but now Williams & Wilkins had sent us large versions of the book with blank pages in between every pair of printed pages. I made notes, revisions, and reference notations on those blank pages opposite the places where revisions and expansions would have to be made. It ate up a lot of time.

Meanwhile, the October 1953 *Astounding* came out with "Belief,"[4] and the October 1953 *Galaxy* came out with the first of the three parts into which *The Caves of Steel* had been divided for serial purposes. Not only that, but also (at my suggestion) *F & SF* had agreed to reprint my story "The Fun They Had." On this occasion, I heard from the magazine's new managing editor, Robert P. Mills, who wrote to suggest lunch.

Much less pleasant than any of this was the fact that McGraw-Hill was showing definite interest in the student-nurse textbook. They had a woman, M. Kolaya Nicholas, who was working on such a book but who felt she needed help. McGraw-Hill thought we might help her and, worse, Walker thought we might—so I was stuck with it.

17

I drove into New York late in October to oblige Sam Moskowitz, who by now (and ever since) was a good friend of mine. He was giving a class in science fiction at City College[5] and wanted me as guest lecturer. The trip was noteworthy since we finally dared leave David in the back seat alone. (It was a two-door car; he could not get out.)

I gave my two-hour talk to Sam's class on October 23, 1953. I remember very little about it except that I drew detailed diagrams on the board to exemplify my notions of novel structure. Sam remembers it more glowingly than I do. He has never ceased bemoaning the fact that it never occurred to him to tape the talk.

18

For some time now, I'd been suffering from a plague of boils, like Job. They tended to be, more often than not, in or near the armpits,

---

[4] See *Through a Glass, Clearly* (New English Library, 1967).
[5] This is a supercommon situation now, but it was not so then. Sam's class may have been the first college class in science fiction.

and they made life very uncomfortable for me. I mentioned it to Dr. Ryan when I took David in for a routine injection. He gave me a penicillin shot and then questioned me closely on diabetes.

It hit home. After all, I had immersed myself in that biochemistry textbook and there was a whole chapter that dealt very largely with diabetes. One of the unpleasant side effects of the disease was a heightened tendency to infections such as boils. I said, "But my urine has been tested any number of times. There's never been any glucose in it."

He said, "That's a late symptom, and you may be in the early stages. What you need is a glucose tolerance test."

That's not pleasant if you don't like having blood withdrawn, and I don't.

You come in fasting. Blood is withdrawn and tested for glucose content. It should be within certain normal limits. You are then forced to drink a large jug of glucose solution, which is sort of sickly sweet. Glucose is the natural sugar of blood, and if you drink it, it is at once absorbed into the blood, the glucose content of which shoots sky-high.

If you're normal, the shock of the glucose entry stimulates the production of insulin, which promotes the conversion of the glucose into a form of starch called glycogen, which is stored in the liver. The blood glucose therefore sinks rapidly. If you are an incipient diabetic, however, the formation of insulin lags and the blood glucose sinks only slowly and doesn't reach normal levels for a long time.

Blood samples have to be withdrawn periodically and glucose content determined. A graph is drawn and from the shape of the curve one can tell whether incipient diabetes seems to be present or not.

Eventually, on November 4, 1953, I had Dr. Walker's technician perform the test and when it was all done, I said, "Well?"

She didn't say anything, but walked into Walker's office. I assumed the worst.

Walker came out and said, "The glucose tolerance test is borderline."

"I'm an incipient diabetic, then?"

"No, not necessarily. This borderline appearance also shows up in obesity. Lose weight and take the test again."

Since I weighed two hundred pounds, I decided it *was* obesity. I tried to lose weight but didn't succeed; even the motivation of possible diabetes wasn't enough.

It might have been if the symptoms had grown worse and if other symptoms appeared—but those things didn't happen. Indeed, the boils became less frequent and finally vanished. I forgot about the matter and remained fat.

19

Stories were simply flooding out of me now.

There were short-shorts like "The Immortal Bard," for instance, in which Shakespeare is brought back to life, takes a course in Shakespeare, and flunks, all in 900 words. This was directly inspired by Gotthard Guenther's remark to me, two years before, that an author need not know anything at all about the meaning of his story.

There were longer stories, like the 6,000-word "The Singing Bell," which dealt with a murder on the moon. I originally submitted it to *Ellery Queen's Mystery Magazine*, which rejected it. There was also the 9,000-word "It's Such a Beautiful Day," about a civilization in which transportation takes place through speed-of-light matter-transference—but one youngster prefers to walk.

"The Singing Bell" introduced my detective character, Wendell Urth, whose appearance I modeled on Norbert Wiener. He didn't like to travel (like myself, but worse) and remained always in his office.

Naturally, I intended to write another novel, but at the moment I had no ideas.

On November 17, 1953, however, I visited the BU Library, found that they had a file of *Time* magazines dating back to 1928 and that, since I was faculty, I could take these out. On impulse, I took out the earliest available volume, January to June 1928, and had a fine anachronistic time reliving the Coolidge boom that was taking place while I was living in Miller Avenue.

After that I returned for the next volume and then the next and so on.[6]

In doing so, however, I noticed in one of the early volumes a line drawing in a small advertisement which, when I saw it quickly out of the corner of my eye, seemed like the familiar mushroom cloud of the nuclear bomb to me. Rather shaken, for the *Time* volume dealt with a period that was half a generation before Alamogordo, Hiroshima, and Nagasaki, I took another look. It was only the Old Faithful geyser of Yellowstone National Park and the advertisement was perfectly ordinary.

But at once I thought: What if that *were* the mushroom cloud? How would a drawing of the nuclear bomb come to be in a magazine that was published many years before 1945? Why should it be there?

I searched for an answer to this question, had to have time travel,

[6] It took me nearly a year to move up into the 1950s to the mingled astonishment and amusement of the librarians who, I understood, called me "the *Time* professor."

had to have a number of things, more and more complicated, and in the end I decided to write a novelette that I named "The End of Eternity" and that I began on December 7, 1953.

20

On November 27, 1953, I received advance copies of the NAL paperback edition of *The Currents of Space*. It was my first real paperback. About then I also received copies of *Lucky Starr and the Pirates of the Asteroids*, my second juvenile.

21

On December 2, 1953, I began my lab sessions with the student nurses. Between that in the morning and my protein class in the afternoon, my time for anything else vanished into nothing. Worse than that was the fact that I found I didn't like laboratory classes, even when I was in charge. In fact, I've forgotten almost everything about that lab, such was my hatred of it, except for one thing.

The girls were going to have to bring in samples of urine—their own, of course—on which they would then run tests. Walker warned me, however, that I must ask those young women who were menstruating not to bring in their own urine, but to use their neighbor's.

I stared at Walker with horror. I was on difficult enough terms with the girls, as it was, since, as their instructor, I had to curb my naturally flirtatious tendencies, and that reduced me to melancholia. I didn't see how I could get this stuff about menstruation across to them.

I said, "How do I tell them that, Dr. Walker?"

He said, "With your mouth," and walked away.

So I did and the young women took it very calmly indeed. I guess menstruation was old stuff to them.

22

On December 16, 1953, a gentleman from Metropolitan Life Insurance Company arrived with a check for $1,007.90 It represented the twenty-year-old annuity policy my father had opened on my behalf when I was thirteen, in lieu of an allowance for me. I had been paying the premiums myself since 1942, of course. Now that I had the cash worth of the policy, I didn't need it. I'd rather have had the allowance when I was young—but who can forsee the future, and my father had meant well.

23

Suddenly I was having a rash of rejections. *Lucky Starr and the Oceans of Venus*, the third of my Paul French series, was encountering serious objections at Doubleday—the first that had developed over those novels.

On the whole, Doubleday was justified, for Lucky Starr, in this particular adventure, was needlessly close-mouthed, allowing his sidekick to think he was an utter bastard, when I was merely trying to keep things from the reader. I had to rewrite in such a way as to keep things from the reader in a subtler fashion and more in keeping with Lucky's character.

"The Singing Bell" was rejected not only by *Ellery Queen*, but also by *Astounding*. Fred Pohl, who was now working with Ballantine, rejected it for one of his anthologies as well. Then *F & SF* rejected "It's Such a Beautiful Day."

Even my appearances in the magazines at this time were minor. The December 1953 *Astounding* contained "The Micropsychiatric Applications of Thiotimoline,"[7] which I thought better than the original thiotimoline article, but which, of course, didn't have the impact of the first.

The December 1953 *Universe* had "Everest."[8] The editors had tried to patch it up very slightly to take into account Hillary's successful conquest of Mount Everest but didn't succeed, so there I was—I had published a story that depended on Mount Everest's *not* having been climbed half a year after it *was* climbed.[9]

24

The year 1953 ended with my having published two more books:

9. *Second Foundation* (Gnome)
10. *Lucky Starr and the Pirates of the Asteroids* (Doubleday)

This was a comedown from the four of the year before. I was not, however, complaining, for the figures on my writing income showed clearly that the whopping earnings of the year before were no accident. In 1953, in fact, my writing income was $9,660, a little over $1,000 more

---

[7] See *Only a Trillion* (Abelard-Schuman, 1957).
[8] See *Buy Jupiter and Other Stories*.
[9] This was no tragedy. I frequently tell the story of the "Everest" fiasco in my after-dinner talks and do so with great success. The story *about* the story has earned me far more money than ever the story itself did.

than the year before and very close to the $10,000 I had long ago estimated to be the absolute most it was possible to earn as a science-fiction writer.

My school income in 1953 was $5,750, slightly above the figure for 1952, but only three fifths of my writing income. The total was over $15,000, a dizzying sum.

25

Though writing was making me wealthy beyond the dreams of Croesus (well, that's how it seemed to me at the time), there was unpleasantness at school. There was, for instance, the case of Bernie Pitt.

As I had suspected might be the case at the very start, Bernie Pitt and Bill Boyd did not, in the long run, get along.

For months, it had been clear to me that Bernie disliked Bill, disapproved of his easygoing ways and of his occasional drinking, and utterly discounted his intelligence. As for Bill, his reaction to Bernie seemed to me to be one of increasing anger. Bernie's sardonic humor apparently rubbed him raw.

I kept gloomily apart from this, doing my best to remain detached and noncommittal when either criticized the other to me. I was unhappily aware that I might have warned Bill or Bernie, or both, at the start and that I had refrained from doing so out of the fear that I might have been wrong. But suppose I had warned each of them? Would either have believed me? And if they had, and had the association not been made, how could I have known for certain that things would have turned out as I had predicted?

By December, Bernie reported to me that Boyd had delivered an ultimatum to him to the effect that he had "two months to change his ways."

I was stirred by curiosity to ask, "What ways?"

Bernie shook his head. He didn't know.

I privately thought that Bernie would not be gone in two months, that Bill would not be that arbitrary, and that Bernie would have to the end of the fiscal year to find another position. I was wrong. Bill fired Bernie on January 7, 1954, with pay to the end of the month. Bernie had been on the job for 2¼ years.

The episode showed me the wisdom of my determined and, finally, successful drive to get out from under Lemon. He could no longer force me to undergo the humiliation of being fired out of hand.

To be sure, I had a similar problem. Dean Faulkner, hearing about all the writing I was doing, was annoyed at my neglecting my research.

How he found out about it and what made him annoyed, I don't know. Lemon both knew and was annoyed and might, conceivably, have told Faulkner of it in order to make trouble for me, but I have no evidence of that.

In any case, Faulkner asked me to come see him, and on December 29, 1953, we had a forty-five-minute talk. I explained the nature of the nonfiction I was doing—showed him my articles in the *Journal of Chemical Education*—explained my views on the importance of teaching, and won him over. At least there were no more complaints on how I spent my time—from Dean Faulkner, that is.

26

I was thirty-four years old on January 2, 1954, and I celebrated my birthday two weeks later by finishing that blasted revision of *Biochemistry and Human Metabolism* and sending it off on January 15. I use first-person singular, but that doesn't imply that Walker and Boyd were not involved in the revision. Certainly, however, they were involved to a far smaller extent than I was.

And on January 22, I started on my share of the student-nurse textbook, which we decided to call *Chemistry and Human Health.*

It was a depressing January. It was the coldest stretch of time since I had arrived in Boston, and I had trouble starting the car in the morning, especially when there was snow—and there was lots of it. The car, as it happened, had to sit in the driveway exposed to the elements because there was no garage attached to the house, and there were times when the engine was simply too cold to start—and at least once I ran down the battery trying.

I finished my protein-structure course that month but decided I didn't like lecturing *that* much—not when it meant I taught both semesters, with the student nurses thrown in. And I had to do more with the student nurses than with the laboratory portion of the course. Walker was supposed to do the lecture but he was frequently unable to come in. He had abandoned his city home and moved out to his wife's family farm since his father-in-law was too old to live there by himself. It meant a long commuting distance of forty miles, and in bad weather he was reluctant to try. Sometimes, even in good weather, problems kept him at home. One time, a horse was sick—and when he didn't come in, I had to give a lecture on some subject on short notice.

Then, too, Marty Greenberg sent me a statement (at last) that carefully worked out my total earnings, over and above what small sums I had been paid, at no more than $950. This seemed low to me, considering that it covered four books, but unless I had an accountant go over Marty's ledgers there was nothing to do but take his word for it.

What's more, he only sent me the figures; not a check. He might have felt that sending both figures *and* a check might have induced a heart attack in me, and he was far too concerned about my health to risk that.

Oh well, the February 1954 *F & SF* contained "The Fun They Had," which now appeared for the first time before a science-fiction audience. The February 1954 *Astounding* included the first part of "Sucker Bait,"[10] which Campbell had converted into a two-part serial, the fourth serial I had had in *Astounding*. The first part got the cover.

"The Singing Bell" was rejected by *Argosy*, its fourth rejection, and with a printed rejection slip, yet. It was a humbling experience.

However, January did see advance copies of *The Caves of Steel* in book form arrive, and this was the book that, up to that time, I felt most satisfied with. And on February 2, Fred Pohl accepted "It's Such a Beautiful Day" for an anthology of original stories he was doing for Ballantine.

27

On February 6, 1954, I finished "The End of Eternity." It was about 25,000 words long and I was very pleased with it. I sent it off to Horace, and on the ninth he called me. It was a complete rejection. He talked revision but what he wanted was a *complete* revision. It would have amounted to jacking up the title and running a new story under it. I refused point-blank to do this, and that was that.

The depression over this lasted long enough to mute my pleasure at having survived to the last day of the student-nurse course on February 17. My general annoyance with Horace, in fact, made it easier for me to be annoyed with Walker over the student nurses and to make up my mind firmly that I would not give the course again. My full salary, *all* of it, would have to come out of the school budget or I would quit.[11]

28

On March 17, we all drove to New York, and on the two days following, I went through my routine of visiting editors. In particular, I

10 See *The Martian Way and Other Stories*.
11 Stanley was, by now, an instructor at the college level, too. He was giving a news-writing course at New York University. I can imagine how my father felt with *both* sons "professors."

handed in a totally revised *Lucky Starr and the Oceans of Venus* to Margaret Lesser, Doubleday's juveniles editor.

I also dropped in to see Marty Greenberg to ask for money. My diary notes I was "demanding" dough. Marty promised he would pay in weekly installments. He always paid *some*, just enough to whet one's appetite for one's own money without really satisfying it.

Most important, I visited the Henry Schuman Company, or, rather, the company it had been transmuted into. Schuman, who was not making money as a publisher, had sold out to Lew Schwartz of Abelard Press, and the combined firm was now Abelard-Schuman. Both Schuman and Washton were completely out, and my editor was now Lillian McClintock. I thought I had better meet her and find out if *The Chemicals of Life* had met with the same disaster that my earlier attempts at non-fiction had.

Not so! Lillian insisted that she thought very highly of the book.

One more thing I did was to leave "The End of Eternity" with Brad in order that he might decide whether it had possibilities as a novel.

When I got home on March 22, I found that Tony Boucher was willing to consider a revised "The Singing Bell," and after all its rejections, I was eager enough for an acceptance to agree to that. (In fact, I usually agreed to reasonable revisions, except in the case of Horace. He was simply too abrasive to make agreement easy, or sometimes possible.)

Meanwhile, the May 1954 *Universe* came out with "The Immortal Bard."[12]

29

It was time for a new car. My first car was nearly four years old and it had some thirty-three thousand miles on it. It was still good for much more, but it was a gear-shift car and it seemed to me that some sort of fluid drive would be better. Besides, if we eliminated the clutch, it might make Gertrude more confident about taking lessons herself. She had never taken further lessons in all the time I had owned the car.

Since the Plymouth had given me good service, I stayed with it, and, on March 26, 1954, I brought home a 1954 Plymouth with "Hydrive." This was a kind of drive that allowed you to stay in third just about all the time, though it still had the clutch. It also had power steering.

It was a nice-looking car in my eyes, pink with a white top, but,

[12] See *Earth Is Room Enough*.

alas, it was a lemon. All the Hy-drives were. I think they were only made for half a season and then proved so complicated and so bound to break down that they were abandoned.

I had all kinds of trouble with my Hy-drive Plymouth, but I stubbornly kept on having it repaired and adjusted until, out of sheer weariness of seeing the inside of a garage, the car decided to settle down.

All the Hy-drives except mine were speedily traded in or junked, and I do believe that for years and years mine was the only one on the road. The old car, by the way, I gave to John Blugerman, and the Blugermans used it for many years.

30

Having sold "It's Such a Beautiful Day" to Fred, I thought I ought to sell him other stories, too. I wrote a 5,000-word short story called "The Portable Star" and mailed it to him on April 5. I got it back on April 14 with a rather long letter telling me, with what I thought unnecessary vehemence, that it was bad.

I tried both Campbell and Gold after that, and both rejected it quite decidedly.

On the other hand, Brad liked "The End of Eternity," liked my suggestions for fleshing it out to novel length, and by April 7, had told me that a contract was in the works. The advances offered me for novels had now grown to $1,250, and I accepted that as a measure of the increasing confidence Doubleday had in me.

On April 26, I received a copy of an August Derleth anthology of original stories that contained "The Pause."[13]

31

Every once in a while the television set proved to be more than a medium of entertainment and also became a method for involving one's self with the world in a way that would have been impossible before television.

In 1954, Senator Joseph R. McCarthy, who was all-powerful because so many Americans were dupes and so many others were cowards (and who had easily survived my own satire of him in "The Martian Way"), tangled with the Army. The Army, backed up against the wall and trembling with fear, had no choice, at last, but to fight back, accusing McCarthy of attacking the Army out of revenge for their having inducted a protégé of his.

[13] See *Buy Jupiter and Other Stories*.

Considering that McCarthy was destroying the United States (and one can easily argue that it was his legacy that led to a number of wrongheaded decisions on the part of the American government, including those that involved us in the disastrous Vietnam War), it was in the highest degree ironic that the point at which the line was drawn was over whether McCarthy was trying to pull strings to get some pampered youngster out of the Army or not. That, however, was the point over which the Army dared fight.

The hearings that resulted were on every day, and there were summaries every night. I watched them during the day when I could and I never missed the summaries at night. It seemed to me that surely there was no way on Earth that any sane person could fail to see McCarthy's gangsterism, and I trembled over the possibility that Americans would prove obstinately irrational and cling to the monster. Fortunately, McCarthy was, unwittingly, on my side. Through his own persistent and unbelievable display of unpalatability and the smooth work of Attorney Joseph Welch, McCarthy was destroyed.

Yet I couldn't *see* that was happening. Night after night I went to bed in a mental argument with McCarthy, reliving the events of the day, trying to find the comments that the various investigating senators *should* have made, and I was certain that never in my life would I ever dislike any American in public life as *intensely* as I disliked McCarthy. (I was wrong there.)

32

I had never gone farther than Philadelphia to attend a science-fiction convention, but Marty Greenberg persuaded me to attend the 1954 Midwescon ("Midwest Convention"), which was to be held in Bellefontaine, Ohio. He would drive.

On May 19, I drove Gertrude and David to New York, and the next morning I went to the Golds'. Marty intended to come there and pick up Evelyn Gold. Also in the car was Marty's accountant, a very nice fellow who must have had difficulty remaining sane if he seriously tried to handle Marty's books.

Though Marty might be a reluctant disburser of money, he was an excellent driver, and he got us to Bellefontaine on the twenty-first with no trouble.

I had a marvelous time at the convention, exchanging comic patter with Randall Garrett and also with Robert Bloch (whom I now met for the first time and with whom I thereafter carried on a prolonged correspondence).

It would be impossible for me to explain the flavor of the long session a group of us had in some bar that first evening (with everyone but myself drinking steadily), but it seemed to us at the time that no group in the history of the world had ever been so consistently and devastatingly funny as we all were. We could hardly talk for laughing.

I can remember only one remark of that session. Someone mentioned that the duckbill platypus had a forked penis. I don't know whether this is true or not, but the statement was made. Whereupon I said, owlishly, "It is for that reason that a female platypus, on awaking in the morning with a male platypus in her bed, cries out, 'Good heavens, I've been forked.'"

It's no use telling me that this is not a very funny play on words, or even that you don't get it. That fact is that twenty-five people laughed for twenty-five solid minutes, and I don't care if most were drunk with alcohol and all were drunk on previous laughter, it was, as far as the effect went, one of the most successful witticisms I ever invented.

There was a serious moment at this meeting from which I greatly benefited. Randall, Phil Farmer, and I were interviewed by a reporter who asked us how we kept up with science. Randall and I were rather flip, but Phil very seriously described his techniques. One of them was his subcription to *Scientific American.*

I may be flip, but I listen. It was soon after my return that I subscribed to *Scientific American* myself, and I have maintained that subscription to the present day to my infinite benefit.

I wanted to leave on Sunday the twenty-third, but neither Marty nor Evelyn Gold were ready to go yet, so I drove back with Dave Kyle and two other fellows. We had a marvelous time talking McCarthy. Kyle (who had been Marty's partner when Gnome Press was started, and might still have been at this time) could imitate the McCarthy style perfectly and undertook to cross-examine me on my behavior at the Midwescon. In no time at all, he had me fruitlessly and unconvincingly denying any sexual misbehavior. Although I was completely innocent of any such thing, he made me sound as guilty as Hitler.

We had started late in the day, and Kyle drove grimly through the night. I settled back beside him in the front seat to sleep, but I found myself talking steadily through the hours.

At one point, I said, "I'm sorry, Dave. I must be boring you to madness."

"No, no," said Kyle, "keeping on talking. In the first place, you're interesting, and in the second, it helps keep me awake and alert."

Then as dawn was breaking, he stopped the car and said, "Your turn, Isaac," and we switched places.

I got behind the wheel with a certain alarm. Up to that point I had never driven a car that wasn't my own, and this one was a decrepit old station wagon with, Kyle himself admitted, defective brakes. Since I had been awake all night, I peered ahead through a gray streak of road between two banks of mist and felt very woozy indeed.

"Your turn to talk and keep me awake, Dave," I said as I eased the car into the road and picked up speed. This was met with silence, and when I looked quickly to my right, I found that it was too late. Kyle was already asleep. I drove across the Pennsylvania Turnpike till breakfast time. How I kept from destroying the car and everyone in it, I don't know.

We got back to New York at 2:00 P.M. on May 24, and my first action on reaching the Blugerman apartment, after giving everyone a feeble hello, was to remove some of my clothes and tumble into bed and oblivion.

33

The next day, May 25, I made my rounds. I visited the offices of *Thrilling Wonder* for the first time since I had stormed out with the rejected "Grow Old with Me" seven years before. Merwin was no longer there, of course. The editor was Sam Mines, a tall, husky fellow with a strong jawbone.

I gave him "The Portable Star" and he read it and bought it on the spot.

I then picked up the galleys of *Lucky Starr and the Oceans of Venus* at Doubleday, and finally went off to dinner with Bob and Ginny Heinlein. I hadn't seen either of them in nine years, not since the end of the Navy Yard days, and this was the first occasion on which I met them as a married couple.

While I suppose Bob was glad to see me on my own account, he had a purpose for the dinner. He knew that Pohl had quit the agency business and he also knew that I had been working agentless since then. As it happened, Bob drew me aside to urge me to become a client of his own agent. He told me very earnestly that his income had quintupled, thanks to his agent. I thought of my own writing income quintupling, and the thought of fifty thousand dollars per year had a vague Olympian quality about it that was endlessly appealing.

I wanted no agent—on principle. Money could not move me.

At least, that was the theory. But fifty thousand dollars a year! I could feel my principles softening about the edges, and I was glad that the agent would be joining us at dinner. Maybe—if he seemed pleasant —and competent—maybe—just maybe—well, after all, why not . . .

My principles were melting further.

What I needed was something that would jolt me back to my right mind, and fortunately it was supplied me.

I was seated next to the agent's wife, a very talkative woman. She talked about everything in a stream-of-consciousness manner that would have quickly driven me insane if I had listened to her. Fortunately, I had long since learned that one can detach one's self completely in such cases and merely make little moaning sounds at odd intervals to indicate one's attention is riveted, and the speaker is thoroughly satisfied.

I had ordered Shrimp Diabolo and was squaring away, quite prepared to eat with gusto, when the agent's wife, eyeing my dish with interest, said, "Well, what have you there, my, that looks good, I've always been interested in shrimp, been eating them ever since I was so high, but I don't seem to recognize this way of cooking them, it smells good, what do they call it, where's the menu, I wonder why I didn't notice it on the menu when I was ordering, does it taste good, let me see what it tastes like . . ."

And at this point, she speared one of my shrimps and carried it off.

I stared at her with horror. I *hate* having anyone sample my plate. I don't sample yours, you don't sample mine is my way of looking at meals.

There are some principles that even the thought of fifty thousand a year won't affect. Once she had speared my shrimp there was no longer a chance in Hades that Bob's agent could have me as a client. My heart hardened, my mind closed, and I settled back to my mere ten thousand a year.

And I never again got even that close to considering a literary agent.

34

On my rounds earlier that day, Mac Talley had told me that NAL had paid Marty Greenberg a $500 advance for the paperback rights to *I, Robot*. It seemed to me that Marty had never mentioned this in any of his discussions of my earnings.

I called him up on the twenty-sixth therefore and said, "Hey Marty, what about the $500 you got from Mac Talley?"

It may have come as a surprise to Marty to find out that I knew about this. At any rate he started yelling at me and calling me a variety of bad names.

I survived the barrage and insisted that he pay me—and he did in small, slow installments.

35

On June 16, 1954, I got my first speeding ticket. I believe I was trying to make it home to catch the last of the McCarthy hearings (it came to an end the next day after two months of national trauma).

On June 18, I took David to Norumbega Park, and while there I held out a peanut to a squirrel who seemed to be looking at me wistfully. I didn't throw it at him but wanted him to take it from my hand.

The squirrel came over cautiously and stretched out its head to the peanut, while I smiled at it with loving paternalism. Then, ignoring the peanut and for no reason whatever, the little fiend seized one of my fingers and bestowed a hard bite on it, drawing blood.

I yelled, squeezed as much blood out of it as I could, then went off to the park office for some iodine. I brooded over the possibility of tetanus and even rabies. I got myself a tetanus booster at school from Derow, just in case, and nothing developed.

I have never offered food to an animal again. I have *thrown* food, yes, but I've carefully kept my hands to myself. It was disillusioning to see a mere beast act in so typically human a fashion as to bite the hand that fed it.

36

"The Singing Bell" had been at *F & SF* for two months, and finally, on June 21, it was taken. I felt that to be a triumph, for it had been making the rounds without success for an unconscionable time.

Another story, "The Last Trump," which was a fantasy, I had sent off to Horace, hoping that it would be my second entry into *Beyond*. Horace wrote me to the effect that *Beyond* wasn't buying stories for six months, but if I wanted to revise it then, he would take it—and meanwhile he would hold the story.

I didn't want to wait till then because a six-month suspension of buying probably meant an end to the magazine. (I was right.) I therefore asked him, rather stiffly, to return the story, and he did. Other markets turned it down, however.

One sale I made, which pleased me enormously, was a parody of a poem by William S. Gilbert. In *Patience*, the poet, Bunthorne, sings a very effective solo that begins, "If you're anxious for to shine in the high aesthetic line . . ."

I parodied this with a poem I called "The Foundation of S.F. Success," which began, "If you ask me how to shine in the science-fiction line . . ."

It was a parody of myself and of the Foundation series, in which I openly admitted my debt to Roman history in the second verse, which goes:

"So success is not a mystery, just brush up on your history, and borrow day by day.

"Take an Empire that was Roman and you'll find it is at home in all the starry Milky Way.

"With a drive that's hyperspatial, through the parsecs you will race, you'll find that plotting is a breeze,

"With a tiny bit of cribbin' from the works of Edward Gibbon, and that Greek, Thucydides."

F & SF occasionally published poetry, and it was Tony Boucher who bought the parody. He was delighted and wrote to tell me he thought it the cleverest bit of self-parody since Swinburne. He paid me $15 for it—not much, but it was the first poetry I'd ever sold.

To be sure, it was not really poetry, but only comic verse; but then, comic verse is the limit of my poetic muse. Fortunate is the man who knows his own limitations.

37

At the moment, in fact, I was but too aware of my own limitations and was quite convinced I had risen to the highest level made possible by them.

The year was 1954. I was thirty-four years old. And . . .

As far as my chemical career was concerned, I had gone as far as I could. I had my doctorate, I had my professorial status. I might achieve another trivial promotion or two, but I could not honestly expect that I would ever be a great biochemistry teacher outside my own immediate classroom. The absolute failure of the textbook had made that plain.

As to my other career, science fiction, there, too, I had gone as far as I could. I might do things that were better than "Nightfall," *The Foundation Trilogy, I, Robot,* or *The Caves of Steel,* but surely not much better. These were already recognized as classics, and I had been writing for fifteen years and I had yet to make more than ten or eleven thousand dollars a year as a writer.

I didn't see how I could ever do better than that, especially since there was bound to come a time soon when a new and younger group of writers would take over and sweep myself and my contemporaries from the field—as we had done to the writers of the 1930s.

This volume of my autobiography, then, is the tale of my moving in, deeper and deeper, into the specialized world of biochemistry and science fiction, until I reached the dead-end wall that marked my limit. Taking into account my starting point at ground level, I had every right to count myself a success; but I was a very modest success indeed, and I was left ruefully unsatisfied.

Yet where could I find a way of moving out as I had moved in, but to a much higher level? What on earth could I do besides my biochemistry and my science fiction?

I had been writing straight science, of course, but some of it had been for the science-fiction magazines and was bound up entirely with my science fiction. Some of it had been for chemical journals and went nowhere. A good deal of it had gone into the textbook and had failed ignominiously.

That left my little book *The Chemicals of Life*, which was just being published. It actually represented my first move out, though I surely didn't recognize this at the time.

How, beginning with that book, I overleaped the blank wall I faced—not without trouble and controversy—and how I succeeded in reaching heights I was utterly unable to foresee in 1954, and how I reached the point, in fact, where Doubleday could actually make itself believe that the world might be interested in two fat volumes of autobiography by me, will be the tale of that second volume.

Catalog of Books
Isaac Asimov

Note: The numbers preceding the titles of books refer to the order in which they were published.

PART I—FICTION

A *Science-fiction Novels*

1. *Pebble in the Sky* Doubleday, 1950
3. *The Stars, like Dust—* Doubleday, 1951
4. *Foundation* Gnome (Doubleday), 1951
5. *David Starr: Space Ranger* Doubleday, 1952
6. *Foundation and Empire* Gnome (Doubleday), 1952
7. *The Currents of Space* Doubleday, 1952
9. *Second Foundation* Gnome (Doubleday), 1951
10. *Lucky Starr and the Pirates of the Asteroids* Doubleday, 1953
11. *The Caves of Steel* Doubleday, 1954
12. *Lucky Starr and the Oceans of Venus* Doubleday, 1954
15. *The End of Eternity* Doubleday, 1955
17. *Lucky Starr and the Big Sun of Mercury* Doubleday, 1956
20. *The Naked Sun* Doubleday, 1957
21. *Lucky Starr and the Moons of Jupiter* Doubleday, 1957
26. *Lucky Starr and the Rings of Saturn* Doubleday, 1958
67. *Fantastic Voyage* Houghton-Mifflin, 1966
121. *The Gods Themselves* Doubleday, 1972

B *Mystery Novels*

28. *The Death Dealers* Avon, 1958
172. *Murder at the ABA* Doubleday, 1976

C *Science-fiction Short Stories and Short-story Collections*

2. *I, Robot* Gnome (Doubleday), 1950
14. *The Martian Way and Other Stories* Doubleday, 1955

23. *Earth Is Room Enough*   Doubleday, 1957
29. *Nine Tomorrows*   Doubleday, 1959
60. *The Rest of the Robots*   Doubleday, 1964
82. *Through a Glass, Clearly*   New English Library, 1967
87. *Asimov's Mysteries*   Doubleday, 1968
98. *Nightfall and Other Stories*   Doubleday, 1969
113. *The Best New Thing**   World Publishing, 1971
125. *The Early Asimov*   Doubleday, 1972
146. *The Best of Isaac Asimov*   Sphere, 1973
150. *Have You Seen These?*   NESRAA, 1974
164. *Buy Jupiter and Other Stories*   Doubleday, 1975
167. *The Heavenly Host*   Walker, 1975
170. *The Dream, Benjamin's Dream, Benjamin's Bicentennial Blast*   Private print., 1976
174. *Good Taste*   Apocalypse, 1976
176. *The Bicentennial Man and Other Stories*   Doubleday, 1976

D   *Mystery Short-story Collections*

155. *Tales of the Black Widowers*   Doubleday, 1974
178. *More Tales of the Black Widowers*   Doubleday, 1976
190. *The Key Word and Other Mysteries**   Walker, 1977

E   *Science-fiction Anthologies (edited by* Isaac Asimov)

47. *The Hugo Winners*   Doubleday, 1962
52. *Fifty Short Science-fiction Tales* (with Groff Conklin)   Collier, 1963
76. *Tomorrow's Children*   Doubleday, 1966
110. *Where Do We Go from Here?*   Doubleday, 1971
115. *The Hugo Winners,* Volume II   Doubleday, 1971
147. *Nebula Award Stories Eight*   Harper, 1973
151. *Before the Golden Age*   Doubleday, 1974
186. *The Hugo Winners,* Volume III   Doubleday, 1977
192. *One Hundred Great Science-fiction Short-short Stories* (with Martin Harry Greenberg and Joseph D. Olander)   Doubleday, 1978

PART II—NONFICTION

A   *General Science*

31. *Words of Science*   Houghton-Mifflin, 1959
36. *Breakthroughs in Science**   Houghton-Mifflin, 1960

B Mathematics

C Astronomy

D   *Earth Sciences*

E   *Chemistry and Biochemistry*

83. *Is Anyone There?*   Doubleday, 1967
88. *Science, Numbers, and I*   Doubleday, 1968
103. *The Solar System and Back*   Doubleday, 1970
109. *The Stars in Their Courses*   Doubleday, 1971
119. *The Left Hand of the Electron*   Doubleday, 1972
138. *Today and Tomorrow and—*   Doubleday, 1973
144. *The Tragedy of the Moon*   Doubleday, 1973
148. *Asimov on Astronomy*   Doubleday, 1974
157. *Asimov on Chemistry*   Doubleday, 1974
159. *Of Matters Great and Small*   Doubleday, 1975
163. *Science Past—Science Future*   Doubleday, 1975
171. *Asimov on Physics*   Doubleday, 1976
175. *The Planet That Wasn't*   Doubleday, 1976
183. *Asimov on Numbers*   Doubleday, 1977
187. *The Beginning and the End*   Doubleday, 1977
193. *Quasar, Quasar, Burning Bright*   Doubleday, 1978
198. *Life and Time*   Doubleday, 1978

I   History

54. *The Kite That Won the Revolution*   Houghton-Mifflin, 1963
63. *The Greeks*   Houghton-Mifflin, 1965
71. *The Roman Republic*   Houghton-Mifflin, 1966
81. *The Roman Empire*   Houghton-Mifflin, 1967
86. *The Egyptians*   Houghton-Mifflin, 1967
91. *The Near East*   Houghton-Mifflin, 1968
92. *The Dark Ages*   Houghton-Mifflin, 1968
94. *Words from History*   Houghton-Mifflin, 1968
96. *The Shaping of England*   Houghton-Mifflin, 1969
106. *Constantinople*   Houghton-Mifflin, 1970
116. *The Land of Canaan*   Houghton-Mifflin, 1971
126. *The Shaping of France*   Houghton-Mifflin, 1972
137. *The Shaping of North America*   Houghton-Mifflin, 1973
149. *The Birth of the United States*   Houghton-Mifflin, 1974
156. *Earth: Our Crowded Spaceship*   John Day, 1974
161. *Our Federal Union*   Houghton-Mifflin, 1975
189. *The Golden Door*   Houghton-Mifflin, 1977

J   The Bible

44. *Words in Genesis*   Houghton-Mifflin, 1962
49. *Words from the Exodus*   Houghton-Mifflin, 1963

93. *Asimov's Guide to the Bible*, Volume I   Doubleday, 1968
99. *Asimov's Guide to the Bible*, Volume II   Doubleday, 1969
127. *The Story of Ruth*   Doubleday, 1972
195. *Animals of the Bible**   Doubleday, 1978

K   Literature

41. *Words from the Myths*   Houghton-Mifflin, 1961
104. *Asimov's Guide to Shakespeare*, Volume I   Doubleday, 1970
105. *Asimov's Guide to Shakespeare*, Volume II   Doubleday, 1970
130. *Asimov's Annotated Don Juan*   Doubleday, 1972
154. *Asimov's Annotated Paradise Lost*   Doubleday, 1974
181. *Familiar Poems Annotated*   Doubleday, 1977
191. *Asimov's Sherlockian Limericks*   Mysterious Press, 1977

L   Humor and Satire

112. *The Sensuous Dirty Old Man*   Walker, 1971
114. *Isaac Asimov's Treasury of Humor*   Houghton-Mifflin, 1971
166. *Lecherous Limericks*   Walker, 1975
177. *More Lecherous Limericks*   Walker, 1976
185. *Still More Lecherous Limericks*   Walker, 1977
197. *Limericks: Too Gross* (with John Ciardi)   Norton, 1978

M   Miscellaneous

100. *Opus 100*   Houghton-Mifflin, 1969
200. *Opus 200*   Houghton-Mifflin, 1979**

N   Autobiography

200. *In Memory Yet Green*   Doubleday, 1979**

* for children
** tie for 200th place

Title Index

Italicized items are published books.

Name Index

LEE COUNTY LIBRARY
SANFORD, N. C.

LEE COUNTY LIBRARY SYSTEM

3 3262 00106 6338

B
Asimov
Asimov
In memory yet green

LEE COUNTY LIBRARY
SANFORD, N. C.